CONCISE COLLEGE TEXTS

"A" LEVEL LAW

OTHER BOOKS IN THIS SERIES

Tort, by C. D. Baker
Law for Retailers, by Jennifer Brave
"O" Level Law, by W. J. Brown
Press Law, by Robin Callender Smith
Contract, F. R. Davies
Sale of Goods and Consumer Credit, by A. P. Dobson
Labour Law, by C. D. Drake
The English Legal System, by K. J. Eddey
Hotel and Catering Law in Britain, by David Field
Gill: The Law of Arbitration, by Dr. Enid Marshall
Family Law, by Grant and Levin: Jennifer Levin
Introduction to Commercial Law, by C. Hamblin and F. B. Wright
Land Law, by W. Swinfen Green and N. Henderson
Shipping Law, by Robert Grime
The Law and Procedure of Meetings, by Matthew Moore
General Principles of Law, by C. R. Newton
Criminal Law, by P. Seago
Construction Law, by J. Uff
Patents, Trade Marks, Copyright and Industrial Designs, by T. A. Blanco White and Robin Jacob

AUSTRALIA AND NEW ZEALAND
The Law Book Company Ltd.
Sydney : Melbourne : Perth

CANADA AND U.S.A.
The Carswell Company Ltd.
Agincourt, Ontario

INDIA
N. M. Tripathi Private Ltd.
Bombay
and
Eastern Law House Private Ltd.
Calcutta and Delhi
M.P.P. House
Bangalore

ISRAEL
Steimatzky's Agency Ltd.
Jerusalem : Tel Aviv : Haifa

MALAYSIA : SINGAPORE : BRUNEI
Malayan Law Journal (Pte.) Ltd.
Singapore

PAKISTAN
Pakistan Law House
Karachi

CONCISE COLLEGE TEXTS

"A" LEVEL LAW

BRIAN HOGAN, LL.B.
Of Gray's Inn, Barrister,
Professor of Common Law, University of Leeds

PETER SEAGO, J.P., LL.M. (Nottingham)
Senior Lecturer in Law,
Dean of The Faculty of Law, University of Leeds

GEOFFREY BENNETT, M.A.
Of the Inner Temple, Barrister,
Lecturer in Law, University of Leeds

LONDON
SWEET & MAXWELL
1983

Published in 1983 by
Sweet & Maxwell Limited of
11 New Fetter Lane, London.
Computerset by Promenade Graphics Limited, Cheltenham
and printed in Great Britain by
Richard Clay (The Chaucer Press) Limited,
Bungay, Suffolk.

British Library Cataloguing in Publication Data

Hogan, Brian
A-Level law.—(Concise college texts)
1. Law—England
I. Title II. Seago, Peter
III. Bennett, Geoffrey IV. Series
344.2 KD661

ISBN 0-421-29790-5
ISBN 0-421-29800-6 Pbk

PREFACE

When we began to plan this book we at first thought to cover the syllabuses of all the Boards offering law at "A" level. We were soon obliged to abandon this apparently attractive plan and for two connected reasons. One was that to produce a book which dealt adequately with the disparate syllabuses of the various Boards would have resulted in a text apt for no one. The other was the constraint of producing a book of manageable dimensions at a reasonable price.

In the result this book caters most obviously for students taking the examinations of the Oxford Board and the Northern Universities Joint Matriculation Board on whose syllabuses it is based. We followed these syllabuses because they are the most traditional in scope and accordingly deal with matters basic to any course in "A" level law. We have also included an appendix which lists texts for supplementary reading and reference; these texts should also cater for the special demands of other syllabuses.

If teachers of "A" level law encounter difficulties or shortcomings in the use of this book, we would be glad to enter into direct correspondence with them; and, indeed, we would welcome correspondence on any aspect of teaching law at "A" level. In this way, we hope, future editions will continue to meet the demands of teachers and students.

We owe thanks to many. To our publishers for their forebearance, courtesy and help. To Mrs. Christine Taylor and the secretarial staff for their first rate service, and to colleagues who have advised us on various parts of the text.

We have endeavoured to state the law as it was on March 31, 1983.

July 1, 1983

BRIAN HOGAN
PETER SEAGO
GEOFFREY BENNETT

CONTENTS

PART THREE: CONTRACT 313

TABLE OF CASES

TABLE OF STATUTES

Part One

THE LEGAL SYSTEM

CHAPTER 1

LEGAL CONCEPTS AND LEGAL REASONING

In this chapter an attempt is made to explain in outline how law works, how lawyers approach problems and how the courts resolve them. Issues raised in this chapter will be taken up in more detail in later chapters; the idea here is to give the essential flavour of law. One of the aims of this chapter is to assist a student who is minded to study law at "A" level to decide whether law is likely to interest him and whether he feels confident to study it.

Suppose B returns from holiday to find that during his absence an unsolicited parcel containing a book has been delivered to his home. With the parcel is a letter from the Ace Book Company offering to sell the book for £25 and the letter concludes, "If we hear no more from you in 14 days we will consider that you have bought the book." The 14 days elapsed while B was on holiday. Is B bound to pay for the book?

B knows no law but his instinctive feeling will surely be that he is not bound to pay; B will think it unfair if a bargain can be foisted on him against his will. However, B subsequently receives several aggressive demands for payment and thinks it wise to seek legal advice; after all B has read somewhere that the law can be a bit assinine at times. So B consults C, a solicitor. Before C gives legal advice he will first of all wish to get the facts as clear as he can. He will want to know whether the book was really unsolicited and did not arrive as the result of B responding to some advertisement, or because B was a member of a book club operated by the Ace Book Company. If B appeared to look young enough, C would also ask his age because if B is under 18 he is in law a minor and is accordingly in a privileged position under the law which regulates contracts. Of course, C cannot definitively establish the facts at this stage. No doubt B is telling the truth as he sees it but it may be that the Ace Book Company takes another view of the facts. Hopefully the Ace Book Company will accept B's version of the facts; if they do not, it may be that after some argument through correspondence the parties can agree what the facts were. If there is still no agreement, it may be necessary to take the matter to court where it will be for the judge, after hearing evidence, to decide what the facts were.

Most cases involve disputes about the facts rather than the law. Once the facts are determined the law, *i.e.* the legal consequences following from those facts, is *usually* clear. A major area of civil litigation these days arises from road accidents. It must not be thought that this is owing to any great uncertainty in the law. The law is well settled and relatively straightforward; if the plaintiff (the party bringing the action) establishes that the defendant drove his car negligently (that is failed to measure up to the standards of the reasonably competent driver) and as a result caused injury to the plaintiff then the plaintiff is entitled to compensation. The difficulty of such cases lies in the facts. What the court has to determine is whether the lights were red when the defendant crossed them, or whether his brakes were properly maintained, or whether he failed to signal his intentions and so on. Once the facts are established there is normally no difficulty in applying the law. The same is true of criminal cases. The difficulty in a shoplifting case is much more likely to concern the facts (for instance, did X deliberately or absent-mindedly take the tin of salmon) than a complex issue in the law of theft.

Notice, incidentally, that in a civil case it is for the plaintiff to establish the facts and for the prosecutor in a criminal prosecution. The plaintiff and the prosecutor normally bear what is called the burden of proof. In a civil case the plaintiff has to establish his case on what is called the balance of probabilities, that is that his version of the facts is more likely to be true than the defendant's version. In effect the plaintiff has to make the running. In a criminal case it is the prosecutor who has to make the running but it is not enough for him to prove his case on balance of probabilities. A criminal conviction is a serious matter so the standard required of the prosecutor is that he must prove the accused's guilt so convincingly that there can be no serious doubt about it. Today, judges tell juries to convict only if they feel sure that the accused is guilty; this may be generous to the accused but a criminal conviction is so serious a matter that a very high standard of proof is required.

In a civil action against a motorist the plaintiff succeeds if he establishes that it was probable that the motorist went through the lights at red. But if on these same facts the motorist is charged with careless driving it is not enough to establish that it was probable that he went through the red light. It is quite possible to form the view that an event probably happened while retaining a real doubt whether it did happen, and in that event a man cannot be convicted of crime. Take a case which was decided in 1966 when the accused was charged with murdering a woman by strangulation. The accused admitted that he had gone to bed with the woman and claimed that he must have strangled her in his sleep. Had this been so the accused was entitled to an acquittal because no man is liable for what he does when he is asleep. The doctors who gave evidence said they had never come across a case where a man had in his sleep strangled another. Nevertheless the jury acquitted. From the medical evidence it may have appeared probable that the accused had deliberately strangled her but the jury was still left with a real doubt, probably because while the doctors knew of no such cases they could not rule them out as a possibility. It may seem strange but a jury in a criminal case must acquit a man whom they think to be probably guilty if they think there is a real possibility that he may be innocent. But had the woman's dependants brought a civil action for compensation it seems clear that the evidence which was insufficient to establish the accused's guilt on the criminal charge would have been enough to establish his civil liability.

In the practice of law the establishment of the facts is of paramount importance. The law student because he is studying the law and therefore concentrating his attention on cases which raise legal issues, may get the impression that every dispute raises an issue that requires litigation to resolve it. This is far from being the case; only a fraction of disputes ever reach the courts and, as we have seen, most of these are likely to turn on disputes of fact rather than law. Even so there are still areas of doubt and difficulty in the law and there is a vast body of law to be learned.

To go back to B's case with the Ace Book Company. C, the solicitor, can assure B that, on the facts as B has presented them, B has nothing to worry about. The law in this instance (as most often it does) accords with commonsense for it is only fair that B's silence in response to an offer of which he was entirely unaware should not constitute an acceptance of the offer. But if C is asked why he has formed the opinion he has, he will not reply that it is because it is the "commonsense" or "fair" result. C knows that he must have legal authority for his statement to be found in a statute or a decision of the courts. In this instance his authority would be the (to lawyers) well-known case of *Felthouse* v. *Bindley* decided in 1862.

What happened in that case was that John Felthouse was about to sell his farming stock by auction, and Paul Felthouse, John's uncle, was anxious to buy a horse forming part of the stock. A misunderstanding arose over the price, John thinking he had sold the horse for 30 guineas, Paul thinking he had bought it for £30. So Paul wrote to John offering to split the difference and said, "If I hear no more about him, I consider the horse mine at £30.15s." John did not reply but he was clearly satisfied with the offer because he told the auctioneer, Bindley, to withdraw the horse from the sale. Unfortunately, Bindley forgot this instruction and sold the horse. Paul sued Bindley claiming that at the time of the auction the horse had already been sold to him by John so that Bindley had sold Paul's horse.

It was held by the court that Paul's claim against Bindley failed because there was no concluded contract between himself and John before the auction took place. One judge, Willes J, said that while it was clear that John intended to accept his uncle's offer, "he had not communicated such his intention to his uncle, or done anything to bind himself."

The case of *Felthouse* v. *Bindley* is not exactly the same as B's case with the Ace Book Company but C must be right in saying that if the court held there was no concluded bargain on the facts of *Felthouse* v. *Bindley* it necessarily follows that there was no concluded bargain between the Ace Book Company and B. Indeed, B's case is clearer than *Felthouse* v. *Bindley* because B never had any intention of accepting the offer of the book and was entirely unaware of the offer until he returned from holiday.

In advising B, C would also take account of the Unsolicited Goods and Services Act 1971. This Act was intended to deal with the mischief of "inertia selling," that is of foisting unsolicited goods on another and purporting to treat the other's inaction as an acceptance. It is now a criminal offence for a person (including a company) who, not having reasonable cause to believe there is a right to payment, makes a demand for payment for what he knows are unsolicited goods. The Ace Book Company may have committed an offence under this section but not necessarily so. It may be, for instance, that D played a practical joke on B by responding to an advertisement by the company in B's name. In such a case the company might in good faith believe that the goods were solicited by B, and hence would not be guilty of an offence. The Act also specifies a procedure whereby the recipient may, if the goods are not collected within six months or after notice by the recipient, treat the goods as an unconditional gift to him. No doubt C would consider whether in the circumstances B may avail himself of this procedure. But the Act does not in any way modify the law of contract. C will consider separately (i) B's contractual position; and (ii) any rights which B may have under the Act.

What the lawyer does, then, when presented with a problem is to consider the relevant legal rules to be found in the statutes and the decisions of the courts. He cannot rely on his own (or even abstract) notions of fairness and justice as guides for these would be much too uncertain and it is fundamentally important that the rules which regulate our social and business life should, so far as possible, be known and applied in a predictable way. Hence the lawyer's respect for precedent, that is he seeks to solve problems consistently with earlier cases which are similar to the case in hand. Moreover, as we shall see in more detail later, lower courts are bound by the decisions of higher courts so that certainty and predictability of result can be maximised. Obviously it would not do if lawyers had in every instance to advise their clients to take their cases to court to see what the judges thought was a "fair" result.

Sometimes, however, the lawyer does have to tell his client that the law is uncertain and that it will be necessary to take the matter to court in order to resolve it. We are never likely to reach the stage where the law is so developed and comprehensive that it provides an instant solution to every problem that arises; life is too complex for that. What we hope for is that the law is sufficiently comprehensive and developed to solve most disputes without undue difficulty, but at least some cases are bound to arise where even judges in appellate courts can differ as to the proper result.

The problem B presented to C was for C an easy one. But we can pose more difficult problems. Suppose that the insurance policy on B's motor cycle expired on April 30. On April 29, B received from his insurers a cover note valid for 15 days. B intends to renew his policy but, being pressed for money, he decides that he will make payment on May 14, just before the cover note expires. In the meantime B takes his cycle on the road; on May 10, he is stopped by a policeman and is subsequently charged with driving without insurance. This is a criminal prosecution and not an action for breach of contract but the law of contract is relevant because if B had a valid contract of insurance on May 10, he has a defence to the charge.

Felthouse v. *Bindley* is again in point. The prosecution will point out that the cover note was an offer to renew the insurance but was an offer B had not accepted by May 10. Like John Bindley, B intended to accept the offer but had done nothing to communicate his acceptance nor done anything to bind himself.

As it happens, while this particular problem has never been *decided* by any court, it has in fact been *considered* by Lord Parker C.J. in *Taylor* v. *Allen* (1965). In the doctrine of precedent courts are bound only by what other courts decide is the law applicable to the decision (called the *ratio decidendi*) and not by the opinions (called *obiter dicta*) which judges might express on issues which do not fall to be determined in that case. Such opinions can be persuasive and the opinion expressed, as it was in this case, by the Lord Chief Justice is bound to carry a lot of weight. Lord Parker said that it might be said in such a case as this that the motor-cyclist had accepted the offer by conduct (*i.e.* by taking his cycle on the road) in reliance on the offer made and without any formal communication. Lord Parker was aware that *in general* silence in response to an offer cannot be taken as an acceptance but was no doubt thinking that there was no reason why, if it suits him, the offeror should not dispense with communication.

What Lord Parker was prepared to do, it seems, was to *distinguish Felthouse* v. *Bindley*. He was not questioning the actual decision in that case, merely saying that the motor-cyclist's case was sufficiently different to permit an exception to the general rule that silence is not acceptance. If Lord Parker is right, the question arises as to what the result would have been in *Felthouse* v. *Bindley* if John had sued his uncle Paul for the purchase price of the horse. Suppose that John's instructions for the withdrawal of the horse had been complied with but the following day, and before John had communicated with Paul, Paul had written to say he was no longer interested in the horse. Would Lord Parker have been inclined to say that there was a contract because (a) Paul dispensed with the need to accept; and (b)in reliance on that John withdrew the horse from an auction at which it might otherwise have been sold? It is worth noting that in *Felthouse* v. *Bindley* itself one judge, Keating J, said that while he agreed that Paul failed in his action against Bindley, "Had the question arisen between the uncle and the nephew, then probably there would have been some difficulty."

Some writers (writers do not make, though they may influence, the law) have therefore questioned whether *Felthouse* v. *Bindley* was correctly decided. These writers are not questioning the principle that *in general* silence cannot constitute acceptance (and all of them would certainly agree that the Ace Book Company cannot treat B's silence as an acceptance) but they are saying that if the offeror chooses to dispense with acceptance *and* the offeree acts in reliance on what the offeror says, then the offeror ought to be bound. It is of course open to higher courts (the Court of Appeal or the House of Lords) to overrule *Felthouse* v. *Bindley*. The case has stood for over 100 years but that does not mean it cannot be overruled if it is thought to be wrong.

It seems that Paul Felthouse's lawyers were not entirely happy with the decision because they advised an appeal. While the appellate court affirmed the view of the trial court, there was next to no argument on this issue because it was held that Paul failed on another ground, namely, there was no sufficient written evidence to satisfy the Statute of Frauds 1677. At that time (this is no longer the law) the statute required that any contract for the sale of goods of £10 and upwards should be in writing and there was no sufficient writing in this case. So it might be said that Paul lost his case on a "technical" point which had nothing to do with the real merits of the case.

Cases can be lost and won on so-called technical points which, to the layman at least, seem to have nothing to do with the justice of the case. The creation of the offence of driving a motor vehicle with a blood/alcohol concentration above the prescribed limit (the "breathalyser" law) spawned a series of cases in which motorists were acquitted, or had their convictions quashed on technical points. The law is a complex one requiring, among other things, that the breath test be administered by a constable in uniform, that the breathalyser be of a type approved by the Home Secretary, that the test be administered at or nearby the place where it was required. So it follows that a motorist cannot be convicted where the constable is not in uniform, or where the breathalyser is not so approved, or where the test is administered a mile away from where it was required. This is so even though the motorist is clearly over the legal limit and is a menace to other road users.

A more dramatic example is provided by *Dyson* (1908). Dyson was charged with the manslaughter of his baby daughter who had died in March 1908 following brutal assaults by Dyson in November 1906 and December 1907. The judge had directed the jury that Dyson might be convicted of manslaughter if satisfied that death was caused by the assault in 1906 or accelerated by the assault in 1907 and the jury found Dyson guilty. This seems a sensible verdict and, you may think, the sentence of 10 years' penal servitude was fully deserved. But it so happens that before anyone can be convicted of homicide (whether murder or manslaughter) it must be proved that death occurred within a year and a day of the injury causing death. This rule was introduced many centuries ago probably because in those days, medicine being an even less precise science than it is now, the judges were understandably reluctant to attribute the cause of a death to an event occurring over a year before the death occurred. It is arguable that the rule is no longer necessary, but it is still a rule of law and it therefore followed that the trial judge had misdirected the jury in telling them that they could convict on the basis of the 1906 injuries which occurred 15 months before the death. Dyson's conviction was accordingly quashed. To some this might appear unjust because Dyson had unquestionably killed his daughter in circumstances where condign punishment was called for. But to the lawyer any other result is unthinkable. The rule requires death to occur within one year and one day of the injury. The rule may be indefensible in modern conditions, it may be that Parliament should abolish it, but while it stands the courts must apply it. That is what justice according to the law requires. In such circumstances it may be that the defendant can be convicted of some other offence (Dyson was convicted of common assault in respect of the two attacks on his child) but it also happens that some defendants escape scot free on a "technical" point even though their conduct would be regarded by all as reprehensible.

It must not be thought from these examples that the law is concerned only with technicalities, with notions of fairness and justice taking a back seat. Parliament seeks to enact fair laws which will command the respect of thinking people and the courts seek to apply the laws sensibly in order to produce fair results. But lawyers must act within the framework of the rules, must seek to apply the rules in a predictable and not capricious way. It must not be thought, however, that laws can be applied like mathematical formulae in order to produce the "right" result. Frequently more than one solution is possible and the judges may differ sharply as to what is the preferable solution.

Consider the case of *Morgan* (1975). A number of men charged with rape claimed that they believed that the victim had consented when as a matter of fact she had not. The trial judge, three Lords Justices of Appeal in the Court of Appeal and two Law Lords in the House of Lords took the view that an honest belief in the victim's consent was not a defence unless that belief was based on reasonable grounds. But three of the Law Lords held that an honest belief in the victim's consent was a defence even if it was an unreasonable belief. These three judges, since they constituted a 3–2 majority in the House of Lords which is the highest court, established the law though if judicial heads were to be counted there was a 6–3 majority the other way. All nine judges, however, were considering the same authorities and using the same techniques of reasoning but this happened to be a case where either view of the law was tenable.

The interest of the case does not end there. *Morgan* provoked such a storm of controversy (some critics thought it amounted to a rapist's charter) that the Government set up an Advisory Group to consider whether any changes in the law of rape were desirable. The approach of the Advisory Group was entirely different to the approach of the courts. Courts have to decide what the law *is* and in so deciding are confined to a consideration of legally relevant authorities. In deciding what the law *ought to be* the group's inquiry was much more wide ranging. The group issued a public invitation and received opinions from, among many others, the Association of Police Surgeons, the Mothers Union and the British Broadcasting Corporation. In the result the group recommended that the law relating to consent as a defence to a charge of rape should remain as the three Law Lords had stated it so that an honest, even though unreasonable, belief in the consent of the victim should be a defence. In no sense was the group deciding that the three were "right" while the view expressed by the six was "wrong." For all we know the members of the Advisory Group may have been privately of the opinion that, in view of the authorities, the opinion of the six was the preferable view. But the group was not sitting as a sort of further court of appeal to decide whether the decision of the House of Lords was in law the correct one. They were deciding, in the light of all the evidence presented to them, what would be the best rule to operate for the future.

Courts cannot possibly approach their task by soliciting views from members of the public on what the law ought to be. The judges are aware that the proper application of law can sometimes produce an injustice. Hence in some cases the judge will express regret about the decision he is constrained to make and may even recommend that the law which he has to apply ought to be changed by Parliament. Changing the law is, however, the function of Parliament and is not the prerogative of the courts. It has to be said that some judges are bolder in their approach to authorities than others and are more willing to remould the law to achieve what they see as being a fair result. But even the boldest judge seeks to work within the framework; he may be able to recast the rules but he cannot, as it were, destroy the mould and start again. The advantage of the bold approach is that the law can be better adapted, as the judge sees it, to modern conditions; the disadvantage is that the outcome of cases becomes less predictable so that the lawyer is that much less certain in advising his client. The law student will have to decide for himself whether he prefers the conservative or the progressive approach to the development of law but he can only make an informed choice in the matter after much study of the subject.

Chapter 2

INSTITUTIONS OF THE ENGLISH LEGAL SYSTEM

1. The Constitution in Outline

Britain has no written constitution which neatly defines the respective spheres of the Sovereign, Parliament, the Executive (the Government), and the Judiciary. Historically there has been adjustment and readjustment. The Sovereign once firmly holding the reins of government is now largely confined to a titular role and ceremonial duties. Parliament once little more than a sounding board is now the supreme legislative body; once dominated by the Lords it is now dominated by the Commons. The Judiciary who once developed large areas of the law of their own initiative and once even asserted, though never established, the supremacy of the common law now accept the supremacy of Parliament. And Parliament itself is in practice dominated by the Government which formulates the policy of the day and can in large measure ensure the legislation to implement it. Nor is the end of change in sight. There are moves to abolish the House of Lords, or to severely truncate its powers, or to replace it with a differently constituted chamber. There are moves also, perhaps prompted by the fear of an all powerful Commons, to introduce an entrenched Bill of Rights which would ensure that certain fundamental rights could not be readily abrogated by Parliament.

Some political theorists have argued for a rigid separation of powers between the legislature, the executive and the judiciary. The idea is that no one branch ought to be paramount and that liberty is best ensured by a system where each arm acts as a check on the others. Such a system is most nearly maintained in the United States. The President may propose legislation to Congress but it is Congress which has the power of disposal. While Congress has the exclusive law making power, the courts, who have to a degree assumed the power which the English courts once hankered after, may invalidate legislation on the ground that it is contrary to their written constitution—the fundamental law.

We have no such rigid separation but it has to be said that our constitution works tolerably well and, if the absence of violent revolutionary change is taken as the measure, has in the past adapted itself to change with less trouble than many constitutions elsewhere. It may be asked what is meant by saying that our constitution "works" and an answer to that can only be given in relation to the values which people seek to preserve. At the risk of oversimplification it may be said that our constitution, at the public level, seeks to ensure freedom of political action so that by free and fair elections we may have the Government of our choice; and, at the private level, to ensure equality of treatment before the law and freedom from arbitrary action by the authorities of the state. To most of us these appear to be values which are worth having and preserving.

Just how does the constitution guarantee these and other rights? Parliament is supreme and there are only theoretical limits on its law making power. It may be, for instance, that Parliament could not pass a law binding its successor not to repeal that law. But Parliament can pass a law to continue its own life notwithstanding that the Parliament Act 1911 states that five years shall be the maximum duration of a Parliament. Parliament could pass a law which would retrospectively make illegal that which was legal when it was performed. Parliament could pass a law authorising arbitrary action by the police. Thus, in theory, a Government commanding a majority in Parliament could almost overnight establish a police state. However, and quite apart from practical restraints on actions which might provoke a constitutional crisis or even violent reaction, there are constraints imposed by constitutional conventions and by respect for the rule of law.

(1) Constitutional conventions

In its essential respects our constitution is governed by conventions. These conventions are not rules of law which must be followed but they are practices which are normally regarded as obligatory; only in exigent circumstances may they be modified or ignored. Thus the Sovereign in whom great legal powers are vested might, for example, dismiss and appoint Governments, prorogue Parliament, or refuse the Royal Assent to Bills passed by Parliament. By convention, however, the Sovereign accepts the advice of his or her Ministers in these and many other constitutional matters. In turn the Government is a slave to convention. By convention a Government which cannot command a majority in the Commons will advise the Sovereign to dissolve Parliament and call an election, or nominate to the Sovereign someone who can form a Government which will command a majority. There is no law which requires Ministers of the Government to be members of the Houses of Parliament but it is a conventional requirement that they be so in order that Ministers can answer in Parliament for the conduct of their Ministries.

The advantage of conventions is that they provide a flexibility not given by rules of law. It might be countered that since Parliament is supreme it may just as easily alter a law as a convention, and perhaps the only adequate counter to that is that we have found it preferable to maintain the constitution more by convention than by law. Take the law, just noted, which limits the life of a Parliament to five years. There is no law which says that Parliament cannot repeal this law but there is a convention that this is not done, and in ordinary circumstances no Government would seek to prolong its life for this would provoke a constitutional crisis. In ordinary circumstances, note. During both World Wars Parliaments were continued beyond five years and, for obvious reasons, no constitutional crisis was caused.

In practical terms the difference between convention and law is slight. Conventions are regarded as binding in all but highly exceptional circumstances. Law, of course, binds even in the exceptional circumstances. Nevertheless when exceptional circumstances do arise people just as readily accept a change in the law as they accept a modification of the conventional practice.

(2) The rule of law

The rule of law means something more than rule in accordance with the law. The most terrifying dictatorship can rule in accordance with law by enacting laws to give effect to its policies, however inhuman these may be. The rule of law in the sense it is used here really involves certain presuppositions about law itself. The nature and extent of these presuppositions is open to argument but most would agree that the rule of law requires that all power and authority in the state be derived from law, and the notion of equality before the law.

In a dictatorship judges might be understandably reluctant to question the legal basis upon which the dictator and his designates act. In a parliamentary democracy there is no such reluctance. Thus ministerial powers, however widely phrased, are generally subject to review by the courts and if a minister has acted *ultra vires* (beyond the powers of) his authority, his action is invalid even if done in complete good faith and in accordance with the public interest. If the police effect an arrest or search premises without the legal powers to do so, the arrest or search is illegal and it will not help the police to show that their action was reasonable or that it was done to prevent greater harm.

Equality before the law requires that like should be treated as like. We accordingly accept that differences of sex, religion and race are not proper factors to be taken into account when it comes to questions of political rights, criminal liability or job eligibility. But equality is a slippery concept. Only in this century have women secured political parity. Our forebears, incidentally, probably did not see the denial of the vote to women as a breach of the principle of equality; they did not see women in this respect as "like" to men. We accept that for many purposes the young may be treated more favourably in law than those of mature judgment but the age at which equality of treatment is accorded is for most purposes 18 and not 21 as it was only a few years ago. So our notions of equality change but we accept that arbitrary (unreasoned) exceptions to equality of treatment before the law are intolerable.

If past practice is a guide, it is safe to assume that parliamentarians approach their affairs with an awareness, and acceptance of, the rule of law. Parliamentarians may not have identical definitions of the rule of law but there would be substantial accord on legal accountability and equality. In Germany in 1935 an Act was passed stating that persons should be punished if their acts were "deserving of punishment according to fundamental conceptions of a penal law and sound popular feeling." This Act was unquestionably a law and the judges were bound to apply it. Even in the exigent circumstances of war it is inconceivable that any British Parliament would find such a law even remotely acceptable. That Parliament has the power to pass such a law is clear; but legislation so vague and oppressive in its terms would be thought to violate the rule of law which informs our thinking about law.

The point about the British constitution is that the limitations within which it is operated are largely self-imposed. With the doctrine of parliamentary supremacy the potential for abuse is great but the traditions to which we subscribe have ensured that Parliament does not abuse its power. The cynic might say, as the man who jumped off a skyscraper was heard to say as he passed the twentieth floor, "It's been all right so far."

2. The Common Law

"Common law" has several meanings. When asked what it means a lawyer is most likely to reply that it refers to the law as developed by the judges since the Norman Conquest. When William I established himself he did not seek to impose on the English an entirely new system of law. There was no very developed Norman law which he could impose and, in any case, the imposition overnight of an entirely new system of law could only have caused legal and administrative chaos. So William was content to endorse the Saxon laws subject to such changes necessary to secure his own position.

The Normans were great administrators (Domesday Book bears witness to that) and they set out to centralise and regularise the government of the country. While local courts and local laws continued to flourish, the central government appointed its own judges (*justiciars*) to look after its own interests. A principal interest of the Crown was to secure its own revenues so it is no accident that the Court of Exchequer was the first to emerge as a distinct court. As the Crown's interest became more pervasive the central courts expanded at the expense of local ones, an expansion accelerated by their superior procedures and remedies.

In developing the law the judges no doubt made use of customary law, both Saxon and Norman, adapting these to the needs of a developing society. In so doing the lawyers used the technique of developing the law by reference to judicial decisions; arguing the case in hand by reference to decisions in similar cases after the fashion outlined in Chapter 1. Much of our law was developed in this way with relatively little legislative interference until the nineteenth century. So long as the pace of social change was slow, as it was until the Industrial Revolution, the judges could adapt the law to that change. Once the pace of change quickens the development of the law solely by judicial decision cannot keep abreast. Legislation becomes increasingly necessary, for legislation can do overnight what may take the courts years to accomplish. Although substantial parts of our law are still to be found in the decisions of the courts, most of our law is now to be found in statutes. But this has not entailed the demise of the common law; much of it has been little more than restated in statutory form and the common law technique—that of arguing deductively from like cases—continues to govern our legal reasoning.

3. Equity

As we saw in Chapter 1, judges are not free to decide cases on the basis of fairness but only on the basis of the established laws. Sometimes the proper application of the law can lead to an unfair or harsh result. In such cases the judge may draw the matter to the attention of law reform agencies with a view to legislative change of the law. In the formative era of the common law there were no such law reform agencies. Litigants who were dissatisfied with the outcome of litigation took to petitioning the Crown, as the fount of all justice, to redress their grievances. The Crown, in turn, assigned such petitions to the Lord Chancellor. It is sometimes said that this was because the Chancellor, invariably an ecclesiastic in early times, was the keeper of the King's conscience and thus peculiarly well qualified to determine issues of right and justice. The real reason may have been more practical. The Chancellor would inevitably be familiar with the law; he was in fact intimately connected with its early development, and was a legal adviser to the King's Council (the *Curia Regis*). Moreover he had a secretariat (the Chancery, later to become the Court of Chancery) which had the all important administrative machinery to deal with such petitions.

Suppose, for instance, that A had agreed to sell land to B but had reneged on his promise. In the common law courts B could get damages (compensation in money) for the breach of contract but B might find damages less than adequate; what B wanted was the land itself and he could see no reason why A should not be kept to the terms of his promise. To us it may seem strange that the common law courts failed to respond by ordering A to convey the land but they did so fail and it was the Chancellor who intervened to give B a decree of specific performance (see *post*, p. 452). Similarly if A built a wall which interfered with the light to B's house, what B required was not monetary compensation but an order to take down the wall; the Chancellor was prepared to give that order—the injunction. The common law for all its innovation and flexibility became rigid and unresponsive to the needs of certain situations; the Chancellor was not so inhibited and could act on the conscience of the parties, ordaining what he thought to be fair (equitable) in the particular case. But what is "fair"? One Chancellor might take one view, his successor another. Hence the seventeenth century jibe that equity varied with the length of the Chancellor's foot.

Inevitably there was conflict between the court of Chancery and the courts of common law since the Chancellor was recognising rights and granting remedies not accorded at common law. Moreover the Chancellor made the claim, true but for that reason no less galling to common lawyers, that he dispensed a superior justice; and, worst of all, he was even prepared to issue an injunction to restrain a ligtigant from enforcing his legal rights in the common law courts if it was against "conscience" to do so. Nor was the litigant well served by the division between the court of equity and the courts of common law; he could be involved in the burdensome and expensive task of going to the common law courts to establish his right and then going to Chancery to get the appropriate remedy.

In the end, though the end was a long time in coming, the supremacy of equity was acknowledged in the ruling, first made by James I but subsequently endorsed in the Judicature Act 1873, that where rules of equity and law conflict, equity prevails. By that same Act the common law courts and the court of Chancery were united in the Supreme Court of Judicature and henceforth *all* judges were enjoined to apply both law and equity in the resolution of cases. And by this time equity no longer merited the old jibe; Chancellors such as Nottingham, Hardwicke and Eldon systematised the rules of equity so that equity became as predictable and rigid as the common law. Chancellors had always claimed that equity was to supplement, not supplant, the common law; by the nineteenth century that claim was a reality. Courts now administer the law and that law includes both common law and equity; law and equity have at last been fused. Nevertheless, the distinction between law and equity remains important for more than merely historical reasons, and equitable remedies (because they have their basis in conscience) may still be denied a party even though his right at common law is unimpaired.

This is not to suggest that the law (the rules of common law and equity) has reached a stage where it is incapable of improvement, nor to say that the proper application of the law is now incapable of producing a harsh or unfair result. But it is true to say that most judges, faced with a case in which the application of the law produces what appears to be an unfair result, will content themselves by drawing attention to the apparent injustice in the expectation that Parliament, after appropriate inquiry and consultation, will put the matter to rights. Some judges, however, are bolder and will not wait on legislative reform so that even in recent years there have been some striking judicial innovations, an example of which is provided by equitable estoppel (*post*, pp. 344–349).

4. The Courts

The courts exercising civil and criminal jurisdiction may be diagramatically shown as on page 19.

While this diagram conveys the essential structure of the courts, it is both inaccurate and incomplete. It is inaccurate in suggesting a precise distinction between civil and criminal jurisdiction. While the jurisdiction of the High Court is primarily civil, the Queen's Bench Division exercises an important supervisory jurisdiction in criminal cases (*post*, p. 33); and while the jurisdiction of the Crown Court is primarily criminal, it has some civil jurisdiction such as licensing appeals from the magistrates' courts. It is incomplete in that it does not show the Court of Justice of the European Communities. While this court is not part of the English legal system it has jurisdiction in matters of Community law and its decisions take effect here (*post*, p. 124). Nor are tribunals (*post*, p. 37) part of the recognised court system though the collective jurisdiction of these is immense.

In fact the court system cannot be precisely categorised. It is common to refer to courts exercising appellate jurisdiction and

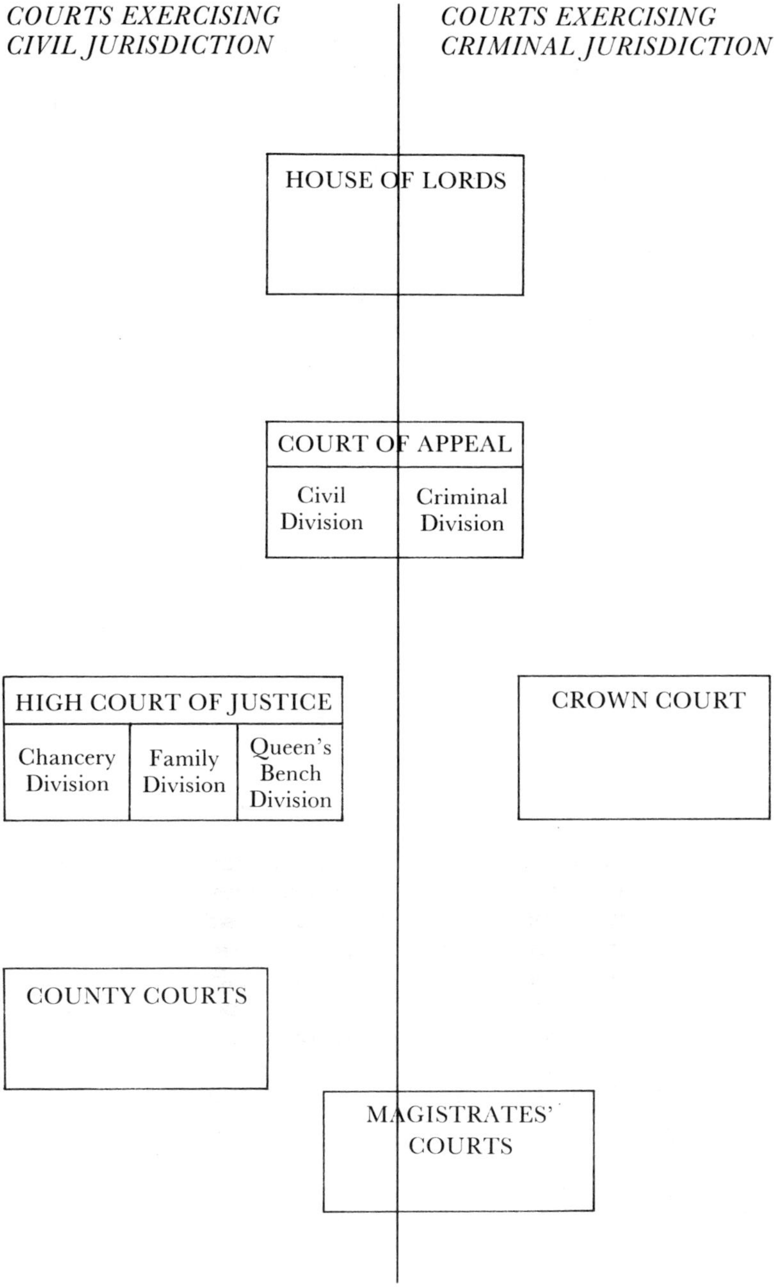
COURTS EXERCISING CIVIL JURISDICTION
COURTS EXERCISING CRIMINAL JURISDICTION
HOUSE OF LORDS
COURT OF APPEAL
Civil Division
Criminal Division
HIGH COURT OF JUSTICE
Chancery Division
Family Division
Queen's Bench Division
CROWN COURT
COUNTY COURTS
MAGISTRATES' COURTS

courts exercising original (trial) jurisdiction but it has to be recognised that some courts (the High Court, the Crown Court) exercise both. Another distinction is between superior courts (House of Lords, Court of Appeal, High Court, Crown Court) whose jurisdiction is unlimited, and inferior courts (county courts, magistrates' courts) whose jurisdiction is limited to a particular geographical area or by the amount claimed in civil proceedings or by the seriousness of the offence in criminal proceedings. One test of an inferior court is whether it is subject to the prerogative orders (*post*, p. 33) of the High Court but the Crown Court is recognised as a superior court although it is so subject when exercising its appellate jurisdiction.

So classification has only a limited value. The court structure, after all, is not one which has been modelled and imposed by logicians. It has evolved over a long period and has been frequently adapted to meet changing situations where convenience often requires solutions that do not make for neat categorisation.

5. The Personnel of the Law

(1) Magistrates

There are over 20,000 lay magistrates in England and Wales and some idea of their importance may be gleaned from the simple fact that over 90 per cent. of criminal cases begin and end in magistrates' courts. This heavy reliance on laymen in the administration of justice may appear odd and the reasons for it are historical and practical. It might have been possible to keep the administration of justice entirely in the hands of lawyers but in the fourteenth century, and probably in response to a crime wave, it was decided to accord judicial powers to lay justices of the peace. At this time the justices would have been drawn from the ranks of the knights and squires and down to the twentieth century magistrates were drawn mainly from the ranks of the upper and middle classes.

The formal qualifications are few. On appointment a magistrate must be over 21 and under 60 (50 in the case of the juvenile court bench), and must normally reside within 15 miles of the area in which he is to act. There is no formal requirement for good character (other than that bankruptcy and conviction for treason are disqualifications) though the process of selection ensures that only persons of good character who possess the qualities required for the discharge of the office will be appointed. They must retire at 70 (65 in the case of the juvenile bench) and may be removed for misconduct.

Justices of the Peace are appointed in the name of the Crown under the hand of the Lord Chancellor or, in Lancashire, the Chancellor of the Duchy of Lancaster. The Chancellors are assisted by local advisory committees which interview and assess candidates and make recommendations. The responsibility for appointment, however, lies with the Chancellors and it must not be assumed that they rubber-stamp the recommendations made by local committees.

In 1966 Lord Gardiner, then Lord Chancellor, caused something of a stir by directing local committees *not* to disregard the political affiliations of candidates. This may seem surprising but what Lord Gardiner was, and was properly, concerned to do was to ensure that the magistracy was truly representative of all sections of society and all shades of opinion within it. What we do not want is a middle-aged, middle-class, male-dominated magistracy, all with similar social and political values.

No knowledge of law, still less legal qualification, is required. Newly appointed magistrates are required to attend courses of instruction designed to familiarise them with the essentials of law and procedure and to acquaint them with judicial technique. In court magistrates receive expert guidance on matters of law and procedure from the clerk to the magistrates. At one time the clerk was literally that, a mere scrivener who kept the books. Nowadays clerks must be legally qualified (as a barrister or solicitor of five years standing) and will ordinarily have a much more thorough knowledge of law, procedure and evidence than the magistrates. Nevertheless they *advise* the magistrates; the ultimate responsibility lies with the magistrates and not with their clerk.

(2) Stipendiary magistrates

A stipendiary magistrate is a professional lawyer (a barrister or solicitor of seven years standing) who receives a salary (hence "stipendiary" for lay magistrates are unpaid) and works full-time. The number of stipendiaries who can be appointed at any one time is by statute limited to 40. In the past stipendiaries have often been appointed in response to local dissatisfaction with the lay magistracy. There is no demand for the general replacement of lay magistrates by professional stipendiaries and as a practical matter the professions could hardly provide even the more limited number of full-time professionals which would be required to replace over 20,000 part-time lay magistrates. Additional stipendiaries are now likely to be appointed only where there is a shortage of lay magistrates.

(3) Recorders

A recorder is a part-time judge of the Crown Court and must be a barrister or solicitor of 10 years standing. Since a recorder is appointed on a part-time basis for a fixed term the appointment may be used, in effect, as an apprenticeship; there is the opportunity both for the recorder to demonstrate judicial ability and for his ability to be assessed with a view to his permanent appointment as a circuit judge.

(4) Circuit judges

The circuit judge was introduced in 1971 following radical revision of the courts system. All county court judges, who were till then exclusively concerned with civil work, became circuit judges and were additionally assigned to the Crown Court where the bulk of the work is criminal. Circuit judges are appointed from barristers of ten years standing or from recorders who have held office for five years. So a solicitor who, as we have seen, is eligible for appointment as a recorder, may become a circuit judge. The maximum number of circuit judges is fixed from time to time by the Lord Chancellor who will obviously have regard to the volume of civil and criminal work; where the pressure of work is a temporary one the Chancellor may appoint deputy circuit judges from barristers or solicitors of ten years standing. At present there are some 300 circuit judges. Circuit judges retire at 72 and may be removed by the Chancellor for incapacity or misbehaviour.

(5) High Court Judges

The judicial personnel mentioned above all have limitations on their jurisdiction, as we shall see in more detail later. Judges of the High Court (often called "puisne"—inferior or subordinate—judges) have no limits on their jurisdiction and are knighted on appointment. The appointment is made on the recommendation of the Lord Chancellor and confined to barristers of 10 years standing which means that solicitors, who may be appointed as stipendiary magistrates, recorders or circuit judges, cannot become High Court judges. The maximum number of puisne judges is presently fixed at 75 but in order to deal with pressing business the Lord Chancellor may appoint deputy High Court judges who must also be barristers of 10 years standing and who, for the duration of their appointment, have the same powers as High Court judges.

Puisne judges hold office during good behaviour and may be removed only by the Crown on an address by both Houses of Parliament. From time to time Members of Parliament have put down a motion critical of a judge's conduct in particular cases but it is rare for such motions ever to reach the stage of debate and no judge has been removed from office this century. Judges of higher rank than puisnes are also dismissible only in this way, except for the Lord Chancellor who holds his office on the same terms as other ministers of the Government. All judges appointed since 1959 must retire at 75.

(6) Lords Justice of Appeal

Lords Justices of Appeal who sit in the Court of Appeal are appointed on the recommendation of the Prime Minister after consultation with the Lord Chancellor, and must be barristers of 15 years standing or judges of the High Court. Their number is presently limited to 16.

(7) Lords of Appeal in Ordinary

Lords of Appeal in Ordinary who sit in the House of Lords are appointed on the recommendation of the Prime Minister after consultation with the Lord Chancellor from holders of high judicial office (*e.g.* High Court judges, Lords Justices of Appeal) or barristers of 15 years standing, and on appointment are created life peers. Normally, but not invariably, Lords of Appeal in Ordinary are appointed from the Lords Justices of Appeal. Their number is presently limited to eleven of whom two are normally appointed from similarly qualified Scottish lawyers—the House of Lords being the final court of appeal from Scottish courts in civil matters.

(8) The Lord Chancellor

The Lord Chancellor holds the highest judicial office and is also Speaker of the House of Lords where (unlike his Commons counterpart) he is the Government's principal spokesman. He is a Minister of the Crown and usually a cabinet minister. The judicial duties are considerable. We have seen that he recommends most judicial appointments and is consulted in all others. He is the *ex officio* head of the Chancery Division, President of the Court of Appeal (though he rarely sits in either), and presides over judicial sittings in the House of Lords and Privy Council. The increasing burdens of the office have been such that for a period after the second world war Lord Chancellors sat only infrequently on appeals but recent Chancellors have somehow managed to reverse the trend.

Oddly enough there are no formal qualifications for the office, any doubt whether a Roman Catholic could become Lord Chancellor being removed by statute in 1974. He is now invariably a lawyer and in the nature of things a lawyer of considerable experience and standing; not infrequently he will have served the Government as a law officer (Attorney-General or Solicitor-General).

(9) Lord Chief Justice

The Lord Chief Justice is next in judicial rank to the Lord Chancellor. The appointment is made on the recommendation of the Prime Minister after consultation with the Lord Chancellor. A person qualified for appointment as Lord Justice of Appeal, or who is a judge of the Court of Appeal, is qualified for appointment as Lord Chief Justice.

The Lord Chief Justice is, in the absence of the Lord Chancellor, President of the High Court; he is also President of the Queen's Bench Division and presides over the Criminal Division of the Court of Appeal. In practice the Lord Chief Justice is to be found in one of two appellate courts, the Court of Appeal or the Queen's Bench Divisional Court. Sometimes he sits as a trial judge, but this is now much less common than it was.

(10) Master of the Rolls

The appointment of, and qualification for, this office are as for the Lord Chief Justice after whom the Master of the Rolls next ranks. He presides in the Civil Division of the Court of Appeal.

So far as the development of law is concerned, the Lord Chief Justice and the Master of the Rolls occupy key positions. Although the House of Lords is the final appellate court the number of civil appeals heard by the House in an average year is less than 50 while it is nearer 500 in the Civil Division of the Court of Appeal; the comparable figures for criminal cases are 5 and 2,500. Figures can be deceptive, but it can be appreciated that in practical terms the influence of the Court of Appeal outweighs that of the House of Lords. In the Court of Appeal the Lord Chief Justice and the Master of the Rolls are the dominant figures—hence their importance in the legal system.

(11) President of the Family Division

He is responsible for the organisation and management of his division, sits in the division and is also an *ex officio* member of the Court of Appeal.

(12) The Vice-Chancellor

As we have seen, the Lord Chancellor is the president of the Chancery Division, but he now rarely sits in that court; he may, and ordinarily he does, appoint a Vice-Chancellor who is responsible to him for the organisation and management of the business of the division.

(13) The Attorney-General

The Attorney-General is the principal legal adviser to the Crown (the Government) and is invariably a Member of Parliament and of the Government. The Government may require legal advice on a wide range of problems but perhaps especially on issues of constitutional law and international law, and the Attorney is expected to advise the Commons on legal issues. The Attorney exercises a large measure of control over criminal proceedings; prosecutions for certain offences (*e.g.* under the Official Secrets Act 1911) cannot be commenced without his consent, and by entering a *nolle prosequi* (be unwilling to proceed with) he may summarily terminate any prosecution which has been commenced. By tradition he represents, though in an impartial manner, the interests of the Crown in the courts; accordingly he conducts certain cases (*e.g.* prosecutions for treason or for serious breaches of the Official Secrets Act) where the Crown has a special interest, or cases (*e.g.* certain prosecutions for murder) where the "public interest" appears to require it.

(14) The Solicitor-General

The foregoing brief review of the Attorney-General's duties indicates that he has a burdensome office. The Solicitor-General (who is a barrister and, like the Attorney, will normally be both a Member of Parliament and of the Government) assists the Attorney in the discharge of these duties, and may deputise for the Attorney during his absence or a vacancy in the office.

(15) Director of Public Prosecutions

There is not, nor has there ever been, a system of publicly controlled and centrally administered prosecutions. Most prosecutions are now initiated by the police which people often think of, wrongly, as "public" prosecutions for these are private prosecutions and are not initiated by an agency of the Crown. In the nineteenth century the system of private prosecutions led to widespread abuse so the office of Director of Public Prosecutions was established in 1879. The Director, who acts under the general supervision of the Attorney-General, may initiate prosecutions and may give advice to chief officers of police, clerks to the justices and others concerned with criminal proceedings. The police are required to inform the Director of certain offences (*e.g.* murder, manslaughter, abortion, certain sexual offences) and in other cases (*e.g.* certain homosexual offences, theft by one spouse from the other) the consent of the Director is required before a prosecution may be commenced.

On the face of it the Director has extensive powers. He may take over any private prosecution and, by offering no evidence at the trial, he may terminate any criminal prosecution. In practice the Director conducts relatively few prosecutions, usually in serious or difficult cases where the "public interest" is involved, and the vast majority of prosecutions are still conducted by the police though the importance of the Director's guidance to them on matters of prosecuting policy must not be underestimated.

The Director, who must be either a barrister or solicitor of 10 years standing, is appointed by the Home Secretary.

(16) Barristers and solicitors

In the popular mind, the distinction between barristers and solicitors is that the former are concerned with advocacy in court while the latter are concerned with legal work out of court. This is not quite the case. Barristers are primarily concerned with advocacy and they have an exclusive right of audience in the High Court, the Court of Appeal and the House of Lords; but they are not confined to advocacy and may devote a deal of their time to giving expert opinions on legal matters. Nor are solicitors exclusively concerned with out-of-court work for they have a right of audience in magistrates' courts, county courts and, in some instances, in the Crown Court.

This division of the legal profession is a curious one and is unknown even in many Commonwealth countries which might have been expected to adopt the English professional model along with their adoption of the common law. The education of both barristers and solicitors has much in common. Both will normally complete the academic stage of their legal education by obtaining a law degree, though a law degree is not the only way to complete the academic stage. Both undergo a vocational stage though here the differences are more marked. The barrister takes the Bar Examination under the aegis of the Inns of Court School of Law while the solicitor takes the Final Examination under the aegis of the Law Society and in these examinations the emphasis differs to take account of their different roles. Both must complete a period of apprenticeship; pupillage in the case of barristers served under a pupil master (an experienced barrister), and articles in the case of solicitors served under an experienced solicitor. Here, at this "practical" stage, the difference is perhaps most marked since the day-to-day work of the barrister is quite different to the office routine of the solicitor.

The difference, however, is one of function rather than purpose. It is the purpose of both to ensure that the citizen has available sound professional services and advice to enable him to order his business and social life. When a citizen consults a lawyer it is more likely to prevent matters going wrong (*e.g.* he wishes to form a company, or to organise his business affairs to attract the minimum of tax, or to make a will) than because matters have gone wrong (*e.g.* he is threatened with civil or criminal proceedings). Only exceptionally will the citizen require the specialist services of the barrister hence practising barristers number some 4,500 as against some 38,000 solicitors. But even a distinction between the "specialist" barrister and the "generalist" solicitor can be misleading; many barristers, particularly in their early years at the Bar, may take whatever cases come their way, and many solicitors, especially those in large firms, may specialise in a particular area of law.

That the fusion of the two professions is *possible* is demonstrated by experience in similar common law jurisdictions elsewhere. Whether it is *desirable* is another matter. The acid tests must be whether fusion would secure for the citizen an improved standard of legal services or whether it would significantly reduce their cost. The Royal Commission on Legal Services (1979) took the view that the public interest was best served by retaining the existing division, and that legal services would not be improved, nor costs significantly lowered, by fusion. The Commission was, however, inclined to think that there should be a common education for barristers and solicitors so that entrants to the legal profession could make the decision as to which branch of the profession they should join after the completion of their apprenticeship and not, as now, at the outset of their professional careers.

6. The Courts: Composition and Jurisdiction

(1) Magistrates' courts

For most purposes a magistrates' court must be composed of two justices (a stipendiary has the powers of two lay justices) though normally the bench will be composed of three. A single lay justice has very limited powers (*e.g.* issue of summonses or warrants of arrest) but a single justice may determine whether a person is to be tried summarily or on indictment.

(a) *Criminal jurisdiction*

Some offences are so serious (*e.g.* treason, murder, manslaughter) that they can be tried *only* on indictment (hence they are known as indictable offences) at the Crown Court before a judge and jury; and some offences are so minor (*e.g.* many traffic offences such as driving without due care, speeding) that they can be tried *only* summarily (hence summary offences) by the magistrates. But there is an intermediate type of offence where the seriousness turns upon the circumstances (*e.g.* theft may involve property valued at only a few pence to property worth many thousands of pounds) and these offences may be tried either summarily or on indictment (hence they are known as offences triable either way).

If the offence is one which is triable only on indictment or only summarily the accused has no choice as to the mode of trial. If the offence is triable either way the accused may always insist on being tried on indictment, and it is not uncommon to have cases of shoplifting involving trivial sums being tried at the Crown Court. But the accused cannot insist on being tried summarily for such offences; it is for the magistrates, having regard to the circumstances and representations made, to decide whether the case is suitable for summary trial. In making that decision the magistrates will consider whether the maximum punishment they can inflict (which is usually six months imprisonment, or a fine of £1,000, or both) would be adequate to deal with the case. If the magistrates decide that they can properly deal with the case they must then (a) tell the accused that he may consent to be so tried or that he may be tried by jury; and (b) that if on conviction following summary trial it appears from his antecedents (*i.e.* his previous convictions of which the magistrates will be unaware at this stage because such evidence is generally excluded in criminal cases) that the case calls for a higher sentence than the magistrates can impose, he may be committed to the Crown Court for sentence.

If the accused consents he will be tried summarily. If not the magistrates proceed as *examining justices* with a view to deciding whether to commit the accused to trial at the Crown Court. And, of course, if the accused is charged with an offence triable only on indictment the magistrates must proceed as examining justices. The purpose of these proceedings is to determine whether there is a prima facie case against the accused, and the function of the magistrates is not to determine guilt or innocence but merely whether, having regard to the evidence against him, the accused ought to stand trial.

Before 1968 committal proceedings were conducted orally. This was time-consuming and therefore expensive and was hardly justified if, as was usually the case, the accused was not going to contest the committal and was reserving his defence for the trial itself. Moreover, the Press were at liberty to report such proceedings and this, especially in notorious cases which were widely reported, could work to the prejudice of the accused because potential jurymen might have read these reports and formed a view about the accused's guilt. A new style of committal proceedings was accordingly introduced in the Criminal Justice Act 1967 whereby the accused, provided he is legally represented, may be committed for trial without any hearing by the magistrates. What happens is that the prosecution tenders its evidence in writing and if the accused, whose legal representative will have seen the evidence, agrees to being committed, the magistrates may so commit him without themselves considering the evidence. Most committals now take this form though the old style of committal is still available to an accused and is obligatory if the accused is not legally represented.

Whatever form a committal takes the same Act imposed severe restrictions on reporting by the Press; the Press may now report only such matters as the names of the accused, the charges and the decision to commit. But it is open to the accused to insist on these restrictions being lifted in which case reporting becomes admissible. Such a course might be advantageous to the accused where, for example, he hopes that the publicity might bring forward witnesses whose evidence may prove favourable. Until recently an accused could insist on reporting restrictions being lifted even though he was charged with co-accused who believed that publicity would be prejudicial to their case. The Criminal Justice (Amendment) Act 1981 now provides that where there are two or more accused and one objects to the lifting of restrictions, the court may order that restrictions be lifted only if satisfied that it is in the interests of justice to do so.

(b) *Civil jurisdiction*

The magistrates' courts have odds and ends of civil jurisdiction including such matters as enforcing demands for rates and investigations into shipping casualties. The most important, and homogenous, aspect of civil jurisdiction relates to domestic proceedings. This jurisdiction is extensive (extending to such matters as maintenance orders in favour of either spouse or their children, exclusion of either spouse from the matrimonial home for the protection of the other spouse and children, custody and access orders, adoption orders, affiliation orders) but is generally subject to financial limits. This has led to the criticism that there is a secondary system of domestic courts for the poor; the better off using the county courts and High Court which are staffed by professional and highly qualified judges. To meet this criticism it is now provided that magistrates sitting in domestic cases must be drawn from a panel of specially qualified magistrates and that of the three magistrates comprising the bench at least one must be a man and one a woman.

(c) *Juvenile courts*

The juvenile court bench, like the domestic bench, is drawn from a specially qualified panel of magistrates, and of the three magistrates at least one must be a man and one a woman. As we have seen, a magistrate must be under 50 at the time of appointment to this panel and must retire at 65.

A juvenile is a child (person under 14) or young person (under 17). There are special rules governing the criminal liability of children, but quite apart from these there has evolved a special system for dealing with juveniles governed by the notions: (i) that they should be dealt with separately from adults; (ii) that "care proceedings" rather than criminal proceedings are more suitable; and (iii) that courts should act for the welfare of the child.

Subject to certain exceptions (*e.g.* where the charge is homicide) a juvenile must be brought before a juvenile court which must sit in a separate court room or a room where no ordinary criminal proceedings have been held for a least an hour. Other than the court officials, the parties, their legal representatives and parents, and authorised members of the Press, no one may be present unless authorised by the court. Nor may the Press, without the direction of the court or the Home Secretary, identify any person under 17.

Criminal proceedings against juveniles are in process of being replaced by care proceedings under the Children and Young Persons Act 1969. Only certain authorised persons (*e.g.* the local authority, the police) may bring a juvenile before the court and then only if there are reasonable grounds for believing that the court may make one of the orders under the Act. To make an order the court must be satisfied that certain conditions are met such that the juvenile's proper development or health is being avoidably neglected, or that he is beyond the control of his parents, or that he is guilty of an offence other than homicide. Satisfied that such grounds exist, the court may order parents to enter into a recognisance (which is a bond to pay a certain sum, in this case not exceeding £200, in default) to take proper care; or may make a supervision order, a care order, a hospital order, or a guardianship order.

So where a juvenile commits a criminal offence, he may (and should whenever practicable) be made the subject of care proceedings, or he may be prosecuted before the juvenile court in the ordinary way. In the latter case the power to order the detention of young persons is restricted to cases where it is necessary for the protection of the public.

(d) *Administrative functions*

Apart from the foregoing, magistrates also perform administrative, or quasi-judicial, functions. The best known of these is liquor licensing which probably found its way into the hands of the magistrates because of the close connection between drunkenness and breaches of the peace.

(2) County courts

County courts are concerned exclusively with civil work and their jurisdiction is entirely statutory. Set up in 1846 to replace with a uniform system an uneven provision of local courts, their purpose was to provide a cheap process for minor civil claims. They are sometimes regarded as courts for the recovery of small debts but this is an entirely misleading index of their importance. Their jurisdiction extends to claims up to £5,000 in most actions and includes undefended divorce actions, and for every proceeding commenced in the High Court at least three are commenced in the county court.

In the work of the court the circuit judge is assisted by a registrar (solicitor of seven years standing) who, apart from attending to the administration of the court, has jurisdiction to hear actions involving claims not exceeding £500. Even so the cost of pursuing small claims can be disproportionately expensive and in some parts of the country voluntary arbitration schemes have been introduced to provide even cheaper redress. Under this scheme as it operates in Manchester, for example, consumer claims (*i.e.* claims arising from consumer transactions such as the purchase of a washing machine) up to £500 can be entertained. Both parties must agree to the procedure and an arbitrator (who receives a nominal fee and is usually a solicitor) decides the dispute after considering the cases presented by the parties who are bound by the arbitrator's award. Such schemes are cheap to the litigant but they are subsidised both by the local authority and by the arbitrators who provide their services at nominal rates. A similar arbitration scheme has now been introduced within the county courts whereby the registrar may refer cases involving less than £200 to an arbitrator even if (unless the case involves an allegation of fraud) one of the parties objects.

(3) The High Court

The High Court was established by the Judicature Acts 1873–75 to overcome with a single court the problems caused by separate courts with differing procedures, and in particular the separate administration of equity and law. All judges of the High Court accordingly have the same jurisdiction and the same powers. For administrative reasons, however, and to take account of the nature of the work and the expertise of the judges, the Court is made up of various divisions which are now the Chancery, Family, and Queen's Bench divisions. But note that administrative changes do not affect the authority of decisions; for example, the authority of *Felthouse* v. *Bindley* (discussed in Chapter 1) is unaffected by the fact that it was decided by a court, the Court of Common Pleas, which in name has long since ceased to exist.

(a) *Chancery division*

This division deals with those matters (such as the administration of estates, trusts, mortgages, actions for specific performance and injunctions) which were formerly dealt with by the Court of Chancery together with certain other business (such as revenue and company matters) which have been assigned to it.

(b) *Family division*

The business of this division extends to all defended matrimonial causes, to proceedings concerning wardship, adoption and guardianship of minors, and to the settlement of property disputes between spouses.

Since the magistrates' courts and county courts also have jurisdiction in family matters, matrimonial business is shared by three courts and this, it has been argued, leads to an unevenness in the handling of matrimonial causes. Proposals have therefore been made for a unified family court which would not only standardise the legal approach but which would also integrate the social services involved in domestic matters. These proposals enjoy wide support but the cost involved has ruled them out of serious practical consideration.

(c) *Queen's Bench division*

The business of this division extends to all civil matters (mainly actions in contract and tort) not falling within the purview of the other divisions. Within the division there is a court, designated the Commercial Court, to deal specifically with commercial matters; and a court, designated the Admiralty Court, dealing with shipping matters. Obviously judges are assigned to these courts who have a special expertise in commercial or admiralty law just as judges are assigned to the divisions of the High Court itself.

(d) *Appellate jurisdiction of the High Court*

Although the principal appellate courts are the Court of Appeal and the House of Lords, the High Court also has an important, if limited, appellate jurisdiction. All three divisions may constitute courts, somewhat confusingly called Divisional Courts, where the quorum (*i.e.* number of judges required to be present) is usually two puisne judges but, for some minor matters, may be constituted by a single judge. Thus, for example, the Chancery Divisional Court hears appeals from the county courts in bankruptcy matters; the Family Divisional Court hears appeals from the magistrates' courts in matrimonial matters; and the Queen's Bench Divisional Court hears appeals from certain tribunals.

The Queen's Bench Divisional Court also exercises an important supervisory jurisdiction. The Court may issue orders of mandamus (*e.g.* to require a person to carry out a public duty imposed by law), certiorari (*e.g.* requiring an inferior court to transfer a cause to the High Court for speedy trial), prohibition (*e.g.* requiring an inferior court to desist from hearing an action in which it has no jurisdiction), and habeas corpus (*e.g.* requiring someone who holds another in custody to show cause that the imprisonment is lawful). Another very important aspect of this supervisory jurisdiction is where on a case stated (which is explained *post*, p. 46) the Court advises magistrates' courts on issues of criminal law.

(4) The Crown Court

The Crown Court was established by the Courts Act 1971 to replace the former courts of assize and quarter sessions whose jurisdiction was essentially local, with a single court (though of course it sits in many different places) having jurisdiction throughout England and Wales. When the Court sits in the City of London it is known as the Central Criminal Court (popularly, the Old Bailey) and while the titles of Recorder of London and Common Serjeant are retained the persons holding such offices are Circuit judges. The jurisdiction is mainly, though not entirely, criminal; it has exclusive jurisdiction over trials on indictment, hears appeals from magistrates' courts and deals with committals for sentence.

The jurisdiction and powers of the Crown Court may be exercised by any High Court judge, any Circuit judge or recorder; or any of the former sitting with justices of the peace. Where there is an appeal to the Crown Court from a decision of the magistrates or a committal for sentence by them, at least two and not more than four justices *must* sit with the judge or recorder; in such cases the justices have an equal say in the decision but in the event of the court being equally divided the judge or recorder has a casting vote.

Cases coming before the Crown Court vary enormously in seriousness and complexity. Offences are accordingly classified from those (Class I offences such as treason and murder) which are reserved for trial by High Court judges to those (Class IV offences which include all offences triable either way) which are listed for trial by a Circuit judge, and there are intermediate offences (Classes II and III) where provision is made for a degree of interchangeability. Court centres are also ranked according to volume of business from first tier centres which provide for all Crown Court business together with High Court civil work to fourth tier centres which provide only for offences triable either way. The responsibility for the administration of the new legal system lies in each circuit (of which there are six) with the circuit administrator.

(5) The Court of Appeal

Another effect of the rationalisation of the courts system introduced by the Judicature Acts 1873–75 was the replacement of the Court of Appeal in Chancery and the Court of Exchequer Chamber by a single Court of Appeal to deal with civil appeals. There was not at this time a similar court for the hearing of appeals in criminal cases (though judges could reserve points of criminal law for consideration by the Court for Crown Cases Reserved) and it was not until the Criminal Appeal Act 1907 established the Court of Criminal Appeal that a general right of appeal was accorded in criminal cases. The Court of Criminal Appeal functioned as a separate court until it was abolished by the Criminal Appeal Act 1966 and its jurisdiction transferred to the Court of Appeal. There is now a single court with civil and criminal divisions.

The *ex officio* membership of the Court of Appeal comprises the Lord Chancellor, former Lord Chancellors, Lords of Appeal in Ordinary, the Lord Chief Justice, the Master of the Rolls and the President of the Family Division but of these only the Lord Chief Justice and the Master of the Rolls, who preside in their respective divisions, sit regularly. Lords Justice of Appeal are ordinary members of the Court. The Lord Chancellor may request any ex-Lord Justice or ex-High Court judge to sit in the Court and may require any High Court judge to do so.

Certain minor matters apart, three judges are required to make a quorum. Where a case is considered to be one of great importance it is not uncommon for the Court to be composed of five judges; such courts are referred to as full courts but a full court has no more authority and power than a court of three members.

(a) *The civil division*

A court in the civil division will normally consist of either the Master of the Rolls sitting with two Lords Justices, or three Lords Justices. The jurisdiction of the court extends to all appeals from the High Court, appeals from the county courts in common law and equity matters, and appeals from many tribunals.

(b) *The criminal division*

The Lord Chief Justice, after consultation with the Master of the Rolls, may require judges of the Queen's Bench Division to sit as judges in the criminal division; in practice he regularly does so and a court in the criminal division is normally comprised of the Lord Chief Justice sitting with two puisne judges, or a Lord Justice of Appeal sitting with two puisne judges. The reason for this is the day-to-day familiarity which the judges of the Queens's Bench have with criminal cases; they can provide a particular expertise perhaps especially in relation to sentencing. The jurisdiction of the court almost entirely concerns appeals following trial on indictment in the Crown Court.

(6) The House of Lords

By the Appellate Jurisdiction Act 1876 an appeal may not be determined by the House of Lords unless at least three (in practice it is normally five) of the following are present: the Lord Chancellor, the Lords of Appeal in Ordinary, and peers who have held high judicial office (*e.g.* ex-Lord Chancellors). Strictly, all members of the House may vote on an appeal but by convention do not do so.

The House of Lords has both original and appellate jurisdiction. The original jurisdiction, not of much practical importance, extends to contested claims to peerages, and, in theory, it is still open for the Commons to impeach any person before the Lords. The appellate jurisdiction extends in civil cases to appeals from the Court of Appeal and (by what is known as the "leapfrog" appeal described *post*, p. 50) from the High Court; and in criminal matters from the Court of Appeal and the Divisional Court of the Queen's Bench Division. The House of Lords is also the final court of appeal for Northern Ireland and, except for criminal matters, for Scotland.

(7) The Privy Council

The composition of the Judicial Committee is similar to that of the House of Lords when hearing appeals, and as in the House five members usually sit though the quorum is three. The bulk of its work is done by the Lords of Appeal in Ordinary and the Lord Chancellor frequently sits, but it is not uncommon for a member of the Privy Council who holds a designated judicial office in specified Commonwealth countries to sit as a member of the court.

The Judicial Committee has jurisdiction to hear appeals from British Colonies and Protectorates and from independent Commonwealth countries though the latter have increasingly availed themselves of their right to exclude appeals to the Privy Council. Its jurisdiction also extends to appeals from the Admiralty Court of the Queen's Bench Division in prize cases (which concern the ownership of vessels captured during hostilities), certain appeals from ecclesiastical courts, and certain appeals from the disciplinary committee of the General Medical Council.

(8) Tribunals, inquiries and administrative law

Administrative law has been defined (de Smith, *Constitutional and Administrative Law*, 4th ed., p. 521) as concerning—

> "the day-to-day adminsitration of the country at central and local level and putting into practice constitutionally decided policies. Administrative law regulates that process. It relates to the organisation, composition, functions and procedures of public authorities and special statutory tribunals, their impact on the citizen and the legal liabilities and restraints to which they are subject. It controls the making of subordinate legislation by public authorities."

It will be appreciated, therefore, that any comprehensive treatment of the subject would be of enormous dimensions so that what follows here is only the barest outline.

We might begin by supposing that the Government has decided to build an additional airport to serve London. Legislation will be required to empower the appropriate Minister to decide on the best site, to authorise him to acquire land compulsorily, to authorise him to engage contractors and so on. These are not matters which can be decided by the courts for they involve issues of policy entirely unsuitable for resolution by judges. No doubt the residents of north London would prefer the airport to be sited in south London while those in the south would prefer it to be the north, but their differences of view could not be satisfactorily resolved by a court.

On the other hand, members of the public will demand a forum where their views can be aired, where they can argue about the suitability of particular sites, about the effect of the environment, even about the consequences for wild life. People whose property is compulsorily purchased will want a forum where they can challenge the Minister's decision or his assessment of the value of their property. The contractors need to be assured that, in the event of a dispute with the Minister, their complaints will be impartially determined. In theory the Government might by legislation empower the Minister to site the airport without regard to the interests of the public and to acquire land compulsorily without compensation. But in practice this is unthinkable. Most likely the legislation would provide for public inquiries as to the siting of the airport where, although the final decision would remain with the Minister, this would be after individual or collective representations of members of the public have been heard. The legislation would also likely provide that disputes as to the valuation of compulsorily acquired property would be settled by the Lands Tribunal while contractual claims could be left to be settled in the ordinary way by the courts.

Thus the critical decision—the location of the airport with all its social, economic and environmental consequences—is an administrative one. Important decisions relating to compensation are made by a tribunal rather than a court because it is felt that a specialist tribunal is better equipped for this task than a court. It would be possible to set up a specialist tribunal to deal with contractual claims but these can be left to resolution in the courts which are well able to deal with them.

The pattern may be repeated at local governmental level where the local authority must make decisions about new roads or new housing developments. Or a local authority may be concerned with the licensing of taxi-cab operators; on the face of it a purely administrative matter but it can be appreciated that the grant or withholding of a licence can vitally affect the livelihood of particular people.

The Government may also decide that certain matters are best adjudicated by a specialist tribunal rather than by the ordinary courts. In fact Governments have increasingly resorted to tribunals, especially in relation to the administration of the welfare state, as a means, not only of providing specialist expertise, but also in the interests of cost-effectiveness and expedition. So great has been the proliferation of such tribunals that the man in the street is much more likely to have some dispute resolved by a tribunal than by a court.

Tribunals are not all of the same pattern. At the one extreme is the high-powered tribunal of inquiry (such as the inquiry conducted by the Lord Chief Justice into the events of "Bloody Sunday" in Northern Ireland in 1972, or the inquiry conducted by Lord Scarman into the Brixton riots of 1981) where the judge has power to subpoena (*i.e.* compel the attendance of) witnesses and require the production of documents. At the other extreme a householder may be seeking planning permission for a garage or a porch. Some tribunals may be set up to deal with a particular issue, some may be established on a permanent basis; some may have an exclusively legally qualified membership, some may have lay membership. It may be helpful to consider the composition and jurisdiction of just three such tribunals though it must not be thought that all tribunals follow the pattern shown by these.

(a) *Criminal Injuries Compensation Board*

It will be appreciated that where X is deliberately injured by Y, X is usually entitled to claim compensation from Y; such a claim may be brought, depending upon the amount claimed, either in the county court or in the High Court. Whether it is worth X bringing such a claim will depend on the means of Y and Y may be of such limited means (a "man of straw") that X's right to compensation is worthless, or it may be that X's assailant is never identified.

To deal with this sort of problem a scheme—the Criminal Injuries Compensation Scheme—was introduced in 1964 under which victims of crimes of violence who have suffered personal injuries may claim compensation from public funds. A person so injured may apply to the Board (all of whose members are legally qualified) for compensation and this application is in the first instance considered by one member who normally makes his decision solely on the basis of the papers submitted to him and without seeing the applicant. Some 90 per cent. of claims are settled in this way, but if an applicant is dissatisfied with the decision of the single member the case is referred to a panel of three members which then conducts a hearing at which the applicant and witnesses are heard and examined. From the decision of this panel there is no appeal but an applicant may apply to the High Court for an order of *certiorari* to quash the decision of the Board where it is alleged to be wrong in law.

Arguably there ought to be an appeal against decisions of the Board on questions of fact or of mixed fact and law. Arguably the scheme ought to be better publicised because many who could claim fail to do so out of ignorance of its existence. But what is clear is that the Board itself carries out a desirable policy in an exemplary way. Whatever criticism may be levelled against it, it performs its business in a cheap and expeditious manner. Nearly all its cases are settled by a single member to the satisfaction of, and at virtually no cost to, the applicant. The pluses of the scheme far outweigh the minuses.

(b) *Industrial tribunals*

No one of sense needs to be reminded of the cardinal importance of maintaining good industrial relations and the consequent importance of ensuring that employees are treated with fairness and dignity. What the lawmakers have to do is to ensure a fair balance between the interests of the employer and those of the employee. While there can be no question of paramountcy for either, it would be right to say that successive Governments in this century have sought to redress in favour of the employee a balance which formerly very much favoured the employer. In recent years there has been legislation aimed at protecting the employee against discrimination, against unfair dismissal, and against the consequences of redundancy. It would, of course, have been possible for this law to have been administered by the courts but instead the task has been assigned to tribunals. Tribunals have the advantages of informality, low costs and expedition not matched by the courts. Moreover, such tribunals may be staffed by members having a particular knowledge of, and expertise in, the area of law which they administer.

Hence industrial tribunals were established in 1964 at first with a limited, but now a growing, jurisdiction. The tribunal is constituted by three members, a legally qualified chairman with two lay members who are appointed after consultation with organisations of employers and employees but in no sense do the persons appointed represent these organisations. The lay members have an equal voice with the chairman and decisions are by majority.

Appeal lies to the Employment Appeal Tribunal (E.A.T.) which is composed of a High Court judge sitting with two lay members. The lay members are again appointed after consultation with organisations of employers and employees but once appointed they are independent members and decisions are by majority. Appeal lies on questions of law under a variety of enactments and, in some cases, on questions of fact or law. It appears that appeals are made against the decisions of industrial tribunals in about 4 per cent. of the cases heard; it is also worth noting that only exceptionally are the decisions of the E.A.T. not unanimous, and that on occasion the judicial member has found himself in the minority.

Other than on a question of fact appeal lies from the E.A.T. to the Court of Appeal and from thence to the House of Lords.

(c) *Social welfare tribunals*

The growth of the welfare state, especially since the end of the Second World War, has necessarily required a vast bureaucracy in order to administer it. Successive Governments have created rights to family allowances, child benefits, disablement allowances, unemployment benefits, supplementary benefits, industrial injuries compensation, and many other rights besides. In some cases the amount involved can be significant, but the fact that in most cases the amount claimed is modest does not mean that it is less than important to the claimant.

Social security is administered by the Department of Health and Social Security (D.H.S.S.) and in the first instance claims are handled by officials, the insurance officers, of the D.H.S.S. Inevitably, however, disputes will arise between the citizens and the state concerning entitlement to, or the amount of, benefit. To deal with these a variety of procedures has been adopted.

Most usually, however, a claimant who is dissatisfied with a ruling by an insurance officer may appeal to a local national insurance tribunal. The tribunal is an entirely independent body with a legally qualified chairman appointed by the Secretary of State for the D.H.S.S. and two lay members, one drawn from a panel consisting of employed earners and one from a panel consisting of employers and others. In general a claimant may appeal as of right and at the hearing the claimant, the insurance officer, interested parties and the Secretary are entitled to be heard. While the proceedings are informal, parties may produce evidence and examine witnesses in the ordinary way. The proceedings are not, however, conducted as a contest but as an inquiry, hence the members of the tribunal may play an active role in the presentation and conduct of the case.

A further appeal by either the claimant or the insurance officer on an issue of law or fact lies to a Social Security Commissioner except that where the tribunal is unanimous either its chairman or a Commissioner must give leave. The Commissioners must be barristers of ten years standing and are appointed by the Crown on the advice of the Lord Chancellor. Their decisions are final except to the extent that their decisions and those of the local tribunals may be subject to judicial review (*post*, p. 41).

Unlike Industrial Tribunals which are concerned with claims between private individuals, this system deals with claims made by the citizen against the state. It is interesting to note that the total amount of benefit now disbursed amounts to some £10,000 million, that some 20 million claims are made each year of which some 30,000 are taken by way of appeal to local tribunals while a further 2,000 are taken by way of appeal to the Commissioners.

Appeals against decisions relating to supplementary benefit are heard in a similar way by the Supplementary Benefit Appeal Tribunal. The majority of the chairmen of these tribunals are not lawyers. A further appeal lies against their decisions to the Social

Security Commissioner but only on a point of law and with his leave.

(d) *The supervision of administrative action and tribunals*

As we have seen, administrative action is essential if the airports, the roads, the hospitals, the schools and a thousand things besides which are necessary to the functioning of modern society are to be provided within a reasonable timescale. But decisions about these matters may vitally affect the interest of any of us. We are all in favour of roads and hospitals until our private interests are affected. While roads and hospitals cannot be built without adversely affecting someone's interests, we need a system which ensures a measure of fairness for all. Similarly with tribunals. We can see the need for specialist tribunals, with their advantage of expertise, expedition and informality, but we need to be assured that their decisions, like those of the courts, are subject to correction by appeal. In fact many tribunals are substantially indistinguishable from courts. Decisions of Industrial Tribunals, as has been shown, are subject to review by the Employment Appeal Tribunal from which appeal lies to the Court of Appeal and the House of Lords. But we have also seen that in the case of the Criminal Injuries Compensation Board there is no such constituted system of appeal while the system for social welfare has a two-tier system of appeals within its own administrative framework. These instances show that tribunals have not been created in pursuance of a master plan but in response to the expanding needs of a complex society. Not surprisingly, the solution adopted for one sort of problem may differ markedly from that adopted for another. The acid test is whether tribunals "work."

To ensure that they do, and independently of judicial control which will be examined below, the Tribunals and Inquiries Act 1958 set up a Council on Tribunals whose function it is to keep under review the constitution and workings of specified tribunals. The Council, which consists of up to 15 members appointed by the Lord Chancellor, works part-time and has no power directly to interfere with the decisions or the workings of tribunals. Nevertheless, the reviews which it conducts and the reports which it produces have proved invaluable in securing what are considered to be the essentials of administrative justice, namely, openness, fairness and impartiality. There is in this country a deep commitment to these ideals, even if they can be only imperfectly defined, and a government ignores an informed opinion only at its peril.

Nor have the courts been prepared to play a spectator's role. They have of course recognised the need for administrative action and where legislation confers upon a particular person or body the power to make policy decisions, no court would assume to substitute its own view. But the courts will intervene on various grounds, the process being known as judicial review, which is largely accomplished by the use of prerogative orders (*ante*, p. 33). Strictly judicial review does not operate to overturn the administrative decision itself but to question the procedure by which that decision has been reached. The distinction can be a fine one. Consider *Secretary of State for Education and Science* v. *Metropolitan Borough of Tameside* (1976). In 1975 a local education authority (at this time Labour controlled) submitted proposals to the Secretary for introducing a system of comprehensive education which would have given admission to schools without reference to ability and which would have resulted in the abolition of five grammar schools. The Secretary approved these proposals but before implementation a local election resulted in control of the education authority passing to the Conservatives. They decided to modify these proposals by retaining the grammar schools but their proposals to the Secretary were rejected by him on the grounds that the authority was acting unreasonably, and he required them to implement the original proposals. It was held by the House of Lords that even though the Secretary might legitimately take the view that the subsequent proposals were misguided and wrong, there were no grounds on which he could find them to be unreasonable because, given the expected willingness of the teachers to co-operate with the revised plan, there was nothing to suggest that it could not operate satisfactorily. Strictly this decision was given on procedural grounds but its effect was substantive because the Secretary had no other objections to allege and the new proposals were accordingly implemented.

In this case it was held that the Minister had acted *ultra vires* (outside the powers). It will be appreciated that an authority given by statute to do one thing may carry with it powers to do that which is implicit in carrying out that authority, but that it cannot carry powers to do something else. To take an obvious, if far-fetched example, a Minister who was by legislation authorised to build an additional airport for London would be restrained from using these powers to build a motorway between Leeds and Manchester. A good example is provided by *Bromley L.B.C.* v. *Greater London Council* (1982). The G.L.C. was by statute under a duty to provide "integrated, efficient and economic transport facilities" for London and was empowered to perform its function with due regard to "efficiency, economy and safety of operation." The G.L.C., having decided that it was in the best interests of the service to reduce fares, did so by 25 per cent. This increased the operating deficit and in order to balance the books the G.L.C. issued a supplementary rate demand to all London boroughs. This demand was successfully challenged by Bromley L.B.C., the House of Lords holding that although the G.L.C. had a wide discretion in the management of transport services it was nevertheless obliged to run them on ordinary business principles. The G.L.C. thus acted *ultra vires* in reducing fares by an arbitrary amount without regard to the ordinary business principle that the service should pay for itself by self-generated income.

Another ground for judicial intervention is where a person or body has powers which require him or it to act "judicially." In such a case the courts will intervene to quash a decision reached without regard for the rules of natural justice which, at the very least, require that the parties be given a fair hearing. An example is provided by *R.* v. *Hull Prison Board* (1979). Following riots at Hull Prison, disciplinary proceedings were instituted before the Board of Visitors which resulted in the prisoners being punished by way of losing remission on their sentences. The prisoners moved to quash the proceedings, alleging that the Board was in breach of natural justice in that it refused to allow them to call and cross-examine witnesses. Notwithstanding that these proceedings were of an internal disciplinary character and that the applicants were at the time incarcerated, the Board was exercising a judicial function and was bound to observe the rules of natural justice. "The courts," said Shaw L.J. "are in general the ultimate custodians of the rights and liberties of the subject whatever his status and however attenuated those rights and liberties may be as the result of some punitive or other process."

This observation by Shaw L.J. may be said to typify the modern judicial attitude to administrative action. Where standards of "fairness" have not been observed the courts have shown an increasing willingness to intervene, even where the relevant legislation has purported to exclude review by the courts. In *Anisminic* v. *The Foreign Compensation Commission* (1969) Lord Reid said that if a statute provided that a certain order could be made by a person holding specified qualifications and further provided that such an order could not be questioned in a court of law, an order which was alleged to be a forgery or to have been made by a person not possessing the specified qualifications would nonetheless be open to review by the courts. Thus in the *Anisminic* case itself a statutory provision saying "The determination by the Commission of any application made to them under this Act shall not be called in question in any court of law" did not prevent the House of Lords from reviewing the Commission's declaration when it appeared that in making the determination the Commission had taken into account a factor which it had no right to take into account. "Determination" meant a real determination properly arrived at and did not extend to a purported determination which had been arrived at improperly.

(e) *Conclusions*

In this brief review we have seen that administrative action is necessary and that while decisions on matters of national and local policy are rightly not matters for courts to determine, the courts are ever ready to intervene where private rights are affected to ensure that the procedures followed are essentially fair. Even where Parliament purports to oust the jurisdiction of the courts, the courts show an increasing willingness (even ingenuity) to review decisions arrived at by procedures which do not comply with the essential standards of fairness which the courts would require of their own procedures.

Where administrative tribunals are constituted on a regular basis (such as industrial tribunals) there is an increasing tendency to provide for appeal to the courts so that intervention by judicial review becomes much less important. Such tribunals have the advantages of informality, cheapness and expedition but it may be that they lack certain qualities which are available in the courts. One commentator, Professor Harry Street, has likened the courts to a Rolls-Royce system of justice while tribunals provide the Mini; the Mini is not as good a car as the Rolls but more people can afford it.

(f) *The Parliamentary Commissioner for Administration* (*Ombudsman*)

English courts and tribunals do not provide a remedy for all wrongs and every grievance. There are of course extra-legal avenues for airing grievances (*e.g.* letters to the Press, programmes on television and radio, complaints to local councillors or Members of Parliament) which not infrequently lead to a remedy, and these extra-legal avenues should not be discounted. Nevertheless they have their limitations, perhaps especially so when the citizen is dealing with the powerful bureaucracy of the State. For the citizen there may be no redress in the courts and extra-legal procedures may have failed to penetrate the secrecy with which bureaucrats, almost by instinct it seems, shroud their actions from public scrutiny. To meet this sort of case the Parliamentary Commissioner Act 1967 established the office of Parliamentary Commissioner for Administration (popularly called the Ombudsman following the innovation of the office in Denmark) to investigate complaints by citizens who claim to have suffered injustice as a result of "maladministration" at the hands of Government Departments.

The P.C.A. is appointed by the Crown on the advice of the Prime Minister and holds office until 65. There are no professional qualifications for the office; while the present holder is a lawyer, the office has also been held by ex-civil servants whose familiarity with administration may be both an advantage and a disadvantage. The P.C.A. cannot act of his own initiative, nor directly on a complaint by a member of the public; he can act only on a written complaint made on behalf of the complainant by a Member of Parliament. Thereafter the P.C.A. conducts his inquiry in private but he has the necessary powers to penetrate official secretiveness. He has no powers to alter decisions nor to compel redress of any maladministration he finds to be proved and is confined merely to publishing a report of his findings.

The results have not been spectacular and have led to the accusation that the P.C.A. is an Ombudsmouse. On the other hand, and given that our civil servants, though wedded to secrecy, do prize integrity and efficiency, it is not surprising that maladministration is more frequently found not proved than proved, and that when proved rarely establishes alarming shortcomings. What is more surprising is that his findings have sometimes been hotly contested by the Minister on behalf of the Department to which they apply, and the *ex gratia* payment which he has recommended only grudgingly given. In the end, though, the P.C.A. has provided a means of redress where other avenues have been closed. He has, for example, persuaded the Inland Revenue (a frequent subject of complaint) to modify or forgo tax demands which, though legal, are oppressive or would cause hardship; and in the Sachsenhausen Case (1967) he found maladministration on the part of the Foreign Office in dealing with claims for compensation by former prisoners-of-war.

In 1974 the Local Government Act established a Commission for Local Administration in England which provides for Local Ombudsmen to consider complaints about maladministration in local authorities in much the same way as the P.C.A. does with central government. The local Commissioners cannot directly handle complaints which must be ordinarily referred to them by a local councillor on behalf of the complainant. Like the P.C.A. they cannot directly interfere with decisions but are confined to making reports which are concerned not with the merits of particular decisions but the way in which they are arrived at. Most complaints relate to planning and housing matters and only a minority of complaints result in a finding of maladministration. As with central government so in local government the report and recommendations of the Local Commissioners are not always greeted with unqualified acceptance by the local authority. In such a case Local Commissioners may issue a second report which, especially if given Press coverage, will be even more persuasive. In the end, though, the Local Commissioners cannot enforce their recommendations on a local authority which is prepared to dig in its heels. This is, however, the exception and normally local authorities comply with the recommendations of the Local Commissioners.

7. The Courts: Appeals

(1) Criminal cases

As we have seen a person charged with crime may be tried summarily in a magistrates' court or be tried on indictment in the Crown Court and the system of appeals differs accordingly.

(a) *Appeal following summary conviction*

A person convicted in a magistrates' court (*e.g.* of careless driving, shoplifting, assault) may appeal to the Crown Court as of right (i) against any sentence imposed if he pleaded guilty; and (ii) against conviction and/or sentence if he pleaded not guilty. In the Crown Court the appeal will normally be heard by a circuit judge sitting with two to four magistrates (other, of course, than magistrates concerned in the trial) and each member has an equal vote except that if the court is equally divided the circuit judge has a second or casting vote.

The appeal is by way of re-hearing. In effect it is a re-trial with the prosecution and the defence calling witnesses and adducing evidence even though not called or adduced at the trial. The Crown Court may if it decides to convict, impose any sentence which the magistrates' court *might* have imposed on that charge so that the defendant may have imposed on him a sentence more severe than that imposed by the magistrates.

(b) *Appeal by way of case stated*

Quite independently of the foregoing right of appeal to the Crown Court, it is additionally open to the defendant *or to the prosecutor* to request the magistrates' court or the Crown Court to state a case for the opinion of the Divisional Court of the Queen's Bench Division on the grounds that the decision is wrong in point of law or is in excess of jurisdiction. It is necessary for the stated case to identify the point of law so it is necessary for the magistrates or the Crown Court to provide a statement of the facts which is agreed to by the parties. Typically a stated case involves a case where the facts are not in dispute but the issue is whether those facts disclose an offence. For example, in *Fagan* (1969) it was common ground that the defendant had while parking his car inadvertently driven on to a police officer's foot but, having been told by the officer of this, he deliberately left his car there for a few moments before switching on his engine and releasing the officer. These facts raised a nice question of law as to whether the defendant had assaulted the officer (see *post*, p. 152) and hence a case was stated to resolve the legal issue.

On a case stated a further appeal is possible from the Divisional Court to the House of Lords provided that the Divisional Court (i) certifies that a point of law of public importance is involved; and (ii) that either the Divisional Court or the House of Lords gives leave to appeal (see *post*, p. 49). Thus a case which is tried in a magistrates' court may end in the House of Lords and may involve three, or even four if it goes to the Crown Court, separate hearings. But such cases are highly exceptional. In practice appeals from the decision of magistrates (both to the Crown Court, or by way of case stated) are taken in less than 0·5 per cent. of cases. This may seem a surprising statistic but it has to be remembered that the vast majority charged before magistrates plead guilty; and of those others who may feel aggrieved by a verdict of guilty, many would rather avoid the possible expense, publicity and embarrassment which may be involved in an appeal.

(c) *Appeal following conviction on indictment*

A person so convicted may appeal to the Court of Appeal (i) as of right on a point of law alone; and (ii) with leave of the Court of Appeal on a question of fact alone or of mixed law and fact. Unless the sentence is one fixed by law (*e.g.* the mandatory life sentence on conviction for murder) the defendant may, with leave, appeal against sentence. On such an appeal, the Court of Appeal cannot impose a more severe sentence than that imposed by the Crown Court though, as we have seen, the Crown Court on an appeal from a magistrates' court can impose a sentence more severe than that imposed by the magistrates.

A person convicted on indictment may apply to the Home Secretary to have his case referred to the Court of Appeal, and the Home Secretary may so refer a case without any application. In practice such references are made in cases which continue to excite public disquiet long after the trial has taken place; the Home Secretary may refer a case notwithstanding that there has already been an unsuccessful appeal or notwithstanding that the defendant has since died.

The Court of Appeal may allow an appeal against conviction if the conviction is unsafe or unsatisfactory (*e.g.* where the verdict cannot be supported by the proved facts); if there is a wrong decision on a question of law (*e.g.* a misdirection on the burden of proof); or a material irregularity in the trial (*e.g.* improper disclosure of the defendant's previous convictions). An appeal against sentence will be allowed only where the sentence is wrong in principle or manifestly severe; the Court will not interfere merely because it might have passed a different sentence.

Though the Court of Appeal finds there are grounds for allowing an appeal, it may dismiss the appeal if it is satisfied that no miscarriage of justice has occurred. To apply this provision—something which the Court finds difficult—it has to be satisfied that notwithstanding the error at the trial, no reasonable jury would have failed to convict the defendant. An example is provided by *Whybrow* (1951) (*post*, p. 214) where, notwithstanding the trial judge's misdirection on the mental element required on a charge of attempted murder, the Court upheld the conviction because, on the evidence in the case, there could be no doubt but that Whybrow intended to kill.

(d) *Appeal following an acquittal*

In general the prosecutor cannot appeal against the acquittal of the defendant even though the weight of evidence in the case clearly points to the defendant's guilt. One exception to this we have already noted; while the prosecutor cannot appeal to the Crown Court against the acquittal of the defendant by the magistrates, he may ask the magistrates (or the Crown Court following an appeal by the defendant) to state a case for the Queen's Bench Divisional Court. A further exception, though of a limited nature, was introduced by the Criminal Justice Act 1972. Notwithstanding an acquittal in a trial on indictment, the Attorney-General may now refer any point of law which has arisen in the case for the opinion of the Court of Appeal. The purpose of this power is to enable the Court of Appeal to review a potentially false ruling before it gains too wide a circulation in trial courts. Strictly it is not an appeal because though the defendant may be represented thereat, he is not identified and his acquittal remains unaffected even if the point of law is decided against him.

Curiously, there is one case where the defendant may appeal against his own acquittal. This occurs when the defendant has been found not guilty by reason of insanity. This verdict, though one of acquittal, involves indefinite detention in a secure hospital so it is not really so curious that the defendant may seek to avoid this effect of his acquittal. Somewhat similarly, the defendant may appeal against a verdict that he is unfit to plead. Such a verdict denies the defendant a trial and again involves indefinite detention in a secure hospital; it is accordingly thought right that he should be allowed to appeal against such a verdict though it involves no decision about his guilt.

(e) *Appeal to the House of Lords*

An appeal lies either from the Court of Appeal or from the Queen's Bench Divisional Court to the House of Lords. Such an appeal lies only where (i) either the Court of Appeal or the Divisional Court have certified that a point of law of general public importance is involved; *and* (ii) either of those courts or the House of Lords gives leave to appeal. There can be no appeal against a refusal to certify a point of law under (i) but in the event that a point is certified while leave to appeal is refused (which may be done where the Court of Appeal or the Divisional Court is confident of the correctness of its decision) a party may ask the Appeals Committee of the House of Lords for leave to appeal.

In a sense all points of criminal law, since they involve the liberty of the subject, are of public importance but the point must be one of *general* public importance and in practice less than 10 cases a year reach the House of Lords. In dealing with an appeal the House has powers substantially similar to those of the Court of Appeal.

(2) Civil cases

Depending on the nature of the subject matter and the amount involved, civil actions may be commenced in the magistrates' courts, the county courts or the High Court.

(a) *Actions commenced in magistrates' courts*

As we have seen (*ante*, p. 29) magistrates' courts have limited, but significant, civil jurisdiction, particularly in relation to domestic proceedings. In general appeal lies to the High Court (and it is also possible for the magistrates to state a case under the procedure outlined at p. 46, *ante*) and in domestic matters appeals are usually determined by a Divisional Court of the Family Division. From the High Court appeal lies, with leave, to the Court of Appeal and the House of Lords. In some minor civil matters and in affiliation proceedings, appeal lies to the Crown Court.

(b) *Actions commenced in the county courts*

While the general rule is that an appeal lies to the Court of Appeal on matters of law and fact, there are important exceptions where leave (either of the county court or the Court of Appeal) is required; for example, where the sum claimed is less than half the jurisdictional limit (*i.e.* less than £2,500 in most cases). The Court of Appeal considers the case on the basis of the notes made by the trial judge or other sufficient evidence of the proceedings, and it may affirm, vary, or reverse the judgment of the County Court. Appeal lies from the Court of Appeal to the House of Lords with leave of either court.

(c) *Actions commenced in the High Court*

In general appeal lies as of right to the Court of Appeal. Nearly all actions in the High Court are tried by a judge (*i.e.* the judge finds the facts as well as determining all issues of law) but some civil cases (though now less than 1 per cent. of cases in the High Court) are tried by judge and jury where issues of fact are the province of the jury. The Court of Appeal is very reluctant to disturb a jury verdict and will do so only where there is no evidence which can reasonably support their verdict, or where an award of damages is obviously excessive. The Court of Appeal is less unwilling to intervene where the trial is by judge alone; since the trial judge has the advantage of observing the demeanour of witnesses giving their evidence, the Court of Appeal will hardly ever question his findings about their veracity and reliability as witnesses but is much more willing to differ from the trial judge on the inferences to be drawn from primary facts.

(d) *Appeal to the House of Lords*

Appeal lies from the Court of Appeal to the House of Lords with the leave of either court. While the appeal may concern matters of fact or law, appeals to the House of Lords are nearly always concerned with important issues of law.

In certain circumstances it is possible to appeal to the House of Lords direct from the High Court, thus avoiding the additional expense of a hearing in the Court of Appeal. This procedure (colloquially known as the leap-frog appeal) was introduced by the Administration of Justice Act 1969 and enables a judge to grant a certificate for leave to appeal to the House of Lords if a point of law of general public importance is involved which relates to the construction of any statute or is one in respect of which the judge is bound by a previous decision of the Court of Appeal or the House of Lords. All the parties must consent to the grant of the certificate and the House of Lords must give leave to appeal. The use of this procedure is exceptional; typically it is used in revenue cases where a particular decision has taxation implications of general application.

In dealing with appeals, the powers of the House of Lords are similar to those of the Court of Appeal.

Chapter 3

SOURCES OF LAW AND THE DOCTRINE OF PRECEDENT

Anyone might be forgiven for thinking that a book about law would begin with a definition, or at least a description, of what law is. This book began with an introduction to legal reasoning and then described the institutions and workings of the English legal system but has not so far attempted to define law. One reason for this may simply be tradition; this being the traditional way in which lawyers approach their subject. But another and more compelling reason is that lawyers find it extraordinarily hard to define what is law. They can tell you, as we saw in Chapter 1, how lawyers approach problems and they can tell you as we saw in Chapter 2, who administers the law and how it is administered. Nevertheless, they find it impossible even after hundreds of years of thought, to come up with a definition of law that all accept as authoritative. The question: "what is law?" still awaits an answer.

Hence most books of this kind examine the *sources* of law; they are more concerned with where the law is to be found than with what it is. Such books will describe, as the primary sources of law, legislation and precedents (*i.e.* the decisions of the courts) and, as secondary sources of law, such things as custom, textbooks, or even something as vague as the principles of right reason.

Suppose we begin with legislation, with Acts of Parliament. A moment's reflection tells us that an Act of Parliament is not a *source* of law: *it is law*. The decisions of the courts might be said to be rather different. It is not every word of a judgment, which may comprise many thousands of words, that is law. Ony such words as constitute the reason for the decision (the *ratio decidendi*) are law; the rest, though it is all part of the process of reasoning, is strictly surplusage (*obiter dicta*). So a judgment might be said to be a source of law because we search through it to find what legal proposition the case established, just as we looked through *Felthouse* v. *Bindley* (*ante*, p. 5) to discover for what legal proposition it was an authority. We do not look through a statute to discover which parts of it are authority for a legal proposition because the whole of a statute is law. But a *ratio* (*i.e.* the legal proposition which is determined in a case) is no more a *source* of law than a provision in a statute; the source of both is the process by which we identify these as rules of law.

It may be helpful to compare statutes and cases with the writers of textbooks. Some writers on law (*e.g.* Coke, Hawkins, Lindley) have achieved such eminence that their opinions on law are frequently cited as authorities on law. But such opinions, however eminent the author, are persuasive only and are not themselves law; they become law only when adopted by a judge as the reason for his decision in a case. Though the judge who adopts the opinion of the writer may never aspire to the intellectual eminence of the writer, it is the judge, and not the writer, who declares the law of the land.

1. Legislation

Legislation, as we have seen (*ante*, p. 13), is the supreme law in that by legislation all law, including previous legislation, can be altered. Courts must give effect to the sovereign will of Parliament as expressed in its statutes. Judges may be critical of Acts of Parliament, they may even in their judgments suggest ways in which they might be improved, but it is not open to them to decline to apply them because they are thought to be unconscionable or to give them meanings which they cannot reasonably bear.

But no statute can escape the process of interpretation by the courts. We might take a very simple example. Under section 9 of the Theft Act 1968 burglary is defined as entering a "building" as a trespasser with various intents, most commonly the intent to steal (*post*, p. 294). The word "building," like most words in the English language, is capable of a number of meanings. Most people would not call a boat or a caravan a building and, realising this, Parliament specified in the Act that the reference to "building" should apply to an inhabited vehicle or vessel—the entry of a thief into your dwelling is no less serious because you happen to live in a boat or caravan. Otherwise Parliament did not attempt a comprehensive definition of "building" so it is for the courts to decide whether a person is guilty of burglary where he enters a telephone kiosk to steal the contents of the meter, or enters a park bandstand to steal a trombone, or on his hands and knees enters a battery shed in order to steal eggs. Parliament might have specifically provided for these cases just as it has specifically provided for inhabited vehicles and vessels. So Parliament might have resolved a possible problem of interpretation by including, or excluding, telephone kiosks and bandstands. But there are certain difficulties. One is that it is in practice impossible to anticipate all cases in which there might be an argument as to whether a particular structure is a building. The other is that if, say, telephone kiosks and bandstands were to be included in the definition, further definitional problems arise as to what is a telephone kiosk or what constitutes a bandstand.

Hence the process of interpretation is inevitable. And that process becomes more complicated with the complexity of the subject matter. It may be assumed that only occasionally will the definition of "building" trouble the courts for in 999 cases out of 1000 it will be as clear as can be that a particular structure is or is not a building. But other cases are less straightforward. Consider *London & North Eastern Railway Co.* v. *Berriman* (1946). Mrs. Berriman sued the L.N.E.R. Co., claiming damages for an alleged breach of statutory duty resulting in the death of her husband. By statute railway companies were bound to provide a look-out man whenever a railwayman was engaged on "repairing or relaying" the permanent way, but no look-out man had been provided for Berriman whose job it was to top-up the oil-boxes which lubricated the points in the line. In the result Berriman was killed by an approaching train of which he had no warning as he was attending to his work. In enacting this legislation, as must be clear, Parliament had it in mind to protect by the provision of a look-out man any railwayman whose work made it impossible always to be on the look-out for his own safety and thus "intended" to protect Berriman. But Mrs. Berriman lost her case; the House of Lords holding by a majority of three to two that while Berriman was engaged in *maintaining* the line, he was not engaged in *repairing* or *relaying*. Maintenance was not the same activity as repairing.

We might of course argue forever about *Berriman's Case*—the decision after all caused an acute difference of opinion among the judges. Some of us might take the view that "repair" is not the same function as "maintenance"; we do not say we have repaired a car because we have kept the oil topped-up. Some of us might say that Parliament really intended to protect the railwayman who could not look out for himself and thus an extended definition of "repairing" ought to have been taken. What must be clear, though, is that the judges in *Berriman's Case* were not taking sides in the sense of being in or out of sympathy with Mrs. Berriman but their function was to apply the law as they found it, *not* to guess at how Parliament would have provided for this situation had Parliament thought about it.

Thus it happens that sometimes (it must not be thought that this is a matter of daily occurrence) the courts give to a statute a meaning which it was never intended to bear by the legislature. This sometimes leads to the accusation that the courts are usurping the functions of Parliament or flouting the will of the people; an accusation which was made, for example, following the decision of the Court of Appeal and the House of Lords disallowing the subsidising of transport fares by the G.L.C. *Bromley L.B.C.* v. *Greater*

London Council (1982). It would be idle to pretend that in such cases the courts are always "right" and their critics always "wrong." What is clear is that, even among lawyers, legitimate differences of opinion may exist as to whether a telephone kiosk is a building for the purpose of the law of burglary, whether maintenance is embraced by repairing, or to what extent a statute permits the subsidising of fares at the expense of the ratepayer.

It might help in the resolution of such problems if the courts could look at the debates in Parliament to determine what was really intended by the words used, or even call Ministers responsible for the legislation to explain what they really wanted to achieve. Such an approach has its attractions but it also has its dangers and the courts are generally opposed to admitting such extrinsic evidence in the interpretation of statutes. "In determining the meaning of any words or phrase in a statute," said Lord Reid in *Pinner* v. *Everett* (1969), "the first question to ask always is what is the natural and ordinary meaning of that word or phrase in its context in the statute." This—the so-called literal rule—is the starting point of all judicial interpretation though its application does not mean that all judges end with the same view.

Even so the application of the literal rule does not result in frequent conflict between Parliament and the courts. Language is not so imprecise, and the art of draftmanship so amateur, that experienced craftsmen (Parliamentary Counsel) cannot ensure that in most cases the words say what they mean. But with the increasing complexity of subject-matter (taxation provides the most extreme example) it is impossible for draftsmen to ensure that the words used always mean what they were intended to mean. In this matter it must not be thought that the courts are completely unhelpful, that they will hold to the literal meaning however absurd the result. In *Pinner* v. *Everett* (1969) Lord Reid went on to say, "It is ony when that [*i.e.* the literal] meaning leads to some result which cannot reasonably be supposed to have been the intention of the legislature that it is possible to look for some other possible meaning of the word or phrase."

At first sight this may seem a somewhat grudging exception to the literal rule but it is hallowed by lawyers as the "golden" rule. A good illustration is provided by *Allen* (1872). Allen had been indicted for bigamy under section 57 of the Offences against the Person Act 1861 which provides that "whosoever being married shall marry again" during the lifetime of the former spouse shall be guilty of bigamy. It was proved that Allen had married W1 and had then "married" W2 while W1 was still alive but Allen took the point that he could not "marry again" W2 because such a marriage was necessarily invalid since it was bigamous and thus he had not "married" again! Had Allen's literal view of the statute been taken, it would have meant that no one could ever be convicted of bigamy; the court held that such an interpretation made an absurdity of the statute and that the words "shall marry again" must be read to mean "shall go through a ceremony of marriage" even though that ceremony could not produce a valid marriage. Another example is provided by *Adler* v. *George* (1964). George had entered on a prohibited place where he obstructed a member of H.M. Forces. He was charged under section 3 of the Official Secrets Act 1920 which provides that no person shall "in the vicinity of" a prohibited place obstruct any member of H.M. Forces. His argument that he was not "in the vicinity of" a prohibited place because he was *in* the prohibited place was rejected; the court held that the expression must be read to mean "*in or* in the vicinity of" because it would be absurd to suppose that Parliament intended to proscribe such conduct outside but not inside the prohibited place.

But it must not be thought that the so-called golden rule is used by the courts to resolve ambiguities and doubts in favour of the meaning intended by Parliament, however the intention is to be determined. The rule is used only exceptionally and only where the application of the literal rule would render the statute virtually nugatory. That the intention of Parliament is largely defeated, that Parliament will be put to the trouble of passing amending legislation are not in themselves sufficient reasons for applying the golden rule. Take *Fisher* v. *Bell* (1961) for instance. Following a number of incidents in which flick-knives had been used to cause injuries, Parliament decided to proscribe them. In the Restriction of Offensive Weapons Act 1959 it was made an offence to "sell or offer for sale" any flick-knife. The defendant had flick-knives in his shop-window and he was charged with offering these for sale. It was held that "offers for sale" must be given its ordinary contractual meaning (see *post*, p. 319) and that his was not an offer for sale but a mere invitation to treat so it followed that the defendant had committed no offence. Nothing could be clearer than that Parliament intended to proscribe the defendant's conduct but the wrong words had been used to proscribe it. Parliament was thus put to the trouble of passing amending legislation in 1961. It is, therefore, a nice question of judgment wether a result is so absurd that it cannot reasonably be supposed to have been the intention of the legislature.

In *Pinner* v. *Everett* (1969) Lord Reid spoke of interpreting words or phrases in their context in the statute. It is obviously important to have regard to the context of the statute as a whole. Consequently it was held by the House of Lords in *Beswick* v. *Beswick* (1967) that sections in the Law of Property Act 1925 which literally might have entitled a stranger to *any* contract to enforce its provisions must be confined to contracts affecting real property. No word or phrase can be read in a vacuum. It must at least be read in the context of the statute as a whole, and the statute itself must be read in the context of its time—in its contemporary historical and social setting. This received expression in the sixteenth century when in *Heydon's Case* (1584) the judges decided that it was proper to look beyond the four corners of the Act itself. They said it was permissible to consider: (i) what was the common law before the Act; (ii) what was the defect for which the common law did not provide a remedy; (iii) what remedy Parliament had resolved on to cure the defect; and (iv) what was the true reason for the remedy.

This has come to be known as the "mischief" rule and its precise status is open to doubt. On a conservative view (and this must be the least for which the rule allows) a judge is entitled to have regard to the history of the statute. All events, including Acts of Parliament, have a context, historical, social and political; and the judge, unless he abjures books, newspapers, radio and television, can hardly be unaware of, and can hardly be uninfluenced by, this context. Judges do not try to work against Parliament and society but with them and the framework of their law is fashioned by their experience. At the other extreme the mischief rule might accord to the judge the prerogative of carrying out Parliament's intention however imperfectly this might have been expressed in the words used—an idea that was expressed in *Heydon's Case* itself.

In the latter sense the mischief rule has been rarely used. Not surprisingly it was used in this sense by Lord Denning when in *Magor & St. Mellons* v. *Newport Corporation* (1950) he said that it was the function of courts to find out the intention of Parliament and Ministers and that this was best done by filling in the gaps and making sense of legislation than by opening it up to destructive analysis. But in this same case Lord Denning was taken to task by the House of Lords (1951) where his approach was described as a "naked usurpation of the legislative function under the thin guise of interpretation."

The mischief rule, then, cannot be used to carry out the *spirit* of the law when the *letter* of the law cannot reasonably bear the meaning which will carry out its spirit. Judges apply the law but do not make it; and though the line between the two can be a fine one, it is a line which must be observed.

Thus the mischief rule was not used in *Fisher* v. *Bell* (*ante*, p. 56) though it must have been clear that the court's interpretation of "offers for sale" rendered the enforcement of the statute almost impossible. Placing flick-knives in a shop window was clearly within the "mischief" which Parliament intended to proscribe but the words used failed to express this. On the other hand the mischief rule was used in *Smith* v. *Hughes* (1960) when a prostitute maintained that she was not soliciting "in a street or public place" contrary to the Street Offences Act 1959 when, sitting in her own house, she solicited men through the window. She herself was not *in* the street when the soliciting took place but Lord Parker C.J. said regard should be had to the mischief at which the Act was aimed. The purpose of the Act was to enable people to walk the streets without being solicited and they were just as much solicited though the source of the solicitation came from private premises.

The so-called literal, golden and mischief rules must not be thought of as separate approaches to statutory interpretation as though conservative judges held to the letter while liberal judges adopted the spirit. All judges approach statutes in the same way; they seek to declare the law as it was intended to be declared but they are inevitably, and rightly, constrained by the words used and by the context in which they are used. They can do a good deal with words in order to give them their intended effect (and perhaps some judges are more "flexible" in this respect than others) but they cannot stand words on their head. They can, and indeed must, take account of the internal context of the statute (the title, preamble, headings, punctuation, etc., may all provide valuable internal aids) and they must take account too of the ordinary rules of the English language.

But at the end of the day the interpretation of statutes cannot be reduced to a set of scientific principles the automatic application of which would lead all judges to the same conclusion. Some years ago the Law Commission examined the interpretation of statutes (Law Comm. Working Paper No. 14 (1967)) and had "little hesitation in suggesting this is a field not suitable for codification." This was not to say that the present position was beyond improvement. The Law Commission found that there was "a tendency to an undue degree of literalism" and, among other cases, cited *London & North Eastern Railway* v. *Berriman* (*ante*, p. 54) as an example of this. To remedy this, the Commission proposed a more liberal use of internal aids, and of external aids such as the reports of official bodies leading to the legislation and explanatory material accompanying the bill during its passage through Parliament. The Commission also canvassed the advantages and disadvantages of allowing references to Parliamentary debates but made no firm recommendation on this matter.

2. Case Law

There is no positive provision of English Law which requires a judge to give reasons for his decision; it would suffice for the judge merely to conclude that he finds the plaintiff's case not proved, or that he finds it proved and assesses the damages at a specified sum. Nowadays judges always give reasons for their decisions though they may be very shortly stated (the early volumes of the Criminal Appeal Reports abound with cases where the judgment is expressed in two or three lines) or may be stated at great length (the judgment in *Tito* v. *Waddell* (*No. 2*) (1977) extends to nearly 200 pages and is prefaced by a table of contents).

Usually a judgment contains: (a) a statement of facts; (b) a review of the authorities applicable to those facts; and (c) the reason which is given for the decision (*ratio decidendi*) in the case. Some judges may even insert headings in their judgment which can be of considerable assistance to the reader, especially the student, in digesting the case. A very good example is provided by the judgment of Lord Denning in *Broome* v. *Cassell & Co. Ltd.* (1971) a libel action arising from the German attack on the British convoy PQ17 taking supplies to Russia in 1942. Lord Denning's judgment (though it did not escape severe criticism in the House of Lords) sets out the facts with dramatic force, identifies and examines the issues with great clarity, and ends with a conclusion identifying the *ratio* of the judgment.

It is of the first importance to indentify the *ratio* in a case for while a court may be bound to follow the *ratio* of a previous decision, it is not bound to follow other propositions of law asserted in that decision (*obiter dicta*) which do not form part of the reason for the decision. Sometimes it is an easy matter to find the *ratio*, as where in a single judgment the court shortly and clearly disposes of the point at issue. But the fact that there is a single judgment does not mean that the determination of the *ratio* is necessarily straightforward. Take the case of *Smith* (1960) which was concerned with the mental element required on a charge of murder and in which a single judgment was given by the House of Lords. There was acute controversy as to what was the *ratio* of this case; so much so that in *Hyam* v. *D.P.P.* (1974) Lord Hailsham L.C., having admitted that *Smith* had given rise to a "series of wholly irreconcilable interpretations" declined to overrule it because "it is difficult to know exactly what one is overruling."

Where more than one judgment is given in a case each judgment may give a different ratio; one judge may reach the same conclusion as another but for quite different reasons. Consider *Hyam* v. *D.P.P.* (*ante*, and see *post*, p. 225) which, like *Smith*, was concerned with the mental element required on a charge of murder. The trial judge had directed the jury that Mrs. Hyam could be convicted of murder not only if she intended to kill or cause serious bodily harm to the deceased but also if she had foreseen that death or grievous bodily harm was "highly probable." In the House of Lords, where Mrs. Hyam's conviction for murder was affirmed by a majority of three to two, the affirming judges gave different reasons for their decision. Viscount Dilhorne contented himself with approving the direction of the trial judge that foresight of high probability sufficed. Lord Cross went further; he thought that "highly" should be deleted from "highly improbable" so that foresight of a probability was enough. Lord Hailsham L.C., thought that the criterion of "high probability" was too vague for juries to apply; he thought that the test should be whether the accused intended to create a "serious risk" of death or serious bodily harm. It is not entirely clear what Lord Hailsham meant by this; arguably any risk of death is a serious risk even if it does not amount to a probability.

The problem of determining the *ratio* of Hyam fell to the Lord Chief Justice of Northern Ireland in *McFeely* (1977). McFeely was involved in a typical terrorist incident. A package was placed in a bar and the customers warned that it contained a bomb; the customers vacated the bar and the police were called and it was when a police officer was examining the parcel that he was killed as the bomb exploded. The Lord Chief Justice was satisfied (there is no trial by jury for such cases in Northern Ireland) that McFeely knew the bomb was to be planted and that a warning would be given. In such circumstances people usually clear the building so that *usually* no one is killed. Turning to *Hyam* the Lord Chief Justice considered that case to establish that death or serious bodily harm must be foreseen by the accused as *probable* before he could be convicted of murder; since McFeely did not foresee death as a probable result, but only a possible result, he could not be convicted of murder.

In considering the various propositions of law advanced in *Hyam*, the Lord Chief Justice sought to deduce a proposition which was *common* to all three judgments and he concluded that all three were agreed that the trial judge had been too restrictive in requiring high probability and that probability sufficed.

Those who have attempted to formulate a test for determining the *ratio* of a case are generally agreed that the ratio must be a proposition of law which is *necessary* to the decision reached. One writer (Professor Goodhart) rightly reminds us that the first step must be to determine the facts treated by the judge as *material*, for his judgment relates only to the material facts. But determining what facts are material can be difficult. While judges normally include in their judgments a statement of the facts, only by a consideration of the judgment, as a whole is it possible to determine which facts the judge considered material. In the great case of *Donoghue* v. *Stevenson* (1932) the plaintiff suffered gastro-enteritis when, having consumed half the contents of an opaque bottle of ginger-beer purchased by a friend, she discovered a decomposed snail in the remaining half. It was held by the House of Lords that even where there is no contractual relationship between a manufacturer and a consumer, the manufacturer owes a duty to the consumer to take reasonable care that his product will not injure the consumer when that product is sold in such a form that there is no reasonable possibility of intermediate examination by the consumer (see *post*, p. 481). Here we can see that while the opacity of the bottle was a material fact, for it was this that denied the plaintiff the opportunity to inspect the contents before consumption, it was not material that the product was ginger-beer for the case must have been decided in the same way had the contents been whisky or water. Nor was it a material fact that the product was sold in a bottle, nor that it was a food. The material facts were simply that a manufactured article had been used by a person whom the manufacturers could reasonably foresee would use it, that the consumer could not reasonably be expected to spot its defects and had suffered damage as a result of its use.

Donoghue v. *Stevenson* is entitled to be called a "great" case because its mundane facts resulted in the declaration of a principle capable of being applied to a vast field of commerical activity. But extensive though the principle is, it may fairly be asked whether it extends beyond manufactured *chattels*. Does it, for example, extend to houses which because of negligence in building cause harm to someone not in a contractual relationship with the builder? Does it extend to negligent statements which cause someone, again not in contractual relationship with the maker, to suffer economic loss? In fact the courts have made the negligent makers of both houses and statements liable for resulting loss but this has been by analogy with the *Donoghue* v. *Stevenson* principle, not because the *ratio* of that case necessarily *requires* that result.

Courts may use *material* differences of fact to distinguish a decision which could otherwise bind them. As we have seen, *Donoghue* v. *Stevenson* could not be distinguished on the grounds that the product was whisky or water but it could fairly be distinguished on the grounds that it is applicable only to manufactured chattels. Another example may be taken from the law of contract. Ordinarily an acceptance of an offer must be communicated to the offeror before a contract comes into existence but in the nineteenth century the courts modified this rule in connection with acceptances *by post* which were held to create a contract from the time of posting even though the posted acceptance might be delayed or even never reach the offeror (see *post*, p. 325). In *Entores Ltd.* v. *Miles Far East Corporation* (1955) the court had to decide whether the postal acceptance rule applied where a Telex machine was used. The postal rule for acceptance was held inapplicable because when the Telex is used communication is virtually instantaneous; it was thus to be likened to the case where the parties were in direct oral communication and was thus distinguishable from cases applying the postal rules of acceptance. This view was confirmed by the House of Lords in *Brinkibon Ltd.* v. *Stahag Stahl* ((1982) *post*, p. 326).

This discussion will have served to show that the determination of the *ratio* of a particular case may often prove a difficult task. Yet the process of determining the *ratio* is one in which lawyers (including law students) are *constantly* involved. No two cases are ever exactly alike and the lawyer's art is to determine whether the cases are sufficiently alike so that the principle for which the one is authority applies to the other, or whether the cases are sufficiently unalike so that a different solution may be sought.

3. Custom

In the judicial oath a judge promises to do right according to the "laws and usages of this realm." Usage, or custom, was of cardinal importance in the formation of the common law. Mediaeval judges did not, as it were, pluck laws from the air; they had regard to what was the actual practice of people and the extent to which these practices were regarded as obligatory. But once a custom received judicial recognition by incorporation as the *ratio* of a decision, lawyers thereafter looked to that case as the relevant authority, not to the antecedent custom. Over the course of centuries customs were, in effect, made the subject of a take-over bid by the courts so that custom has ceased to be a creative source of law.

On the other hand it is still possible to rely on a local, as opposed to a general custom even though it constitutes a derogation from the common law. Such customs must meet stringent tests. They must have existed since time immemorial (strictly 1189 but in practice such period as the memory of man does not run to the contrary), they must be reasonable and certain, they must be regarded as obligatory, and they must not be against any statutory provision. Thus an alleged custom that at a particular place a pound of butter should weigh 18 ounces was rejected because statute had provided that a pound should weigh 16 ounces everywhere. And in a nineteenth century case the courts rejected a parson's claim to a customary right to a fee of 13 shillings on the celebration of a marriage because 13 shillings would have been wholly exorbitant fee in the Middle Ages. But courts have accepted rights based on custom to use common land for the playing of sports, to dry fishing nets on private property, and to establish rights of way.

4. Textbooks

When a lawyer needs to inform himself on some aspect of law he will usually turn in the first place, not to the statutes and cases themselves, but to a textbook where the law will be set out in a convenient and accessible form. The work may be a monograph or a multi-volume encyclopedia and its authority will turn upon the reputation its author or editor has acquired for it. When lawyers consult such works they know that they do not contain the law but contain the *opinions* of their authors, based upon their interpretation of the relevant statutes and cases, as to what the law is believed to be. The persuasiveness of such opinions varies according to the standing of their authors but such opinions can become law only by virtue of their adoption by a court as part of the *ratio* of a decision. Judges vary in the attention and deference they pay to textbook writers, but the citation of such "sources" of law before courts is now a commonplace and reference to them in judgments is far from uncommon.

5. The Operation of the Doctrine of Precedent

Since so much of our daily lives is regulated by law it is obvious that law must usually be certain and predictable. The man in the street does not as a matter of course see his daily routine as being regulated by law but this is in fact the case. So soon as he takes his car on the road a whole host of laws govern his activity, and by the average day's end he has concluded not less than a dozen contracts all of which have legal obligations for himself and the other party. The man in the street usually only consciously adverts to law when things go wrong; when, for example, he is involved in a collision with another motorist or when the goods he buys do not measure up to the standards he expects of them. When such unfortunate events occur it would be intolerable if the invariable advice of his lawyer was that he would have to have his dispute tried by a judge and that there was no means of predicting what the outcome might be.

In practice the law achieves such a high degree of certainty that only a small proportion of disputes ever go to trial, and most of these concern the facts rather than the law. Given a particular set of facts, a lawyer can usually, having regard to the authorities, state with confidence what the legal outcome will be. Hence the broad justification for the system of precedent whereby lower courts are bound to follow the decisions of higher courts and whereby like cases must be decided alike. This doctrine of *stare decisis* (keep to what has been decided) is fundamental to our legal system. Of course our system does not achieve complete certainty of result and can probably never do so; we are light years away from a legal system that has an obvious answer to every legal problem that can possibly present itself.

(1) The House of Lords

Decisions of the House of Lords bind all lower courts. In *London Street Tramways* v. *L.C.C.* (1898) the House went further and stated that the House of Lords itself was bound by its own previous decisions. Even if the earlier decision was now thought to be wrong it would be followed. At this time the House put the highest value on certainty and predictability of result and said it was for Parliament to remedy any erroneous decision by legislation.

There are, however, certain exceptions. First (strictly not an exception) the House of Lords is bound not to follow a previous decision which cannot stand with subsequent legislation. Second, the House is not bound to follow a decision given *per incuriam* (through carelessness), that is where that decision was made in ignorance of a relevant statutory provision or of a relevant prior decision of the House of Lords. In fact no clear instance of either form of carelessness has yet arisen. Third, where "public policy" is an element in a decision (as it is in connection with contracts in restraint of trade, *post*, p. 419) a decision with reference to the public policy of one age does not bind the House when considering the public policy of a later age.

The attitude to precedent expressed in *London Street Tramways* v. *L.C.C.* governed the practice of the House of Lords for nearly seventy years but in 1966 the House issued a statement ([1966] 3 All E.R. 77) saying that while the House acknowledged the importance of certainty in the law and would *normally* follow its own previous decisions, it would depart from a previous decision "when it appears right to do so."

What this statement immediately reveals is that rules concerning the operation of precedent are rules of *practice* and not rules of law; the House of Lords changed from the practice adopted in *London Street Tramways* v. *L.C.C.* and is free to make further changes in its practice. What has become clear since is that the House will overrule previous decisions only exceptionally (there have been only three clear instances so far). It is not enough that the earlier decision was reached only by a narrow majority, that the House might now have taken a different view (especially where the earlier decision relates to a matter of statutory interpretation), or even that the decision is considered wrong. Before the House will overrule itself there must be some very good reason, such as that the earlier decision is productive of clear injustice or that it seriously hampers the development of the law. Nevertheless the introduction of the new practice has been generally welcomed; Parliament cannot always respond rapidly to remedying what are now seen as bad decisions and it is as well that the House should be able to put matters to rights when there is a clear and pressing need to do so.

When a prior case is overruled, whether by the House of Lords or by some other court, it should be noted that the effect of the overruling is not to change the law but to state what the law has always been. Suppose, for example, that the case of *A* v. *B* in 1900 decided that a certain form of words would create a certain kind of interest,, say a life estate in land. If in *C* v. *D* in 1982 the decision in *A* v. *B* is overruled the effect is that the *A* v. *B* form of words was *never* effective to create that interest, not that it is ineffective from 1982. The effect of overrulling *A* v. *B* is thus retrospective. Now it may be that between 1900 and 1982 many lawyers, relying on the correctness of *A* v. *B*, have used that form of words to create a life interest. Because of this effect of overruling their Lordships said in their statement in 1966 that they would bear in mind the danger of disturbing retrospectively the basis on which contracts, settlements of property and fiscal arrangements had been entered into. One advantage of legislative change as opposed to judicial overruling is that the law can be changed *prospectively* thus avoiding any retrospective effect.

One last point in connection with the House of Lords is the extent to which inferior courts are entitled to avail themselves of the exception available to the House and not to follow its decisions. May the Court of Appeal or a High Court judge decline to follow a decision of the House because: (i) it has been overruled by statute; (ii) it was given *per incuriam*; (iii) that public policy has changed; or (iv) the case is one where the House might overrule a previous decision of its own? It is clear that in (i) an inferior court must prefer the subsequent legislation to the earlier decision, and it is equally clear that in (iv) it would not be open to an inferior court, in effect, to second-guess the House of Lords. So far as (ii) is concerned the House of Lords has decided (*Broome* v. *Cassell* (1972)) that it is for it to determine whether one if its decisions was given *per incuriam* and the Court of Appeal 1971 was forthrightly admonished for declining to follow a decision of the House (in *Rookes* v. *Barnard* (1964) where, in the view of the Court of Appeal, that decision was given *per incuriam*.

In *Broome* v. *Cassell, Rookes* v. *Barnard* was said to have been decided *per incuriam* because the House had failed to consider certain previous *decisions*; a different view might have been taken if the ground for the decision being *per incuriam* had been that a statutory provision had been overlooked. As to (iii) there appears to be no binding authority but it would seem that lower courts must judge "public policy" in its contemporary context and would be free not to follow decisions of the House of Lords reached in a social or economic context that is no longer apropos.

(2) The Court of Appeal (Civil Division)

The decisions of the Court of Appeal bind all inferior courts, including Divisional Courts. As has been seen, the Court of Appeal is bound, subject to certain limited exceptions, to follow decisions of the House of Lords. What is still not entirely settled is how far the Court of Appeal is bound by its own decisions.

The starting point is provided by *Young* v. *Bristol Aeroplane Co.* (1944). Here the Court of Appeal decided that it was bound by its own decisions and that for this purpose a "full" court (there were five members in the instant case) had no greater powers than any division of the court properly constituted (normally three). The court then went on to spell out three exceptions.

The first is that where there are two conflicting decisions of the Court of Appeal, the court is entitled to choose between them, thus impliedly overruling the one not followed. Apparently the Court of Appeal does not consider itself bound to prefer the earlier decision on the ground that the latter is *per incuriam* and this introduces an element of uncertainty in that a lawyer cannot advise his client which of the two decisions will be preferred.

The second is that the Court of Appeal is bound *not* to follow a previous decision of its own which cannot stand with, even if not expressly overruled by, a *subsequent* decision of the House of Lords. Where it is alleged that a Court of Appeal decision (*C* v. *D*) cannot stand with an earlier decision (*A* v. *B*) of the House of Lords, the Court of Appeal should follow *C* v. *D* at least if *A* v. *B* was considered by the Court of Appeal in *C* v. *D*. If *A* v. *B* was not considered in *C* v. *D* it may be that the case would be considered under the third exception.

The third exception is where a decision of the Court of Appeal was given *per incuriam*. In *Young* the court gave the example of a decision reached in ignorance of a statutory provision but it would presumably also extend to the example just given where the prior

House of Lords decision in *A* v. *B* was not considered by the Court of Appeal in *C* v. *D*.

This was the position in the Court of Appeal until Lord Denning assumed office as Master of the Rolls. During his tenure (1962–82) he frequently expressed his dislike for the principle of *Young's* case and took the view that the Court of Appeal should be free, as the House of Lords had made itself free, to overrule prior decisions which were now seen to be wrong.

Viewed as a matter of principle it can be appreciated that there are arguments either way. If the Court of Appeal is so free it adds to the uncertainty and makes it that much more difficult for the lawyer to predict the outcome of litigation. Moreover the Court of Appeal while following its own decision can always indicate where it believes a decision to be erroneous, thus leaving it to the House of Lords to deliver the coup de grâce to the bad decision. But this ignores the fact that relatively few cases go to the House of Lords (it has been said that only the very poor and the very rich can afford to take a case there) so that if the Court of Appeal cannot overrule a decision thought to be wrong that decision may remain authoritative for many years.

Matters came to a head in *Davis* v. *Johnson* (1979) where in a full court of five members, three expressed the view that earlier decisions could be overruled while two held to the principle of *Young's* case. Of the three, Lord Denning M.R. thought that an earlier decision could always be overruled if it was thought to be wrong but the other two judges expressed the power more narrowly. Shaw L.J. thought the power should be exercised only in cases involving an element of "emergency"; he was prepared to exercise it in the instant case because the subject matter (Domestic Violence and Matrimonial Proceedings Act 1976) concerned the exclusion from the domestic premises of a partner who was doing physical violence to the other. On the other hand, said Shaw L.J., the public interest would suffer no mortal blow if, say, a decision on a financial or commercial matter was allowed to stand even if thought to be wrong.

The House of Lords while approving the decision in *Davis* v. *Johnson* on the merits, was unanimously and strongly of the view that the Court of Appeal should adhere to its previous decisions subject only to the limited exceptions given in *Young's* case. But in the Court of Appeal, Lord Denning, no doubt anticipating just this view, had said that since rules relating to the operation of the doctrine of precedent were rules of *practice* only, nothing said by the House of Lords could stop the Court of Appeal from adopting its own rules of practice.

And there the matter rests for the time being. While there can be little doubt but that Lord Denning would have continued unrepentant in his views, his retirement may mark a return to more orthodox views with the consequent re-adoption of *Young's* case.

(3) The Court of Appeal (Criminal Division)

In their statement in 1966 the House of Lords said that in adopting its new policy on precendent it would have regard to "the especial need for certainty as to the criminal law." This contrasts oddly with the practice of the Criminal Division of the Court of Appeal (following the practice of its predecessor the Court of Criminal Appeal) which has adopted a more flexible policy than that adopted in *Young's* case. Thus in *Gould* (1968) Diplock L.J. said that if the court was satisfied that the law had been misunderstood or misapplied in an earlier decision, the court was entitled to depart from it even if it could not be brought within any of the exceptions in *Young's* case. In this regard a decision of a full court of five members has no more power than any properly constituted division of the court; in *Gould* a court of three members overruled a decision given by a court of five members.

(4) Divisional Courts

Divisional Courts of the High Court exercise appellate jurisdiction in both civil and criminal matters. In the exercise of civil jurisdiction it is accepted that a Divisional Court is bound by its own previous decisions subject to the exceptions in *Young's* case: *Huddersfield Police Authority* v. *Watson* (1947). It is similarly accepted (*Younghusband* v. *Luftig* (1949)) that a Divisional Court is bound by its own decisions in criminal cases subject to the *Young* exceptions. In relation to criminal cases it has never expressly claimed the more flexible policy which has been adopted by the Criminal Division of the Court of Appeal, but nor has it expressly disclaimed that policy.

A Divisional Court is of course bound by decisions of the House of Lords. In the exercise of civil jurisdiction it is bound by decisions of the Civil Division of the Court of Appeal, and in the exercise of criminal jurisdiction by the Criminal Division. In the (unlikely) event of conflicting decisions of the civil and criminal divisions of the Court of Appeal, a Divisional Court would presumably follow the decision of the Court of Appeal in which it was exercising jurisdiction.

(5) The High Court

While judges of the High Court are bound by the decisions of all superior courts, they are not bound by each other's decisions. Lord Goddard C.J. no doubt correctly stated the practice when in

Watson's case (above) he said that a judge of first instance would, unless he was convinced that the judgment of a fellow judge was wrong, follow it as a matter of comity. No doubt inferior judges (circuit judges and magistrates) would feel even more constrained to follow the judgments of High Court judges but there exists no direction that they are formally bound to do so.

Chapter 4

THE LEGAL SYSTEM IN OPERATION

From time to time all of us are involved in disputes which raise issues of law as well as of fact. Neighbours may dispute the boundary which separates their properties, a purchaser may allege that a washing-machine is faulty, a motorist may claim that his car has been damaged by the carelessness of another and so on. Such disputes involve issues of civil law but at least some of us will also come into contact with the criminal law which is much more likely to be in connection with our operation of a motor vehicle than with any other activity.

1. Civil Actions

So far as disputes concerning civil law are concerned, experience shows that only a very small fraction of these ever come before a court for resolution, and it can be confidently asserted that the vast majority are resolved without either party even seeking professional legal advice. Most disputes are settled without any overt reference to law, the parties reaching a settlement which strikes them as "fair"; the dispute concerning the faulty washing-machine will most likely be resolved though neither party has a working knowledge of the Sale of Goods Act 1979, or has even heard of its existence. The parties know that it is in their best interests to reach a speedy and acceptable settlement without recourse to lawyers and the courts because of the expense that will be incurred and, just as important, the time and worry involved. Even if the dispute is pressed to the point of taking legal advice, the solicitor will be of the same mind. He will always seek to obtain an acceptable settlement for his client long before he talks of issuing a writ.

(1) Costs

What it will cost to take a case to court depends upon such factors as its complexity, the time taken by the trial and the number and eminence of the lawyers involved. In a protracted libel action in the High Court the costs may run to tens of thousands of pounds while an undefended divorce in the county court may cost about £120, and much less than that if the petitioner can handle the matter himself without legal representation. Better guidance comes from a survey conducted by Professor Michael Zander (*Cases and Materials on the*

English Legal System (3rd ed.), p. 336). His survey, based on a sample of personal injuries actions contested in the High Court, showed that the average claimed costs was £1,027 and that in no less than 40 per cent. of the cases in the sample the claimed costs were more than the amount awarded for the injuries involved! Costs in the county court are much less but, where a party is represented, even the simplest case will leave little change from £100.

These figures relate to the costs incurred by one party. The other party, or parties, will incur similar costs and it has to be noted that an unsuccessful party (whether plaintiff or defendant) must usually pay the costs of the successful party; in general costs follow the event or, if you like, winner takes all.

Hence it is no light decision to take a dispute to court. If the amount claimed is less than, say, £100 (as it will be in the many disputes which involve defective goods) it can hardly be worth taking the matter to court at all unless, perhaps, use of the very cheap procedure mentioned above (p. 31) is available. On the other hand a claimant may be insured against costs. It is safe to assume that most, if not all, of the personal injuries cases used in Professor Zander's survey related to claims arising from motor vehicle accidents and that many of the parties were insured. Here the costs will be borne by the insurer and not the assured. Similarly a policy commonly taken out by householders may insure the householder in respect of costs and damages arising from a legal liability incurred in the use of the property. It is in fact possible to insure against a wide variety of legal liability; newspapers insure against liability for defamation, a policy exists for employers to insure against the consequences of their unfairly dismissing employees, and many professional people can insure against the consequences of their own professional negligence.

So there will be some cases where a party need have no financial worries about the consequences of litigation. We have also seen how a wide range of disputes are now handled by tribunals which are much less expensive than courts. An unrepresented claimant before a tribunal will usually incur no costs even if his claim is unsuccessful. In an industrial tribunal, for example, an order for costs will be made against a party only where the proceedings have been instituted frivolously, vexatiously or otherwise unreasonably. On the other hand, if a party to such proceedings does engage professional legal representation this will have to be paid for and legal aid is not usually available in respect of proceedings before tribunals.

Nonetheless, there remain many cases where the claimant faces the daunting expense of litigation. A client or a patient may allege that he has suffered damage as the result of the negligent advice of a solicitor or a doctor and this negligence is denied. Win or lose the professional man will normally be insured but loss to the claimant will mean that he must bear the costs and these might even prove ruinous.

(2) Legal aid and advice

For the person of poor means, litigation would prove to be impossible, and even before litigation is contemplated professional legal advice will be required. But there has long been a measure of assistance for poor persons and the matter is now regulated by the Legal Aid Acts 1974–1979 and Regulations made thereunder.

Legal advice is available under what is called the "green form scheme" up to a normal limit of £40, the legal aid committees having power to increase the amount in appropriate cases. This would ordinarily cover such services as writing letters or negotiating a settlement but also extends to non-contentious legal matters such as making a will. In order to qualify an applicant must: (a) have a disposable income of less than £93 per week, *or* be in receipt of supplementary benefit or family income supplement; *and* (b) his disposable capital (disposable income and capital is determined after making deductions for such things as income tax, rent, maintenance of dependants) does not exceed £655. Where an applicant's disposable income is below £44 a week the advice given is entirely free but where such income exceeds £44 a week an applicant is required to make a contribution to the costs according to a graduated scale. The figures given here are the current figures and they are subject to periodical review.

In relation to legal proceedings, legal aid is available in the county and higher courts and in respect of certain domestic proceedings in magistrates' courts but there are certain exceptions (*e.g.* defamation actions and undefended matrimonial causes). As with advice, there are financial limits and provisions governing the contribution to be made by the applicant. In order to qualify for aid the applicant's disposable income must not exceed £4,440 a year but such an applicant may be refused legal aid if his disposable capital exceeds £2,725 and it appears he could proceed without legal aid. There are further conditions, the most important of which is that the applicant must show to the local legal aid committee that he has reasonable grounds for bringing or defending or being a party to the proceedings.

Where a legally aided litigant is successful in an action against an unassisted party, costs awarded against the unassisted party are paid directly to the Legal Aid Fund and not to the assisted party.

Conversely, where the unassisted party is successful and an award of costs is made in his favour, those costs are normally recoverable from the Legal Aid Fund.

As we have seen, various deductions are made to arrive at an applicant's disposable income so that in practical terms a person may be entitled to legal aid (covering the whole or part of his costs) with a gross annual income of the order of £8,000. The scheme may not be described as generous but in prevailing economic conditions it is not niggardly. A more serious criticism is that it is largely confined to actions before the courts; there is a case for extending legal aid to at least some tribunals especially where (an obvious example is the Mental Health Review Tribunal) legal representation becomes especially crucial.

It is worth noting, as an index of the use and growth of legal aid in both civil and criminal cases, the levels of expenditure involved. Civil legal aid in 1970 cost the country £6·3 million and in 1983 is expected to reach £50 million. In 1974 the green form scheme cost £1·3 million and this is expected to reach £30 million by 1983. Legal aid in criminal cases, which cost £8 million in 1970, is by 1983 expected to top £100 million. Making every allowance for inflation these are very substantial real increases in expenditure and appear fully to support the Lord Chancellor's (Lord Hailsham) claim that during this period legal aid has been the fastest growing of the social services.

(3) Course of proceedings and trial

Whether a civil action is to be commenced in a county court or the High Court normally depends, as has been shown, on the amount involved. In this section what is described is the procedure governing actions in the High Court; it needs to be noted, however, that while the procedure governing county court actions is broadly comparable, there are some significant differences.

(a) *Proceedings before trial*

Civil procedure is governed by Rules of the Supreme Court, These, together with explanation and comment can be found in a publication called *The Supreme Court Practice* (the "White Book") and a notion of the size and complexity of the subject can be deduced from the fact that the White Book runs to some 3,500 pages. The comparable work for the county courts (the "Green Book") runs to nearly 2,000 pages. The description which follows here is accordingly only the barest outline.

The purpose of rules of procedure is to ensure that the case comes to court with the issue or issues clearly defined, with what is agreed or what is disputed clearly delineated so that the trial can be conducted as expeditiously and efficiently as possible. The proceedings between the issue of the writ and the commencement of the action are called *interlocutory proceedings*. Obviously difficulties and disputes will arise in connection with the rules of procedure themselves; guidance and rulings on these are given by officers called *Masters* in London and *District Registrars* elsewhere.

One thing that law students tend to forget is that clients in real life do not appear with their problem set out in the form of an examination question on contract. The client may not even know what remedy he wants let alone what branch of substantive law is involved. Assume, for instance that P (the plaintiff) tells his solicitor that he has suffered a substantial loss as a result, as P sees it, of D's (the defendant's) failure to deliver goods which were promised. From the facts given him by P, the solicitor will want to satisfy himself (if only provisionally at this stage) that P has a cause of action. He will thus consider whether there was a completed contract between P and D, whether there has been an actionable breach of that contract, and what remedies are available. He will also note when the cause of action arose because there are limitation periods (*i.e.* the period from the accrual of the cause of action within which the writ must be issued) which must be observed. These are now contained in the Limitation Act 1980 and the limitation period for an action based on simple contract is six years. It must not be assumed of course that the solicitor immediately thinks in terms of litigation. If a relevant limitation period has almost run its course when the solicitor is apprised of the cause, he may issue a writ to prevent the action being barred. Otherwise he will normally think of an out-of-court settlement. To this end he may conduct negotiations with D, or with D's solicitors, on a "without prejudice" basis. This means that the negotiations are conducted without prejudice to any possible litigation, and what is said or written in such negotiations cannot be used as evidence in the litigation. On the other hand, if one of the parties alleges that the "without prejudice" negotiations have resulted in an agreement to settle the action, a court may look at the correspondence to determine whether such an agreement has been reached.

At this stage and throughout the proceedings the solicitor may well advise his client that although on paper they appear to have a good case, nothing is certain until final judgment and that if costs are awarded against him, he could be in a far worse position than he is as a result of the breach of contract. Of course, if legal aid is available these considerations may well be irrelevant. If the client is determined to press on, then his solicitor will have to determine who are likely to be parties to the proceedings. It is assumed here that only P and D are involved in the action; it will be appreciated that the joinder of further parties is in itself the subject of further law, much of it very complicated.

Actions in the High Court are commenced either by *writ* or by *originating summons* or *motion*, of which the first is the most common. Originating summons procedure is often convenient when the sole or principal question is likely to be one of construing an Act, or a deed, or is a pure question of law, or where there is unlikely to be any substantial dispute over facts. Any action may be commenced by writ and certain actions must be. To issue the writ the plaintiff takes two copies to the Central Office in London or a local district registry. One copy is signed by the plaintiff or his solicitor, sealed, stamped and filed at court. The second copy is sealed and returned to the plaintiff. For purposes of limitation periods the action is now commenced. The plaintiff must either include in the writ his statement of claim (see below) or a brief statement of the nature of the claim and the remedy sought.

Once the writ has been issued it remains valid for a period of 12 months and during this time it may be served on the defendant. There are various methods which would constitute satisfactory service but the most normal would be to ensure that a copy is placed in the hands of the defendant or the defendant's solicitors. Once the defendant has received his copy of the writ he has fourteen days within which to acknowledge service. If the defendant does not acknowledge service or indicates that he does not intend to fight the action then the plaintiff may proceed to obtain judgment in default of acknowledgment.

Assuming that the defendant intends to contest the action and that he has acknowledged service, the next stage is for the solicitors for both sides to get the action into a suitable form for trial. This is done through the *pleadings* and allied procedures. At this stage the plaintiff submits his *statement of claim* (if he has not already included this in his writ). The statement of claim is a formal document in which the plaintiff outlines the facts upon which his claim is based, together with the remedy he is seeking. Just as the plaintiff may proceed to obtain judgment if the defendant does not acknowledge service, so too the defendant may apply to have the plaintiff's action dismissed for want of prosecution if his statement of claim is not lodged within 14 days of the defendant's acknowledgment. Indeed these remedies are available to the parties at various stages of the proceedings as a penalty for undue delay. In practice the specified periods for the service of documents are often extended by mutual agreement where this suits the convenience of the parties.

Once the defendant has received the statement of claim, he must reply in a document known as the *defence*. The defendant must (except for damages alleged which are presumed to be denied) deny or refuse to admit all the allegations in the statement of claim which he intends to contest, otherwise he will be taken to have admitted them. The plaintiff may issue a *reply* to the defence but this is not normally necessary since he is presumed to deny any allegations in the defence. Even at this stage there may remain ambiguities and uncertainties in the allegations of the parties. In order to resolve these either party may apply to the other for further and better particulars. Since the aim of the pleadings is to clarify the issues it is important that each party should know, as precisely as possible, the case he has to meet.

Occasionally the defendant may include a *counterclaim* or *set-off* in his defence. A counterclaim is a cross action independent of the plaintiff's action, but which may conveniently be tried at the same time; here the plaintiff will be the defendant to the counterclaim and the counterclaim is then, in effect, governed by the same procedural requirements as govern the original claim. A set-off is confined to money claims, and is a claim by the defendant to set-off against the plaintiff's claim a sum of money owed by the plaintiff to the defendant and arising directly from the plaintiff's claim.

The defence (or sometimes the reply) is normally the last of the formal documents and at this stage the pleadings are said to close. At any stage either the writ or the pleadings may be amended. Sometimes this may be done without the court's leave if it is before the pleadings have closed, but otherwise, and whenever a substantial change is to be made, leave of the master will be required. It is possible that the pleadings do not give one side enough information upon which to answer the claims and in this event he may, through the agency of a master, be able to compel the other side to provide further and better particulars. Answers to such questions are then attached to and become part of the pleadings.

It is quite conceivable, especially in commercial cases, that much will depend upon the construction of various documents that have passed between the parties. Within fourteen days of the close of pleadings both sides must send to the other a list of documents he has which relate to the action. The rules provide that each side must indicate in one list those documents which he has in his possession and does not object to producing for inspection; a second list comprising those documents which he does object to producing and the reason for the objection (*e.g.* privileged document); and finally a list showing those documents which he no longer possesses. The master may make an order for *discovery of documents* if he feels that either side has not made a full disclosure or if he rejects the reason for objection to disclosure. A failure to make discovery may be punished by the master ordering the plaintiff's action to be dismissed or striking out the defendant's defence.

A further procedure which is available to enable the clarification of the issues with consequent savings in costs concerns *admissions* and *interrogatories*. Interrogatories are written questions which may be served by one party on the other with the leave of the master. They must be answered in a sworn document (affidavit). They are to enable the parties fairly to dispose of the issues or to save costs. The answers, for example, may enable the plaintiff to work out on what basis the action will be defended, and so enable him to concentrate on the contested issues. The answers do not form part of the pleadings, though they may be used at the trial. Either side can serve a notice to admit facts and this will enable the issue that has been admitted to be dropped from the trial and thus time and therefore expense will be saved.

Within one month of the close of the pleadings the plaintiff must take out a *summons for directions*. The idea behind this part of the proceedings is for the master to hold a sort of stocktaking of the case so far. It is to enable him to see that the pleadings have eliminated as many non-contentious issues as possible and that the remaining issues are ready for trial. It is the time at which such interlocutory proceedings as discovery should be ordered if this has not already been done. The summons for directions in effect amounts to a pre-trial review. The plaintiff obtains a formal document entitled summons for directions which contains a list of 29 matters upon which the parties may require directions. Each side can indicate upon this form what action the master should take. When the master is satisfied that all is ready he will indicate on the document the time and place for the trial.

Occasionally it may be possible to move for what is known as summary judgment under Order 14. Briefly this procedure may be used where the defendant is thought to have no answer to the plaintiff's claims. It cannot be used in actions for defamation or malicious prosecution, false imprisonment or actions based on an allegation of fraud. Where the defendant can show that he has a defence which ought to be tried or that there is a good reason for there to be a trial, the master will give him leave to defend and will then give the parties directions for the future conduct of the action. Otherwise the master will award judgment for the plaintiff which will be final if the damages are liquidated (*e.g.* it is an action concerning a dishonoured cheque where the amount of money in question is not disputed) or interlocutory if the damages are unliquidated; in the latter case the actual amount of the damages will be settled by trial.

The issue of a writ in no sense commits the parties to a trial of the action and at any stage (even during the trial itself) the parties may reach a settlement. At various stages the parties may take stock of the position to decide whether it is worth pressing the matter to litigation. In this connection the defendant may decide that he will meet part of the plaintiff's claim but not the whole of it. If the plaintiff finds this offer unsatisfactory, the defendant may make *payment into court* of that sum. If in the subsequent action the plaintiff recovers no more than the sum paid in then the plaintiff, though he is successful in the action, can recover costs only up to the time of the payment into court and will ordinarily be ordered to pay the defendant's costs incurred thereafter.

(b) *The trial of the action*

A civil action is normally heard by a single judge who determines the facts of the case as well as resolving any issues of law. Strictly, trial by jury is available for a wide range of civil actions since the judge has a discretion to direct jury trial; in practice the discretion is almost invariably exercised to exclude jury trial. For most kinds of civil actions the courts take the view that jury trial is unsuitable: trial by judge alone is said to produce a predictability and uniformity of result which would not be achieved by jury trial. Another important factor, most especially in personal injury claims, is that the assessment and award of damages is best left in the experienced hands of a judge rather than to the instinctive reaction of a jury which has no detailed experience in the matter.

There are, however, some cases where there is a right to jury trial and these include defamation actions, false imprisonment and cases involving an allegation of fraud. The right is not absolute in these cases because if the action is likely to involve issues unsuitable for jury trial (such as an extensive examination of documents or scientific issues) trial by judge alone may be directed. The decline in jury trial for civil actions has been a remarkable one; less than 150 years ago nearly all civil cases were tried by jury, now less than 1 per cent. are so tried. In those cases where jury trial is directed, eligibility for jury service, summonsing and empanelling is the same as in criminal cases tried on indictment (see *post*, p. 106).

A civil action is normally opened by the plaintiff who adduces evidence, which may be real (for instance, the goods alleged to be defective) or testimonial. Witnesses (including the plaintiff) may be called who will be examined by counsel for the plaintiff, and may be cross-examined by counsel for the defendant and then re-examined by the plaintiff's counsel. The plaintiff also normally carries the burden of proof which is usually expressed by saying that he must establish his case on the balance of probabilities. This means that the plaintiff must satisfy the judge (or, exceptionally, the jury) not that his allegations are necessarily true, but that they are *more likely* to be true than the defendant's allegations. The burden on a plaintiff in a civil action is thus less exacting than the burden on a prosecutor in a criminal case (see *post*, p. 102). Sometimes, an obvious example is where a counterclaim (see *ante*, p. 76) is involved, the defendant carries the burden of proof on an issue or issues and in such a case it is for the defendant to establish that his allegations are more likely to be true.

At the close of the plaintiff's case the defendant may submit that he has no case to answer, that is that the plaintiff has failed to adduce evidence on which the judge (or jury) could find for the plaintiff. Where this submission is made in a trial by judge alone, the judge will not rule on it unless the defence elects to call no evidence. The purpose of this election is, in effect, to prevent the defendant from having two bites on the cherry; it is not right that the judge should rule on the evidence (for that is the effect of a no case submission) until all the evidence is in. Where a civil action is tried by jury the judge has a discretion as to whether he will put the defendant to his election before passing on the submission. In a criminal trial the accused is not put to his election in this way (see *post*, p. 102).

If no submission is made then the defendant proceeds to adduce his evidence and his witnesses are subject to examination, cross-examination and re-examination. At the close of the case the judge, if he is hearing the case alone, will announce his decision. Normally he will rehearse the evidence and state which facts he finds to be proved, apply the relevant law to those facts and make a determination in favour of the plaintiff or the defendant; if he finds in favour of the plaintiff he will order the appropriate remedy together with making an order for costs. If the case has been tried with a jury then the judge will sum-up the case bearing in mind that while he gives any relevant directions as to law, the finding of the facts lies within the province of the jury.

While in broad outline the course of a civil action is similar to that of a criminal prosecution, there are important differences. Apart from those already noted in this section, three further distinctions may be mentioned. One results from the elaborate system of pleadings (see *ante*, p. 75) which governs civil, but not criminal, cases. By the time a civil action comes to trial each side will know a great deal of the other's case and the issues in the case will have been delineated. In a criminal prosecution this is far from being the case. In a summary trial the defendant may know no more than the details of the charge and equally the prosecutor may know nothing of the defendant's case. In a trial on indictment, the defendant will know something of the prosecution's case from the evidence tendered by the prosecutor in the committal proceedings (see *post*, p. 104) but this does not prevent the prosecutor from tendering additional evidence at the trial. If, however, the prosecutor does wish to adduce additional evidence at the trial he must send a copy of the additional evidence to the defendant and to the court. The defendant will then know the essentials of the case he has to meet, but for his part he is not similarly obliged (other than that he must give notice of the essential details of an alibi if he proposes to rely on one) to give notice of his defence to the prosecutor. It is thus possible for the prosecutor to be caught off guard by the line of defence, leading to what one commentator has called trial by ambush.

A second distinction relates to the law of evidence. In criminal cases hearsay evidence is in general excluded. This means, in substance, that the actual witness of an event or the actual maker of a statement must be produced to prove this event or statement; it is not possible for someone who was informed by the actual witness or maker to relate what he was told was seen or said. There are several reasons for the rule against hearsay, one being that as A repeats what he has seen to B, and B to C, and C to D, the more unreliable the account becomes. But we commonly treat hearsay as having at least some reliability and for civil, but not criminal cases, first hand hearsay (that is, what A said to B) is generally admissible if proper notice has been served. If the trial is, as usually it will be, by judge alone, the judge, by reason of his experience, will know what weight to attach to a hearsay statement.

A third difference concerns the defendant as witness. In a criminal case the defendant cannot be compelled to testify (see *post*, p. 102) whereas in a civil case he has no such privilege. Somewhat similarly, a spouse who is not in criminal proceedings ordinarily a competent or compellable witness against the other spouse (see *post*, p. 103) is in civil litigation competent and compellable against the other spouse.

2. Criminal Proceedings

In our country the investigation and prosecution of crime lies mainly in the hands of the police. But in law (subject to certain exceptions where the consent of the Attorney General or the Director of Public Prosecutions is required) it is open to any citizen to prosecute crime. A "private" (*i.e.* non-official) prosecution is no different from a "public" prosecution in its incidents. Private investigation and prosecution, though dwarfed by prosecutions conducted by public agencies, should not be dismissed as unimportant. Many institutions employ security staff and though their role is mainly preventive they will necessarily investigate crime though they will usually consult with the police over the critical question of prosecution.

Nevertheless, the substantial responsibility for the enforcement of the criminal law lies with the police. For this purpose the constable has somewhat, but by no means immensely, greater powers than the private citizen. In the exercise of these powers a constable (all police officers are constables whatever their rank within the force) is answerable to the law and not to his superiors. A senior officer of police may properly direct his subordinates where and when to patrol but he cannot lawfully order him not to enforce particular laws or not to enforce the law against particular individuals.

A constable has a legal duty to enforce the law and if, without lawful authority or reasonable excuse, he fails to do so he is guilty of an offence. This does not mean that a constable must necessarily prosecute for every infraction that comes to his notice. Life would become intolerable for both the citizen and the constable if the latter did not occasionally turn a blind eye or issued a friendly caution. But in 1978 a constable was fined on a charge of misconduct as a police officer where he deliberately refrained from intervening in a brawl outside a club when from the cries and screams it was clear that someone was being done a serious injury (*Dytham* (1979)). The court said that his failure to act in this situation, where life itself was at risk, was such as to injure the public interest and to call for condemnation and punishment.

(1) Police powers: general

While the police are better trained and equipped than the private citizen for the investigation of crime, their legal powers are not significantly greater.

When a crime has been committed, indeed when any event has occurred, any person is at liberty to ask questions of participants or witnesses, and any participant or witness is equally at liberty to refuse to answer any such questions. In practice the police usually secure the co-operation of witnesses and, contrary to the image fostered in detective fiction, most crime is uncovered by information volunteered by members of the public. The informant thus plays a central role in the detection and prosecution of crime. Most of us are informants at one time or another, perhaps reporting a theft or burglary or volunteering evidence concerning a road traffic accident.

Socially we draw a distinction between the *informant* who

volunteers his information disinterestedly except for an interest in the proper enforcement of the law, and the *informer* who trades his information for some advantage to himself which may be financial or otherwise. To take the matter a stage further, the informer may affect to join the participants in their criminal enterprise only to inform on them, or may even (and at this stage he is referred to as an *agent provocateur*) incite or instigate crime by others.

These are muddy waters. In dealing with terrorist organisations bent on the wholesale destruction of life, few would question the propriety of undercover police infiltration for the purpose of securing the conviction and punishment of the terrorists. But what of the inspector who orders a drink after hours with a view to entrapping the friendly publican? Or the woman police officer who affects to be pregnant to secure evidence against an alleged back-street abortionist? Or the agent who has "laid-on" a robbery so that his principals may be caught red-handed?

The courts have ruled unequivocably that "entrapment" is not a defence to the perpetrators. On the other hand the courts have recognised that law enforcement should not overstep the mark. This mark is ill-defined and it may be that the mark for offences of terrorism is not the same as it is for offences of shoplifting, but the courts are strongly inclined to reduce an otherwise appropriate sentence where it appears that the participants might or would not have committed the offence but for instigation by an agent. The Law Commission considered this matter (Law Comm. No. 83) and proposed that it should be made an offence positively to instigate, incite or persuade another to commit an offence but no action has been taken on this recommendation.

Another general problem concerns the interception of communications. Clearly eavesdropping is lawful; if X on a bus relates to Y in a loud voice his part in a murder, he has only himself to blame if a police officer sitting behind him hears all. In one case (*Maqsud Ali* (1965)) the police placed two men suspected of murder in a room which contained a concealed microphone and the court allowed the taped recording, tantamount to a confession, to be given in evidence.

This leads on to a consideration of telephone tapping and interference with mail. It might be argued that if X uses the mail or his telephone to organise a crime there is no good reason why his communications should not be intercepted to provide evidence against him. Against that it might be said that we do not know whether X plans a crime until we intercept his communications. Should we intercept all communications on the basis that they will disclose evidence of crime against at least some of us?

In practice the interception of postal and telephonic communications is authorised only exceptionally (so the Government of the day assures us) and then only under a warrant issued by the Home Secretary. Such a warrant is issued only where the suspected offence is serious (that is, likely to result in a conviction involving imprisonment for at least three years) and where conventional methods of investigation have failed. The legality of such warrants has been questioned but the matter has never been tested in the courts. Since our courts take the view that illegally obtained evidence is in general admissible the point is somewhat moot.

(2) Police powers: interrogation

It has been pointed out that everyone is at liberty to refuse to answer questions whoever poses the questions. If a man has nothing to hide, however, he is normally more than willing to answer questions whether put by the police, the press or his next-door neighbour.

But if a man is, *or is thought to be*, a participant in events that might show him in a discreditable light (most obviously a crime) then he would be best advised to stay silent at least until he receives professional legal advice. Our law has long recognised this right of silence *and* has additionally taken the view that no adverse inferences may be drawn from an accused's refusal to answer questions. Hence no deduction of guilt may be drawn from an accused's silence in response to police questions or from his refusal to give evidence in court.

The law may thus be said to be favourable to the suspect or accused. And it goes further than this. A confession is not admissible against a defendant unless it is proved to be *voluntary*, that it has not been obtained by fear of prejudice, nor by hope of advantage held out by a person in authority, nor by oppression. Not only is the rack proscribed but also a confession obtained by a promise of bail or other favourable treatment is equally inadmissible.

But if this is the law, the reality is somewhat different. Few can resist the urge to communicate with a fellow human being even if he happens to be a police officer whose interest lies in securing evidence, most especially a confession, about a crime which the suspect is thought to have committed. The contest of wits may not be an equal one. The suspect (unless he is an old hand) is in foreign territory, his movements are controlled and he is dependent on his captors for his means of existence. He may have been stripped, for reasons of evidence or security, of possessions which are important to his dignity. The police officer, on the other hand, is entirely familiar with the environment and has all the trappings of control and authority.

It is probably the case that no interrogation is entirely "fair" as any errant schoolboy brought before his headmaster will testify. The headmaster brings the pupil to *his* office, unfamiliar territory to the pupil, and will subtly use the trappings of his office to erode the boy's confidence. The headmaster who needs to resort to beatings or threats or inducements to obtain damaging admissions cannot have read any worthwhile books on his trade in the last half century.

But a confessional statement is not inadmissible simply because the parties are not on equal terms. An admission may yet be considered voluntary even though the interrogator enjoyed certain psychological advantages over the suspect. Consider *Prager* (1972). The police, who suspected Prager of offences against the Official Secrets Act 1911, arrived at Prager's house with a search warrant at 8.00 on a Sunday morning. They asked Prager if he would accompany them to the police station for questioning in relation to a serious matter and he agreed. At the station he was questioned from 9.15 to 12.30, from 17.45 to 19.40 and from 19.40 to 23.30, a total of nine hours. At 19.40 he made a damaging admission and in the final session made further admissions culminating in a confession which he dictated at 23.30.

During this time Prager was fed and allowed to rest but he did not see a solicitor until much later and he then retracted his confession which he said had been obtained by fear. In the result his confession was admitted. The Court of Appeal, accepting that a confession obtained by "oppression" was not admissible, held there was no evidence of oppression here. The court thought that the crucial question was whether Prager's will had crumbled under the weight of the questioning or whether he had taken a conscious decision to tell the truth. The Court of Appeal was clearly influenced in reaching this conclusion by the facts that the jury had reached the conclusion that the confession was voluntary and that Prager was a tough minded individual.

Another point that was made in *Prager's* case was that the confession was obtained in breach of the Judges' Rules. The judges have long realised that interrogation is a matter requiring regulation and early in this century they issued guidelines on interrogation, the essential feature of which is the necessity to caution the suspect, at the time of his arrest and at the time a decision is made to charge him with an offence, that he is not obliged to say anything. The Judges' Rules are not rules of law but evidence obtained in breach of them may be held inadmissible.

From the reported cases, however, it seems that the judges only rarely exclude evidence obtained in breach of the Rules. There was a clear breach of the Rules in *Prager's* case because, though the police had reasonable grounds for suspecting him of various offences under the Official Secrets Act, at no stage did they remind him of his right to remain silent. Prager's confession was found to be voluntary and the proved technical breaches of the Judges' Rules did not make it inadmissible.

(3) Police powers: arrest

General powers of arrest are to be found in section 2 of the Criminal Law Act 1967. Broadly, this section authorises any person, whether a constable or not, to arrest without warrant: (i) anyone who is, or who is reasonably believed to be, in the act of committing an arrestable offence; and (ii) where an arrestable offence has been committed, anyone who has, or is reasonably believed to have been guilty of the offence.

The section then confers further powers on constables who may additionally arrest a person; (iii) where there are reasonable grounds for believing that he has committed an arrestable offence; and (iv) where a person is, or is reasonably believed to be, about to commit an arrestable offence. Moreover, a constable, but not a private citizen, is authorised to enter (if needs be by force) any place where the suspect is or is reasonably believed to be for the purpose of effecting an arrest.

So the powers of a constable are somewhat more extensive than those of a private citizen. Under (iv) a constable has a prophylactic power; he may arrest a man whom he reasonably believes to be about to throw a brick through a shop window while the citizen must wait until the window is broken. The additional power conferred on a constable under (iii) may be simply illustrated. Suppose a bookshop manager sees a shopper behaving in a way that reasonably leads the manager to believe that the shopper has taken a copy of Hogan, Seago and Bennett's *"A" Level Law* from the shelves and secreted it in his coat. In fact the shopper had been bent on stealing this priceless work but, guessing that he was being observed, had changed his mind. The manager follows the shopper into the street where he arrests him. In these circumstances the manager is not protected by the section because *no arrestable offence has in fact been committed* and is thus liable to pay damages for the unlawful arrest (false imprisonment). Had the manager communicated his reasonable suspicions to a passing constable and had the constable effected the arrest then neither would be liable; the manager because he has not made the arrest, and the constable because he is protected by (iii), (see *Walters* v. *W.H. Smith*, (1914)).

Had the manager arrested the shopper at the very shelf where the manager reasonably believed he was stealing then the manager would have been protected by (i) which protects the manager even if the theft has not been committed so long as he reasonably believes the shopper to be in the *act of committing*. But once the shopper has left the premises he can no longer be said to be in the act of committing the theft.

It may seem odd that a citizen may be liable for an unlawful arrest even though he has acted reasonably on the available evidence. Not surprisingly the so-called "citizen's arrest" is very much the exception; it is usually possible, and certainly safer, to leave these matters to the police.

An arrestable offence is defined as any offence for which an offender *may* be sentenced to a term of imprisonment for five years. It thus includes serious offences against the person (grievous bodily harm, wounding, rape, for example) and all offences of theft and criminal damage. But extensive as the definition of an arrestable offence is, it does not extend to all cases where a power of arrest is necessary if the law is to be effectively enforced. Take the protection of wild birds, for example. Since we do not wish such birds as the osprey to disappear from our shores it has been made an offence to take them or their young or eggs. But such an offence could hardly be punished with five years' imprisonment and generally the maximum for an offence of this sort is a fine of £1,000. On the other hand, if a police officer could not without a warrant arrest or search on the spot a person whom he reasonably suspected of being in possession of an osprey's egg, the law would be a dead letter; by the time a warrant could be obtained the evidence would be removed. So there are many cases (about 70 in all) where, though the offence is not serious enough to merit the five years' imprisonment that would bring it within the definition of an arrestable offence for the purposes of section 2 of the Criminal Law Act 1967, nevertheless a statutory power of arrest has been thought necessary for effective enforcement of the law.

Two points might be made about statutory powers both of arrest and search. One is that they have been created from time to time as circumstances appear to have demanded without thought to any overall strategy or plan, and as a consequence anomalies abound. So, for example, while a constable may arrest a person for obstructing the highway, he cannot arrest him for obstructing the officer in the execution of his duty. And while there is a power to search premises for stolen goods, there is no power to search for a body believed to be that of the victim of a murder. The other point is that these powers are expressed in different terms so that it is not an easy matter for a constable, and still less for a citizen, to know precisely when a power of arrest exists.

In relation to arrest without warrant, mention must also be made of the common law power of a constable to arrest for a breach of the peace committed in his presence. A breach of the peace is conduct which involves, or threatens, violence to the person or involves significant harm to property. Fighting in the street provides a common occasion for the exercise of the power and here the constable does not have to pass upon the merits; he may properly arrest all the combatants though it turns out that one or more of them was acting lawfully in self defence.

All powers of arrest are conditioned by the requirement that reasonable grounds must exist for the suspicion on which the arrest is based. Reasonable cause cannot be defined in the abstract and has to be related to the circumstances of the case. Clearly a constable is not required to have an open-and-shut case against the suspect because it is his *suspicion* that he must justify, not prove that the suspect committed the offence. But deprivation of liberty is a serious matter and can be justified only where good grounds exist for the suspicion. This requires, at the least, that the officer be open-minded and that he makes such inquiries as are practicable in the circumstances. The officer may act on information provided by third parties if it has every appearance of being reliable and leads to a reasonable inference of the suspect's guilt. It would, for example, be reasonable for the officer to rely on a report given him by a store-detective whom the officer knows to be experienced and reliable, but not on an anonymous tip-off given hurriedly over the telephone. One exception, of little practical importance, to the requirement for reasonable cause is where the officer's suspicions, though unfounded on any evidence available, turn out to be right. If, for example, an officer following a report of a burglary arrests X just on a hunch, he will be liable in damages if his intuition is wrong but will not be liable if it turns out that X did in fact commit the crime.

An arrest is lawful only if the suspect is given a *valid* reason for it. The suspect is entitled to know why he is being deprived of his liberty so that he can meet the case against him. In *Christie* v. *Leachinsky* (1947) police found Leachinsky in possession of stolen cloth and arrested him under the Liverpool Corporation Act (it might be noted in passing that powers of arrest may be conferred by local as well as general statutes) on a charge of unlawful possession. This Act did confer a power of arrest for unlawful possession but only when the identity of the suspect was unknown and Leachinsky was well known to the officers concerned. It was held by the House of Lords that a suspect is entitled to know the valid ground for his arrest and since Leachinsky was given no such valid ground he was entitled to damages. It appears in this case that the police might have had reasonable grounds for suspecting that Leachinsky had received the cloth knowing it to be stolen and might have validly arrested him under the then Larceny Act 1916 which conferred an arrest power whether the suspect's identity was or was not known. But an arrest cannot normally be justified by showing that a power did exist if only the police had remembered it; and still less by showing that the suspect had committed some other arrestable offence.

In *Christie* v. *Leachinsky* it was said that the party arresting need not use technical language so long as the suspect knows for what he is arrested. The police are well advised to use unmistakable language, *e.g.* "I arrest you for stealing this watch/murdering your mother-in-law." But, and so long as the import is clear to the suspect, it would do to say "You're nicked laddie for lifting this watch/doing away with your dear old mother-in-law."

If the suspect is not so informed the arrest is unlawful unless: (a) it is patently obvious to him why he has been arrested; or (b) he makes it impossible, as by running off or by violence, for the police to provide the grounds; or (c) there are other compelling grounds (such as the deafness of the suspect or his inability to speak English) which make it impossible for the police immediately to communicate with him. In cases (b) and (c), however, the suspect must be informed as soon as practicable.

Apart from powers of arrest without warrant, an arrest may also be effected under warrant. Warrants of arrest are usually issued by a magistrate after hearing evidence on oath and may be issued for both arrestable and non-arrestable offences. A warrant may be executed anywhere within the jurisdiction and reciprocal arrangements exist with Scotland, Northern Ireland and the Irish Republic. A constable who in good faith executes a warrant according to its terms incurs no liability to the suspect even though the warrant proves to be unlawful. The officer need not have the warrant in his possession but the suspect must be shown it as soon as practicable.

Two basic criticisms may be made of the law relating to arrest. The first is that it is far from clear and simple (mainly owing to the plethora of differently expressed statutory powers of arrest) and a restatement is therefore required. The second is that arrest is often authorised for trivial infractions of the law; an arrest is permissible, for example, in the case of any theft or act of criminal damage however trivial the subject matter. The Royal Commission on Criminal Procedure (1981, Cmnd. 8092) recognised these shortcomings and proposed a code based on a so-called "necessity" principle. Their proposals are wider than the existing law in that they would permit an arrest for any offence punishable by imprisonment or for any other offence committed in a constable's presence. They are narrower in that arrest would be authorised only where it was necessary to prevent repetition of the offence, or to prevent harm to person or property, or to secure evidence or make further inquiries, or to obtain evidence of the suspect's identity. These proposals have in turn been criticised on the grounds (a) that they would produce even further uncertainty because there are some 7,000 criminal offences and not even a high court judge, let alone a citizen, can know which of these is imprisonable, and (b) they give the police virtually a free hand in that they can always claim that further inquiries would be necessary.

(4) Police powers: search

It cannot be pretended that the law relating to search is, as it should be, clear, certain and simple. There is, as with arrest, a rag-bag of statutory powers supplementing uncertain common law powers.

Several statutes authorise search of the person. Usually the power is restricted to constables but it may occasionally be given to others. For example, where upon conviction magistrates have imposed a fine which the convicted person claims he does not have the means to pay, they may order him to be searched to determine whether he has the wherewithal. Powers exist to stop and search, upon reasonable suspicion, for such things as poaching equipment, dangerous drugs, protected birds and plants.

A general power of search of the person attaches where a suspect is lawfully arrested and the constable has reasonable grounds for believing the suspect has on him evidence of the crime, or the wherewithal of doing mischief to himself or another, or the wherewithal to effect an escape. Thus a power of search does not automatically attach to an arrest. If, however, the suspect is not released unconditionally or on bail and is required to spend the night in custody, it appears to be the invariable practice of the police to conduct a search to make sure that he has nothing on him which might be used to cause harm and to take safe custody of his valuables. This practice is of very doubtful legality but has not been directly challenged though the courts have said that the police would not be justified in removing personal articles, such as jewellery or a wristwatch.

Where a search of the person is authorised it would be permissible to search a briefcase or handbag in the possession of the suspect. It seems also permissible for the police to search any vehicle of which the suspect is in charge at the time of the arrest. But sometimes the police go much further than this by taking the suspect to his house which they proceed to search. This practice is also of doubtful legality but the courts have disapproved it only where there are no reasonable grounds for believing that a search of the suspect's house will turn up evidence implicating the suspect *in the crime for which he is arrested.* Thus if the police arrest the suspect for breaking a shop window, it would be unreasonable for them to assume that evidence relating to that crime would be turned up by a search of his house. On the other hand, if the suspect is arrested for receiving stolen property or for murder it might be reasonable to suppose that stolen goods or evidence of the murder would be found on search of his house. But if this is lawful, and some cases suggest that it is, the oddity is that in the case of stolen goods the police can thus circumvent the normal requirement for obtaining a warrant; and in the case of the murder may search his house for evidence although there is no power, either with warrant or otherwise, to search premises for evidence even of serious crimes.

While it *may* be lawful in the foregoing circumstances to search the suspect's premises, it would not be lawful to search the premises of a third party even if the suspect resides there. So if the police arrest a son at his father's premises where the son resides, they may search the son and seize articles in the son's possession; they may not then search the father's house.

It might be argued that if the police are acting reasonably in the enforcement of the law that their conduct ought to be accounted lawful. But in this area of the law there is no such general principle. In order to justify the serious invasions of liberty which arrest, search and seizure involve, the police must be able to cite chapter and verse for it, that is some statutory or common law rule which authorises their conduct.

Powers to search premises (other than the parasitic power following arrest which has just been discussed) arise entirely under statute and may be accorded with or without warrant. The most commonly used power relates to stolen goods; a magistrate (and in some circumstances a senior officer of police) may issue a search warrant to a constable where there are reasonable grounds for believing that stolen goods may be found at specified premises. There are of course other powers besides, such as the powers, on reasonable suspicion, by warrant to search premises for obscene articles or for the purpose of detecting offences against the Official Secrets Act 1911.

(5) The suspect in custody

Other than by authority of law (almost invariably following arrest) no one can be compelled to go to a police station and, still less, can he be compelled to give evidence against himself. It is not uncommon to hear or read following a report of a crime that a man is at a certain police station "helping the police with their inquiries." It is of course open to suspects voluntarily to attend a police station and submit to questioning but such public-spiritedness in suspects is very much the exception. A person can be lawfully detained only following a valid arrest; there is no obligation on him to help and the police have no general power to detain him for questioning. If a person is held against his will, that is it is made clear to him that he is not a free agent, he is unlawfully detained unless he has been given a valid ground for his detention.

As appeared from the section on interrogation, the suspect in custody is not ideally placed to take a course of action in his own best interests. It is open to him at any stage to ask to see a solicitor and the Judges' Rules state that a suspect *should* be able to communicate and consult privately with a solicitor provided that the processes of investigation are not thereby unreasonably delayed or hindered. But many suspects may be unaware of this privilege (note that it is not a *right*) and the police are not legally required to remind them of it. Moreover, a confession, provided it is accounted voluntary, will not be rendered inadmissible because the suspect was improperly denied access to legal advice.

Under the Criminal Law Act 1977, s.62, a person held in custody is *entitled* to have intimation of his arrest and the place where he is held sent to one person reasonably named by him without delay or, where some delay is necessary in the interests of the investigation or prevention of crime or the apprehension of offenders, with no more delay than is necessary. Again, the police are not legally obliged to inform the suspect of this entitlement but guidance given by the Home office states that the terms of the section should be drawn to the suspect's attention when he is taken into custody. Nor does the suspect have any apparent remedy if he is denied this entitlement and its denial is hardly likely to render involuntary any statement made by him. Section 62 is most likely to be used by a suspect to inform next of kin of his or her whereabouts and, though a solicitor may be a person reasonably named by the suspect, it gives no substantive right to legal advice. Nevertheless, it was passed only by a narrow majority in the Commons and against the advice of the Home Secretary!

A person taken into custody may of course be released unconditionally if it turns out that further inquiries reveal that there is no case against him. If, however, there is a prima facie case against him, he may be charged with an offence. In this event he may be released on bail (see *post*, p. 95) or he may be kept in custody to appear before the magistrates. No timescale is laid down except that once a suspect is taken into custody he must be brought before the magistrates as soon as practicable, and, if it is not practicable to do so within 24 hours, he should be released on bail unless the crime is a serious one.

(6) Complaints against the police and police accountability

Inevitably policing attracts complaints and it is essential to both the police and the public that a fair system should exist for airing and investigating these complaints. The police themselves are well aware that in a democratic society their effectiveness depends in large measure in securing the confidence, and therefore the cooperation, of the public.

A complaint at the one extreme may involve little more than an allegation of incivility and, at the other, may involve an allegation of a serious criminal offence. A complaint may be made about the conduct of a particular officer or it may be made about policing in general. Examples of the latter might be an allegation that blacks are being subject to harrassment by the police, or a complaint that an area is insufficiently policed resulting in soliciting by prostitutes becoming an intolerable nuisance. The procedures which govern complaints against the police and complaints about policing have overlapping elements but call for separate discussion.

(a) *Complaints against the police*

Procedures for dealing with complaints against the police have existed almost since the creation of the police, and are now mainly regulated by the Police Act 1964 and Regulations made thereunder. Where a chief officer of police receives a complaint against any member of his force, he must (unless the complaint relates to an offence with which the member has already been charged) record the complaint and cause it to be investigated; and for this purpose he may (and must if so directed by the Home Secretary) request another chief officer of police to provide an officer to conduct the investigation. Such an investigation may result in: (i) criminal proceedings against an officer; or (ii) disciplinary proceedings within the force; or (iii) the dismissal of the complaint. The report of the investigation must be sent to the Director of Public Prosecutions unless it is clear that no criminal offence has been committed.

Complaints run at some 15,000 a year and their investigation obviously takes up a good deal of police time. The very fact that complaints are investigated by officers of a force whose fellow officers are under investigation has led to demands for an independent element in the investigative process. To meet these, the Police Act 1974 created a Police Complaints Board comprised of not less than nine members appointed by the Prime Minister and who must not be, or have served as, constables. The Board is substantially concerned with the oversight of disciplinary proceedings since criminal charges fall within the purview of the Director of Public Prosecutions.

The Board receives a report from the chief officer of police whenever the investigation has *not* resulted in the bringing of any disciplinary charge, and where disciplinary charges have been made which are disputed by the officer concerned. Where the chief officer of police has decided not to prefer disciplinary charges, the Board may, if it disagrees with his decision, recommend (and in the last resort direct) that disciplinary proceedings be instituted. The Board may also direct where there are exceptional circumstances affecting the case (these are not defined but might include cases attracting great public interest, or a fear of local bias) that the case shall be heard by a disciplinary tribunal chaired by the chief officer of police who would otherwise discharge this function together with two members of the Board. Appeal lies from a decision of this tribunal to the Home Secretary.

It has been said (by Professor Harry Street) that the 1974 Act satisfies nobody; the police resent lay interference in something they feel best equipped to handle, and by lay critics as being ill-equipped for its task. Certainly the Board has no independent investigative machinery but it is difficult to see who, other than the police, have the powers and expertise that are necessary for the conduct of investigations.

(b) *Complaints about policing*

The last section dealt with complaints against the police in the narrow sense under procedures governed by the Police Acts 1964 and 1974. These by no means exhaust the procedures, both formal and informal for dealing with complaints about the police which may range from a criticism in a letter written to a local newspaper to a high level tribunal of inquiry.

By way of introduction it is necessary to know something of the constitutional position of the police. As we have seen (*ante*, p. 81) a constable's primary duty is to keep the peace and in the exercise of his functions he is answerable to the law. So it is essentially with a chief constable, except that his responsibilities are general as well as particular. The office is one of enormous power for it is the chief constable who decides upon the disposition of his force, the allocation of resources, the determination of priorities as between the various police functions, the methods of policing to be used and so on. With these immense powers come immense responsibilities. He has to balance the requirements of law enforcement against a wider, if ill-defined public interest which includes the maintenance of strict impartiality in his force and the retention of public confidence in it. He must decide upon the strategies for dealing with pickets at the factory gate, demonstrations outside an embassy, or rioters on the streets; it will be for him to indicate when and what force may be used.

In this he is subject to the law as *R.* v. *Metropolitan Police Commissioner, ex p. Blackburn* (1968) shows. The Commissioner had issued a directive to his force which, in effect, said that the Gaming Act was not to be enforced since its provisions were virtually unworkable. In the result the Commissioner withdrew this instruction but the Court of Appeal was clear that, had he not, mandamus would have issued to compel him to do so. It was not open to a chief constable to refuse altogether to enforce particular legislation because he thought it unworkable and a waste of valuable police time.

But too much must not be read into this decision for its practical effect is limited. The indefatigable Mr. Blackburn (one of life's natural litigants) brought a further action (*R.* v. *Metropolitan Police Commissioner, ex p. Blackburn* (*No.* 3) (1973)) to compel the Commissioner to enforce the laws against obscenity more vigorously in central London. The court refused to interfere; there was no suggestion that the Commissioner had abdicated his responsibility for enforcing the obscenity laws and it was for him to decide, along with all other competing demands on the police resources, what priority to accord the enforcement of these laws.

Of more importance as a practical matter is "political" control. At the national level the Home Secretary has considerable potential for control in that he has power to withhold the grants payable from central funds to police forces and there are fewer more potent controls than the financial one. The Home Secretary may also call upon a chief (or a deputy or assistant) constable to retire in the interests of efficiency though an inquiry must be held if the officer concerned wishes to dispute the matter. Finally, the Home Secretary may cause a local inquiry to be held "into any matter connected with the policing of any area." Such inquiries in the past have been concerned with particular allegations of misconduct, such as fabricating evidence or using violence against suspects in custody, but could be used to investigate matters of policing policy.

At the local level there is the police authority which is comprised (except for London where the Home Secretary is the police authority) as to two-thirds from the elected councillors for that area and as to one third from magistrates for that area. It is the duty of the police authority "to secure the maintenance of an adequate and efficient police force" for the area, to appoint the chief constable, and to determine the number of persons in each rank which is to constitute the establishment of the force.

But on the critical question of the relationship between the chief constable and the police authority, the legislation says next to nothing. The chief constable is required to make an annual report to his authority "on the policing during that year" and the authority may from time to time require reports on matters connected with policing; but information which it is not in the public interest to divulge or which is not needed for the authority to discharge its functions may be withheld by the chief constable on the authority of the Home Secretary. The result is that the divisions of functions and authority as between the police authority and the chief constable is highly uncertain. On more than one occasion this has led to confrontations which have not been satisfactorily nor authoritatively resolved.

To conclude this section on the police, their powers and responsibilities, it may fairly be said that the law is far from being free from obscurity and uncertainty. This matters less if the police enjoy public confidence and goodwill, if they are seen to act disinterestedly and to enforce the law with common sense and compassion. The police draw their strength, and indeed their very authority, from the community and it is certainly not unreasonable that the community, through its elected representatives, should have both a more clearly defined and more authoritative role in matters of policing policy. And it is equally not unreasonable that the citizen, most especially where he falls under suspicion of crime, should know how he stands. The police have enough advantages without adding to them the dimension of uncertainty.

(7) Bail

Where a person is charged with a criminal offence it is obvious that there will normally be a delay before the prosecution will be ready to proceed with trial. What, therefore, happens to the accused in the meantime? There are various possibilities. At one extreme it may be necessary to keep the accused in custody pending the verdict; at the other it will suffice simply to give him a date on which he is to present himself before the magistrates court. In between these two extremes are cases in which the accused is remanded on bail which may be unconditional or conditional.

(a) *When the question of bail arises*

The bail question may arise at any time between the initial arrest of the accused up till and including the final appeal in the case.

If the accused has been arrested under the authority of a warrant issued by a magistrate then this warrant may have been "backed for bail." In this case the accused will be arrested and immediately bailed by the police under the terms of the warrant. In the case where the warrant is not so backed, and in cases where the accused is arrested without warrant, bail may be granted by the police at the police station.

Where the police have decided not to grant bail to the accused, it is their duty to produce him before a magistrates' court at the earliest opportunity, which in practice is usually the following morning. The magistrates will normally grant the prosecution's application for the case to be adjourned, and the bench will then have to decide whether or not the accused should remain in custody or be released. If he is to be remanded on bail he will simply be told to appear before the court at a future date, often a month to six weeks later and will be warned of the consequences of failure to attend. If he is to be remanded in custody the adjournment of the case can be for no longer than eight clear days. In other words if the remand takes place on a Monday morning he must appear again no later than the Wednesday of the following week. Following the decision of the Divisional Court in *R.* v. *Nottingham Justices, ex p. Davies* (1981) unless there is a change in circumstance the accused may make only one application for bail; this is to prevent the courts having to go through the same applications every week. In practice the court will not count the first application he makes on the morning after his arrest as his proper application since neither he nor his counsel will be fully prepared and so he will be allowed to make another application on the second appearance. After this, however, he will have to point to a change in the circumstances before the court will allow a further application. The Criminal Justice Act 1982 now provides limited powers to make further remands in custody in the absence of the accused. If his application for bail fails he has the right of appeal to a high court judge in chambers, or to the Crown Court.

After conviction the convicted person may apply for bail pending appeal. In this case the application may be made either to the court from which, or the court to which, he is appealing, or both; but as will appear he no longer has the benefit of the presumption (which applies only before conviction) that bail should be granted.

(b) *How the bail decision is reached*

The factors to be considered by the adjudicating body may vary depending upon the stage at which the application is made and upon the nature of the offence, but in each case there is the need to balance the right of a person to be at liberty until he is convicted against the need to protect the community. The problem is best illustrated by examining the way the decision is handled by the magistrates court when the accused makes his full application to them. In many cases the prosecutor will say that bail is not opposed and this will normally mean bail is granted (though the bench is not thereby obliged to grant bail). Where bail is opposed, the accused has the right to apply for it.

Under section 4 of the Bail Act 1976 the accused has a right to be granted unconditional bail unless one of two conditions is satisfied. The first is that he was arrested for absconding while on bail or for failing to comply with a condition of bail; or the bench is of the opinion that he needs to be kept in custody for his own protection; or he is already serving a custodial sentence. The second is where the magistrates find proved one or more of the exceptions to the right to unconditional bail. These are, in the case of *imprisonable* offences, the bench believes that he would fail to surrender to his bail, or that he would commit further offences while on bail, or that he would interfere with witnesses or would obstruct the course of justice, or that there has been insufficient time to gather information about him, or that (after conviction) it would be impracticable to prepare a report on him if he were on bail; or (in the case of *non-imprisonable* offences) the bench believes he has previously failed to surrender to bail and is unlikely to surrender this time.

The Act also provides a list of grounds for finding one or more of the above exceptions proved. The grounds most commonly relied upon are: (i) the seriousness of the offence; (ii) the accused's previous record and present community ties; and (iii) previous responses to the granting of bail. Thus the bench could hold that he would fail to surrender to bail on the ground that he has failed to obey the terms of a previous granting of bail; or that he would commit further offences on bail because of his previous record. These findings must be recorded by the bench and given to the accused.

Once the bench has considered that there is an exception to the accused's right to unconditional bail, they should consider whether the desired result (*e.g.* that the accused should appear on the prescribed day or should not commit further offences before his trial) could be achieved by conditional bail rather than a remand in custody. There is no list of what conditions may be imposed but it is common to impose such conditions as (i) that the accused undertakes to reside at a particular place; (ii) that the accused undertakes to be at that place between, for example, 7 p.m. and 7 a.m. (a curfew can sometimes be useful in cases where the accused is most likely to commit further offences at night); (iii) that the accused undertakes to report so many times each week to his nearest police station. In addition (iv) sureties may be required. Since the Bail Act it is no longer possible to demand that the accused put up money as a guarantee that he will appear on the appointed day (except where there is a likelihood that he may leave the country), but it is still possible for the bench to say that they are willing to grant bail if the accused can provide the name (or names) of persons who are willing to stand as surety for him. This means that if, for example, a father stands surety for his son in the sum of £200, part or all of that sum may be forfeited if the son fails to attend court for his trial. Furthermore it is an offence, punishable by imprisonment, for the accused to fail to answer to his bail.

Conditions as to bail can be imposed only to ensure: (a) that the accused appears on the appointed day; (b) that the accused commits no further offences whilst on bail; (c) that the accused does not interfere with witnesses or otherwise obstruct justice; and (d) to ensure that the accused is available for the preparation of any report which is to be completed.

(8) Legal aid and advice

As with legal aid and advice in civil cases, legal aid and advice in criminal cases is governed by the Legal Aid Acts of 1974 and 1982 together with the various regulations made under these Acts. Legal advice is accordingly available in criminal cases under the "green form" scheme in the same way as in civil cases (*ante*, p. 72). In addition most court centres operate what is known as the duty solicitor scheme. This scheme provides for local solicitors to be present in the courts to give advice to unrepresented defendants. In the past this service has been operated without funding but the Legal Aid Act 1982 authorises the Lord Chancellor to make arrangements for this service and to provide remuneration for the solicitors who operate it.

An application for legal aid in criminal cases is normally made directly to the court itself, and in the case of appeals may be made either to the court from which or to which the defendant is appealing. The initial application will usually be made to a magistrates court where it will be processed by the Clerk. While the Clerk has authority to *grant* legal aid, only the magistrates have power to *refuse* legal aid and in certain cases (where the charge is murder for example) the grant of legal aid is mandatory. Formerly there was no appeal against a refusal to grant legal aid but the 1982 Act provides for the making of regulations to enable a person refused aid to appeal to such other court or body (most likely the body will be the local legal aid committee) as may be specified.

Unless the grant of legal aid is mandatory, a court in determining whether to grant aid has regard both to the means of the defendant and the requirements of justice. In the past the relevant means test has been such that less than 10 per cent. of defendants have been required to make any contribution and their contributions have realised only £2 million against an expenditure of £100 million. The 1982 Act empowers the Lord Chancellor to introduce new regulations and his expressed intention is to introduce contribution arrangements broadly comparable with those applicable in civil legal aid (*ante*, p. 72) though one significant difference will be that the court will be empowered, upon conviction, to remit contributions not yet due.

As well as the means requirement, the court considering an application must consider whether the needs of justice require that legal aid be granted. It is now provided by statute that an unrepresented defendant cannot be sent to prison for the first time unless he has been informed of his right to apply for legal aid and has refused. In addition guidance given to the courts following upon the report of a Departmental Committee on Legal Aid (the Widgery Committee, 1966) indicates that the grant of legal aid is in the interests of justice when: (i) the charge is serious (i.e. that the accused is in danger of losing his liberty, livelihood or of suffering serious damage to his reputation); or (ii) a substantial question of law is involved; or (iii) the accused is incapable of following the proceedings or of stating his case (either from mental or physical disability or simply because he cannot speak English); or (iv) the case involves the tracing or interviewing of witnesses or will involve a detailed cross-examination of a prosecution witness; or (v) legal representation is desirable for other reasons (for example, the case will involve the cross examination of a child witness in a sexual case).

(9) Plea bargaining

Most people who are charged with a criminal offence plead guilty, and in magistrates' courts an overwhelming majority does so. Strictly, every defendant could plead not guilty and put the prosecution to the trouble of proving its case. Were this to be done by all defendants the results would be catastrophic so far as the administration of criminal justice is concerned. There is an old aphorism that delay defeats justice; if all defendants pleaded not guilty delay would become endemic and the administration of justice would be at least seriously impeded and might even grind to a halt.

It could be said, therefore, that the state has an interest in having the majority of defendants plead guilty. This is not to suggest that there is a deliberate policy aimed at curtailing not guilty pleas. Of those who plead guilty, most do so because they face an open-and-shut case where there is little point in prolonging the agony and where no steps have been taken by the prosecution to induce a guilty plea. Even in these cases the defendant knows, or will be so informed by his attorney, that he will get a lesser sentence by pleading guilty. If the tariff (see *post*, p. 112) for a particular offence is "x", the practice is to give "x-y" where the defendant pleads guilty. The defendant is, in effect, rewarded for saving time and money and, perhaps, possible embarrassment and even humiliation of witnesses.

But then there are cases where some form of persuasion is brought to bear to secure the defendant's agreement to a guilty plea. This process is called plea bargaining, but it is important to note that the initiative for a plea bargain might be taken just as readily by the defence as by the prosecution. Bargains take many forms but may be reduced to two types: bargains as to plea and bargains as to sentence. An example of the former might be where X is charged with the serious offence of causing grievous bodily harm with intent and also with the less serious offence of malicious wounding; the prosecution and the defence may agree that in return for the accused pleading guilty to the less serious charge, the prosecution will drop the serious charge. An example of the latter might be provided by a charge of indecent assault on a very young child; in return for a plea of guilty, thus sparing the victim and his family the embarrassment of a trial, it might be indicated to the accused that he will receive a sentence lighter than he would have received on conviction after trial.

There is a difference between bargaining as to plea and bargaining as to sentence. The former can be done without the participation of the judge. A judge (or magistrates) normally accept bargains as to plea. Though it is open to the judge to insist that the prosecution proceeds with the more serious charge, this is done only exceptionally; in the case of Peter Sutcliffe (the so-called Yorkshire Ripper), for example, the judge insisted that the charge of murder be proceeded with though the Attorney-General had indicated that the prosecution was willing to accept a plea of guilty to manslaughter on the grounds of diminished responsibility. A bargain as to sentence, on the other hand, necessarily requires the participation of the judge. It is, of course, perfectly proper for an accused's counsel to tell him that the likelihood is that he will get a lighter sentence if he pleads guilty but the circumstances in which the judge should enter into such a bargain are severely, if uncertainly, prescribed. Appellate courts have indicated that it is only in the most exceptional cases that the judge should be involved in such discussions and that, whenever possible, such discussions should be conducted in the presence of both sides and in open court. It is never proper for a judge to indicate that in the event of a guilty plea he will impose a lighter sentence for this is necessarily coercive and deprives the defendant of his unfettered choice to plead guilty or not guilty. But it may be permissible for the judge to indicate that in any event he will not impose a custodial sentence.

Bargains, whether as to plea or sentence, raise serious issues. On one view there is something in it for all parties. The prosecution gets a conviction without the delay and expense of a trial, the police can close their files on the case, and the defendant gets off more lightly than he might otherwise have done. But there are dangers. An accused, even though innocent, might be tempted to plead guilty to a charge, or to a lesser charge, because he fears the consequences of being found guilty and thus exposing himself to a more severe sentence. And it is obviously important that judges should not be seen to be involved in what are essentially compromises. The function of the judge is to act as an impartial referee motivated only by the dictates of the law; it is not proper that he should be influenced by notions of expediency.

There is no doubt, however, that plea bargaining is extensively practised and that it is seen as having advantages both to the prosecution and the defence. To an extent it must be recognised as a useful device to ensure the smooth running of the criminal justice system. But it has certain dangers and thus far the courts have been unable to articulate guidelines which give rise to complete confidence in the propriety and fairness of its practice.

(10) Course of trial

A person charged with a criminal offence may be tried on information summarily before a magistrates' court, or on indictment at the Crown Court. The essential difference between the two is that trial on indictment involves trial by jury. In a summary trial the magistrates determine the facts as well as the law; in a trial on indictment it is for the jury to determine the facts while questions of law are the province of the judge.

Otherwise the law and procedure is substantially similar whether the trial is summary or on indictment. The same general rule applies that it is for the prosecution to establish the guilt of the accused and not for the accused to prove his innocence (*ante*, p. 4). This used to be expressed in the time-honoured phrase of proof beyond reasonable doubt but this particular expression has fallen out of favour and the standard is now expressed by saying that the judges of fact (the jury or the magistrates as the case may be) must be completely satisfied, or feel sure, of the accused's guilt. There are, however, numbers of exceptions (mainly created by statute) to this principle where the burden of proving particular facts falls upon the accused. When this occurs the accused is not required to prove the matter to the same strict standard as applies to the prosecution; it is enough to establish the matter on the balance of probabilities (see *ante*, p. 4).

Normally the prosecution opens the proceedings by outlining the case against the accused and by adducing evidence (which may include real evidence such as fingerprints or the murder weapon, as well as testimonial evidence) to prove that case. The witnesses called and examined by the prosecution may be cross-examined by the defence and may, in turn, be re-examined by the prosecution.

When the prosecution has completed its case it is open to the defence to submit that there is no case to answer. In effect the accused is asserting that, on the basis of the evidence given so far, no reasonable jury (or bench of magistrates) could find the charge against him proved. If the submission is upheld the judge will direct the jury to return (or the magistrates will return) a verdict of not guilty.

If no submission is made or if the court rules against it, the defence then adduces its evidence; its witnesses will in turn be examined and may be cross-examined and re-examined. The accused, however, is in a special position. While he is free to give evidence, he cannot be compelled to do so. If he chooses to do so he is subject to examination in the normal way except that he cannot usually be compelled to answer questions tending to show that he has committed offences other than the one with which he is charged. Until recently an accused who chose not to give evidence was able to make an unsworn statement from the dock. The value of such statements, since they were not subject to cross-examination, was probably small and now by the Criminal Justice Act 1982, s.72, the right is substantially abolished. This is, however, without prejudice to an *un*represented accused making an address to the court or jury which, were he represented, his counsel or solicitor could have made on his behalf. Furthermore, the accused upon conviction may make an unsworn statement in mitigation before sentence is passed.

The accused's spouse is also in a special position. In general a spouse is not a competent witness for the prosecution subject to certain exceptions, for example where the charge relates to violence done to the spouse. A spouse is a competent witness for the defence but may normally be called only on the application of the accused spouse.

At the conclusion of the defence case and following closing speeches by the prosecution and the defence, the judge, in a trial on indictment, sums up the case to the jury. In his summing-up the judge will review the evidence and direct the jury's attention to the salient points of the case but he must not trespass upon the jury's function of finding the facts. He will always instruct the jury on the burden of proof and may direct them on any matters of law affecting the case.

Magistrates in a summary trial do not direct themselves in this fashion. They may reach a conclusion on guilt or innocence without leaving the bench or they may retire to give the case more detailed consideration.

(11) Form of trial

Whether a person is to be tried summarily or on indictment depends upon a number of factors. Some crimes (numerically by far the largest class) are of such a minor nature that they may be tried only summarily. Nearly all motoring offences are summary only as are most offences involving a failure to possess a necessary licence (for a television receiver or a dog, for example) and a host of other offences. At the other extreme there are offences which because of their seriousness are indictable only. These include such offences as treason, murder, manslaughter, infanticide, rape and robbery. In between are offences where the seriousness depends not upon the nature of the offence but the particular circumstances of it. An obvious example is theft which may involve property to the value of a few pence or property to the value of millions of pounds. Such offences are made triable either way.

Where an offence is summary only or where it is indictable only, the accused has no choice as to the form of trial. Where the offence is triable either way it is in the first place for the magistrates to decide (having regard to such things the nature of the case, the punishment which they can inflict if the accused is found guilty) whether the case is suitable for summary trial. If they decide that it is not so suitable, the accused cannot gainsay their decision and they proceed to consider whether there is sufficient evidence to commit him for trial on indictment. If they decide that the case is suitable for summary trial, they so inform the accused and tell him that he may consent to summary trial or that he may insist on trial by jury. They must further inform him that if he consents to summary trial and is convicted he may be committed to the Crown Court for sentence if it appears on hearing information about his character and antecedents (for the magistrates will learn of these only *after* conviction) that a greater punishment should be imposed than the magistrates have power to impose.

The above classification and procedure was introduced by the Criminal Law Act 1977 and represents a considerable simplification of the previous position. It may be that it is not entirely logical in that, for example, an accused cannot insist on jury trial for such offences as assaulting a police officer in the execution of his duty nor for driving with a blood-alcohol concentration above the prescribed limit. Both might be thought to be relatively serious offences but both are classified as summary only. On the other hand, if an accused is charged with theft, and even if the value of the property involved is only a few pence, it will be open to him to insist on trial on indictment though summary trial is more appropriate. The Government attempted to meet this difficulty in the Criminal Law Act by proposing that where an offence of theft involved property worth less than £20, it would be triable only summarily. This proposal was overwhelmingly defeated in Parliament though Parliament did accept that for offences of criminal damage, where the damage does not exceed £200, the offence should be summary only. Parliament's reasoning appeared to be that where the offence reflected upon a man's honesty (as theft does while criminal damage does not) he should be entitled to be tried by his peers. In practice minor cases of theft are usually dealt with summarily because the accused consents to being so tried but it is by no means uncommon for cases involving trifling amounts to be tried by judge and jury.

If the accused is charged with an offence which is indictable only or if he is charged with an offence triable either way and the magistrates decide that the case should be tried on indictment, it is the function of the magistrates to decide whether the accused should be committed for trial.

In such proceedings the magistrates sit as *examining magistrates* and conduct a preliminary inquiry into the case against the accused. At one time the prosecution conducted these proceedings much as at the trial on indictment itself, outlining the case and calling witnesses who after examination might be cross-examined and re-examined. This had certain advantages for the accused; he would know the case he had to meet at the trial and might even secure a ruling that he had no case to answer. The latter was, however, unlikely in the extreme because no prosecutor was likely to advise in favour of proceedings unless there was, at the least, a prima facie case and thus the elaborate oral procedure was really a waste of time and money. That was also a possible disadvantage to an accused, especially when the case was one to attract great public interest, that extensive press coverage of the prosecution's case at the committal stage might predispose potential jurors to think him guilty.

Accordingly a new style of committal was introduced by the Criminal Justice Act 1967. It is now possible for magistrates to commit a person for trial "without consideration of the evidence" if all the prosecution's evidence consists of written statements. In practice, the accused's solicitor will have been shown these statements and have satisfied himself that there is a prima facie case. If he is not so satisfied he may submit that there is no sufficient case for committal and in this event the magistrates will consider the evidence to determine whether a prima facie case is made out. So far as the press are concerned they may publish only specified information such as the name of the accused (unless the charge is rape where the accused's anonymity must normally be preserved), the charge and the decision to commit.

It is, however, still possible for an accused to insist upon the old-style of committal proceedings but this is only rarely done. It might be done, for example, where the defence believes that cross-examination of the prosecution's witnesses will quickly discredit the prosecution's case. As with the new-style committals, the press is similarly restricted in reporting the proceedings, but it is open to the accused to insist that reporting restrictions be lifted so that the proceedings can be fully reported. This is sometimes done where the defence believes that the publicity given to the case will bring forward witnesses who might help the defence case. Until recently an accused could insist on the lifting of reporting restriction even though he was charged with co-accused who were opposed to this course; but the Criminal Justice (Amendment) Act 1981 provides that where one of the co-accused objects to the lifting of restrictions, the court shall make an order for lifting restrictions only if satisfied that it is in the interests of justice to do so.

While committal proceedings, in effect, serve notice of the prosecution's case against the accused, the accused is not obliged to reveal to the prosecution his line, or lines, of defence. One important modification of this principle is that the accused will be told by the magistrates that he will not at his trial be able to adduce evidence tending to establish an alibi (that is that he was somewhere else at the time of the crime) unless he gives particulars of the alibi to the prosecutor within seven days of the order for committal. This is to enable the prosecutor (through the police) to check the alibi and to prevent an accused from springing upon the jury an alibi of doubtful provenance at the eleventh hour which the prosecution has no opportunity to counter.

Nearly all trials on indictment follow from committal by magistrates but it is possible to circumvent this procedure by what is known as a voluntary bill of indictment. The prosecution may apply to a High Court judge for leave to prefer an indictment and, in substance, the judge performs the functions normally performed by examining magistrates in determining whether there is a prima facie case. This procedure is only exceptionally used. It may be used, for example, where the magistrates have refused to commit but the prosecutor believes that the case is strong enough to justify trial. Or it may be used where the prosecution have evidence implicating A, B and C in a robbery and have secured the committal of A and B while C still remains at large; if C is subsequently apprehended the prosecutor may apply for a voluntary bill so that he can be tried with A and B. In such a case the judge has to balance the disadvantage to C in being brought speedily to trial against the hardship to A and B involved in delay.

(12) Trial by jury

Trial by jury is the only form of trial for offences tried on indictment. The system has many defenders and some critics but before any appraisal is attempted it is necessary to know the mechanics of the system which are now for the most part contained in the Juries Act 1974.

Every person between the ages of 18 and 65 is qualified for jury service provided: (i) that person is registered as a parliamentary or local government elector; (ii) has been ordinarily resident within the United Kingdom for any period of at least five years since reaching the age of 13; and (iii) is not ineligible or disqualified for jury service.

Disqualification extends to any person who within the United Kingdom has (a) been sentenced to imprisonment for life (or to be detained during pleasure) or to a term of five years or more; or (b) served any part of a sentence of imprisonment of three months or more during the last ten years, or has been detained in borstal.

Of those rendered ineligible by the Act the largest class comprises those who are connected with the administration of the law. For obvious reasons, judges, magistrates and police officers are ineligible but so too are many people (clerks and secretaries for example) who are employed (for instance by the Lord Chancellor's Office, the Director of Public Prosecutions, the police) in the day-to-day administration of justice. The other categories of ineligible persons extends to persons in holy orders and the mentally ill.

There is a further category of persons who, though eligible, may claim to be excused as of right. This category recognises that certain people (for example, Members of Parliament, doctors, nurses) may have more important duties than jury service and they may, if they wish, excuse themselves from it.

The next step is to get together a panel from which juries may be chosen for particular cases. This is done by a person, designated as appropriate officer, who works under instructions issued by the Lord Chancellor. The panel is selected at random but no particular method of selection is prescribed. Any party to proceedings in which jurors may be called is entitled to inspect the panel from which the jurors are to be drawn. This affords no more information than the names and addresses of the persons comprising the panel but it is in theory open to a party to conduct his own inquiries into the backgrounds of these persons to determine whether they are likely to be sympathetic or unsympathetic to his case. In practice this is *rarely* done, partly because the considerable expense involved in investigating what may be 100–150 persons forming the panel and partly because the parties will normally be confident that the random system of selection will ensure a reasonably impartial jury. This is not to say that it is never done and in a limited class of case ("political" offences involving terrorism and breaches of the Official Secrets Act, and serious offences committed by a gang of "professional" criminals) the Director of Public Prosecutions may authorise the police to check the names on the panel with certain specified sources to ascertain whether a potential juror is a known associate of the accused or is known to be sympathetic or antagonistic to the accused's cause.

That this practice, known as jury vetting, is legal is clear; whether it is desirable is hotly debated. The Juries Act contains no disqualification of persons who might be subject to improper pressure, nor of persons of extreme political views, and it is argued by some that this form of vetting constitutes a deliberate interference with the principle of randomness which governs jury selection, and that in the nature of things it is a facility available to the prosecution but not to the defence. On occasion, however, the defence has been granted legal aid to make its inquiries into the panel. In one case where prison officers were charged with various offences following a prison riot this was permitted to determine whether there might not be persons on the panel who, though not formally disqualified, from some previous prison experience might be expected to be very hostile to the defendants.

Jury vetting must not be confused with jury challenges though the two are connected in the sense that the information gleaned from vetting might lead to a challenge.

Once the accused is arraigned the charge (or charges) is read to him and he is asked in relation to each charge whether he pleads guilty or not guilty. A plea of guilty to be acceptable must be unequivocal and if it is not, or if the accused refuses to plead, a plea of not guilty is entered. If the accused pleads not guilty, or if such a plea is entered, he is told that the jury will now be called and that if he objects to any of them he must do so as they are called to be sworn.

The accused may challenge: (i) all or any of the jurors for cause, and (ii) not more than three jurors without assigning any cause. In practice challenge, whether with or without cause, is uncommon. Most people have prejudices of one sort or another but these are not likely, bearing in mind that they are constrained by the collective nature of the jury's discussion and decision, to significantly affect their impartiality in the ordinary fare of criminal prosecutions. But in some cases prejudice can obtrude sufficiently to undermine impartiality. An obvious example is racial prejudice which, at least in some, runs so deep that a black defendant could not expect his case to be heard fairly by people having such prejudices. Then there are types of case such as sexual assaults on young children where the defence might think it preferable not to have on the jury mothers with young children of their own. On the other hand, in a celebrated obscenity case, counsel challenged male jurors in the hope of getting additional female jurors because he thought females would be more dispassionate in dealing with such an issue.

The defence is not limited in the number of challenges it may make for cause. The defendant may challenge the whole of the panel (sometimes called a challenge to the array) on the grounds that it has not been selected randomly and impartially. Such a challenge would succeed if, for example, it could be shown that the appropriate officer had selected a panel from people likely to be prejudiced against the defendant or his cause. Such challenges are now almost unheard of. Recently such a challenge was made on the grounds that the panel did not fairly reflect the proportions of whites to blacks known to exist in the area from which the panel had been drawn but the challenge was disallowed; so long as the panel is selected at random it is not a valid ground of challenge that it produces a disproportionate number of whites—or blacks come to that.

Challenges of individual jurors for cause are less rare. "Cause" has never been comprehensively defined but means any cause which is likely to unfit a juror for the performance of his duties. Most obviously this would extend to any cause which is likely to affect his impartiality (for instance, that he is related to the defendant or belongs to an extreme political organisation opposed to the defendant's cause) but also extends to other matters obviously affecting his fitness (such as that he is hard of hearing or that he has an insufficient command of English to follow the proceedings). The defence cannot examine a juror with a view to determining his suitability, as by questioning him about his attitudes to the offence in issue, or on his racial attitudes and so on. This practice has become established in the United States where the selection of a jury may occupy days of the court's time but it has never been allowed to take root here.

The defendant may also challenge without assigning cause (often called peremptory challenge) but he is limited to three such challenges. Where there is only one defendant the use of such challenges is unlikely to affect the composition of the jury to any significant extent, but as the number of defendants is increased so is the number of peremptory challenges. In one case nine black defendants were charged with various public order offences so that between them they had twenty-seven peremptory challenges. Their request to be heard by an all-black jury was refused; all they could do was to use their twenty-seven challenges in the hope of securing some black representation on the jury.

The prosecution cannot challenge jurors but it can ask jurors to stand-by. This is virtually indistinguishable from challenge in its effect except that the prosecution is not required to assign cause until the number left in the panel falls below the number required to compose a jury. It is then a virtually unlimited power of challenge.

But it is again necessary to emphasise that challenge, or stand-by, is very much the exception. It is also necessary to make the point that challenge and stand-by are not used by the defence and prosecution to secure a jury favourable to their respective causes but merely to eliminate from the jury persons who are likely to be biased one way or the other.

During the course of a trial the judge may discharge the jury or any individual juror. The former may occur when it is accidentally disclosed to the jury that the accused has previous convictions since this would prejudice the accused's case (*ante*, p. 28); in such circumstances the trial is recommenced with a different jury. The latter is most likely to occur where a juror falls ill but it may also occur where some impropriety by a juror (in one case the fact that a juror was giving the accused a lift in his car to the court each morning was found to be such an impropriety) has occurred; but discharges must not reduce the number of jurymen below nine.

On completion of the case the jury will retire to consider their verdict. They will be instructed to reach, and ordinarily do, a unanimous verdict and thereafter they must communicate with no one other than the judge in open court.

This is still the general rule but in 1967 the law was altered (it is now contained in the Juries Act 1974) to permit the judge to accept a majority verdict in certain cases. If the jury cannot agree after a reasonable period of deliberation having regard to the complexity of the case (the period must not be less than two hours but the judge may allow much, much longer in a difficult and protracted case) the judge may direct them on a majority verdict. The judge may then accept a verdict; (a) in a case where there are not less than 11 jurors, 10 agree, or (b) in a case where there are 10 jurors, 9 agree.

The theory behind the majority verdict is the danger that is said to exist in some cases of a juror being bribed or threatened to hold out against his fellow jurors, or of a juror holding out simply because of his extreme and intractable views. Formerly a single such juror could provoke a disagreement leading to the expense of possible re-trial; this risk is now very much reduced. In the nature of things it is difficult to produce affirmative proof of the arguments which led to the adoption of the majority verdict but there are certain types of case in which threats are made to jurymen, or are likely to be made, and from time to time judges order special police protection for the jury.

It is not an easy matter to make an informed judgment about jury trial. As an institution it is hallowed by its very antiquity and must be the sole institution which unites in its approval judges, Members of Parliament and the National Council for Civil Liberties. It is popular with the public but the police are less unflagging in their support. Critics point out that trial by jury has been virtually eliminated in civil cases without any harmful (and arguably only beneficial) effects, and that the vast majority of criminal cases are tried summarily without a jury.

The problem is that the vital information is lacking. We do not know how the jury works. No one is allowed to sit in on their deliberations so that no systematic study can be made. Indeed it is now a contempt of court to obtain or disclose any particulars of a jury's deliberations in any legal proceedings.

This legislation will ensure that disquieting instances which have come to light in the past where it is evident that jurors have not understood the issues in the case or have reached their decision more on prejudice than reason, will no longer surface to embarrass the faith of those who support the institution.

The arguments for and against are accordingly replete with slogans and shibboleths rather than with facts and statistics. Lord Denning has said that where a man's honour is at stake trial by jury has no equal; yet the same judge believes that juries are entirely unsuitable for a civil negligence action. It is sometimes said that the jury is a bulwark of liberty by which is presumably meant that oppressive prosecutions by the state or the police is divined and checked by juries. While there have been famous historical instances of this, serious research finds little to support the thesis that the jury acts as an effective check on the arbitrary use of power.

One difference, perhaps the critical one, between trial by judge alone and trial by jury is that the judge makes a detailed and explicit finding of fact while the jury returns an "inscrutable" verdict which simply finds in favour of one party or the other. The former is much more open to review by appellate courts because the findings and the inferences of the trial judge can be tested. But when the appellate court is faced, as it is in the case of jury trial, simply with a conclusion it must support that conclusion if there is *any* reasonable view of the evidence which leads to it. The former system is rational, the latter instinctive. If we had never devised trial by jury it must be doubtful whether judges, Members of Parliament and (though possibly less so) the National Council for Civil Liberties would now be clamouring for the replacement of the developed and professional expertise of the judge by the amateur and instinctive reaction of a randomly selected group of laymen. On the other hand not all successful institutions owe their acceptance to reason: faith plays an important part.

(13) Sentencing

The framework for sentencing a convicted defendant is now almost entirely prescribed in legislation and within that framework the actual sentence is fixed by the court. Exceptionally Parliament prescribes a fixed penalty (life imprisonment in the case of murder for instance) which the court has no option but to impose; but more usually Parliament prescribes only the maximum punishment in the definition of an offence (life imprisonment for rape, 10 years' imprisonment for theft, five years' imprisonment for reckless driving, a fine of £100 for dropping litter in a public place and so on) leaving it to the court to decide whether to impose the maximum or some lesser sentence. Parliament has also placed certain general limitations on the sentencing powers of magistrates' courts which may usually not impose a sentence of imprisonment exceeding six months nor a fine exceeding £1,000. The offence creating provision normally expresses the maximum in terms of a period of imprisonment and/or a fine of a certain amount but other legislation provides for alternative measures such as absolute and conditional discharges, probation, suspended sentences and hospital orders.

(a) *Sentencing in general*

The sentencer thus often has a range of measures which he can use to deal with the case in hand. In practice the sentencer is nearly always a magistrates' court and the sentence imposed is most often a fine. For the run-of-the-mill offences which come before magistrates (soliciting, careless driving, drinking after hours, operating a television receiver without a licence, and the like) the almost invariable response is a fine since, and for obvious reasons, other penalties are entirely inapropos.

In fixing a fine the sentencer usually follows the tariff, that is he fixes the amount by reference to what he knows from his experience other courts will impose for a similar offence. Normally the fine will fall within a certain band between the maximum and the minimum; the sentencer will impose a fine above or below this band only if there are recognisable aggravating or mitigating circumstances. It is the same with imprisonment where this is decided upon. There is a band within which the "normal" case falls which may be departed from only if there are recognisable circumstances of aggravation or mitigation. If rape is taken as an example the band within which most sentences fall is four to seven years though the maximum punishment is imprisonment for life.

Quite how this tariff is arrived at is a matter of conjecture. We know that one sentencer follows the tariff because all other sentencers do and that appellate courts may reduce (they cannot usually increase) a sentence not in accordance with the tariff. But this does not explain why four to seven years imprisonment is thought appropriate for most cases of rape or why a fine in the range £20 to £40 is thought apt for someone dropping litter in a public place.

In practice sentencers probably rarely ask themselves fundamental questions about the nature of punishment. It may be just as well that they do not because there are no very satisfactory answers. At first sight there are a whole range of seemingly obvious explanations. We punish a man because he has done wrong and deserves to be punished for it (retribution), or because punishment will ensure that he and others do not commit like crimes (deterrence), or because he will learn from his punishment the folly of his ways (reformation), or simply to keep him out of harm's way (protection of the public).

None of these theories is entirely convincing though this is not to say that they are entirely without validity. If retribution is given as the reason, how do we rationally fix the "right" retribution for stealing a sheep? At one time it was thought to be death but nowadays, for a first offender, it would hardly attract more than a modest fine. As for deterrence it seems attractive to assert that the imposition of punishment deters the offender and that the threat of it deters the rest of us. But if punishment was an effective deterrent none of us would ever commit crime. It might be countered that the only reason we are not deterred is because the punishment is not sufficiently severe. Experience is, however, against this; people did not stop stealing sheep though their lives were forfeit for it.

Reformation is an attractive idea because it is not an atavistic response and appeals to humanitarian motives. Some of the measures available to courts may be genuinely reformative in their intent (probation and the community service order for example) but there is no evidence that imprisonment is reformative and a good deal of evidence that it is not.

The dominant consideration in sentencing, most especially where imprisonment may be imposed, is probably protection of the public. This view, which emphasises deterrence, requires the sentencer to have regard to the interests of the community at large. Thus the Lord Chief Justice has recently reaffirmed (*Roberts* (1982)) that, other than in wholly exceptional circumstances, rape requires the imposition of an immediate custodial sentence; this, he said, is required to mark the gravity of the offence, to emphasise public disapproval, to serve as a warning to others, and, last but by no means least, to protect women. Sentencers accordingly emphasise the public interest in securing what is felt to be the appropriate penalty. No doubt it is true to say that the public (and women especially) would be deeply disturbed if rape did not ordinarily attract a custodial sentence but it does not follow from this that a custodial sentence is the "right" or "best" response, nor does it offer any guidance on the length of the term of imprisonment which should be imposed.

If the notion of protection of the public was taken to its logical conclusion then it would seem to follow that a rapist, a burglar, or a shop-lifter should be incarcerated until it was evident that he would no longer repeat his crimes, that he was no longer a danger to the public. But such a policy would require sentences far in excess of what is normally thought apt for the particular crime. No one, for instance, would want a shop-lifter to be imprisoned for life even if it could be shown beyond a shadow of a doubt that on release he would immediately recommence stealing from shops. The tariff for a crime cannot, therefore, be fixed exclusively by the notion of protecting the public. It is a nice idea that there should be a punishment to fit the crime but we have no formula which can precisely tell us what punishment fits what crime.

(b) *The information required for sentencing*

Much of the information required for sentencing is revealed by the case itself. In a simple case of speeding, for example, it will be revealed by how much the defendant exceeded the speed limit, whether it was on a busy road at rush hour or a deserted road at night, whether the defendant was speeding for the sheer joy of it or because he was taking a sick relative to hospital and so on. All these factors will be taken into account by the sentencer when he fixes the fine. But the trial will not reveal the previous convictions of the defendant and the sentencer *may* need to take these into account depending upon their relevance to the instant case, and upon conviction the prosecution normally tenders evidence of previous convictions. In the case of a man convicted of theft it would not be relevant that he has a previous conviction for careless driving while it would be highly relevant that he has two previous convictions for burglary.

While the case itself together with previous convictions will reveal much of the information required for sentencing, there are certain kinds of case where it may be advisable for the sentencer to have much more detailed information concerning the background of the defendant and the mechanism for this is the *social inquiry report.* Obviously a social inquiry report is not required where the defendant is charged with routine road traffic offences; equally obviously it will usually be necessary in the case of a juvenile or a first offender charged with serious offences, or in many cases where upon conviction a custodial sentence is likely.

The social inquiry report is made by a probation officer and may, with the consent of the accused, be made before trial. In his report the probation officer gives information concerning the background of the accused, including such matters as family circumstances, educational record and employment prospects. The probation officer may also give his views on what he considers to be the appropriate sentence, in particular whether he believes that probation would or would not be a suitable method for dealing with the case.

A final matter that needs to be noted in this connection is the power of the court to defer sentence. This power was introduced by the Powers of Criminal Courts Act 1973 and enables a court to defer passing sentence for a period up to six months following conviction. The Act contains no guidelines on the use of the power other than that it can be exercised only with the consent of the offender and that it would be in the interests of justice to exercise the power. The power is intended to be used where the sentencer has reason to believe that, within the period for which he defers the sentence, the circumstances will materially change so that less, or even no, punitive measures may be called for at the time of sentence. Such material circumstances might be that the offender makes reparation to the victim or settles down to employment or otherwise demonstrates that he has changed his ways for the better.

(c) *The sentencing measures available*

Among the sentences which a court may impose, the following may be briefly described.

Absolute and conditional discharges. An absolute discharge may be given where though in law the defendant is guilty of an offence, the circumstances are such that it would not be right to impose any punishment. It is impossible to catalogue all the circumstances in which such a discharge might be given but broadly it may be said that it would be appropriate where no reasonable person would attach any blame to the defendant's conduct. A conditional discharge is quite different in that, and although the defendant receives no immediate punishment for the offence, he remains liable to be punished for that offence if within a stated period which must not exceed three years he commits another offence. It might be given where there are mitigating circumstances which are not quite strong enough to merit an absolute discharge, or it might be given even for an offence meriting imprisonment where the sentencer thinks that the mere threat of punishment will cause the offender to mend his ways. Absolute and conditional discharges may be granted for any offence other than an offence for which the penalty is fixed by law.

Fines. A fine may be imposed for any offence other than murder and it is by far the most common punishment imposed by the courts. The amount of the fine is, within the maximum prescribed, determined in relation to the gravity of the breach involved and it may be fixed to reflect the profit that the offender has made from his crime. But a magistrates' court must (and the Crown Court in practice does) have regard also to the offender's means to pay. It is wrong, however, to impose a substantial fine on a rich offender where the offence properly requires a custodial sentence; just as it is wrong to imprison a poor offender where the offence properly requires a substantial fine which the offender cannot pay.

Disqualification. Various statutory provisions authorise disqualification as a penalty. Thus a person who is convicted of cruelty to animals may be disqualified from keeping a dog and a person convicted of corrupt or illegal practices at an election is for a period of five years from his conviction disqualified from voting and from being elected to the Commons. But the most common use of disqualification arises in connection with motoring offences. For certain driving offences (most notably driving with a blood/alcohol concentration exceeding the prescribed limit—the "breathalyser law") disqualification for twelve months is mandatory unless there are special reasons. For other driving offences (such as careless driving, speeding) immediate disqualification, though possible, is unlikely; but there is a scale of penalty points and disqualification follows when an offender incurs twelve points within a prescribed period.

Compensation, etc. Courts may order an offender to pay compensation (up to £1,000 in a magistrates' court, unlimited in the Crown Court) in respect of any personal injury, loss or damage provided it does not arise from a road traffic accident. A court may order the restitution of stolen property or, if the stolen property has been disposed of, it may order that compensation be made to the victim from any money taken from the offender when arrested. Where an offender has used property for criminal purposes (a car used in connection with a robbery for instance) he may be ordered to forfeit that property. An even more far reaching provision is that for criminal bankruptcy. Such an order may be made by the Crown Court against an offender whose offences have caused loss or damage exceeding £15,000 and who has significant assets, the idea being to prevent him or his family enjoying ill-gotten gains.

Probation. The rationale underlying probation is that certain persons who commit crime (most obviously the young and the inexperienced) will respond to guidance under professional supervision and that this is much more likely to restore them as good and useful citizens than a more severe way of dealing with them. It is thus an alternative to a custodial sentence and accordingly a probation order is not appropriate where some lesser sentence (such as a fine) is called for.

Except where the sentence is fixed by law, the court, if of the opinion that it is expedient to make a probation order rather than pass a custodial sentence, may make an order in respect of any person who has attained 17 and who has expressed his willingness to comply. The offender is told that if he fails to keep the order or commits another offence whilst on probation that he is liable to be sentenced for the original offence.

Community service order. This was introduced to provide an alternative way of dealing with offenders who would otherwise have been sentenced to a short term of imprisonment. The general conditions for making such an order are much the same as for a probation order and it is in fact supervised by a probation officer. The order requires the offender to perform within 12 months a specified number of hours (between 40 and 240) unpaid work for the benefit of the community and thus the making of such an order is dependent upon a community service scheme being available and a place for the offender on it. Such schemes are in operation involving such things as work on conservation projects, archaeological sites and canal clearance.

Custodial sentences. A custodial sentence is always the last resort of the sentencer. While it may be imposed on a first offender, a person given a custodial sentence has typically run the gamut of lesser punishments.

Custodial sentences may take the form of imprisonment, detention in a detention centre or youth custody. In general, imprisonment is available only for persons over 21 and, following the implementation of the Criminal Justice Act 1982, sentences of youth custody are available (in both the magistrates' and Crown courts) for persons between the ages of 15 and 21. Where a term of youth custody is considered appropriate, the court will fix a term which is not less than four months and not more than the maximum term of imprisonment available for an adult offender charged with the same offence. If the offender is under 17 the maximum term of youth custody must not exceed 12 months. A sentence of youth custody for life may be imposed on offenders convicted of an offence carrying life imprisonment if committed by an adult offender; such a sentence will be mandatory for those offenders between 18 and 21 who are convicted of murder. The actual conditions of youth custody will vary according to what is considered necessary for the particular youth. It may take a form similar to the former borstal training, or it may more closely resemble imprisonment, and it is intended that all institutions will provide training.

The detention centre also provides for young offenders (aged 14–21) and is to cater for those whose offences merit only a short period of confinement. Under the Criminal Justice Act 1982, a person cannot be sentenced to a detention centre for a period less than 21 days nor more than four months. This reduces the term formerly available and is in line with the theory of a short, sharp shock rather than the reformation of the offender.

The suspended sentence. A sentence of imprisonment may be

suspended in whole or in part. A court which sentences an offender to a term of imprisonment not exceeding two years may suspend the sentence for a period between one and two years. If the sentence which is suspended is for more than six months the court may make a supervision order placing the offender under the supervision of a probation officer for a period up to that of the suspension. The thinking behind the suspended sentence appears to have been a sort of sword of Damocles theory, the offender being encouraged to (or coerced into) mending his ways by the threat of activation of the sentence.

The *partially suspended sentence* is significantly different. Where a court imposes a sentence of not less than six months and not more than two years it may order that he spends part of the sentence in prison while the remaining part (which must not be more than three quarters nor less than one quarter of the whole term) is suspended in the normal way.

Other powers. The foregoing by no means details all the powers possessed by courts for dealing with offenders but gives some indication of the principal powers available. Two general points emerge. One is that we have gone a long way in providing the sentencer with alternatives to imprisonment and many of the alternatives have been bold and imaginative. Few believe that imprisonment is in any sense reformative and merely operates (in some cases rightly operates) to keep some people out of society's way for a period of time. So imprisonment is rightly regarded only as a last resort, to be imposed if none of the whole panoply of non-custodial measures is appropriate. The other point is a sobering one. Notwithstanding these developments the prison population has not significantly diminished and our prisons are in fact over-crowded. On one view this could be said to reflect a growing lawlessness, a more ready resort to violence, in our society and does not indicate any unwillingness on the part of the sentencers to utilise non-custodial measures. On another view there seems to be a sort of Parkinson's Law which dictates that the number of prisoners rises to meet the number of cells available for them.

Chapter 5

THE LEGAL SYSTEM AND THE EUROPEAN DIMENSION

This chapter examines the effect on the English Legal System of the United Kingdom's membership of the European Communities and its ratification of the European Convention on Human Rights.

1. The European Communities

It is tempting to view the various European Communities as an embryonic United States of Europe; especially when we hear politicians talk of the importance of European unity in forming a united restraint on the Eastern powers. However it is important to realise that Europe is a very long way from becoming anything like the United States. When the original 13 American states resolved to form what is now the United States of America, they were intent on forming a political as well as economic entity. They were prepared to yield as much of their own sovereignty as would be essential to allow the newly formed national government to operate as a single international political force. A balance was therefore struck in the constitution to allow the individual states as much self-government as possible while ensuring that, for example in military matters, the central government spoke for all. It is true that today one still hears the odd dispute over state sovereignty and attempts to return some power to the individual states, but no-one would challenge the fact that, on matters external to the United States, the Government in Washington represents the sole policy-making body.

In Europe it is quite clear that many people would like to see a political union of the countries since this would produce a formidable international military force. However it is equally clear that while there might be some unified political action flowing from the European Communities (such as was seen over Europe's response to the British involvement in the Falkland Islands dispute), the Communities were intended as purely economic entities in the first place. Membership almost certainly involves some loss of national sovereignty, but the United Kingdom could probably leave the community by a simple majority vote in the Westminster Parliament, something which no state in the United States could lawfully do. We are still a very long way from a single Parliament for Western Europe with powers to make political decisions for all.

(1) The composition of the European Communities

In 1951 six founding countries (France, West Germany, Belgium, Luxembourg, Italy and the Netherlands) signed the Treaty of Paris which created the first of the three European Communities—the *European Coal and Steel Community*. Later in 1957 the same six countries signed two further Treaties (the Treaties of Rome) to create the *European Economic Community* and the *European Atomic Energy Community*. Over the next eight years the principal governing institutions of these three bodies were gradually unified so that they covered all three communities. There thus emerged the Council, the Commission, the Assembly (now unofficially called the European Parliament) and the Court of Justice of the European Communities. The functions of each body are described and governed by the relevant treaty. Of the three, the European Economic Community (EEC) is by far the most significant and is the subject of this chapter.

In 1973 the United Kingdom, by virtue of the European Communities Act 1972, became a signatory to the three Treaties. Ireland and Denmark joined at the same time. Greece joined in 1981, and Spain and Portugal are at present negotiating membership. Under section 2(1) of the 1972 Act the United Kingdom agreed that existing and future community law was to be given legal effect in the United Kingdom without the need for further legislation:

> "All such rights, powers, liabilities, obligations and restrictions from time to time created or arising by or under the Treaties, and all such remedies and procedures from time to time provided for by or under the Treaties, as in accordance with the Treaties are without further enactment to be given legal effect or used in the United Kingdom shall be recognised and available in law, and be enforced, allowed and followed accordingly; and the expression 'enforceable Community right' and similar expressions shall be read as referring to one to which this subsection applies."

Membership of the EEC involves participation in all of the major institutions of the Community and we must now briefly examine their functions. From the outset it should be emphasised that while comparisons can be made with domestic institutions (*e.g.* it is tempting to compare the Commission with the civil service and the Assembly with Parliament) these comparisons are misleading.

(a) *The Council*

Although the four major institutions are supposed to be of equal importance the Council of Ministers is the supreme legislative body, though its power is curtailed by the fact that on most issues it can only proceed on a proposal emanating from the Commission. The Council is comprised of ministers from the national governments of Member States and its presidency rotates amongst them every six months. These ministers may be the foreign ministers of each country or the ministers responsible for the subject matter under discussion. Thus the agriculture ministers will spend much time debating the Common Agriculture or Fisheries policies. The Council's Regulations, Directives and Decisions form part of the law of the EEC, though this is often referred to as secondary legislation to distinguish it from the contents of the Treaties. Decisions may be taken on a simple majority vote or on what is called a qualified vote. In this latter case each country has a certain number of votes, (France, Germany, Italy and the United Kingdom 10; Belgium, Greece and Netherlands 5; Denmark and Ireland 3; Luxembourg 2) and a decision can only be taken on the basis of 45 votes which means that the big four cannot outvote all the other countries. Under what are known as the Luxembourg Accords a practice has grown up under which, on any important issues concerning the national interests of a member state, decisions shall be taken only by a unanimous vote. This practice is of doubtful authority and was allegedly broken by a vote in 1982 against the United Kingdom.

The Council may be questioned by the Assembly, but the chief control is exercised by National governments over their ministers who attend the council.

It is now normal practice for the heads of government of the Member States to meet to discuss crucial issues and the name given to such meetings is European Councils.

(b) *The Commission*

It is tempting to see the Council and the Commission as the legislative and executive branches of the Community, and while there is some truth in this analogy, it is misleading because the Commission has legislative powers and the actual implementation of EEC policy is carried out, not by the Commission, but by the institutions of the Member States. On the other hand the Commission does in some respects act as the Civil service of the Community. Whereas the Council is comprised of ministers who are likely to take nationalistic standpoints, the Commission is the voice of the Community. It is comprised of 14 members who are each appointed for four years by general agreement with the Member States. From this number a President and Vice President are appointed to serve for a period of two years.

> "The Commission is the guardian of the Treaties; it is the executive arm of the Communities; it is the initiator of Community policy and exponent of Community interest in the Council." (Noel, *The European Community: How it Works*).

That basically summarises the functions of the Commission within the Community.

Although it is the Council which must enact measures above a certain level of importance, the initiative must come from the Commisson. Further once a proposal has been sent by the Commission to the Council, the Council may only amend the proposal by a unanimous vote. Thus the Council must either take a majority decision (or unqualified majority) on the proposal as a whole, or unless a unanimous agreement to change the proposal can be reached it will have to try to persuade the Commission to alter the proposal. The Commission is thus involved at all stages of the procedure and will be represented on the Council when the proposal is discussed.

It is the Commission which will see that the obligations laid down in the Treaties are observed. Thus under Article 169 a procedure is laid down to deal with breaches of Treaty obligations by Member States. Where the Commission decides that the Treaty has been infringed (the investigation may have been prompted by a Member State, a government or by an individual) it first gives the state the opportunity to submit observations, and then delivers a reasoned opinion. The state is then given a chance to comply with the opinion after which time the Commission may take the matter before the Court.

The Commission is given a large amount of legislative and executive powers by the Treaties and the Commission may also be invested with powers to ensure the enforcement of decisions made by the Council. The Commission also represents the Community in its dealings with non member states and with international organisations, and is responsible for the administration of Community funds. In order to protect the independence of the Commission it is made answerable to the Assembly alone.

(c) *The European Assembly*

The Assembly is now normally, but unofficially, called the Parliament. It often comes as a surprise to discover that the Parliament is not the supreme law making body of the community, though it is hoped that since the introduction of direct elections it will assume more importance. Originally members of the Parliament were nominated directly to it by the national governments of the community members and many were in fact national M.P.'s. In 1979 each member country conducted elections to elect a new Parliament and on this occasion the citizens of the member states were able to choose the new European M.P.'s. The new Parliament met on July 17, 1979. There are 410 seats in the Parliament of which the division is as follows: France, Germany, Italy, United Kingdom 81 each; Netherlands 25; Belgium 24; Denmark 16; Ireland 15; Luxembourg 6; Greece 24.

To a large extent this is a consultative body which considers proposals from the Commission before they are discussed in the Council of Ministers. However it has considerable powers in relation to budgetary matters and can reject the whole community budget; it may question the activities of both the Council and the Commission and has the power to dismiss the Commission.

Although the Council is not bound to heed the Parliament's opinion, any action taken by the Council would be open to challenge if it had failed to seek Parliamentary opinion when required.

(d) *The Court of Justice of the European Communities*

The Court of Justice is responsible, *inter alia*, for ruling on the validity and interpretation of Community law. It operates as a constitutional supreme court in the sense that it has the power to interpret Community law or to declare invalid any law which has been passed illegally by the Council or Commission. Its decisions, though not binding on itself, can be changed only by its own subsequent decision or by an amendment of the Treaty which would require the unanimous approval of Member States through their own Parliaments. It is thus unlike any court within the English Legal System and in this respect more closely resembles the Supreme Court of the United States.

Under the Treaty there are 11 judges each appointed for a period of six years renewable. Every three years there is a partial replacement of the Bench in that either five or six judges shall be replaced or re-appointed. The judges may sit in plenary session or in one of three chambers of three judges. They will sit in plenary session whenever the case is brought by a member state or by an institution of the community or whenever the chambers do not possess the requisite jurisdiction under the Rules of Procedure. The judges will elect one of their members as President of the Court of Justice for a period of three years; he may be re-elected at the end of that period.

The Court of Justice is assisted by five Advocates General whose duty it shall be, acting with complete impartiality and independence, to make, in open court, reasoned submissions on the cases brought before the Court of Justice in order to assist the Court to ensure that in the interpretation and application of the Treaty the law is observed.

The judges and Advocates General must be persons whose independence is beyond doubt and who would be eligible to assume the highest judicial office in their own countries.

(2) The law of the European Economic Communities

The law of the EEC is to be found in the establishing Treaties and in the Regulations, Directions and Decisions of the Council and Commission, and in the rulings of the Court of Justice. According to Article 189 of the Treaty "a regulation shall apply generally. It shall be binding in its entirety and take direct effect in each member state. A directive shall be binding, as to the result to be achieved, upon each member state to which it is directed, while leaving to national authorities the choice of form and method. A decision shall be binding in its entirety upon those to whom it is directed." In addition these bodies issue recommendations and opinions which are not binding.

One of the major questions that must be asked is whether EEC law takes precedence over the domestic law of the individual Member States. One of the features of international law is that it only binds the states themselves and not the individuals of those states. EEC law on the other hand may bind the individual citizens of member states so as to affect their rights and is enforceable before national courts. Where it is held to affect both the states and the individuals of those states it is said to have "direct effect" and laws which have direct effect take precedence over domestic law even if that domestic law was passed later in time. Law which has direct effect is therefore part of the domestic law of the member states. In the United Kingdom this is provided for by sections 2 and 3 of the European Communities Act 1972. Though it is open to the national courts of member states to interpret the provisions of Community Law, the ultimate arbiter is the Court of Justice of the European Communities. Whenever a national court seeks to interpret a particular provision (for example whether a particular law has "direct effect") it should bear in mind the need for consistency of approach throughout the Community. The courts should therefore adopt the approach to interpretation used in the European Court which is based on adherence to principle rather than the literal approach to interpretation of statutes adopted by English Courts (see *ante*, p. 55).

One view of the effect of United Kingdom membership of the EEC on our municipal law was given by Lord Denning in *Bulmer* v.

Bollinger (1974) when he said: "The Treaty is like an incoming tide. It flows into the Estuaries and up the rivers. It cannot be held back." Commenting on this Lord Scarman added:

> "For the moment, to adopt Lord Denning's imagery, the incoming tide has not yet mingled with the home waters of the common law: but it is inconceivable that, like the Rhone and the Arve where those two streams meet at Geneva, they should move on, side by side, one grey with the melted snows and ice of the distant mountains of our legal history, the other blue and clear, reflecting modern opinion. If we stay in the Common Market, I would expect to see its principles of legislation and statutory interpretation and its conception of an activist court whose role is to strengthen and fulfil the purpose of statute law replace the traditional attitudes of English judges and lawyers to statute law and the current complex style of statutory drafting."

The Court has both judicial and advisory functions. In its judicial capacity the court may hear complaints that a member state has failed to fulfil its treaty obligations; such proceedings are normally instituted by the Commission after having given the member state an opportunity to submit its observations. The Court has power to review the legality of acts of the Council and Commission other than recommendations or opinions. These actions may be brought by member states, the Council or the Commission on the grounds of lack of competence, infringement of an essential procedural requirement, infringement of the Treaty or of any rule of law relating to its application, or misuse of powers. Such proceedings may also be instituted by a natural or legal person. If the action is well founded the Court shall declare the act concerned to be void.

It is perhaps its jurisdiction under Article 177 that is of supreme interest to students of the English Legal System. Under this Article the Court of Justice is given power to give preliminary rulings concerning: (i) the interpretation of the Treaty; (ii) the validity and interpretation of acts of the institutions of the Community; and (iii) the interpretation of statutes of bodies established by an act of the Council where those statutes so provide. Where such a question is raised before a court or tribunal of a member state, that court or tribunal may, if it considers that a decision on the question is necessary to enable it to give judgment, request the Court of Justice to give a ruling thereon. Where any such question is raised in a case pending before a court or tribunal of a Member State, against whose decisions there is no judicial remedy under national law, that court or tribunal shall bring the matter before the Court of Justice.

Thus where a national court of a Member State is confronted by a point of EEC law which is said to be of "direct effect" it may seek clarification from the Court of Justice. In this way it is hoped that a uniform approach to interpretation of EEC law can be achieved through the Community. Any court or tribunal may refer a point of law to the Court of Justice for a preliminary ruling which will then enable the national court to reach a decision on the case. It is only where there is no appeal from the national court or tribunal that the reference to the Court of Justice is obligatory and even here there is no compulsion to refer if the national court feels that there is no uncertainty in the interpretation of the point of EEC law.

The Court of Justice also has jurisdiction in several other matters including disputes between the Community and its servants which are known as staff cases.

The Court of Justice in its advisory capacity may give its opinion as to whether proposed Community legislation is likely to offend the Treaties.

2. The European Convention on Human Rights

On December 10, 1948 the General Assembly of the United Nations adopted the Universal Declaration on Human Rights. The Declaration expresses what were thought to be the fundamental rights of mankind and, though the idea of "human rights" has a long history, a precipitating factor was unquestionably the barbaric treatment accorded many millions of people in the Second World War.

Quite what is, or what ought to be, a "human right" is open to argument. In an underdeveloped society pre-eminence is likely to be placed on a right to enough food to sustain life with access to medical care sufficient to preserve it. In a developed society where such things are taken for granted, the emphasis shifts to access to education or, if that too is guaranteed, to sophisticated notions of a fair trial or to rights to privacy. And the most developed societies can experience hard economic times. Should there, then, be a right to a job?

The Universal Declaration makes interesting reading. It does in fact state that everyone has the right to a standard of living adequate for the health and well-being of himself and his family and that everyone has a right to work, as well as to a right to a fair trial and a right to own property. The Declaration, however, binds no one and equally confers rights on no one; it is an expression of ideals.

On November 4, 1950 the Council of Europe adopted the European Convention on Human Rights and the United Kingdom was the first state to ratify this Convention. The Convention is modelled on, just as it was inspired by, the Universal Declaration but there are significant differences. The rights contained in the Convention include the right to life, the right not to be subjected to torture or other inhuman or degrading punishment, the right not to be held in slavery or servitude, the right to liberty and security of person, the right to a fair trial, the right to respect for private and family life, the right to freedom of thought, religion and conscience, the right to freedom of expression, the right to join a trade union and the right to marry.

An impressive list on the face of it but there *might* be thought to be significant omissions. There is no mention of a right to an adequate standard of living though this might be said to be superfluous in modern western European conditions. There is no reference to a right to work though some might argue that this is more fundamental to the dignity of man than the niceties of a fair trial. The European Convention is nevertheless an important document which affects public standards as well as private rights.

It should be noted that these rights are not expressed in absolute terms and they are qualified by limitations. Thus the right not to be held in servitude does not prevent a state from imposing a period of conscription in its armed forces, nor does the right to marry invalidate laws against bigamy or incest.

The Convention further established machinery to protect these fundamental rights—a *Commission of Human Rights* and a *Court of Human Rights*. Where any state which is a party to the Convention feels that another member state is in breach of the Convention it may report that state to the Commission which then tries to reach a friendly "out-of-court" solution. If this fails the matter may be referred to the Court. If the member state fails to comply with the report of the Court the ultimate sanction is suspension from the Council of Europe. Private citizens of member states may also cause a case to come before the Court. The private citizen will first report the alleged breach through the Council of Europe to the Commission, which will investigate the complaint and may refer it to the Court. Recent examples have included complaints against dismissals from employment through failure to join a trade union, complaints concerning corporal punishment, and the rights of imprisoned persons to have access to legal advice.

While the United Kingdom has ratified the Convention and has thereby agreed to abide by the principles stated therein, no steps have been taken (as they have by some other signatories) to incorporate the provisions of the Convention in English domestic law. Lord Scarman wondered whether the effect of our joining the EEC was not to lead to the incorporation in English law of the

Convention's provisions without further action by Parliament, but the better view is probably that of Lord Denning M.R. when he said (*R.* v. *Chief Immigration Officer, ex. p. Bibi* (1976)):

> "The position, as I understand it, is that if there is any ambiguity in our statutes or uncertainty in our law, then these courts can look to the Convention as an aid to clear up the ambiguity and uncertainty, seeking always to bring them into harmony with it. Furthermore, when Parliament is enacting a statute or the Secretary of State is framing rules, the courts will assume that they had regard to the provisions of the Convention and intended to make the enactments accord with the Convention, and will interpret them accordingly. But I would dispute altogether that the Convention is part of our law. Treaties and declarations do not become part of our law until they are made law by Parliament."

A good example of the practical result is provided by *Malone* v. *Commissioner of Police of the Metropolis* (*No.* 2) (1979). In criminal proceedings against the plaintiff it was disclosed that the police, acting under a warrant issued by the Home Secretary, had tapped his telephone and in a subsequent civil action the plaintiff alleged that the tap was unlawful both under English domestic law and by virtue of Article 8 of the Convention which conferred on him "the right to respect for his private and family life, his home and his correspondence." Megarry J. held that the telephone tap was not unlawful under domestic law; he did take the view that there had been a breach of Article 8 but since the Convention was "plainly not of itself law in this country" the plaintiff's remedy had to be pursued with the European Commission.

Part Two

CRIMINAL LAW

INTRODUCTION

The student of criminal law is often puzzled by the fact that the greatest part of his time is taken up with an investigation of so called general principles of criminal liability rather than with a study of specific crimes. The reason for this is quite simple. Although there are obviously hundreds of different criminal offences, there are features common to all prosecutions. Such questions as who can be a party to a criminal offence, how many people can be involved in one single crime, does the prosecution have to prove that the accused intended to bring about the prohibited result, what defences are open to him, are questions which can be asked about nearly every crime and in many cases the answers will be the same whether the crime involved is murder, stealing or assault. Thus in the first chapters we shall examine these general principles. The final chapters will examine certain specific offences.

CHAPTER 1

THE INGREDIENTS OF A CRIME: ACTUS REUS AND MENS REA

Let us start by considering a particular offence, namely that of rape. Suppose that X has been charged with raping Y. What does his criminal prosecution entail? It is a basic principle of English law that the prosecution must establish the guilt of the accused and that the accused is not expected to establish that he is innocent. Thus the prosecution must prove to the court's satisfaction that the accused, X, raped Y. But what exactly does that mean? In every crime there is what amounts to a set of ingredients which must be established before a verdict of guilty can be returned. The ingredients of rape are to be derived from section 1 of the Sexual Offences Act 1956 and section 1 of the Sexual Offences (Amendment) Act 1976. They are (1) that the accused had unlawful intercourse (2) with a woman (3) without her consent. In addition the prosecution must establish that (4) at the time of the act of intercourse he either knew that she was not consenting or that he was reckless as to whether she was consenting. Factors (1)–(3) are sometimes called the external features of the crime or *actus reus* (literally "guilty act"). Number (4) represents what is called the internal features of the crime or *mens rea* ("guilty mind").

Whatever the crime (whether it be murder at one extreme or dropping litter at the other) there can be no exception to the requirement that the prosecution establish the *actus reus*. So in the case of rape the prosecution must establish sexual intercourse, which in the case of rape means that there must have been at least slight penetration of the vagina by the penis. If this cannot be established then the charge of rape must fail, however revolting the circumstances. Equally if the woman was actually consenting even though the man thought that she was not, then there can be no conviction for rape. The requirement that the intercourse be "unlawful" has been taken to confirm the common law rule that a husband cannot rape his wife during the subsistence of marital cohabitation.

The reason for this strict requirement is that the law has set its face against imposing criminal liability simply on the basis of the accused's intentions; the law requires, in addition, strict proof of all the elements which the law says constitutes the crime.

The reason for the second requirement—of a certain state of mind—is even more obvious. A broad distinction needs to be drawn between persons who deliberately cause harm and those who cause harm unavoidably and accidently; the former, it may be supposed are rightly brought within the purview of the criminal law, while the latter are not. In relation to "serious" crimes (sometimes referred to as crimes *mala in se*) this is normally the postition; but in relation to "minor" crimes (crimes *mala prohibita*) criminal liability is frequently imposed even though the accused has not deliberately brought about the harm (the *actus reus*). Where liability is imposed though the accused is not at fault, the crime is known as an offence of strict (or absolute) liability. These crimes, and the policies which are claimed to justify their existence, are dealt with later in Chapter 2, though some incidental mention will be made of them in this chapter.

Even if the prosecution establish these two requirements (*viz*. the forbidden act deliberately brought about by the accused) it does not necessarily follow that a crime has been committed. Take a case where the accused is charged with murdering another and pleads that he was acting in self defence. The prosecution may have no difficulty in establishing that the accused has caused the forbidden act and that he did so deliberately; but the accused claims that he killed the victim because, had he not done so, the victim would have killed him. Killing, even deliberate killing, is not always a crime. This is true of other crimes also; the law admits of certain circumstances in which even the deliberate causing of a forbidden act is held to be justified.

Obviously not every case raises an issue of justification but where the issue is raised it is not for the accused to prove the justification, but for the prosecution to negative it. The prosecution will have to prove beyond reasonable doubt that the accused acted without grounds which in law would justify his act (see *post*, p. 190). This is because lack of justification is regarded as one of the ingredients of the crime—the definition of many offences contains the phrase "without lawful authority or excuse"; for murder the killing must be "unlawful."

As to whether circumstances of justification form part of the *actus reus* or *mens rea* no general agreement exists. What is clear, however, is that unless the prosecution can *prove* that there was no justification it will not obtain a conviction. It is also safe to say that where the accused raises the issue of justification the prosecution must prove that at the time he is alleged to have committed the offence the accused was unaware of the existence of the circumstances of justifiction. (*Dadson* (1850)).

In *Miller* (1983) Lord Diplock said that it would be conducive to clarity in analysing the ingredients of a crime that was created by statute, as the great majority of criminal offences now were, if one were to avoid bad Latin and instead to think of and speak about the conduct of the accused and his state of mind at the time of that conduct, instead of speaking of *actus reus* and *mens rea*. Clearly to translate *actus reus* and *mens rea* as "guilty act and guilty mind" would be misleading. However most lawyers regard the terms as useful symbols for the various elements of a criminal offence, and their disappearance from common usage seems rather unlikely.

1. Actus Reus

Actus literally means "act" but while most crimes require that the accused commits a certain act this is not always the case. Criminal liability may also arise through failure to act and so *actus* can cover an omission as well as an act. Perhaps it would be better to speak of conduct since conduct can be taken to include commission and omission. Even this enlarged meaning of *actus* may not cover all cases since on occasion, as we shall see (*post*, pp. 137–138) criminal liability may be imposed for a state of affairs without any requirement for conduct on the part of the accused.

A crime, however, requires more than conduct: the *actus* must be *reus*. If X fires a rifle he is engaged in conduct but to fire a rifle, without more, is not a crime. Suppose then that X aims his rifle at Y and deliberately kills him. X has now brought about a consequence which consequence is normally proscribed by the law of murder—*normally* but not always. Whether or not X will be guilty of murder depends upon the circumstances surrounding the killing. X will not be guilty of murder if Y is an enemy in time of war or if X is acting in circumstances of self-defence. Thus we can say of any crime that it usually involves (a) some conduct (b) a prohibited consequence and (c) certain surrounding circumstances. At first sight it may appear puzzling why one should want to analyse an *actus reus* in this way, but the reason will shortly appear (see *post*, p. 158).

(1) Voluntary nature of the act

Ordinarily the prosecution must prove that the accused voluntarily brought about the *actus reus* of the crime. To put it another way the act or omission must have occurred because of a conscious exercise of will on the part of the accused. Thus there would be no voluntary act where the act alleged to constitute the crime was performed by the accused while he was asleep, or suffering from concussion caused by a blow on the head. In these types of case it is usualy said that the accused is acting in a state of automatism (or more accurately non-insane automatism; see *post*, p. 136). But these are not the only situations in which the action of the accused may be said to be involuntary. For example if X were to hold Y's hand and force him to stick a knife in Z, Y's act could not be said to have been a voluntary one on his part. It is necessary to distinguish the requirement for a voluntary act from the requirement in many, but not all crimes, that the accused intentionally caused the *actus reus*. Whereas the prosecution will always fail if it cannot prove that the accused acted voluntarily, in certain crimes (crimes of strict liability) it will be excused from the need to show that the accused acted intentionally. Suppose that A is charged with failing to stop at a red traffic light, it will be no defence for him to say that he had not seen any traffic lights let alone that they were showing red; this is an offence of strict liability which does not require that the police prove that he knew the lights were red. However a plea that he suffered a blackout just before his car reached the lights would, if accepted, mean that there was no voluntary act of driving and this would be fatal to the prosecution's case. It is pointless to worry about whether voluntariness is rightly described as part of the *actus reus* or part of the *mens rea* of a given crime; the point to remember is that it is an essential part of every crime.

Consider the following hypothetical situations:

(i) A pushes B so that B loses his balance and falls against C;
(ii) While driving his car D is attacked by a swarm of bees; in instinctively brushing them away from his face he loses control of his car which mounts the pavement and injures E;
(iii) While driving his car F is subject to an epileptic fit which causes him to lose control of the car which then mounts the pavement;
(iv) While asleep H stabs and kills J, his wife;
(v) K suffers from arteriosclerosis which causes a blackout. During the blackout K hits his son L, with a hammer.
(vi) M is under the influence of alcohol to such an extent that he is no longer aware of what he is doing. In this state he strikes his friend, N, with a beer mug.

In each of these situations a criminal charge may be laid and in all of them the accused might raise the same defence, namely that there was no voluntary conduct of his which caused the *actus reus*. But it does not necessarily follow that the same result would be reached in all six examples.

In example (i) A may well be liable for assaulting both B and C, but B has not assaulted C since there is absolutely no voluntary conduct at all on B's part. This would clearly result in an absolute acquittal.

Example (ii) differs in that D is the only human agent involved, but his action is purely reflexive and the view would no doubt be taken (*cf. Hill* v. *Baxter* (1958)) that it was not a volunatry act—or a sufficiently voluntary act—for D to incur criminal liability either for injuring E or for driving the car without due care and attention.

In example (iii) F is prima facie not guilty for the same reasons. There is no truly conscious control of movements by F during the epileptic fit and thus he cannot be said to be driving the car (see *Sullivan* (1983)). But here it becomes necessary to consider F's knowledge of the nature and frequency of his spasms. If this was the first fit suffered by F then he would incur no liability (but see below, *e.g.* (v)), but if F was aware that he was frequently subject to fits there would be no difficulty in saying that, by virtue of taking the risk of a fit whilst driving, he was guilty of careless driving—from the moment he started to drive. So in *Kay* v. *Butterworth* (1945) the accused was found guilty of careless driving even though he had fallen asleep at the time when the accident occurred; his culpability consisted of continuing to drive when he knew he was feeling drowsy. A more refined example is provided by *Jarmain* (1946) where in the course of a robbery J pointed a loaded pistol at a cashier knowing that it had no safety catch and required only a light touch on the trigger to fire. The cashier, a brave woman, told him to go away and this so disconcerted J that, according to his version of the facts, while he was trying to work out what he should do he involuntarily pressed the trigger and the cashier was killed. The court declined to regard J's last action separately from the rest of the transaction. The death was caused by pointing a loaded pistol at the cashier at point blank range, and there was no doubt that this had been done voluntarily.

Example (iv) is straightforward. Acts done in a state of somnambulism are evidently not voluntary. Cases of killings done by persons in such a state are rare but they have occurred and resulted in acquittals. In *Cogdon* (1951), Mrs. Cogdon a woman with a record of bizarre dreams and of excessive worry over her 19-year-old daughter, Pat, on the night in question dreamt that the Korean War was taking place all round her house and that a Korean soldier was attacking Pat who was in bed. In a state of somnambulism she took an axe and attacked the "Korean" thereby killing her daughter. At her trial for murder she pleaded that her act was an involuntary one and she was acquitted.

The case posed in example (v) is more complicated. There is no doubt that K is entitled to an acquittal but the real question is whether he is entitled to a verdict of not guilty or to a verdict of not guilty by reason of insanity which would result in commitment during her majesty's pleasure. It will be appreciated that K's case, unlike those of B and D, raises the possibility of repetition. Of course, it is just possible that on some future occasion B may again be pushed by A or that D might again be attacked in his car by a swarm of bees, but these are contingencies against which no precautions can be taken. With K it is different. The prognostication may be that he will have further blackouts leading to further impulsive and motiveless violence.

What the courts have done is to draw a line, as best they can, between the sane and insane automatism. Both forms of automatism result in an acquittal but only the former enables the defendant to leave the court a free man. Example (v) would no doubt result in a verdict of not guilty by reason of insanity because K would be held to be suffering from a disease of the mind within the M'Naghten rules. These rules are amplified below (pp. 192–197); for now it is important to note that there is an important practical distinction between automatism which is based on a disease of the mind (insane automatism) and other forms of automatism (non-insane automatism). It may seem odd that the somnambulist who has killed in his sleep will be acquitted and subject to no further restraints, especially since there may be reason to believe that if he can kill once in his sleep he can do it again. The explanation is simply that somnambulism, as such, is not a disease of the mind.

Example (vi) is given to draw attention to the fact that automatism arising from the non-medical and voluntary consumption of alcohol or drugs is not generally a defence. There are said to be special policy reasons for treating such cases in an exceptional way (see *post*, p. 197).

In the result automatism is a defence of limited application. Thus Lord Denning felt able to say that it was confined to "acts done while unconscious and to spasms, convulsions and reflex actions" (*Bratty* (1963)). A claim by an accused that he did the prohibited act during a blackout is an easy one to make and it may be extremely difficult for the prosecution to rebut (since we have said that voluntariness is a part of the ingredients of every crime it is up to the prosecution to prove beyond reasonable doubt that the accused did voluntarily cause the *actus reus*). This has led the courts to rule that when automatism is raised the accused must lay a sufficient foundation for his claim before the prosecution will be expected to prove beyond reasonable doubt that the accused was acting involuntarily. This will normally mean that the accused will be expected to produce some evidence, possibly medical, to support his claim that he was acting under a blackout. If he fails to do this then the court will assume that he was acting voluntarily and will not expect the prosecution to deal specifically with the issue of voluntariness. (See burden and standard of proof; *ante*, p. 4.)

(2) Criminal liability in the "state of affairs" cases

While there is notionally no criminal liability unless the *actus reus* is brought about by some voluntary act or omission on the part of the accused, there is no rule of law which says that criminal liability cannot be imposed without some such voluntary act by the accused. Parliament could, for example, make it a criminal offence to be over six feet tall. In such an unlikely event it would be no defence for the accused to claim that he had no control over the mechanisms in his body which had caused him to be over six feet in height. While it is inconceivable that Parliament would create such an offence it has to be acknowledged that it is theoretically open to Parliament to do so and there are, as it happens, some crimes which might be taken to impose criminal liability without proof of any voluntary act on the part of the accused.

Under section 1 of the Road Traffic Act 1974 for the purposes of ensuring that certain fixed penalties such as parking fines, are paid, "it shall be conclusively presumed . . . that [the owner] was the driver at that time . . . that acts or omissions of the driver of the vehicle at that time were his acts or omissions." Thus if the accused's son has parked the accused's car illegally, the accused will be liable even though he is sleeping in a bed in New York at the time. It is, however, a defence for the accused to show that the car was in the possession of the other person without the consent of the accused; thus liability is incurred only if the accused consented to the possession of the car. Nevertheless, given an actual consent to possession, the accused is liable for certain crimes committed thereafter without any proof of any voluntary act on his part. It is easy to appreciate what led Parliament to take this unusual step. Many parking tickets were left unpaid and when the police served a summons on the owner they would be met by the impossibility of proving whether it was the owner, his wife or some other member of the family who had been responsible for the illegal parking.

A much more extreme case is provided by *Larsonneur* (1933). A French woman, L, went from England to Ireland where she was arrested by the Irish police and sent back to England where she was taken into police custody. She was charged with being an alien who was "found" in the United Kingdom without permission. Strictly speaking, of course, she was "found" in this country the moment she set foot off the boat from Ireland. However she did not want to come back to England but she was forced back by the Irish police. Once the boat docked here she had no alternative but to get off on to

British soil—straight into the arms of the English police—at which stage she was "found" here without permission. There was no voluntary action on her part and nothing she could do to prevent herself stepping on to British soil. Nevertheless she was convicted of the offence. Her conviction was upheld because she literally came within the prohibition. She was "an alien" to whom permission to land was refused and she was "found" here. As a matter of fact her conduct was not involuntary (conduct is not involuntary merely because it is done under duress) but the implication in the judgment is that she would have been convicted even if she had been physically carried into England by the police.

The decision in *Larsonneur* has been justly and universally condemned. It can be defended only by a very literal approach to statutory interpretation. Statutory offences rarely specify that such issues as insanity and duress should be a defence but these are implied as a matter of course; it would be no more difficult to read in the fundamental requirement that the *actus reus* must be caused by some voluntary act of the accused. Of course, if, as is the case with section 1 of the Road Traffic Act 1974 (referred to above), Parliament has patently dispensed with the need to prove that the *actus reus* was caused by some conduct of the accused, then that has to be accepted. Miss Larsonneur was improperly convicted of the offence with which she was charged; had she left her car with her sister in London she would now unquestionably be liable to pay the fine incurred by her sister for illegal parking even though she was in a Liverpool police cell at the relevant time.

(3) Liability for failing to act

In most criminal prosecutions the prosecutor will be seeking to prove that a prohibited situation or result has been brought about the acts of the accused. However in certain situations it will be the fact that the accused failed to act that led to the prohibited event occurring. For example, if A pushes B under the water in a swimming pool and holds him there until B is dead then it is clear that A's actions have caused B's death. On the other hand if A sees B drowning in the swimmimg pool in a situation where it would be easy to rescue B, but A does nothing, the result will be the same—B will die. However this time B would have died whether or not A had been there. Should the law therefore hold A responsible for B's death? It would be easy to say yes, for most of us would find the picture of A simply watching B drown morally abhorent. Yet if we hold, in principle, that A should be liable for failing to act, we would probably cause more problems than the law could handle. It would be easy to hold that A should be liable for the death of B where B is a small child drowning in about two or three feet of water, but such straightforward cases are unlikely to occur. The water may be much deeper, or there may be strong currents, or A may only be a modest swimmer. How much of a risk can the law expect A to take with his own life in order to save another from death or lesser injury? The answer that he should take such risks as the court deems reasonable in all the circumstances would merely involve the courts in a minute examination of all the surrounding factors and possibly A's appreciation of them.

For these sorts of reasons most jurisdictions, including our own, have not adopted a general principle of liability for failing to act. Instead the law has enumerated certain factual situations in which persons shall be under a duty to act, and if they fail to act in these situations thereby causing a prohibited criminal result, they shall be liable for that result. Where the law imposes such a duty to act, this duty forms part of the *actus reus* for that particular charge and the prosecution will have to prove not only the existence of the duty to act, but also that the accused unreasonably failed to act.

The situations in which such duties are imposed can be found in both statute law and in the decisions of the courts. Examples of stautory crimes which will be committed by a failure to act include certain failures by drivers to report a road traffic accident caused by the presence of their vehicles on the road (see *e.g.* the Road Traffic Act 1972, s.25); failure by a motorist to provide a police constable with a specimen of breath for a breath test (the Road Traffic Act 1972, s.8(3)). Where statute has made it an offence to perform a certain act without first obtaining the necessary authority (for example operating a television without a licence) there is both an act and an omission, but the crux of the offence is the act and so these are not true examples of omissions.

Certain persons are liable to act because of their status. For example sea captains are under a duty to take reasonable steps to protect the lives of their passengers and crew. Parents are under an obligation to look after the welfare of their children and guardians their wards, though the guardian's duty probably arises as much out of the specific undertaking by the guardian. (See *Sheppard* (1980).)

It is possible to bring oneself under a duty to act through contractual obligations. The leading case in this area is *Pittwood* (1902) where the accused who was under a contractual obligation to look after a railway level crossing negligently left his post with the gates in such a position to suggest to road users that no trains were coming. As a result a man was killed when his cart, which was crossing the railway lines, was struck by a train. Clearly the action of the accused could be regarded as grossly negligent and clearly his negligent conduct had lead to the death. He argued that he owed no duty to the users of the level crossing; his contractual obligations lay solely with the railway company. The court, however, held that this contractual undertaking was sufficient to place him under a duty to the road users and thus the prosecution were able to establish the remaining part of the *actus reus* and the accused was convicted of manslaughter.

The courts have also found a duty to exist where the accused has voluntarily assumed responsibility for another's care and then simply failed to fulfil that undertaking. One example of this is the case of *Instan* (1893) where the accused undertook to look after her aged and helpless aunt, but then caused her death by failing to provide for her or summon help when she was ill. Although there may be a contractual situation in relation to the food, the court held that there was also a duty arising out of the voluntary undertaking to look after the aunt.

In some jurisdictions the courts have held that where a person has created a dangerous situation, he is under a duty to take reasonable steps to avert the danger. Thus, whereas A, who comes upon a burning house, is under no obligation to take any action to extinguish the fire, if it was he who caused the fire, he would be under an obligation to do his best to get the fire extinguished. A similar situation arose recently in *Miller* (1983) where the accused had fallen asleep while smoking a cigarette. He awoke to find that his mattress was on fire, but instead of taking steps to put the fire out, he simply moved to another room leaving the mattress to burn. The House of Lords decided that common sense dictated that he should bear responsibility for the result of his failure to avert the danger and it was necessary to formulate an approach to such cases which Crown Court judges could explain clearly to lay jurors. Thus it was held that where an accused had unwittingly created a risk that the property of another would be damaged or destroyed, he should bear the responsibility for the resulting damage if he subsequently became aware of the risk and failed to take steps to avert it. The prosecution would, of course, have to show that the failure to take action was accompanied by the necessary *mens rea* (see *post*, p. 149).

Once the prosecution have proved that the accused failed to act in a situation where the law imposes a duty to act then the general principles of criminal liability operate as in any other case. The prosecution will have to establish any remaining elements of the *actus reus* together with any requirements relating to the state of mind of the accused. It is very tempting in situations where the accused has failed to look after someone properly as a result of which the person has died, to say that this will at most amount to manslaughter. However if the prosecution can establish that the accused deliberately withheld food so that the victim would suffer serious bodily harm or death, then this is a proper case for a conviction for murder (see *Gibbins and Proctor* (1918)).

This is not intended to be an exhaustive list of duty situations; the courts may well add further categories. The law in this area is, possibly of necessity, imprecise. There is little authority on just how much of a risk people under a duty to act must take in order to perform their duty, but the majority of cases are concerned with situations where no risk at all is involved and the accused has simply abandoned his responsibility. In some American states where there has been codification it has been common to include in the provisions dealing with liability for omissions some such phrase as "or the omission to perform a duty which the law imposes upon him and which he is physically capabable of performing," and this is probably implicit in the English decisions.

(4) Causation

Not every crime requires that the prosecution prove that the accused brought about a particular prohibited result. Take careless driving, for example. A person may be convicted of this offence though no harm is caused to person or property; it is only his conduct in driving the car that matters. Murder on the other hand requires a result; namely that the accused has killed someone and in crimes such as these the prosecution must prove that it was the unlawful act of the accused which resulted in the victim's death. This all seems very simple and indeed in most cases it is, but we shall see that complex situations can arise.

For any given result, there will normally be several contributing causes [often described as factual causes], and our task is to determine what can, in law, be held to be the cause of the prohibited result. For example, I might invite X to my house for dinner and on the way to my house he is run overy by Y and killed. You could say that but for my invitation X would not have been killed. Equally you could say that it was the careless way X stepped off the path in front of Y, or the fact that Y was not concentrating or that the road surface was slippery, or that X could have been saved by a more competent surgeon. If we decide to prosecute Y on a charge of causing death by reckless driving we shall have to prove that his reckless driving was, at least, a factual cause of X's death; in other words the jury must find that but for Y's reckless driving X would not have been killed. If the jury reaches the conclusion that even the most careful of drivers would have been unable to avoid hitting X, then the prosecution will fail (*Dalloway* (1847)). If we are prosecuting the surgeon for manslaughter in that he caused X's death by gross negligence, then we must show, at least, that a reasonably competent surgeon would have saved him.

It is, of course, a question for the jury to decide whether the accused caused the death of the victim. But the judge must rule on which of the various factual cuases is capable, in law, of amounting to a cause of the victim's death. In the general run of case this presents no problems. It is important to note that in early homicide cases lawyers did not have the benefit of advanced medical testimony as to what medically speaking caused the victim's death. They therefore developed a rough and ready causal test under which the prosecution would have to prove that the death of the victim occurred within a year and a day of the last injury inflicted by the accused. This requirement still exists today and so even if you could establish that X infected Y with a form of slow growing cancer from which X died two years later, X could not be charged with Y's murder (though he could be charged with an offence under section 18 of the Offences Against the Person Act 1861 which carries life imprisonment).

Just as there can be several factual causes of a result, so can the judge instruct the jury that they are entitled to find that, in law, more than one factor is responsible. Thus if X and Y attack Z who dies as a result of the combined wounds inflicted by both X and Y, both X and Y can be held responsible as principal offenders in the homicide. One can think of many possible variations, but in the end the test is largely one of common sense. Should the law really hold X's action to be a cause of Z's death? Thus if X poisons Z, but before the poison has any chance to take effect Y shoots and kills Z, only Y will be held liable for the homicide, though X may be found guilty of attempted murder. Most of these problems occur when there is an event which intervenes between the act of the accused and the prohibited result. The question is then whether this intervening event breaks the chain of causation which would otherwise link the accused's acts with the prohibited result. Although the possible factual situations are infinite, certain general principles are discernible.

In the first place the accused may well escape liability if the intervening act is unforseeable. For instance, if X renders Z unconscious and leaves him on a beach where the tide is coming in, Z's subsequent death by drowning is easily foreseeable, but the position would be different if Z were blown up by an undiscovered land mine on the beach.

It is also clear that to a certain extent the accused must take his victim as he finds him. Thus if X injures Z and Z dies partly as a result of those injuries, and partly as a result of failing to take proper care of himself, then X will be held liable for the resulting death. This principle has been recently extended to a case where the victim, a Jehovah's Witness, died as a result of stab wounds inflicted by the accused, because she refused, on religious grounds, to have a blood transfusion (*Blaue* (1975)).

A particular example of these principles involves medical treatment. In *Smith* (1959) the accused stabbed the victim in a barrack room brawl puncturing his lung. The victim was then carried to the medical officer's tent where, due to pressure of work, the doctor failed to notice the severity of the injuries. As a result he prescribed totally inadequate treatment and the victim died two hours after the initial wound. It was held that the initial stab wound was still an operative cause of the death despite the poor treatment administered. Only where the medical treatment is so grossly negligent that the initial wound becomes merely the setting in which the real cause of death (the medical treatment) occurs, can one say that the chain of causation has been broken. In such a case the initial injury becomes more like the invitation to dinner which caused the victim to be at a place where he was struck down by a car. (See *Jordan* (1956)). In some respects, as we said before, it is often a question of common sense in choosing between various competing factual causes.

2. Mens Rea

No only must the prosecution show that the accused brought about the *actus reus* of the crime, but they must also, in most cases, prove that he caused the *actus reus* with *mens rea*. Literally translated *mens rea* means "guilty mind," but the expression "guilty mind" is both misleading and too imprecise as a yardstick of liability. This is well demonstrated by the case of *Cunningham* (1957) where a Miss Wade lived in a house which had been divided into two apartments, the cellar being divided by a wall of loose stone rubble. When visiting Miss Wade, his girlfriend, Cunningham noticed that the other apartment was unoccupied. One night Cunningham entered the empty apartment and wrenched the gas meter off the cellar wall in order to steal its contents and in so doing he fractured a gas pipe causing gas to percolate through the rubble wall and into Miss Wade's apartment. As a result Miss Wade, who was asleep at the time, was partially asphyxiated. He was charged with "unlawfully and maliciously" administering a noxious thing to Miss Wade contrary to section 23 of the Offences Against the Person Act 1861.

The judge directed the jury that "malicious" meant "wicked—something which he (Cunningham) has no business to do and perfectly well knows it." In this sense Cunningham undoubtedly had a guilty mind. He knew that he was up to no good and there was no doubt that he had committed the crime of theft and possibly burglary into the bargain. Nonetheless this was held, on appeal, to be a misdirection. "Malicious," said the Court of Criminal Appeal, required either that (i) Cunningham intended to administer the noxious thing or (ii) without intending to administer it, he foresaw that by fracturing the pipe he might cause gas to seep through the house to the injury of Miss Wade. In *Sheppard* (1980) Lord Diplock held that the word "wilfully" imported the same notions.

Cunningham shows that *mens rea* must not be confused with having a bad motive. Conversely the fact that the accused has the best of motives does not mean that he cannot have *mens rea*. In a tragic case (*The Times*, October 7, 1965), Mr. Gray killed his 11-year-old son by administering an overdose of drugs and then gassing him while he was asleep. Mr. Gray was a devoted father and had done this because his son was dying from an incurable cancer and was in such pain that he could not even bear the weight of his bed sheets. On Mr. Gray's conviction for manslaughter (the charge was murder but this was reduced to manslaughter on account of diminished responsibility; see *post*, p. 195. The judge said to Mr. Gray, "I am perfectly certain that there is not a single person inside this court who will feel that you are in any sense a criminal." One can see what the judge meant but, as the conviction for manslaughter proved, Mr. Gray had committed a crime; he had caused the *actus reus* of an unlawful homicide and in intending to kill his son he had the necessary *mens rea* for murder or manslaughter.

What then, precisely, does "*mens rea*" mean? In *Cunningham* the court was defining "malicious" for the purposes of section 23 of the Offences Against the Person Act 1861 but the test which the court articulated provides us with a good definition of *mens rea*. We can confidently say, *in general*, that an accused has *mens rea* where:

(a) he intends to bring about the elements which constitute a crime; or
(b) though not intending to bring about those elements which constitute a crime, he realises that there is a risk that his conduct may bring them about and he unreasonably decides to take that risk.

These two mental states, commonly called intention and recklessness, need some elaboration.

(1) Intention

Many crimes can be committed if the accused acts either intentionally or recklessly. Section 23 of the Offences Against the Person Act 1861, just discussed, provides us with an example; offences of criminal damage (Criminal Damage Act 1971), provide another. In such cases there is no need to pursue a refined distinction betwen intention and recklessness. But there are many crimes which can be committed only intentionally. Examples of such crimes include any attempt to commit a substantive offence (see *post* p. 214) and wounding with intent to cause grievous bodily harm contrary to section 18 of the Offences Against the Person Act 1861. Where these crimes are concerned it becomes necessary to define intention and draw the line between it and recklessness.

Where a consequence is desired, wanted or aimed at for its own sake, there is no difficulty in saying that the consequence is intended. Nor do we have any difficulty in saying that a man can intend consequences though he realises that the chances of achieving them are less than certain. A terrorist who shoots at a member of the security services even at point blank range would realise (if he thought about it) that the death is not certain. The bullet might not strike a vital part of the body or the victim's life might be saved by a surgeon. So it is never 100 per cent. certain that intended consequences will occur. However we have no difficulty in saying that the terrorist intends to kill the victim. What, however, if the terrorist is shooting beyond the known range of accuracy of his weapon and rates his changes of even hitting the victim at about 1 per cent.? Still we would have no difficulty in concluding that the terroist acted deliberately if the death of his victim was what he desired, or wanted or aimed to bring about when he fired.

Difficulties begin to arise when the consequence is not wanted for its own sake. In *Steane* (1947) the accused, who had given broadcasts for Germany during the Second World War because of threats to the safety of his family if he did not do so, was charged under regulation 2A of the Defence (General) Regulations with "doing an act likely to assist the enemy with intent to assist the enemy." Delivering the judgment of the court Lord Goddard C.J. referred to British prisoners-of-war who had been forced by their brutal Japanese captors to work on the Burma Road, and considered what the position would have been had they been charged under the same regulation. In such a case, said Lord Goddard, "it would be unnecessary surely . . . to consider any of the niceties of the law relating to duress, because no jury would find that merely by doing his work they were intending to assist the enemy." He concluded, allowing Steane's appeal, that the jury should have been instructed that they could find that Steane lacked the necessary intent if they found that he did what he did in subjection to the power of an enemy.

It is easy to sympathise with Lord Goddard's conclusion. No one would want to see those British prisoners-of-war subject to the risk of even a charge, much less a conviction. However, it is an old adage that hard cases make bad law. It is tempting, but wrong, to say that a man who acts under duress does not act intentionally. The prisoners did not choose to build the road but they did built it and they knew that their acts would undoubtedly assist the Japanese. It would certainly be odd to say that they acted unintentionally. What Lord Goddard did was to confuse intention and motive; he talked of an "innocent" and "criminal" intent, but whether conduct is intentional is not determined by the motive with which it is done. The exculpation of such prisoners, and Steane, should be sought in the defence of duress, not in lack of intention.

The same is true where A desires to take an inheritance under the will of his grandfather. He knows the money will be coming to him sooner or later but is desperate to get his hands on it immediately. He is very fond of his grandfather and if there was a way of getting the money without killing the old man he would take it, but there is not and so he poisons him. On a subsequent charge of murder it would be of no avail for him to say that he did not intend to kill his grandfather, because he did not desire the old man's death. He deliberately killed his grandfather and the killing was an intentional one.

Further difficulties arise where the accused intends consequence B but realises that if he brings about B then consequence C may follow from it. B is clearly an intended consequence, but is C? This problem differs from the one concerning the killing by the accused of his grandfather, just discussed, in that here it is not inevitable that consequence A will be necessarily brought about in order to achieve consequence B. In the following hypothetical cases a terrorist has placed a bomb in a bank timed to explode at noon. His intention is to destroy the bank as a protest against capitalism and he sincerely hopes that no one will be killed.

(1) He gives no warning and realises that it is virtually certain someone will be killed. X is killed.
(2) He telephones a warning at 11.55 a.m. He knows that he is cutting it fine. He hopes that it will allow sufficient time to clear the bank but realises that someone will probably be killed. Y fails to get out of the bank in time and is killed.
(3) He telephones his warning at 11.45 a.m. He believes that this

should allow sufficient time for the bank to be cleared but that there is a possibility that someone might be killed. Z is killed.

The question we are asking is not whether the terrorist will be guilty of murder, but whether we can say that the terrorist intended to kill X, Y and Z. Although there is no case directly on point there is general agreement that the terrorist intentionally kills only X, the deaths of Y and Z being caused recklessly. This means that a line has to be drawn between that which is foreseen as virtually certain to happen and that which is merely probable or highly probable. This would seem to be supported by the decisions in *Mohan* (1976) and *Belfon* (1976).

As we have seen earlier the *actus reus* may consist of both consequences and circumstances. Whereas we can say that an accused intended to bring about a given consequence it is rather inelegant to say that he intended a circumstance. For this reason in relation circumstances "know" is the equivalent of "intend." Thus we should say that the accused knew or was virtually certain that a given circumstance existed.

(2) Recklessness

You will remember that in *Cunningham* (*ante*, p. 143) the Court of Criminal Appeal said that the jury should have been directed that in order to convict the accused they should be satisfied that either (i) he intended to administer the noxious thing or that (ii) he had foreseen that there would be a risk of fracturing the gas pipe. This second state of mind is traditionally known as recklessness and it normally serves as the basis of most, but not all, crimes. It is often referred to as deliberate risk taking. This type of *mens rea* suffers from the fact that the word "recklessness" is an everyday word often used to mean negligence (failure to see risks that reasonable people would have seen—see *post*, p. 150). The word is to be found in several modern statutes (Theft Act 1968, Sexual Offences Amendment Act 1976, Criminal Damage Act 1971) and recent decisions of the Court of Appeal had tended to support the definition given in *Cunningham* of conscious risk taking (see *e.g. Stephenson* (1979)).

That recklessness involved conscious risk taking appeared to be settled until the decision of the House of Lords in *Caldwell* (1982), where Lord Diplock, stated that where the word "recklessly" or "reckless" was used in a modern statute it ought to be given a wider, less artificial meaning. Speaking in the context of the Criminal Damage Act 1971, Lord Diplock said that it means that (i) the accused does an act which, in fact, creates an obvious risk that property will be destroyed or damaged and that (ii) he *either* has not given any thought to the possibility of there being any such risk *or* he has recognised that there was some such risk and yet has carried on with his actions.

Let us consider exactly what this means in the context of a trial. Suppose that X is charged under section 1(1) Criminal Damage Act 1971 with damaging Y's car. The jury must, of course, be satisfied that the accused caused the damage to the car (*actus reus*). But what *mens rea* must the prosecution show? The statute says that the prosecution must prove that X intended to cause the damage or was reckless as to causing the damage. After *Caldwell* this will mean that the prosecution will only have to show that the accused created an obvious risk of damage to the car. If this is established it matters not whether or not the accused foresaw this risk. Lord Diplock's holding that it is sufficient that the accused did not give any thought to the possibility entirely swallows up any need to show he did foresee a risk. With respect to Lord Diplock this is more closely akin to a definition of gross negligence (see below) and his view was vigorously criticised in the dissenting speech of Lord Edmund Davies.

We are, however, obliged to accept the decision of the House of Lords. The question is how far it applies to other crimes. Clearly it applies throughout the Criminal Damage Act 1971 and in *Lawrence* (1981) a similar definition was applied to the crime of reckless driving (Road Traffic Act 1972, s. 2). Lord Diplock appears to say the wider definition should apply wherever "reckless" appears in modern statutory provisions. In *Pigg* (1982) it was held by the Court of Appeal to apply where "reckless" appears in the definition of rape (see *post*, p. 249). The word also appears in section 15 of the Theft Act 1968 (obtaining property by deception) but here the prosecution must also prove that the accused was acting dishonestly and it is difficult to see how a jury could find that the accused was acting dishonestly when he was unaware that the statement he was making was false (see *post*, p. 281)).

The wider meaning will not apply to older offences where the word "maliciously" is used (such as the offence in *Cunningham* and the Offences under sections 18 and 20 of the Offences Against the Person Act 1861 see *ante*, p. 240. It is unlikely to be applied to general assaults which have no statutory definition but which are said to require either intentional or reckless conduct. And in *Miller* ((1983) *ante*, p. 140) Lord Diplock said that where recklessness was being used as the basis for liability in a case in which the accused was being prosecuted for his failure to avert a danger he had unwittingly created, he thought that the jury should be directed that the accused was liable "if, when he did become aware that the events in question had happended as a result of his own act, he did not try to prevent or reduce the risk of damage by his own efforts or if necessary by sending for help . . . and the reason why he did not was either because he had not given any thought to the possibility of there being any such risk or be ause having recognised that there was some risk involved he had decided not to try to prevent or reduce it". this is a complex direction. Stripped to its essentials it acknowledges that an accused in Miller's position may be convicted only if he consciously takes a risk. Had Caldwell inadvertently started the fire it would, presumably, be necessary to prove that at some stage *he realised that there was a risk* of further damage to property, or to life, before he could be committed of an offence. Since Caldwell started the fire deliberately it was enough to prove that the fire created a serious risk to property or life and that Caldwell had given no thought to these risks.

Whatever the eventual outcome of the present debate, recklessness will continue to be risk taking (either conscious or unconscious), and we should finally note that the risk must be a risk you are not justified in taking. Whether or not the risk is one you are justified in taking will depend upon how the court measures the social utility of the accused's actions. Many doctors operate knowing that the patient might die as a result of the operation. They are therefore taking a conscious risk of killing the patient. But in nearly every case the risk is a justifiable risk, and thus if the patient dies the doctor will not face a charge of murder. On the other hand, if X drives his car down a High Street at 90 m.p.h. in order to evade police capture he risks killing pedestrians and this risk is not one he is justified in taking since there is no social utility in his action. Nor would it be a justifiable risk for the driver of an ambulance to risk killing pedestrians in order to get his patient to hospital quickly.

(3) Other mental states

Although the term *mens rea* was traditionally used to indicate that the prosecution had to establish intention or recklessness on the part of the accused, it has come to include "negligence" which is not really a state of mind of the accused at all. Further we have already mentioned that there are now a great many crimes where the accused may be convicted in the absence of intention, recklessness or negligence on his part. Thus it is important to explain two further "states of mind" which an accused might possess in relation to a particular *actus reus*. These are negligence and blameless inadvertence.

(a) *Negligence*

In the civil law the classic definition of negligence is that given by Alderson B. in *Blyth* v. *Birmingham Waterworks Co.* (1856). "Negligence is the ommission to do something which a reasonable man, guided upon these considerations which ordinarily regulate the conduct of human affairs, would do, or doing something which a prudent and reasonable man would not do."

It is thus not a defence in a civil action for the defendant to show that he did not foresee the harm if a reasonable man would have done so; nor even to show that his failure to foresee was due to physical or mental limitations not shared by the reasonable man. Nevertheless it seems probable that the defendant's physical and mental defects may be taken into account in determining whether he is negligent to the extent that they make it impossible for him to take the necessary precautions. Thus it would not avail a man with defective eyesight to attribute a car accident to his inability to judge distances, but if the same man were to fall over and injure the plaintiff's prize poodle when walking along the pavement, the appropriate test would be whether, for a man with defective eyesight, he had taken reasonable care.

So far as the criminal law is concerned there is, of course, no general crime of negligently causing harm. There are, however, particular crimes of negligence. At common law the only instance of a crime of negligence appears to be manslaughter though there, as we shall see (see *post*, p. 234) the negligence must be "gross." Parliament, has, however, thought it appropriate to create certain crimes of negligence. Possibly the best known of such crimes is careless driving contrary to section 3 of the Road Traffic Act 1972.

Where the crime is one of negligence the test to be applied is probably the same as that in civil cases though in a criminal case (a) the standard of proof required is more stringent (see *ante*, p. 4); and (b) generally there is no need to prove actual harm to person or property. Thus on a charge of careless driving where the accused is a learner driver his driving will be considered careless if he fails to measure up to the standard of the reasonably experienced driver and no allowance is made for the fact that he is a learner: *McCrone* v. *Riding* (1938). In that case Lord Hewart C.J. said "That standard is an objective standard, impersonal and universal, fixed in relation to the safety of other users of the highway. It is in no way related to the degree of proficiency or degree of experience attained by the individual driver."

Crimes of negligence are exceptional in our law. Sometimes, however, Parliament will create a crime and then make the absence of negligence a defence. Under section 7 of the Sexual Offences Act

1956 it is an offence for a man to have intercourse with a mental defective but by section 7(2) it is provided that the accused does not commit the offence if he does not know and has no reason to suspect the girl to be a defective; the Court of Criminal Appeal made it clear that the accused bore the burden of proof on this defence. Construing this provision in *Hudson* (1966) the Court of Criminal Appeal said that the trial judge was wrong to direct the jury that the test was wholly objective (*i.e.* would a reasonable man have believed that the girl was mentally defective?); the jury should have been instructed to consider whether it was reasonable for Hudson not to have realised that the girl was a defective. This is different from the wholly objective test approved for careless driving in *McCrone* v. *Riding*. The test in *Hudson* is still objective in the sense that it would not avail an accused to show that he was in fact unaware that the girl was a defective, but it will avail him to prove that persons sharing his limitations, whether physical or mental, would not have realised that the girl was a defective. Under section 7, therefore, a conviction is possible only if the jury conludes that the relevant standard could have been attained by the accused; with careless driving the accused may be convicted even though the relevant standard was unattainable by him.

It must not be thought that whenever a statutory offence is defined with a defence of no negligence, it inevitably follows that the court will adopt the subjective-objective form adopted in *Hudson*. The precise wording of the provision is all important. Under section 7 it is a defence if "*he* does not know and has no reason to believe" (italics supplied) that the girl was a defective. Had the provision been worded, for example, "it shall be a defence to prove that a reasonable person would not in the circumstances have realised that the girl was a defective" the trial judge's direction would almost certainly have been upheld.

Although, manslaughter apart, there are no crimes of negligence at common law, negligence has, at least in the past, had relevance in connection with the defence of mistake of fact. Sometimes courts have held that a mistake of fact is a defence only if it is honestly made *and* that there were reasonable grounds for making it. The result of this can be, in effect, to make negligence a ground of liability even in connection with serious crimes. The matter of mistake is a highly complicated one and is dealt with below (*post*, p. 155).

(b) *Blameless inadvertence*

On principle, it might be thought, a man who causes harm inadvertently and without a scintilla of fault on his part ought not to be convicted of a crime. Thus A should not be guilty of homicide when in driving his car with every care he causes the death of a pedestrian who suddenly steps into the path of his car. Nor should B be guilty of receiving goods which are, in fact, stolen, which he buys in good faith from a reputable dealer. Nor should C be guilty of abducting a girl under 16 if he reasonably believes that she is 18; nor D guilty of selling unsound meat if he has employed a qualified analyst who certifies the meat to be sound. In all these situations the accused would lack *mens rea*, at least as we have defined it, in that he does not intentionally recklessly nor negligently bring about the elements which constitute the crime.

In reality the position is not quite so straightforward. In the illustrations given A would not be guilty of unlawful homicide; B would not be guilty of receiving stolen goods; but C can be convicted of abduction and D of selling unsound meat. On the face of it this is very unfair to C and D and so some explanation is called for.

What has happened is that as to the quality of the meat and the age of the girl the law has dispensed with the need for *mens rea* and liability on these elements of the crime is said to be strict (or sometimes absolute). These crimes are therefore known as crimes of strict (or absolute) liability. The accused is blamelessly inadvertent as to the quality of the meat or the age of the girl, but he is nonetheless convicted. We shall return to these crimes in the next chapter.

3. Actus Reus and Mens Rea: How do They Relate to Each Other?

Where *mens rea* is required the prosecution must establish that the *actus reus* and the *mens rea* were concurrent. Suppose that the accused intended to shoot X on Friday afternoon, but, for some unforeseen reason, failed to do so, and then on Saturday morning ran over and killed X completely accidentally without realising whom he had hit. Should we allow the prosecution to say that he had the necessary *mens rea* on Friday and performed the *actus reus* on Saturday morning and thus he should be convicted of murder? Clearly not. The prosecution must show that the accused perpetrated the *actus reus* and at that time possessed the necessary mental state. The courts have allowed a certain degree of flexibility, though not sufficient to cover the above case. In *Fagan* (1969) the accused accidentally drove his car onto a policeman's foot and when asked to remove his car from the foot refused to do so immediately. The objection to any charge involving an asault on the policeman is that in this case the *actus reus* would consist of the infliction of unlawful personal violence by Fagan upon the policeman, and the *mens rea* would be that the accused intentionally or recklessly applied force to the person of another (see *post*, p. 238). Now it is clear that unlawful personal violence was inflicted by Fagan upon the policeman, but at the time when he drove onto the foot he neither intended to do so nor did he realise that there was the risk of so doing. When he realised what he had done and decided to get some fun out of it, it could be argued that the act of inflicting violence was already over. However the court took a common sense view of the situation and resolved that an assault was a continuing offence, in this case beginning when he drive onto the policeman's foot and continuing up to the time when he drive off, and that if *mens rea* was proved to exist at any time during the continuance of the assault, the prosecution had made out its case.

A more extreme example is provided by those cases where the accused has attacked another with the appropriate *mens rea* for murder but has failed to kill the victim and has then disposed of the "body," the act of disposal in the end killing the victim. In *Thabo Meli* v. *R.* (1954) the accuseds had attempted to kill the deceased by beating him over the head. They had then rolled his "body" over a cliff in an attempt to make it look as if he had died from accidentally falling over a cliff. Medical evidence, however, revealed that he had in fact died from exposure and not from the beating. The problem facing the court was the fact that at the time the accused possessed the necessary malice aforethought for murder they failed to achieve their objective and when they rolled the body down the cliff they believed that the victim was already dead. However the court held that it was impossible to divide up what was really one series of acts in this way. The court seemed to base its decision upon the idea that there was an antecedent plan and that the victim died as a result of that plan, albeit in a way not anticipated by the accused. However, in subsequent cases the doctrine has been applied in situations where there was no antecedent plan. It has been suggested that the answer is possibly that the accused will be liable if he kills during the continuance of the "transaction" in which he acted with *mens rea*; and that transaction is continuing as long as D is covering up the homicide or other offence he believed he has committed. In *Thabo Meli* the court was concerned with a charge of murder; the principle has been held to apply also in cases of manslaughter (*Church* (1965)).

It was clear in *Thabo Meli* and *Church* that the victim had been killed as a result of the second of the two acts. In *Attorney-General's Reference* (*No.* 4 *of* 1980) (1981) the Court of Appeal was faced with a variant on the problem. There the accused had slapped his girlfriend on the face and this had caused her to fall down the stairs, banging her head. He then put a rope around her neck and dragged her up the stairs, placed her in the bath and then drained off all her blood. Finally he sawed up her body into disposable pieces. The victim died either from the fall, or due to being strangled, or due to having her throat cut; it was not, however, proved exactly how she died as very little of her body was found. The Court of Appeal held that if the jury were satisfied that culpability had been established in respect of all the acts which might have caused the victim's death, then they were entitled to convict him of manslaughter. If, however, they were not satisfied that culpability had been established on all of the acts which might have caused death then they would be bound to acquit.

However, these rare cases aside, the rule remains that the prosecution must prove that the accused caused the *actus reus* with the necessary *mens rea*.

4. Transferred Malice

Let us imagine a situation in which X intends to kill Y and to this end shoots him. The bullet misses Y but hits and kills Z. What view should the law take of this? On the one hand you might argue that he only attempted to kill Y and that unless you could find the necessary *mens rea* for a charge in relation to Z (for example that he was reckless or grossly negligent as to the fact that his shot might kill others) there should be no conviction. On the other hand in deliberately trying to kill one man he has unlawfully caused the death of another and should therefore be treated as if he had killed Y. In fact the law adopts the second approach. It is said that the malice X bears towards Y is transferred to Z. X can therefore be convicted of murdering Z even though he only intended to kill Y and was possibly even unaware of Z's presence (see *Latimer* (1886)). But suppose that the bullet had missed Y and had struck, not Z, but Z's pet labrador, killing it. Clearly the killing of a dog does not constitute any offence against the person, though it might constitute an offence of criminal damage to Z's property. Can we still join X's *mens rea* against Y to the *actus reus* of destroying Z's property? In *Pembliton* (1874) in the course of a fight outside a public house the accused picked up a stone and threw it at someone, but succeeded only in breaking a window behind his intended victim. He was charged with (the then equivalent of) the offence of criminal damage to property, but his conviction was quashed on the ground that you cannot join the *mens rea* of an offence against the person with the *actus reus* of an offence against property. Does this mean the Pembliton and X in our hypothetical example must go free? In our hypothetical example it is quite probable that you would be able to bring a successful charge against X for attempting to murder Y. Alternatively you might be able to charge X with criminal damage to Z's dog, but on the basis that he recklessly caused damage to the dog and not on the basis that he intended to kill a human being.

5. Mistake: Its Effects on Mens Rea

In some respects the question of mistake ought to be left to the general chapter on defences to criminal charges. On the other hand the defence of mistake is so closely bound up with the *mens rea* of the crime in question, that discussion of it will be included in this chapter. A lot of confusion is caused in relation to the defence of mistake by rather ill-defined use of terminology. The basic rule is, it is suggested, fairly simple. If the accused makes a mistake, the effect of which is to deprive him of the necessary *mens rea* required for that crime, then the mistake is capable of affording him a defence. From this it follows that if the accused makes a mistake as to an issue for which no *mens rea* is required then the mistake will not afford him a defence. Thus, for example, we have seen that the offence of abducting unmarried girls under the age of 16 (Sexual Offences Act 1956, s. 20) does not require that the prosecution prove that the accused knew, or was indifferent as to the fact, that the girl was under 16. Thus a mistaken belief, however reasonably held, that the girl was 17 would afford no defence. On the other hand a mistake by a man charged with murder to the effect that he thought he was shooting at an escaped bear would mean that the prosecution would not be able to prove that he intended to kill a human being. We shall see later that complications are caused by the fact that the courts do not seem to be able to make up their minds as to whether the mistake must be an honest mistake or an honest and reasonable mistake (see *post*, p. 157). Another type of mistake often made is the fact that the accused did not know that what he was doing was a criminal offence. For example, in one case the accused told the court that buggery was not an offence in his country and that as a result he was unaware that it was in this (*Esop* (1836); but see now Sexual Offences Act 1967, s. 1). Clearly the accused made a mistake, but it was not a mistake that would affect the necessary *mens rea* of the offence. The prosecution would have to establish that the accused had sexual connection with the other man and that was what he intended to do. It is not part of the prosecution's case to establish that the accused knew that buggery was an offence. It is often put in the form that the prosecution must prove that the accused was aware of the facts which made the action criminal, but not that he knew that it was criminal. For example in the crime of handling stolen property the prosecution would have to prove that the accused deliberately received the goods knowing or believing that they were stolen. The prosecution do not have to prove that the accused knew that the handling of stolen goods is a criminal offence. Unless it were part of the offence that the accused knew he was committing a crime this type of mistake will not suffice since it does not relate to the *mens rea* of the crime. Hence the general rule that mistake or ignorance of law is no defence to a change of crime.

If, then, it is appreciated that the mistake is one which affects the *mens rea* of the accused, then it will be possible to apreciate that the mistake may take several forms. In the first place it may be one that clearly relates only to factual issues. For example in *Rose* (1884) the accused was charged with the murder of his father. He said he had thought that his father was about to kill his mother and that was why he had killed him. The court found that although his father was not intending to kill the accused's mother, the accused's belief was an honest one (and indeed a reasonable one). If the facts had been as the accused believed them to be he would have had a good defence to the killing (see now Criminal Law Act 1967, s. 3 *post*, p. 207). This was purely a mistake of fact; there was no mistake as to any legal issue whatsoever. On the other hand the accused's mistake might refer to some legal concept which relates to the *actus reus* of the crime. For example where the accused is charged with bigamy (Offences Against the Person Act 1861, s. 57) the prosecution must prove that, being married, he married another. It would be a defence for the accused to show that he believed that his first wife was dead, and this would be a mistake of fact. On the other hand he might say that he had been through certain procedures at a solicitor's office and that he believed that as a result his marriage had been dissolved or annulled. Such a belief would be a defence. The mistake, in one sense, is a mistake of fact, namely that he believed that he was a single person. On the other hand it is a mistake as to the effect of certain legal processes and to that extent is a mistake of law. Whichever view is taken the mistake means that the accused did not intend, being a married person, to marry another; his intention was, as a single person, to marry. To reiterate a point made earlier, a mistake that bigamy was not a criminal offence would be no defence whatsoever. Both these mistakes are in a sense mistakes of law; the difference being that one affects the *mens rea* that has to be proved by the prosecution, the other does not. It is for this reason that it is suggested the second type of mistake, that is "I did not realise bigamy was a crime," be called ignorance of the law.

If it is accepted that a mistake which deprived the accused of the necessary *mens rea* can be a defence to a criminal charge, then we can turn to one of the most difficult aspects of the subject. Is it sufficient that the accused genuinely (or honestly) acting under a mistake which meant that he did not, in fact, form the *mens rea* required, or should we only allow him the benefit of his mistake if it was a mistake that a reasonable person could have made in the circumstances? Obviously when a jury is trying to decide whether the accused genuinely made a mistake it will ask itself "would we have made such a mistake?" This is because if the mistake was the sort that any reasonable person could have made, then it is more likely that the accused did in fact, make it himself. It is, however, quite another matter to instruct a jury that they may only consider the mistake as a defence if they consider it to have been a reasonable mistake. In *Cogan and Leek* (1976), for reasons which need not concern us here, the jury were asked to say whether they thought that the accused; (i) honestly thought that the woman was consenting to intercourse, and (ii) whether this was a reasonable mistake for him to have made. The jury held that it was an honest but unreasonable mistake and, on the state of the authorities at that time, the accused was convicted of rape. Since that time in *Morgan* (1976) the House of Lords has held that such mistakes need only be honestly made and this ruling has now found statutory effect in section 1 of the Sexual Offences (Amendment) Act 1976. *Cogan and Leek*, however, shows that such a distinction can be and was, in that case, crucial.

Wherever the prosecution has to show that the accused either intended or was reckless as to a certain act, circumstance or result, then if the jury believe that the accused thought that he was shooting, *e.g.* at a bear and not at a human being, then the prosecution have failed to show that he intended to kill a human being; equally he was not reckless as to this. If the judge directs the jury that the accused's mistake must be a reasonable one, he is, in effect, telling the jury that the prosecution need only prove that a reasonable person would have known that he was shooting at a human being and this is imposing liability for negligence. The logic of all this is that wherever a crime is said to require intention or recklessness (in the way that that was defined in *Cunningham*) then an honestly held mistake on this element of the *actus reus* should suffice. Unfortunately the House of Lords in *Morgan* did not provide that an honest mistake which negatives the *mens rea* will always suffice. In bigamy cases the prosecution must prove that the accused, being married, married a second time, but it is a defence for the accused that he thought he was free to remarry (*e.g.* because his wife was dead), but here the mistake needs to be honest and reasonable. So what is the difference? Why does the mistake about whether the woman was consenting to intercourse have only to be honest? Where does this leave other crimes? It is suggested that certain generalisations can be made. You will recall that we said an *actus reus* comprises certain conduct, surrounding circumtances and results. Where the mistake relates to a result (such as the killing of a human being for murder) the mistake will need only to be one which the accused honestly made (this would seem to follow from section 8 of the Criminal Justice Act 1967; see *post*, p. 159). Where, however, the mistake relates to anything else the position is less clear. In *Morgan* the House of Lords seems to take the view that in every crime there is a central core (the prohibited act) and if the mistake relates to this then it suffices that the mistake was honestly made. Thus in rape the issue of consent is central to the prosecution's case and thus it sufficed that the accused honestly, if unreasonably, thought that the victim was consenting. This is further illustrated by the more recent case *Albert* v. *Lavin* (1980) where the accused was charged with assaulting a police officer in the execution of his duty. The court accepted as proved the fact that the police officer had acted correctly in restraining the accused in order to prevent a breach of the peace, that the accused had then punched the police officer in the stomach and that at the time he honestly but unreasonably believed that the person he was punching was not a police officer. The court held, following *Morgan*, it was necessary to distinguish betwen the *mens rea* required for the basic elements of the offence and the mental element required for a defence. In the former an honest but unreasonable mistake may negative the *mens rea*, whereas in the latter only an honest mistake based upon reasonable grounds sufficed. In rape the element of lack of consent was a basic element of the offence, hence the mistake need only be honest. In an assault, whereas the question of whether the victim is consenting to the assault is a basic element, a mistake that his victim had no right to detain him relates to a defence and hence the mistake must be both honest and reasonable.

6. Proof of Actus Reus and Mens Rea

Probably more than with any other branch of substantive law the student of criminal law finds it difficult to keep theoretical problems of criminal liability apart from the practical problems of proving a case in a court. Very soon he will ask the question, "this is all very well, but how do you prove that he intended to kill?" It could be argued that in some ways it is the failure to keep these two issues apart that had led to so much of the uncertainty in, for example, the cases on mistake. We will conclude this chapter with a look at the problem of proving *mens rea*.

By and large the proving of the elements of the *actus reus* presents little problem. The basic *actus reus* of most crimes consists of elements which can be perceived by the senses and can therefore be testified to in court by witnesses. Even where the *actus reus* includes a mental element such as the lack of consent on the part of the victim, this will rarely cause difficulties since the victim will be ready to testify. However, proof of the *mens rea* of a given criminal offence is, on the face of it, an impossiblity without the confession of the accused. How can you decide whether the accused intended permanently to deprive the victim of his wallet in the crime of theft? The answer is that, in the absence of a confession by the accused, the *mens rea* will have to be proved by circumstantial evidence; the jury will be given factual evidence which has been perceived by a witness and will be asked to draw the necessary conclusions from that evidence. For example if the accused has been charged with murdering Z by shooting him, then if a witness testifies that he saw the accused level the gun at Z and pull the trigger, this will be direct evidence that the accused committed the *actus reus* of murder. It will also be circumstantial evidence that the accused intended to kill Z. Of course we will never know that he did intend to kill Z, but if the witness says that he accused took careful aim and did not appear surprised when the gun went off, the jury would be entitled to draw the conclusion that the accused intended to kill. If the accused were to take an axe and decapitate Z the natural consequence would be that Z would die. There grew up a maxim that a man must be taken to intend the natural and probable consequences of his actions. Clearly it is permissible for a jury in trying to decide what was going through the mind of the accused at the time he committed an *actus reus* to use a principle of common sense that if a certain act normally has a certain result, then in the absence of evidence to the contrary a person who did that act probably intended to produce that result. Unfortunately the courts began to direct juries that they were bound to infer that if the results were the natural and probable consequences of the accused's actions, they were bound to infer that the accused intended those results. Once again what was a useful tip for juries as to how to decide what a man intended became a mandatory direction.

In 1967 by section 8 of the Criminal Justice Act Parliament provided:

> "A court or jury in determining whether a person has commited an offence,

(a) shall not be bound in law to infer that he intended or foresaw a result of his actions by reason only of it being a natural and probable consequence of those actions; but

(b) shall decide whether he did intend or foresee that result by reference to all the evidence drawing such inferences from the evidence as appear proper in the circumstances."

It is important to understand the effect of this section. It is concerned only with those crimes where the law requires that the accused be proved to have intended or foreseen a given result or consequence. The law of murder requires that the accused intend or foresee death or serious bodily harm; section 8 thus applies and controls the question of how the jury shall decide that issue. The law of manslaughter by gross negligence does not require that the accused foresaw death or any other result and so section 8 has no application. It certainly does not alter the substantive law of murder and manslaughter.

If the given crime does require that the accused—has intended or foreseen a particular result then section 8 does not prevent the jury from drawing the conclusion that people generally intend the natural and probable consequences of their acts, it merely prevents the judge from forcing them to draw that conclusion. They are entitled to consider any relevant evidence which they feel may help them decide what the accused actually intended. Another relevant piece of evidence would be motive; we have seen that motive is rarely directly relevant, but indirectly it may help the prosecution to prove that the accused actually intended a certain result. It would seem to follow that if they believe that the accused was honestly mistaken about the result of his acts they should acquit and that, at least in relation to results, an honest mistake will suffice (see *ante*, p. 157).

It might have been arguable that the jury should be entitled to consider the fact that the accused was under the influence of alcohol, since this is likely to be a factor relevant to the assessment of what the accused actually intended. However, special policy considerations have led the courts to adopt a harsher attitude towards self-induced intoxication (see *post*, p. 198).

CHAPTER 2

STRICT LIABILITY

In the last chapter we noted (*ante*, p. 152) that on occasion the law imposes liability even though the accused lacks *mens rea* in the strict sense, and that these crimes are called crimes of strict liability. We said that the accused is convicted even though, as to one element at least of the *actus reus*, he is blamelessly inadvertent.

It is worth considering whether it is necessarily unfair to impose criminal liability even though the accused lacks *mens rea* in the strict sense. Let us consider a rather fanciful illustration. In murder the prosecution must establish that the victim died within a year and a day after the last injury inflicted by the accused. Suppose that H poisons W, his wife, using a poison that a brilliant chemist had assured him would take 18 months to take effect. In fact, owing to W's curious metabolism, W dies just inside the year and a day period. Is it to be said that H ought to be acquitted of murder or manslaughter because he did not intend or foresee that death would occur within a year and a day? On a strict application of the *mens rea* doctrine he must be acquitted of murder. But should we go this far? After all, H does intend to kill—he intends the prohibited act—and is merely inadvertent to a circumstance. Moreover that circumstance has no moral content; it does not alter the fact that H deliberately killed W and there is much to be said for the view that H should take his chances on the death occurring inside or outside the stated period.

Although the above problem might be thought to be far fetched, it was essentially the problem that arose in *Prince* (1875). William Prince eloped with Annie Phillips, who was aged 13, and was subsequently charged with an offence under section 55 of the Offences Against the Person Act 1861 which provided "Whosoever shall unlawfully take or cause to be taken any unmarried girl, being under the age of sixteen years, out of the possession and against the will of her father or mother or of any person having the lawful care or charge of her, shall be guilty . . . " (see now Sexual Offences Act 1956, s. 20). The jury concluded that Prince honestly and reasonably believed that Annie was 18 years old but a conviction was directed by the trial judge and that conviction was affirmed by the Court for Crown Cases Reserved. One view that was taken, expressed by Bramwell B., was that Prince did intend to do the prohibited act. He intended to take a girl, not a woman, whom he knew to be in the possession of her parents and further he was aware that he had no lawful authority for the taking. The only factor he was unaware of was the circumstance that she was under 16. Bramwell B. accordingly felt able to hold that Prince had *mens rea*. It is worth noting that when Prince eventually came up for sentencing he was given six months' imprisonment with hard labour; evidently the trial judge was of the opinion that, despite his mistake as to Annie's age, Prince had acted wrongly.

Did Prince get justice? Does not the fact that Prince believed Annie was over 16 take the carpet out from underneath Bramwell B.'s argument? Had Annie been, as Prince supposed she was, 18, Prince would have needed no one's consent—other than Annie's which had been readily given—to take her away. On the other hand Prince knew that her parents would disapprove—why else did he elope with her without telling them? Whether you approve or disapprove of Prince's conviction indicates what you think *mens rea ought* to mean.

It is, however, important to remember that even in crimes of strict liability some mental element will be required. Had Prince believed that Annie was a prostitute and thus not in the care of her parents, he would have been acquitted since in *Hibbert* (1869) the Court for Crown Cases Reserved held that *mens rea* was required on the aspect of the girl being in the control of her parent or guardian. So *Prince* does not decide that no *mens rea* at all is required, only that, in the case of *Prince*, once the prosecution established that he intended to take a girl out of the possession of her parents, then a conviction was possible even though he reasonably believed that she was 18. You may well wonder why such a distinction was drawn between the various elements of the *actus reus* in *Prince*. The answer is probably that these two elements came for discussion at different times and a different mood existed amongst the judges. There can be no logical defence of the distinction.

1. How Can You Identify Crimes of Strict Liability?

It is relatively simple to show how strict liability operates, the difficulty is in being able to identify which crimes will attract strict liability.

With very few exceptions (public nuisance, criminal libel and contempt of court) crimes of strict liability are statutory offences. It is highly unlikely that we shall see the creation of any new common law crimes of strict liability. In practice we can say that strict liability operates only in respect of statutory crimes. Thus the principles of statutory interpretation operate and the courts are supposed to try to discover the intention of Parliament from the wording of the statute. One principle of statutory interpretation is that in statutes creating criminal offences there is a presumption that *mens rea* will be required even where it is not specifically mentioned. An example of a crime which expressly provides for *mens rea* is section 1 of the Sexual Offences (Amendment) Act 1976 where in the crime of rape it is expressly provided that the accused must either know that the woman was not consenting to sexual intercourse or be at least reckless as to this fact. On the other hand many offences contain no reference at all to the requirements of *mens rea* and here the courts should start from the principle that *mens rea* is required. Thus common assault under section 47 of the Offences Against the Person Act 1861 contains no reference to *mens rea*, but the courts have held that the prosecution must prove that the accused either, intended to cause the victim to apprehend immediate and unlawful violence or that he was reckless as to whether his actions would have this effect.

However this presumption in favour of *mens rea* is rebuttable and we must now examine the factors which are likely to cause its rebuttal.

(1) The wording of the Act

As with any other statute the court's first duty is to try to ascertain the intention of Parliament, not from any extraneous sources, but from the wording of the Act itself. At present there is no guarantee that any given form of wording will create an offence of strict liability. On the other hand there are one or two discernible patterns. Thus certain words have received fairly consistent interpretations as requiring or dispensing with the need for *mens rea*. We will now have a look at some of these "key" words.

(a) *Permitting or allowing*

Where it is an offence to permit or allow another to do a certain act, the prosecution will normally be expected to prove that the accused was aware of the circumstances which made the act unlawful or deliberately avoided finding out. Thus under a statute creating an offence of permitting or allowing another to drive a motor vehicle with defective brakes, the prosecution would have to prove that the accused knew that his vehicle's brakes were defective before he permitted or allowed the other to drive it (see for example, *James & Son Ltd.* v. *Smee* (1955)). You must remember, however, that he does not have to know that it is illegal to permit or allow another to drive a vehicle with defective brakes (see *ante*, p. 155). On the other hand where the statute makes it an offence to drive or use a vehicle with defective brakes the courts have tended to say that the prosecution need not prove that the driver or user knew that the brakes were defective (see for example *Green* v. *Burnett* (1955)).

(b) *Cause*

Where statutes create an offence of causing something to happen, the courts have tended to impose strict liability. Thus in *Alphacell* v. *Woodward* (1972) the House of Lords decided that the defendants were guilty of the offence of causing the pollution of a river even though the pollution was owing to circumstances beyond their control.

(c) *Possession*

There are many offences which are defined in terms of "being in possession" of prohibited items. Drugs, explosives and plates for forging currency are three examples. The question we have to ask here is what does the word "possess" mean. Can you possess something, the existence of which you are totally unaware? (see, *e.g.* *Woodman*, *post*, p. 262. Suppose that Y, an innocent pedestrian, is stopped by the police and discovered to have a packet of cannabis in his pocket which has been placed there by a drug addict, who thought he was being watched by the police. Does Y possess the cannabis? The courts have tended to say that the word "possess" requires some mental element—in these types of offences, you must be aware that you are in possession of a substance. Thus Y, in our example, would not be said to be in possession of a prohibited substance. Suppose, however, that Y knew that he had a substance in his pocket but erroneously thought it to be a lemon sherbert. The House of Lords has taken the view that although you can now be strictly said to be in possession of the substance, you have a defence if you can show that you were mistaken as to the nature rather than the quality of the substance: *Warner* v. *M.P.C.* (1969). In our example the mistake would be as to the nature of the substance; lemon sherbert and cannabis are totally different commodities. If on the other hand you thought you had aspirins and the tablets were L.S.D. then this would be a mistake as to the quality; you thought you possessed a drug your mistake was simply as to which type of drug it was.Many of the problems relating to drugs are now covered by the Misuse of Drugs Act 1971 but cases such as *Warner* are still authority on the meaning generally of the word "possession." Possession therefore has certain mental elements, but it falls far short of requiring full *mens rea* as to the substance possessed.

(d) *Knowingly*

One would think that the word knowingly could cause few problems and that it would indicate an express requirement for *mens rea*. This is true to the extent that it clearly requires *mens rea* as to the clause it qualifies, but it is not always easy to identify the clause it does qualify. For example in *Hallam* (1957) the accused was charged with knowingly possessing explosives. Does this mean that the accused knows that he is in possession of a substance which is later identified as an explosive even though he thought it was soap powder, or does it mean that he must be both aware that he possesses a substance and that he further knows the substance to be an explosive? In the case cited the court held that the prosecution must prove that the accused knew that the substance was an explosive. Indeed to have held otherwise would have been to render the word "knowlingly" superfluous since as we have seen the word "possess" is usually held to require at least the knowledge that the accused has something in his possession. It would have been better had Parliament defined the offence as possession of goods knowing them to be explosives.

In older statutes the words "wilfully" and "maliciously" have been interpreted to require intention or recklessness (see *Cunningham, ante*, p. 143).

The word "knowingly" has been used by the courts indirectly to indicate strict liability. In certain offences the word knowingly appears in one section but not in the next, or in some but not all subsections of a given section. Where this happens it is tempting to say that this is a clear indication that Parliament must have intended those sections which do not contain the word "knowingly" to impose strict liability: *Cundy* v. *Le Coq* (1884); a case in which the absence of the word "knowingly" was used to exclude *mens rea*. Although this may be a pointer it is not conclusive. Thus in *Sherras* v. *De Rutzen* (1895) the accused was charged with selling alcohol to a police constable on duty. The defence submitted that the constable had removed his duty armband and so it was impossible for the accused to know that he was on duty. Against this it was argued that whereas other surrounding provisions of the statute used the word knowingly, section 16(2) of the Licensing Act 1872 did not. The Divisional Court quashed the conviction largely on the basis that, without the requirement of knowledge, the accused would be defenceless, since he would be convicted even if he had asked the constable whether he was on duty and the constable had told him falsely that he was not.

It is important to stress that these sort of "key" words are useful guidelines, but you must not expect complete consistency from the courts.

(2) Crimes and quasi crimes

In *Warner* v. *M.P.C.* (1969) the issue of strict liability received attention for the first time from the House of Lords in a case relating to possession of drugs. The House of Lords gave its approval to the notion of strict liability. In *Sweet* v. *Parsley* (1970) four of the same Law Lords appeared to be suggesting a much stronger adherence to the presumption of *mens rea*. The *Sweet* case was not, however, in any sense a denial of strict liability. What their Lordships said was that there were two types of criminal offence: the first were those which could truly be said to be criminal such as murder, rape, theft and assault. These were to be distinguished from those which are not criminal in any real sense, but are acts which in the public interest are prohibited under a penalty. Crimes of this second type have been called regulatory offences, quasi crimes or crimes *mala prohibita*. In other words when Parliament makes regulations to govern the better running of society—such as regulations to ensure that food and drink are sold and served under hygienic conditions or regulations to prevent industry from polluting the environment—then it is common to sanction breaches of such regulations with a penalty, though no one really thinks of the offenders as criminals. The significance of the distinction is that in the former category (true crimes) the presumption in favour of *mens rea* should rarely, if at all, be rebutted, whereas in the second category it is easier to infer that Parliament intended the presumption to be rebutted. Thus whereas in *Sweet* v. *Parsley* the offence of "being concerned in the management of premises which are used for the purpose of smoking cannabis" was treated as a true crime (*mala in se*) and thus requiring *mens rea*, in *Alphacell Ltd.* v. *Woodward* the House of Lords treated the offence of "causing polluted matter to enter a river" as a regulatory offence and dispensed with the requirement for *mens rea*. The result was that the defendants in *Alphacell*, who had taken great care to ensure that they did not pollute the river, were convicted.

If this distinction is now seen as crucial we must be able to distinguish between true crimes and regulatory offences.

It would be impossible to say with any degree of certainty which crimes will be classified as quasi crimes, but the following examples should serve to provide some indication:

(a) *Sale of food and drink*

Here they are many complicated regulations designed to ensure that hygiene prevails and also to ensure that customers are not given short measure. This area extends to the rules concerning the licensing of public houses. These crimes are prime examples of "regulatory offences" (see *Meah* v. *Roberts* (1977)).

(b) *Laws governing the environment*

Like clothing, strict liability has its fashions. At times of economic crises we see strict liability being applied in regulations designed to help the economic situation. In the sixties the concern seemed to be with drugs, while in the seventies pollution of the environment became one of the main topics of concern. The argument here seems to be that there is a form of activity which is causing grave public concern and that breaches of the regulations designed to help the community should be subject to sanctions irrespective of whether the transgressor did it innocently or culpably. Such severe action, it is said, will serve to keep people on their toes.

(c) *Drugs*

As mentioned in the previous paragraph increasing concern over drugs led to strict liability being imposed in the field of possession, etc., of dangerous drugs, but the recognition by the House of Lords that some of these offences fall into the category of true crimes has led to a softer approach being adopted by the courts and by the legislature in the Misuse of Drugs Act 1971.

(d) *Road traffic*

Many road traffic offences are created by regulations and provide sanctions for breaches of rules designed to ensure that the vehicles are in a roadworthy condition; it is a good bet that most of these offences will be interpreted as imposing strict liability. Another group of offences deals with the way in which the vehicles are actually driven on the road. Into this category fall the offences relating to driving whilst under the influence of alcohol. Although these latter offences are now purely summary, the penalties can be severe and nearly always include a year's disqualification, but as we have already said the courts have interpreted these offences as imposing strict liability. Speeding is clearly a crime of strict liability; careless driving is crime of negligence; reckless driving and causing death by reckless driving which carries up to five years' imprisonment are crimes requiring some form of *mens rea*. Thus it would seem that as the maximum penalties grow the less likely the courts are to impose strict liability.

(3) Smallness of the penalty

Another pointer to the way in which a court will interpret a given offence is the size of the penalty available. As a general rule the larger the penalty the less likely the court is to treat it as a crime involving strict liability. The reasoning behind this is that a heavy maximum penalty is an indication of Parliament's intention that the accused should be shown to be blameworthy. Whereas you can impose fines on blameless individuals, imprisonment should be reserved for those whose conduct is blameworthy.

At the end of the day there is no sure test to discover whether a statute has imposed strict liability. The above principles have been taken from cases. They are not applied consistently but provide some indication of how the courts will react when confronted with a new criminal offence.

2. Defences to Offences of Strict Liability

If we say that the offence is one of strict liability does this mean that the accused can have no defence to it? No, for that would be going too far. We have already said that where an offence is held to be one of strict liability, this usually means that the court has dispensed with the need to prove intention, recklessness or negligence as to one element of the *actus reus*. The practical effect is that on that one element the accused cannot raise the defence of mistake of fact, *even if his mistake was reasonable*. It possibly also means that the defence of impossibility will not apply to that element; thus where the accused is charged with failing, as the owner of a vehicle, to display the excise licence, it will be of no defence to show that it happened without any default of his own while he was away from the vehicle. However mistake of fact may well apply to other elements of the *actus reus* and the remaining general defences such as infancy, duress, necessity and automatism are possible defences to a charge. Let us consider a hypothetical example. The offence of driving with the level of alcohol in the blood being over the prescribed limit requires that the prosecution prove that the accused was driving on a road or other public place. The notion of driving involves a mental element or at least the concept of voluntary conduct. Thus if the accused were to show that he had received a blow on the head immediately before he started to drive and this had produced a state of automatism, then he would be able to say that he was not "driving" the car. On the other hand a defence that he was unaware that he had consumed any alcohol since a friend had laced his drinks would fail; liability on this element is strict and mistake of fact is no defence.

In Australia the courts have made attempts to lessen the rigours of strict liability by allowing the accused to plead by way of defence that he had taken all reasonable care. If we consider the example of a butcher who sells bad meat (an offence contrary to the Food and Drugs Act 1955, s. 8), if such an approach were to be adopted, the prosecution would at first prove that the butcher had sold meat and that this meat had turned out to be bad. If nothing further is said then the butcher will be convicted. However if he can prove, on a balance of probabilities, that he had taken all reasonable precautions to ensure that the meat sold in his shop was sound, then he would be acquitted. Of course, this would be an exception to the rule in *Woolmington's* case which says that it is for the prosecution to prove guilt and not for the accused to prove his innocence. However if the alternative is strict liability with no such defence, then it is clearly an improvement from the point of view of the butcher. It would be an even greater improvement if the butcher merely had to introduce evidence that he had taken all reasonable care, leaving the prosecution to prove that he had not taken all reasonable care.

We have not adopted such a general midway position in offences of strict liability. Occasionally the courts have held that a statute, which might have been expected to impose strict liability, did not, in fact impose strict liability, because there was nothing the accused could have done to protect himself. Thus in *Sherras* v. *De Rutzen* the court held that a statute making it an offence for a licensee to sell alcohol to a policeman on duty did not impose strict liability since this would have left him defenceless had the constable deliberately lied about being off duty. Similarly in *Lim Chin Aik* v. *R.* (1963) the Privy Council took the view that the imposition of strict liability is pointless unless there is something that the accused can do to prevent himself breaching the regulation.

It is becoming more common today for statutes which impose strict liability to contain express defences. Thus one type of defence consists of allowing the accused to escape conviction if he can prove that the contravention of the regulation was due to the fault of a third party and that he, the accused, took all reasonable precautions against breaking the regulations (see *e.g.* the Food and Drugs Act 1955, s. 113). More generally statutory defences take the form of casting the burden on the accused to prove that he was not negligent; thus we do specifically for some crimes what the Australian approach would suggest we should do for all crimes of strict liability. (See for example Trade Descriptions Act 1968, s.24).

3. Conclusion

There seems no really convincing reason for the perpetuation of these offences. The same result could be achieved by means of imposing liability for negligence; in other words a failure by the accused to take reasonable care. In any event Parliament should make it totally clear in the drafting of legislation, exactly what sort of liability is being imposed.

Chapter 3

PARTIES TO CRIMINAL OFFENCES

1. Principal and Secondary Offenders

When a criminal offence is committed attention is primarily focused on the perpetrator. In a case of murder the police will look for the killer, in a case of burglary the person who entered the building as a trespasser, in a case of criminal damage the person who caused the damage and so on. However a moment's reflection tells us that if the criminal law were concerned only with the perpetrator it would be seriously defective. Someone who helps the perpetrator (for example by providing the gun for a killing, or a key for burglary) ought also to incur liability for the crime. In some cases the helper may indeed have played a much more significant part than the perpetrator for he may have been the one who conceived and planned the offence. On the other hand a point is reached at which the assistance given is so remote that it would be unfair or unrealistic to make the helper a party to the crime. In a well-known civil case (*Lloyd* v. *Johnson*, (1798)) it was held that a laundress could recover from a prostitute the cost of washing expensive dresses and some gentlemen's nightcaps though the laundress knew well that the dresses were used for the purpose of enticing men in public places. In such circumstances the laundress could hardly be regarded as a party to the prostitute's offence of soliciting. Once again the task of the law is to draw the line at the appropriate place.

Our starting point should be section 8 of the Accessories and Abettors Act 1861 (as amended by the Criminal Law Act 1977). This provides "Whosoever shall aid, abet, counsel or procure the commission of any indictable offence whether the same be an offence at common law or by virtue of any Act passed or to be passed, shall be liable to be tried, indicted and punished as a principal offender." There are similar provisions in relation to summary offences. Until 1967 offences were either felonies or misdemeanours and in the case of felonies various degrees of participation were identified. The actual perpetrator of the offence was known as the principal in the first degree, anyone who was present at the scene of the crime and gave assistance was known as the principal in the second degree, while anyone who gave assistance before the commission of the crime but who was not present at the scene was designated an accessory before the fact. A person who gave assistance to the felony after the offence was called an accessory after the fact. With the passing of the Criminal Law Act 1967 the distinction between felonies and misdemeanours was abolished and section 8 of the Accessories and Abettors Act became applicable to all indictable offences, with the resulting disappearance of the above classifications. Today it is more normal to refer to the actual perpetrator of the offence as the principal offender and all the others who assisted in the commission of the offence as the secondary parties, or accessories, and these are the terms we shall use in this chapter.

From a procedural point of view it is not necessary to distinguish in the indictment between principal and secondary offenders—all can be indicted as having committed the offence—provided that at the trial the prosecution can prove that the offence was in fact committed by someone and that those on trial are either principal or secondary parties. Once convicted they are all liable to the same penalty. This was brought home in a dramatic way by the case of *Craig and Bentley* (1952) where following a rooftop chase Bentley was arrested by police officers following a robbery. He called out to Craig "Let him have it Chris" and Craig shot and killed a police officer. Both were indicted and convicted of murder. Craig was too young to face the death penalty and he was sentenced to life imprisonment, but Bentley, who was in police custody at the time of the killing, was hanged.

Three points should be noted before we go any further. Firstly, a person does not become a secondary party to a crime until a crime is either committed or attempted by the principal. If B supplies A with a gun in order to kill X, B becomes a party to the murder only when A kills X, though he will be a party to an attempt if A attempts to kill X and fails. Secondly, both section 8 of the Accessories and Abettors Act 1861 and the Criminal Law Act 1967 were designed to improve criminal procedure and not to affect substantive criminal liability. Thus the old cases are authoritative on the question of who is a participant in a given crime. Today, however, we do not need as a general rule to distinguish between the various types of secondary participation. Thirdly, with the abolition by the Criminal Law Act 1967 of felonies, the old offence of being an accessory after the fact to a felony automatically lapsed. However section 4 of the Act introduces a new offence of assisting arrestable offenders which has similar features to the old offence.

(1) The principal or perpetrator

Suppose that A, B and C are charged with murder of X. The evidence establishes that they had agreed to kill X, that all were present at the time of the killing, and that X was killed by a single stab wound. All deny striking the fatal blow and the evidence does not establish which was the perpetrator though it was clearly one of them. It would be the height of absurdity if the law provided in such a case that all three should be acquitted and of course it does not. All three may be convicted of murder and on conviction all three must be sentenced to imprisonment for life.

In this illustration there is no need to isolate the principal, but sometimes this is necessary because the rules relating to his liability differ from those of secondary parties. Suppose in our illustration, that A, B and C all claimed that D had threatened to kill them unless they killed X. Duress is a defence to one who is a secondary party to murder, but it is not available to the principal offender (see *post*, p. 202). If the jury come to the conclusion that all three were in real fear for their lives if they did not kill X, then to secure a conviction for murder the prosecution must be able to identify the one who inflicted the fatal stab wound, for only he is denied the defence of duress. If the prosecutor cannot identify the perpetrator then all three would have to be acquitted.

Another situation in which it is necessary to draw a sharp distinction between the principal offender and secondary party is where the offence is one of strict liability (see *ante*, p. 161). We have seen that a person may be made liable for certain offences even though he lacks *mens rea*. But strict liability is imposed only on the principal offender and is not imposed on secondary parties. In *Callow* v. *Tillstone* (1900) the principal offender was a butcher who was charged with exposing bad meat for sale. He had got a vet to examine a carcase of a heiffer which had eaten yew leaves. The vet passed it fit for sale and relying on the vet's certificate the principal offender put it up for sale. The offence was one of strict liability and the principal offender was therefore convicted. The justices also convicted the vet as they found that he had been negligent in issuing the certificate. On appeal the vet's conviction was quashed since he did not know nor was he reckless as to the meat being bad. It may strike the reader as a trifle odd that the principal offender was held liable even though he was entirely blameless while the secondary party (the vet) was not liable though he was at fault in the sense that he was negligent. However the courts have taken the view that strict liability applies only to the principal offender. The reason for all this is that liability for secondary participation arises at common law and criminal liability at common law generally requires *mens rea*. You could argue that this is illogical since if there are good policy reasons for imposing strict liability on the principal there are equally good reasons for imposing it on the secondary offenders—but the law is not always logical.

So how is the principal to be marked off from the secondary parties? Normally this presents no problems. A shoots and kills X with a gun provided by B. A is the principal and B is a secondary party. C enters a building to steal while D keeps a watch outside; C is the principal offender in the burglary and D is the secondary party. However it is not always as clear as this. Suppose that E holds Y while F stabs him (these are part of the facts of *Abbott*, discussed below, p. 202) and Y dies as a result. Is E a principal offender or a secondary party? It is, of course, possible to have more than one principal offender. If E had merely decoyed Y to the place where F stabbed him, then E would clearly only be a secondary party. Does he become a principal by holding Y so that Y cannot defend himself against F's murderous attack? This case is clearly right on the borderline. If the crime had been rape and E had held Y down while F had intercourse with her, you could hardly say that E was the perpetrator of the rape—you could not really say that E raped Y. On the other hand if E holds Y while F punches him you could say that E and F are co-perpetrators of an assault since for E to hold Y against his will is in itself an assault. But where E holds Y so that F can stab him it may be unrealistic to say that E killed Y: what he has done is to help F kill Y.

The principal offender is, therefore, any person (or persons) who by his own conduct directly brings about the *actus reus* of the crime. This formulation may not, however, suffice for all cases. Suppose that A puts poison in X's medicine knowing that B a nurse will innocently administer the poison to X in the course of her duties. Or suppose that C persuades D, a nine year old boy, to steal from Y. Neither B, since she lacks *mens rea*, nor D, since he is under the age of criminal responsibility can be charged as parties either to killing of X or the stealing from Y. In both cases it might be said that A and C did not directly bring about the *actus reus* of the respective crimes. Common sense, however, tells us that A killed X and C stole from Y and the formulation at the beginning of this paragraph should be taken to include such cases. In such cases, B and D are often referred to as innocent agents; thus we say that A killed X through the innocent agency of B. It is proably safer and simpler to ask—can we drop B out of the picture and say A killed X?

(2) Secondary parties

From the discussion in the preceding section we can say that a secondary party (sometimes called an accessory) is, broadly speaking, someone who helps to bring about the crime without being the actual perpetrator. Such a broad definition, though it will probably suffice for most cases, is not sufficiently refined to deal precisely with all the cases that can arise.

It might be thought that the position of a secondary party was exactly the same as that of a principal. After all section 8 of the Accessories and Abettors Act 1861 provides that he is liable "to be indicted and tried as if he were a principal offender." However this is not really so and the liability of the secondary party turns out to be rather more complex than that of the principal. Suppose that A and B are charged with a crime and it is alleged that A is the perpetrator and that B is the secondary party. Against A it has to be proved that he by his own conduct directly caused the *actus reus* with the appropriate *mens rea*. Against B it has to be proved that:

(i) he knew that A would cause the *actus reus* with the appropriate *mens rea*, *and*
(ii) that he helped A to commit that crime knowing that his conduct would be of assistance to A.

You may say that proposition (ii) includes proposition (i), but this way of setting out the requirements in relation to B serves to emphasise that the *mens rea* of a secondary party extends not only to knowledge of the principal's *mens rea* but also requires a further intention to help the principal; and, in the case of the secondary party, not only has it to be shown that the *actus reus* of the crime was brought about but also that there was some conduct of the accessory which helped the commission of that crime.

If follows, therefore, that B cannot be convicted as an accessory to A's crime merely because he knows that A will commit the crime. B may learn that A plans to murder X or burgle Y's premises but this knowledge alone is not enough to make B a party to the killing of X or the burgling of Y's premises. It can make no difference that, on learning of A's intention, B is secretly delighted because he will inherit under X's will or because Y is someone he hates. An even more extreme illustration is provided by the case of *Allan* (1965). Allan was present when some of his friends became involved in a fight. He knew that his friends were committing a crime, but not only did he approve of their conduct, he had secretly resolved to help them should they require his aid. His conviction, however, as a party to the crimes committed by his friends was quashed because knowledge of the principal's crime coupled with an intention to aid is not enough unless there is also some conduct of the accessory which helps the principal.

So what exactly has to be proved against the accessory to make him a party to the principal's crime? Simply put, it must be shown that with knowledge of the principal's crime the accessory did something to help in its commission with the intention of assisting, though in detail the position may be more complicated.

(a) *Knowledge of the type of crime*

First, the requirement of knowledge of the principal's crime does not require that B should know of every detail of A's planned crime. Take a case where A plans to steal money from a safe at a particular factory and needs cutting equipment for this purpose. He contacts B and purchases this equipment from him making no mention whatever of his plans. B, however, knows that A has a record for burglary, that he has no legitimate business for which such equipment could be required and guesses (correctly) that it is required to break into a safe on some premises or other. Nevertheless B supplies the equipment. B may be convicted as an accessory to the burglary committed by A though B has no idea when or where the crime is to be committed. The point is that he knows the essentials of the crime. But *Bainbridge* (1960) on which the last illustration was based shows that it is not enough to make B liable that he knew that A was up to no good—that would be far too vague. It was also accepted in that case that B would not be liable if his only suspicion was that A planned to commit some different type of crime, such as receiving stolen metal and that the cutting equipment was to be used to break it up.

So the accessory will not escape liability saying that it was a case of no-questions-asked if he in fact, realised what the principal was up to. Moreover, it is enough that the principal commits one of a range of crimes which was in the contemplation of the accessory. In *D.P.P. for Northern Ireland* v. *Maxwell* (1978) Maxwell's task had been to lead Northern Ireland terrorists to a public house in a village where they left a bomb. He claimed that he could not be convicted as a party to the bombing since he did not know what the terrorists had planned to do. The House of Lords decided that from his knowledge of the organisation he knew that the mission would take one of a number of forms and it was sufficient that the actual deed that night fell within the bounds of one of the offences he, in fact, contemplated.

In most cases the test propounded in *Maxwell* will provide a ready answer. However one or two questions remained unanswered. For example if B suspects A is about to commit burglary and the equipment he has supplied will be used to force open the windows of the premises will he be liable if A's plan, which he carries out, is to rape a girl who lives there? Your immediate reaction will be to say that this is an entirely different crime from the one B contemplated. However where A enters the house as a trespasser with intent to rape someone inside this is burglary contrary to section 9(1)(*a*) of the Theft Act 1968 (see below, p. 294) and burglary is the very crime B contemplated. Perhaps the courts would take a common sense view in these sorts of case and hold that B should not be convicted as a party to a particular variant of burglary he almost certainly would not have contemplated. Another problem is that once B has supplied the equipment A can go on using it for the type of crime B had in mind indefinitely. Does B become a party to all the future crimes A commits with the equipment? This may seem rather hard on B but there is nothing technically to stop such liability arising.

We have said so far that the secondary party must know that the principal offender will commit a particular offence or one of a known group of offences. Knowledge here includes wilful blindness and so B would be liable if he guesses that A is about to commit a burglary with the equipment he is supplying and deliberately asks no questions so that he can say that he did not know what A is about.

(b) *Liability for unforeseen consequences*

It follows from the foregoing discussion that while B may be liable for such crimes committed by A as were in B's contemplation, he is not liable for crimes committed by A that he does not contemplate at all. We have just seen that where B supplies cutting equipment to A knowing of its use in connection with a burglary, that B becomes an accessory to the burglary. Suppose then, that as part of the burglary, A attacked X, a nightwatchman, and rendered him unconscious. B is not a party to the assault on X which was uncontemplated by him; the fact that B contemplated one crime (burglary) and that during the commission of that crime another (assault) was committed is not enough to make B liable as a party to the further crime. In relation to the assault B is totally lacking in *mens rea*.

In this example it is assumed that B supplies the equipment some days before the burglary and is not present at its commission. Does it, therefore, make any difference if B accompanies A on the burglarious expedition? The answer is that it makes no difference whether B is present or absent from the scene of the crime. B is liable only for such crime or crimes of A that he contemplates A will commit, intending to assist in their commission. Thus if B had accompanied A but had been totally unaware of the presence of the nightwatchman and had never contemplated that force would be used on any person, he could not be a party to A's assault.

In general terms, therefore it can be said that B (even if he accompanies A for the purposes of carrying out the crime) is not a party to other crimes committed by A which were unforeseen by B. This does not mean that B escapes liability because A has deviated from the precise terms of that plan. If B counsels A to kill X by poisoning and A shoots X, B will be a party to the murder of X. If B counsels A to steal X's silver plate and A steals X's gold plate, B will be a party to the theft. Moreover B may be liable for a consequence unforeseen by him if that consequence is one for which A is liable even though it was equally unforeseen by him. Suppose that B counsels A to kill X, A shoots at X, misses and kills Y. As we have seen, A will be liable for the death of Y (*ante*, p. 154) by virtue of the doctrine of transferred malice. Since A is liable for the death of Y even though that consequence was unforeseen by him, B will be liable as an accessory even though Y's death was also unforeseen by him.

Now we can have a look at a rather more complex example. Suppose that A, B, and C plan to burgle X's house in the night at a time when the occupants are expected to be asleep. They plan to steal certain valuable antiques. A and B are to enter the house and C is to remain outside in his car with the engine running. B knows that A carries a loaded revolver; C does not know this but knows that A has a reputation for violence. A and B enter the house. During the enterprise B commits various acts of vandalism by slashing furniture and furnishings with a razor. As they are about to leave they are surprised by X. A fires at him, misses and the bullet travels through the door killing Y, X's wife, who was standing behind it. If we consider the various crimes in turn:

(i) *The burglary.* This presents no problems. A and B are joint principals and C is an accessory. Though the point is unimportant A and B are also joint principals in theft. Could C say that he was not a party to the theft if some of the articles taken were not antiques? Probably not. (He could not deny liability for burglary since this arose the moment A and B entered the house with the intent to steal). He could do so if the compact was for the taking of antiques and nothing else but this is unlikely in the extreme. If C contemplated that other articles would be taken (and he would surely contemplate that A and B would appropriate any money they found lying about in the house) he will be a secondary party to the theft of articles other than the antiques.

(ii) *Criminal damage.* B is the principal offender here. Whether C will be held to be an accessory depends upon whether he knows of B's proclivities. It is not at all uncommon for burglars to be given to vandalising the premises they burgle; if C knows that B is given to this activity, he is a party to the criminal damage if there is an understanding that B will damage property in the house. (See *C* v. *Hume* (1979)). If C has no such knowledge then he cannot be a party to the criminal damage. A's position as an accessory to criminal damage is essentially the same. (It should be noted that under s.9(*b*) it is burglary, having entered premises as a trespasser, to commit criminal damage to the property. Thus the unresolved point discussed at p. 175 above could arise here. Both A and C contemplate burglary and this has occurred though in a form they did not contemplate).

(iii) *Murder and manslaughter.* By virtue of the doctrine of transferred malice A is liable for the death of Y and will be liable to be convicted of murder or manslaughter depending upon his *mens rea*; murder if he intended to kill or cause serious bodily harm; manslaughter if he merely intended to frighten X. As for C, it is clearly not enough to make him liable in respect of Y's death that he knew that A was given to violence. But suppose that C contemplated that the householders might be awakened by the burglary and contemplated that A would use force against anyone who disturbed him. Here the fact that C is unaware of the gun is crucial. In *Davies* v. *D.P.P.* (1954) there was a fight between two rival gangs on Clapham Common. Basically what started as a punch-up ended with a member of one gang, Davies, stabbing to death a member of the rival gang. It was held by the House of Lords that Lawson, another member of Davies' gang, was not an accessory to the murder since he did not know that Davies had a knife. It is clear that Lawson was not an accompliace in the manslaughter either since it was said that he was not an accomplice "in the use of the knife." If, however, the death had occurred as a result of a blow struck by Davies's fist, then Lawson would have been an accessory to the manslaughter. As we have seen a secondary party may be liable for a consequence unforeseen by him if the crime is one in which the principal is liable for that unforeseen consequence. Manslaughter by an unlawful act is such a crime (*post*, p. 235) so that Lawson becomes a party to manslaughter if he is a party to the form of violence which causes the death.

It follows in our example that C's ignorance of the gun insulates him from liability for the death of Y.

B's position is quite different because he knew that A had loaded the gun. If B realised that in the event of their being surprised by anyone, that A would use the gun to kill or cause grievous bodily harm, then B is a party to murder. If B realised that A would use the gun to frighten and A so used it, then B would be a party to manslaughter. In neither case does it make a scrap of difference that Y's death may have been unforeseen.

Suppose that B thought that A had taken the gun to give himself

Dutch courage and that A would not use it. Strictly speaking B would not be a party to the death of Y. As a matter of fact, though, any jury is likely to give short shrift to such a claim by B when he knew of the loaded gun and knew that they were burgling occupied premises in the night. More realistically B may claim that he thought that the gun would only be used to frighten and that A would not use it with intent to kill. What then if it is accepted that B realised that the gun would be used to frighten and A then used it with a deliberate intent to kill or cause serious bodily harm? B cannot be guilty of murder because he does not share, and indeed is quite unaware of A's intent to kill. But surely, it might be said, that B is guilty of manslaughter because he had sufficient *mens rea* for that crime and there is an *actus reus*. *Anderson and Morris* (1966) however suggests otherwise. Following an attack by Welch on Anderson's wife, Anderson armed himself with a knife and, accompanied by Morris, went in search of Welch. When Welch was found he was attacked by Anderson who stabbed him to death. The judge instructed the jury that if they were satisfied that Morris took part in the assault they could convict him of manslaughter even if he was unaware that Anderson had a knife. This was clearly wrong and Morris's conviction was quashed but the Court of Criminal Appeal went on to indicate that even if Morris was aware that Anderson had the knife and that he planned to assault Welch, Morris would incur liability neither for murder nor manslaughter if, unbeknown to Morris, Anderson formed an intention to kill. This may seem a very generous result so far as Morris was concerned; after all, if Anderson had used the knife with an intent to frighten Welch and had accidentally caused his death, Anderson would have been convicted of manslaughter and Morris would have been an accessory. But the decision can be defended; Morris may have been prepared to help Anderson to assault Welch without being at all prepared to help Anderson to kill him.

(c) *Aids, abets, counsels or procures*

In addition to providing that the secondary party knew of the crime the principal intended to commit, the prosecution must prove that the secondary party helped the principal with intent to do so. In fact section 8 uses neither the words "help" nor "assistance" and imposes liability where the accessory "aids, abets, counsels or procures" the crime. Basically these verbs convey the idea of help or assistance but in the end we have to consider the precise interpretation of the words used in the statute itself. This was the important point made by the Court of Appeal in *Attorney General's Reference* (*No.* 1 *of* 1975) (1975) when it was said that these words must be given their ordinary meaning. Obviously the words overlap to some extent. If A and B meet X and B encourages A to assault X we may indifferently say that B aids, abets, counsels or procures A to assault X. On the other hand each word may contain nuances of meaning not conveyed by the others; *Attorney General's Reference (No. 1 of 1975)* illustrates the point. B added alcohol to A's drink without A's knowledge and A's subsequent driving of a car resulted in him being prosecuted under the breathalyser provisions. It was held that B had procured the commission of the offence by A. The court rejected an argument that the secondary participation always requires communication between the accessory and the perpetrator and held that a crime could be procured (*i.e.* brought about by endeavour) though there was no communication between the secondary and principal offenders. The court did not attempt an exhaustive definition of the remaining verbs but it would now be unwise to assume that they are synonymous.

(i) *Conduct amounting to aiding, abetting, counselling or procuring.* At all events there must be some conduct of the secondary party which can properly be said to amount to an aiding, etc. *Allan* (*ante*, p. 174) shows that a secret intention to assist without any assistance in fact is not enough. On the other hand very little assistance may, in fact, be required, and words alone may suffice. It would have been enough had Allan shouted encouragement to the principals or even if he had said "give me a call if you need a hand." This necessitates consideration of two particular problems.

Presence as aiding, etc. If a shout or two of encouragement is enough to constitute aiding, why should not mere presence suffice? A may be just as much encouraged by the presence of B as by a word of encouragement. Clearly B's accidental presence cannot suffice but the reason for this is that B would then lack any intention to aid. But what if B then stays to watch? Recently terrorists seized the Iranian Embassy in London and their illegal activities were closely watched for some days by hordes of newsmen and, through the medium of television, by many millions of viewers. In a very real sense the terrorists drew encouragement from this for one of their primary aims was to secure publicity for their cause. Common sense tells us that the newsmen were not accessories to the continued imprisonment of the Embassy staff and the case of *Clarkson* (1971) strikingly bears this out. In that case B and C did not become secondary parties to rape merely because, to satisfy their prurient interests, they watched fellow soldiers repeatedly rape a girl in their barracks.

Presence, however, if it is not accidental constitutes some evidence of aiding, etc., though it must be considered along with all the other evidence. Thus presence coupled with evidence of a previous conspiracy between the parties to commit the crime will suffice. In *Coney* (1882), however, it was held to be a misdirection to direct a jury that (non-accidental) presence at a fight was conclusive evidence of aiding. No doubt this decision was right, but presence at an illegal activity which requires spectators if it is to prosper at all may more readily give rise to an inference of aiding and abetting than presence at other illegal activities. In *Wilcox* v. *Jeffrey* (1951) B was convicted of aiding and abetting A (the celebrated jazz saxophonist Coleman Hawkins) to play in public contrary to the conditions on which he was allowed to enter England. The Divisional Court thought it right in such a case to invite the jury to infer aiding from presence throughout the illegal performance together with the fact that B had met A at the airport and had written an account of the performance in the newspaper for which he worked. Suppose then that in *Allan* the trial judge had directed the jury that Allan's continued presence at the fight could be regarded as evidence of aiding, and that the jury had convicted him. Would the Court of Appeal have quashed his conviction?

Aiding, etc., by omission. The last question raises another problem. Is B liable for A's crime because he fails to intervene to prevent it or to put a stop to it? The general answer must be No, because there is no general duty to prevent the commission of crime by others. Exceptionally there may be circumstances where B is under a duty to take positive steps to prevent the commission of a crime by A. In an Australian case *Russell* (1933) it was held that a father was a secondary party to the homicide of his children where he stood by and watched the mother drown them. In *Du Cros* v. *Lambourne* (1907) it was held that B could be convicted of aiding A to drive dangerously where A was driving B's car with his permission and was, to B's knowledge, driving it dangerously.

(ii) *The mental element in aiding, etc.* It has been pointed out that a secondary party's *mens rea*, in a sense, requires two elements: (i) knowledge of the principal(s *mens rea* and (ii) an intent to aid the principal in the commission of his crime. The former of these requirements has been examined in some detail above; it is now necessary to say something more about the latter. Clearly B does not become a party to A's crime if, knowing of it, he accidentally helps in its commission as where B, knowing that A intends to steal from C's safe, absentmindedly fails to lock the safe. The words "aids, abets, counsels or procures" suggest purposive conduct on B's part.

Suppose, however, that A plans to burgle X's house and he asks B to drive him to a specified destination. B does so and A burgles the house. B's liability may be considered on various hypotheses:

(1) If B believes that A's enterprise is an innocent one then B cannot incur criminal liability.

(2) If B knows what A plans and is willing to drive him to and from the scene of the crime he is evidently a party to A's crime.

(3) B is a taxi driver who A has engaged at the normal commercial rates. B knows that A plans to burgle C's home but considers that this is none of his business. B reasons that if he refuses his services then another taxi driver (who does not have B's knowledge of A's intentions) will be readily found by A. Why, B asks himself, should he lose a fare when the crime will be committed anway? A problem similar to this arose in *National Coal Board* v. *Gamble* (1959) where the defendants, the National Coal Board, had supplied X with coal. The procedure was that X's drivers filled up their lorries at the Coal Board's depot and then drove the loaded lorries on to a weighbridge. If the weight shown was correct the weighbridge operator issued the driver with a ticket at which time the court held that ownership of the goods passed to X. Under the Motor Vehicle (Construction and Use) Regulations it is an offence to drive a lorry on a public road when the load exceeds a certain weight. On the occasion in question the weighbridge operator saw that the lorry was over loaded and commented on this fact to the driver. The driver replied that he would take the risk and a ticket was issued. The driver committed the offence immediately he drove onto the road, but the difficult question was whether or not the Coal Board was liable as a secondary party (through the action of their employee). It seems clear that although the weighbridge operator did not want to help the driver commit an offence: he could not have cared less whether the driver was picked up for contravening the regulations or not. On the other hand he did know all the facts which constituted the offence and his action in issuing a ticket enabled the driver to commit the offence. The Divisional Court held that this was enough to make the weighbridge operator (and therefore the Board) a secondary party. Thus it is sufficient that X performs an act which he knows will assist Y in the commission of a crime.

(4) Now suppose that B hopes that A will be unable to commit the burglary let's say that he hopes that on arrival at X's house they will discover that it is occupied and that A will thereupon call off the enterprise. It seems that this will not save B. In *D.P.P. for Northern Ireland* v. *Lynch* (1975) Lynch drove some terrorists to a place where they shot and killed a man. Lynch said that he was hoping that the crime—or any crime—would not be committed but it was said that

this would be no defence. Would it make any difference that B spent the journey to X's house trying to persuade Z not burgle the house? *Fretwell* (1864) suggests that it might, for there B was held not guilty for the self-murder by A where he gave her the wherewithal to procure an abortion whilst earnestly entreating her not to use it. This decision is, however, questionable. In *N.C.B.* v. *Gamble* Devlin J. thought, surely correctly, that if B sold a gun to A knowing that A intended to murder his wife, B would be an accessory to the murder even though his interest was only in the profit he would make on the sale and was utterly indifferent to the fate of A's wife. It is unlikely that Devlin J. would take a different view of B's participation if B had sold the gun to A with a plea for matrimonial reconciliation. This brings us full circle to the case we were discussing at the outset of the laundress who washed and returned clothes to a prostitute knowing that she would use them to ply her trade in public. It seems unlikely that we should convict the laundress as a party to the prostitution and therefore a line has to be drawn. Of course in these cases B can always refuse to sell the gun and wash the clothes, but what if A is asking for the return of the gun he lent to B? If B refuses can he be sued for wrongful retention of A's property? It is unlikely that a civil court would uphold such an action and in any case *Garrett* v. *Arthur Churchill (Glass) Ltd.* (1970) would imply that such a plea would be no defence to B if he returns the gun. How then do we distinguish between the sale of the gun and the washing of the clothes. The only really practical solution is to say that liability in these type of situations will depend upon the severity of the contemplated crime. Thus if B returns the gun to A knowing that he plans to shoot his wife he will be liable, but not if he knows that A plans a bit of illegal poaching. This hardly seems satisfactory but it is submitted it is the only practicable solution.

(3) Victims as parties to an offence

When A is charged with raping B we can say that in a very real sense that B is the victim of the crime and no one would suggest that B is a party to rape. On the other hand, if A is charged with having unlawful sexual intercourse with his 15-year old girl friend, B is again the victim, but this time a very willing one and so why should she not be charged as an accessory to A's crime? The reason why B cannot be so charged is the rule in *Tyrell's* case (1894) which provides that where a statute is designed to protect a certain class of individual, then such an individual cannot be held to be a party to the crime however willing she was for the crime to be committed against her. The scope of the rule is uncertain but it has been applied mainly in the sexual area. It only protects, however, the victim of the particular crime. If B, a 15-year old girl helps A to have intercourse with C, another 15-year old girl, then B can be charged as a party to that intercourse, but C cannot.

(4) Repentance by a secondary party before the crime is committed

As we have said, the secondary party becomes liable only when the principal commits the offence in question or attempts to commit it. There may be, therefore, a fair amount of time between the act of assistance rendered by the secondary party and the commission of the offence by the principal. Is it therefore possible for the secondary party to escape subsequent liability by washing his hands of the crime?

The least that B, the secondary party, can do to avoid liability is to communicate his withdrawal from the enterprise to the principal offender, A. It is not sufficient that he secretly decides to have nothing more to do with A. Even if he does communicate his repentance to A, he may still be in difficulties. In the first place, he may already have committed the crimes of incitement or conspiracy and he will remain liable for these. Secondly, if he has supplied A with a gun to kill his wife, he must ensure that A does not carry out the plan, by force, if necessary. If communication is impossible or if he cannot prevent A from harming his wife, B's only way out would seem to be communication of the plan to the police (see *Becerra* (1976)).

2. Vicarious and Corporate Liability

We shall conclude this chapter with a look at the way in which a master can be prosecuted for the crimes of his servants and a limited company can be prosecuted as if it were a human defendant.

(1) Vicarious liability

In civil actions a master (usually covered today by the word "employer") is liable for the wrongs of his servants (employees) which were committed by the servants during the course of their employment. This usually enables the victim of the torts to sue a defendant who is more likely to be able to pay should liability be proved. There is no general application of vicarious liability in criminal law where we are normally trying to attach liability to the people directly responsible for the commission of a criminal offence and where compensation of the victim is not the primary concern. However, it does occur in the following situations:

(a) *Express statutory vicarious liability*

Occasionally Parliament provides expressly for the imposition of vicarious liability. For example, section 163 (1) of the Licensing Act 1964 provides: "A person shall not, in pursuance of a sale by him of intoxicating liquor, deliver that liquor, either himself or *by his servant or agent*, from any van, barrow, basket or other vehicle or receptacle. . . . "

(b) *Implied vicarious liability*

In some cases the courts treat the acts of the perpetrator as the acts of his employer. This they will do when the word used in the statute is one which, without too much of a strain on its meaning, can be interpreted to cover persons other than the actual perpetrator. Such words as "sell," "supply" and "use" have frequently received this extended meaning. Thus when a lorry driver takes a lorry out for his employer, it is not unreasonable to say that both the driver and the employer "use" the lorry. So both could be said to have used a lorry with defective brakes. This form of vicarious liability is found only in cases where the statute imposes strict liability. It cannot be used, in offences requiring *mens rea*, to transfer the *mens rea*, of the actual perpetrator to his employer.

In *James & Son Ltd.* v. *Smee* (1955) the offence in question was using, or causing or permitting to be used a vehicle in contravention of the Motor Vehicle (Construction and Use) Regulations 1951. The Divisional Court held that there were in effect three different crimes of which permitting to be used clearly required *mens rea* and using clearly did not. Thus if A, an employee, sets out in one of his employer's lorries which has defective tyres, the employer, B, can only be convicted of permitting the use of the vehicle if he knows that the tyres are defective, whereas A can be charged with using the vehicle even if he is unaware of the defect. Furthermore, if the police rely on the "using" offence they can hold B vicariously liable—they can, in effect, say that B was using the lorry. They may charge both A and B in which case they will be co-principals. If, however, the regulations had provided that it was an offence to drive a vehicle with defective tyres, then the police could charge only A as a principal offender. B could not be held vicariously liable since the word "drive" is not really capable of an extended meaning—you could not really say that B had driven the lorry. In this case it would only be possible to charge B as a secondary party and then only if he had knowledge of the defect. (See also *Coppen* v. *Moore (No.* 2) (1898))

(c) *The delegation cases*

Most people are aware that before a public house can sell alcohol to the public there will have to be a licence obtained from the local magistrates permitting such a sale. This licence has to be issued to a person and not to a company so it will be issued either to the tenant of the pub or, in most cases today, the manager who draws his salary from one of the breweries. The sale of alcohol is governed in the main by the Licensing Act 1964 under which there are many offences which can only be committed by the holder of the justices' licence. This means that he will have to be named as the principal offender and if he does not commit the offence then the offence is not committed which means that there is no chance of charging the actual perpetrator (*e.g.* a barman) as a secondary party. There are not many pubs or establishments operating under these licences where the licensee is the sole person working. Most places employ staff and so there is a good chance that it will be these staff that perpetrate the acts which if done by the licensee would be an offence. Thus without vacarious liability many offences would be virtually unenforceable.

Some of the offences under the Licensing Act are offences of strict liability and where this is the case it may be possible to hold the licensee vicariously liable under the principles discussed in section (*b*) above; *e.g.* selling alcohol to a person under the age of 18 years. The courts, however, do not seem to have taken this course in licensee cases. On the other hand some of the offences are offences requiring *mens rea*. We saw in Chapter 4 (*ante*, p. 165) that the offence of selling alcohol to a policeman on duty requires that the offender knows that the policeman is, in fact, on duty. The offences of permitting drunkeness and permitting prostitutes to congregate also require *mens rea*. The courts have not allowed the type of vicarious liability we saw in the previous section to be used where the offence requires *mens rea*. Thus the courts have developed a second type of vicarious liability which is now used almost entirely to impute the guilty mind of the licensee's employees to the licensee himself. This operates only when the licensee has delegated general responsibility to his staff for at least part of the pub and is himself not present in that part when the offence is committed. The principle is not restricted to the Licensing Act, but this is where it has been largely developed.

We can see how this delegation principle works in relation to an offence requiring *mens rea*. Let us suppose that members of the local rugby club are in the lounge celebrating a victory that day. They are now all well and truly drunk. It is an offence for the licensee to permit drunkeness on the licensed premises (the Licensing Act 1964,

s. 172(1)). B who is the senior barman on duty in the lounge has been instructed by A that under no circumstances must he permit such behaviour. B, however, knows most of the players and consequently does nothing. Has an offence been committed? This will depend upon whether we can impute B's knowledge to A under the delegation principle. This raises two questions. Has A delegated authority for the general running of the lounge to B and is A absent? Of course, if he has gone out for the night and he will have delegated authority to someone and he will not be present. But is it enough that he is simply in another room. Most of the cases on this topic suggest that it is sufficient that the licensee is not in the room in question at the time the offence is committed and that in his absence another is in charge (see *Howker* v. *Robinson* (1973)). However in *Vane* v. *Yiannopoullos* (1965) the House of Lords held that there had not been delegation when the licensee of a restaurant was not in the room in question, but had gone up onto another floor. Since there was no delegation the House of Lords did not give a final ruling on the delegation principle, but their comments suggested that they were not altogether happy about the idea of imputing *mens rea* to a licensee in this way. As Lord Donovan said "If a decision that 'knowingly' means that 'knowingly' will make the provision difficult to enforce, the remedy lies with the legislatute." But the lower courts have continued to apply the delegation principle.

If the drunken men were in the room where A was clearly in charge then the delegation principle does not operate. So, in our example, if the drunken men were in the bar and only D is aware of their state. D's knowledge cannot be imputed to A. In such a case the prosecution will have to prove that it was A who personally permitted the drunken men to remain and that he knew that they were drunk.

One final point can be made here. Suppose that various customers continue to drink after closing time with the knowledge of the bar staff. The point to remember is that the offence is drinking after hours and not permitting customers to drink after hours. Thus it is the customer who is the principal offender. Any of the staff who knowingly permit this to continue will be liable as secondary parties, but if A is absent the knowledge of his staff cannot be imputed to him under the delegation principle; you cannot be vicariously liable as a secondary party (*Ferguson* v. *Weaving* (1951)).

(2) Corporate liability

Limited companies possess what is known as legal personality. This means that the company can hold property as if it were an ordinary human being and that it can sue and be sued in the civil courts in its own name. The question for us to consider now is whether the company can be a party to criminal proceedings. Of course when a criminal offence is committed, the actual act must have been perpetrated by an ordinary human being and he will be liable as an individual for the criminal act, but the courts have held that in certain circumstances the limited company can also be held liable in the criminal law for the acts of one of the member individuals.

There are two ways in which a limited company can be held liable for criminal acts:

(i) The company can be held to be vicariously liable for the crimes of its employees in just the same way that a human employer can be held responsible for the crimes of his employee. Thus, as we saw earlier (*ante*, p. 185) this will only apply in statutory crimes of strict liability where the court has been able to give an extended meaning to words such as "sell" or "use."

(ii) The company can be held liable by what is known as the doctrine of identification. What this means is that in each company the court recognises certain senior individuals as being the company itself and the acts of these individuals when acting in the company's business are treated as the acts of the company. It has been said that certain members of the company can be regarded as its brain and the others as its hands. This tells us that we are looking for people who have the power to control the company's actions. Thus in most companies we can say that the managing director and the other directors will be regarded as being in a position of control and this might even extend to the company secretary and non-director managers if they have sufficient executive power. But the line is not easy to draw with any degree of certainty and this was illustrated by the case of *Tesco Supermarkets td.* v. *Nattrass* (1972). In that case an old age pensioner was trying to buy a packet of soap powder at the reduced price being offered by one of Tesco's shops. He could not find any packets priced at the lower price and the shop refused to sell him a packet at anything other that the full price. He complained to the inspector of weights and measures who brought a prosecution against Tesco Supermarkets Ltd. under the Trade Descriptions Act 1968, s.11(2). Tesco sought to put the blame on the branch manager who had failed to ensure that packets at the reduced price were on display, despite the control exercised by the firm and its detailed instructions to managers as to how to deal with such matters. One of the issues confronting the House of Lords was whether or not the store manager could be identified as the company. If this was the case then Tesco would liable for the offence. The House of Lords held that because of the strict controls exercised by the company over its branch managers they were left with so little power that they could not be regarded as part of the "brains" of the company. This meant that Tesco Ltd. was able to show that the offence was, in fact, committed by a third party—namely their manager—and thus it could rely on section 24 of the Act which provided that it would be a defence to a person charged under the Act to show that the commission of the offence was due to the act or default of another person and that he himself took all reasonable precautions to prevent the commission of such an offence by himself or any person under his control. (See defences to strict liability *ante*, p. 168). This is not a true example of the third party defence since there is no need for the third party to be joined in the proceedings. It is sufficient that the defendant can give sufficient information to the prosecution to enable the true culprit to be prosecuted.

(a) *Liability of individual*

If the firm is held to be liable because of the acts of one of its members, can the member be joined as a party to the proceedings? The answer to this is clearly Yes. In both types of corporate liability he may be joined as co-principal.

(b) *Are there any crimes a company cannot commit?*

A company can be convicted of any offence provided that the sentence can be in the nature of a fine. You clearly cannot send a company to jail, let alone hang it. Thus the penalty must take the form of a fine which will fall upon the shareholders. The only crimes where this will not be possible are treason, murder and some forms of piracy where imprisonment is mandatory.

Theoretically this means a company can be convicted of all offences against the person except for murder. There is no reason why a company should not be liable for manslaughter, when, for example, its managing director electrifies its perimeter fence against vandals, killing a small child who accidentally touches the wire. It is however difficult to imagine that a company director acting in furtherance of his company duties could ever render the company liable for rape. However if Z, the managing director of X Co. Ltd., a film company, supervises the filming of intercourse between M, an 18 year old male with N, a 15 year old girl, there is no reason why Z and hence the film company should not be convicted as secondary parties to the unlawful sexual intercourse.

Chapter 4

GENERAL DEFENCES

Although specific crimes may be provided with special defences of their own, there are several defences which are of general application to criminal offences and these will be examined in this chapter. Most defences are, in fact, allegations by the accused that the prosecution has failed to establish one or more elements of the *actus reus* or *mens rea*. In some cases the defence relates to a part of the *actus reus* or *mens rea* that is so central that the accused does not even have an evidential burden to discharge before the judge is bound to leave it for consideration by the jury. Thus if X is charged with the murder of Y and he says either that it was another man who shot Y or that the gun went off accidentally, he is doing nothing more than saying that the prosecution cannot prove that he caused Y's death or that he had the *mens rea* needed for murder. Both of these issues are issues upon which the prosecution have the duty to introduce evidence and also the duty to prove their case to the court's satisfaction. It would obviously be advisable for the accused to introduce any evidence he possesses in support of such defences, especially where the prosecution appears to have a good case. On the other hand if the prosecution's case is weak he may be advised to say nothing, since the judge is bound to direct the jury that the prosecution must prove that the accused was the man who pulled the trigger and that he did so with the necessary *mens rea*. A second group of defences although relating to the *actus reus* or *mens rea* of the crime are not so central to the prosecution's case and here the accused may well bear an evidential burden, which means that unless, by the end of the case, there is evidence which could create a reasonable doubt, the judge will not give the jury any direction on that issue. This is the case with the defences of self-defence, provocation, duress, necessity, automatism and intoxication. Finally there are those defences in which the accused bears not only an evidential but also a legal burden; here the accused will not only have to introduce evidence of this defence, but he will also have to prove to the jury that it was more likely than not that factors amounting to such a defence existed. Under this category come the defences of insanity, and diminished responsibility (there are others but these are by far the best known).

If we discount for the moment those defences in the third category, it is probably not inaccurate to say that in order for the prosecution to secure a conviction, it must prove *actus reus*, *mens rea* and absence of a defence. Thus if X is charged with the murder of Y, the prosecution will have to prove the *actus reus* of the crime and this will include proof that the killing was unlawful. If X gives no evidence and the prosecution establish that X shot Y and that Y died as a result, the jury would conclude that the prosecution had also proved that the killing was unlawful. On the other hand if X believes that he acted in self-defence the judge will only direct the jury to consider whether the prosecution have failed to rebut self-defence beyond reasonable doubt if, by the end of the case for the defence, there is some evidence to support such a finding. It does not matter whether this has been raised specifically by the defence or whether it has emerged from various sources during the course of the trial so long as there is evidence adduced upon which a jury could entertain a reasonable doubt.

1. The Mentally Abnormal Offender

(1) Unfitness to plead

When we talk of the defence of insanity we normally mean a plea by the accused that at the time he was alleged to have committed the offence he was suffering from a state of mind which fell within the legal definition of insanity. Before we discuss that, however, we should first note that many of those who may well fall within the legal definition of insanity are not, in fact, tried at all. Where it is obvious that the person charged is suffering from a really severe mental abnormality which would make it impossible to conduct any sort of meaningful trial, he may well be committed to a mental institution by the Home Secretary using his powers under sections 72 and 73 of the Mental Health Act 1959. Clearly this should only be done where a trial is out of the question, and even then, if the accused later recovers he should be tried for the offence. Where the condition is not so obviously one in which no trial should be attempted, and the accused is brought before the court, a question might arise as to whether or not he is fit to stand trial. If the court comes to the conclusion that the accused cannot stand trial he is said to be unfit to plead.

What does unfitness to plead mean? A person is unfit to plead when he is unable to understand the charges that have been brought against him and is unable to appreciate the difference between a plea of guilty and a plea of not guilty. If he is able to understand these issues then he is fit to stand trial even if he is unable to recall any of the events to which the charges relate (*Podola* (1960)). This emphasises that it is the state of the person's mind at the time of the trial that is in issue. Podola by the time of the trial was clearly able to understand the charges that had been brought against him and knew the difference between pleading guilty and not guilty. In his case, if his claims were true, his difficulty lay in knowing whether to plead guilty or not guilty since he could not recall what had happened.

Who raises this issue, and when? Unfitness to plead can be raised by the accused, the prosecution or even the judge. Where it is raised by either the judge or the prosecution, it is then up to the prosecution to prove that the accused is unfit to plead and the standard of proof required is the criminal standard—beyond reasonable doubt. Where the accused claims that he is unfit to plead he bears the burden or proof and must prove on a balance of probabilities that he is unfit to plead. Like insanity, which will be considered below, this is a clearly recognised exception to the rule that the prosecution bears the burden of proof on all issues in criminal cases.

Where the issue of unfitness to plead is raised, the trial judge will empanel a special jury to determine whether or not it has been proved and the decision will normally be made right at the start of proceedings. However, where the question of fitness to plead is raised by the prosecution against the desires of the accused, in a case where the accused feels that he has a substantive defence or that the prosecution case is very weak, a decision that he is unfit to plead will have the effect of depriving him of the opportunity of clearing his name. Thus under section 4 of the Criminal Procedure (Insanity) Act 1964, the judge is given a discretion to postpone any decision on fitness to plead until after the case for the prosecution has been closed. If he then feels that there is no case to answer he can direct the jury to acquit the accused. It may still be that the accused's condition is so bad that he will need to be confined in a mental institution, but this will not then be under suspicion of having committed a crime.

What is the effect of a successful plea? The accused will not be tried. He will be committed to a mental hospital and his release can be secured only with the consent of the Home Secretary.

(2) The defences of insanity and diminished responsibility

Now we can look at the true defence of insanity, under which the accused claims that because of his mental state at the time he allegedly committed the offence, he was not truly responsible for his actions. The defence of insanity is of common law origin and its requirements are to be found in what are known as the M'Naghten Rules 1843 (from *M'Naghten's Case* (1843)). We shall see that insanity is a relatively narrow defence and does not provide for many mentally abnormal offenders. This led Parliament in the Homicide Act 1957 to provide a special defence, applicable only to murder, known as diminished responsibility which, when successfully pleaded, means that the accused will be convicted, not of murder, but manslaughter.

(a) *Insanity*

The word "insanity" is not a medically recognised term which describes a particular mental state; it is a legal term for a legally defined state of mind which will lead in any criminal offence to a verdict of not guilty by reason of insanity.

The starting point is the presumption that the accused is presumed sane until the contrary is proved. The burden of proving insanity lies on whoever wishes such a finding to be made by the jury. Thus if the accused raises the defence he must prove that it is more likely than not that he is insane. If the accused pleads diminished responsibility the prosecution will be entitled to argue that the accused was insane. If the jury decide that the accused was insane they will return a verdict of not guilty by reason of insanity. Since this is technically an acquittal it is provided by section 12 of the Criminal Procedure (Insanity) Act 1964 that the accused may appeal against the verdict.

The side bearing the burden of proof must prove that the accused was, at the time he committed the act, "labouring under such a defect of reason, from disease of the mind, as not to know the nature and quality of the act he was doing, or if he did know it, that he did not know he was doing what was wrong." Thus there are various elements which must be established.

(i) *Disease of the mind.* The basis of the defence is that the accused's state arose from a disease of the mind. On many occasions the accused may argue that a particular medical condition affected his ability to form the *mens rea* of the crime in question without any thought of pleading insanity (see *Clarke* (1972) *post*, p. 195). But where the court is of the opinion that the condition amounts to a disease of the mind, the person may be taken to have raised the defence of insanity. So what constitutes a disease of the mind? Clearly, the term is apt to cover any physical condition which is directly affecting the brain, such as inflammation of the brain or a brain tumour. The case of *Charlson* (1955), where the court held that a brain tumour was not a disease of the mind must now be regarded as questionable; *Bratty* v. *Att.-Gen. for Northern Ireland* (1963). It has been also held to cover such illnesses as diabetes, arteriosclerosis and some forms of epilepsy. The court, it would seem, should be looking for something in the nature of a permanent cause rather than a transitory condition which has been caused by a blow on the head or the taking of drink or drugs. In *Quick* (1973) the accused had inflicted actual bodily harm on a hospital patient where he worked as a nurse. He wished to plead that he suffered from diabetes and that as a result of a hypoglaecemic condition he was totally unaware of what he was doing. In other words, he wanted to plead that he was acting in a state of automatism. The trial judge ruled that the condition resulted from a disease of the mind and that the correct plea was therefore insanity. At this point, Quick, not surprisingly, changed his plea to one of guilty. He appealed against his conviction and the Court of Appeal held that the trial judge should have left his defence of automatism to the jury. The blackout had been caused not so much by his diabetes, but by the effect of alcohol and absence of a proper meal on the drugs he was taking. This should not be taken as saying that alcohol or drugs cannot lead to insanity. Where the accused has become an alcoholic or drug addict then a court may well be entitled to say that he is suffering from a disease of the mind.

(ii) *Defect of reason*. The disease of the mind must have led to such a defect of reason that the accused did not know the nature and quality of the act he had committed or, if he did know, that he did not know that what he was doing was wrong.

The reference to nature and quality of his acts is basically another way of saying that the accused did not intend to do what he did nor was he reckless. Traditional examples given include the man who cut a woman's throat thinking that it was a loaf of bread and the nurse who put the baby on the fire, thinking it was a log of wood.

If the accused is relying on the second limb—that he did not know he was doing what was wrong—then it seems he must prove that he did not know that it was legally wrong (*Windle* (1952)). Thus, even though the accused believed that what he was doing was morally abhorrent and that people in general would not approve, he is entitled to a verdict of not guilty by reason of insanity if he can show that he thought that it was legally permissible. It is useful to remember at this point that in the case of a sane adult, it is no defence to prove that he was unaware that his actions constituted a criminal offence (see *ante*, p. 155). Thus if X's disease of the mind caused him to think that three of his friends, A, B and C were members of an assassination squad who had to be killed before they could kill him, then he would succeed on a defence of insanity, because his delusion caused him to think that he was legally entitled to kill A, B and C. If, on the other hand, his disease of the mind caused him to think that he was Jack the Ripper and so led him to go round killing prostitutes, he would not succeed with a plea of insanity because, as Jack the Ripper, he would know that he was not entitled to kill random prostitutes. He might now, however, be able to plead diminished responsibility.

(iii) *Insanity as a defence today*. Although insanity is technically available as a defence to any crime, it is almost entirely restricted, in practice, to murder cases, and with the advent of diminished responsibility it has all but disappeared. However it may arise indirectly. Suppose that X has been charged with theft and pleads by way of defence that she blacked out. The judge will want to know what caused the blackout, and the explanation might tend to suggest that the accused was suffering from a disease of the mind. If this is the case then the judge will be forced to rule that the accused is pleading insanity and that it is for the accused to prove it. In practice such a ruling will almost certainly cause the accused to drop the plea of automatism altogether (see *Clarke*, *ante* p. 193).

Thus a defence counsel who wants to plead lack of *mens rea* and who wants to give some medical explanation for this (such as pre-menstrual tension, depression, etc.) should tread cautiously lest he inadvertently describes a disease of the mind.

(b) *Diminished responsibility*

Such was the narrowness of the legal test for insanity that Parliament introduced a special defence which would apply to charges of murder only. This was known as diminished responsibility and a successful plea leads to the accused being convicted of manslaughter rather than murder. As with insanity, the burden of proof lies on the accused to prove that it was more likely than not that he was suffering from diminished responsibility at the time he committed the offence. In effect, it is rather like provocation in that it enables the jury to return a verdict of guilty of manslaughter but not a complete acquittal. Once the jury has returned a verdict of guilty of manslaughter, the judge then has a wide discretion over what should happen to the accused. He can commit him to prison for up to life, he can have him detained in a mental institution, he can put him on probation or even give him an absolute discharge. The net result is that diminished responsibility has almost entirely replaced insanity as a defence. In reality, insanity was only raised as a defence to a charge of murder and we shall see that any state of mind that can constitute insanity would also amount to diminished responsibility. With a finding of not guilty by reason of insanity, the judge is bound to commit the prisoner to an indefinite stay in a mental hospital such as Broadmoor whereas, following a successful plea of diminished responsibility, there is every chance that the judge will pass a determinate prison sentence.

What, then, must the accused prove in order to establish the defence? Section 2(1) of the Homicide Act 1957 provides:

> "Where a person kills or is a party to the killing of another, he shall not be convicted of murder if he was suffering from such abnormality of mind (whether arising from a condition of arrested or retarded development of mind or any inherent causes or induced by disease or injury) as substantially impaired his mental responsibility for his acts and omissions in doing or being a party to the killing."

This looks all very technical. What is the judge supposed to do? Is he to try to define the terms of the section for the jury? The Court of Criminal Appeal eventually resolved that it was wrong for a trial judge simply to read the section to the jury and leave them to make what they could of it. He should give them whatever guidance they require to understand it (*Byrne* (1960)). Basically, three factors have to be established:

(i) *The accused must have been suffering from an abnormality of mind.* In effect, the judge should ask them whether the accused's mind seems normal—would they say that he appeared to them to be normal. If he appears "mad" or "insane" (as a layman would use these words) then he can be said to be suffering from an abnormality of mind. Thus it was apt to cover the accused in *Byrne* (1960) who had strangled a young girl and had then horribly mutilated her body. His defence was that from early years he had suffered from overwhelming perverted desires which he found very difficult—if not impossible to resist. He submitted that he had killed the girl under the influence of such an urge. It is interesting to pause here for a moment. Could Byrne have successfully pleaded insanity? The answer is that he could not. Whether or not he could have established that he was suffering from a disease of the mind, the evidence suggested that not only did he appreciate what he was doing, but that he also realised that it was wrong. His trouble was that he found it very difficult to stop himself.

(ii) *Cause of the abnormality of mind.* The abnormality of mind must have arisen from a condition of arrested or retarded development of mind or any inherent causes or must have been induced by disease or injury. This is clearly a very wide provision. Is it wide enough to cover an abnormality of mind caused by excessive drink or drugs? It would seem for this to be possible, the accused would have to argue that the alcohol had injured his mind; possibly, therefore, a condition such as alcoholism caused by long-term drinking might be covered, but not an accused who was simply drunk at the time he committed the offence.

(iii) *Effect of the abnormality of mind.* The accused must prove that the abnormality of mind substantially impaired his mental responsibility for his acts and omissions in doing or being a party to the killing. In *Byrne*, the accused had relied on perverted sexual urges which he alleged caused him to kill the girl. Clearly, if the evidence had shown that he found these urges to be irresistible, the defence would have been established. But this would amount to a total impairment of his responsibility and the Acts says that he need only prove a substantial impairment. What, therefore, does the Act mean by "substantial?" This is clearly a question of fact and degree for the jury. If Byrne found his urges no more difficult to resist than the lusty male finds it to resist leaping on every attractive female he sees, then this would not be enough. In other words his urges must be so strong so as to deprive him of any real self control.

(3) Hospital orders

We should mention here that when a person is proved to have committed a criminal offence (other than murder), the court has power, under section 60 of the Mental Health Act 1959, to make a hospital order under which he will be committed to the care of a mental hospital. Where the court, in such a case, feels that the accused is particularly dangerous, it can make a restriction order which has the effect of necessitating the consent of the Home Secretary before he can be moved or released.

2. The Intoxicated Offender

You will recall that under section 8 of the Criminal Justice Act 1967, where the definition of the offence requires that the prosecution prove that the accused intended or foresaw that a given result would be a consequence of his action (*i.e.* that sticking a knife into Y would cause Y's death) then the jury should be entitled to take into account any evidence which may help them reach such a conclusion. The same sort of proposition should be true in relation to knowledge or foresight of circumstances. One such factor immediately springs to mind, namely that the accused has drunk so much alcohol or has taken such a large quantity of heroin that he really could not have been fully aware of what he was doing. Is this therefore a factor the jury are entitled to take into account? Why should it be any different from any other factor which might affect the accused's ability to form the necessary *mens rea* required? One reason is that many members of society would find it abhorrent that a person who has caused the *actus reus* of a criminal act should escape liability because he has got himself into such a state that he did not know what he was doing. Should the law, therefore, allow such a defence only if the court is satisfied that the accused was not at fault in becoming intoxicated or drugged; if, for example, his drinks had been laced? We shall examine first of all those situations in which the accused has knowingly consumed alcohol or drugs and seeks to adduce this as evidence that he should not be held responsible for the act he committed. After that we shall look at the situation where the intoxication was involuntary. (In this section we shall use the word intoxication to cover both drink and drug induced states.)

(1) Voluntary intoxication

If the basic common law principle of requiring the *actus reus* to be accompanied by the necessary *mens rea* before there could be a conviction were to apply in relation to defendants who had consumed quantities of alcohol, then it would follow that if the accused has consumed so much alcohol that he did not form the requisite *mens rea* for the offence he should be acquitted. But as we have already said, such a rule would be unacceptable to many. Objection could be taken on the ground that such a defence would be easy to raise and hard to rebut, or simply that people who get drunk should learn to accept the consequences, and possibly this last notion is at the base of the uneasy compromise that has been drawn by the courts in this area.

Over the last few decades increasing attention has been drawn to a distinction which is said to exist between crimes of specific intent and crimes of basic intent. In *D.P.P.* v. *Majewski* (1976) the House of Lords has finally agreed with the proposition that voluntary intoxication which deprives the accused of the requisite *mens rea* can only be a defence to crimes of specific intent. The ruling makes it clear that we must be able to identify those crimes which the House calls crimes of specific intent and those which it calls crimes of basic intent. There is no sure guide that can be given here. In general, those crimes in which, at least as to one element, intention and nothing less is required, can be regarded as crimes of specific intent. Thus offences under section 18 of the Offences Against the Person Act 1861 (*e.g.* wounding with intent to cause grievous bodily harm), theft, burglary and attempts in general are crimes of specific intent. On the other hand, crimes in which it is sufficient for the prosecution to prove either intention or recklessness as to each element of the *actus reus* can be regarded as crimes of basic intent. Examples of such crimes include offences under sections 20 and 47 of the Offences Against the Person Act 1861 (*i.e.* unlawful wounding, assault occasioning actual bodily harm and basic assault), manslaughter, and rape. The decision of the House of Lords in *Caldwell* (*ante*, p. 147) does at least bring some logical basis for the treatment of so-called crimes of basic intent. This is because if recklessness means failing to foresee an obvious risk, the reason for the failure is irrelevant. We are simply asked (i) was there an obvious risk and (ii) did the accused fail to foresee it? But you must not get the impression that there is a watertight rule. Murder, for example, might from the above discussion appear to be a crime of basic intent in that the prosecution will succeed if they can prove that the accused intended to kill or cause grievous bodily harm or that he foresaw death or grievous bodily harm as likely. However, the courts have, for the purposes of the defence of intoxication, described murder as a crime of specific intent. It is therefore safest to say that a crime of specific intent is one in which the courts have actually allowed the defence of intoxication to rebut the requisite *mens rea* and the examples given above have been so tested. It is possible to see a sort of policy working behind these decisions. In the case of a murder charge, where the defendant raises the defence of intoxication, the jury will be entitled to find him not guilty of murder because his self-induced state of intoxication prevented him from forming the requisite *mens rea* for murder. However, they would not be entitled to acquit him of manslaughter (which is an alternative verdict on a murder indictment) on the basis of intoxication since manslaughter is a crime of basic intent and self-induced intoxication is no defence. The overall effect is that intoxication provides the accused with a partial defence, but still brings him within the net of the criminal law. The same is true of charges under section 18 of the Offences Against the Person Act 1861 (such as wounding with intent to cause grievous bodily harm); the jury will be entitled to acquit him on the section 18 charge but would be able to bring in an alternative verdict of guilty of unlawful wounding contrary to section 20 of the same Act. It would be more satisfactory if the courts would admit that this concept of crimes of specific and basic intent is a rather devious way of saying that voluntary intoxication can be a defence to some crimes but not to others and that in crimes where the defence is not available it means that the prosecution will gain a conviction even if the intoxication means that the accused did not form the *mens rea* that would be required of a sober man.

Let us now consider how these principles work in practice. Let us suppose that D has been charged with the murder of his wife. If D wishes to rely on intoxication as a defence it will be up to him to introduce evidence of the defence and if this is done it will be up to the prosecution to prove that the intoxication either did not exist or, if it did, that it did not rob the accused of the requisite *mens rea* at the appropriate time. It would be of no use for the accused to say that he had wanted to kill his wife for months but it was the four double brandies which eventually gave him the necessary courage to do the deed. If that were the situation then he would still have the necessary *mens rea* and the presence of the alcohol would be irrelevant. To succeed the jury must, at least, be left in reasonable doubt as to whether the accused actually intended to kill or cause his wife serious bodily harm or foresaw that that was the likely result of the act he was committing. Though, of course, the jury may still convict him of manslaughter.

If, on the other hand, D was charged with an assault occasioning actual bodily harm on Y it would be of no avail to show that due to intoxication he had no intention to hit Y. This is a crime of basic intent to which the defence of voluntary intoxication does not apply. If follows that if D staggers, blind drunk, from a pub, knocking Y into the road where he is then run over and killed, that not only is D liable for an assault on Y, but also for constructive manslaughter (this seems to be the logic of *Majewski*). Now in these cases if there were no question of intoxication the prosecution would have to prove that the accused either intended to or was reckless as to causing Y to apprehend immediate and unlawful violence (see *post*, p. 238). It would seem that where D raises the defence of intoxication, the effect is to relieve the prosecution of the need to prove *mens rea*. In other words a rule that intoxication shall be no evidence that the accused did not form the necessary *mens rea*, comes to mean that the prosecution can rely on the evidence of the intoxication to prove the completed assault. Does this mean that the prosecution, where they suspect that an accused has been drinking, can introduce evidence of his intoxication as a means of avoiding the need to prove *mens rea*? There is no clear-cut answer to be found in *Majewski*, but it would seem to be reasonable that the prosecution should only make use of such evidence once it is raised by the accused except, of course, in cases where the intoxication is the basis of the offence, such as in drinking and driving offences.

Should the accused, having formed the intention to kill another person, drink in order to give himself courage to perform the deed and thereby pass into a state in which, although he is no longer capable of forming the intent to kill, he kills that person, then he will not be able to rely on his mental state as a defence (*Att.-Gen. for Northern Ireland* v. *Gallagher* (1963)). Thus if X determines to kill his wife, drinks half a bottle of whisky to steady his nerves and thereby brings to the surface his quiescent insanity, he may not rely on the insanity as a defence.

(2) Involuntary intoxication

Finally, we must consider the case of the person who commits a criminal act whilst under the influence of alcohol or drugs but where he was not responsible for that condition. He my have got into such a condition because his friends laced his drinks or got him to take drugs without his knowledge. Equally, the accused may have been forcibly injected with a drug or forced to consume alcohol. Finally, there are those situations in which the accused is on a prescribed course of medical treatment and he does not know the effect the drugs will have on him, and in particular, the effect it will have if combined with alcohol. There is little authority on such a condition as a defence to a criminal charge. However, one of the main factors in the judicial unwillingness to allow intoxication as a general defence to all crimes, namely the fact that the accused was responsible for his condition, is missing here. It is suggested that a plea of involuntary intoxication should be a defence to any crime if it means that the accused did not form the necessary *mens rea*. There should be no place here for the classification of crimes of basic and specific intent. Where involuntary intoxication leads an accused to commit a crime he would not have committed when sober (for example he rapes a woman) but does not deprive him of the requisite *mens rea* then it should be no defence, though it will be presumably taken into account in mitigation. Involuntary intoxication is no defence to driving whilst over the prescribed limit though it may well lead to the driver not receiving the automatic disqualification.

3. Duress and Necessity

Duress and necessity are rather similar concepts from the point of view of defences to criminal charges. Both envisage that the accused is confronted by a dilemma in which he feels compelled to commit a crime in order that he may prevent some occurrence which he considers to be worse than the crime he will commit. In duress the dilemma is imposed by another human being, whereas in necessity it is the surrounding circumstances which have created the problem. In both cases he may be said to have acted "involuntarily," but this does not mean that he will have the sort of defence described earlier (*ante*, p. 133); here he deliberately performs an act which is a criminal offence.

(1) Duress

English law has long recognised the defence of duress—but its scope has recently received attention from both the House of Lords and Privy Council. The general basis of the defence is that the accused, who is alleged to have committed a criminal offence, claims that he did so because of threats made against him by another. Thus two questions need to be answered; (i) is duress a defence to all charges of crime, and (ii) what constitutes duress?

(a) *The scope of the defence*

Duress is now a defence to all crimes except, *possibly*, murder and treason to one charged as a principal offender. In *D.P.P. for Northern Ireland* v. *Lynch* (1975), the House of Lords held that where the accused drove terrorists to a place where, as he knew, they planned to kill someone, fearing that, if he did not, he would be killed, the trial judge was wrong to withdraw the defence of duress from the jury. The House was divided on whether the defence was available to a principal offender and in *Abbot* v. *R.* (1976) the Privy Council held that it was not. Abbott fearing, as he claimed, that his mother would be killed if he did not obey X who had ordered in the victim's killing, held the victim while she was stabbed by others. The victim, who was still alive, was then buried by Abbot and others, her death being caused partly by the stab wounds and partly by asphyxiation. It was held that Abbot, being a principal in the killing, could not avail himself of the defence of duress.

The Privy Council did not say whether Abbott was a principal by virtue of holding the victim or by helping to bury her. On the former hypothesis he was strictly a secondary party (see *ante*, p. 173) but on the latter he could be properly regarded as a principal. From a common sense point of view Abbott's liability should not turn on the fine distinction which may be drawn between a principal and a secondary party. Suppose, for instance, that in this case X, who had given the order to kill the victim and had allegedly threatened to kill Abbott's mother if he did not obey, had himself been threatened by Y that he would be killed if he did not procure the victim's death. It would seem that X, as a secondary party, would have available the defence of duress, even though he planned and directed the killing, while Abbott would not.

Graham (1982) illustrates the difficulties. Graham, a practising homosexual, lived with his wife, W, and another homosexual, H. H was a violent man and was jealous of W and planned to kill her. Graham, as he claimed in fear of H, helped H to execute his plan. When H strangled W with a piece of flex, H told Graham to hold one end of the flex which he did but, as Graham claimed, so soon as he exerted pressure on the flex, the plug on the end of the flex came off so he was unable to keep up any pressure. The prosecution conceded that it was open to Graham to raise duress and did not seek to contend that the defence was not open to a principal. The Lord Chief Justice, Lord Lane, appeared to agree with this view. He said that a jury would surely be puzzled to learn that whether Graham, assuming he was acting under duress, could or could not be convicted of murder might depend on whether the plug came off in his hand when he began to pull.

It can be argued that if the defence of duress is allowed to the actual killer then terrorists might, in effect, confer immunity on the agent they employ for a killing by threatening him with death if he does not do their bidding. Strictly this must follow if the defence is accorded to a principal in murder. But it has been held in Northern Ireland (*Fitzpatrick* (1975)) that one who has voluntarily put himself in a position where he is likely to be exposed to pressure to commit criminal acts (for example, by joining an organisation which uses violence to achieve its ends), cannot plead the duress, to which he realises he is exposing himself, as a defence.

(b) *What constitutes duress?*

Where the accused seeks to rely on the defence of duress he bears the burden of introducing evidence on it and it is then up to the prosecution to prove beyond reasonable doubt that the accused was not acting under duress. Many of the statements on what constitute duress speak of the need for the will of the accused to have been overborne by threats of death or serious personal injury so the commission of the alleged offence was no longer the voluntary act of the accused. Whatever the earlier courts may have meant by the use of the word "voluntary" it is now clear that it is not to be used in the sense we saw it used in relation to automatism in the sense of an act he was not really in control of. What we are concerned with is a situation in which the accused was faced with a choice of two evils and under that pressure he chose what to him seemed the lesser of the two and deliberately committed a crime. The question is whether the court should take account of the pressures and if so what sort of pressure should be needed.

In *Graham* (1982) the Court of Appeal recommended the following approach. First was the defendant, or may he have been, impelled to act as he did because, as a result of what he reasonably believed the threatener to have said or done, he had good cause to fear that he might be killed or seriously injured? Secondly, if so, have the prosecution made sure that a person of reasonable firmness sharing the same characteristics as the accused (*cf. Camplin, post*, p. 231) would not have responded in the way that the defendant did?

In *Graham* the court was considering duress as a defence to murder. Where a lesser crime (criminal damage, for example) is committed under duress it may be that threats less than to kill or cause serious bodily injury would suffice; the test being: would the particular threat have overborne the will of a reasonable person to make him act as the defendant did. Probably, however, the threat must be one of physical harm to the defendant and threats of other kinds (to damage the defendant's property or ruin his business, for example) would not suffice. But it would seem clear that threats to members of the accused's family would be sufficient and possibly against anyone with whom the accused has a special relationship. For example, a threat by a group of terrorists that they would kill hostages one by one until X did what they wanted would suffice as a defence for X. On the other hand, it is unlikely that the courts would be willing to entertain a plea of duress based on a threat to destroy property belonging to the accused.

A further restriction is that the defence of duress should not be open to the accused if it was open to him to avoid the threatened consequences of not committing the criminal act. Thus, if there is an opportunity for him to place himself under police protection, even if he does not believe that the police will be able to protect him, then failure to avail himself of the opportunity will mean that the defence of duress will fail. A rather benevolent application of this rule was seen in the case of *Hudson* (1971) where two girls were charged with committing perjury. They claimed that they had been threatened with injury if they made certain statements at the trial in question, and that during the course of the trial they had seen one of the men who had made the threats in the public gallery. Of course, they would have been able to have asked, then and there, for police help, but the Court of Appeal held that the defence of duress should have been left to the jury. The decision seems to have been based upon the notion that police protection could not guarantee to be effective and that the threats were no less immediate because they could not be carried out until the girls had left the courtroom. However, police protection will rarely, if ever, be able to guarantee permanent protection and the decision seems to be understandable. The Law Commission recommend that the defence should not be available where the accused has had an opportunity to seek official protection and this would presumably overrule *Hudson*.

Does such a rule mean that if a man's daughter is being held hostage and threatened with death if he does not join the kidnappers on a robbery that because there will be a chance to call in the police, he cannot rely on the defence of duress? It would seem at present that a defence of duress would be available in these circumstances, but the Law Commission have recommended that in this situation the defence of duress should not be available. It may seem a harsh recommendation, but it must be seen against the policy argument that to widen the scope of the defence is to provide villains with even more incentive to use threats to gain their ends. If a person subjected to threats knows that he will have no defence to a criminal prosecution, then he is less likely to yield to those threats.

Finally, duress is available as a defence only where the defendant is threatened with some harm unless he perpetrates the crime at the behest of the person making the threat. It is not sufficient that the defendant commits an offence in order to escape from men he believes are threatening him. Thus in one case the defendant was sitting in a car when he was approached by two men who were in fact police officers. He thought he was about to be attacked and so he drove off at full speed to the nearest police station where he ran inside for protection. He was charged with dangerous driving. It was held that the defence of duress was not available to him; he may have believed that he was about to be attacked but there was no suggestion that the "attackers" wanted him to drive dangerously (*Jones* (1963)).

(2) Necessity

The basic question here is whether A, confronted by a choice between committing a criminal offence or allowing what he considers to be far worse to occur, would have any defence if he chooses to commit the criminal offence. In some situations it would seem just that he should have a defence. For example, if the accused is charged with failing to stop at traffic lights we might be very tempted to say that he should have defence if the reason for this failure was that he could see someone in need of immediate help in a burning building beyond the lights. We might wish to be satisfied that he exercised all reasonable care in the circumstances, but otherwise this seems to be an excellent case for a defence of necessity. Suppose, however, that A and B were out mountain climbing. Suddenly B, who is roped to A, loses his footing and falls. A realises that he will soon be pulled off the mountain unless he cuts the rope holding B, but equally that this will result in B's certain death. The case for a defence of necessity may now seem less clear cut. The number of such hypothetical examples is limitless. But what does English law say of this?

We cannot say that the law never recognises a defence of necessity because the well known defences of duress and self-defence are, in reality, species of necessity, though they are cases where the necessity is imposed by a deliberate human agency. Where the necessity is not of this kind English law appears to have set its face against such a defence.

The leading case is *Dudley and Stephens* (1884) where the two accused together with another crew member and a cabin boy were forced to take to the lifeboat. After 20 days adrift, the last eight of which were without food, Dudley and Stephens killed the cabin boy and the three survivors fed on his flesh and blood. The cabin boy was by this time by far the weakest and most likely to die if help did not arrive soon. Four days after the killing they were rescued. They were later tried for murder, though their death sentences were commuted to six months imprisonment without hard labour.

The case is not noted for the clarity of the ruling which emerges from it. It is difficult to tell whether the court took the view that there was, in fact, no necessity for the killing or whether, even if such necessity existed, English law did not recognise necessity as a defence. It is, however, usually regarded as authority for the proposition that there is no defence of necessity in English Law.

This approach certainly has the advantage of simplicity since it does not force us to consider such questions as who decides when the necessity exists and if it does which of the crew is to be killed should lots be drawn? If necessity was recognised as a defence would the cabin boy have had the right to defend himself?

The Law Commission has recommended that no such defences should be introduced into English Law (Report No. 83; 1977), but possibly some compromise could be achieved. It could be introduced as a defence to all crimes save murder and possibly serious offences against the person. It could operate along the lines of provocation to reduce a charge of murder to manslaughter. Of course the moral dilemma that such a defence might raise may be a strong argument against it. It is very tempting to say that it can be left to the discretion of the police not to prosecute in cases such as the accused who has failed to obey a traffic signal in an attempt to save another's life. But this is rarely a satisfactory solution. In any event it would be difficult to avoid a prosecution in such cases as *Dudley and Stephens*—but was it right to convict them of murder?

4. Self Defence

The term "self defence" is loosely used to cover several allied defences common to which is the concept of necessity; necessity to take action to prevent: (i) crime; (ii) injury to oneself or others; (iii) loss of or damage to property. Such defences are most usually raised where the accused has been charged with an offence involving injury to another, and in each case the accused bears an evidential burden which he must discharge before the prosecution will have the burden of disproving the defence beyond reasonable doubt.

(1) Prevention of crime

This was originally covered by common law rules, but is now covered by section 3 of the Criminal Law Act 1967 which provides

> "(1) A person may use such force as is reasonable in the circumstances in the prevention of crime, or in effecting or assisting in the lawful arrest of offenders or suspected offenders or of persons unlawfully at large."

The crux of the provision is determining what is reasonable in the circumstances of the particular case being tried, and this is a question of fact to be determined by the jury. Thus where the accused is charged with assaulting another and seeks to rely on section 3, the question for the jury is whether they are "satisfied that no reasonable man (a) with knowledge of such facts as were known to the accused or reasonably believed by him to exist (b) in the circumstances and time available to him for reflection (c) could be of the opinion that the prevention of the risk of harm to which others might be exposed if the suspect were allowed to escape, justified exposing the suspect to the risk of harm to him that might result from the kind of force that the accused contemplated using." (*Reference under s.48A of the Criminal Appeal (Northern Ireland) Act 1968* (*No.* 1 *of* 1975), *per* Lord Diplock interpreting a provision identical in terms with s.3). Thus in *Cousins* (1982) the Court of Appeal held that, in appropriate circumstances, it could be reasonable to threaten to kill another when, for example, it is believed that this would forestall a planned attack on oneself. Whether or not such a threat is reasonable is always a question of fact for the jury. Clearly a threat to kill may be reasonable in circumstances where the implementation of such a threat would not be.

What, then, if the accused was mistaken in thinking that the man he assaulted was about to commit a crime? Suppose that X was drinking in a bar when he saw Y pick up a broken glass and wave it menacingly in front of Z. It would not be unreasonable for X to suppose that Y meant to harm Z and for him to take action to prevent such injury to Z. However, it turns out that Y was just telling Z of an incident which had happened in the bar on the previous evening. Lord Diplock's statement would indicate that the jury must consider the facts as they were known to X or as he reasonably believed them to be. Thus, in our example, if the jury considers that X honestly and reasonably thought that Y was about to attack Z, they should proceed to consider whether it was reasonable for him to have acted in the way he did, (see below for problems relating to the case of excessive force).

(2) Self-defence and defence of others

Although in many cases where the accused pleads self-defence the situation could be covered by section 3 in that if the accused's story is correct he is merely trying to prevent the other man from committing a crime—namely attacking the accused—this is not necessarily so. If D is attacked by a child he knows to be below the age of criminal responsibility then he cannot say that the force he used on the child to stop the attack was force used in the prevention of crime. He would, however, be able to rely on the common law defence of self-defence. It is clear that the common law defence of self-defence survives section 3, but since the area of overlap is, to all intents and purposes, total, it would be absurd if the common law defence were to be governed by principles different from those controlling section 3. It is therefore submitted that where the accused, who is charged with an offence against the person, relies on the common law defence of self-defence, the court will approach the question in the same way as a defence brought under section 3.

Under the common law rules relating to self-defence the accused was expected to retreat before resorting to force; he was also expected to show that the expected violence was imminent and not a mere threat of what might happen at some time in the future. It is now suggested that these are now merely facts which the jury should take into account in assessing whether the accused's use of force was reasonable in the circumstances (see *Browne* (1973) and *Cousins* (1982)).

(3) Defence of property

Again this is probably covered sufficiently be section 3 and the same principles will apply; was the force used by D to protect his property reasonable in the circumstances? Can it ever be reasonable to kill in order to defend your property? (See *Hussey* (1924)).

(4) Excessive force

Now that we have looked at the various forms of self-defence, we can turn to a problem that has been hinted at in the preceding sections. We have seen that if the accused mistakenly believes that there is a need for force, he will be able to rely on the defence provided that he used only so much force as was reasonably necessary in the circumstances he reasonably believed to exist. Thus, if the accused rightly believes X is about to attack him, but wrongly believes, though on reasonable grounds, that X plans to use a knife, the amount of force which would be reasonable will be assessed on the facts the accused believed to exist. But the more difficult problem is the one in which the amount of force used was unreasonable even in the circumstances he believed to exist. Two types of problem may arise here:

(i) X believes that he is about to be attacked by Y and reasonably decides to shoot Y in the leg as he approaches. Unfortunately, his aim is bad and Y is killed. If X is charged with murder, the first thing to remember is that the prosecution must prove that X had the necessary *mens rea*. That aside, the jury should be asked to consider the reasonableness of what the accused contemplated doing. In our case, they should ask whether it was reasonable for X to try to shoot Y in the legs to prevent the attack (see the passage of Lord Diplock, *ante*, p. 207).

(ii) X believes that poachers are taking trout from his lake during the night. He therefore lies in wait with a twelve-bore shotgun and when he sees Y taking trout from the lake he shoots at him and kills him. In other words, we have a situation in which the jury would have probably sanctioned the use of some force, but not the killing of Y. Where does X stand now? Does this finding mean that he has no defence at all? The problem is only likely to be acute in the cases where the charge is murder, since in all other cases, if it is held that excessive use of force means that the defence fails, the judge can take the facts into account when passing sentence. However, where the accused is charged with murder, if the defence fails the accused will be convicted of murder, if the prosecution establishes the necessary *mens rea*, in which case he receives life imprisonment. In Australia, for example, (see, *e.g. McKay* (1957)) the courts have adopted a half-way house. Where the accused has pleaded self-defence to a charge of murder, but the jury has decided that although he was entitled to use some force, he used too much force, they are entitled to acquit him of murder but return a verdict of guilty of manslaughter. This line of approach has been rejected in this country (see *McInnes* (1971) and *Palmer* (1971)). In England and Wales, therefore, self-defence and defence of property and the defence under section 3 are either complete defences in that they lead to acquittal or they are no defence at all. This may seem rather harsh but the recent case of *Shannon* (1980) shows that this harshness is tempered with leniency. In that case the judge had left the jury with the simple question "Are you satisfied that the appellant used more force than was necessary in the circumstances?" On its own, this would give the jury the impression that they should simply take a detached look at the facts and decide what force would have been reasonable in the circumstances. However, the Court of Appeal said that they should have been reminded of Lord Morris' qualification to this test which he propounded in *Palmer*, namely, that, if they concluded that the appellant honestly thought without having to weigh things to a nicety, that what he did was necessary to defend himself, they should regard that as "most potent evidence" that it was actually reasonably necessary. "In other words, if the jury concluded that the stabbing was the act of a desperate man in extreme difficulties, with his assailant dragging him down by the hair, they should consider very carefully before concluding that the stabbing was an offensive and not a defensive act, albeit it went beyond what an onlooker would regard as reasonably necessary." What the court is saying is that the test is reasonableness taking into account the circumstances in which the decision had to be made. The 14th Report of the Criminal Law Revision Committee favoured the introduction of a partial defence so that where the accused honestly miscalculates the amount of force needed he would be convicted of manslaughter and not murder.

Chapter 5

THE INCHOATE OFFENCES

In Chapter 3 we saw that a secondary party to a criminal offence could be held liable for acts of assistance he had performed sometime before the commission of the offence; but his liability does not arise until the offence is actually committed or attempted. The law would be seriously deficient if liability only arose when the offence was actually committed. It would mean that if the police were aware that X intended to assault Y they would have to choose between preventing the offence and prosecuting X. Obviously we would not wish to prosecute a man simply for dreaming up criminal plans in his head, but as soon as he begins to commit overt acts which evidences his intention to put the plan into operation it is arguable that the law should be able to intervene. This, basically, is the role of the inchoate offences of incitement, conspiracy and attempt. Consider, for a moment, the following set of events: (i) X conceives in his mind a plan to burgle Barclays Bank; (ii) he approaches Y and tells him of his plans; (iii) he encourages Y to help him and to find a getaway driver; (iv) Y agrees to help and they formulate a plan in collaboration with Z who will be the get-away driver; (v) on the night in question they render the alarm on the outside of the bank inoperative; and (vi) they enter the bank.

Clearly at stage (vi) they commit the completed offence of burglary the moment they enter the bank with intent to steal from it. No offence is committed at stage (i) for our law does not punish a man for his thoughts; nor at (ii) in disclosing his thoughts to Y does X commit a crime because this is still too remote from the commission of the contemplated crime. But at stage (iii) X oversteps the mark; in seeking to persuade Y to join him he commits the crime of incitement. At stage (iv) the agreement reached by X, Y and Z is a crime; they have conspired to commit burglary. At stage (v) they are probably guilty of attempting to burgle the bank. When the prosecution gain a conviction for inciting, conspiring or attempting to commit a criminal offence the convicted person is generally speaking liable to receive the same penalty he would have incurred had he been convicted of the completed offence.

It is important to remember that these offences do not exist in the abstract; the indictment must always contain reference to the completed offence. Thus it would be wrong to say in the indictment

"X is charged with conspiracy" it should be "X is charged with conspiracy to murder, steal, etc."

1. Attempts

The law relating to attempts is now covered by the Criminal Attempts Act 1981.

Occasionally statutes expressly prohibit attempted conduct (*e.g.* driving or attempting to drive a motor vehicle . . . contrary to section 6 of the Road Traffic Act 1972), but these few offences apart, the general rule is that whenever a new statutory offence is created there automatically arises liability for attempting to commit the completed offence. Thus, when in 1968 Parliament replaced larceny with theft under section 1 of the Theft Act 1968, attempted theft automatically became a possible common law charge. By and large the mode of trial and possible sentence is that of the completed offence. Indeed a verdict of not guilty of the substantive offence, but guilty of an attempt to commit it is always an alternative verdict for the jury and there is no need specifically to charge the accused with the attempted offence.

It is possible to attempt to incite another to commit a substantive offence, but it is no longer possible to attempt to conspire (Criminal Law Act 1977, s.5(7)). It is possible to be convicted as a secondary party to an attempt, but it is thought that it is not possible to be charged with attempting to become a secondary party.

What therefore constitutes an attempt? In simple language we are looking for situations in which X has tried to commit a crime, but has failed. Certain questions arise: how close must X get to comitting the crime before we can convict him of an attempt? In every day language when we say X attempted to kill Y we mean he intended to kill Y, but failed. What is the *mens rea* of an attempt? Does it matter that X was attempting to do something which was impossible? We will now look at these questions in turn.

(1) Proximity

Suppose that X wishes to kill Y. He buys a gun, loads it, goes to Y's house, rings the door bell, points the gun at Y and pulls the trigger. If the bullet strikes and kills Y then X will be convicted of murder. Suppose however, that either Y does not die from the wounds, or that X is stopped before he can pull the trigger. At what stage can we say that he has attempted to kill Y? The 1981 Act says that he must do an act which is more than merely preparatory to the commission of the offence. This may seem unduly vague and not particularly helpful, but the view is held that it is for the jury and not for the judge to decide whether the accused can be said to have attempted to kill. It would be wrong for a judge to say to the jury "if you find the following acts proved, then you will find that the acts of the accused go beyond mere acts of preparation." This would be usurping the jury's function (*D.P.P.* v. *Stonehouse* (1978)). On the other hand the judge may tell the jury that certain acts are mere acts of preparation and not sufficiently proximate to the completed offence to constitute an offence. We thus cannot say in advance that a given set of facts constitutes an attempt, but we can make a calculated guess on the basis of principles applied in earlier cases. One test that provides a fairly simple and reliable guide is to ask whether the accused has done all that is required of him—*i.e.* has he done the last act? If he has and he has been charged as a principal offender then he will be convicted of an attempt. Thus in our example when X pulled the trigger, this was the last act required to be done by X in order to shoot Y—there is nothing more for him to do. When on the other hand he purchases a gun, there is clearly a lot more for him to do and the purchase of the gun in everyday language would be a mere act of preparation; no juror would say that he has by the purchase attempted to kill Y. In *Comer* v. *Bloomfield* (1971) where the accused hid his car, and enquired whether he could submit a claim to his insurance company, it was held that his action was not sufficiently proximate to constitute an attempt, though whether the same result would be reached under the Criminal Attempts Act 1981, remains to to be seen. In *D.P.P* v. *Stonehouse* (above) the accused having set up an insurance policy in favour of his wife, faked his own death. It was held that a jury was entitled to find that this constituted an attempt. There was nothing left for him to do.

Three reservations must be placed on this "last act" guide:

(i) where the accused is not the principal offender, it may produce a false result. Thus if X hires Y to shoot Z, X has done the last act required of him, but he is surely not guilty of attempted murder at this stage.

(ii) You must not be led by the "last Act" doctrine into thinking that an attempt is committed *only* when the accused does the last act required of him. For example, where the accused is in the process of killing his wife by a series of poison doses, he could be convicted of attempted murder before he administers the last dose.

(iii) It is important to remember that at the end of the day it is the jury who decides whether or not there has been an attempt. A judge is entitled to say that there is no evidence upon which

> the jury could find that there has been an attempt, but he must not say that the jury will find that certain facts, if proved, amount to more than mere acts of preparation.

(2) What mental state is required?

Section 1(1) says that the prosecution must prove that the accused did the act with the intention to commit an offence to which this section applies. . . . It would therefore appear that attempts are crimes where the prosecution must prove that the accused intended, with full knowledge of the circumstances, to commit the prohibited act. Thus in *Whybrow* (1951) the accused was charged with attempted murder. It was held that although an intention to inflict grievous bodily harm would have sufficed had the charge been murder, only an intention to kill would suffice for attempted murder. Thus it is submitted that in rape the prosecution must prove that the accused intended to have intercourse with the woman knowing that she did not consent. Similarly if Prince (*ante*, p. 161) were to be charged with attempted abduction he would have to be acquitted since he was unaware that the girl was under 16.

This may all look rather strange, but the reason lies in the whole notion of the word "attempt." Whereas it is considered reasonable to convict X, who is trying to cause Y grievous bodily harm, of murder should Y die, it is considered odd to say that X attempted to kill Y if Y does not die. Unless X actually wanted Y dead, it simply looks strange to say that X was trying to kill Y.

Although it is clear that intention (or knowledge) is required as to the central core of the crime (the prohibited act) it is not clear whether or not it is required on every aspect of the *actus reus*. Would the prosecution fail on a charge of attempted murder if it could not prove that the accused intended that the victim should die within a year and a day?

(3) Attempting the impossible

As we have said before, attempt normally implies the failure of the accused to achieve his objectives, but that his objectives were at least feasible. Thus X is prevented from killing Y by the timely intervention of Z. But what if the objective was not possible in the first place? For example, it is not possible for a pickpocket to steal from an empty pocket, or for an assassin to kill a victim who is already dead. Over the last few years the courts have managed to make this area of law particularly complex. Suffice it to say that the 1981 Act effects a great simplification here. We can look at the present position through examination of the various types of situation.

(i) X is trying to open a bank safe using a can opener which would never make the slightest impression on the safe. There never has been any problem here; failure to achieve one's objective through use of inadequate means is no defence to charge of attempt. Thus if X tries to shoot Y using a rifle whose range is wholly inadequate he can be convicted of attempt.

(ii) Consider a case where X is a pickpocket who has resolved to steal from Y's pocket. He puts his hand into Y's pocket but it is empty. At this stage he is arrested. Can he be charged with attempting to steal from Y's pocket? There are many variations on this theme including stealing from an empty safe, and trying to kill a person who is already dead. The average man in the street would almost certainly be amazed if you were to say that, in our illustration X was not attempting to steal, but until the 1981 Act that was the position (*Haughton* v. *Smith* (1975)). Now under section 1(2) of the Act it is not a defence that the facts are such that commission of the offence is impossible. X would thus be liable to conviction for attempted theft.

(iii) What is the position if B has intercourse with G believing that she is 15 when, in fact, she is 16? If the facts were as he supposed them to be he would be guilty of a criminal offence (see *post*, p. 249). Clearly he cannot be guilty of the completed offence since the prosecution would be unable to establish the *actus reus*. Can we therefore say that he attempted to commit the offence? The effect of section 1(2) and (3) is that he can be convicted of an attempt in these circumstances. This overrules the actual decision in *Haughton* v. *Smith* (1974) where the House of Lords held that the accused could not be convicted of attempting to handle stolen goods since, unknown to the accused, the goods had ceased to be stolen. The type of impossibility described in paragraph (ii) is known as attempting the physically (or factually) impossible, whereas the situation described in paragraph (iii) is known as attempting the legally impossible. The effect of the new legislation is that neither type of impossibility can be used as a defence to a charge of attempt.

(iv) Consider a situation in which D has intercourse with his 17 year old girl friend believing that it is a crime to have intercourse with girls under the age of 18. This is not an offence since there is no known crime he is attempting to commit.

2. Conspiracy

While a decision by one person to commit a crime, even if there is clear evidence of his intention, is not an offence, it has long been the law that an *agreement* by two or more to commit a crime is an offence. Perhaps the reason is that where two or more persons have agreed on a course of action it is much more likely that the planned course of action will be carried out. Certainly courts have taken the view that confederacies are especially dangerous. So dangerous, in fact, that criminal conspiracies were not restricted to agreements to commit crimes. In *Kamara* v. *D.P.P.* (1974) for example, it was held by the House of Lords that an agreement to commit the tort of trespass to land, if accompanied by an intention to inflict more than merely nominal damage, was indictable as a criminal conspiracy.

That it should be a crime in certain circumstances even to agree to commit a civil wrong was thought by many to be objectionable. The Law Commission considered the matter and at first the Commission essentially expressed the idea that only agreements to commit crimes should be indictable as conspiracies. This proposal was in turn criticised as being too narrow. In particular it would have restricted the operation of conspiracy to defraud because, on the common law view of this crime, there could be a conspiracy to defraud even though there was no conspiracy to commit a crime. Take *Scott* v. *Metropolitan Police Commissioner* (1975) for example. Here A, B and others made copies of films without the consent of the copyright holders with a view to making a profit for themselves by showing the films without paying the copyright holders. In such a case as this it may have been difficult to prove that A and B had committed some crime under the Theft Acts. They did not steal anything from the copyright holders nor was there any deception of the holders. But it was held that their conduct fell within the wide net of conspiracy to defraud—"an agreement by two or more by dishonesty to deprive a person of something that is his or to which he is or would be or might be entitled and an agreement by two or more by dishonesty to injure some proprietory right of his."

The Law Commission therefore proposed that criminal conspiracy should extend to: (i) agreements to commit crime, and (ii) that the common law conspiracy to defraud should be retained, at least for the time being. Had this proposal been accepted all common law conspiracies other than conspiracy to defraud would have ceased to be criminal. But the government of the day thought it best to postpone a final decision on conspiracies to corrupt public morals and conspiracies to outrage public decency pending the outcome of another review. The result, not altogether a happy one, is embodied in the Criminal Law Act 1977. The Law Commission's proposals have been implemented to create statutory offences of conspiracy but the common law conspiracy to defraud was retained and agreements to corrupt public morals and outrage public decency were excepted from the statutory scheme as well. We thus have statutory conspiracies and common law conspiracies.

(1) Mens rea

It was established by the House of Lords in *Churchill* v. *Walton* (1967) that conspiracy at common law involves *mens rea* in the full sense—strict liability does not apply. Thus if in *Prince* ((1875) *ante*, p. 161) Prince and another agreed to take the girl out of the possession of her parents, both believing she was over 16, neither could be convicted of conspiracy to abduct.

Section 1 of the Criminal Law Act was intended to embody the identical principle for statutory conspiracies and provides:

> "1.—(1) Subject to the following provisions of this Part of this Act, if a person agrees with any other person or persons that a course of conduct shall be pursued which will necessarily amount to or involve the commission of any offence or offences by one or more of the parties to the agreement if the agreement is carried out in accordance with their intentions, he is guilty of conspiracy to commit the offence or offences in question.
>
> (2) Where liability for any offence may be incurred without knowledge on the part of the person committing it of any particular fact or circumstance necessary for the commission of the offence, a person shall nevertheless not be guilty of conspiracy to commit that offence by virtue of subsection (1) above unless he and at least one other party to the agreement intend or know that that fact or circumstance shall or will exist at the time when the conduct constituting the offence is to take place."

These are complex provisions but they should be interpreted to reflect the common law position. Thus in the example just given Prince and his friend are not guilty of a statutory conspiracy. Section 1(2) makes it clear that even if the completed offence can be committed without knowledge of a "particular fact or circumstance" (in this case that the girl is under 16) there can be no conviction for conspiracy unless that fact or circumstance is known to those charged with conspiracy.

Section 1(1) is intended to make it clear that on a charge of conspiracy, *e.g.* to murder or to cause criminal damage, it must be shown that the alleged conspirators had agreed on a course of conduct which will necessarily result in murder or criminal damage if the agreement is carried out in accordance with their intentions. There is no difficulty whatever if A and B agree to kill X by poisoning or to break Y's windows. But suppose that A and B agreed to "knee-cap" X. A and B would here be guilty of a conspiracy to cause grievous bodily harm and if X dies they would be guilty of murder since an intention to cause grievous bodily harm forms part of the *mens rea* of murder (see *ante*, p. 226). Are A and B thus guilty of conspiracy to murder? The answer is No. The course of conduct they have agreed on will not necessarily result in death; indeed it is rare for death to occur as a result of "knee-capping." Another example could be where, in a street fight, A and B agree to attack X and Y by throwing stones at them, both realising that they might miss X and Y and break windows in the street. A and B are guilty of a conspiracy to assault X and Y but they are not guilty of a conspiracy to commit criminal damage. In other words conspiracy is an intentional crime in the same sense as attempt (see *ante*, p. 214).

(2) Actus reus

The *actus reus* of conspiracy consists in an agreement by two or more persons: (i) to commit a crime; (ii) to defraud; (iii) to corrupt public morals; or (iv) to outrage public decency. The Criminal Law Act governs conspiracies falling within (i), but (ii), (iii) and (iv) are common law conspiracies.

It is common ground to both statutory and common law conspiracy that there must be an agreement by two or more persons.

As to the latter of the requirements it is a truism to say that a man cannot conspire with himself. It was accordingly held in *McDonnell* (1966) that A, the managing and sole director of A Ltd., could not be convicted of conspiring with A Ltd. even though A Ltd. could have been convicted of the substantive crime committed by A (see *ante*, p. 187). On the other hand it is perfectly possible to convict A, A Ltd. *and* B on a charge of conspiracy; or to convict A Ltd. of conspiring with B Ltd.

For reasons of policy one spouse cannot be convicted of conspiring with the other spouse if these are the *only* parties to the agreement. So husband and wife do not commit a crime in agreeing to murder X but if their son, A, becomes a party to the agreement then all three are guilty of conspiracy. This was the rule for common law conspiracies (*Mawji* v. *R.* (1957)) and by section 2(2)(*a*) of the Criminal Law Act 1977 the same rule is applied to statutory conspiracies. It is also provided in section 2(2) of the Act that a person cannot be convicted of conspiracy if the *only* other party is (*b*) a person under the age of criminal responsibility; or (*c*) an intended victim of the offence. There is no common law authority on agreements falling within (*b*) or (*c*); the Law Commission was of the view that at common law a conviction for conspiracy was at least theoretically possible in both cases. The Law Commission further proposed that a person should not be liable for conspiracy if the only other party was himself or herself exempt from liability for conspiracy to commit the offence in question. Had this proposal been implemented it would have reversed the decision in *Duguid* (1906) where it was held that A could be convicted of conspiring with B to abduct a child from his guardian even though B, as the mother of the child, was exempt from liability. Since it was not implemented it continues to be the law that a non-exempt party can conspire with an exempt party even though the exempt party cannot be convicted.

As to the former requirement, the agreement, what is required is a compact. Negotiations, however far advanced, will not suffice without a compact to effect a criminal purpose. Nor is it enough that A gives help to B knowing of his criminal purpose. In *Bainbridge* ((1960) *ante*, p. 175) B in knowingly supplying oxygen cutting equipment to A became a secondary party to the burglary committed by A, but, on those facts alone, it could hardly be said that B had agreed with A to commit burglary.

In relation to statutory conspiracy, section 1 requires that A and B should have agreed on a course of conduct which if it is carried out as planned will necessarily amount to a crime. Suppose that A and B agree to go on a shoplifting expedition tomorrow. Between now and tomorrow many things may go wrong and thwart the plan. They may fall ill, or the shops may be closed by a strike or by a power failure. Have they, then, agreed on a course of conduct which if carried out in accordance with that intention will *necessarily* result in the commission of a crime? Of course they have and the fact that their intentions are thwarted for some reason cannot affect the matter. Nor are they any the less guilty of conspiracy to steal because they have not decided upon the particular shop or shops from which they will pilfer, nor because they have not yet specified the goods they will steal.

When A and B are the only parties to the alleged conspiracy it is necessary to show a meeting of their minds. But if there are three or more parties it is unnecessary to show that each conspirator was in contact with every other conspirator. A agreed with B to rob X leaving it to B to get someone to provide transport and B engaged C in the enterprise. A and C have now conspired to rob X though neither may have met or even know of the other's identity, provided

C knew he was joining such an enterprise and that there were other members of the gang even if he did not know their names. On the other hand, there must be a nexus between A and C in relation to the conspiracy charged. If A and B plan to kill X as well as rob him but only the intention to rob X is disclosed to C, A has conspired with C to rob X but there is no agreement between them to murder X.

Criminal conspiracies are now confined to agreements: (i) to commit crime; (ii) to defraud; (iii) to corrupt public morals; and (iv) to outrage public decency. For the sake of completeness it should be added that an agreement (v) to commit murder abroad is indictable here though not agreements to commit other crimes abroad.

Little needs to be said of (i). We have seen (*ante*, p. 216) that (ii) is wider than (i) in embracing certain dishonest activity which would not be a crime if perpetrated by one person. As to (iii) and (iv) these seem to go much further than (i) in embracing all sorts of vague conduct which would not necessarily be a crime if committed by one person. But this may not be so. There is almost certainly a substantive offence of outraging public decency (*Knuller* v. *D.P.P.* (1973)) and if this is so (iv) adds nothing to (i). It is not clear whether there is a substantive offence of corrupting public morals (see *D.P.P.* v. *Withers* (1975)) but if there is then (iii) adds nothing to (i). These are matters which still await judicial decision or, for preference, clear statutory restatement.

As with attempts, so with conspiracy, issues of impossibility arise (see *ante*, p. 214); it is possible for persons to agree to steal from a safe which is, in fact empty, or to receive goods which are no longer stolen. By section 5 of the Criminal Attempts Act 1981 the law of conspiracy on this point is brought into line with the new law on attempts; there can be a conviction for conspiracy in both of these cases.

3. Incitement

We saw at the beginning of this chapter that if X were to conceive in his mind a plan to burgle Barclays Bank and even if he were to outline his plan to Y he would commit no offence. However if the prosecution can prove that he tried to persuade Y to join him in the venture this would amount to the common law offence of inciting Y to commit, in this case, burglary. The basis, therefore, of incitement is an attempt to persuade another to commit an act which, if committed by that other, would amount to a criminal offence. As with the other inchoate offences incitement is divisible into *actus reus* and *mens rea*.

(1) Actus reus

The prosecution must establish that the accused by word or deed encouraged another to commit a criminal offence. One who incites another to commit a criminal offence will become a party to the offence when it is committed by that other, but the reverse is not necessarily true. If X supplies Y with a gun to kill Z, X will be a party to the killing, but he is not necessarily guilty of incitement since this requires that he urged Y to kill Z. Thus if Y approached X for the gun telling him that he was thinking about killing Z, but he had not yet made up his mind, and if X then tries to remove the lingering doubts in Y's mind X will be guilty of both incitement immediately and murder when the crime is committed.

The persuasion can be by both words and deeds and it can take the forms of encouragement or threats. It can be to a particular person or to people in general. Thus even though the government has approved the use of citizen's band radios it would constitute incitement for a seller to advertise his radios by saying that the problems of police radar speed traps were almost eliminated by careful use of the equipment. In such an advertisement there would be implied encouragement for motorists to break the speed regulations.

(2) Mens rea

As with conspiracy and attempts, incitement requires that the accused has *mens rea*. Thus the prosecution will have to show that the accused intended that as a result of his persuasion another person would commit an act which would be a criminal offence, though, of course, there is no need to prove that the accused knew that the act in question was a crime (*ante*, p. 155).

In the following examples it is accepted that X has tried to persuade Y to receive some watches and to sell them.

(i) If we assume first that the watches are, in fact, stolen at the time of the incitement then if X is unaware of this fact he cannot be guilty of inciting Y to handle stolen property since X is unaware of the fact which would make Y's receiving of the watches a crime. Similarly if X does not tell Y that the watches are stolen and has no reason to suppose that Y knows this then this will not be incitement by X since Y will not be guilty of any criminal offence—in other words the act incited is not a crime.

(ii) If we assume that the goods are not, in fact stolen, and if X, believing them to be stolen, tells Y that the watches are stolen and encourages Y to receive them he will be inciting Y to do an act which will not, in fact, be a crime since the watches are not stolen property. This, of course, is incitement's equivalent of attempting the legally impossible. It would seem from the case of *Fitzmaurice* (1982) that if the crime is capable of being committed at the time of the incitement, then even though it subsequently becomes impossible to commit, the accused may be convicted of incitement. Where, however, the crime is incapable of being committed at the time of the incitement there can be no conviction. It is suggested that in our example (i) X cannot be convicted of inciting Y to receive stolen goods.

Chapter 6

UNLAWFUL HOMICIDE

Homicide simply means the killing of a human being by a human being and there is no crime called homicide. It is homicide where one person kills another in lawful self-defence but this is not a crime. So what the law does is single out certain homicides which are considered to be unlawful or unjustifiable or inexcusable and makes crimes of these. These homicides are called variously murder, manslaughter, infanticide and causing death by reckless driving. In this section we shall look at the crimes of murder and manslaughter.

In this country we have seen fit to attempt to reflect the varying degrees of heinousness of unlawful homicides by dividing them into two categories; murder and manslaughter. By our definition of these two offences we try to classify as murder those killings which we consider to be the most heinous, and as manslaughter those killings which are less serious but still deserving of punishment. Until 1965 we subdivided murders into those which attracted the death penalty and those which were punished by life imprisonment. Today, following the abolition of the death penalty all convicted murderers are sentenced to life imprisonment. This means that they will stay in prison until the Home Secretary orders that they may be released on licence. The trial judge may, in very serious cases, impose a recommendation that the Home Secretary should not review the case for a minimum number of years. Those convicted of manslaughter may receive any sentence up to life imprisonment. It is a sign of the times we live in that we have a special offence of causing death by reckless driving to cover cases of unlawful killings which result from road accidents (Road Traffic Act 1972, s.1 as amended); juries were reluctant to convict motorists of manslaughter. The present position is that the *actus reus* for murder and manslaughter is the same; the distinguishing feature is the *mens rea*.

1. The Basic Elements Common to Murder and Manslaughter

In all cases of murder and manslaughter the prosecution will have to prove that the accused unlawfully caused the death of a human being who was within the Queen's peace and that the victim had died within a year and a day of the last act causing death performed by the accused. Murder and manslaughter are exceptional crimes in that any citizen of the United Kingdom and Colonies who is alleged to have committed murder or manslaughter may be tried in this country wherever the killing was alleged to have occurred. Our courts also have jurisdiction over any such crimes alleged to have been committed by non-British subjects in the United Kingdom or on a British ship or aircraft.

(1) Human being

In the normal run of events it will be obvious whether the accused has killed another human being. Difficulties may, however arise at each end of life's spectrum. At what precise moment does a child come under the protection of the law of homicide? It is established that the child must be expelled entirely from the mother's body and that it must have an existence of its own. It is difficult to be any more precise, for although there are authorities to suggest that the after-birth need not have been expelled or severed, there are authorities which say that the child must have breathed and others which say that independent breathing is not required since this may start several minutes after the child has been expelled from its mother. There are, of course, separate offences to deal with the killing of a child not yet independent of its mother. Further, the injuring of a child in the womb which is then born alive, but later dies of the injuries may be murder or manslaughter (see *West* (1848)).

At the other end of life it is not difficult to think of problems which might occur as to the precise moment at which a human being died and thus ceased to be capable of being murdered. Is a person dead when his heart stops beating or only when a surgeon states that it cannot be restarted? There is no authoritative answer to many of the questions though it is likely that in the not too distant future courts will be called upon to decide whether for example a person whose bodily functions are being sustained solely by mechanical means is capable of being murdered.

(2) Queen's Peace

If the accused has killed an enemy during the heat of war and in the exercise thereof the killing will not be an unlawful homicide.

(3) Death within a year and a day

The old definitions of murder and manslaughter provide that the prosecution must prove that the victim died within a year and a day of the wounds inflicted by the accused and if this was a series of wounds within a year and a day of the last. This rule still persists today (see *Dyson* (1908) and *ante*, p. 9).

(4) Unlawful

The inclusion of the word "unlawful" indicates that the courts recognise that there are certain situations in which the killing can be said to be justified. Thus where the accused kills X because X was about to kill the accused, the accused's killing of X may be said to be "not unlawful," and hence he may be acquitted. (See *ante*, p. 206 and Chapter 4.)

2. Murder

In addition to proving that the accused caused the death of another human being without lawful excuse or authority, the prosecution will have to prove that at the time he caused the death he possessed a certain state of mind. This state of mind, which has traditionally been described as the malice aforethought of murder, has been differently defined at different times in our history, and even now there still remains uncertainty to the precise definition of malice aforethought for murder. Obviously it includes an intention to kill, but it also includes mental states other than an intention to kill. Precisely what those other mental states are was considered by the House of Lords in *Hyam* v. *D.P.P.* (1975) and it says something of the difficulty of the subject that the House divided three to two.

Hyam provides us with a useful starting point in our consideration of the malice aforethought of murder. In that case Mrs. Hyam found herself with a rival for the affections of Mr. Jones. She made several unsuccessful attempts to break up the relationship between the other woman, Mrs. Booth, and Mr. Jones. Eventually one evening she drove to the house where Mrs. Booth lived with her son and two daughters. She poured about half a gallon of petrol through the letter box and then tossed in a lighted newspaper. She made no attempt to warn the occupants of the house, nor the local fire brigade. As a result of the ensuing fire the two daughters were killed by asphyxiation, though Mrs. Booth and her son escaped. When the police questioned Mrs. Hyam she admitted to setting fire to the house, but said that her only desire was to scare Mrs. Booth away from the neighbourhood; she certainly did not intend to kill her or cause her any serious harm. In his summing up to the jury Ackner J. said:

> "The prosecution must prove, beyond all reasonable doubt, that the accused intended to (kill or) do serious bodily harm to Mrs. Booth, the mother of the deceased girls. If you are satisfied that when the accused set fire to the house she knew that it was highly probable that this would cause (death or) serious bodily harm then the prosecution will have established the necessary

intent. It matters not if her motive was, as she says, to frighten Mrs. Booth."

The jury convicted Mrs. Hyam who then appealed unsuccessfully to the Court of Appeal and finally to the House of Lords. Since juries in this country do not give reasons for their decisions we must conclude that they found that the prosecution had established that when Mrs. Booth set fire to the house she did so with one of the four states of mind listed by Mr. Justice Ackner in his summing up. It is clear that of the four the most culpable is that Mrs. Hyam intended to kill Mrs. Booth and the least is that she foresaw that it was highly probable that her action would cause Mrs. Booth serious bodily harm. It is quite possible that the jury based their guilty verdict on this least culpable state of mind and therefore if the House of Lords was to uphold the conviction it would have to do so on the basis that that state of mind sufficed as the basis for murder. In the result the House of Lords upheld the conviction and in the light of the speeches in the House it would seem that an accused has the necessary malice aforethought for murder if at the time he kills the victim he:

(i) intends to kill;
(ii) intends to cause grievous bodily harm;
(iii) foresees that death is a (highly) probable consequence of his conduct;
(iv) foresees that grievous bodily harm is a (highly) probable consequence of his conduct.

Each of the above propositions now requires further consideration.

(1) Intent to kill

In certain crimes there is the need to prove that the accused intended to produce a certain result. In those crimes it is necessary to define exactly what is meant by "intention" since nothing less will suffice. In murder, however, it is clear from *Hyam* that several states of mind less culpable than an intention to kill will suffice and it is therefore unnecessary to spend a lot of time defining the limits of intentional conduct. We can safely say that a person intends to kill if he desires the death of another and is deliberately taking steps to accomplish his purpose. The doctrine of transferred malice (*ante*, p. 154) applies and, indeed, *Hyam* is an example of its application.

(2) Intention to cause grievous bodily harm

Under section 1 of the Homicide Act 1957 the so-called felony murder rule was abolished. Under this rule a man who, intending to commit certain violent crimes, killed another during the commission of that violent crime was guilty of murder. In these situations the prosecution simply had to establish the *mens rea* of the violent crime. Obvious examples of such crimes were rape and robbery. It was also murder for a man intending to resist arrest to cause the death of an officer of justice. These were both types of felony murder or what is sometimes called constructive murder and they were both abolished by the Homicide Act of 1957. However it has long been held to be murder if a person intentionally inflicts grievous bodily harm on another and that other person dies. Now on the face of it this looks like an example of constructive murder since the death is the result of the commission of another crime, namely the intentional infliction of grievous bodily harm (section 18 of the Offences Against the Person Act 1861) but in *Vickers* (1957) the Court of Criminal Appeal confirmed that an accused who caused the death of another intending to cause that person grievous bodily harm was guilty of murder. This category of malice aforethought was different from constructive malice which was abolished in 1957. This was the view taken by the majority in *Hyam*, but there was a strong dissent from Lords Diplock and Kilbrandon who thought that the distinction drawn in *Vickers* was not supported by the previous authorities. In view of the very ambivalent judgment of Lord Cross, this strong dissent left a question mark over this category of malice aforethought. However this has now been removed by the House of Lords in *Cunningham* (1982) where the correctness of *Vickers* was confirmed.

The phrase "intention to cause grievous bodily harm" was defined by the House of Lords in 1961 where it was said that bodily harm needs no explanation and "grievous" means no more and no less than "really serious" (*D.P.P.* v. *Smith* (1961)). What actually constitutes really serious bodily harm will thus be a question of fact and degree for the jury to decide.

(3) Foresight of death

Since the House of Lords upheld the direction of the trial judge it seems safe to say that D is guilty of murder where he foresees the death of his victim as highly probable. In fact all five judges would have supported such a direction. However difficulties may arise in the future because even within the majority in the House of Lords differences of degree are apparent. At one end Viscount Dilhorne agreed with the wording used by the trial judge and would therefore hold that the prosecution must prove that the accused did foresee that the death of the victim was *highly* probable. Lord Cross, on the other hand, felt that the use of the word "highly" was too favourable to the accused. Lord Hailsham thought that juries might have difficulties assessing degrees of probabilities and so he thought the test should be "did the accused intend to expose the victim to a serious risk of death (or grievous bodily harm)?" This could be interpreted as imposing an even lower test than the "probable test" of Lord Cross because a risk that it is less than probable—say one in four—could be regarded as a serious risk. In the recent case of *McFeely* (1977) the accused had planted a bomb in a pub and had given the occupants a 10 minute warning. Lord Lowry C.J. said that the resulting killings amounted to murder only if the risk of death was foreseen as probable, and in this type of case it was less than probable that death would be caused. Thus the accused was acquitted of murder.

However the test is worded it is clear that we are talking about conscious risk taking (the objective approach in *Caldwell* has no place here), and, as we saw in Chapter 1 the risk that is taken must be one the accused is not justified in taking. Whether or not a risk is justifiable is determined by the jury partly by reference to the social utility of the action. Thus a surgeon will usually, but not always, be justified in performing an operation where there is the risk of death, whereas participation in a game of Russian roulette will never be justifiable.

(4) Foresight of grievous bodily harm

Little need be said of this since the meaning of grievous bodily harm has been explained and foresight examined above. It might, however, be useful to note that the effect of this category is to give an extremely extensive meaning to malice aforethought. Thus if D foresees that it is (highly) probable that his conduct will cause really serious bodily harm to his victim, he is guilty of murder if death results, even though neither he nor even reasonable men would have foreseen that death was likely.

Voluntary Manslaughter

Although we tend to divide unlawful homicide into two categories, namely murder and manslaughter, there are in effect at least three categories since manslaughter can be divided into voluntary and involuntary manslaughter. Voluntary manslaughter is the term given to those situations in which the accused would be convicted of murder, that is he possesses the necessary *mens rea* but because of some mitigating factor he is only convicted of manslaughter.

Examples of these mitigating factors are provocation, diminished responsibility, suicide pacts. In the first the accused kills another but at the time of the killing he has been provoked by, for example, the victim to such an extent he has lost control of himself. Diminished responsibility is the legal term applied to an accused whose mental powers have been disturbed by some diagnosible mental illness so that he is not fully to be held accountable for his actions (this has been considered in the section on insanity and diminished responsibility *ante*, p. 192). The term suicide pact covers those situations in which the accused has deliberately killed another but can prove that the killing was in pursuance of an agreement whereby the accused was to kill both the deceased and then himself (Homicide Act 1957, s.4). In our jurisdiction it is normal to refer to killings in this category as voluntary manslaughter, though in some jurisdictions the term "mitigated murder" is preferred.

(1) Provocation

The first question to ask is what is meant by provocation? The classic definition is usually taken to be that of Devlin J. in *Duffy* (1949) where he said "Provocation is some act, or series of acts, done by the dead man to the accused, which would cause in any reasonable person, and actually causes in the accused, a sudden and temporary loss of self-control, rendering the accused so subject to passion as to make him or her for the moment not master of his mind". We shall see later that this definition has been somewhat modified by subsequent legislation and cases but it nevertheless provides us with a useful starting point. We are concerned here with, for example, a situation in which A insults B about B's deformed nose, a characteristic about which B has very strong feelings. B loses his self-control and smashes A over the head with a beer glass he happens to be holding, thereby killing A. Two preliminary points should be noted. In the first place provocation is only a defence to the crime of murder and a successful defence of provocation results not in an absolute acquittal but in a conviction for manslaughter. The policy behind this rule is quite straightforward; the only sentence a judge is able to pass after a jury has returned a murder conviction is life imprisonment. Thus provocation serves to reduce the charge and conviction to one where the judge has a discretion to impose what sentence he considers suitable up to a maximum of life imprisonment. In fixing this sentence he will take account of the provocation. This is not to say that the defence would not raise the issue of provocation on any other charge, but on all other charges involving offences against the person, the judge has a discretion as to what sentence he imposes and can thus take account of the provocation in fixing that sentence. So when we say the provocation is only a defence to murder we mean that only in a case of murder does it actually alter the actual conviction. It is not a defence even to attempted murder.

Secondly, you must not lose sight of the need of the prosecution to establish the necessary malice aforethought of murder; the defence only becomes necessary if the jury find that the killing was done with the *mens rea* for murder.

The defence of provocation is now regulated by section 3 of the Homicide Act 1957 which provides that:

> "Where on a charge of murder there is evidence on which a jury can find that the person charged was provoked (whether by things done or by things said or by both together) to lose his self-control, the question whether the provocation was enough to make a reasonable man do as he did shall be left to be determined by the jury; and in determining that question the jury shall take into account everything both done and said according to the effect which, in their opinion, it would have on a reasonable man."

The statute clearly provides that once the judge has reached the conclusion that on the evidence before him there is evidence that the accused was provoked he must leave the issue of provocation to the jury. This does not mean that the judge must be satisfied that the accused was in fact provoked or that reasonable people would have been provoked: it is sufficient that there is some evidence on which a reasonable jury could be entitled to find that the prosecution had not proved beyond reasonable doubt that he was not provoked. Before the passing of the 1957 Act the judge was entitled to withdraw the issue of provocation from the jury on the ground that even if the accused had himself been provoked no reasonable man would have reacted in the way he did to the provocation. This led to cases where the judges held that a reasonable man only lost his self-control when he found his wife in the act of adultery and not when he had been told of it; that a reasonable man who was provoked by fists did not retaliate with a knife but only with fists; that reasonable men would not lose their self-control when taunted about a peculiar characteristic, *e.g.* impotence, since reasonable men did not possess that characteristic; and reasonable men would cool off after a certain period of time and regain their self-control. It is quite clear that in so far as the judges before 1957 were entitled to withdraw the issue altogether from the jury on the basis of these rules, section 3 has removed that power. The judge must leave the issue to the jury if there is evidence that the accused was provoked to lose his self-control however unreasonable his actions might appear to the judge. It is necessary also to remember that the defence of provocation might not have been specifically pleaded by the defendant who may, for example have been relying on the defence of self-defence. If, however, the judge feels that there is evidence of provocation, he is duty bound to leave the issue with the jury.

However, once the judge has decided that there is an issue of provocation he must leave two questions with the jury. First, he must direct them to consider whether the accused himself was actually provoked. It will not avail the accused for the jury to come to the conclusion that he was not provoked, although most reasonable men would undoubtedly have been. Secondly, the jury will be directed to consider whether a reasonable man so provoked would have responded in the way that the accused did. This could have provided the judges should they have so wished, with an opportunity to return to all the pre-1957 cases on what reasonable men do in the face of provocation. Clearly it would no longer be possible for a judge to tell a jury that reasonable men do not get provoked by things said to them alone, since this is now expressly covered by the section but he could tell the jury that reasonable men do not get worried about taunts as to their impotence, since reasonable men are not impotent. Admittedly it would be possible for a jury so directed to ignore the judge's ruling, but this is not a satisfactory way for the law to operate. The position has recently been examined by the House of Lords in the case of *D.P.P.* v. *Camplin* (1978). In *Camplin* the accused who had been drinking went to the house of a middle-aged Pakistani, K, whom he had been blackmailing over a homosexual relationship K was having with a friend of the accused. While he was there the accused was buggered by K, according to the accused, by force. After the act of buggery the accused claimed that he was overcome with remorse and shame, especially when he heard K laughing over his sexual triumph. He hit K over the head twice with a heavy chapati pan, thereby killing him. The accused was charged with murder and at his trial rested his defence solely on the issue of provocation, thereby seeking to reduce the offence to manslaughter. From the point of view of the case the major factor in dispute was whether the jury should have been advised not to pay any regard to the fact that at the time of the killing the accused was only 15 years old. In the event the jury were directed to apply the criterion of whether a reasonable man of full age would in like circumstances have acted as the respondent had done. The accused was convicted of murder but this was reduced on appeal to a conviction for manslaughter. The Court of Appeal certified that there was a point of law of general public importance involved in the case namely "whether on the prosecution for murder of a boy of 15, where the issue of provocation arises, the jury should be directed to consider the question, under section 3 of the Homicide Act 1957, whether the provocation was enough to make a reasonable man do as he did by reference to a 'reasonable adult' or by reference to a 'reasonable boy.' "

In the eventual appeal the House of Lords confirmed the decision of the Court of Appeal. Their Lordships took the view that if the accused possesses one characteristic which is relevant to the provocation the jury must be able to take it into consideration. Lord Diplock suggested that the proper test for a jury would be as follows: "The judge should state what the question is, using the very terms of the section. He should then explain to them that the reasonable man referred to in the question is a person having the power of self-control to be expected of the person of the sex and age of the accused, but in other respects sharing such of the accused's characteristics as they think would affect the gravity of the provocation to him, and that the question is not merely whether such a person in like circumstances would be provoked to lose his self-control, but also would react to the provocation as the accused did."

In *Newell* (1980) the Court of Appeal returned to the question of what "characteristics" a jury was entitled to consider in deciding whether the accused had responded to the provocation in the way a reasonable man would have responded. The court said that the characteristic must have a sufficient degree of permanence to make it part of the individual's character or personality. Furthermore there must be some real connection between the nature of the provocation and the particular characteristic of the offender by which it is sought to modify the reasonable man test. Thus the fact that the accused was a homosexual would have a sufficient degree of permanence to render it a characteristic, but it would be relevant only if the provocation was in some way related to the trait; it would be totally irrelevant if the provocation had taken the form of insulting the accused's talents as a pianist. Alcohol will rarely ever be relevant. It has long been held that it is no defence for the accused to suggest that he reacted more violently because he was drunk. This is partly because of the general policy of the law in relation to self-imposed drunkenness, and also because there is no sufficient degree of permanence here for the condition to be regarded as a characteristic. The position might possibly be different if the accused was suffering from a more permanent form of alcoholic illness and the provocation was directed against that condition.

There is a very great tendency in this area of law to refer back to the pre-1957 cases. These may often provide useful factual illustrations, but they must always be read in the light of section 3. Thus *Bedder* (1954) which decided that a jury should take no account of the accused's impotence when deciding how a reasonable man would react to taunts about impotence, cannot stand in the wake of *Camplin*, and is expressly overruled in that case. *Holmes* v. *D.P.P.* (1946) which decided that reasonable men were not provoked by words alone is expressly overruled by section 3 of the Act. The reasonable relationship rule (a man who is provoked by fists does not respond by using a knife, *Mancini* v. *D.P.P.* (1942) should be seen today, not as a hard and fast rule, but as a factor which the jury might consider in deciding whether a reasonable man would have acted as the accused did.

(2) Self-induced provocation

Suppose that X is blackmailing Y. On one occasion X goes to collect payment from Y who finally breaks under the strain and attacks X. X hits and kills Y. If X is charged with murder should he be entitled to say that he was provoked by Y? In *Edwards* v. *R.* (1973) the Privy Council said that a blackmailer should not be entitled to rely on provocation caused by his blackmailing activities unless the reaction to the blackmail goes to extreme lengths. But if there was evidence that the blackmailer was, in fact, provoked by his victim then section 3 would seem to leave the judge no discretion—he must leave the issue of provocation to the jury, though he would presumably be entitled to refer to the accused's blackmailing activities as one of the factors the jury should consider when deciding whether a reasonable man would have acted in the way that the accused did.

4. Involuntary Manslaughter

This title is used to cover those unlawful homicides where the courts have decided that the accused should be held to be criminally liable for the death of another, but where the accused does not possess the necessary mental state to be convicted of murder. With the exception of causing death by reckless driving and infanticide we have deposited all unlawful homicides into the two categories of murder and manslaughter with the result that both crimes have tended to embrace widely differing types of killings.

Some countries have adopted a third category which they have called negligent homicide. The use of this term has enabled murder to be restricted to those situations in which the accused actually intended to cause death or foresaw that it was likely, and manslaughter to be used where the accused actually foresees serious bodily harm. At present we shall see that it is possible for an accused to be convicted of manslaughter even though he may not have foreseen even the slightest harm befalling the victim.

Basically involuntary manslaughter falls into two categories: killing by gross negligence and constructive manslaughter.

(1) Manslaughter by gross negligence

In the civil law an action lies at the suit of a person injured as a result of the negligence of another. In general we are looking for a situation in which the person responsible for the injury failed to exercise the care that a reasonable person would have exercised. To put it another way, the defendant has failed to foresee what would be the consequences of his actions, consequences reasonable persons would have foreseen. For our purposes it is better to describe negligence as failing to exercise the care a reasonable person would take in a given situation. If it is expressed this way then it is easy to see that there can be degrees of negligence. To take a simple illustration; if it is generally accepted as safe to drive at 30 m.p.h. in certain conditions then the more you exceed that speed the more negligent you can be said to be. At 40 m.p.h. we could say that there was a further increase in the likelihood that you would injure someone and at 60 m.p.h. that likelihood has significantly increased. At 80 m.p.h. we could probably say that it would be a miracle if you did not injure someone. At some stage along this line the courts hold that it is no longer sufficient that the victim can be compensated in damages for his injuries, the law should be able to punish the driver for the totally irresponsible way in which he has behaved and for the injuries he has caused. At this point his negligence can be described as gross or criminal negligence (see *Bateman* (1925)).

Just as in the crime of murder we said that the prosecution had to prove that the accused either intended or foresaw death or serious bodily harm, so in the crime of manslaughter the prosecution will have to prove that the accused was grossly negligent. Also just as the terms intention or foresight are related to some existing circumstance or result so the term negligence must be related to some consequence. The main difference is that we are not concerned with what the accused foresaw, since if he foresaw death it would be murder, we are concerned here with what a reasonable man placed in the same situation would have foreseen. Thus in the crime of manslaughter by gross negligence the prosecution must prove that the reasonable man would have foreseen that had he acted in the way the accused acted he would have very likely killed someone.

What, in effect, the jury are asked to say is that the accused's actions were such that death was a very great probability. If the jury can only find that death was only a possibility then the negligence is not sufficiently gross for a conviction of manslaughter. To put this into a concrete example suppose that the accused is on the top of a cliff at the seaside and he has a large rock in his hand which he throws onto the beach below. Clearly if he intends to kill or seriously injure someone on the beach or foresees that throwing the rock down will probably have this effect then he will be convicted of murder. If however, this possibility does not occur to him even though the beach is crowded then we can say that he ought to have realised that he would very likely kill someone and this would be sufficient for a conviction of manslaughter. If the beach were practically deserted and he has no reason to suspect that there will be persons below, then his actions may be described as negligent in the sense that reasonable persons would never take such risks, but since the likelihood of killing another is remote the jury should not convict him of manslaughter.

Foresight by the reasonable man of any consequence short of death (or possibly grievous bodily harm) will not suffice as the basis for gross negligence manslaughter.

All this may seem to be very unsatisfactory. The jury is being asked to decide an issue of fact and degree without really being given much guidance as to where on the scale the critical point is reached and the negligence becomes gross. Equally it is at least arguable that the criminal law should only punish an accused where he has deliberately brought about a result either intending to produce that result or at least seeing that that is likely to be the consequences of taking an unjustifiable risk. There is no satisfactory explanation. At present it is the policy of the criminal law to impose liability for gross negligence in the case of manslaughter, on the basis that it will serve to make persons take more care.

(2) Constructive manslaughter

We have already mentioned that there existed a doctrine known as felony murder. Under this doctrine killings in the course of committing (violent) crimes were automatically murder, the only mental state the prosecution had to prove being that of the felony. Alongside this doctrine grew up a similar one for killings that occurred during the commission of lesser wrongs; this has been named constructive manslaughter, unlawful act manslaughter or misdemeanour manslaughter. In this country during the last century the accused could be convicted of manslaughter by this doctrine if he caused the death of another whilst committing any unlawful act including wrongs which were tortious but not criminal. Eventually the doctrine was modified so that it can now be confidently asserted that the unlawful act has to amount to a crime; and during this century it has been further qualified by decisions that the act must be an act likely to cause some harm. The doctrine receives its clearest statement in the judgment of Edmund Davies L.J. in *Church* (1966), where he said "the unlawful act must be such as all sober and reasonable people would inevitably recognise must subject the other person to, at least, the risk of some harm resulting therefrom, albeit not serious harm."

What therefore must the prosecution prove to make out a charge of manslaughter under this doctrine?

In the first place they must prove that the accused committed an unlawful act; it would appear that failure to act will not suffice as the basis for constructive manslaughter, *Lowe* (1973); though it may be prosecuted as gross negligence manslaughter. This act must be an act which is unlawful in itself and not one that would have been lawful but for the negligent way in which it was performed. For example, driving a car is a lawful act, but if the car is driven negligently then it becomes a criminal offence. This is not the sort of unlawful act which would suffice for the doctrine of constructive manslaughter. If the driver kills someone while driving badly the prosecution will have to charge him either with causing death by reckless driving or with manslaughter by gross negligence described above (*Andrews* v. *D.P.P.* (1937)). On the other hand an assault is an unlawful act in itself and indeed most cases of constructive manslaughter will be based on some form of assault. Another reason why negligent driving cannot form the unlawful act for purposes of constructive manslaughter is provided by the case of *Dalby* (1982) where the Court of Appeal held that the unlawful act had to be directed at the victim and likely to cause immediate harm. Negligent driving is not directed at a victim. Similarly the supply of controlled drugs by A to B is not, in itself, an act which is likely to subject the victim to the immediate risk of injury. In the drugs type of case the Court of Appeal appears to be saying that the offence—namely possession of controlled drugs—is not the real cause of the injury. It does not necessarily follow that because a person possesses drugs he will administer them to himself. In other words the offence is too remote from the injury. This "aimed at" or "directed at" test is clearly inappropriate for gross negligence manslaughter. Once you have established that the accused committed the unlawful act, the next step is to prove that it was the unlawful act which caused the death of the victim. The final step is to prove to the court's satisfaction that sober and reasonable people would inevitably recognise that the act would subject the other person to, at least, the risk of some harm, albeit not serious harm (*Church* (1966)). It must be noted that it is not necessary to establish that the accused himself foresaw the possibility of any harm to the victim. Since the decision in *Church* there have been instances where it was thought that the Court of Appeal was saying that the accused himself must foresee that his actions would harm the victim, but the House of Lords in *D.P.P.* v. *Newbury* (1976), where youths had thrown paving slabs from a bridge on to a passing express train thereby killing the guard, re-affirmed the law as expressed by Edmund Davies L.J. in *Church.*

Now that we have outlined both doctrines we can look at an example to see how they operate in practice. In *Lamb* (1967) two young men were playing with a revolver. Lamb pointed it at his friend and pulled the trigger. The gun fired and the friend was killed. Lamb was charged with manslaughter. The Court accepted that he knew that there were two bullets in the chambers but that both men believed that revolvers revolve after they have been fired and not, as actually happens, before the firing pin strikes the bullet. On appeal against conviction, the Court of Appeal held that there could be no finding of constructive manslaughter since, because of his belief, the victim did not anticipate harm and Lamb did not intend even to frighten the other man, and so there could be no assault to form the unlawful act. As to gross negligence manslaughter the court appears to accept that if the jury had been properly directed they would have been entitled to convict the accused on the basis that they considered his view as to there being no danger was formed in a criminally negligent way. This is clearly a finding that the test to be applied is objective and not subjective. However the Court of Appeal went on to say that the accused was entitled to have the jury consider the fact that he honestly believed that the gun would not fire and that three experts testified to the fact that this was understandable in view of the fact that the accused was unskilled in the art of guns.

CHAPTER 7

NON FATAL OFFENCES AGAINST THE PERSON

In this chapter we shall examine a selection of the many offences against the person. The first section covers the more common assault type offences and the second section outlines certain sexual offences.

I. *ASSAULTS*

1. ASSAULT AND BATTERY

At common law there were two basic offences of assault and battery. Technically assault is the offence of causing another to apprehend immediate and unlawful personal violence. Thus if X puts up his fists to strike Y, if Y apprehends that he is going to be hit then we can say that X has assaulted Y. When Y is, in fact, hit on the nose, this constitutes a battery. However over the years lawyers have come to use the word "assault" to cover both situations, and indeed the offence of common assault under section 47 of the Offences Against the Person Act 1861 covers both assaults and batteries. In *Att.-Gen.'s Reference* (*No.* 6 *of* 1980) (1981) the Court of Appeal approved with a slight addition the definition of assault given by James J. in *Fagan* v. *Metropolitan Police Commissioner* (1969); "the actual intended use of unlawful force to another person without his consent (or any other lawful excuse)."

(1) Assault

In order to establish the offence of common assault contrary to section 47 of the Offences Against the Person Act 1861 the prosecution must establish that the victim was put in fear of immediate and unlawful personal violence (the immediate fear of future violence would not be enough), and that the accused either intended to cause such an effect or was reckless that his actions would have that effect. It is a crime of basic intent to which drunkenness is no defence (see *ante*, p. 200). For the purpose of common assault the personal violence is not unlawful if the accused was acting in self-defence or if the defence of consent is available (see *post*, p. 245). There is some authority for the view that words alone cannot constitute an assault, but it is suggested that in appropriate circumstances there is no reason why they should not. For example, if X, a prostitute, was walking home in the dark one evening when a man said to her "I am continuing Jack the Ripper's crusade against prostitutes," it would be absurd if this was not capable of amounting to an assault.

It is the effect X intentionally or recklessly creates on the victim that is central to the offence; it does not matter that the accused had neither the intention or the ability to carry out the threat. Thus if X holds up Y, a cashier at the bank, with a water pistol, if X intends that Y should be afraid for his personal safety and Y is so affected then X is guilty of assault. It is no defence for X to say that there was no assault because Y was in no danger. It is generally accepted that in all the assault offences the word reckless should be confined to the meaning given in *Cunningham* (*ante*, p. 144) namely the deliberate and unjustified taking of a risk of which the accused is aware. The wider meaning given to recklessness in *Caldwell* (*ante*, p. 147) should not be adopted.

In *Lamb* (1967), where two men were playing with a revolver, it was held that there was no assault when Lamb pointed the gun at the other man, since Lamb did not intend to cause any fear of immediate personal violence and the other did not expect any (see *ante*, p. 237).

(2) Battery

Here the prosecution must prove that the accused inflicted unlawful personal violence on the victim, and that he intended to do so or that he was reckless as to his conduct having that effect. There is no need to show that the amount of force was great; in fact any touching of another without that other's consent amounts to a battery (see consent, *post* p. 245), but consent is generally implied in the sort of bodily contact that happens in ordinary everyday life. Thus people are taken to accept that if they walk about in the street that others will bump into them; that others may tap them on the shoulder to attract their attention; and that in the course of conversation there are people who need to touch them to emphasise what they are saying.

The most simple examples of batteries are those cases in which the accused hits his victim either with a fist or with an object he is holding. But it is also a battery to dig a hole for someone to fall into or to cause people to fall down stairs by turning the lights out (*Martin* (1881), *post*, p. 241).

There is no need for the victim to be aware that he is about to be struck, nor even that the accused formed the *mens rea* before the battery occurred. In *Fagan* (1969) where the accused accidentally drove onto a policeman's foot and then refused to drive off, it was held that assault (including battery) was a continuing offence and it sufficed that the accused formed the *mens rea* during its continuance.

2. Assault Occasioning Actual Bodily Harm

Under section 47 of the Offences Against the Person Act 1861, it is an offence for a person to assault another thereby causing that other actual bodily harm. The offence is punishable with up to five years' imprisonment. In order to gain a conviction for this offence the prosecution must prove that the accused was guilty of an assault or battery as described above and that this caused actual bodily harm. Thus the *actus reus* consists in the *actus reus* of assault or battery which led to actual bodily harm, and the *mens rea* is the *mens rea* of assault or battery. The only question that remains to be considered is what amounts to actual bodily harm. According to the House of Lords in *D.P.P.* v. *Smith* (*ante*, p. 227) which was examining the phrase "grievous bodily harm,"the words "bodily harm" needed no explanation and "grievous" means really serious. Thus it follows that actual bodily harm is something less than really serious, and possibly any degree of bodily injury may suffice however slight, even an injury to the state of a person's mind.

3. Offences Against the Person Act 1861, s.20

> "Whosoever shall unlawfully and maliciously wound or inflict any grievous bodily harm upon another person, either with or without any weapon or instrument, shall be guilty of an offence triable either way and being convicted thereof shall be liable to imprisonment for five years."

The first thing that should strike you about this offence is that although it sounds far more serious than that under section 47 (assault occasioning actual bodily harm) it carries precisely the same maximum penalty. This is a result of the Offences Against the Person Act being a haphazard consolidation of offences, but it does make the law look a trifle illogical.

Actus reus

The prosecution must establish that the accused unlawfully inflicted grievous bodily harm or that he unlawfully wounded the victim. The word unlawfully means that the offence is not committed if the accused was acting in self-defence or possibly that the victim had consented (see *post*, p. 245). Wounding will rarely cause problems; here the prosecution must prove that as a result of the accused's actions the inner and outer skin of the victim were severed. Would it suffice therefore that the accused has caused internal bleeding in his victim? If, for example, the accused has caused bleeding inside the accused's mouth this will be classified as a wounding, but probably not if he has caused a rupture of the victim's stomach lining or a bruise. The difference is that the inside skin of the lips and cheeks are readily accessible from the outside; you can trace the continuity of the skin with your finger. In no way is this true of the stomach lining. The matter is not likely to cause many problems since an attack which caused internal bleeding is likely to be said to have inflicted grievous bodily harm—or at least actual bodily harm in the case of a bruise.

We have already seen that grievous bodily harm means that the victim suffers bodily harm which can be described as really serious. Here there need be no breaking of the skin, and it is a question of fact for the jury whether the harm is or is not really serious. However it will be seen that in section 20 the accused must be shown to have "inflicted" grievous bodily harm, whereas under section 18 he must be shown to have "caused" grievous bodily harm. Is any significance to be drawn from the use of these different verbs? The answer is that no such distinction may have occurred to the original drafters of the provisions, but in interpreting them the courts have more often than not held that the word "inflicts" means that the act of the accused which results in the grievous bodily harm must itself be an assault. In the majority of cases this causes no problems since the accused usually produces the grievous bodily harm by striking the victim with his fists or a weapon. In *Clarence* (1888), however, the accused who was suffering from a communicable form of venereal disease had intercourse with a woman without revealing his condition to her. It was held that he could not be convicted of "inflicting grievous bodily harm" on her since she had consented to the intercourse and hence there was no assault (see *post*, p. 246 for meaning of consent). Recently in *Wilson* (1983) the Court of Appeal has held that the word "inflicts" did not necessarily include an allegation of assault. This still leaves open the question of whether the word "inflicts" has a meaning different from "causes" and it is possible that "inflicts" might be held to require the application of some force, whether by an assault or not, and may not therefore cover a situation in which grievous bodily harm has been caused by the secret administration of poison.

Whatever the eventual decision in cases of poisoning and cases such as *Clarence*, the decision in *Wilson* removes doubts from other earlier cases in which convictions under section 20 had been upheld despite the absence of any obvious assault. Thus in *Martin* (1881) the accused had caused panic in a theatre as the audience was leaving after a performance, by extinguishing all the lights on the stairs and placing a bar across the doors at the bottom. In the ensuing chaos several persons were injured when crushed against the doors which would not open. The court seems to have assumed that there was an assault, though it is difficult to see how they were placed in fear of immediate and unlawful violence. Possibly there was a battery of the type involved where a pit is dug for somebody to fall into. If, however, the word "inflicts" does not require proof of an assault there will be no difficulty in holding that the accused has inflicted grievous bodily harm on the victims. Similarly many of the problems of holding that there has been an assault in cases in which the victim has caused grievous bodily harm upon himself in trying to escape from the accused will disappear. In *Halliday* (1889) the accused advanced in a threatening manner towards his wife who tried to jump out of an upstairs window. Her daughter prevented her fall by trying to hold on to her, but the accused ordered her to let go whereupon her mother fell to the ground below. It was held that the father had inflicted grievous bodily harm. In that case it would be possible to say that there was an assault since both the mother and daughter were put in fear of immediate harm; but this is more difficult in the case of *Lewis* (1970) where the husband who was threatening the wife was on the other side of a locked door. Again the court held that there was an assault although the wife was not in fear of such immediate harm because of the locked door. The decision in *Wilson* means that a conviction in such cases as these can be upheld without the need to give unduly wide meaning to the requirement in assault that the accused should place the victim in fear of "immediate" harm.

Mens rea

The prosecution must prove that the accused acted maliciously. We have already seen that maliciously does not mean that the accused acted from evil motives; it generally indicates that *mens rea* will be required (*Cunningham, ante,* p. 144). If this is the case then one would have supposed that the prosecution would have to prove that the accused intended or foresaw that his actions would wound or inflict grievous bodily harm. However in *Mowatt* (1968) the Court of Appeal held that it was sufficient if the accused foresaw that some physical injury would be caused to some person albeit of a minor nature. The accused did not have to foresee that it would be a wound or grievous bodily harm. The effect of this is to reduce the *mens rea* of section 20 to the same level of culpability required for assault occasioning actual bodily harm, and this seems to be indefensible. Admittedly both offences through an accident of history carry the same sentence, but section 20 is clearly intended to be the more serious and sense can only be made of the two offences if a higher degree of culpability (namely foresight of grievous bodily harm or wounding) is required under section 20. However, at present this is not the requirement.

Thus in conclusion if X punches Y and foresees that Y will suffer slight harm, X will be guilty of an offence under section 20 if Y is wounded or if he suffers really serious bodily injury as a result of the punch. He also commits an offence under section 47.

In *Sullivan* (1980) the Court of Appeal confirmed the correctness of the decision in *Mowatt,* and went on to hold that an intention to frighten the victim, without more, would not suffice as the *mens rea* for section 20. Where, for example, A drives his car perilously close to B intending to scare him, A may well realise that he might cause some injury to B. Unless, however, he does realise that there is a risk of injury there is no offence under section 20, though there may be an offence under section 47.

4. Offences Against the Person Act 1861, s.18

> "Whosoever shall unlawfully and maliciously by any means whatsoever wound or cause any grievous bodily harm to any person with intent to do some grievous bodily harm to any person, or with intent to resist or prevent the lawful apprehension or detaining of any person, shall be guilty of an offence, and being convicted thereof shall be liable to imprisonment for life."

The maximum possible sentence of life imprisonment clearly shows that this offence is reserved for the most culpable of offenders against the person.

Actus reus

The *actus reus* of this offence is to a large extent identical to that of the offence under section 20. It should be noted however that this section speaks of the accused "causing" rather than "inflicting" grievous bodily harm, and thus there is no question of the need to show an assault here.

Mens rea

The prosecution must prove (i) that the accused intended to do grievous bodily harm or intended to resist arrest, and (ii) that he acted maliciously.

(i) The prosecution must prove that the accused caused the *actus reus* with the intention either of doing grievous bodily harm to some person or with the intention of resisting or preventing the lawful apprehension or detaining of any person. *Belfon* (1976) makes it clear that nothing short of intention will suffice on this part of the *mens rea*; thus the prosecution must establish that the accused wanted to achieve one of these ends or that he knew that his actions would certainly have that effect. We need say nothing more about an intention to do grievous bodily harm. In relation to intention to resist, etc., we can safely say that if the accused believes that the arrest is unlawful and it is, in fact, unlawful, he will have a defence. The position is less clear if he believe the arrest is unlawful, but it is, in fact lawful. On principle he should have a defence as long as his belief is genuine. This would seem to follow from *Morgan* (*ante*, p. 157) but there is old authority to the contrary (*Bentley* (1850)).

(ii) In addition to the intent described in (i) above the prosecution must establish that the accused was acting "maliciously." In *Mowatt* (1968) the Court of Appeal said, *obiter*, that this word is superfluous in section 18, presumably thinking of a case in which the accused is charged with maliciously causing grievous bodily harm with intent to do grievous bodily harm. And similarly it would not add much to wounding where this was charged coupled with an intent to do grievous bodily harm. Where, however, the accused is charged with wounding or causing grievous bodily harm with intent to resist arrest it has a full part to play. Consider a situation in which X, in trying to resist lawful arrest pushes the arresting officer who falls and is seriously injured. If the word malicious is given no role to play it means that the only *mens rea* required of X would be his intent to resist arrest and this would be satisfied even if he used only the slightest force to break away. This would surely be wrong. Thus the word maliciously should be employed so as to require that in addition to the ulterior intent the prosecution should also have to prove that the accused at least foresaw grievous bodily harm or a wound whichever was specified in the indictment. Thus in our illustration X would only be liable on an indictment charging him with causing grievous bodily harm with intent to resist arrest if he did intend to resist arrest and if he also foresaw that his act would cause grievous bodily harm. The extended meaning given to maliciously by the Court in *Mowatt* for section 20—*i.e.* foresight of any degree of injury—should not be applied to section 18, however inconsistent this may appear.

5. Domestic Violence

Special problems are raised by violence within the family unit, for example, wife and child battering. Of course, the ordinary remedies of civil and criminal law apply. The assailants are clearly guilty of the various forms of assault, but this is not a satisfactory answer. In the case of child abuse the problem of detection is acute. If the abuse is detected there are no shortage of remedies; the child can be taken into the care of the local authority and the assailant can be prosecuted. In the case of a battered wife problems are caused by the reluctance of the spouse to testify in court against the other and by the reluctance of the police to enter the home to settle a domestic dispute. In any case the prosecution of the aggressor is not a satisfactory solution to most domestic problems. The wife will often feel the need for continuing protection against her husband and may desire his exclusion from the home. Such protection may be gained under the Domestic Violence and Matrimonial Proceedings Act 1976 and the Domestic Proceedings and Magistrates' Courts Act 1978.

6. Consent as a Defence to Offences Against the Person

The questions we must ask in this section are whether consent can ever be relied upon as a defence to offences against the person and, if so, what does the criminal law mean by the term "consent"?

(1) Is consent any defence to a charge involving an offence against the person?

It has been said that the least touching of another without his consent amounts to a battery. Put another way we can say that an element of battery is lack of consent. Clearly everyday life requires that you consent to others touching you; if this were not so you would not be able to visit the hairdresser without being the victim of a battery. When you walk down the crowded high street you impliedly consent to other pedestrians bumping into you. But can you consent to more violent contact? Again a moment's thought will show you that you can. For instance most of us pay painful visits to the dentist from time to time and thousands of people engage in sporting activities where bodily contact can be quite violent. If we were not allowed to consent to such activities we should not have sports such as rugby or boxing. In such sports the participants consent to the amount of violence that is legally permissible under the rules of the game and also to fouls that occur in normal games. However, it would be no defence where a member of one team violently punched a member of the other team in a game of rugby to say that it was all in the game.

Equally we know that in some sports very serious harm or even death can result. Does this mean that you can consent to the possible infliction of really serious harm? The general policy has been recently reviewed by the Court of Appeal in *Att.-Gen.'s Reference* (*No.* 6 *of* 1980)(1981). There it was held that, contrary to one line of argument put forward, it mattered not whether the act occurred in public or in private; "it is an assault if actual bodily harm is intended and/or caused." The Court of Appeal, however, added that their decision was not intended to cast doubt upon the accepted legality of properly conducted games or sports, lawful chastisement or correction, reasonable surgical interference, dangerous exhibitions, etc. Of these lawful chastisement is the exercise of a legal right and the remainder can be justified on the ground of being for the public good.

Thus the position would appear to be that where actual bodily harm is not intended or is not actually caused, lack of consent is an essential ingredient of the crimes of assault and battery. Where, however, actual bodily harm is intended and/or caused, consent is irrelevant unless the act falls within one of the exceptions such as a properly conducted sport. Here the victim's implied consent to the risks of the sport will be a defence to any allegation of assault. It would seem that little scope is left for the concept of consent.

In the field of sexual offences consent plays an important role. For example it is obvious that persons over the age of 16 can consent to sexual intercourse and their consent is a complete defence to a charge of rape. Girls who are under 16 can clearly give consent to intercourse, provided they understand the nature of the act, (*post*, p. 247) and this will be a defence to a charge of rape, but not to a defence of unlawful sexual intercourse which is an offence to which consent is irrelevant. (See *post*, p. 249).

(2) What is consent?

It is often said that to constitute a defence the consent must be real. This means that if the person submits to some act because of duress, there is no real consent. Equally the law takes the view that some children are too young to give any meaningful consent. A 15-year-old girl's consent to intercourse may save the man from a charge of rape if not unlawful sexual intercourse, but if the girl was much younger then the court is likely to discount the fact that she agreed to what was being done. There is no rule of thumb about the age at which a person can give meaningful consent, it depends on the facts of the case and the actual child.

More problematical are the cases where consent is procured by fraud. In *Bolduc and Bird* (1967) a doctor permitted a friend who was a jazz musician to attend a vaginal examination. He introduced his friend to the woman as a medical student and asked if she minded his presence. She said she did not mind and so the examination took place. When she learned the truth she was, not surprisingly, furious, and the doctor and his friend were prosecuted for an assault. Now obviously if the woman consented to being examined there was no assault; but can you say that she really consented when it is perfectly clear she would not have consented had she know of the true facts. The criminal courts take a rather simplistic approach to such problems. If the act which follows the consent is the act which the person was consenting to, then it is irrelevant that the person would not have consented had he or she known of all the surrounding circumstances. Thus in *Bolduc and Bird*, the woman consented to the doctor performing a vaginal examination and that is what he did. It was irrelevant that the woman would not have consented had she known his friend was a voyeur and not a student. Similarly in *Clarence* which we discussed earlier (*ante*, p. 241), the woman consented to intercourse and that is what took place albeit in circumstances that would have led her to withdraw her consent. In *Williams* (1923) a singing master was charged with the rape of a girl of 16. The prosecution's case was that he had told her her voice need improving and that he could help her. She then let him have intercourse with her. If the prosecution could establish that she was totally unaware of sexual matters and that she thought this was some form of operation to improve her voice, then there would be no consent. If, on the other hand she knew that he was proposing sexual intercourse but wrongly believed him when he said that this would improve her voice then there would be effective consent.

II. *SEXUAL OFFENCES*

Although non-consensual sexual offences might be subsumed under the general category of non-fatal offences against the person, many sexual offences have the unusual feature that they may be committed even where the conduct was consensual. It is therefore customary to treat sexual offences as a separate category and a further justification may lie in the fact that sexual *offenders* constitute a special category of offenders.

The law relating to sexual offenders is at present under review by the Criminal Law Revision Committee, though it is likely to be several years before a new code on sexual offences emerges.

Among the plethora of sexual offences the following need to be noted.

1. Rape

Under section 1 of the Sexual Offences Act 1956 it is an offence for a man to rape a woman. The definition of rape is to be found in section 1 of the Sexual Offences (Amendment) Act 1976 which was passed as a result of controversy following the decision of the House of Lords in *D.P.P.* v. *Morgan* ((1976); the Act supported the decision of the House of Lords. See *ante*, p. 157).

Actus reus

In a prosecution for rape the prosecutor must prove—

First, that the man had sexual intercourse with the woman and for this purpose the slightest penetration of the vagina by the penis suffices (Sexual Offences Act 1956, s.44).

Secondly, that the woman did not, in fact, consent to have sexual intercourse. It does not have to be proved that intercourse was achieved by force or threats of bodily harm. Thus in *Olugboja* (1981) it was held that where a girl submitted to intercourse through fear of what might happen if she did not, even though no specific threats had been made, the intercourse was non-consensual. There is no requirement that the woman should put up at least some resistance. The prosecution would also succeed if it could prove that intercourse was achieved by fraud, provided that the fraud resulted in the woman being mistaken either as to the identity of the man or as to the nature of the act performed (see *Williams* (1923)). Where the woman is too young, too drunk or too mentally deficient to be able to give a meaningful consent, intercourse would be held to have taken place without her consent.

Thirdly, that the man is not the husband of the woman. At the present time the common law rule that a husband cannot rape his wife prevails. He can, of course, be charged with assaulting his wife if he forces her to have intercourse with him and the force satisfies the normal requirements of one of the assault offences (see *ante*, p. 238). The rule does not apply if the spouses are living apart or if a decree nisi of divorce or annulment has been granted. Furthermore the rule does not apply to persons who are cohabiting but who are not husband and wife.

Fourthly, that the man is over the age of 14. There is an irrebuttable presumption that males under the age of 14 are incapable of having sexual intercourse. It follows, therefore, that they cannot be the principal offender in any offence which requires sexual intercourse, including sodomy. They can, however, be charged as secondary parties to such offences or with the offence of indecent assault.

Mens rea

The prosecution must prove that, at the time of the intercourse, the man *either* (i) knew that the woman was not consenting *or* (ii) was reckless as to whether or not she was consenting. The first of these two alternative requirements presents no problems. In view of the recent decision of the Court of Appeal in *Pigg* (1982), (ii) requires elucidation. In *Pigg* the Court of Appeal said, obiter, that the word "reckless" was to be given the meaning ascribed to it by the House of Lords in *Caldwell* (see *ante*, p. 147). It follows that under the second requirement the prosecution would succeed if it can prove *either* that the accused was aware that there was a risk that the woman was not consenting *or* that the accused had not adverted to the possibility that the woman was not consenting in circumstances where there was an obvious risk that she was not consenting. However if the accused genuinely holds the belief that the woman is consenting then he cannot be convicted of rape (*per* the House of Lords in *D.P.P.* v. *Morgan* (1976)).

2. Unlawful Sexual Intercourse

In seeking to protect young girls from what are seen as the adverse social and psychological effects of having sexual intercourse at an early age the law provides that it is an offence, punishable with two years imprisonment, for a man to have sexual intercourse with a girl who is under the age of 16 (Sexual Offences Act 1956, s.6). Where the girl is under the age of 13 the man is guilty of a more serious offence which carries life imprisonment (Sexual Offences Act 1956, s.5). Since the purpose of the law is to protect young girls against these adverse effects it is irrelevant that she consented to the intercourse; though, of course if she did not consent the man would also have committed the offence of rape.

It is no defence for the man to plead that he thought that the girl was older than she in fact was, since liability on the age element of the *actus reus* is strict. However in relation to the less serious offence under section 6 there are two statutory defences. Under section 6(2) it is a defence for the accused to show that he had gone through a form of marriage with the girl and that he honestly and reasonably believed that she was his wife. Under section 6(3) it is a defence for the accused to show that at the time of the intercourse he was under the age of 24, that he honestly and reasonably believed that the girl was over the age of 15 and that he had never been previously charged with such an offence. In keeping with the principle which underlies the defence under section 6(3) it is probably safe to say that where the offence is committed by a young man who himself is not much over the age of 16 it is more likely that he will be cautioned by the police rather than prosecuted. As the age gap widens between the parties, prosecution becomes more probable.

3. Indecent Assault

The offence of indecent assault can be committed by both men and women against both men and women (Sexual Offences Act 1956, ss.14 and 15). As far as the seriousness of the offence is concerned, this depends upon the victim. Where the indecent assault is against a woman the offence carries up to two years imprisonment unless she is under the age of 13 when the offence carries five years. If the indecent assault is upon a male then the maximum sentence is ten years.

In order to obtain a conviction the prosecution must prove firstly that there was an assault or battery and secondly that the assault or battery was committed in circumstances of indecency.

(1) An assault or battery

It is clear that the prosecution must prove an actual assault or battery within the normal meaning of these terms (see *ante*, p. 238). Consent will therefore be a defence unless it was obtained by fraud either as to the nature of the act proposed or as to the identity of the accused. Consent will not be a defence where the probable or intended consequence of the assault or battery is the infliction of bodily harm (see *ante*, p. 246). The position is further complicated by the fact that for purposes of indecent assault certain persons are treated as being incapable of consenting to the proposed acts, namely person under the age of 16 and persons who are mentally deficient.

In *Fairclough* v. *Whipp* (1951) the accused exposed his penis to a nine year old girl and invited her to touch it. At no stage did he give any indication that he would touch her. It was held that no indecent assault had occurred, and rightly so, since although his motives were highly indecent there was nothing which could be classed as an assault or battery. In *D.P.P.* v. *Rogers* (1953) the accused put his arm around his 11 year old daughter and led her upstairs so that she could masturbate him. It was held that there was no hostile act against the girl and so the accused was acquitted. It is submitted that this requirement of a hostile act is misconceived; the accused clearly touched his daughter and in these circumstances her consent was irrelevant since she was under the age of 16 (see *Faulkner* v. *Talbot*, below).

We saw earlier that it is an offence under section 6 of the Sexual

Offences Act for a man to have intercourse with a girl who is under the age of 16. There is, however, no corresponding offence where a woman has intercourse with a boy who is under the age of 16. The woman may commit an indecent assault, if she does anything during the act of intercourse which constitutes an assault. Thus if she lies perfectly still while the boy has intercourse there would be no indecent assault. If, on the other hand, she touches his penis in order to arouse him, this would constitute an assault since the boy's consent would be irrelevant. These were the facts of *Faulkner* v. *Talbot* (1982) and the Court of Appeal held that the woman had indecently assaulted the boy. There was however nothing in the nature of a hostile act and it is suggested that the decision of the Court can be treated as an indication that this is no longer a requirement of the offence.

(2) Circumstances of indecency

In *Beal* v. *Kelley* (1951) the Court approved the rule that the assault must be accompanied by circumstances of indecency on the part of the prisoner. It is impossible to give a watertight definition of what this means, but it is probably safe to say that the accused must have committed the assault in a way which clearly indicates an overt sexual element in the assault together with sexual motivation on the part of the accused. Thus where in *George* (1956) the accused tried to remove a girl's shoe to satisfy his perverted sexual desires, the court held that there was no evidence of any circumstances of indecency since the indecency was all in the mind of the accused. On the other hand in *Beal* v. *Kelley* (1951) the accused exposed his penis to a 14 year old boy and asked him to handle it. When the boy refused the accused grabbed the boy's arm and pulled him nearer. Although the act of pulling the boy nearer was not, on its own indecent, it was held that it had to be viewed in the light of all the facts, and there was thus clear evidence of indecency.

Before leaving the offence of indecent assault we should note two points. First, if a man is charged with having unlawful sexual intercourse with a 15 year old girl (Sexual Offences Act 1956, s.6), we have seen that he will have a defence if he can prove he was under the age of 24, believed her to be over 15 and had never been charged with such an offence before; but this defence is not available on a charge of indecent assault. Thus if the police charge him with indecently assaulting the girl (by having intercourse with her) he will not be able to raise such a defence. The defence under section 6(2) (*ante*, p. 249) is, however, available on a charge of indecent assault.

Secondly, the law has provided for the *Fairclough* v. *Whipp* type of case, where the accused is acquitted because there is no actual assault. The Indecency with Children Act 1960 makes it an offence for any person to commit an act of gross indecency with or towards a child under the age of 14 or to incite a child under that age to such an act with him or with another. Thus mere incitement may constitute the offence. The accused in *Fairclough* v. *Whipp* would now commit an offence under this Act. This would also have been the appropriate charge to have been brought against the accused in *Sutton* (1977). Sutton had taken photographs of naked and partially clad boys in poses designed to draw attention to their genital organs. He had only touched them on their arms, legs and torsos so as to indicate a pose. The Court of Appeal held that the touching was not of itself indecent and so there was no indecent assault. The use of the word "gross" to qualify "indecency" suggests that the act must be more indecent than that required for an indecent assault and is probably confined to activity concerning the genital region.

4. Indecent Exposure

It is an offence under section 4 of the Vagrancy Act 1824 for a man wilfully and indecently to expose his penis, in public or in private, with intent to insult any female. If the man indecently exposes any other part of his body in a public place he may be guilty of a common law offence.

CHAPTER 8

OFFENCES UNDER THE THEFT ACTS 1968 AND 1978

The Theft Acts of 1968 and 1978 provide us with a fairly comprehensive list of offences which broadly speaking involve the dishonest dealing with other people's property. Taken together with the Criminal Damage Act 1971 and the Forgery and Counterfeiting Act 1981, it may be said that there is now a code dealing with all the principal offences against property.

The Theft Act 1968 represents an overhaul of the existing assortment of offences which had become rather complex and unwieldy. The 1978 Act created three new offences to replace a subsection of the 1968 Act which had been found to be unworkable. Between them the Acts have produced a simplification of the law in this area and we can say from the outset that the great majority of cases brought under them present very few difficult legal problems. However it is probably impossible to construct a totally simple code for property offences. Take theft for example; this consists in the interference with the property rights of another. These property rights are controlled at the outset by the civil law and so in theft cases it is sometimes necessary to take account of difficult civil law rules before criminal liability can be sorted out. Occasionally judges have said that complex rules relating to property rights have no place in the criminal law, but it would be impossible to divorce the law of theft from the property rights it is seeking to protect.

In this chapter we shall concentrate mainly upon the offences of theft and deception and the chapter will conclude with a summary of the other well-known offences.

I. *THEFT*

The offence is defined by section 1 of the Theft Act 1968.

> "(1) A person is guilty of theft if he dishonestly appropriates property belonging to another with the intention of permanently depriving the other of it; and "thief" and "steal" shall be construed accordingly."

Sections 1 to 6 of the Act amplify the meaning of words and phrases used in this definition and section 7 provides that the offence of theft shall be punishable with a maximum of 10 years imprisonment. It should be borne in mind that the offence of theft covers all cases of stealing whether it be of a great or small sum; we have no division into petty theft and grand theft; though theft is an offence which is triable either way (see *ante*, p. 103). There is no separate offence of shoplifting; this is a colloquialism which is used to describe a particular form of theft which has the unfortunate tendency of suggesting that there is a separate less serious offence.

From the definition in section 1 we can see that the *actus reus* comprises (a) an appropriation (b) of property (c) which property belongs to another. The *mens rea* requires (a) dishonesty and (b) an intention permanently to deprive the other of property.

As is usual in the criminal law there is no difficulty in applying the definition of the offence to the typical, or everyday, case. But cases do arise which lie at the edge of the definition where complexities can occur. In this context it might be noted that there is a close relationship—indeed there is an overlap—between the offence of theft under section 1 and the offence of obtaining property by deception under section 15. In this grey area great care needs to be taken to determine whether the facts will best support the elements of the offence of theft or the offence of deception. Facts which might easily establish the one offence may only doubtfully, or not at all, support the other. The classic instance of this is *Lawrence* (1971), discussion of which will be taken up (*post*, p. 282) after the elements of both theft and deception have been considered. The moral is plain: faced with a particular set of facts (whether in an examination paper or a solicitor's office) it pays to give careful consideration as to whether those facts will prima facie support *all* the elements of the offence which is to be charged.

The Actus Reus of Theft

(1) Appropriates

This requirement is defined in section 3(1) of the Act as follows: "any assumption by a person of the rights of an owner amounts to an appropriation." Thus the prosecution must prove that the accused, by some conduct of his, treated himself as the owner of someone else's property.

To illustrate this we can consider the most commonly occurring form of appropriation, the case of appropriation by taking. A enters B's bookshop and takes a book belonging to B; C enters D's room and takes D's watch; E puts his hand in F's pocket and removes F's wallet. In these cases it is as clear as can be that A has appropriated the book, C the watch and E the wallet. A, C and E are treating themselves as owners of property which belongs to B, D and F.

But two things need to be noticed. The first is that although taking is so far the most common mode of appropriation that laymen still think of theft as a taking, it is not the *only* mode of appropriation. The definition says that "*any*" assumption of the rights of an owner amounts to an appropriation. Strictly, therefore, it amounts to an appropriation to destroy another's property. Thus if A pushes B's car over a cliff and thereby destroys it, it can properly be said that he has appropriated the car. Most laymen would not recognise this as a case of theft (and no doubt A would be charged under the Criminal Damage Act 1971), but a charge of theft could be supported on such facts. This is clearly an appropriation (what could be a clearer assumption of B's rights than destroying his car?) and section 1(1) makes it clear that the prosecution does not have to establish on a charge of theft that A intended to make any gain from his action.

The second point to note is that while the layman might think that, in the examples first given, A, C and E appropriate the property when they take it *away*, *i.e.* when they remove the goods from the control of B, D and F into their own control, in law the appropriation has occurred at an earlier stage. When, for example, E put his hand on the wallet inside F's pocket, and *before* he removes it, he may be said to have appropriated because, at that instance, he is assuming the rights of the owner, F. It is F's right to enjoy the undisturbed possession of his wallet; in asserting a right to possess in himself, E is assuming F's rights. This point may be further illustrated by reference to *Corcoran* v. *Anderton* (1980). A and B attacked a woman intending to take her bag. A got his hands on her bag and there was a struggle for its possession during which the bag fell to the ground. A and B then ran off empty handed. This to the layman might look like a case of *attempted* robbery because the youths failed to get what they were after but they were convicted of the full offence. Robbery is theft accomplished by force (*post*, p. 292) and the theft was complete when the handbag was appropriated, *i.e.* when A grabbed it and tried to take it from her—that conduct was an assumption by A of the owner's rights.

An appropriation, therefore, may be said to be something done in relation to the property that only the owner can properly do, *and* the doing of which shows that the accused is treating himself as owner. It follows on this view that if the owner authorises the accused to deal with the goods in a certain way, the accused cannot appropriate the goods by dealing with them in the *authorised* way. Suppose, for instance, that B authorised A to push B's car over a cliff because B had it in mind to perpetrate a fraud on the insurers. Whatever else A might be charged with, he could not be charged with stealing the car even if he knew of B's dishonest intent. In doing what he is authorised by B to do, A cannot be assuming any of B's rights as owner. The point is made by *Skipp* (1975), where the accused, posing as a genuine haulage contractor, was instructed to pick up three loads of oranges from different places in London and to deliver them to Leicester. All the time he was collecting the oranges he intended to abscond with them, thereby depriving the owner permanently of his property. The Court of Appeal, however, held that he did not appropriate the property until he did an act inconsistent with the owner's instructions even though the owner would not have let him take the oranges had he known of his intentions. Thus while he was on the designated route he had not appropriated the property; when he left the designated route, however, he appropriated the property for by that unauthorised act he was assuming the rights of the owner.

In line with *Skipp* is *Eddy* v. *Niman* (1981). A and B went into a supermarket with the intention of stealing goods and in pursuance of this plan they took goods from the shelves which they placed in the receptacle provided by the store. B then had a change of heart and left the store. It was held that he could not be convicted of theft because there was nothing that could be described as an appropriation; in doing what he was authorised to do, albeit with a dishonest intention, he had not yet assumed the rights of the owner. It would have been different, however, if A had put the goods, not in the receptacle provided, but in his pockets with a view to passing through the checkout without accounting for them; such an act would have shown that he was treating himself as owner of the goods (*McPherson* (1973)). It might be noted in passing that an appropriation may occur before a customer leaves the store. For practical reasons (such as to negative a possible defence of forgetfulness or mistake or accident) store detectives do not usually challenge the customer until he has left the store but the appropriation occurs not when he leaves the store but when he assumes the rights of the owner.

But more recently the courts have favoured another, and broader, view of appropriation. In *Monaghan* (1979) a checkout cashier was seen to place money given her by a customer for the purchase of goods in the till but without ringing up the purchase. When questioned she admitted that she was acting dishonestly and that it was her intention to take from the till an equivalent sum of money at a *later* stage. It was held that she had appropriated the money when she failed to ring it up and she was convicted of theft. It is difficult to reconcile this with the *Skipp* view of appropriation. In relation to the money she had done exactly as she was bidden by placing it in the till, so how could it be said that she had assumed the owner's rights to the money?

In line with *Monaghan* is *Anderton* v. *Wish* (1981). *Anderton* v. *Wish* concerned a very common supermarket fraud which involves switching the price-tags on goods; the customer switches (or covers) a high price-tag with a lower price-tag and then proceeds to buy the article at the checkout at the lower price. There is no difficulty whatsoever in dealing with this fraud if the customer is charged with obtaining, or attempting to obtain, the goods by deception contrary to section 15 of the Act because the cashier is deceived into selling the goods at less than their true value. In *Anderton* v. *Wish*, however, the customer was charged with stealing the article on which she had substituted a lower price-tag and it was held that she was rightly convicted of theft. The court said that she appropriated the article when she switched the labels because that was an act which could be lawfully done only by, or on the authority of, the owner. At first sight this may seem attractive reasoning. The customer knows perfectly well that he or she is not authorised to switch price-tags and still less that he or she is authorised to do so with a view to defrauding the owner. But section 3 does not say that any unauthorised act constitutes an appropriation; it says that assuming the owner's rights constitutes an appropriation. In *Anderton* v. *Wish* the consumer manifestly planned to defraud the owner when she switched the price-tags, but how could it be said that she had assumed the rights of an owner when, *after* the switch, she offered to buy those goods from the owner?

In *Morris* (1983), which also concerned the switching of price-tags, the Court of Appeal recognised that there were two schools of thought on appropriation. There was the *Skipp* school of thought which required some conduct inconsistent with the owner's rights, and the *Anderton* v. *Wish* school which required no more than taking possession without any requirement that the taking should be in any way antagonistic to the owner's rights. The court preferred the latter, and broader, view. It follows that a customer who takes goods from the shelves in a supermarket with the intention of depriving the owner of them, appropriates (and accordingly steals) the goods the instant he takes them from the shelves. Such subsequent conduct as switching price-tags or placing the goods in the customer's own bag or pocket is merely evidence of dishonesty for he has already stolen the goods when he removes them with dishonest intent.

On the *Morris* test it follows that Skipp stole the oranges when he took delivery of them and his later deviation from the authorised route was merely evidence of dishonesty. It also follows that in *Eddy*

v. *Niman* A ought to have been convicted of theft because he had taken the goods from the shelves with dishonest intent and it could make no difference (except as evidence of dishonesty) whether he placed the goods in the trolley provided or in his pocket. The fact that A changed his mind and left the store without the goods would also make no difference because it could not undo the theft that had already been committed.

The *Morris* test is, however, open to criticism on the ground that it appears to assume that the doing of an unauthorised act in relation to the goods necessarily constitutes an assumption of the owner's rights. No doubt the defendants in *Monaghan*, *Anderton* v. *Wish* and *Morris intended* dishonestly to deprive the owner of his property but section 3 does not say that it is an appropriation to *intend* to assume the owner's rights. An appropriation is effected, and theft is accomplished, only by an assumption of the owner's rights. It is peculiarly difficult to see how a customer, however dishonest he is in trying to get the goods at less that what he knows to be their true price, has assumed the owner's rights when his intention is to take those goods to the owner (or to the owner's agent at the checkout) and, in effect, say, "Please may I buy *your* goods."

Thus far it has been suggested that an appropriation requires some *conduct* on the accused's part. Certainly it is difficult to see how a pure omission could amount to an assumption of the user's rights. If, for example, A has mislaid his umbrella, B could hardly be said to have appropriated it because he knows where it is and fails to tell A—even if B hopes that A will fail to find it so that he, B, can make off with it later on. On the other hand section 3 goes on to say that there is an appropriation where X has come by the property (innocently or not) but without stealing it and has asumed a right to it " . . . by keeping it or dealing with it as owner." This is meant to deal with the sort of case where A "comes by" (A may have borrowed it, or found it or had it delivered to him by mistake, etc.), B's property and decides to keep it. A's mental resolution to keep it is probably not enough; the section says that A must keep it "as owner." Suppose then that A borrows B's lawn mower or bicycle or book for a week. At the end of the week A fails to return the goods and his intention is never to do so. Probably this will not make A a thief; but A will become a thief if, with the necessary intent, he removes the lawn mower to his new premises, or he continues to drive the bicycle, or he writes his name in the book.

Where however A receives the property in good faith from B for consideration, if it later turns out that B had no right to sell the property, no assumption of the rights of an owner by A over that property can amount to an appropriation for the purposes of a charge of theft (see s. 3 (2)). Thus if A buys a car from B in circumstances where A believes that B is the lawful owner of the car, then if he is later told that C is the rightful owner of the car and that B had stolen it, A's refusal to restore the car to C would not amount to theft. Strictly A has now appropriated C's car but it was felt that to make a thief of a person who has purchased goods in good faith would be too harsh a rule.

(2) Property

The definition of what can amount to property for the purposes of being stolen is to be found in section 4. The general position is covered by section 4 (1) which provides that "property" includes money and all other property, real or personal, including things in action and other intangible property. The reference to real property means that land is included in the definition of property, but subsection 2 specifically provides that with one or two exceptions land cannot be stolen (it can, however, be obtained by deception; see p. 282). Before we look at the special problem with land we ought to mention one or two points in relation to the general definition. The effect of subsection 1 is that virtually all tangible property with the exception of land is capable of being stolen. One or two difficulties may, however, arise:

(a) *Gas, water and electricity*

Gas and water are clearly within the definition of property in section 4 (1) and are thus capable of being stolen. Electricity, on the other hand, does not constitute property and cannot therefore be stolen. There is a separate offence to deal with the unlawful abstraction of electricity in section 13.

(b) *Intangible property*

Section 4 (1) makes it clear that choses in action and other intangible property are capable of being stolen. Choses in action are rights which can only be enforced by taking legal action. Thus if X owes Y £50, X can sue Y for the £50 and this right to sue is known as a chose in action. Other examples of choses in action are copyrights, trademarks; patents are not choses in action but they are clearly a form of intangible property. It is perhaps not immediately apparent how such things can be stolen, but if X purports to sell a copyright which belongs to Y, he will have stolen that copyright.

(c) *Intellectual property*

In *Oxford* v. *Moss* (1978) a student borrowed an examination paper and photographed the questions. He could not be charged with stealing the question paper since he intended to return it and the court held that he could not be charged with theft of the confidential information since this did not amount to property under section 4 (1). It would seem to follow that trade secrets are not property which is capable of being stolen.

(d) *Land, wild plants and wild creatures*

While property is widely defined in section 4(1), certain modifications to the generality of the definition are made by section 4(2)–(4) which provides—

> "(2) A person cannot steal land, or things forming part of land and severed from it by him or by his directions, except in the following cases, that is to say—
>
> (*a*) when he is a trustee or personal representative, or is authorised by power of attorney, or as liquidator of a company, or otherwise, to sell or dispose of land belonging to another, and he appropriates the land or anything forming part of it by dealing with it in breach of the confidence reposed in him; or
>
> (*b*) when he is not in possession of the land and appropriates anything forming part of the land by severing it or causing it to be severed, or after it has been severed; or
>
> (*c*) when, being in possession of the land under a tenancy, he appropriates the whole or part of any fixture or structure let to be used with the land.
>
> For purposes of this subsection "land" does not include incorporeal hereditaments; "tenancy" means a tenancy for years or any less period and includes an agreement for such a tenancy, but a person who after the end of a tenancy remains in possession as statutory tenant or otherwise is to be treated as having possession under the tenancy, and "let" shall be construed accordingly.
>
> (3) A person who picks mushrooms growing wild on any land, or who picks flowers, fruit or foliage from a plant growing wild on any land does not (although not in possession of the land) steal what he picks, unless he does it for reward or for sale or other commercial purpose.
>
> For purposes of this subsection "mushroom" includes any fungus, and "plant" includes any shrub or tree.
>
> (4) Wild creatures, tamed or untamed, shall be regarded as property; but a person cannot steal a wild creature not tamed or ordinarily kept in captivity, or the carcase of any such creature, unless either it has been reduced into possession by or on behalf

of another person and possession of it has not since been lost or abandoned, or another person is in course of reducing it into possession."

The general effect of this provision is that land, as such, can be stolen only in exceptional circumstances. Apparently it is not unknown for purchasers of building plots to move the boundary markers in order to enlarge their plots at the expense of neighbouring plots; this practice, though dishonest, does not constitute theft. Nor do people who pick mushrooms or wild growth become thieves unless they do it for gain; strictly they appropriate property of another but it was considered too harsh to make such conduct theft. The last exception, in effect, favours poaching; poachers cannot steal the wild animals that they take though they may commit other offences.

(3) Belonging to another

The prosecution must establish that at the time of the appropriation the property belonged to another. This seems an obvious requirement as theft is generally understood to be the taking of someone else's property. What then do we mean by the phrase "belonging to another"? Clearly it must include the case where the property is owned by the victim at the time when the accused takes it. But that alone would be too restricting. Suppose that X dishonestly appropriates a television set which A rents from B. Does X steal the set from A or from B? If we said that belonging to another meant only "owned by another" then the indictment would have to charge X with stealing the television from B. This might present few problems in our illustration, but there will be cases where the true owner would be hard to indentify. In any case a law of theft which in our example would allow X to defeat a charge of stealing from A on the ground that A was not the real owner would be open to ridicule. Suppose that it was B, the owner of the television set, who secretly took it back from A, intending both to resell the set and claim the cost of a new set from A. Should we not in such a case be able to charge B with stealing the set from A? It is for reasons such as these that the phrase "belonging to another" receives a much wider definition in section 5 of the Act.

Section 5 (1) provides "Property shall be regarded as belonging to any person having possession or control of it, or having in it any proprietary right or interest (not being an equitable interest arising only from an agreement to transfer or grant an interest)."

Thus property can be stolen from a person who owns, possesses or has control over it. In the example of the television set it can therefore be stolen from either A, who has possession of it under a rental agreement or from B who owns it. If A takes the set to C for repairs it could also be stolen from C while it was in his premises awaiting repairs. But then the question arises, "can one of the persons with a recognised interest in the property steal it from one of the others?" If A, the person renting the set, sold it and told B that it had been stolen, could A be charged with stealing it from B? If B, the owner, took it from A and claimed that A had lost it and was therefore under a contractual obligation to pay for it, could B be charged with stealing it from A even though B is the owner? The answer to both of these questions is clearly yes. In *Turner* (1971) the accused had left his car for repair with a garage. Later he returned after it had been repaired and took it from outside the garage intending not to pay the bill. Despite the fact that the car belonged to Turner it was held that the garage had sufficient control of it to come with the phrase "belonging to another," and so Turner's conviction for theft was upheld.

Does the victim need to be aware of the property? It is obvious that most people have property in their homes they have long forgotten that they possess.

In *Woodman* (1974) the X company were running down one of their factories and sold off a quantity of scrap metal to Y company. This gave Y company the right to enter the factory and remove the metal. Y company did, in fact remove most of the scrap metal but left some there as not being worth the cost of salvaging it. X company remained owners of the site and put up a barbed wire fence and notices to discourage trespassers. It became clear that X company was not aware that any scrap remained at the site. Some two years after X company's business had ceased at the factory, Woodman entered the site and took some of the scrap metal. He was charged with stealing the metal from X company. The trial judge took the view that there was no case to go to the jury on the basis that X company owned or possessed the property, but that there was a case of theft which could be left to the jury on the basis that X company controlled the property. The accused was convicted and appealed on the basis that X company could not be said to control the scrap metal since they were under the impression that it had all been removed by Y company. The Court of Appeal held that in the ordinary case if "it is once established that a particular person is in control of a site such as this, them prima facie he is in control of items on the site even though they were unaware of the existence of specific items." It might be that if the scrap metal had been placed there by a third party after the barbed wire had been erected then a different result could follow, but that was not the case here. In one sense the property was abandoned, but at least in relation to Woodman the X company can be said to be in control of it.

Subsections 3 and 4 of section 5 provide for two further situations in which the phrase "belonging to another" is given an extended meaning in order to widen the scope of the offence in section 1. It should be remembered that in both cases the provisions of section 5 enable the accused to be prosecuted for the offence of theft under section 1; they do not create separate offences of theft; the tendency to speak of charging the accused under section 5(4) is therefore inaccurate.

Section 5 (3) provides "Where a person receives property from or on account of another, and is under an obligation to the other to retain and deal with that property or its proceeds in a particular way, the property or proceeds shall be regarded (as against him) as belonging to the other."

The subsection and the problem it is supposed to solve are probably best explained by looking at the facts of one of the leading cases: *Hall* (1973). The accused ran a travel agency and in the course of business had taken various sums of money from customers in return for which he promised to book them on flights to America. Later he was forced to tell these customers that his business was in trouble, that he had not booked the flights and that there was no money with which he could refund their deposits. He was charged with stealing the money from the customers. Now it was not alleged that he had all along intended to default on his obligation towards these customers, otherwise he could have been charged with obtaining their money by deception (contrary to Theft Act 1968, s. 15 see below). The appropriation relied on was the misuse of the money and it is here that the difficulty arises. The appropriation must be of money *belonging to another.* Thus at this point we must consider the civil law. When a customer hands over his money to a travel agent it is quite clear that the agent becomes owner of the property and can pass a good title to it on to a third person. Thus since Hall became owner of the money, when he later misused it he was appropriating money which belonged to himself. Section 5 (3) provides that even where the accused has become owner of the property before it is appropriated he can none the less be regarded as appropriating someone else's property if, but only if, he is expected to deal with that property in a particular way. At first it may appear that this will cover the travel agent, but, unfortunately, it is not as simple as that. When a customer hands over his deposit to the agent he cannot expect that the agent will put the money in a marked envelope and use it solely to book that customer's flight. If the customer thought for a moment, he would realise that all the receipts from all customers go into the business account and money is drawn from that account as needed to make bookings. The customer's only right is that he can expect that a booking will be made or an equivalent amount of money will be returned. Thus the Court of Appeal held that Hall was not covered by the provisions of section 5 (3). So what sort of situation would be covered by section 5 (3)? It applies only where ownership in the property has been transferred to the accused and where he must use that very property in a particular way. The property will nearly always be money, so we are looking for a situation in which the accused was expected to use *that* money for a particular purpose. Thus if the accused is painting A's house and asks A for £5 to buy more paint, it is likely that the court will hold that he was expected to use that £5 note to buy the paint. Similarly the treasurer of a social club might be held to receive money which he is to put in a special fund for the club purposes only. If this is the case, any appropriation of that money will be theft.

The section says "that property or its proceeds"; the inclusion of the words "or its proceeds" is meant to cover a situation where the property is converted into equally identifiable property which is to be used in a particular way. Thus if X is sent by his employer to change a £100 note at the bank, the cash he receives from the bank will be caught by section 5 (3), and can be stolen by the employee.

Whether or not an obligation arises is a matter of law for the judge since the obligation referred to is a *legal* obligation. While it is for the jury to find the facts, it is for the judge to rule on which facts give rise to an obligation.

Section 5 (4). This is possibly one of the most complex provisions of the entire Act yet arguably one of the least needed. It is supposed to cover the situation in which due to a mistake by the victim "ownership in the property passes to the rogue before any act of appropriation" so that when the appropriation occurs he is appropriating his own property. The subsection provides:

> "Where a person gets property by another's mistake, and is under an obligation to make restoration (in whole or in part) of the property or its proceeds or of the value thereof, then to the extent of that obligation the property or proceeds shall be regarded (as against him) as belonging to the person entitled to restoration, and an intention not to make restoration shall be regarded accordingly as an intention to deprive that person of the property or proceeds."

It might be easiest to understand the workings of the subsection if we first consider the case of *Moynes* v. *Coopper* (1956) which it was designed to overrule. In that case the accused was given an advance on his wages during the course of a week. At the end of the week the wages clerk paid him his full salary totally unaware that he ought to have made a deduction for the amount already advanced. When Moynes later discovered the error he decided to keep all the money.

At this point it is necessary to consider the *civil* law. No one can doubt but that Moynes was acting in a thoroughly dishonest way but, as we have just seen, dishonesty is not enough. So far as the civil law is concerned the fact that the person delivering property makes a mistake does not necessarily prevent ownership from passing and, of course, if ownership passes the recipient cannot steal the property because it is his own property. Generally, a mistake will prevent ownership from passing only where the deliveror is mistaken as to the identity of the recipient or the identity of the property. The clerk in *Moynes* v. *Coopper* was mistaken in neither of these senses: he intended to pay to Moynes the exact amount he in fact paid.

Prima facie, therefore, Moynes was merely a dishonest debtor—he owed his employers the amount of money (some seven pounds) which had been overpaid—but the law stops short of making thieves out of dishonest debtors. Moynes, however, was not quite like other dishonest debtors. He did not merely owe seven pounds to his employers: he was under a quasi-contractual obligation to restore either the actual seven pounds or its *proceeds or its value*. Section 5 (4) is there to deal with this sort of case. It is not there to deal with the case where A is under an obligation to pay money to B (because that would make thieves of all dishonest debtors) but only where A is under an obligation to restore to B the *very* property which he received from B or the proceeds or value of *that* property. Whether A is under such an obligation can be a very complicated question but the complications arise in the civil law not the criminal law. For our purposes it is enough to note that section 5 (4) will be necessary in very few situations, primarily because in most cases the mistake will have been caused by the defendant's fraud and hence the more appropriate charge will be obtaining property by deception.

2. Mens Rea

The Act provides that the prosecution must prove that the appropriation of property belonging to another was dishonest and that at the time of the appropriation the accused had the intention of permanently depriving the other of the property. There is no requirement that the accused did it for personal gain; it would be theft if the accused smashed the victim's valuable Ming vase (s. 1 (2)).

(1) Dishonesty

Dishonesty is peculiarly difficult to define. Dishonest conduct is conduct which is regarded by people generally as dishonest. In most cases, of course, there is general agreement as to what is viewed as honest or dishonest. No one doubts but that it is dishonest to take goods from a store without paying for them, or to surreptitiously remove books from a library, or to get goods from a machine by using a washer instead of coinage, and so on. But cases can arise, and arise not infrequently, where views may differ as to whether particular conduct is dishonest.

The Theft Act does not attempt a comprehensive definition of dishonesty. Section 2 provides only a partial definition and details three cases where a person's conduct is not to be regarded as dishonest. Before these are examined, it will be noted that in addition it is provided by section 2(2) that a person's appropriation of property *may* be dishonest notwithstanding an intention to pay for it, and by section 1(1) that it is immaterial that the appropriation is not made with a view to gain. Suppose A wants to purchase a painting from B which B refuses to sell; A may be convicted of theft if he takes the picture though he leaves in its place money which more than represents its value. Alternatively A may wish merely to deprive B of the painting without intending to enjoy it himself or to sell it for his own profit; A may be convicted of theft because he intends the painting to be lost to B though he has no view to a gain for himself.

Section 2(1) states that an appropriation is not to be regarded as dishonest in three cases: (i) where he believes that he has in law the right to deprive the other of it on behalf of himself or another; (ii) where he appropriates the property in the belief that he would have the owner's consent; and (iii) where he appropriates the property in the belief that the owner cannot be traced by taking reasonable steps.

(a) *Belief in legal right*

The only belief that is relevant here is a belief in *legal* right. That A feels that he has a moral claim to the property, or that he is in some vague way justified in taking it, is not relevant under this head though it may be otherwise relevant to the issue of dishonesty. If A believes he has a *legal* right, his conduct cannot be accounted dishonest though his claim is entirely unreasonable or even though the claim is one which the law does not recognise. An honest belief in legal right, however arrived at, is inconsistent with dishonesty (see *Robinson* (1977) *post*, p. 292).

(b) *Belief in consent*

If A honestly believes that B, the owner, would have consented to his appropriation, his conduct cannot be regarded as dishonest. That A's belief is unreasonably arrived at is irrelevant except to the extent that it may cast doubt on the honesty of his belief.

(c) *Belief that owner cannot be traced*

This provision essentially deals with property which is found by A; he is not to be treated as a thief if he appropriates that property in the belief that the owner cannot be traced by taking reasonable steps. If, for example, A finds a £1 note in the street it could only be exceptionally that he would believe that the owner can be traced so that in appropriating it he would not be guilty of theft. If, however, A finds in the same street Goya's portrait of the Duke of Wellington, he is unlikely to believe that the owner cannot be traced by taking reasonable steps. Nevertheless, if A is a Philistine who regards the painting as worthless so that it does not occur to him to take steps to trace the owner, he cannot be convicted of theft. If it does occur to A that the owner might be traced, he may be convicted of theft if he fails to take *reasonable* steps. He is not required to take every conceivable step; no doubt the most usual reasonable step would be to hand the property to the police on the assumption that the owner, if he cares about his loss, will have reported it to them.

(d) *Dishonesty in other cases*

The partial definition does not of course provide for all cases and the question arises as to how dishonesty is to be defined in circumstances not falling within the partial definition. The courts have considered the matter in a number of cases (*Feely* (1973); *Boggeln* v. *Williams* (1978); *Landy* (1981); *McIvor* (1982)) and in *Ghosh* (1982) the Court of Appeal, recognising that the law was in a complicated state, attempted a restatement.

Whether conduct is to be regarded as dishonest is a matter for the jury to determine. The judge should, however, direct the jury that A acts dishonestly if (a) his conduct would be regarded as dishonest by the ordinary standards of reasonable people; and (b) A realises that his conduct is so regarded. If (a) and (b) are satisfied then (c) A's conduct is dishonest however he might regard his conduct; A cannot set up a personal standard which he knows to be at variance with the general standard.

As to (a) the issue is one for the jury who have only their own knowledge and experience to guide them. No doubt on any given set of facts most juries would reach the same decision, but on certain facts juries may reach different conclusions. Take cases where A "borrows" money from B without permission. A may take 75p from B's, his employer's, till to pay a taxi driver because he has no small change; C may take £5 from B's till to lay a wager on a horse (*Feely* (1973)); D may take £200 from B's safe to pay a deposit on his holiday (*McIvor* (1982)). All intend to pay the money at a later stage but, of course, the money which they take is not "borrowed" but is appropriated since B is deprived permanently of the notes and coins taken.

Would any or all of these takings be regarded as dishonest by the generality of reasonable people? No doubt the jury would wish to consider such factors as whether B had expressly forbidden "borrowing", the extent to which A, C and D had an ability to repay, whether the borrowing was done openly or secretly and so on. It seems difficult to lay down a general principle for such cases (but see Elliott [1982] Crim.L.R. 395) so it may be that different juries would reach different conclusions.

As to (b) the jury is concerned to find whether the defendant is generally regarded as dishonest. It is generally regarded as dishonest to travel on buses with intent to avoid paying the fare but, as the court pointed out in *Ghosh*, a person who came from a country where public transport was free, would not act dishonestly if he boarded a bus here believing that public transport here was similarly free.

If, then, a modern Robin Hood thought it was right for him to rob the rich in order to feed the poor, he would be acting dishonestly if he realised, as is the fact, that people generally regard such a taking as dishonest. But if he is out of touch with community standards and genuinely thinks that people generally do not regard such conduct as dishonest, then his conduct cannot, it seems, be accounted dishonest. Cases where the defendant is mistaken about the prevailing standards of dishonesty will be exceptional but they may occasionally happen.

(2) With intention permanently to deprive

During the period of debate before the Theft Act 1968 was enacted, it was suggested that the prosecution should no longer have to prove that the accused intended permanently to deprive the other of his property. This would have had the effect of making dishonest borrowing theft. It was finally decided that the requirement should be retained and that cases of unlawful borrowing were better dealt with by the civil law. (But sections 11 and 12 penalise some instances of unlawful borrowing, for example motor vehicles.)

Thus the prosecution must prove that at the time of the appropriation the accused intended permanently to deprive the owner of the property. This ordinarily presents no problems because when A takes money from B's pocket or when C takes a book from D's shop the prosecution is usually not hard pressed to prove that A and C intended to deprive permanently. But *evidential* difficulties can occur. Where C takes the book from the university library, his claim that he intended to return the book at the end of term may be plausible and the prosecution may in such a case have difficulty in proving the intent. It has been known even for law students to take books from the law library without signing for them and then to leave them at the end of term outside the library door. This is a deplorable practice but it is not theft for it is obvious that the miscreant does not intend the university to lose the books permanently. What, then, if the miscreant left the books in the students' union or on the London underground? Given that the books were stamped as the property of the university of X, the probability is that they would be returned to the university in the first case, though this is much less likely in the second. But in either case the test of C's liability is the same: did he *intend* to permanently deprive the university of its books? If C believes that by leaving the books where he does they will be returned to the university he cannot be said to intend permanent deprivation even if he leaves them in a place which makes it highly unlikely that they will ever be returned.

In the normal run of case, then, the intent permanently to deprive raises only evidential problems. But in exceptional cases it can raise legal problems. Such cases tend to be those where A takes property of B's which, in a sense, he returns to B but only after A has treated himself as owner of that property. It is for these exceptional cases that section 6 is there to provide:

> "A person appropriating property belonging to another without meaning the other permanently to lose the thing itself is nevertheless to be regarded as having the intention of permanently depriving the other of it if his intention is to treat the thing as his own to dispose of regardless of the other's rights; and a borrowing or lending of it may amount to so treating it if, but only if, the borrowing or lending is for a period and in circumstances making it equivalent to an outright taking or disposal."

Consider the following examples:

(1) A is a shopkeeper who stores empty bottles, on which he has paid the refund, in his yard. B enters the yard, takes some bottles and then enters A's shop where he gets a refund on the bottles. Such a case as this is perhaps best treated as obtaining by deception, but

B may alternatively be convicted of stealing the bottles. In a sense he intends that A should get his bottles back but only after A has paid for them. B is clearly treating the bottles as his own to dispose of regardless of A's rights; A can get his own bottles back only by paying for them.

(2) D, a first year medical student, takes a copy of Gray's *Anatomy* from the Library intending to return it on completion of his course in five years time. Can it be said that D has treated the book as his own to dispose of regardless of the other's rights? According to the second part of section 6(1) a borrowing can only be so treated if it is equivalent to an outright taking. Five years is a long time, so can it be said that D's "borrowing . . . was for a period and in circumstances which made it equivalent to an outright taking or disposal?" The difficulty with this view is that it could leave the courts with an impossible task in determining what period of borrowing would be so equivalent. The section says it must be *equivalent* to an outright taking. Borrowing for a fixed term falls short of being so equivalent. Thus the courts have held it to be a misdirection for a judge to direct a jury that X may be convicted of stealing Y's goods where X intends to keep those goods indefinitely (*Warner* (1970)). A taking or borrowing is equivalent to an outright taking only where all the value of the property is consumed. So if X takes Y's season ticket to a football ground, intending to use it for *all* the games for which it is valid and then return the ticket to Y, X has stolen the ticket, for the borrowing is now equivalent to an outright taking.

(3) H hires a car from J for a week. K takes the car, uses it for a week and then returns it to J. No doubt K would be charged under section 12 (taking a conveyance) but he may also be guilty of theft. He has not stolen the car from J but so far as H is concerned he has deprived H of the whole of his interest.

(4) A takes B's silver goblets and pawns them. He keeps the money he receives from the pawnshop intending to redeem it later. This is covered by section 6 (2) which gives a further extended meaning to the phrase "with the intention permanently to deprive."

> "If any person in possession of another's property (whether lawfully or not) parts with that property under a condition he may not be able to perform he may be regarded as treating the property to dispose of regardless of the other's rights."

(3) Conditional intention

A problem which has caused much controversy in recent years has been that of so-called conditional intent. In a sense all intention may be said to be conditional. A may set out with the firm intention of stealing B's painting but his intention will be subject to certain conditions such as that he will be able to effect an entry to the place where the painting is kept or that B will not be guarding the painting. But it would be quite unrealistic to say that if A leaves empty handed because he cannot effect an entry or because B was on guard that he therefore did not intend to steal the painting.

But what if the painting is not in the building at all because B has moved it to another place? Until recently this sort of case caused a problem because of a House of Lords ruling (in *Haughton* v. *Smith* (1975)) that a person could not be convicted of attempting to commit a crime which was physically impossible of achievement. This ruling has been reversed by the Criminal Attempts Act 1981 (*ante*, p. 212) and now a person may be convicted of an attempt even though, in the circumstances, he could not have effected the complete crime. So if A is found in the room where the painting used to hang he may be convicted of attempting to steal it; moreover in entering the building with intent to steal it he commits the crime of burglary.

A somewhat similar problem arose where A has not yet made up his mind whether and what to steal. Take the case of the rogue, A, whose practice it is to search other people's cars to see whether there is anything that takes his fancy. In B's car he finds nothing at all; in C's car he notices that there is a copy of the bible but he is not interested in that; in D's car he finds a handbag but having ascertained that the contents (lipstick, handkerchief, nail file) are of no value to him he returns the handbag to its place. In none of these cases can A be convicted of theft since he has stolen nothing. Now that the rule in *Haughton* v. *Smith* has been changed by statute, A may be convicted even though it was impossible for him to commit the completed crime (theft) owing to the fact that there was nothing he was remotely interested in stealing. But there is another matter to consider. A cannot be charged with stealing nothing, nor with attempting to steal nothing. He must be charged with attempting to steal some property belonging to another. Nor can he be properly charged with attempting to steal property which he just does not intend to steal. A cannot be charged with attempting to steal C's bible or the lipstick from D's handbag because his conduct proves that he had no intent to steal these.

But when A saw the handbag in D's car he no doubt hoped that it would contain money and, had it done so, it is certain that he would have taken it. If so, A can be charged with and convicted of attempting to steal money from D. In the other two cases it may be that A had no expectation of finding money, nor did he find anything else that took his fancy. But if A had found something that had taken his fancy he would certainly have taken it, and in such a case it is proper to charge him with attempting to steal "property belonging to" B or C without specifying any particular property (*Bayley* v. *Easterbrook* (1980)).

II. *OFFENCES INVOLVING DECEPTION*

So far we have been considering the offence of theft which is concerned largely with those situations in which the accused has taken property belonging to another. In this section we shall be concerned with those situations where the accused has, by fraud, induced the victim to act in a way he would not, but for the fraud, have acted. Under the Theft Act 1968 there are two basic offences of deception. Under section 15 it is an offence to obtain property by deception and under section 16 it is an offence to obtain a pecuniary advantage by deception. Common to both offences is the need to establish that the property or the pecuniary advantage was obtained as a result of the deception practised by the accused. The need for two sections arises from the fact that Parliament saw it necessary to distinguish between those situations in which the accused obtained property and those in which he obtained a financial advantage but nothing tangible. For example, if you go into a car rental agency and by showing false driving licence and insurance you induce him to rent you a car for the day, you will have obtained possession of the car by deception and this is clearly the obtaining of property. If, however, when it comes to paying for the car which the garage has already let you take away you trick the owner in giving you time to pay then you have not obtained any property by deception, you have gained a financial advantage—namely more time to pay. Under the Theft Act 1968 "pecuniary advantage" was defined to mean three things under section 16 (2) (*a*) (*b*) and (*c*). Unfortunately section 16 (2) (*a*) gave rise to so many difficulties that it was thought better to repeal it and replace it with three new offences to be found in the Theft Act 1978. Under the new Theft Act it is an offence to obtain services by deception, to evade liability by deception and to make off without paying. The resulting position is that there are now four offences of deception and these are the dishonest obtaining by deception of:

(i) property (Theft Act 1968, s. 15);
(ii) pecuniary advantage (the unrepealed parts of section 16 of the Theft Act 1968—*viz.* 16 (2) (*b*) and (*c*) which deal with defined cases and which have as yet given rise to few problems);
(iii) services (the Theft Act 1978, s. 1);
(iv) evasion of liability (the Theft Act 1978, s. 2).

Finally there is the offence of dishonestly making off without paying (the Theft Act 1978, s. 3—but this offence does not require any deception). In this section we shall first consider the elements common to the deception offences and then examine the four things which have to be obtained. We shall then consider the offence of making off.

1. Elements Common to Deception Offences

There are three basic elements which the prosecution must prove in all four crimes, namely (i) deception; (ii) that the deception was instrumental in the obtaining of, *e.g.* the property; and (iii) dishonesty.

(1) What constitutes deception for the purposes of the Theft Acts?

In the majority of cases it will be quite clear that the accused has deceived the victim into handing over some property or into performing some task and there will be no problem over the definition of the word "deception": the accused will have made a statement of fact which he well knows to be false. Thus if A, a well-known art dealer, tells B, a customer, that the picture he is interested in is a genuine Constable, when he knows full well that it is a reprint, then this will be a deception within the meaning of the Acts. If this is so, then what about the television commercial which says that X soap powder washes whiter than any other brand? Are we saying that if A buys this brand because of the advert and discovers that it washes no whiter than any other brand, that the advertisers obtained his money by deception? If not, what is the difference between this case and the art dealer? There are two points to be made here. In the first place, we should note that section 15 (4) says that "deception" means any deception (whether deliberate or reckless) by word or conduct as to fact or law. . . . " This means that in relation to commercials the deception must involve a false statement as to an issue of fact. It could be argued that television commercials are statements of opinion and not of fact. If A therefore falsely tells B that he believes one car to be better than another this is a statement of opinion and not of fact and is not within the definition of deception. However, many statements of opinion are simply statements of fact expressed as opinion. For example, in the case where A tells B that he thinks that one car is a better buy than another he may have no factual basis for saying this. On the other hand, he may be aware of facts which make one car better than the other; for example, he may be aware that the second car's engine will need replacing in about a thousand miles. If, knowing this, he deliberately tells B that he thinks that the car with the faulty engine is a better car and B buys on the strength of that opinion, then he should be held to have deceived B. To the purchaser of a car from a salesman, the statement "This car is a better buy than the other one" implies to the buyer that the seller is saying that he is not aware of any facts which would prove otherwise.

The second point to note concerning commercials is that in today's world there is the general assumption that most Television watchers are immune to sales pressures through adverts and there is the general view that no one actually believes the inflated claims of the advertisers. However, this does not mean to say that in appropriate circumstances commercials could not be the basis of a deception charge. Much greater care can rightly be expected where the adverts are directed at children. Equally, if it can be shown that the advert makes a false statement of fact, such as "X Co. ball point pens last longer than Y Co. ball point pens," then if it can be shown that viewers were induced to buy the product for this reason, there is no reason why a deception charge should not be made. (See *Bryan* (1857)).

(a) *Misrepresentation of law*

It is quite clear from the definition of deception in section 15 (4) that a deliberate or reckless misrepresentation of law can amount to a deception for the purposes of these offences. Thus if a solicitor deliberately misrepresented the effect a certain clause in a will would have, so that he became a beneficiary under the will, he would, on receipt of the legacy, have obtained property by deception.

(b) *Statement of intention*

X offers to paint Y's house for £100 cash in advance. He intends all along to abscond with the money without painting the house. This is a statement of intention of what he will do in the future if Y gives him £100, and not a statement of fact. Under the pre-1968 law this could not amount to a deception, but section 15 (4) concludes that deception includes "a deception as to the present intentions of the person using the deception or any other person." Thus in our example X's present intentions are to take the money and leave and thus the statement is capable of amounting to a deception within the Act.

(c) *Does there need to be words; will conduct suffice?*

We have already seen above in the definition of deception under section 15 (4) that conduct can amount to a deception. This will be conduct which the accused knows or believes will cause another to draw certain conclusions. Thus in *D.P.P.* v. *Ray* (1974) the House of Lords held in a case where Ray left a restaurant without paying for a meal he had just eaten, that there was evidence which could support a finding that by staying in his seat after forming the intention not to pay, Ray had caused the waitress to leave the room, enabling Ray to walk out. Similarly, if you were to drive into a self-service station intending not to pay when you had filled up your tank, then you would be inducing in the attendants, by your conduct, a belief that you would be paying when you had got your petrol. When you sit down in the hairdresser's chair you are impliedly telling him that you will be paying for the haircut.

What of the accused who tenders a cheque or cheque card in payment? Let us consider the straightforward unaccompanied cheque first. Following the decision in *M.P.C.* v. *Charles* (1977) it would appear that, in the absence of any statement to the contrary, a person who tenders a cheque is impliedly stating that to the best of his knowledge, the cheque will be met when it is presented to the bank. This is not without its difficulties, since you are really saying that your bank manager will authorise payment of the cheque when he sees it. As we have already said, the deception must be as to a question of fact or present intentions and this is a statement concerning how you believe someone else will act in the future. Nevertheless, it does represent a statement of the presenter's present beliefs. He is saying that at that precise moment he has no reason to think that the cheque will not be met. Thus, for example, if he knows that he no longer has an account at that bank or that the manager has specifically told him that all future cheques presented will be dishonoured, it is suggested that this will amount to a deception within the meaning of the Act.

We shall see that cheque cards and credit cards present special difficulties owing to the way in which they operate (see *post*, p. 278). It is suggested, however, that the presenter of such a card is stating that he has the authority to use it.

(d) *Can there be a case of deception by silence?*

In many cases of sales the seller is aware that the buyer labours under a misapprehension as to the qualities of the goods he is about to purchase. Is the seller therefore guilty of obtaining property by deception if he fails to correct the buyer's misapprehension? There exists at civil law, the motto *caveat emptor*, which translated means, "let the buyer beware"; in other words, he must take the risks. It would be odd if the criminal law were to punish the seller for simply following a civil law maxim. However, the seller must do nothing to actively promote the mistake. If the customer were to say "I am going to use this for outside work" and the shopkeeper knew it was extremely unsuitable for that purpose, his silence could be taken as an implied statement that the product was suitable for outside work. It is suggested that this should amount to a deception within the Act. Similarly, if X warrants that the car he is selling Y is roadworthy but discovers before Y pays him the money that there is a serious defect in the car which makes it extremely unsafe, X would be guilty of obtaining the money by deception if he failed to draw this to the attention of Y before he received the money.

(e) *Can you deceive a machine?*

The simple answer to this quetion is: not for the purposes of these four offences. The deception must cause a human being to act in a way he would not have done but for the deception. Thus, if you insert a valueless metal disc into a cigarette machine for the purpose of getting cigarettes out for nothing, then you have stolen the cigarettes just as much as if you had forced the machine open with a crowbar, but you have not obtained them by deception. However, if the machine is used to deceive a human being, there may be a deception. For example, if X takes the afternoon off work and alters the machine which prints his time of leaving so that his record card shows that he left at the proper time, when he gets paid his full amount at the end of the week it will be because he had used the machine to deceive his employers. Thus he will be guilty of obtaining property from his employers by deception.

(2) The causal link

It is not sufficient for the prosecution to prove that the accused practised a deception on the victim and that he then obtained an item of property from the victim. They must prove that the deception was the reason why the accused obtained the property. In other words there must be a causal link between the deception and the obtaining of the property. A few illustrations will help to make this clearer.

(a) A offers to sell B his copy of *Smith and Hogan's Criminal Law*. He tells B that it is the current edition when he knows full well that there has just been a new edition and that B will need the new edition for his classes. The jury should only convict A of obtaining the property (*i.e.* the sale price) by deception if they are satisfied beyond reasonable doubt that B would not have bought the book but for the deception. If, on the other hand, they find that B knew the book was out of date but that he had some reason for still wanting to buy it, then despite A's belief that he has duped B, his attempt to deceive B did not cause B to buy the book and so the purchase price was not obtained by A's lies. In *Laverty* (1970) the accused sold B a stolen car on which he had changed the number plates. The prosecution alleged that P was induced to buy the car because of the accused's representation by his conduct that this was the original car with those number plates. However, the Court of Appeal held that P bought the car because he thought that the accused was authorised to sell it and that there was no evidence to prove that B would have been in any way influenced by the knowledge of the change of number plates.

(b) C drives into a petrol station. He intends to fill up with petrol and then drive off without paying. If the jury are satisfied that his representations caused the petrol station attendants to believe that C intended to pay and thus allowed him to fill his car then clearly C has obtained the petrol by deception.

(c) D writes begging letter to E saying that she is the impoverished widow of a sailor who was drowned at sea. E knows whom the letter is from and that it is an attempt to trick him. Nevertheless E sends D the money in an attempt to trap D. Care is needed here. D has told E lies and E has sent D some money, *but* it was not D's deception which caused the money to be sent because E was aware it was a trick (*Hensler* (1870)). That was a relatively easy case in which to see the absence of causal link between the deception and the obtaining, but it is not always so simple. Let us consider a case in which A and B who are travelling on a train from London to Leeds, go to the buffet car for a snack. In the buffet car a bystander tells them that he suspects that the attendant is selling his own sandwiches and keeping the money. A says that he will only buy a sandwich if it is a British Rail sandwich, for which the money will have to go in the till. B, on the other hand, says that he could not care less who made the sandwich as long as it is fresh. They ask the attendant whose sandwiches are on sale and he falsely tells them that they are British Rail sandwiches. Both are deceived by the attendant, but the deception is material only to A since B would have bought the sandwiches even if the attendant had told them that he had made the sandwiches himself. The attendant obtains property only from A by deception.

A similar situation may arise where credit or cheque cards are used. You will know that one common feature of these cards is that a shopkeeper who sells goods to a person using one of these cards is guaranteed payment provided that he has fulfilled the regulations relating to them. In the case of credit cards these regulations require that the shopkeeper checks the signatures, checks that the card number is not on a stop-list, and telephones the company if the money involved is over a certain amount. In the case of cheque guarantee cards the seller must ensure that the signatures are in order. In both cases he should not actually be aware that the customer is no longer authorised to use the card. Where a person uses such a card he is impliedly representing that he is authorised to use the card. Thus if the shopkeeper is induced by a false representation that the card holder is authorised to use the card to sell the goods, the holder has obtained the goods by deception. Before the introduction of such cards many shopkeepers were reluctant to accept cheques or grant credit. One purpose of the cards is to remove his fears that he will not be paid for the goods. As long as he is not actually aware that the authority to use the card has been withdrawn by the bank or credit card company, he will be paid. It is no longer necessary for him to ask embarrassing questions to ensure the customer's bona fides. He is, in theory, allowed to be like B on the train; he need not care whether the customer is authorised to use the card, so long as he does not actually know that the authority has been withdrawn. So when he accepts a cheque from X backed by a cheque guarantee card does he do so because of X's implied assertion that he is authorised to use the card, or because he knows that he will be paid whether or not X is in fact authorised to use the card? If the prosecution cannot prove that he was influenced by the implied assertion of authority to use the card there is no causal link between X's deception and the obtaining of the property.

There have been two recent cases on this issue. In *Charles* (1977) the House of Lords was concerned with cheque cards and in *Lambie* (1982) with a credit card. In both cases the accuseds had pretended to be authorised users of the cards, when they both knew that this was not the case. In both cases the evidence that there was any causal link between the deception and the obtaining was extremely weak. In *Charles* the House upheld a conviction of obtaining (a pecuniary advantage) by deception, but in *Lambie* the Court of Appeal found a distinction between cheque cards and credit cards (based on the differences in the way the each secure payment for the shopkeeper) and held that this enabled them to distinguish *Charles* and hold *Lambie* not guilty because there was no evidence that the shopkeeper had been influenced by the implied representation that the accused was authorised to use the card. Suffice it to say that the House of Lords, in *Lambie*, held that there was no relevant distinction to be drawn between cheque cards and credit cards. The question then remained of whether Lambie had obtained a pecuniary advantage by holding herself out as an authorised credit card user. The House took the view that had the shop assistant been asked whether, if she had known that Lambie was acting dishonestly and had no authority to use the card, she would have completed the transaction, she would obviously have answered "No." The House found this answer irresistible. But it is not at all clear from the reports that this answer was irresistible. The effect of this decision appears to be that the Courts will fictitiously imply that all those who permit their customers to use credit and cheque cards do so motivated by a belief that their customers are authorised to use the cards.

(d) X buys a book from Y and hands Y a cheque in payment. The following day X discovers that the cheque will not be met by the bank, but he does not inform Y. There is no obtaining of a book by deception since no deception was practised before the book was obtained. If however X did not take possession of the book until after he has discovered that the cheque will not be met then his silence would amount to a deception in that he would be impliedly representing that there is no reason to think that Y will not get his money and this would cause Y to hand over the book.

(e) X sells Y a car and makes several representations about its qualities. All of the representations are true except for the one in which X tells Y that the car has never been involved in a serious accident. Could X defend himself against a charge of obtaining property by deception on the basis that Y bought the car acting on representations most of which were true? This is a question of fact for the jury. If they are satisfied that Y would not have bought the car had he known about the serious accident then the charge is made out.

(f) X drives into a petrol station intending to pay. When he has filled the tank he discovers that he has left all his money at home. He therefore simply drives off without paying. Even if you could find any form of deception here it would be at a time when the ownership in the petrol had already passed to X (it passes to him when he puts it in the tank) and so it would be impossible to say that he obtained the property by deception. Nor is it theft because the property in the petrol has already passed to him before he dishonestly appropriates it. This fraud is now dealt with by the Theft Act 1978, s. 3 (*post*, p. 289.)

(3) Dishonesty

All deception offences require dishonesty. The partial definition of dishonesty which is provided in section 2(1) for the purposes of theft is not made applicable to the deception offences. Obviously this partial definition is for the most part inapt for deception offences but otherwise the concept of dishonesty is the same for the deception offences as it is for theft. So a person would not commit a deception offence if he used a deception with a view to obtaining something to which he believed he was legally entitled. But just as a person's conduct may be accounted dishonest for the purposes of theft notwithstanding an intention to pay for the property, so too a person may dishonestly obtain though he gives full value for what he obtains. If, for example, A sells Christmas cards by pretending that the profits will go to charity, he may be convicted of obtaining by deception though his cards are fair value for the price charged (see *Potger* (1970)).

The foregoing constitute the common elements in deception offences. Their differences lie in the nature of what is obtained. In order to constitute a deception offence it must be proved that as a result of the deception the accused obtained:

(1) property (Theft Act 1968, s. 15); or
(2) a pecuniary advantage (Theft Act 1968, s. 16); or
(3) services from another (Theft Act 1978, s. 1); or
(4) the evasion of liability (Theft Act 1978, s. 2).

2. Obtaining Property by Deception

The most common of the deception offences is that under section 15 of deception by dishonestly obtaining property belonging to another with the intention of permanently depriving the other of it.

(1) Property

Property for the purpose of section 15 is as defined by section 4(1), that is *without* the exceptions which apply in the case of theft by virtue of sections 4(2)–(4). This means, for example, that while wild mushrooms cannot usually be stolen, they may be obtained by deception. For practical purposes, however, the important point to note is that land, which in general cannot be stolen, may be obtained by deception.

Property is obtained for this purpose when A obtains ownership, possession or control of B's property with the relevant intent. Thus if A by deception causes B to lend him property (for example, he procures the hire of a television receiver) A is guilty of this offence *if* he intends to deprive B permanently of it. Merely to obtain a loan by deception is not an offence under this section (though it will usually be an offence under section 1 of the 1978 Act) if A intends to return the goods at the end of the period of loan or otherwise has no intention of permanently depriving the owner of it.

(2) Mens rea

Apart from (i) dishonesty which has been discussed above, it must also be proved that (ii) the deception was deliberate or reckless; and (iii) that there was an intention permanently to deprive.

As to (ii) there must be a representation which is in fact untrue which the maker knows to be untrue or which he makes not caring whether it be true or false. This requirement is really an essential adjunct of the requirement for dishonesty. It follows that D does not commit the offence where he is merely negligent for no amount of negligence can make an honest man a dishonest man. It would appear clearly to follow that the objective test of recklessness endorsed in *Caldwell* (*ante*, p. 147) can have no place in this context.

(3) Is there an overlap between the offences of theft and obtaining property by deception?

It should be noted at the outset that there is no reason why there should not be an overlap between these offences. The fact that in particular circumstances the defendant might be convicted of either theft or deception is of no great consequence.

Suppose, then, that A obtains a television set from B on hire-purchase terms, and that A has no intention of paying the instalments and makes off with the set. This looks like, and is, a case of obtaining by deception contrary to s. 15. It is also a case of theft. Under a hire-purchase transaction the purchaser gets possession but does not get ownership of the goods hired. The ownership here remains in B so when A makes off with (*i.e.* appropriates) the set he is then appropriating property belonging to B. So there are at least some cases in which the defendant may be convicted of theft or deception. What we need to explore is the extent of this overlap.

The first question that arises is whether *all* cases of theft can be charged as deception. The answer must be an obvious No. If A put his hand in B's pocket and abstracts B's wallet this is theft, but by no stretch of the imagination can it be said to be an obtaining of the wallet by deception. Thus by far the most common form of theft (*i.e.* theft by taking) cannot fall within deception—because there is no deception.

The second question is whether *all* cases of deception can be charged as theft. It would certainly be surprising is this turned out to be the case, if only because the Criminal Law Revision Committee, though it anticipated some overlap, can hardly have thought that the offence of deception was entirely superfluous. Sometimes, though, statutory provisions do not always have the effect they were intended by their framers to have and there is Court of Appeal authority, though the statement was obiter, that it might be the law that all cases of deception can be charged as theft. This opinion by the Court of Appeal is obviously wrong in at least one respect. The range of property which is capable of being obtained by deception is wider than the range of property which can be stolen. Land, for example, can be obtained by deception but it cannot be stolen (see *ante*, p. 260). If, then, A obtains Blackacre from B by deception he may commit the offence under section 15 but not the offence of theft under section 1 of the 1968 Act. The court's opinion, therefore, can only be applied to cases where the property involved can be both obtained by deception and stolen. Even in such cases the view is still a surprising one and needs a word or two of explanation, so we might look at the case of *Lawrence* (1971) where this view was expressed. Occhi, an Italian student arrived at Victoria station with little knowledge of English and even less of the breathtaking rapacity of certain of our taxi drivers. He asked Lawrence, the driver of the taxi, to take him to a certain address in Ladbroke Grove which was written on a piece of paper. Lawrence told him that that was a long way and would be expensive. Occhi opened his wallet and took out a pound note which he gave to Lawrence who then took a further £6 out of the wallet which was still open. Lawrence then drove Occhi to his address in Ladbroke Grove for which the correct fare would have been about 50p. He was charged with and convicted of theft of the £6.

Had Lawrence been charged under section 15 the case could hardly have given rise to difficulty, for he had falsely represented that the address was a long way off and that £7 was the correct fare. But for some reason Lawrence was charged with theft and of course the prosecution had to substantiate that charge. Lawrence's argument appears to have been that Occhi *consented*, but the important question is: *consented to what?* If the student had consented to the appropriation of the £7 that would presumably be a complete defence to a charge of theft since Lawrence would not then be appropriating property belonging to *another*. If the student had consented to the *taking* that would not *necessarily* be a defence to a charge of theft. It is not at all clear in which sense the Court of Appeal was referring to consent. The court went on to say, rightly enough, that Lawrence might have been convicted on a charge under section 15, but then concluded, as something of a non sequitur, that it might be that as a result of their decision that any facts which would support a charge under section 15 would also support a charge under section 1 of the 1968 Act.

The decision of the House of Lords does little to clarify the matter. It was there said, again rightly enough, that *some* cases of deception might be charged as theft but the House of Lords did not commit itself to the view that all cases of deception could be charged as theft, but neither did it say that such a view was wrong.

It is submitted that *Lawrence* is an unsatisfactory and inconclusive case, and that not all cases of deception can be charged as theft. Take what might be thought to be a paradigm case of deception that of *King's Norton Metal Co. Ltd.* v. *Edridge* (1897). A rogue called Wallis persuaded King's Norton to sell him some brass rivet wire by falsely representing that he ran a reputable business and was creditworthy. Clearly Wallis's fraud would fall within section 15 but would it also fall within section 1? The action was a civil action between the owner of the wire (King's Norton) and the purchaser (Edridge) who had bought in good faith from Wallis. It was held, and this is the important point, that Edridge received a good title. No doubt King's Norton would not have dealt with Wallis had they known he was a rogue but they did intend to deal with Wallis and, notwithstanding Wallis's fraud, *ownership* passed to Wallis by the contract. If, then, ownership passes it is difficult to see how the rogue can steal that property because the rogue *cannot appropriate his own property*. Thus, it is thought, if by his fraud the rogue gets the victim to transfer ownership to him he may well be guilty of the deception offence but not of theft.

To go back to *Lawrence*. Did ownership of the £7 pass to Lawrence? If it did then, on the view expressed here, Lawrence could not be guilty of stealing the money. The House of Lords did not decide this point but held that even if ownership had passed Lawrence could still be convicted of theft. The House of Lords did this by taking what might be thought an ingenious point. It will be recalled that though Occhi *gave* Lawrence the first £1, Lawrence himself *took* the other £6 from his wallet. While the money was in the wallet it was still Occhi's and *at the very instant Lawrence put his hand on it he was appropriating property which was still Occhi's.*

But this view creates problems in another respect. In what sense did Lawrence *appropriate* the £6? As we have seen an appropriation has to be an *unauthorised* act (*ante*, p. 255) and it looks as though Occhi authorised the taking by allowing Lawrence to take the notes without protest. An answer to that, which is hinted at in the House of Lords' decision, is that Occhi was so confused he did not know what Lawrence was taking so the case might be likened to that where by sleight of hand A gets property from B which B does not realise he is getting and such a case would amount to theft.

In summary therefore we can say that some cases of deception will amount to theft, but that where D has, by deception, induced P to transfer ownership to him before he does any act which could constitute an appopriation, this should not amount to theft. It might well be that Megaw's suggestion that all cases of deception should amount to theft would be a simpler solution, but it is submitted that this is not the proper interpretation of the present statute.

3. Obtaining a Pecuniary Advantage

If X goes into a hairdresser's and allows the hairdresser to cut his hair intending not to pay when the haircut is over, you could say that he has obtained the haircut by deception. But is a haircut property? Clearly not within the definition of section 4 of the Theft Act 1968. Of course, if shampoos, or conditioner have been used you could say that he obtained those items by deception. It would, however, be absurd to say that liability should depend upon whether the haircut involves the use of shampoos. Similarly if A gives false information on an application form for a job and as a result of that false information he obtains the employment, what has he obtained by deception? So far he has obtained the right to work for the firm. At the end of the month when he is paid, this will be for the work he has done during the month and not because of the deception, so does he commit no offence?

These examples should show that whereas theft can be limited to items of property (albeit a widened definition to cover such property as things in action) the definition of property is just not suitable to cover the examples given above. It was therefore felt necessary to include a separate offence to cover situations where the accused by his deception obtains some form of financial advantage. Thus section 16 provided a criminal offence of obtaining a pecuniary advantage by deception. The phrase pecuniary advantage was defined in three ways by section 16(2)(*a*)–(*c*). Paragraphs (*b*) and (*c*) provided for a fairly restricted range of situations and these will be discussed below. Paragraph (*a*) was a wide ranging definition of pecuniary advantage which was intended to cover, for example, the cases like the hairdresser described above. Unfortunately this section caused the courts so many problems, being described at one stage as a "judicial nightmare," that Parliament repealed this one small part of the Theft Act and replaced it with three new offences under the Theft Act 1978. The end result is that the offence of dishonestly obtaining a pecuniary advantage survives in section 16, but the definition of pecuniary advantage is now limited to paragraphs 16(2)(*b*) and 16(2)(*c*). There is, of course, only one offence under s. 16.

(4) What therefore is a pecuniary advantage for the purposes of section 16?

(*a*) *Section 16(2)(b)*:

> "He is allowed to borrow by way of overdraft, or to take out any policy of insurance or annuity contract, or obtains an improvement of the terms on which he is allowed to do so;"

Thus if X falsely tells his bank manager that he is expecting a cheque from his father in five weeks time and as a result is allowed to create an overdraft, then even before he has begun to take advantage of the overdraft facilities he has committed the offence under section 16 of obtaining a pecuniary advantage by deception. It is the obtaining of the facility that is the crux of the offence.

If Y gives false information about his state of health and thereby obtains a life insurace policy, he has committed an offence at the time he is granted the policy.

(*b*) *Section 16(2)(c)*:

> "He is given the opportunity to earn remuneration or greater remuneration in an office or employment, or to win money by betting."

Our earlier example of the applicant for a job who gives false information on the application form which induces the employer to give him the job will be caught by this definition of pecuniary advantage. Similarly a university lecturer who gains promotion by supplying the university with a false list of publications would also commit the offence under section 16.

4. Obtaining Services by Deception

Section 1 of the Theft Act 1978 provides:

(1) A person whom by any deception dishonestly obtains services from another shall be guilty of an offence.

(2) It is an obtaining of services where the other is induced to confer a benefit by doing some act, or causing or permitting some act to be done, on the understanding that the benefit has been or will be paid for.

This offence is based on the notion that a man's services have a value and that it is wrong by deception dishonestly to cause him to confer the benefit of his services on another where there is no intention that he shall be recompensed. "Services" are widely defined and extend to any act, or causing or permitting some act to be done. The operation of this section may be explained by reference to a number of examples.

(i) X deliberately allows a hairdresser to cut his hair, fully intending to leave without paying. Clearly the barber is "induced to do some act" by the deception and there is obviously an understanding that the service will be paid for when it is completed and before the customer leaves the shop. If he decides to leave without paying only after the haircut is completed then he will commit an offence under section 3 (see *post*, p. 289).

(ii) The following example is based on a recent newspaper report. E was a student at school Y where he was studying for his A level examinations. He was dissatisfied with the instruction he was receiving in history and so, putting on the school tie of Z school, he attended the history lessons at that school. The history master at Z school did not realise that there was an interloper in the class and gave the lesson. Did E commit an offence under section 1?

(a) Is he dishonest? This is a question for the jury (see *ante*, p. 267). His wearing of Z school tie tends to suggest that he knows he has no right to be there. But is that enough?

(b) Is there a deception? Clearly he wears the tie to deceive the authorities at Z school into allowing him on to the premises.

(c) Does he obtain a service by the deception? Presumably F was going to deliver his class that day for his own pupils, in which case it would be rather straining the section to say that E's deception deceived F into conferring a benefit upon E. If F had spotted E before the class he would no doubt have expelled E, but that does not seem to be the same as saying that E caused F to perform the act. There is a further difficulty. The Act says that the act must be done on the understanding that it has been or will be paid for. Now F will be paid by the Local Authority (if it is a state school) for his work as a teacher. He therefore gives each class on the understanding that he will be paid. It is submitted, however, that this is not what the Act means. It surely means that an understanding exists between the deceiver and the deceived that there will be payment though not necessarily payment made by the deceiver. If X were to go to a car repairers and falsely tell them that he worked for a firm which had an account with that garage, when the mechanics repaired the car it would be because the deception had created in their minds the understanding that they would be paid, not by the rogue, but by his firm. In our school example no such understanding exists and it is submitted that no offence under section 1 is committed.

(iii) A visits B, a prostitute, for the purpose of having sexual intercourse and intends to walk off without paying. It is submitted that an offence under section 1 is committed; the section makes no reference to the payment needing to be one which is legally enforceable. If he so decides after the act of intercourse he would not commit an offence under section 3 of the Theft Act 1978 (see *post*, p. 289).

5. Evasion of Liability by Deception

Section 2 provides an offence to cover the situation where the accused dishonestly and by deception evades a financial obligation. Although the sections contain only one offence it may be committed in one of three ways and the prosecution would be expected to make clear in the indictment in which of the three ways it was alleged the accused committed the offence.

Section 2 (1) (*a*) covers the situation where D, by any deception, "dishonestly secures the remission of the whole or any part of any existing liability to make payment, whether his own liability or another's."

D's girlfriend, E, is £45 in arrears in the rental payments on her flat. D goes to her landlord and falsely tells him that E's mother is slowly dying and that E is having to spend nearly all her money in travelling to care for her mother and this is the reason for her rental arrears. Out of kindness the landlord tells D that he will accept £20 in full settlement of the arrears.

D has committed an offence within the meaning of section 2 (1) (*a*). The subsection makes it clear that it does not matter whether the liability evaded is his own or another's. The £45 rental arrears is an existing liability which D has dishonestly tricked the landlord into reducing. Most commentators seem to suggest that the use of the word "remit" in section 2 (1) (*a*) indicates that there must be an agreement by the person deceived either to wipe the slate clean as far as the existing liability is concerned or to make a reduction in the amount of money that will have to be paid. It would not be sufficient that the landlord is tricked into believing that he has already been paid. (This might amount to inducing the landlord to forego payment under s. 2 (1) (*b*)). He must be aware that there is an existing liability and decide to extinguish or reduce that liability. If the landlord also says that he will accept half rent until the situation alters, this would be an offence under section 2 (1) (*c*) (*post*, p. 289).

Section 2 (1) (*b*) covers the situation where by any deception the accused "with intent to make permanent default in whole or in part on any existing liability to make payment, or with intent to let another do so, dishonestly induces the creditor or any person claiming payment on behalf of the creditor to wait for payment (whether or not the due date for payment is deferred) or to forego payment."

(i) A has rented a television set from B Ltd. for the last four years, paying monthly instalments. He is now five months in arrears of payments and the shop manager has called round to tell him that if he does not give the money owed they will take immediate possession of the set. A is about to emigrate to Australia in three days' time, but is very eager to see the Cup Final on his set the day before he leaves the country. He therefore hands the manager a cheque for the full amount, knowing full well that he has closed that account and that the cheque will be dishonoured. He believes, however, that by the time the cheque is returned to the television company, he will have seen the Cup Final and have left the country for good.

Has he dishonestly and by deception induced the manager to wait for payment on an existing liability? Has he not, in fact, paid the manager by the cheque? Section 2 (3) expressly provides for a case in which the creditor is given a cheque in payment; he is to be treated not as one who has been paid but one who has been induced to wait for payment. The answer to the initial question is, therefore, yes. There is, however, one more requirement; the accused must have the intention to make permanent default in whole or in part on any existing liability. In our example, this condition is clearly met. He is simply buying himself time so that he can get out of the country and avoid payment altogether. If, on the other hand, A was short of money and not about to emigrate and so sent his son to the door to tell the manager that his father was away for a few days, intending to pay the bill when he received his monthly salary, then this would not amount to an offence since he had no intention to make permanent default. This is a difficult area. The father who sends his son to the door to tell the rent collector that "dad is out" is clearly dishonest, but should he be treated as a criminal? Parliament decided that he should not be so treated unless the deception was practised with the intention that the debt would never be paid.

(ii) Let us imagine another type of debt situation but one in which the liability A evades is to a prostitute C, for services rendered. Unfortunately for C, A commits no offence under section 2 because liability is defined in section 2 (2) as "legally enforceable liability" and under the law (see *post*, p. 422), the prostitute could not sue A for the recovery of the money owed for her sexual services. And this applies to all three types of evasion of liability under section 2.

(iii) X, while driving his car, runs into the back of Y's car, causing about £5 of damage. X denies that he was to blame, but he tells Y that to save any bother he will give him a cheque for £30, knowing that the cheque will not be met. Section 2(2) provides that throughout section 2, liability does not include a liability which is not accepted or established to pay compensation for a wrongful act or omission. Since X has not accepted that he was to blame for the accident, there is no offence committed under section 2.

(iv) A, who owes B's bookshop £20, dishonestly and falsely tells them that he has paid them already. The manager accepts that his sales staff have made a mistake and enters "paid" in the accounts. This would be an example of dishonestly and by deception inducing another to forego payment.

Section 2 (1) (*c*) covers the situation where the accused by any deception "dishonestly obtains any exemption from or abatement of liability to make a payment."

In Y town, senior citizens are carried free of charge on corporation buses when they show the driver a pass card. Z, who is 59, borrows his friend's pass card and shows it to the driver and he is then carried free of charge.

Unlike the other two types of evasion in paragraphs (*b*) and (*c*) this provision makes no reference to an existing liability. It is therefore suitable to cover a situation in which the deception is practised before any liability is incurred with the result that either the liability which is eventually incurred is less than it should have been or that no liability at all is incurred. Thus in our example of the bus pass Z never became liable to pay the proper fare because his deception induced the bus driver to admit him at no charge; but this is exactly what section 2 (1) (*c*) is designed to cover.

III. *MAKING OFF WITHOUT PAYMENT*

Before the Theft Act 1978 came into effect there was a common, and quickly growing, fraud for which the 1968 Act made inadequate provision. The fraud was simplicity itself and consisted merely in making off without paying for goods or services provided. Typical examples are provided by the motorist who, having filled up his tank with petrol, drives away without paying; or by the customer who, having consumed a meal in a restaurant, runs off without settling his bill. If the goods or services are obtained by deception there will usually be an offence under section 15 of the 1968 Act or under section 1 of the 1978 Act (formerly there may have been an offence under section 16 (2) (*a*) of the 1968 Act) but if no deception is made before the goods are obtained or the service provided then these provisions are inapplicable.

On the other hand the law does not in general make it an offence for a debtor dishonestly to resolve not to pay his debts. It is not an offence dishonestly to resolve not to pay the quarterly gas or electricity bill. But since the gas and electricity boards know with whom they are dealing, they can be left to pursue their *civil* remedies and there is no need to make a crime of such conduct. Moreover, if such conduct was made criminal there is a real danger that people who cannot pay, as opposed to those who will not pay, would find themselves in the criminal courts.

Section 3 is accordingly not aimed at dishonest debtors in general but at the kind of debtor who, if he cannot be brought to book on the spot may never be traced and made to pay. Hence the offence of making off is made an arrestable one because without a power of arrest it would, as a practical matter, be impossible to give effect to the section.

Section 3 (1) provides "a person who, knowing that payment on the spot for any goods supplied or service done is required or expected from him, dishonestly makes off without having paid as required or expected and with intent to avoid payment of the amount done shall be guilty of an offence."

Again we can examine the working of the offence in relation to some hypothetical examples.

(i) A eats a meal at a restaurant fully intending to pay. At the end of the meal he discovers that he had no money and so he simply runs out intending to avoid payment. Before the Theft Act 1978 the prosecution would have had to try to find some deception which enabled him to make his escape. Now such mental acrobatics are no longer required. All that the prosecution need prove is that he did make off without paying where he knew payment on the spot was required and that this was done dishonestly in order to avoid payment. It would not avail him to argue that he intended to send in the money the next day. The Act does not require an intent to make permanent default. Nor would it avail him to argue that, since the restaurant accepted diner's cards and credit cards, "payment" on the spot is not required or expected. Payment on spot must include situations where delayed payment facilities are offered—Professor Griew suggests that it covers situations where the customer knows he must make some deal with the (for example) restaurant owner before he leaves the restaurant; either to pay in cash or by some other means.

From a practical point of view it may be easier to use this offence even where you suspect that the accused intended to avoid payment even before he ate the meal. Technically he should be charged with obtaining property by deception which carries a much higher penalty. On the other hand where it is obvious that no use will be made of this greater sentencing power, it may well prove attractive to the prosecution to avoid the need to prove that the deception was made at the outset. Similarly where the accused drives off from a petrol station without having paid, he may well have committed offences of theft, deception and making off, but the prosecution may well settle for the making off conviction.

(ii) X travels each evening between Leeds and Menston on a local pay train (on such trains the guard issues tickets in the same way that tickets are issued on buses, there being no station staff to collect such tickets at the local stops such as Menston). One evening the train is particularly full and the guard has not reached X by the time the train reaches Menston. X gets out of the train and walks off without paying.

This may seem an obvious example of an offence under section 3, but is it? He clearly makes off without paying (would hiding in the toilet constitute a making off?) and a service has been provided for him when payment on the spot was expected. However the section requires that the accused should have acted dishonestly and with intent to avoid payment. We have already seen (*ante*, p. 267) that dishonestly is to be regarded as a question of fact and that the issue is whether people generally would regard such conduct as dishonest and whether X knew it was so regarded. Further it is rather hard to say that he made off with the intention of avoiding payment. Experience may have taught him that it is not advisable to stay on the train to look for the guard since the train will probably move on as soon as other passengers have dismounted. Clearly if he gets off at an earlier station because he sees that the guard will reach him before the train gets to Menston then it will be possible to say that he has dishonestly made off with intent to avoid payment; or possibly if, when he alights from the train at Menston he sees the guard standing on the platform ready to receive fares from those who have not yet paid and then deliberately avoids taking the opportunity to pay. This problem clearly raises problems as to the duties owed by person travelling on such buses or pay trains; is there a duty to seek out the fare-collector? Considerations such as these will affect how the jury tackles the requirements of dishonestly.

(iii) X has just had intercourse with a prostitute who now requires payment. X simply walks off saying "Take me to court and try and get your money." There is no difference in principle between this example and that in number (i). However section 3 (3) provides that if the supply of goods or the doing of the service is contrary to law, or if the service done is such that payment is not legally enforceable, then the offence is not committed. Here the prostitute would not be able to sue X to recover damages for breach of contract and so X commits no offence when he walks off. However if from the outset he intended not to pay, X probably would commit the offence of obtaining services by deception contrary to section 1 of the 1978 Act, since no such qualification is expressed to section 1.

IV. *ROBBERY*

Section 8 of the Theft Act provides:

"(1) A person is guilty of robbery if he steals, and immediately before or at the time of doing so, and in order to do so, he uses force on any person or puts or seeks to put any person in fear of being then and there subjected to force.

(2) A person guilty of robbery, or of an assault with intent to rob, shall on conviction on indictment be liable to imprisonment for life."

In order to succeed on a charge of robbery the prosecution must establish (a) that the property was stolen; and (b) that the theft of it was accomplished by force. Thus all the defences open to one charged with theft are open on a charge of robbery. If the jury believe that the accused honestly thought that he had the right to take the property they must acquit him of theft, and therefore of robbery. In *Robinson* (1977) the accused was owed £7 by I.'s wife. The prosecution alleged that R and two others approached I in the street and that R. was brandishing a knife. In the course of a fight which followed, I dropped a £5 note. R. picked it up and asked for the remaining £2 he was owed. The judge directed the jury that for a defence under section 2 (1) of the Theft Act the accused should honestly believe he had the right to take the money in the way he did. His appeal against conviction for robbery was allowed by the Court of Appeal. The prosecution had to establish the basic offence of theft and it would be a defence to that charge that the accused honestly believed he had a right in law to deprive I of the money, even if he knew he was not entitled to use a knife to get it. If the prosecution failed to prove theft, then an indictment for robbery must also fail.

What then turns an act of theft into one of robbery? In the first place the prosecution must prove that in order to steal the accused used force on any person or sought to put any person in fear of such force being then and there used on him. It is important to note that the section does not say that the force or threat has to be used to the person from whom the property is stolen. It can be used on any person provided that it is used "in order to steal." Thus if the accused sees Mr. and Mrs. A walking along the street, it would be robbery if he knocked Mr. A unconscious and snatched Mrs. A's handbag. The prosecution must, however, establish that the force was used against a person though very slight force will suffice. It is enough to constitute robbery that there is a struggle for possession of the goods and that A pulls them from B's hands (*Corcoran* v. *Anderton* (1980)).

The Act, however, says that the force or threat of force must be used immediately before or at the time of the stealing, and this raises difficult problems of fact and degree. What does the Act mean by immediately before? If a gang intend to break into a factory and one of the gang knocks out the night-watchman before the main part of the gang break in to steal, this would be robbery. If, on the other hand, they were to threaten the night-watchman with a beating up if he did not draw them a plan of the factory so that they could steal from it a week later, this would not be robbery since the force or threat of force was not used immediately before the stealing.

At the other end of the time span, the Act says that the force must be used (immediately before) or at the time of the stealing. Here it is important to remember the other qualification that the force or threat must be used in order to steal. A strict interpretation would mean that once the theft is complete, in the sense that the accused could be charged with the substantive offence of theft, the use of force will not turn the crime into an offence of robbery. For example, if X is a pickpocket and has got his hands round Y's wallet and is in the process of removing it from Y, we have said that since he has now assumed the rights of an owner over (*i.e.* appropriated) the wallet the offence of theft is complete even though he has not yet removed it totally from Y. If Y now realises what is being done, resists and is hit in the stomach by X, does this mean that it is not robbery because the force is used after X has stolen the wallet? Could X argue that since the theft was complete the force was not used "in order to steal"? Clearly, the words must be given a wider meaning than "up to the time when there is a completed act of appropriation." Similar problems arise in handling (see *post*, p. 302, where the phrase "otherwise than in the course of stealing" appears) and presumably a uniform answer should be given. It must be robbery when the accused uses force on the victim to enable him to get the wallet out of his control, or to get the goods off the premises in a bank raid (see *Hale* (1978)). Even though there is already a completed act of theft when the accused assumed the rights of the owner, it would probably still be robbery if X hit Y to stop him immediately recovering the wallet. On the other hand, if X has got hold of Y's wallet and is running down the street when he is stopped by P.C. Z, force now used on P.C. Z would be after the commission of the theft and would not turn the offence into robbery. "At the time of" committing the theft must be viewed in a commonsense way; the test is whether X can sensibly be said to be stealing the goods when the force is used on Y.

V. *BURGLARY AND AGGRAVATED BURGLARY*

1. Burglary

Burglary is traditionally thought of as breaking and entering a dwelling-house in the night with intent to steal. It was once so defined and separate provision was made for less serious entries where the building was entered by day or where buildings other than dwellings were entered. All these distinctions have been swept away.

Burglary can now be committed in buildings generally, and nothing turns upon whether the entry (for there is no longer any requirement for a breaking) was during the day or night (except the more alarm the burglars cause the heavier the eventual sentence they may receive). Section 9 (1) of the Theft Act 1968 provides for two distinct ways in which burglary may be committed, namely by a person who

> "(*a*) enters a building or part of a building as a trespasser and with intent to commit any such offence as is mentioned in subsection (2) below. (These are stealing from the building or part of the building, inflicting grievous bodily harm on any person therein, raping any woman therein, or unlawfully damaging the building or anything therein), or
>
> (*b*) having entered any building or part of a building as a trespasser he steals or attempts to steal anything in the building or that part of it or inflicts or attempts to inflict on any person therein any grievous bodily harm."

Burglary is, in effect, a form of aggravated trespass. In both types of burglary the prosecution have to prove that the accused has entered a building (or part of the building) either knowing, or being reckless as to the fact that, he is a trespasser. If the charge is brought under section 9 (1) (*a*) the prosecution must, in addition, prove that at the time he entered the building the accused intended (and here recklessness will not suffice) to commit one of the offences specified in section 9 (2) which are listed above. If the charge is brought under section 9 (1) (*b*) the accused must be shown to have actually committed one of the offences specified in paragraph (*b*) and at the time of committing the offence he either knew that he entered as a trespasser or was reckless as to that fact.

We shall now consider the elements which are common to both forms of burglary, namely (1) entry; (2) trespassing; (3) a building; (4) part of a building.

(1) Enters

In both forms of burglary the prosecution must prove that the accused entered the building as a trespasser. Under section 9 (1)*(a)* they must prove that the accused intended to enter and that at the time he either knew that he was a trespasser or was reckless as to that fact. Under section 9 (1) *(b)* the prosecution must prove that at the time of committing the specified offence he knew that he had entered as a trespasser or was at least reckless as to that fact.

The prosecution must prove that the accused actually entered the building in question. As with many elements of criminal offences this will pose no great problems in the general run of cases since the accused will be apprehended in the building or some days later when he has actually removed property from the building. However on occasion it may be difficult to say whether or not there has actually been an entry into the building within the meaning of section 9.

There are various possible views as to what constitutes an entry. One view is that entry requires that the accused, A, should be entirely within the building. On this view, if he still had so much as a foot on the window ledge outside the building he would not be guilty of the complete offence though he would be guilty of an attempt. Another view is that A has entered if any part of his body is within the building; on this view A would be guilty should his hand, or even his fingertips, penetrate beyond the door or window. The one case on this point (*Collins* (1973)) holds that there must be "an effective and substantial" entry which seems to suggest a half-way house between these two views. As a practical test it seems to be less satisfactory than either of the two first suggested tests because it is not clear cut. Whether A's body is entirely within the building or whether any part of his body has penetrated the building, admit of definite answers; but whether enough of his body is within the building so as to constitute an effective and substantial entry must be something on which views may differ.

A further complication is introduced where A employs an innocent agent. A might, for example, employ a boy below the age of criminal responsibility to enter the building and bring out property to him. In such a case it must be tempting to use the innocent agency principle (*ante*, p. 173) and conclude that this is to be treated as an entry by A himself. Suppose, then, that A, while remaining outside the building, uses some instrument to withdraw property from the building. Is it to be said that, by parity of reasoning, the implement is to be regarded like the boy so that its insertion into the building is to be regarded as an entry by A himself? Since burglary may now be committed when there is an entry with intent to do serious bodily harm, is A guilty of burglary when the bullet from his gun, fired from the highway, enters the victim's house?

If regard is paid to the wording of section 9, it would appear that these last two illustrations cannot constitute burglary. A person is guilty of burglary if "he enters" with certain intents, or "having entered . . . he" commits certain offences. To hold that "he" enters or has entered when an instrument is inserted by him would seem to be at odds with what the section expressly requires.

It is further suggested that the natural meaning of the words employed in the section require a complete entry by A. "Enters" or "having entered" means just that; it can hardly be supposed to mean "being in the process of entering" or "having half-entered". If A is in the process of entering he may always be convicted of an attempt.

Where an innocent agent (the boy under the age of criminal responsibility) is employed the same argument should hold good. The "he" referred to in section 9 is the person who is charged with burglary and "he" has not entered the building.

(2) As a trespasser

"Trespass" is a civil law concept. Essentially it requires entry on to property which is in the possession of another without the consent of that other. At civil law it would not be a defence to show that you had entered by mistake. So does this mean that for purposes of burglary the prosecution need show only that the accused was, by civil law definitions a trespasser? Fortunately the Theft Act seems to be one area in which the courts have adopted a subjective approach and in prosecutions under section 9 the prosecution will have to prove that the accused was at least reckless as to the fact of being a trespasser; in other words he was aware of facts which might mean he was trespassing. If the prosecution is brought under section 9 (1) (*a*) of the Theft Act the prosecution must prove that he was reckless as to being a trespasser at the time he entered the building. In the case of a prosecution under section 9 (1) (*b*) the prosecution would have to prove that at the time he committed the offence inside the building he then realised that he had entered the building as a trespasser. If the accused mistakenly thinks that he has the consent of the owner to entering, even if his mistake is unreasonable, he should not be convicted; equally if he believes that he is entering his own house, since then he would not even consider the issue of consent. More problematical is the situation where the accused is invited into the house by a person who has no right to give that consent. Again the answer should be that if the accused honestly believes that he has entered with the consent of someone whom he believes is entitled to give that consent he should not be convicted. So in *Collins* (1973) it was held that Collins was not a trespasser where he accepted an invitation from the householder's daughter to enter the house. The case might have been differently decided on this point had Collins known that the householder would not have permitted him to enter. It is instructive to contrast *Jones and Smith* (1976) where the accused and an accomplice were charged with and convicted of burglary, the offence consisting of stealing TV sets from the house of Smith's father. At the trial it was accepted that Smith's father had given his son a sort of blanket permission to enter his house. So how could you say he entered as a trespasser? James L.J. said that the jury were entitled to hold that the son and his friend were trespassing if they found he had entered the premises of another knowing that he was entering in excess of the permission that had been given to him, or being reckless whether he was so entering. Here it is clear that his father's permission to enter did not extend to entry for the purpose of stealing and the son well knew this.

Usually a trespasser enters by stealth but it is by no means unknown for a person to gain entry by tricking the owner into giving his assent to entry. X may, for example, gain entry to Y's house by pretending to be the gas meter reader. In a way he enters not by stealth but with the consent of the owner, but on the other hand he is fully aware that the owner would not have let him in had he known the truth. It is suggested that there should be no difficulty in saying that X entered knowing that he was a trespasser. Does this mean that if X enters a supermarket intending to steal from within, he commits burglary as he enters? X knows that if the shopkeeper knew of his intentions he would not allow him into the shop and his case is thus not really different from the example of the gas meter reader. The major difficulty here is that the jury will have to be sure that he had that intention when he entered the store; this will be difficult to prove unless X is specially equipped for stealing as where, as once happened, an enterprising rogue inserted false arms in the sleeves of his overcoat so that store detectives would not notice what his real arms were doing.

(3) A building

Under the law before 1969 burglary could only be committed from a dwelling-house. The new Act is not so restricted, and burglary can be committed in a building or part of a building.

Little would be gained here in trying to give an exhaustive definition of what constitutes a building. It is a word generally used to convey some idea of permanence, and probably there is a requirement of a roof, but beyond this no firm guidelines can be given. Clearly burglary can now be committed from such places as offices, barns, garages. A tent, on the other hand, although it may constitute a dwelling is probably not sufficiently permanent to be regarded as a building.

The Act specifically extends the definition of buildings to cover inhabited vessels or vehicles, including the times when the person who inhabits them is not there. The word "inhabited" does, however seem to require that the vehicle at the time of the entry is used as a dwelling, and it would not therefore cover an ordinary car or a dormobile which is being used as a form of transport at the time. But if a family use their dormobile as an ordinary form of transport for 50 weeks in the year but as a holiday home for the other two, it would be an inhabited vehicle for those two weeks.

(4) Or part of a building

The Act provides that the accused must have entered a building or part of a building as a trespasser. This second part is designed to cover situations where the accused is lawfully entitled to be in one part of the building but not in another. For example if X is a student in a hall of residence he will be entitled to enter his own room and those parts of the hall designed for common use and connecting corridors, but he would not be entitled to enter a fellow student's room without permission. Thus if he goes into student Y's room to steal money from his desk, he would enter Y's room as a trespasser. He has therefore entered a part of the building as a trespasser and thus he would commit burglary as well as theft. One problem arising out of the use of the concept of parts of a building, is that where the prosecution are alleging that the accused has entered part of a building as a trespasser with intent to steal, they must prove that he intended to steal from that part. Suppose that X enters a department store intending only to purchase some gardening equipment. While in the store, where he is legally entitled to be, he conceives a plan to steal money from the manager's office. To reach this office he must first pass through the staff common room which like the manager's office is out of bounds. If X is apprehended in the staff room and confesses that he was on his way to the manager's office can we say that he has entered a part of the building intending to steal in that part, or is the manager's office another part? Possibly the most sensible answer in cases such as these is to treat the building as having two parts—one part where customers are entitled to be, and the other part which is for staff only. If this interpretation is adopted, then as soon as X enters the staff room he has entered a part of the building he is not entitled to enter, and this part includes the manager's office. In *Walkington* (1979) the accused was charged with burglary from a till in a department store. The till was standing on a three-sided counter and the questions for the jury were (1) did the management regard the floor area within the three sides of the counter as being restricted to staff; (2) if the answer to (1) was yes, then did the accused realise that this area was so restricted and (3) if he did, did he enter it with the intent to steal from it?

Where the accused is charged with burglary from a part of the building contrary to section 9 (1) (*a*) they must prove that he entered with intent to steal from that part of a building. For such purposes it is probably best to regard the building as having only two parts—a restricted part and a non-restricted part. Thus once he has entered any restricted part with intent to steal from somewhere in the building which is restricted, he can be convicted even though the object of his theftuous intent may be in another room or even on another floor. (Similar sort of problems may arise in relation to flats, apartment complexes and terraced houses).

(5) Mens rea

Apart from a trespassory entry which has already been considered the offence of burglary requires an intention to commit one of the specified offences. Burglary is no longer confined to cases where the intention is to commit theft and it will be noted that this range of specified offences is wider under section 9 (1) (*a*) than under section 9 (1) (*b*).

2. Aggravated Burglary

Section 10 of the Theft Act 1968 provides for the offence of aggravated burglary which carries a possible maximum sentence of life imprisonment. A person is guilty of aggravated burglary if he commits any burglary and at the time has with him any firearm, any weapon of offence, or any explosive. Whereas burglary under section

9 is in some senses a form of aggravated trespass, section 10 is designed both to deter would-be burglars from taking offensive weapons with them when they burgle a house and to enable the court to reflect in the sentence the fact that burglary where offensive weapons are carried is a far more serious offence than when they are not.

VI. *MAKING UNWARRANTED DEMANDS WITH MENACES: BLACKMAIL*

Section 21 of the Theft Act provides:

> "(1) A person is guilty of blackmail if, with a view to gain for himself or another or with intent to cause loss to another, he makes any unwarranted demand with menaces; and for this purpose a demand with menaces is unwarranted unless the person making it does so in the belief—
> (*a*) that he has reasonable grounds for making the demand; and
> (*b*) that the use of menaces is a proper means of re-inforcing the demand."

The word "blackmail" is a word commonly used in everyday language to describe a situation in which X is threatening Y with unpleasant consequences unless Y does what X wants. This is, in fact, the gist of blackmail under section 21, but as we shall see the scope of the offence is somewhat more restricted than the everyday use of the term.

1. There must be a Demand

This will generally present no problems and the word will be given its ordinary meaning. What is required is that the accused acts in such a way as to demonstrate that he wants the victim to do something. It does not matter whether the request is made in the form of an order or a humble plea. The offence is demanding with menaces and so it does not matter whether the request is complied with or even that it was heard, provided that it was made. It is immaterial whether it was made orally or in writing. Where it is made in writing and sent through the post the demand is made as soon as the letter is posted and it continues to be made until it is received. Thus if A posts, in England, a demand to B in America, the demand is made and therefore the offence is committed in England; if the facts are reversed the offence is committed in

England at the latest when the letter reaches England (see *Treacy*, 1971).

2. The Demand must be Accompanied by Menaces

This does not mean that there must be a threat of violence; it is sufficient that something detrimental or unpleasant is threatened. (*Thorne* v. *Motor Traders Association*, 1937.) The use of the word "menaces" however rather than "threats" suggests that there might be certain threats which would be too trivial to be classed as menaces. On the other hand if the victim is unduly timid and the blackmailer knows that a threat which would not make a normal person comply with the demand would probably influence this unduly timid man, he should be caught by the section. Probably the approach that would be taken by the courts is that there is a menace if on the facts known to the accused the threat might influence an ordinarily stable person, or that it would influence this particular individual because of his extraordinary sensitivity. Thus a threat to expose A's sexual perversions would probably influence most stable citizens, but a threat to poison A's pet budgie may be an example of a threat which would only be a menace if the accused knew that A, an old lady, was very timid and devoted to the budgie.

3. The Demand must be made with a View to Gain for the Maker or Another, or with Intent to cause Loss to Another

The words gain and loss are defined by section 34 (2) of the Act as being restricted to gains and losses in money or other property; the gain or loss may be temporary or permanent. Gain includes a gain by keeping what one has, as well as a gain by getting what one has not; and loss includes a loss by not getting what one might get as well as a loss by parting with what one has. Thus if A threatens to expose B's cheating in an examination if she does not have sexual intercourse with him, this will not be a gain under section 21, but if his demand is for the £50 which she owes him then it will be an offence under section 21 even though the money is legally owed to him. If A threatens to expose B to his wife as an adulterer if she does not get promoted, this would be an offence since she expects to make a monetary gain from the promotion. However it may be that the monetary gain can become too remote, as where A threatens Professor B that he will expose him as a homosexual if he does not give him a place as a student in the University Law School. Presumably A will be hoping to earn good money with the law degree he will obtain in a few years' time—but it is possible that the court might hold that this monetary gain is too remote.

4. The Demand must be Unwarranted

If the accused raises the issue that the demand was not unwarranted then the prosecution must prove either that the accused did not believe that he had reasonable grounds for making the claim or, if he did, that he did not believe that it was proper to use menaces as a means of reinforcing the demand. In the majority of cases it is likely that the accused will believe that he had reasonable grounds for making the claim. Even a prostitute or bookmaker who knows that the courts would not enforce the demand may genuinely believe that they have the right to demand payment for a "debt of honour." It is far more likely that the accused will know that he should not have used menaces as a means of reinforcing the demand. In *Harvey and Others* (1981) the Court of Appeal held that no act which the accused believed to be a crime could be considered by him to be a proper means of enforcing the demand. However, even here, it is for the jury to decide what the accused actually believed. Thus, in practice, the more serious the threat, the less likely the jury are to believe that the accused considered his conduct to be "proper."

VII. *HANDLING*

When thieves have got away with their stolen property, the next step is to dispose of it. Clearly, if the stolen property is money there will be no difficulty, but where the property is readily identifiable there is every danger that the thief will get caught trying to sell it or use it. It is for this reason that specialist criminals exist whose function is to dispose of the goods for the original thieves. These are the persons regularly known as "fences." In some respects these people are a greater social menace than the original thieves since without them the thieves would have to dispose of the stolen property personally and might find the whole enterprise less attractive and rewarding. Most fences probably commit theft in relation to the property they deal with, but this is not always the case and this fact coupled with the generally accepted need to be able to punish big time fences more severely than the thieves for whom they act has led to the creation of a separate offence. Until 1968 this was known as "receiving" but under the Theft Act 1968 its scope has been increased and it is now termed handling. The basic offence is defined by section 22 of the Act which provides:

> "(1) A person handles stolen goods if (otherwise than in the course of the stealing) knowing or believing them to be stolen he dishonestly receives the goods, or dishonestly undertakes or

assists in their retention, removal disposal or realisation by or for the benefit of another person, or if he arranges to do so."

It should be noted that while there are about 18 methods of handling stolen goods outlined in this section, there is only one offence.

1. The Actus Reus of Handling

1. Stolen goods

"Goods" for the purposes of section 22 are defined to include "money and every other description of property except land, and includes things severed from the land by stealing" (s. 34(2)(*b*)). Subject to minor exceptions goods which may be handled extends to the same property that may be the subject of theft.

Such goods must be "stolen" and for this purpose goods are not only stolen when obtained in circumstances amounting to theft but also when they are obtained by blackmail or by deception contrary to section 15(1) (s. 24(4)). Provision is also made for goods stolen abroad which are brought to this country.

Not only must the prosecution establish that the goods were at some time "stolen" as defined in section 24, they must prove that they were "stolen" at the time of the handling. Section 24 provides that goods which may have been "stolen" within the meaning of section 24 (4) may cease to be stolen in one of three ways, namely where

(i) they have been restored to the person from whom they were stolen; or
(ii) they have been restored to other lawful possession or custody; or
(iii) the person from whom they were stolen (or anyone claiming through him) ceases to have any right to restitution of the goods.

Other lawful possession or custody in (ii) covers the situation in which the police recover the stolen property. Here and in (i) the major difficulty is to decide when the property has actually been restored either to its owner or to other lawful possession. The problem was considered in *Att.-Gen.'s* Reference (*No.* 1 *of* 1974). A police officer suspecting, correctly as it turned out, that the goods in the back of a car were stolen, immobilised the car and kept watch for the driver. When the driver arrived the officer questioned him and, because the driver's replies were unsatisfactory, he arrested him. It was held that in such a case the jury should be invited to consider whether the officer had taken custody of the goods before the driver returned or whether he had postponed a decision to take custody until he had the chance of confirming or disaffirming his suspicions by questioning the suspect. Merely to prevent the suspect from having access to the goods until questions are asked is not necessarily to take possession of the goods.

Sometimes the owner, or the police, become aware that A has stolen goods but, with a view to catching the handler as well, follow the goods to their destination. Such conduct by the owner or the police does not constitute a resumption of possession and the receiver may be convicted of handling.

An illustration of property ceasing to be stolen under (iii) would be where X has obtained property from Y under a contract which is voidable because of X's deception. If, when he realises what has happened, Y ratified the contract, he would cease to have any rights in the property and at that stage the property would cease to be stolen.

Section 24 (3) contains some rather complex rules concerning the proceeds of stolen goods. Two examples will serve to illustrate the general idea of the section. If X steals a car and then sells that car, the money he receives in exchange will be stolen goods and so will the car. Equally, if the handler of stolen property exchanges it for other property, the newly acquired property will be classified as stolen goods. Where, however, stolen property comes into the hands of someone who is not a thief or handler (for example because he is totally unaware that the property is stolen) then although the property is still stolen property, anything he acquires in exchange for it does not become stolen property.

(2) A handling

The prosecution must prove that the accused handled the stolen property. While goods may be handled in a wide variety of ways, these ways fall into two groups:

(a) *Received or arranged to receive.* This is the clearest example of handling. If the prosecution allege that the accused received the goods they will have to show that he took them into his possession whether personally or by his agents. It is a question of fact and degree for the jury to decide whether the alleged receiver had possession or control of the goods. If the accused has not actually received the goods and has not yet done enough to be charged with an attempt he may nevertheless have arranged to receive. Thus a typical case of arranging to receive would be where the thief has got in touch with a fence and has arranged to deliver the property to the fence who will then dispose of it.

(b) *Undertakes or assists in their retention, removal, disposal or realisation by or for the benefit of another person, or arranges to do so.* This form of handling casts the net very wide. Assist would seem to suggest a situation in which the accused joins forces with the thief or other handlers and works with them; undertakes on the other hand would seem more suitable to cover the situation where the accused has acted on his own. A few illustrations will serve to show how this part of the section works.

X negotiates with Y that Y will buy stolen property from the thief Z.

X has undertaken the disposal of stolen goods on behalf of Z.

X helps Y, the thief, store stolen property in a barn where it will stay until the police search dies down. X will have assisted Y in the retention of the stolen goods.

X lends Y, the thief, a van to take the stolen goods abroad. X has assisted Y in the removal of the stolen goods.

The section, however, goes further; if, X arranges to do any of the above acts he will also be guilty of handling. Thus, in the first example, if X agreed with Z that he would try to find him a buyer, X has arranged to undertake the disposal of the goods for Z.

Where the prosecutor is relying on forms of handling other than receiving or arranging to receive, he must prove that the acts were done by or for the benefit of another person. In each of the examples discussed above the acts were done by or for the benefit of another. On the other hand the person who steals the goods does not become a handler by disposing of the goods for his own benefit even if some benefit incidentally occurs to another. If A steals a car and sells it to B there will, no doubt, be profit in the transaction both to A and B. But the thief is not a handler because some benefit accrues to B, even if he realises that some benefit accrues to B. The words "for the benefit of another" were inserted to make it clear that a disposal of the goods for the thief's own benefit would not constitute him a handler (*Bloxham* (1982)).

(c) *Otherwise than in the course of the stealing.* All forms of handling are subject to the requirement that the act which constitutes the handling must not be in the course of stealing. If these words were not present, it would mean that if X and Y were to burgle Barclays' Bank and X handed Y the money from the safe, Y would be guilty of handling. This phrase is similar to that used in the definition of robbery and it is suggested that it should be given the same interpretation (see *ante*, p. 293). Thus, in our example of X and Y burgling Barclays' Bank, the stealing would presumably be deemed to continue until at least they have left the premises and possibly whilst they are making their getaway.

2. Mens Rea of Handling

A person is guilty of handling if he dishonestly receives, etc., the *stolen* goods knowing or believing them to be stolen. Notice that the goods must be proved to be stolen goods at the time of the handling. A person may believe goods to be stolen even where they are not; such a person cannot be convicted of the completed offence of handling though by virtue of the Criminal Attempts Act 1981 (*ante*, p. 212) he may be convicted of an attempt.

(1) Knowing or believing that the goods were stolen

A person may be said to know or believe that the goods were stolen when the thief tells him that they are or when he has no substantial doubt that the goods are stolen. Where, however, he suspects that the goods may be stolen, as where he is offered a watch for a ridiculously low price, and he deliberately shuts his eyes to the possibility, the courts have held that this does not amount to belief. Belief is stronger than suspicion; you may suspect that goods are stolen yet not believe that they are. The appellate courts appear reluctant to give guidance to trial judges on how to direct a jury on this point. They seem prepared only to say what will not suffice (see *Bellenie* (1980)). The jury must be directed that they should convict the accused only if they are satisfied that he actually believed that the goods were stolen; it is not enough that he ought to have believed that they were.

(2) Dishonesty

This is a question of fact for the jury though it will normally add nothing to the requirement that the prosecution must prove that the accused knew or believed that the goods were stolen. However, if X received goods knowing that they are stolen, but intending to return them to their true owner, the jury would no doubt find that X was not dishonest.

Chapter 9

OFFENCES RELATING TO PUBLIC ORDER

Although we have no formalised Bill of Rights in this country, it is common to hear people talking of basic rights such as the right of free speech and the right to hold meetings and demonstrations. However the exercise by one section of the community of such rights often causes extreme annoyance and sometimes fear to another section of the community and it is often necessary to achieve a fair balance between such competing claims. The offences discussed in this chapter represent an attempt to achieve such a balance.

There are many offences relating to what is generally termed "public order" and there is not the space to discuss more than a few here.

1. The Common Law Offences

(1) Affray

It is generally accepted that in order to secure a conviction the prosecution must prove that there was unlawful fighting or unlawful violence used by one or more persons against another or others or that there was an unlawful display of force by one or more persons without actual violence. This may occur either in a public or private place, but if it occurs in private it must take place in the presence of at least one innocent person who was terrified. Finally the incident must be of such a nature that a bystander of reasonably firm character might reasonably be expected to be terrified (see *Button* v. *D.P.P.* (1966); *Taylor* v. *D.P.P.* (1973)), though if the act occurs in public it is not necessary to prove that there was, in fact, such a bystander.

It would seem that the *mens rea* consists solely in the defendant either intentionally or recklessly fighting or using violence on another.

Such an offence is useful where a large scale fight has occurred and it is very difficult to frame individual charges against the participants. Obviously persons who may be charged with this offence may also be guilty of various offences of assault, but this offence requires that the act is likely to terrify a reasonable bystander.

(2) Riot and rout

The offence of riot is rarely used and the offence of rout seems to be obsolete and will therefore not be dealt with here.

The offence of riot arises mainly now in connection with civil claims for compensation for riot damage which is payable out of police funds under the Riot (Damages) Act 1886; such claims can only succeed upon proof of a riotous and tumultuous assembly. Thus there is a need to define what constitutes a riot. It would seem that this is established where at least three persons who have a common purpose, achieve that common purpose having the intent to help one another by force if necessary against any person who may oppose them in the execution of the common purpose. The force or violence is used in such a way as to alarm at least one person of reasonable firmness and courage.

It would seem that there is a riot when the persons begin to carry out the common purpose. It is probably not necessary to prove that at least one person of reasonable firmness and courage was alarmed; merely that such a person would have been had he been present.

(3) Unlawful assembly

There is no clearly accepted definition of this offence. It is defined by Smith and Hogan as a situation where three or more persons assemble on a public or private place having a common purpose either to commit a crime of violence or to achieve some other objective, whether lawful or not, in such a way that would cause reasonable men to apprehend a breach of the peace. The *mens rea* would appear to be satisfied if the accused intends to use or to abet the use of violence or if he intends to do or abet acts which he knows are likely to cause a breach of the peace.

A major problem is caused where a group of individuals proposes to follow a course of conduct which, although perfectly lawful, they know will almost certainly lead to a public disturbance. Such was the situation in *Beatty* v. *Gillbanks* (1882) where members of the Salvation Army proposed to hold a peaceful march, though they were aware that they would almost certainly be met and opposed by members of a rival association, the Skeleton Army. They held the march, despite an order by local magistrates purporting to prohibit it, and trouble occurred when they were intercepted by the Skeleton Army. A local police officer called on the Salvation Army leader to stop, but he refused and was thereupon arrested. The magistrates ordered that he be bound over to keep the peace. The Divisional Court, however, quashed the order on the ground that the magistrates' order amounted to a ruling that a man may be convicted for doing a lawful act if he knows that it may cause another to commit an unlawful act. The principle of the case has been followed many times though there are cases which appear to conflict (*e.g. Wise* v. *Dunning* (1902)). The decision would almost certainly be the other way if the purpose of the Salvation Army leaders had been to provoke the unlawful act committed by the Skeleton Army.

2. Statutory Offences

(1) Insulting or threatening behaviour

It is an offence contrary to section 5 of the Public Order Act 1936 for any person in any public place or at any public meeting to use threatening, abusive or insulting words or behaviour; or distribute or display any writing sign or visible presentation which is threatening, abusive or insulting, with intent to provoke a breach of the peace or whereby a breach of the peace is likely to be occasioned. This offence is punishable on summary conviction with six months imprisonment and/or a fine or £1,000. The words "threatening, abusive or insulting" are not subject to any specialist legal definition. They are to be given their ordinary every day meaning (*Brutus* v. *Cozens* (1973)). The offence must take place in public, though this would include an accused who, while standing in his front room at home, shouted insulting words at someone passing by in the street (or vice versa). For the purposes of this Act, public place means a place to which the public has or is permitted to have access and in the case of places (such as cricket grounds) where the public have access to part only of the premises, the whole area is deemed to be a public place. The conduct complained of must be either intended to cause a breach of the peace or likely to cause a breach of the peace.

There is a great temptation for prosecutors to use this offence to cover a multitude of sins which it was not intended to cover. For example where the facts reveal that the defendants have committed assaults they should be charged with assault and not a section 5 offence. Equally it is important to remember that the conduct must not just be insulting, etc., it must be likely or intended to cause a breach of the peace.

By section 70 of the Race Relations Act 1976 a new section 5A was inserted into the Public Order Act 1936 to create an offence where in similar circumstances hatred is likely to be stirred up against any group of persons in Great Britain, defined by reference to colour, race, nationality or ethnic or national origins, but not religion.

(2) Binding over

Under common law and under statute magistrates have the power to bind over persons to keep the peace and to be of good behaviour, or to keep the peace or to be of good behaviour. Where this power is exercisable the person must agree to be bound over; if he refuses the magistrates must commit him to prison for up to six months. This is thus a very good means for protesters to make martyrs of themselves. The magistrates will decide for how long the undertaking shall run and the amount of money that shall be pledged by way of security for the promise. Thus they may, for example, ask the accused if he is prepared to be bound over for twelve months in the sum of £100 to keep the peace.

This power may be exercised following a conviction together with the sentence imposed for the criminal offence. However, under the Justices of the Peace Act 1361, a justice may bind over anyone whom he thinks may cause a breach of the peace in the future. In this case the binding over can be done at any stage of the proceedings and the magistrates are not restricted to binding over merely the defendant. Thus in an action brought by one neighbour alleging an assault by another neighbour the bench may take the view that both parties and witnesses in the case should be bound over. It is often used by the police in a form of deal with a suspect. The police offer to drop the charges, if the defendant agrees to be bound over. It should be remembered, however, that the magistrates should only use the power if they feel a breach of the peace is likely; it would rarely be an appropriate course of action for a shoplifter.

(3) Obstructing the police in the execution of their duty

Under section 51(3) of the Police Act 1964 (as amended by the Criminal Law Act 1977) it is an offence to resist or wilfully obstruct a constable in the execution of his duty, or a person assisting a constable in the execution of his duty.

Thus anyone who wilfully obstructs or resists a constable who is lawfully engaged upon his duties of protecting life and property, of protecting the peace and of preventing or investigating crime commits an offence. Anything which makes it more difficult for the constable to carry out his duties constitutes an obstruction, but the prosection must show that the defendant acted with the intention of obstructing the police and that he acted without lawful excuse. The word "resists" probably adds little to "obstructs."

The offence is only committed when the constable is actually acting in the course of his duty. This will rarely cause any difficulties, but occasionally the defendant will argue that the constable had acted in such a way so as not to be in the course of his duty. Thus unless the constable is acting under a warrant or statutory powers he will have no right to enter private property. He will have the right of every ordinary citizen to walk up the path to the front door and to make enquiries. But once he is ordered to leave he will become a trespasser if he remains and as such will not be acting in the course of his duty (*Snooks* v. *Mannion* (1982); the phrase "F—— off" is not necessarily to be taken as a withdrawal of the licence; it may just be a term of abuse. Equally if a constable places a person under arrest he may use reasonable force to take him to the police station. If, however, the arrest is unlawful, or he has not arrested the person, such force may amount to an assault, and thus the constable will no longer be acting "in the execution of his duty."

The police are under a duty to use reasonable force to prevent a breach of the peace. In the exercise of this duty he may forbid a meeting to take place or may enter private premises and remain there despite requests to leave if he has reasonable grounds to believe that a breach of the peace will occur (*Thomas* v. *Sawkins* (1935)).

Part Three
CONTRACT

CHAPTER 1

INTRODUCTION

When a man gives his word he is expected to keep it, and usually he does. Nor should we be so parochial as to think that it is only the Englishman's word that is his bond because the notion that a pledge is to be honoured is understood and accepted by all people and has been so understood and accepted for many thousands of years.

Up to a point promises are self enforcing; even without the enforcement machinery of a legal system most people would honour their promises most of the time. Apart from the feeling that it is dishonourable not to keep one's word, there is the practical consideration that a man is placed at a serious disadvantage in his dealings with others if he acquires a reputation for being untrustworthy.

But in an ordered and developed society rules need to be created and fashioned to regulate the enforcement of promises. Even if everyone was prepared always to honour his word, and of course there are always numbers who do not, it would still be necessary to establish a legal framework. To say that a man's word is his bond is too simplistic. Both parties may subscribe unreservedly to this maxim but they may legitimately dispute exactly what was promised. A says that he understood one thing by his promise, B claims that he understood something else. A may say that he made his promise not to B, but to C, B may claim that C was acting as his agent so that he, B, may enforce the contract. A may say that he was mistaken about the subject-matter of the contract, B may claim that he was misled by A. So it can be seen from these few examples that even parties acting in complete good faith will have genuine differences of opinion about the interpretation of their contract; the law of contract is fashioned to resolve these differences.

It needs to be noted at this introductory stage that our law does not enforce all promises even if they are seriously made and intended to be binding. Our law became imbued, it is not entirely clear why, with the notion that promises were enforceable only so far as they formed part of a bargain. The law is a law of contract not a law of promise. To be enforceable a promise must be "bought." So a promise to sell goods is bought by a promise to pay the price but it must not be thought that promises can only be bought for money. A man may offer one sort of goods in exchange for another, or he may offer services in return for goods or money. These are *bargains* which the law will enforce. But the law will not generally enforce gratuitous promises, that is a promise given for nothing in return. This may seem strange because many (perhaps most) of us would think that a promise seriously given and intended to be binding should be enforceable even though given without any compensating promise from the other party. Keeping my word means keeping my word without thought to some compensating advantage to me. But in English law bargain is fundamental to enforceability and a gratuitous promise is usually enforceable only if it is made in a special solemn form, a deed under seal (see *post*, p. 336).

In the development of contract law, form has always played an important part. Form may range from a simple handshake to an elaborate ritual accompanying the signing of a treaty of peace. Formalities may be used to give added solemnity to the promise, to make it clear that the promise is not casually given and that a breach of it will be considered a very grave matter. Thus a promise may be reduced to writing and sealed by the party making the promise. As we have just noticed, even a gratuitous promise is enforceable if made under seal; the solemn form may be said to make up for the lack of the bargain usually required. But there is another reason for reducing a contract to writing which is that the parties have a record of its terms and thus avoid the problems which arise from the uncertain recollection of an oral bargain. This is not to say that written contracts do not give rise to difficulties of interpretation but they may have obvious advantages over an oral agreement. If a contract is for the sale of a newspaper or a packet of bacon a written contract would be entirely inapropos and would only hamper daily business; if it is for the sale of an aircraft or for chartering a ship it would be highly unusual for the parties, given the likely complexity of the contract, to rely on an oral agreement.

There is no general requirement under the law that a contract should be in a prescribed form, but to this rule there are important exceptions where a contract is required to be made under seal (*post*, p. 336) or where it must be in writing (*post*, p. 486). In practice, however, a contract is likely to be reduced to writing whenever the transaction is one of some complexity while routine everyday contracts are concluded by word of mouth, or even by conduct without a word said on either side.

Suppose, then, we take the case of a contract for the sale of goods when the transaction is concluded by the seller wrapping and delivering the goods in exchange for the price. Though not a word is exchanged a valid contract has been concluded. But what are its precise terms? What if the dress is thought by the buyer's wife to be an unsuitable colour, or the shoes pinch when worn, or the pie is mouldy, or the pork when eaten causes trichinosis?

At one time our law took the view that it was for the parties to specify the terms and if the buyer did not bargain for terms warranting the quality of goods then so much the worse for him: *caveat emptor* — let the buyer beware. This view may be acceptable where the parties have equal bargaining strength and deal at arm's length. It is a less attractive view where one party enjoys a bargaining advantage not shared by the other. Another example is provided by contracts of service. In the famous case of *Somersett* v. *Stewart* (1772) it was held that a slave who was confined in a ship on the Thames about to sail for Jamaica, must be set free. In a ringing judgment Lord Mansfield said that slavery was so odious that nothing could be suffered to support it "and therefore the black must be discharged." Yet throughout the Industrial Revolution the courts and the legislature tolerated appalling working conditions for men, women and children at grossly inadequate rates of remuneration. Such practices could be tolerated in the name of freedom of contract and economic policies of laissez-faire, but with the economic power in the hands of the few it would be idle to pretend that the labourer enjoyed any real freedom of contract.

In the context of sale of goods it is significant that the maxim *caveat emptor* called upon the *buyer* to beware with the inference that the seller would be capable of looking after himself. Recognising this imbalance the courts in the nineteenth century began to imply terms, especially in contracts for the sale of goods, to ensure that the buyer got a fair deal. As Lord Ellenborough (*Gardiner* v. *Gray* (1815)) once put it, it can hardly be supposed that a buyer purchases goods in order to lay them on a dunghill. Consequently terms relating to the fitness and suitability of goods (now to be found in the Sale of Goods Act 1979, *post*, p. 461) were implied by the courts.

But these implied terms could be expressly excluded. The general rule remained that it was for the parties to make the contract. People (most especially corporate enterprises which by the twentieth century had come to dominate the market for the provision of goods, services and utilities) realised that they could draw up a written contract entirely favourable to them which the consumer had little option but to accept, and no option whatever if the provider enjoyed a monopoly.

Faced with this development, the courts could, and did, construe such contracts strictly against the party dictating the terms, and showed not a little ingenuity in finding ways of obviating the grosser forms of exemption clause (see *post*, pp. 359 and 473). But only Parliament could launch the frontal assault necessary to ensure a fair deal for the consumer. This it did in such legislation as the Supply of Goods (Implied Terms) Act 1973, the Consumer Credit Act 1974, the Unfair Contract Terms Act 1977 and the Supply of Goods and Services Act 1982. This legislation is examined in more detail below but the broad effect is to ensure that in contracts for the sale and supply of goods, hire-purchase and credit-sale transactions, and in contracts for the supply of services, the consumer's interests are protected. In the field of employment, the restoration of the employee's bargaining position owes more to trade unions than it does to either the courts or Parliament, but legislation now closely regulates conditions of employment, prohibits discrimination, provides for compensation on redundancy and affords remedies for unfair dismissal. The law of landlord and tenant has been similarly revised by Parliament to afford the tenant more security of tenure and a mechanism for ensuring a fair rent.

Thus "freedom" of contract has been progressively constrained by legislative intervention. The broad aim of such legislation, which is to secure reasonable terms for a party who by reason of social and economic circumstances cannot secure them for himself, is clearly an acceptable one though there is always room for argument about the precise details of such legislation. It is against a background of increasing legislative intervention, which shows little sign of diminishing, that the modern law of contract must be viewed.

Chapter 2

OFFER AND ACCEPTANCE

The English law of contract is dominated by the indivisible trinity of offer, acceptance and consideration. That it should have developed in this way was not inevitable, as the rather different approach of Scots law shows. Sometimes the resolution of a factual situation into these classical terms of legal analysis leads to a degree of artificiality which is somewhat out of touch with modern conditions, but then it might be said that any rule of general application will have to cover marginal areas which will not fit readily into a conceptual framework. The problem which the application of these rules does help to solve, however, is essentially one of identity. When and under what circumstances does a legally enforceable contract arise as opposed, for example, to some preliminary discussion or identity of mutual interest which may only later ripen into a fully fledged legal agreement? If I place a "For Sale" notice on the windscreen of my car, at what point am I irrevocably bound to hand it over to a purchaser? What of an auction or tender to carry out work on my house? It is in identifying the point when the contractual bond is finally tied that the basic rules of offer and acceptance come into play.

1. Offer

(1) Offer and invitation to treat

Not every "offer" in the sense in which that word is often used will constitute an "offer" for the purposes of contract. In particular, an "offer" needs to be distinguished from an "invitation to treat" (or as it is described in some of the older cases, an "offer to chaffer"). In other words the "offer" must show that the offeror intends to be bound by the precise terms of his offer, and is not merely taking a tentative preliminary step towards a later agreement. An illustration of such a mere "invitation to treat" is revealed in *Partridge* v. *Crittenden* (1968). Mr. Partridge placed an advertisement in a periodical which read, "Bramblefinch cocks, bramblefinch hens, 25s. each." As this bird was a member of a protected species, he was charged with unlawfully offering for sale a wild bird contrary to the Protection of Birds Act 1954. The Divisional Court quashed his conviction on the grounds that this was not indeed an "offer for sale" but a mere "invitation to treat." The business reality that may to some extent lie behind this view is that unless catalogues and advertisements were considered in this way, a supplier would find himself in the embarrassing position of being sued if demand for an article ever exceeded supply.

The same principle is illustrated in a different context in *Pharmaceutical Society of Great Britain* v. *Boots Cash Chemists (Southern) Ltd.* (1953). Two customers in a "self-service" shop placed in their wire baskets articles selected from the open shelves. These articles were medicines which it was an offence for Boots to sell except by or under the supervision of a registered pharmacist, who was therefore under instructions to supervise the transaction at the cash desk and if necessary to prevent a customer from removing such an article from the shop. The prosecution case was that the display constituted an "offer" which the customers "accepted" when they put the article in the basket. They alleged a contract was completed at that point, although payment was postponed until the customer reached the cash desk. The Court of Appeal did not agree. They decided that the shelf display was, like an advertisement, merely an invitation to treat. It was the customer who made the "offer" when the article was placed in the basket. The shop accepted the customer's offer only at the cash desk where a pharmacist was available, and accordingly no offence was committed. The result illustrates the fact that, contrary to what one might have thought, it is the customer who makes an offer in a shop which the shopkeeper then chooses either to reject or accept. No-one can demand to buy the contents of a shop.

(2) Offers to the public at large

Most offers will be made to particular people on a particular occasion, for example A offers to sell B his car. This will typically be a so-called "executory" agreement, that is, a promise to sell is matched by a promise to buy. Sometimes a promise is exchanged for an act (on which see later), and is known as a "unilateral" contract. There will nevertheless be other occasions, where a unilateral as opposed to executory agreement is involved, when the offeror may not wish to limit his offer to a particular person or persons. In these cases placing an advertisement is likely to be the only way such an offer can in practice be made, and hence such an action will be regarded as an offer and not a mere invitation to treat. The most famous example of this type of offer is in *Carlill* v. *Carbolic Smoke Ball Co.* (1893). The defendants were the sellers of a medical preparation called "The Carbolic Smoke Ball." They placed an advertisement in the *Pall Mall Gazette* stating that they would pay £100 to anyone who bought and used the ball according to their directions, but still contracted influenza. They mentioned that they had also deposited £1,000 with their bankers to show their sincerity in the matter. The plaintiff used the ball as prescribed and contracted 'flu. She thereupon sued the defendants for her £100. She succeeded. One of the points taken by the defendants was that the advertisement was a "mere puff." The Court of Appeal rejected such an argument and held that this was a true offer. It was an offer made to all the world, which ripened into a contract only with those people who accepted and acted upon the terms of the offer.

Of course the Carbolic Smoke Ball Company could lawfully have refused to sell the plaintiff one of their products in the first place. Before the sale took place, the defendants had merely made an invitation to treat.

2. Acceptance

If A offers his car to B for £800, and B says to A, "I accept," this would clearly be an enforceable contract. Unfortunately, many cases are not as clear cut as this. Often, for example, there will be protracted negotiations in which it is difficult to ascertain when, if at all, a contract was concluded. Accordingly, the legal rules elucidate how an acceptance can be recognised. There must in fact be an acceptance, although the communication of that acceptance may take various forms.

(1) The fact of acceptance

For an acceptance to be valid, it must precisely fit the terms of the offer. If it does not, then it may well be a further step in negotiations, but cannot lead to a firm contract. Sometimes the negotiations are so ambiguous that the existence of a contract can only be inferred from the conduct of the parties, as in *Brogden* v. *Metropolitan Rail Co.* (1877). After Brogden had supplied the defendant company with coal for a number of years without any formal agreement, the parties decided to regularise the situation and draw up a formal contract. The company sent Brogden a draft agreement, and after inserting what amounted to a new term in the agreement, he returned it marked "approved." The company's agent put the draft in his desk drawer, where it remained for the next two years. It might have stayed there but for the fact that eventually a dispute arose between the parties. The difficult question at issue was to discover when, if at all, there had been mutual consent to the terms of the agreement. Clearly Brogden had not accepted unconditionally the terms of the offer as he had inserted a fresh term. But how could the subsequent delivery of coal be explained except with reference to a contract?

The House of Lords therefore decided that an acceptance by conduct could be inferred from the parties' behaviour, and a valid contract came into existence either when the company first ordered a load of coal after the receipt of the draft from Brogden, or at the latest when he supplied the first load.

Other clear examples of acceptance by conduct are provided by so-called unilateral contracts where instead of A exchanging a promise with B, B simply does something on the strength of A's promise. *Carlill* (above) is such a case, as are offers of a reward for the return of some article that has been lost. They are further discussed below under problems related to the communication of acceptance.

When a party makes what one might call a qualified acceptance, as did the plaintiff in Brogden, the party is in reality making a counter-offer, the effect of which is to destroy the original offer. So if A offers to sell his car to B for £800, and B offers £750 for it, then although A and B might be thought close to agreement, as a matter of law there is as yet no contract. The point is illustrated in *Hyde* v. *Wrench* (1840). Wrench offered to sell an estate to Hyde for £1,000. Hyde made an offer of £950 which the defendant refused. Accordingly Hyde wrote saying that he was prepared to pay the original asking price of £1,000, and sued Wrench in an attempt to enforce the sale at that price. The court rejected the plaintiff's claim. Hyde's counter-offer of £950 had destroyed the original offer; there was therefore no longer any offer in existence he could subsequently "accept."

Why, therefore, was there a contract in *Brogden* v. *Metropolitan Rail Co.*, but not in this case? If in *Brogden* the defendants had noticed that the plaintiff had inserted a new term, they could have refused his counter-offer. But they *behaved* as though they had accepted it; Brogden was entitled to assume from their subsequent conduct in taking deliveries that they had accepted his new term. This illustrates the way in which parties can be held bound to a contract by an "objective" view of their actions, that is to say, how their actions would have appeared to a disinterested outsider. This is a theme which needs constantly to be born in mind.

A less obvious but similar type of problem has recently been presented by the "battle of forms" cases. Many commercial concerns seek to save time and money by contracting on standard terms which are printed on their own forms. If the parties terms are identical there is clearly complete agreement, but what if they conflict? This situation arose in *Butler Machine Tool Co. Ltd.* v. *Ex-Cell-O Corp. (England) Ltd.* (1979). The sellers offered to sell one of their machines to the plaintiff on their standard terms, printed on the quotation, which were stated to prevail "over any terms and conditions in the Buyer's order." The buyer replied by placing an order which was stated to be on their own terms and conditions, which *inter alia* contained a crucial clause as to price in conflict with the seller's terms. The sellers acknowledged receipt of the order on the buyers form, and a contract was undoubtedly thereupon concluded. The difficulty arose, on whose terms had the contract been concluded? Was it on those of the buyer or the seller's?

The Court of Appeal applied the principle in *Hyde* v. *Wrench* and held that the buyer's reply on their own form constituted a counter-offer which the plaintiff had accepted by agreeing to supply the goods. Hence, although it will not always be the case, it will often be true in the "battle of forms" the party who fires the last shot wins.

A difficult problem of construction may sometimes arise to decide whether a reply is a counter-offer or merely a request for information. If it is the latter, then the original offer remains open. The point arose in *Stevenson* v. *McLean* (1880). The defendant offered to sell iron to the plaintiffs, the offer to be open until Monday. The plaintiffs replied by asking if they might buy the goods on credit. No reply was received, so on Monday afternoon they telegraphed the defendant accepting the offer. By this time the defendant had sold the goods to a third party, and the plaintiffs sued for breach of contract. Although it could be regarded as a marginal case, the court held that this was "a mere inquiry, which should have been answered and not treated as a rejection of the offer." The defendant's offer, therefore, remained open until it had been effectively revoked which, by that time, it had not been.

A simple and convenient test for distinguishing between a counter-offer and a mere inquiry has been proposed by Professor Smith, namely: could the "enquiry" be accepted? If not, it can hardly be interpreted as an offer. On the facts of *Stevenson* v. *McLean*, it is difficult to see how the plaintiffs message could possibly have been accepted, bearing in mind the rather uncertain and general nature of their request.

(2) The communication of acceptance

It is not enough that a party has made a mental decision to accept a certain offer. There must be something further, an external indication that the party intends to be bound by the terms of the offer. This is sometimes explained by the statement that English law takes an objective rather than subjective view of the transaction. In other words, the law looks at the matter from the point of view of an interested bystander, and draws inferences on the basis of how events would appear to him. The way in which such acceptance can be communicated will nevertheless vary greatly according to the circumstances.

(a) *Silence.* It follows from what has been said that silence alone cannot constitute consent, and the authority usually cited to support this proposition is *Felthouse* v. *Bindley* (1862), the facts of which were earlier outlined (*ante*, p. 5). The court held that there had been no acceptance of the plaintiff's offer, and the action therefore failed. The case shows that even though the nephew appeared to have made a mental reservation to sell the horse to his uncle, the failure to communicate this acceptance in some way meant that the contract was never concluded.

(b) *Waiver.* The facts of *Carlill* (above) show that there may be circumstances in which the offeror waives the communication of acceptance. In that case the waiver was by implication, since it would clearly be a practical absurdity if everyone on seeing such an advertisement were obliged to dutifully write a letter communicating their acceptance. In other cases, it may be expressed directly by the parties. Paradoxically, if the nephew had sued the uncle in *Felthouse* v. *Bindley* (above) it seems he would have succeeded. The uncle had clearly waived the need for communication of acceptance.

(c) *Ignorance of the offer.* What if someone does an act which in fact complies with the terms of an offer, although he is unaware of such an offer? For example, if an insurance company offers £100 for information leading to the conviction of a criminal, and a member of the public supplies it in ignorance that any reward was made, can he claim the money? In principle the answer would appear to be No. The underlying rationale of the rules of offer and acceptance is that there should be an agreement, and agreement hardly seems possible when the respective parties are mutually ignorant of each others intention. There is no clear English authority on the matter. It was a slightly different issue that arose in *Williams* v. *Carwardine* (1833). The defendant had offered a reward for information leading to the discovery of a certain murderer, and handbills were posted in the area where the plaintiff lived declaring the fact.

The plaintiff apparently knew of the offer, but gave the information for a different reason. She believed she had only a short time to live, and wished to ease her conscience. It was held that she was entitled to the reward. She had complied with the terms of the offer, of which she was aware, and her motive was not material. Had she completely forgotten the reward at the time she gave the information, then the result might well have been more difficult to justify, as the Australian decision in *R* v. *Clarke* (1927) indicates. In that case the defendant's only object in giving the information was to clear himself of a murder charge, and at the time he had no intention of claiming the reward. The Australian court accordingly dismissed his claim. The borderline between these two cases is obviously a thin one.

(d) *Prescribed communication.* Whilst an offeror may waive communication of acceptance altogether, he may also on the other hand prescribe the way in which it is to be made. If the offeror made it clear that one and only one method of acceptance was possible, for example telephoning at a precise time and date, then it seems that any other purported mode of acceptance would be invalid. What of the case, however, where A prescribes that B should reply immediately by letter, but B replies a day earlier by telephone instead? It would seem absurd to say that there was no contract in this situation. The general principle would seem to be that if the offeree accepts in the prescribed mode or a manner equally efficacious or better, then the offeror should be bound.

(e) *No prescribed mode of communication.* Where no particular means of communication has been prescribed, then the form of acceptance will depend entirely on the circumstances in which the offer is made. If, to adopt the examples given by Lord Denning in *Entores Ltd.* v. *Miles Far East Corporation* (1955), A shouts an offer to B across a river, and does not hear B's reply because of the noise from a passing aircraft, then no contract is concluded. B will have to repeat his reply so that A can hear it. Equally if B's reply is inaudible because of interference on a telephone line, there is no contract until B has made an effective reply.

(f) *Acceptance by post.* Very commonly the medium of communication will be the post, and the courts have inevitably developed a set of rules which regulate the moment at which acceptance takes place. The almost insoluble dilemma which has to be solved is to balance on the one hand the offeror's need to know whether he is bound by the offeree's acceptance, and the latter's need to know that he has done enough to comply with the offer and can therefore rely on it. The courts' response has been to lay down a rule on the basis of convenience rather than principle. The general rule is that an acceptance by post takes effect as soon as it is posted, and was established in *Adams* v. *Lindsell* (1818). On September 2, 1817 the defendants wrote to the plaintiffs offering to sell a quantity of wool and requiring an answer "in course of post." Unfortunately the defendants misaddressed the letter which consequently did not arrive until the evening of September 5. The plaintiffs posted a reply the same evening which reached the defendants on September 9. It appeared from the evidence that a properly addressed letter would have elicited a reply "in course of post" by September 7. The defendants, having heard nothing at that time, sold the wool to a third party on September 8. The crucial question in the case was whether a contract had been concluded before the sale to the third parties on September 8. The court held that a contract was concluded as soon as the acceptance was posted. Various views have been advanced as to the theoretical basis of the court's decision. The court may have been influenced by the consideration that it was the defendant's fault that the letter had been misaddressed, and that they should therefore bear the burden of any loss. It remains true, however, that any solution to the problem would have tended to operate harshly against one of the parties, and as a practical matter, it is easier to prove the posting of a letter than its receipt, or that it has in fact been brought to the attention of the offeror. What if the letter of acceptance has been misaddressed to the offeror? Although, curiously enough, there is no direct authority on the point, it would seem reasonable to assume that under those circumstances the normal postal presumption would not apply. Acceptance should then be effective only when the wrongly directed letter is actually received.

The logical development of this rule can work very harshly against the offeror as was shown in *Household Fire, etc.* v. *Grant* (1879). In this case the letter was lost in the post and never delivered. Nevertheless, it was still held to be an effective and binding acceptance. "Posting" means placing the letter in a post-box or into the hands of a Post Office employee authorised to receive letters. It is not "posting" if the letter is merely placed in the hands of a postman authorised to deliver letters as happened in *Re London and Northern Bank, ex p. Jones* (1900).

Telegrams are treated similarly to letters. Communication by telex being almost, if not quite completely, instantaneous has been treated by the courts as more akin to a conversation, either direct or by telephone. Consequently, in *Brinkibon Ltd.* v. *Stahag Stahl* (1982) the House of Lords approved the earlier Court of Appeal decision in *Entores Ltd.* v. *Miles Far East Corporation* (1955) and decided that acceptance, as a general rule, takes place when the offer was received and not when it was sent. The underlying rationale would seem to be that once a telegram has been dictated or handed to the Post Office, nothing further can be done to ensure its delivery. In the case of telephone or telex, it should be immediately obvious to the sender of a message if something has gone wrong in its despatch, and so it is only sensible that it is the sendor's duty to ensure that any ambiguity or failure in the message is immediately corrected.

In order to prevent the offeror being unfairly prejudiced, the operation of the postal rules is subject to the consideration that the post must be a means of communication which in all the circumstances is reasonable. Clearly, if an offer comes by post, it is reasonable to employ the post to reply. If the offer was made orally by a next-door neighbour, the post would hardly seem appropriate. An intermediate situation was posed in *Henthorn* v. *Fraser* (1891–94). The plaintiff lived in Birkenhead, and the defendant was based in Liverpool. The defendant handed him an offer in Liverpool, which the plaintiff accepted by posting a letter from Birkenhead. It was held in this case that even though the offer was not made by post, because the parties lived in different towns, the use of the post to reply must have been within their comtemplation. The contract came into being as soon as the plaintiff posted the acceptance.

If a party did not wish to be bound by the postal rules, it would always be possible to spell this out expressly. There may undoubtedly be other circumstances when even if it is not so stated directly, it is quite apparent that the parties did not intend the postal rules to apply, in which case whatever the parties themselves envisaged will have to be complied with.

A difficult point is raised by the situation that arises when B accepts A's offer by post, but then changes his mind and telephones A seeking to withdraw. Can B escape from the contract? Surprisingly, there is no authoritative English decision on the point. In principle it would seem that the contract is concluded, and that it is therefore too late to decline the offer. On the other hand, does permitting withdrawal in this situation lead to either party being put at a disadvantage, since A will not yet know of the 'acceptance'?

3. Termination of Offer

Quite apart from the obvious case of an outright refusal, and the more difficult problem of a counter-offer which has been discussed above, there are a number of ways in which an offer may lapse.

(1) Revocation

It has long been the law that an offer may be revoked at any time before acceptance, but that the revocation must be effectively communicated to the offeree. It is not enough that A has simply changed his mind about contracting with B. In *Byrne* v. *Van Tienhoven* (1880) the defendants in Cardiff posted a letter to New York offering to sell the plaintiffs 1,000 boxes of tinplates. On October 8 they posted a letter revoking the offer. On October 11 the plaintiffs received the first letter and immediately telegraphed their acceptance. The second letter eventually arrived on October 20. It was held that the revocation came too late. The postal rules apply only to acceptance, not to an offer, and by the time the second letter reached the plaintiffs a contract had already been concluded.

Although the revocation must actually be communicated to the offeree, it seems that the information does not have to come from the offeror himself. In *Dickinson* v. *Dodds* (1876) the defendant made an offer to sell a house for £800, "to be left over until Friday, June 12, 9 a.m." On Thursday, June 11, the defendant sold the house to a third party, Alan. The plaintiff came to know of the sale through a fourth man. Before 9 a.m. on June 12, the plaintiff handed the defendant a letter purporting to accept the original offer. The Court of Appeal held that the offer had already been revoked, and there was no contract. Dickinson, it was said, "knew that Dodds was no longer minded to sell the property to him as plainly and clearly as if Dodds had told him in so many words." The case could give rise to difficulties. What if the offeree had merely heard a rumour that the property was no longer for sale? It seems that this would have to be considered as a question of fact in each case as it arose.

(2) Revocation in unilateral contracts

A special difficulty arises in the case of unilateral contracts. If before anyone had had a chance to purchase a smoke ball in *Carlill*, an advertisement had appeared stating that the whole offer was a meaningless publicity stunt then no great harm is done. But suppose A offers B £10,000 to walk from John O'Groats to Lands End, the money to be paid over when the walk is completed. Just as B is limping through Truro, A says that he is revoking his offer. Since it is generally assumed that in cases such as these there is no acceptance until the act is completed, and a revocation can be made at any time prior to acceptance, it might seem that A is within his rights in so acting. There does not seem to be a completely satisfactory solution to the problem, but in *Errington* v. *Errington* (1952) an attempt was made to mitigate the injustice of such a rule. A father let his son and daughter live in a house which he had purchased with the aid of a building society mortgage. He told them that if they paid off the mortgage instalments, the house would then be conveyed to them. They paid the instalments as they became due even though they did not bind themselves to do so. The father later died and his personal representatives sought to withdraw the offer. The Court of Appeal held it was too late. Lord Denning explained this by saying, "The father's promise was a unilateral contract—a promise of the house in return for their act of paying instalments. It could not be revoked by him once the couple entered on performance of the act, but it would cease to bind him if they left it incomplete and unperformed, which they have not done." This suggests that partial performance can amount to acceptance of the contract, although complete performance is the necessary consideration (consideration is considered later in Chapter 3). If this view is correct, then A's purported revocation in Truro would also come too late if B were minded to go on to Lands End.

(3) Lapse of time

If an offer is stated to be open for a specific period, then clearly it will lapse after that time. When no period has been laid down, then the offer will lapse after a reasonable time. Quite what a reasonable time will be depends entirely on the circumstances of the case. An offer to sell fruit which will deteriorate is likely to lapse more quickly than that relating to a piece of antique furniture (see, *e.g. Ramsgate Victoria Hotel* v. *Montefiore* (1866)). There may be difficult questions of fact in between these extremes. The problem is closely related to the earlier discussion of the mode of acceptance which the parties contemplated. If the offeror uses the telephone or telex as a means of communication, a reply by letter might well be thought to be defeated by the fact that the offer has lapsed.

(4) Failure of a precondition

An offer, just like an acceptance, may be conditional. Consequently if the condition fails, then there is no offer capable of acceptance. The point arose in *Financings Ltd.* v. *Stimson* (1962). The defendant, in effect, made an offer to a Finance Company that they should purchase a car. Before the company accepted, the car was stolen and badly damaged. In ignorance of this, the Finance Company signed the agreement. It was held that no contract had been concluded. As Donovan L.J. said: "There must . . . be implied a term that until acceptance the goods would remain in substantially the same state as at the date of the offer; and I think that is both good sense and good law."

(5) Death

The effect of death is more ambivalent in law than in life. It is not the case that an offer automatically ceases with the offeror's death. It seems that the precise effect varies with the subject matter of the contract. If the offer is to provide a service such as performing at a concert, which only the particular person can provide, then the offer must lapse on death. But in the case of something that is not "personal" to the offeror, for example an offer to sell a chair, then if the offeree is unaware of the offeror's death, there seems no reason why a contract is not concluded which can be satisfied from the deceased's estate. A contract of guarantee was held not to be invalidated by the death of the offeror in *Bradbury* v. *Morgan* (1862). There appears to be no English authority on the corresponding effect of the offeree's death, but the prevailing view appears to be that the offer would then lapse.

4. Certainty

A contract assumes that there has been agreement on the central issues of the bargain, and clearly if the "agreement" is in such ambiguous terms as to be without real meaning then there has been no true concensus. One could analyse such a failure in terms of offer and acceptance; in other words an unambiguous offer has not been met by a clear and unqualified acceptance. Since, however, the failure of certainty might equally effect "offer" or "acceptance" it is convenient to consider it as a separate issue.

At one extreme a provision that a sum of money should be paid if a horse proved "lucky" was held to be too vague to be enforceable in *Guthing* v. *Lynn* (1831). A less obvious case was *Scammell* v. *Ouston* (1941) where Ouston wished to acquire a van from Messrs. Scammell "on hire-purchase terms." The House of Lords decided that notwithstanding the courts desire to uphold a bargain if in truth there was one, these terms were too vague to signify an agreement. There were many different permutations on "hire-purchase terms" and it was impossible to say what precisely, if anything, had been agreed. In effect, the parties were still negotiating.

In *Hillas* v. *Arcos* (1932), however, the House of Lords upheld an agreement where Hillas had contracted to buy timber from Arcos for the season 1930, stated to be "of fair specification," with a further option to purchase the following year. The further option contained no specific references to the kind or size of timber, but the House of Lords decided that having regard to the parties' previous course of dealings and "the legal implication in contracts of what is reasonable" that the terms used were sufficiently certain. Wherever possible, as Lord Tomlin observed, the courts are anxious not to "incur the reproach of being the destroyer of bargains." This approach is shown in the later case of *Nicolene Ltd.* v. *Simmonds* (1953) where an agreement to purchase steel was couched in perfectly clear terms except for a reference to the fact that the transaction was subject to "the usual conditions of acceptance." It was found that this phrase was quite meaningless as there were no such conditions. That being so the reference could be ignored. Otherwise, any insertion of meaningless words would effectively allow defaulters to escape from their contractual obligations.

5. Auctions, Tenders and the Sale of Land

The general rules applying to auctions, tenders and the sale of land are no different from those that apply to any contract. Their precise application in these circumstances, however, requires some elucidation.

(1) Auctions

Normally the two parties to an auction sale are the bidder and the owner of the goods who is simply making use of the auctioneer's services.

An advertisement that an auction is to take place at a certain time is not an offer which those who attend at the specified time thereby accept. This was decided in *Harris* v. *Nickerson* (1873), where the plaintiff failed to recover damages for travelling to an auction which was subsequently cancelled. The effect of the advertisement was merely a declaration of intention, not a contractual promise. At an auction, it is the bidder who is the offeror, each bid effectively revoking the previous one, and it is the auctioneer who accepts the offer by the fall of the hammer or in any other customary way (Sale of Goods Act 1979, s. 57(2)). The result is that up until the moment of acceptance, the bidder is free to retract his bid, as is the auctioneer to withdraw the item from sale. There is some doubt as to the legal position of a sale advertised "without reserve," that is a sale where an item does not have a minimum reserve price below which it will not be sold. In *Warlow* v. *Harrison* (1843–60) there are *obiter dicta* to the effect that the auctioneer makes an offer that the lot will go to the highest bidder, and the bidder making his bid relying on this, accepts. There is thus a contract quite separate to the main agreement, for breach of which an action will lie against the auctioneer. If this is the case, it is strange that if no sale at all took place he could not be sued, the basis of *Harris* v. *Nickerson* (above).

(2) Tenders

If A asks B, C and D to tender, for example, to supply coal to a hospital for the next 12 months, then clearly A is not making an offer. He is merely inviting B, C and D to make offers to him. If A accepts B's offer, then the precise legal effect will depend upon what sort of tender is involved. If it is to supply 100 tons on July 1, then clearly A and B are bound to pay and deliver respectively at the due date as soon as A accepts B's offer. If the tender was to supply up to a maximum of 100 tons "if and when" required, then the result is quite different. B has made what is called a standing offer. A may order no coal at all, or spread delivery over several instalments. Each time A places an order, he accepts B's offer, and a separate contract is concluded on each occasion. An example of such a transaction is contained in *Great Northern Rail Co.* v. *Witham* (1873). The result is that B is bound to supply within the terms of the offer as required, but revocation is always possible prior to acceptance by A.

(3) Land

Although land is bought and sold in principle like any other commodity, the application of the rules of contract to its transference are dealt with by the courts in a rather strict manner. An example of this tendency is *Harvey* v. *Facey* (1893). The plaintiffs here telegraphed to the defendants, "Will you sell us Bumper Hall Pen? Telegraph lowest cash price." The reply came, "Lowest price for Bumper Hall Pen, £900." The plaintiffs then telegraphed, "we agree to buy Bumper Hall Pen for £900 asked by you. Please send us your title-deeds." The court held on this evidence that there was no contract. The second telegram was regarded merely as an indication of the minimum price if the defendants eventually decided to sell. It was therefore not an offer which the third telegram could accept. A case which if anything seems to go further than this is *Clifton* v. *Palumbo* (1944). The plaintiff wrote to the defendant *inter alia*, "I. . . am prepared to offer you . . . my Lytham estate for £600,000. . . . I also agree that a reasonable and sufficient time shall be granted to you for the examination and consideration of all the data and details necessary for the preparation of the Schedule of Completion." The Court of Appeal held that this was not on offer to sell, but merely a preliminary statement as to price.

The rationale behind both cases is that in contracts for the sale of land, the courts will require cogent evidence that the parties really had settled a final agreement. This is no doubt derived from the complexity of interests in land, and frequently the size of such transactions.

In negotiations for the sale of land it is common to find the phrase "subject to contract." This is a well understood form of words to denote the fact that neither party is bound unless and until a definitive formal contract is executed. Hence the phrase "Sold subject to contract" or "I accept subject to contract" has no binding effect whatsoever. Although the phrase is most commonly found in the context of land, it can be used in any other form of contract, but if an alternative formula is used, there may be a difficulty of construction over its legal effect.

6. Two Problem Cases

(1) Cross offers

What if A offers to sell his car to B for £900 and B offers to buy it for £900, and the letters cross in the post? Do these cross offers constitute a contract? The point has never been decided but these are *obiter dicta* in *Tinn* v. *Hoffman* (1873) which suggest there is no contract. Although the parties are, unknown to each other, in a sense *ad idem,* they are making offers without reference to each other. This seems to offend against the orthodox view that there must be an offer by one party followed by an acceptance from another. Lord Denning has recently said in *Gibson* v. *Manchester City Council* (1979) that (on the facts of that case) there was, "no need to look for a strict offer and a strict acceptance. You should look at the correspondence as a whole and at the conduct of the parties, and see therefrom whether the parties have come to an agreement on everything that was material." In the case of cross offers there does appear to be a mutual intention to contract on indentical terms in respect of the same subject matter. If the courts were to take Lord Denning's broad approach, would not cross offers lead to a contract?

(2) The "Satanita"—The fringes of offer and acceptance

A classic example of another area at the fringes of the concept of offer and acceptance is provided by the case of *Clarke* v. *Dunraven* (1897). Two yacht owners entered a race and undertook in a letter to the club secretary to obey the rules. These club rules contained an obligation to pay "all damages," caused by fouling. The "Satanita" whilst manoeuvring fouled and sank the "Valkyrie." The owner of the Valkyrie sued the defendant who claimed that he was only liable to pay the lesser damages laid down for such an eventuality by a statute. The plaintiff claimed that by entering the competition in accordance with the rules, a contract had been created between the competitors which obliged him to pay "all damages." Was there a contract between the two owners? The House of Lords answered in the affirmative. A contract was created when they entered for the race, or at least when they sailed. Each competitor had accepted the rules as binding on each other.

It is far from easy to analyse the case in terms of the conventional doctrine of offer and acceptance, although the courts upheld the contract. It is perhaps an illustration of the way in which the courts are prepared in problem cases to descend to some degree of artificiality to produce a result that satisfies the requirement to find a binding agreement. Both in regard to what has been said already, and in the ensuing discussion of consideration, it is important to have in mind Lord Wilberforce's statement in *New Zealand Shipping Co. Ltd.* v. *A. M. Satterthwaite & Co. Ltd.* (1975, P.C.) that: "... English Law, having committed itself to a rather technical and schematic doctrine of contract, in application takes a practical approach, often at the cost of forcing the facts to fit uneasily into the marked slots of offer, acceptance and consideration."

CHAPTER 3

CONSIDERATION

In addition to offer and acceptance English law requires the presence of consideration and an intention to create legal relations before it will enforce an agreement as a binding contract. The latter will be considered in Chapter 4, but we now need to consider the former since it bears a specialised legal meaning which our ordinary use of the term "consideration" does not always reveal.

The term consideration was defined in *Currie* v. *Misa* (1875). It was there stated that: "A valuable consideration in the sense of the law may consist either in some right, interest, profit or benefit accruing to one party, or some forbearance, detriment, loss or responsibility given, suffered or undertaken by the other." The same idea is expressed more concisely if less comprehensively by Patteson, J. in *Thomas* v. *Thomas* (1842) where he declares: "Consideration means something which is of value in the eye of the law, moving from the plaintiff; it may be some detriment to the plaintiff or some benefit to the defendant." The terms "benefit" and "detriment" themselves bear in this context a less than obvious interpretation. The benefit and detriment can be very slight, and are often merely alternative ways of describing the same thing from different view points. For example, if A offers to buy B's car if he will bring it round, and B fails to do so, A can sue B. A's promise to pay B for the car is a benefit to B and a detriment to A. The law would thus regard such a promise as valuable consideration. However, as we shall see, if A had merely offered 50p for the car and B had accepted this would still be adequate to complete the contract.

The existence of the concept of consideration is one which at various times has been criticised by the courts. Doubtless this is due partly to the distaste felt at relieving parties from obligations following promises which might be thought binding in conscience, and partly due to the fact that there is a high degree of artificiality in certain marginal applications. The rationale behind the legal requirement for consideration is tersely expressed in the Yorkshire phrase "owt for nowt" and more elegantly translated into the decent obscurity of a dead language as the need for a *quid pro quo*. In other words, central to the English law of contract is the need for a bargain and the law will rarely enforce a gratuitous promise. There must be something in return for which an offer or promise is made. That "something" is the required element of consideration. The fact that the adequacy of the consideration will not be inquired into reflects the historical reluctance of the courts to inquire into men's bargains once they have been made.

A distinction encountered in reading the cases is made between "executory" and "executed" consideration. In a bilateral contract, in other words a contract where there is a promise in exchange for a promise, the consideration is said to be executory. The promise itself is the consideration, and is "executory" in the sense that it has yet to be fulfilled. "Executed" consideration arises in the case of a so-called unilateral contract where there is a promise for an act or a forebearance to do something. Typically this might be the case of a reward. For example, A offers £10 for the return of his lost dog. If B returns it, then his act is the response to A's offer and the complete act of returning the vagrant animal is the executed consideration. The detriment to B in returning the dog, and the benefit to A in receiving it has actually been carried out. The consideration in this case is executed.

1. Agreement Under Seal

There is a separate category of agreement where there is no obvious consideration which is nevertheless enforceable. This exception to the general requirement is a so-called agreement "under seal" or "by deed." These are described as "formal" contracts, whereas every other type of contract is described as a "simple" contract. The seal is nowadays nothing more elaborate than a red adhesive piece of paper appended to the foot of the document.

The reason for such a class of document is typically to give binding legal effect to what might otherwise be a gratuitous gift unenforceable for lack of consideration. If A promises B that he will give B £100 next week, B cannot compel payment if A subsequently refuses. It is otherwise if the declaration is made "under seal." It is perhaps easier to regard such a transaction as not so much an exception to the need for consideration, as an example of a *sui generis* legal device which produces the consequences of a contract without necessarily containing all the ingredients. Declarations of trust are frequently made by deed.

2. Sufficiency and Adequacy of Consideration

In normal speech most people would not draw a distinction between the meaning of "sufficient" and "adequate" but the law of contract does. Whilst the word "adequate" has acquired no precise legal connotation, "sufficient" is used in a technical way to describe consideration which the law considers sufficient to form the basis of a contract. If in the example already mentioned A pays B 50p for the car, no-one (in all probability) would regard this as an adequate consideration. It would nevertheless be "sufficient" consideration in law. The law merely seeks the presence of *some* consideration; it does not seek to rectify a bad bargain made by the parties. So in *Thomas* v. *Thomas* (1842) the defendants agreed with the plaintiff that she could live in her deceased husband's house provided she paid £1 a year and kept the house in good repair. This was held to be sufficient consideration to enable the plaintiff to succeed in an action for breach of contract.

In the bizarre case of *Bainbridge* v. *Firmstone* (1838) the plaintiff, at the defendant's request, allowed him to weigh two boilers. The defendant agreed to return the boilers in perfect condition, which he failed to do. The plaintiff sued and the defendant claimed there was no consideration for the promise to return the boilers in perfect condition. The court, however, held that the plaintiff had suffered detriment in parting with his boilers, but in any event the defendant had obtained a benefit by being enabled to weigh them. The court was not concerned to investigate what this agreed benefit actually was. The omission to do so, though clearly correct in principle, has done nothing to assuage the curiosity of generations of law students who have wondered why anyone should want to weigh someone else's boilers. A further illustration of the disparity between adequate and sufficient consideration is provided by the reasoning in *Chappell & Co. Ltd.* v. *Nestle* (1960). Nestle's offered a record for sale at a price of 1s. 6d. plus three wrappers from their 6d. bars of chocolate. When the wrappers were received by Nestle's they were thrown away. It was still held that they were part of the consideration for the contract between the record buyers and the chocolate manufacturers. It would logically follow that if these wrappers could be part of the consideration, they could just as easily in an appropriate case be the entire consideration.

3. Consideration must Move from the Promisee

In the typical case of a breach of contract the plaintiff (the promisee) will be suing the defendant (the promissor) for a failure to honour the defendant's promise in some way. To succeed he must prove that consideration moved from (that is to say, was provided by) him. To have a different rule would, it might be thought, enable someone to obtain the benefit of a "gift" rather than the earned consequence of a "bargain." Hence if A, B and C agree that B will mow A's lawn in return for C giving him £10, then this agreement cannot be enforced by A. He has provided no consideration.

A closely related but possibly slightly different situation is provided by the facts of *Tweddle* v. *Atkinson* (1861). William Guy and John Tweddle agreed with each other that they would each provide a sum of money for William Tweddle. Guy died without having paid and so William Tweddle sued his executors. The court held that his action must fail as he was "a stranger to the consideration." In a sense he failed on two grounds, both that he had not provided consideration, and that he was not even the promisee. He was to benefit from the agreement, but he was not the person to whom the promise was actually made.

This case raised a further issue which will be dealt with later, the question of privity (see Chap. 8). It is generally stated that a person who is not a party to an agreement cannot sue on it. Some writers have sought to separate this doctrine from the rule that consideration must move from the promisee. Others, it is thought more realistically, regard the two concepts as different ways of describing the same thing. If the promisee cannot enforce an obligation when there is lack of consideration, then *a fortiori* it cannot be done by someone who is not even a party to the agreement.

4. Past Consideration

It is generally stated that past consideration is not sufficient. It would perhaps be more accurate to say that it is no consideration. It is, however, important not to confuse this with executed consideration discussed earlier. In the case of returning the lost dog, then when B meets A it is true that the consideration is in the past. Nevertheless the law regards this as valid, because it was not 'in the past' when A's original offer was made and on which B relied and acted.

A classic illustration of the rule is the old case of *Roscorla* v. *Thomas* (1842). The defendant had sold the plaintiff a horse without, it seems, any warranty that it was a sound animal. Subsequently, the defendant claimed that it was "sound and free from vice." It seems that this somewhat overstated the horse's virtue, and the plaintiff sued. It was held that the promise was not supported by fresh consideration, and the action therefore failed. If the plaintiff had bought the horse after the statement, then the result would have been different. As it was, the only consideration was the "past consideration" of the sale which had already taken place and was over.

A modern illustration of the same principle is *Re McArdle* (1951), where a man left his house in his will to his wife for life, then to his children. While the mother was still alive the son and daughter-in-law lived in the house and spent money improving it. Later the other children signed a document in which they stated: "in consideration of your carrying out certain alterations and improvements to the property, we hereby agree that the executors shall repay to you from the estate, when distributed, the sum of £488 in settlement of the amount spent on such improvements." The Court of Appeal held that the document did not produce a binding contract. When the letter was signed, the work had already been done. It was therefore "past consideration."

A different situation arises if the act was carried out at the request of the promissor, and the situation is such that it can be assumed that payment was all along contemplated for the act. It seems misleading to describe these cases as ones where past consideration is sufficient. Rather the cases seem to be rationalised upon the assumption that the act was always effectively a response to the promissor's original request.

In *Lampleigh* v. *Braithwait* (1615), Thomas Braithwait had killed a man and asked Anthony Lampleigh to obtain a pardon for him from the King. Lampleigh went to considerable trouble at his own expense "riding and journeying to and from London and Newmarket." Doubtless buoyed up by the euphoria of absolution, Braithwait promised him £100. He failed to pay and Lampleigh sued. The court gave judgment for the plaintiff and explained that whilst "a mere voluntary courtesy" would not have led to liability, the fact that the services were performed at the request of the defendant with, apparently, the tacit assumption that they would be paid for, rendered the transaction a valid contract. A modern illustration of the principle is to be found in *Re Casey's Patents, Stewart* v. *Casey* (1893). A and B owned certain patent rights. They wrote to C saying that in consideration of his services in relation to the patents, they would give him a one-third share of them. Later they claimed that as their promise was made in relation to C's past services, it was "past consideration," and therefore invalid. The court, however, took the view that the services were always meant to be paid for, and rejected A and B's argument. Their statement merely made it easier to fix the level of C's remuneration.

5. Forbearance to Sue

A type of valuable consideration of practical importance is forbearance to sue. Suppose B injures A, with the result that A may recover damages for injury against B if he were to bring an action against him. Instead, A agrees not to sue B if he will pay him £1,000. If B subsequently defaults, A may recover the money. The forbearance to sue is consideration, and contributes to the bargain which the parties have made. One way of looking at it is to say that A has conferred a benefit on B by agreeing not to expose him to the hazards of litigation.

Forbearance to sue will only be adequate consideration when the prospective plaintiff at least has the possibility of bringing on action. Where a claim is totally invalid as in the case of an illegal contract (see Chap. 9), and the plaintiff knows this, he is clearly not giving up anything of value. In such a case, declining to bring an action would be no consideration.

6. Performance of an Existing Duty

We have seen that the requirement of consideration may at times be rather artificial, but it must be regarded as in some way the price of defendant's promise. That is the result of the underlying concept of the bargain. A problem is therefore raised when the purported consideration is in fact the performance of some duty which the plaintiff was obliged to render anyway. At first sight all such cases would appear to fail, since what extra element is the defendant receiving from the bargain? Nevertheless, the courts have sometimes found it possible to discover consideration in such circumstances. The problem is likely to arise under four main headings, of which the fourth has given rise to intense modern development and controversy.

(1) Performance of a duty imposed by law

The general rule would appear to be that where a person, for example a policeman, is merely carrying out his legal duties, then he provides no consideration in so doing, or in agreeing to do so. The point is made in *Collins* v. *Godefroy* (1831). The plaintiff had, in effect, been put under a legal duty to give evidence at a trial. The defendant allegedly had promised to pay him six guineas for his attendance which he failed to do. The plaintiff's action failed because it was said he had given no consideration. He was bound to attend regardless of any inducement from the defendant. There is a suggestion that the case can also be explained as being contrary to public policy (on which see Chap. 9).

This case can be contrasted with the decision in *England* v. *Davidson* (1840), which at first sight seems somewhat surprising. A reward had been offered for information leading to the conviction of a criminal. The plaintiff, a policeman, gave the requisite information but was refused the reward. He sued, and it was argued against him that it was against public policy to make such a reward to a policeman, and that he had only done his duty anyway. The court rejected these arguments. The judgment is brief in the extreme, but the court seems to have assumed in this case that the plaintiff did render services which went beyond the call of duty, and could therefore justify the claim.

Exceeding one's public duty is undoubtedly regarded as consideration. In *Glasbrook Brothers* v. *Glamorgan County Council* (1925) a difficulty arose over adequately protecting a coal mine during a strike. The company requested the police to provide a higher degree of protection than the police considered was reasonably necessary, and they agreed to pay the additional cost of £2,200 thereby incurred. Subsequently the company refused to pay claiming absence of consideration on the part of the police. The House of Lords rejected this defence and gave judgment for the plaintiffs. They said that in providing more protection than they considered necessary, they had provided consideration in return for the promise of extra payment.

The case of *Ward* v. *Byham* (1956) illustrates the willingness of the courts to find evidence of some consideration. The defendant, the father of the plaintiff's illegitimate child, wrote to her offering to pay £1 a week in maintenance "providing you can prove that she will be well looked after and happy and also that she is allowed to decide for herself whether or not she wishes to come and live with you." The mother was at that time under a specific statutory duty to maintain the child in any event. The defendant eventually defaulted on payment, and when sued by the plaintiff, pleaded absence of consideration. The majority of the court held that there was a valid contract, and that she had promised to do more than was required by the statute by agreeing to "Look after the child well" and see that it was "happy." Lord Denning even put forward the view that: "a promise to perform an existing duty, or the performance of it should be regarded as good consideration because it is a benefit to the person to whom it is given." Whilst such a view does not yet seem to represent the law, it may signify a future trend.

(2) Performance of a contractual duty owed to the promissor

Obviously, if A is already bound to carry out certain duties as a result of his contract with B, then A's performance of those duties can not amount to consideration. There is no fresh element of bargain. The point is neatly illustrated by contrasting two nineteenth century shipping cases.

In *Stilk* v. *Myrick* (1809) two seamen deserted from a ship on a voyage from London to the Baltic and back. The captain being unable to find susbstitutes, promised the crew extra wages if they would work the ship back short-handed. They agreed, but were subsequently refused the extra money. It was held that the crew were doing no more than their duty in meeting the normal contingencies of a voyage. Lord Ellenborough expressly stated that he based his decision on lack of consideration. This can be contrasted with the later case of *Hartley* v. *Ponsonby* (1857). A ship left England with 36 crew, but reached Port Philip with only 19. The captain promised the plaintiff extra money if he would help work the ship to Bombay. He agreed to do so, but the defendant subsequently refused to pay. It was held in this case that the plaintiff was entitled to recover the extra money, since he had furnished consideration. The shortage of seamen had made the rest of the voyage so dangerous, that the plaintiff was performing duties well beyond the normal hazards of a voyage. The danger had relieved them from their old contract, and they were therefore free to enter a new agreement in which their promise to serve was the fresh valid consideration.

(3) Performance of contractual duty owed to a third party

It might seem surprising in view of what has already been said that where A makes a promise to B to do something which A is already bound to do by a contract with C, A is nevertheless regarded by the law as having supplied consideration by such a promise is illustrated by *Scotson* v. *Pegg* (1861), a case which was recently approved by the Privy Council in *New Zealand Shipping Co. Ltd.* v. *Satterthwaite & Co. Ltd.* (1975). In *Scotson* v. *Pegg* the plaintiffs had entered into a contract to supply a cargo of coal to X or to the order of X (meaning anyone whom X nominated). X directed the plaintiff to deliver the coal to the defendants. The defendants promised to unload the coal at a stated rate, which they failed to do. The plaintiff sued and claimed that the defendants' promise to unload the coal was matched by their promise to deliver it to him. There was therefore executory consideration. The defendants replied by saying that as a result of the contract with X, they had to supply the defendant anyway. In other words, there was no consideration for their promise to unload. The court upheld the plaintiff's claim. It did so on the basis that either the delivery of the coal was a benefit to the defendant, or that there was a detriment to the plaintiffs. Whatever the theoretical difficulties of such cases, the result is obviously satisfactory from a commercial point of view.

(4) Part payment of a debt

This category is essentially a particular example of the duty discussed in (ii) above. There are, however, certain specific rules which have developed in this area and which therefore make it easier to consider the topic separately.

Suppose A owed B £10. A is in financial difficulties and asks B if he will accept £5 in full and final satisfaction of the debt. B agrees. On the face of it, there is nothing to stop B changing his mind a week later and suing A for the balance of the money. A has given no consideration for B's promise; there is no element of bargain. A has merely obtained a gratuitous promise which, as we have seen, the law will not normally enforce. On the other hand, as a matter of justice or even "fair play" the situation might be thought to bear rather harshly and unfairly on A. The law has therefore developed in a way that tries to reconcile these opposing considerations and inevitably the development has involved legal controversy.

(a) *The rule in Pinnel's case – the common law approach.* The basic legal proposition has become known as the rule in *Pinnel*'s Case (1602).It was there stated that, "Payment of a lesser sum on the day in satisfaction of a greater cannot be any satisfaction for the whole." There is simply no consideration in such a case. The rule was approved by the House of Lords in *Foakes* v. *Beer* (1884). Mrs. Beer was owed £2,090 on a judgment debt by Dr. Foakes. She agreed that if he would pay the money by instalments, she would not "take any proceedings whatever on the judgment." A judgment debt bears interest until it is fully paid, but the agreement made no reference to the interest. Dr. Foakes did eventually pay off all the money, and Mrs. Beer then asked for the interest as well. He refused, pointing to the agreement. She sued, claiming there was no consideration for it. The House of Lords, applying the so-called rule in *Pinnel*'s Case, upheld Mrs. Beer's claim. This decision has never been abrogated, but the situation is somewhat more complex than the result of this case suggests.

(b) *Two exceptions to the rule.* (i) The first exception relates to the fact that if the debtor supplies some new element at the request of the creditor together with or instead of the lesser sum, then the rule does not apply. This much was stated in *Pinnel*'s Case itself, where the court made clear that, "the gift of a horse, hawk, or robe etc., in satisfaction is good. For it shall be intended that a horse, hawk or robe etc., might be more beneficial to the plaintiff than the money in respect of some circumstance, or otherwise the plaintiff would not have accepted it in satisfaction . . . ." Accordingly, if the creditor accepts £5 today for a debt not due until next week, or £5 in London under an agreement to pay £10 in say Newcastle, or a book instead of the £10, in each of these cases the law will not permit the creditor to go back on his word. In effect, the parties have struck a fresh bargain which the courts will enforce, and are not concerned to see that it is also a good bargain for the parties. A further development of the principle applies when the creditor's claim is unliquidated (which means that there is a valid claim against the debtor, but the precise amount is uncertain). If the creditor accepts a lesser sum than he might have hoped to obtain if he had sued the debtor to judgment, this will still lead to a binding agreement. Of course he may have obtained more than he would have got in a completed action, but even if this is not the case, it is clear that there is considerable practical benefit to a creditor in sometimes agreeing to such an arrangement and avoiding the vagaries of litigation.

(ii) A second exception relates to composition agreements with creditors. It not infrequently happens that A owes money to B, C and D and it becomes apparent that A is insolvent and cannot pay everybody what he owes them in full. B, C and D will often therefore agree to take a "dividend" (that is a certain amount in the pound which is less than the full debt) in full and final settlement of their claims against him. Such an agreement has long been held binding by the courts although it is difficult, if not impossible, to see where the consideration comes from. Clearly if one creditor went behind the others and sued for the full amount this would act as a fraud upon the others, but this observation rings more like a justification of a practical rule rather than an adequate theoretical basis.

A similar principle, or perhaps one should say lack of principle, applies when part of a debt is paid by a third party in full satisfaction of the original debt. This was the situation in *Hirachand Punamchand* v. *Temple* (1911). An army officer was indebted to a moneylender. The officer's father sent a draft for a smaller amount "in full settlement" of the debt. The moneylenders accepted the draft, but nevertheless subsequently sued the son for the full amount. The Court of Appeal rejected the moneylenders' claim. It is equally difficult in this case to detect any consideration for the agreement, but is similar to the last case in that it would clearly have been a fraud on the father to have allowed recovery of the balance from the son. Perhaps both cases can be most easily regarded as exceptions to the general requirement of consideration.

(c) *The doctrine of promissory estoppel – Equity's solution.* We have seen earlier that equity has always sought to mitigate the rigour of a common law rule where it might work an injustice. The development over recent years of the doctrine of promissory estoppel, as it has become generally known, serves as an illustration of the way in which this process is worked out in the courts. "Promissory estoppel" essentially means an impediment or bar to action brought about by a promise, but its meaning becomes clearer after reading the *"High Trees"* case later. A study of the relevant cases also provides an insight into both the advantages and disadvantages of our system of judge-made law. On the one hand it provides a flexible response to practical problems. On the other hand, there is the difficulty that as the courts develop or revitalise a new set of principles, there is inevitably doubt about how far these principles extend. In this area, law is still very much in the making. This process is clearly evident in the development and doubts which surround promissory estoppel.

The case which is often regarded as the modern starting point for the doctrine is the decision by the House of Lords in *Hughes* v. *Metropolitan Railway Co.* (1877). In October 1874 a landlord gave his tenant six months to repair the premises, or else his lease would be forfeited. In November the landlord started negotiations with the tenant for the purchase of what remained of the lease. During this time the tenant did nothing about carrying out the repairs, and the negotiations were ultimately broken off at the end of December. At the end of the six month notice period the landlord claimed that the lease was forfeited and brought an action to enforce his claim. The House of Lords, however, took the view that the negotiations between the parties amounted to a promise by the landlord that as long as they continued he would not enforce the notice. It was on this basis that the tenant had failed to carry out the repairs, and consequently the six months notice only ran from the date when negotiations finally failed.

Lord Cairns, holding that the tenant was entitled in equity to relief, made the now famous statement that:

> "It is the first principle upon which all Courts of Equity proceed, that if parties who have entered into definite and distinct terms involving certain legal results – certain penalties or legal forfeiture – afterwards by their own act or with their own consent enter upon a course of negotiation which has the effect of leading one of the parties to suppose that the strict rights arising under the contract will not be enforced, or will be kept in suspense, or held in abeyance, the person who otherwise might have enforced those rights will not be allowed to enforce them where it would be inequitable having regard to the dealings which have thus taken place between the parties."

It is important to note that the tenant was not relieved from his duty to repair, he was merely in effect given extra time to do so.

The principles of the case were applied 70 years later by Denning J. (as he then was) in *Central London Property Trust Ltd.* v. *High Trees House Ltd.* (1956). In September 1939 the plaintiffs had leased a block of flats to the defendants. Due to the ensuing wartime conditions there were many vacancies in the flats, and the landlords agreed in 1940 to accept half-rent only. By 1945 the flats were full again, and the plaintiffs claimed the full rent for the last two quarters of 1945. The last two quarters only were claimed as a 'test case' for all the other monies which the plaintiffs alleged could now be recovered. The court decided in the plaintiff's favour. The 1940 agreement was a temporary expedient to reflect wartime conditions and was no longer applicable. Accordingly, the original rent fixed by the 1939 contract was payable.

The main interest of the case, however, is contained in what Denning J. went on to say *obiter dicta*. He considered that had the plaintiffs tried to recover the rent for the period 1940–45 they would have failed in accordance with the principle in *Hughes* (above) in that the landlord would have been estopped. But a moment's thought shows that this view carries the principle of *Hughes* case one stage further. In the earlier case the landlord's rights were essentially temporarily suspended; in *High Trees* Denning J. asserted that the landlord's claim for the period 1940–45 had been extinguished. If Lord Denning's view is correct, then the landlord had lost his right to claim for arrears of rent, it had not merely been put into temporary abeyance until the tenant found himself in a position to pay. Part, at least, of the reasoning is based on the fact that the traditional concepts of offer, acceptance and consideration, and especially the latter, although appropriate ingredients in the formation of a contract, need not be applied in quite the same way when, as here, the defendants are not seeking to enforce a contract but merely to establish a defence. Such a view might be regarded as part of a wider criticism that contract law tends to be more concerned with the establishment of a strict contract, than with the subsequent practicalities of its discharge or variation.

The doubts and difficulties associated with the doctrine enunciated in *High Trees* have only been partially alleviated by many of the subsequent cases, in which Lord Denning himself has frequently been a leading proponent. In *Combe* v. *Combe* (1951) the court made clear that, in keeping with orthodox doctrine, promissory estoppel can only be used as a defence and not as a means of establishing a new cause of action. Lord Denning explained it thus: "The principle stated in the *High Trees* case . . . does not create new causes of action where none existed before. It only prevents a party from insisting upon his strict legal rights, when it would be unjust to allow him to enforce them, having regard to the dealings which have taken place between the parties. . . . " Hence the principle has been described "as a shield and not as a sword," although such a formulation appears as a simplification in which there is potential for subsequent change or development.

A problem which still remains is whether obligations are merely suspended or extinguished by the doctrine. Lord Denning is of the view that the latter result is produced. He reiterated this view in *D. & C. Builders* v. *Rees* (1966) where he stated that: "the principle may be applied, not only so as to suspend strict legal rights but also so as to preclude the enforcement of them." In the later case of *Alan* v. *El Nasr* (1972) he appears aware of the difficulty, but is still insistent that rights can be extinguished when he commented that the creditor's rights are, "at any rate suspended . . . but there are cases where no withdrawal is possible. It may be too late to withdraw; or it cannot be done without injustice to the other party." Nevertheless, it is difficult to reconcile Lord Denning's view with the orthodox interpretation of the doctrine and hardly seems to fit easily with *Pinnel's* case. In *Hughes* itself the rights were clearly suspended and not extinguished. In *High Trees*, this aspect was not part of the *ratio decidendi* of the decision. The consideration of the issue of promissory estoppel by the House of Lords in *Tool Metal Manufacturing Co. Ltd.* v. *Tungsten Electric* (1955) seems if anything to favour the standard interpretation of *Hughes*. In the Privy Council case of *Emmanuel Ayodei Ajayi* v. *R.T. Briscoe (Nigeria) Ltd.* (1964) the view was expressed that the promise only becomes final and irrevocable if the promisee cannot resume his original position. The result of the cases, and bearing in mind the traditional doctrine of consideration, therefore seems to support the view that rights are suspended rather than extinguished by the doctrine. It would, however, be rash to regard this yet as clearly established law. What if the obligation were suspended until the limitation period had expired? There has yet to be a case on such facts, but if that were to happen, then it seems the Limitation Acts would be an effective bar to further action.

A further unsolved issue is what precisely the promisee must have done to invoke the doctrine. Is it necessary that he should act to his detriment in some way, or is it enough that he has merely acted in reliance upon the promise? If the notions of 'bargain' and 'consideration' are to mean anything at all, it might be suggested that acting to the promisee's detriment ought to be an essential requirement. It was certainly a factor present in the *Hughes* case in that the tenant had acted to his detriment in relation to the landlord in failing to repair. In *Emmanuel Ayodei Ajayi* v. *R.T. Briscoe (Nigeria) Ltd.* the Privy Council talked of the promisee altering his position, and by many this was understood as meaning '*for the worse*'. Lord Denning, on the other hand, has consistently taken the view that acting to one's detriment is not an essential ingredient. In *W.J. Alan & Co.* v. *El Nasr Export and Import Co.* (above) he commented: "I know it has been suggested in some quarters that there must be detriment. But I can find no support for it in the authorities cited by the judge." More recently in *Brikom Investments Ltd.* v. *Carr* (1979) he stated: "The principle extends to all cases where one party makes a promise or representation, intending that it should be binding, intending that the other should rely on it, and on which the other does in fact rely, by acting on it, by altering his position on the faith of it, by going ahead with a transaction then under discussion, or by any other way of reliance. It is no answer for the maker to say: 'You would have gone on with the transaction anyway.' " However, a note of caution in relation to the "new estoppel," as it has been called, was sounded by Lord Roskill who noted; "it would be wrong to extend the doctrine of promissory estoppel, whatever its precise limits at the present day, to the extent of abolishing in this back-handed way the doctrine of consideration." There seems, therefore, to be an obvious difference of approach between the expansionist assertions of Lord Denning in relation to a creature which might be thought to a large extent to be of his own making, and the rather more cautious view of other members of the judiciary towards promissory estoppel. It remains to be seen which approach will ultimately command final approval.

Although the doctrine has often been stated in wide terms, two cases illustrate the way it can be restricted. In *D. & C. Builders Ltd.* v. *Rees* (1966) the plaintiffs were a small firm of jobbing builders who were owed £482 by the defendants. They pressed for payment over several months, but received nothing. Eventually, knowing that they were in financial difficulties, the defendant offered the plaintiff £300 in final settlement saying that if they refused this offer they would get nothing. The plaintiffs reluctantly agreed. They later sued for the balance of the original debt, and the court awarded judgment in their favour. As Lord Denning graphically put it: "The debtor's wife held the creditor to ransom." Under these circumstances it would hardly have been equitable to allow the defendants to succeed in a claim of promissory estoppel. Equity is concerned to do justice between the parties, not to facilitate a settlement procured by intimidation. A second case, which simply serves as an illustration of the way the courts approach the business of examining representations, is *China Pacific S.A.* v. *Food Corpn. of India* (1980). In a complicated commercial dispute there had been considerable correspondence and dealings between the parties. For the defendants it was alleged that a promissory estoppel existed based on a letter and what was said in a discussion between counsel prior to arbitration. The court, on the facts of the case, rejected the defence of estoppel. Megaw L.J. took the opportunity to emphasise that: "for a promissory estoppel, apart from other conditions, it has to be shown that there is something which is a quite unequivocal statement." It seems that the representation relied on must therefore be in clear and unambiguous terms.

(d) *Promissory estoppel and the future of consideration.* Various aspects of the doctrine of promissory estoppel seem somewhat surprising when measured against some notions of legal orthodoxy. One of the interesting facets is that the doctrine has been established more by way of authoritative *obiter dicta* than the clear *rationes decidendi* of cases. Many of the reularly cited authorities on the matter in fact turn on, or are explicable upon, other points of law. It is, unless one takes a very restricted view of the meaning of "law," clear that it is something of an oversimplification to say that our system always proceeds on the basis of building one *ratio decendi* upon another.

Some of the controversial areas of the doctrine expose fundamental difficulties in the English notion of contract. The discussion on the issue of the requirement for merely "acting" or "acting to one's detriment" is a reflection of this. Clearly the latter view seems to reflect more closely established views on the requirement for consideration and the need for benefit and detriment. On the other hand, if the doctrine of promissory estoppel is compared to the phenomenon of the unilateral contract (that is, a promise for an act) the rather artificial nature of "detriment," as it is often used, becomes apparent. In a unilateral contract, it is essentially the act which forms the basis of the contract, and the notion of any real detriment (or sometimes benefit) seems somewhat unreal. The law often seems to be finding a convenient mechanism for enforcing a gratuitous promise. Perhaps no great disservice to the law would be caused by dropping any requirement of 'detriment' from the law of promissory estoppel.

Consideration has often received astringent criticism from the Judges. In the late nineteenth century, Jessel M.R. observed: "According to English Common Law a creditor may accept anything in satisfaction of his debt except a less amount of money. He might take a horse, or a canary or a tom-tit if he chose, and that was accord and satisfaction; but by a most extraordinary peculiarity of the English Common Law, he could not take 19s. 6d. in the pound; that was *nudum pactum*" (*Couldery* v. *Bortrum* (1881)). The contrary view has been put by Professor Hamson when he said: "So far from being an accidental and unnecessary mystery, an accidental tom-tit in an otherwise rational theory of contract, consideration in its essential nature is an aspect merely of the fundamental notion of bargain, other aspects of which, no less but no more important, are offer and acceptance. Consideration, offer and acceptance are an indivisible trinity, facets of one identical notion which is that of bargain.''

The reality is perhaps more subtle than either of these quotations might suggest. Of course consideration is a central ingredient of the notion of bargain that underlies much contract law. However, it is only one strand, albeit a crucial one, in weaving the web of a binding agreement. As we have seen, sometimes the element of bargain looks more fictional than substantial. Moreover, concentrating on the rules relating to the *formation* of a contract may distract attention from considering the very different problems that arise often much later when for some reason contractual performance as originally envisaged becomes mutually inconvenient. In those cases a practical solution to the parties' new situation might be thought to be more in keeping with the tradition of the pragmatic response of English Contract Law to business efficacy than insistence on an often rather technical doctrine of consideration. Quite how the doctrine of promissory estoppel will develop is something only the subsequent case law is likely to show, at least in the absence of some legislative intervention.

Chapter 4

INTENTION TO CREATE LEGAL RELATIONS

Although offer, acceptance and consideration are essential prerequisites, there is a further element which must be present in order to constitute a binding contract, namely an intention to create legal relations. The view was expressed in somewhat ponderous language by Lord Stowell in the early nineteenth century, that contracts, "must not be the sports of an idle hour, mere matters of pleasantry and badinage, never intended by the parties to have any serious effect whatever." The matter can be put more clearly by an example. If I offer to give you dinner tomorrow if you will come and bring a bottle of wine, prima facie all the elements of a contract would seem to be present. I make an offer, and there is acceptance and consideration when you arrive with the wine. However, it would be contrary to commonsense and most people's expectations to say that there was a binding contract here. Nobody would contemplate legal action if I failed to provide dinner after you had turned up with the wine. Consequently, in a situation such as this, the decided cases make clear that there is no binding agreement since there is no intention to create legal relations. Of course many factual situations are more ambiguous than the fictional example, and in order to ascertain whether or not an intention to contract will be assumed by the courts, it is convenient to distinguish between domestic and social agreements on the one hand and commercial transactions on the other. In the case of the former, the court will generally need to be persuaded that formal legal relations were intended. As regards the latter, the presumption is that the parties did intend to bind themselves by their agreement.

1. Domestic and Social Agreements

Although many social and family arrangements are clearly made without thought for legal consequences, difficult borderline cases may sometimes arise. For example in *Merritt* v. *Merritt* (1970) the husband left the wife in order to live with another woman. The husband and wife met to settle various financial arrangements, and eventually the husband signed a piece of paper which stated: "in consideration of the fact that you will pay all charges in connection with the house . . . until such time as the mortgage repayment has been completed I will agree to transfer the property into your sole ownership." The wife duly paid off the mortgage; the husband failed to convey the house. The Court of Appeal upheld the wife's claim. In this case, the couple were not living in amity at the time of the agreement, and the court held that the parties had intended to create formal legal relations. This case can be contrasted with the attitude of the court in *Balfour* v. *Balfour* (1919). The defendant was a civil servant stationed in Ceylon. While on leave in England the wife was taken ill, and it became clear that the husband would have to return on his own. He therefore agreed to pay an allowance of £30 a month as maintenance while he was away. The wife later sued for his failure to pay, but the Court of Appeal refused to uphold the agreement. Lord Atkin commented: " . . . one of the most usual forms of agreement which does not constitute a contract appears to me to be the arrangements which are made between husband and wife . . . and they are not contracts because the parties did not intend that they should be attended by legal consequences." Although as an illustration of a general principle *Balfour* v. *Balfour* is still entirely valid, it probably represents a decision on the legal borderline. Given this and the changes in social assumptions which have taken place since 1919, it is far from certain that on similar facts the actual result of the earlier case would be followed.

Similar types of problems may arise between parent and child as those between husband and wife. In *Jones* v. *Padavatton* (1969), the mother, Mrs. Jones, wished her daughter to give up her job in Washington and qualify as a barrister in England. She therefore agreed to pay the daughter a monthly allowance while she studied. The daughter accepted the offer, and came to England. Mrs. Jones later bought a house in London and the daughter lived there although she persistently failed to complete the Bar examinations. The mother and daughter eventually quarrelled and a dispute arose over possession of the house. There were then two agreements, neither of them in writing. The first was to pay the daughter a monthly sum in return for travelling to England to read for the Bar. The second permitted the daughter to live in the house while she studied. The Court of Appeal considered that neither agreement was intended to create legal relations, it was merely a family arrangement depending upon the good faith of the promisors. One judge, however, thought that although this was true of the second agreement, the first was a binding contract intended to last for a reasonable time which had now elapsed. Having regard to the serious consequences of the daughter's move, there seems much to be said for such a view.

A domestic agreement where the parties were not related existed in *Simpkins* v. *Pays* (1955). A grandmother, grand-daughter and lodger took part each week in a newspaper competition. The entries were actually made in the name of the defendant, and one week she obtained a prize of £750. The plaintiff, the lodger, claimed a third of the sum as his share of the prize. The grandmother refused, claiming there was no intention to create legal relations. The court upheld the claim of the plaintiff, considering that each had contributed to the competition in the expectation of sharing any prize.

2. Commercial Agreements

Because the presumption operates in favour of assuming that the parties do intend to create legal relations, the courts require evidence of a clear contrary intention before holding that no binding agreement exists. Nevertheless, problems may be caused by the extravagant language used in, for example, advertising. It is unlikely that a disappointed customer could sue for breach of every claim that is made in the course of promoting the sale of goods, although naturally everything depends on the facts of an individual case. This was one of the difficulties raised in the case considered earlier (p. 320) of *Carlill* v. *Carbolic Smoke Ball Co.* (1893). Amongst the defences unsuccessfully raised by the defendants was the assertion that their statement was "a mere puff," in other words, an advertising gambit not to be taken seriously. The court rejected this interpretation, saying that the mention of the deposit of £1,000 with their bankers "to show their sincerity" was strong evidence that they did indeed contemplate legal liability when they placed the advertisement.

If the parties expressly make it a term of their agreement that there is no legal liability, then the courts will not interfere. One of the clearest examples of this is the case of *Rose and Frank* v. *Crompton Bros.* (1924). In 1913 the parties made an unexceptional agreement for the sale of goods. There was, however, one unusual feature, the "Honourable Pledge Clause." This stated: "This arrangement is not entered into . . . as a formal or legal agreement, and shall not be subject to legal jurisdiction in the law courts . . . but it is only a definite expression and record of the purpose and intention of the parties concerned, to which they each honourably pledge themselves." In 1919 the defendants terminated the agreement without giving the specified notice, and the plaintiffs sued. The House of Lords refused to uphold the claim. Scrutton L.J. commented: " . . . I can see no reason why, even in business matters, the parties should not intend to rely on each other's good faith and honour, and to exclude all idea of settling disputes by any outside intervention. . . . "

So-called "honour clauses" are frequently found on football pools coupons. Although prima facie the submission of such a coupon would obviously be regarded as part of a commercial transaction, it has been held that the presence of the words "binding in honour only" is sufficient to prevent a disappointed punter being able to sue the promoter. Strange though it may seem, a pools company who uses such a clause is therfore under no legal obligation to pay out money to a winner.

Nevertheless, where there is an ambiguity in the words used, the courts will favour the interpretation which gives the agreement binding effect. An example of this is contained in *Edwards* v. *Skyways Ltd.* (1964). As part of a redundancy agreement the plaintiff's employers promised that they would make him an *ex gratia* payment of a specified amount.Later the employers refused to make the *ex gratia* payment saying that the words used showed that there was no intention to create legal relations. The Court of Appeal rejected such an interpretation. This was a commercial agreement and there was therefore a strong presumption in favour of creating legal relations. All the words *ex gratia* signified was that the employers were not admitting any pre-existing liability; it did not mean that they were not bound by the agreement.

3. Collective Bargaining

One type of commercial agreement, which has frequently led to political controversy, is treated by the law in a rather special way. Collective agreements between employers and trade unions are not generally enforceable contracts. The point was raised in *Ford Motor Co. Ltd.* v. *Amalgamated Union of Engineering and Foundry Workers* (1969). A written and carefully worded agreement was drawn up between the Ford Co. and various trade unions. One clause in effect stated that a strike should not be called before certain negotiating procedures had been carried out. The defendants issued strike notices in breach of the agreement and the plaintiffs sought to restrain them. The court declined to do so, relying mainly on "the climate of opinion voiced and evidenced by the extra-judicial authorities." In other words, public policy was the determining factor. Of course, if terms and conditions of employment negotiated by a trade union are later incorporated into the individual employment contract between an employer and employee then these terms are legally binding on both parties.

The legal position after the *Ford* case has effectively been affirmed by statute. Under section 18 of the Trade Union and Labour Relations Act 1974 a collective agreement is presumed not to create a legally enforceable contract unless it is in writing and the agreement expressly provides that the agreement is to be legally enforceable. In practice it seems that the presumption is rarely, if ever, displaced.

CHAPTER 5

CONTRACTUAL TERMS

The terms of a contract provide the map which delineates the area of subject matter to be covered, and they make clear what duties and obligations will arise at various stages in the performance, or indeed non-performance, of the agreement. At first sight it might seem obvious that in the case of a straightforward written contract the parties will simply agree between themselves what is to be included and what is to be left out. Matters are not always, however, quite so easily dealt with. What if the parties have forgotten to include a crucial term? Can a court repair the omission? What if the parties are not really on an equal footing, can one party "impose" a term on the other? What is the relative importance of different terms? At what stage does a statement become a term of the contract, if at all? Can the law itself imply a term into an agreement, regardless or even against the wishes of the parties? Related to these problems is the effect of so-called "exclusion clauses" on the duties and obligations that might otherwise have arisen.

Many of these problems are considered later (in Chaps. 13 & 14) and consequently what follows must be read in the context of and with an awareness of the further material in later chapters. Two matters will be dealt with at this stage: (a) the incorportion of terms into a contract, and (b) the relative importance of contractual terms.

I. *INCORPORATION OF TERMS INTO A CONTRACT*

The fact that a certain statement is not considered to be a term of the contract does not necessarily rob it of all legal signifiance. As we shall see in Chapter 6, a misrepresentation made before a contract is concluded may well give rise to a remedy which can give relief to the victim of such a statement. Nevertheless, it is only where a term of the actual contract is broken that the plaintiff can sue for breach of contract and claim the appropriate remedy. It must not be forgotten that, with the possible exception of certain terms implied by law, the underlying purpose of deciding whether or not a statement is a term of the contract is to give effect to the intention of the parties. The intention of the parties, however, as we saw earlier in the contect of offer and acceptance, is considered objectively. In other words, the matter is viewed from the position of an interested and reasonable bystander.

The approach of a court to the problems raised in this area will inevitably be affected by whether the contract is written or oral. Where it is completly in writing, then it should be obvious what terms are involved, and it will be for the judge merely to decide as a matter of law what is their effect. Where the contract is oral, there is a preliminary issue of fact whether the relevant statement was made at all. Only when this initial hurdle has been surmounted will the court then go on to consider its effect. Sometimes a contract may be partially contained in a written document, and partly set out in various oral undertakings. In this case the court has to combine elements of both approaches in order to ascertain the intention of the parties.

1. Representations and Terms

The law has long drawn a distinction between "mere" or "non-contractual" representations, for example various statements made in the course of negotiations, and statements which are actual terms of the contract. Although the distinction between them, as we shall see in the next chapter, no longer has quite such significance as in the past, it is still a matter of importance. In an ideal case, the parties might after prolonged negotiations embody their eventual accord in a comprehensive written agreement. Often this does not happen, and so the courts have developed various guide-lines in order to assist in making what may be a difficult assessment of whether a statement is a representation or a term.

(1) Does the representor have special knowledge?

The courts will in general place more weight on the words of an expert than on a similar statement made by an amateur or someone who has no special knowledge. This can be seen by contrasting two cases involving the sale of cars.

In *Oscar Chess* v. *Williams* (1957) the defendant wished to trade-in his Morris car for a new Hillman Minx. Obviously the price allowed for the Morris depended on its age, and relying on the information in the vehicle's registration book (the forerunner to the present car owner's document) the defendant innocently stated that it was a 1948 model. On this basis the plaintiffs allowed him £290. They later discovered that the registration book had presumably been fraudulently altered by someone in the past, and the car was in fact only a 1939 model worth £175. They thereupon sued the defendant for the difference in price between the two valuations on the grounds of breach of a contractual term that the car was in fact a 1948 model. The Court of Appeal rejected their claim. The seller was a private individual who had simply relied in all innocence on the contents of the registration book. The buyers on the contrary were experts who as professional car dealers were in a position, if anyone could, to discover its true age. Consequently, the defendant's statement was not a contractual term.

A different approach was adopted in *Dick Bentley Productions Ltd.* v. *Harold Smith (Motors) Ltd.* (1965) where the defendant was a car dealer. The plaintiffs said they were looking for a "well-vetted" Bentley car, and the defendant stated that this particular car had only done 20,000 miles since it had been fitted with a replacement engine and gearbox. It later emerged that the car was unsatisfactory and had done almost 100,000 miles since then. In this case the Court of Appeal said the defendant's statement was a term of the contract.

(2) Does the representee place special importance on the issue?

If the representee lets it be known that he attaches special importance to some particular fact, then it is not difficult to see that the court may well regard that fact as a term of the contract. This point is illustrated in *Bannerman* v. *White* (1861). A prospective buyer of hops asked the seller if any sulphur had been used in their treatement. He explained that if it had, then he would not even trouble to ask the price. The seller said no sulphur had been used, and a contract of sale resulted. It later transpired that it had been used. The court held that the seller's statement as to the absence of sulphur was a term of the contract, of which he was therefore in breach.

(3) When was the statement made?

Although the cases show that it can be no more than an approximate guideline, it may be a matter of some significance when the statement in question was actually made. If it was made in the negotiations some time before any contract, it is more likely that the court will regard this as a non-contractual statement. For example, in *Routledge* v. *McKay* (1954), the parties had been discussing the sale of a motor-cycle. Both were private persons with no special knowledge, and the defendant relying on the registration book asserted that it was a 1942 model. A week later a written contract was drawn up which did not mention the date. In fact, it was a 1930 model. The buyer unsuccessfully claimed that the date of manufacture was a term of the contract. In this case not only was there a pronounced interval between the negotiations and the ultimte contract, but it was also significant that the date of the model was not part of the later written agreement. If the parties draw up a written contract but fail to include an earlier statement, it may be reasonable to assume that they did not regard it as of great significance.

Nevertheless, if the intention of the parties as gathered from all the evidence shows that they regarded a particular term as of special or indeed of no significance, the courts will not hesitate to regard such general indications of the kind being considered as inconclusive.

(4) How strong was the inducement?

A point can be made with more or less force. If the representor makes a statement with some diffidence, this is less likely to be relied upon as a contractual term than is an emphatic direction. In *Ecay* v. *Godfrey* (1947) the seller of a boat said that it was sound, but suggested to the prospective buyer that he should have it surveyed. The court held that this indicated the statement was not intended to be a term of any contract. This can be contrasted with *Schawel* v. *Reade* (1913). The plaintiff, who wished to buy a horse, started to examine it. The defendant said to him: "You need not look for anything: the horse is perfectly sound." Accordingly the plaintiff stopped his examination. Eventually, three weeks later, the sale was concluded. In fact, the horse was quite unsuitable. The House of Lords were all agreed that under the circumstances the seller's statement was a contractual term. It is note-worthy that in this case the obvious strength and importance of the statement negated any suggestion that the length of time involved between negotiation and sale indicated that this was something other than a contractual term.

2. Incorporating Terms

Even if a statement is made that is clearly intended to be a term, it must of course be apparent to both parties *before* the contract is concluded. One party cannot unilaterally impose terms on another. Where there is no signed contractual document, a term will only be incorporated into a contract if one of two conditions are fulfilled: (a) the affected party knew of the clause or (b) reasonable steps have been taken to bring the term to his notice. If the contract is in writing, we shall see later that different considerations apply. Although problems of notice are often dealt with in the context of "exemption clauses" (see Chap. 14), this may give a misleading impression. What is said about notice applies to any term, regardless of its function.

As one would expect, a considerable body of case law has built up on what are "reasonable steps" in bringing a term to someone's notice. The answer in any case is likely to turn upon two issues: (1) what degree of notice was given, and (2) when was the notice given? If the degree of notice is too little, or the term comes too late, it will not form part of the contract.

(1) The degree of notice

A person will not receive notice if he is handed something which is clearly not a contractual document. If, on the other hand, he is handed a document which is clearly meant to contain contractual terms, then he is likely to be bound even if he fails to read them. This problem arose in *Chapelton* v. *Barry U.D.C.* (1940). The plaintiff wished to hire two of the defendants' deck chairs in order to sit on the beach. A notice requested the public to obtain a ticket from the attendant, and retain it for inspection. The planitiff collected his two tickets which he thrust into his pocket without reading. When he sat down on the chair it collapsed, injuring him. He sued the council who relied on a term printed on the back of the ticket stating that they were not liable in the event of "any accident or damage arising from the hire of the chair." The Court of Appeal held the defendants liable. No reasonable person would have thought he was receiving anything other than a receipt for the hire. If, however, the council had put up a prominent notice warning of this clause, then this could have been regarded as a contractual document giving reasonable notice and so might have exempted the defendants in this case.

Many of the cases on "notice" arose out of nineteenth century decisions on, for example, the contractual effect of railway tickets. Hence they are often referred to as "the ticket cases." One case, however, is generally regarded as being of fundamental importance in eliciting the guiding principle, *Parker* v. *South Eastern Railway* (1877). The plaintiff left a bag in the defendant's cloakroom, paid the 2d. charge and received a ticket in return. The front of the ticket contained details such as opening hours of the office, but also the words: "See back." On the back was a clause limiting the company's liability in the case of loss of the bag to £10. Later that day, when the plaintiff presented his ticket, it was discovered that the bag was lost. The value of the bag was £24–10s, and this was the amount claimed from the railway company. They claimed that liability was limited to the £10. The Court of Appeal said two questions needed to be considered. Did the plaintiff read or was he aware of the term? If the answer was "yes," then the matter was clear. If the answer was "no," then a second question needed to be answered: did the defendant do what was reasonably sufficient to give the plaintiff notice of the term? Accordingly, in each case it will be necessary to consider the facts and see if the test is satisfied. If, for example, the ticket or notice contained terms which were illegible or obscured by an obstruction or obliterating date stamp, then the court is likely to find that the notice was inadequate (see, *e.g. Sugar* v. *L.M. & S. Railway* (1941)).

One way in which a plaintiff may be considered to have notice of a term is through a previous course of dealing between the parties. In *Hollier* v. *Rambler Motors (A.M.C.) Ltd.* (1972) the plaintiff took his car to garage where it was destroyed by fire as a result of the defendants' negligence. On the three or four previous occasions in the last five years when the plaintiff had used the garage, he had been asked to sign an invoice containing the words: "The company is not responsible for damage caused by fire to customers' cars on the premises." The defendants argued that this term was imported into the contract even though on this occasion nothing had been signed. The Court of Appeal held that there was an insufficient course of previous dealing to justify the inclusion of such a clause. One wonders what the position might have been if, say, the plaintiff had used the garage six times in the last two years?

Although the frequency of previous dealing is one fact from which the courts may deduce that a party is aware of a term, this will also be readily accepted if the parties are dealing in the same trade or business. Even if they have not done business before with each other, a knowledge of the usual trade terms can often be assumed. Hence in *British Crane Hire Corporation Ltd.* v. *Ipswich Plant Hire Ltd.* (1975) the hirer of a crane was liable for the expense of extracting it from marshy ground even though at the time when the crane became stuck, the written terms had not reached the hirer. The court held that both parties knew that this was a usual term in the business, and their oral agreement was therefore made with this in mind.

(2) The time when the notice was given

A clause can only become part of the contract if notice of it is given either before or at the time of contracting. If it comes later than this, then it will be without legal effect. This is simply illustrated in the case of *Olley* v. *Marlborough Court Ltd.* (1949). A husband and wife booked into a hotel for a week, and then went up to their allotted room. On the wall was hung a notice effectively excluding the liability of the hotel for loss of guests' property. The wife's property was in fact wrongfully taken, but the hotel relied on the clause contained in the wall notice to exempt them from liability. The Court of Appeal held that the notice came too late. By the time the guests had reached their room, the contract was already completed. A new term could not then be unilaterally imposed on another party.

In *Olley* the gap between contract and term was obvious. A more difficult case, although one that poses similar problems in principle, in *Thornton* v. *Shoe Lane Parking* (1971). In this case the plaintiff wished to use the defendant's car park, to which admission could be gained by way of an automatic barrier. He drove up to the barrier and the machine automatically produced a ticket, and he was permitted to drive in. The ticket referred to various exempting terms, and the defendants pleaded one of these as a defence to a claim by the plaintiff. An immediate problem was to break down this modern feature into the standard analysis of offer and acceptance, and so decide when the contract was complete. The old "ticket cases" were somewhat different, in that there one person was dealing directly with another; here, the "other" was a machine. Lord Denning analysed it in this way. The offer was made by the proprietor of the machine holding it out as ready to receive custom, in this case by the notice at the entrance to the garage. Acceptance took place when the customer through driving up to the machine activated it enabling him to gain entry. The contract was then complete, and the terms printed on the ticket which was thrust at him by the machine came too late. This is obviously a sensible rationalisation of the situation. It would be unrealistic to expect a motorist to stop and read through a large number of terms at the threshold of the garage while he reflected whether or not to contract. By the time he reaches the machine, he is likely to be effectively committed.

The decisions in both of these cases might have been different if the plaintiffs had been regular users of the respective services. Then it might be inferred from the previous course of dealing that the parties were both aware of the relevant terms, and were therefore bound by them.

3. Written Contracts

(1) The rule in L'Estrange v. Graucob

A special rule applies to the effect of terms in a contractual document which has been signed. This is known as the rule in *L'Estrange* v. *Graucob* (1934) after the case in which the rule was strikingly illustrated. Its effect is that a party is bound by the terms in a document which he has signed and it is immaterial that he may never have read the document. He is still bound as though he had and was aware of the contents. In the case itself, the plaintiff bought a vending machine from the defendants by signing a "sales agreement." The machine proved to be unsatisfactory, but the defendants claimed the protection of a clause "in regrettably small print but quite legible." The court held that they were protected by the clause. The plaintiff had signed the document and was bound. The result shows how important it is to read a legal document with the utmost care before signing it.

(2) The parol evidence rule

The effect of this "rule" is that extrinsic evidence cannot be introduced to contradict, add to or vary the contents of a written agreement. The obvious basis of such a rule is that if the parties have taken the trouble to put their contract into writing, then they presumably intend that it should contain all, or at least all the important terms. Accordingly if two statements made by the parties conflict, then that contained in the written agreement will generally be regarded as conclusive.

Nevertheless, it is a "rule" with so many exceptions as to make clear that it is only a common sense starting point. It is qualified by the fact that if, for example, the written evidence is clearly inconsistent with what the parties really agreed, then the agreement can be rectified to reflect this. If the written agreement was never intended to be the whole contract, then again evidence may be admitted to clarify the rest of the agreement. Another important qualification to the rule is the possibility of effectively side-stepping it by the use of a "collateral contract" (on which see p. 366 later). The result is that exceptions to the rule are likely to be just as important as the rule itself.

4. Implied Terms

The express terms of a contract may not contain every particular of the parties agreement. Sometimes a term may be omitted through mere inadvertence, at other times the parties may have tacitly assumed its existence and thought it too obvious to be worthy of mention. In such cases the courts can intervene under certain circumstances to repair the omission. A term may also enter a contract through the operation of a particular statute. There are therefore various ways in which terms may be implied into a contract.

(1) Custom

Custom, especially in the past, was a fruitful source of implied terms. Indeed the common law itself developed as the customary law of the land. In particular, it has played an important part in the development of commercial law. Nevertheless, in consumer and everday transactions, it is somewhat unlikely to be encountered in modern conditions.

We have already considered the effect of a previous course of dealing in incorporating terms into a contract, and this is in a sense merely incorporating into the contract the customary usages as between the parties. Custom, on the other hand, even if it may sometimes be limited to a specific locality, is clearly wider in its effect in that it does not depend upon previous transactions between the particular parties.

(2) Statute

Many terms are implied into agreements by specific statutes. An obvious example is the terms implied by sections 12–15 of the Sale of Goods Act 1979. The other side of the coin is represented by the Unfair Contract Terms Act 1977. Both these areas are considered later in detail (Chaps. 13 & 14) in the context in which they are likely to arise in normal consumer dealing. There are, however, a very large number of statutory interventions of this kind which may be relevant to many different kinds of agreement. To take only one example, many leasehold agreements contain a term that the property will not be assigned (that is transferred to someone else) without the landlord's consent. Section 19(1)(*a*) of the Landlord and Tenant Act 1927 implies a term that "such consent is not to be unreasonably witheld." Such a term is implied even if the understanding of both parties is to the contrary.

(3) Terms implied by the courts

These terms readily fall into two main categories; those the courts will imply into specific classes of agreement, and those which may be implied into contracts generally.

(a) *Specific types of contract*

It would not be possible to catalogue all the cases where a court, always subject to any contrary expression of the parties, will imply a term. For example, it has long been held to be a standard implied term in a contract for the lease of a furnished house that it is reasonably fit for habitation at the beginning of the term. A graphic example in another context was posed by *Samuels* v. *Davis* (1943). The plaintiff, a dentist, agreed to make a set of false teeth for the defendant's wife. The defendant refused to pay for them on the grounds that they were so unsatisfactory that they were unusable. One of the problems that arose, which is dealt with later in Chapter 12, was whether this was a contract for the sale of goods or for services. A contract for the sale of goods would have carried an implied statutory term that the goods were fit for the purpose for which they were supplied. The court held that the distinction was irrelevant. If it was for sale of goods then the statutory term would be implied; if it was for services, then on the analogy of the Act (which was a codification of the earlier common law) a similar term would be implied into such a contract by the court.

(b) *Contracts generally*

Parties who have drawn up a written contract may well have provided in clear terms for the general nature of their obligations, but simply have overlooked or failed adequately to formulate a term to allow for a contingency which later arises. In these circumstances the courts will willingly imply a term to make the contract work, or in the phrase used by judges, to give the contract "business efficacy." This is an aspect of another theme which underlies the law of contract. Where possible, the courts claim to be the upholders of bargains, not the destroyers of them.

A famous case which illustrates the role of the courts is *The Moorcock* (1889). The defendants, who operated a wharf on the Thames, contracted to allow the plaintiff to discharge his vessel at their jetty. Both parties knew that at low tide the vessel would ground. During the unloading, the vessel did settle on the bottom and was damaged by a ridge of hard ground beneath the mud. Their contract did not expressly provide that this was a safe anchorage. Nevertheless, the Court of Appeal implied into the contract a term that the defendants undertook that so far as reasonable care could make it, the river bottom was in such a condition as not to endanger the vessel.

The principle has often been applied by the courts, and was explained by Lord Pearson in *Trollope and Colls Ltd.* v. *North West Regional Hospital Board* (1973) when he said: "An unexpressed term can be implied if and only if the court finds that the parties must have intended that term to form part of their contract: it is not enough for the court to find that such a term would have been adopted by the parties as reasonable men if it had been suggested to them: it must have been a term that went without saying, a term necessary to give business efficacy to the contract, a term which although tacit, formed part of the contract which the parties made for themselves." It follows from this that since it is the presumed intention of the parties which is the underlying rationale, a term cannot be implied if it is inconsistent with some other term agreed by the parties. Equally, if one party is completely ignorant of some fact which is peculiarly within the other's knowledge, a court can hardly imply a term that would result in both parties being bound. Such a term could not be said to be an accurate reflection of their mutual intention (see, *e.g. Spring* v. *N.A.S.D.S.* (1956)).

5. Collateral Contracts

The doctrine of the "collateral contract" is a device developed by the courts which has become increasingly important as a means of varying or supplementing what appear to be at first sight the clear terms of a contract. It may operate in a number of ways. For example, it may provide the mechanism for the avoidance of an exemption clause (on which see Chap. 14 later) or have the effect of importing into a contract a term quite inconsistent with a later written agreement. It may therefore be relevant to the problem of when a statement has become part of the contractual bond, to the effect of terms in an agreement, and to the more specialised problem of exemption clauses. The difficulty of assessing under what head it should most appropriately be considered only emphasises its importance. The point becomes clearer by examining a recent case.

In *City & Westminster Properties (1934) Ltd.* v. *Mudd* (1959) the defendant had been the plaintiff's tenant for some years. The lease related to a shop, and annexed to it was a small room in which, as the plaintiffs knew, the defendant slept. Later on a new lease was negotiated which contained a clause restricting use to business purposes only. The defendant received an oral undertaking that if he accepted the lease, notwithstanding this clause, he could still sleep on the premises. The defendant thereupon signed the agreement, but the plaintiff later sued for breach of the covenant relating to use of the premises. The court held that the defendant had a good defence despite the clear words of the written document; he could plead the collateral contract made before the lease was executed. The landlords could not resile from this earlier agreement.

The term "collateral contract" in this context may be slightly misleading. There was a proper complete contract before the lease was signed which contained all the essential elements of offer, acceptance and consideration. The situation could be analysed in terms of a promise not to enforce the particular term of the lease in exchange for a promise to sign it. The term "collateral" merely draws attention to the fact that in reality the first contract operates to modify or amplify another agreement. It is still, quite clearly, a complete independent contract, the consideration for which is an agreement to enter into another contract.

A slightly different example of the same principle can be seen in *De Lassalle* v. *Guildford* (1901). The parties were negotiating over the lease of a house. The plaintiff refused formally to agree the lease unless he was assured that the drainage system was in order. The defendant declared that it was, and the plaintiff thereupon agreed to the lease. In fact, the drains were defective. The plaintiff successfully sued the defendant for damages. The basis for this action was not the tenancy agreement, the lease not containing any express conditions as to the state of the drains, but rather a prior collateral contract. That again could be stated as deriving from an exchange of promises. You promise that the drains are in order, I therefore (impliedly) promise to execute the lease. The strength of the doctrine is shown in the way that whereas in the first case it was used as a shield so to speak, in the latter it was wielded as a "sword." It is, as can be seen, a device that can be used not only to undermine the effect of the parol evidence rule, but also as an alternative approach to the problems of the distinction between a term and a "mere" or "non-contractual" representation.

II. *THE RELATIVE IMPORTANCE OF TERMS—CONDITIONS, WARRANTIES AND INNOMINATE TERMS*

In any contract some terms are likely to be more important than others, so that breach of a term will not always be regarded with the same degree of seriousness. The law has reflected this by labelling the terms in a contract as being either "conditions" or "warranties" (although as we shall see this is not an exhaustive categorisation) and attaching different consequences according to the type of term which is broken. The discharge of a contract by breach is dealt with in detail later (in Chap. 10) but the essential distinction between the two terms is that whereas for breach of either monetary damages may be recoverable, in the case of breach of a condition the wronged party is entitled to regard the contract as repudiated and so is absolved from future performance. Hence, breach of a condition is regarded as a failure to perform some really important obligation, or at least one which the parties themselves regard as important, whereas breach of a warranty is felt to be a relatively minor failure which can adequately be compensated by an award for damages. It is often said that the contract has been terminated by a breach, but it is important to remember that this is only a shorthand way of describing the situation. Parts of the contract (for example a clause setting out a scale of damages payable on breach) may survive; it is only the innocent party's obligation to carry out his part of the contract that is ended, and this only if he elects to treat the contract as repudiated. A party may treat a breach of a condition as equivalent only to a breach of warranty, and simply sue for damages.

The terms "condition" and "warranty," used in the sense described above, have crystalised as a result of their incorporation into what is now the Sale of Goods Act 1979. In the case of an uncomplicated contract, the employment of these labels to describe the relative importance which the parties attach to their terms is likely to lead to a readily understood and predictable set of legal consequences. There are, however, a number of difficulties which give rise to formidable complications. These stem partly from the fact that "condition" and "warranty" are not always used in the limited way so far described and partly from the fact that the parties themeselves do not always make clear how they regard a particular term. Even if they appear to do so, the courts may regard their labelling of the term as inconclusive. Furthermore, there has recently emerged a third category of term, the "innominate" or "intermediate term." It is these difficulties and developments which now need to be examined.

1. Meaning of "Condition"

In the older cases, especially those decided before 1893 when the forerunner of the present Sale of Goods Act was passed, terms such as warranty and condition were often used without reference to the comparatively clear distinction that is now made between them. Although this difficulty is no longer a source of confusion, there is a sense in which "condition" is still used which is distinct from that so far described. It is sometimes employed to denote the existence of some fact or event which is a pre-requisite to contractual liability arising or continuing. Just as we say passing examinations is a condition for entry to a university, so some eventuality may be a prior condition to the existence of a contract. The case of *Carlill* yet again furnishes an example of this. The purchase of the smoke ball by the customer on the terms of the offer made in the advertisement undoubtedly brought about a binding contract. Nevertheless, no action could arise unless and until the user contracted flu despite using the device. This was a condition precedent to the plaintiff's action for breach of contract.

A modern illustration of the same principle would be an agreement to buy land subject to the vendor obtaining the requisite planning permission. In this sort of case, where satisfaction of the condition lies within the power of one of the parties, the courts are very willing to imply a further promise that the appropriate party must use his best endeavours to bring about fulfilment of the condition.

2. What Sort of Term is it?

If the parties have drawn up a formal written agreement, then the fact that the words "condition" or "warranty" are used to denote the status of certain terms will almost always be conclusive. This is no more than an acknowledgment of what, on the face of it, is the parties' common intention. Nevertheless, there may be rare occasions when even this fails to solve the difficulty. In *Schuler A.G.* v. *Wickman Machine Tool Sales Ltd.* (1973) the parties conculded an agency agreement in which the respondents undertook to visit certain manufacturers at least once a week. This was stated to be a condition of the agreement, although it is clearly the sort of term that could be broken with varying degrees of seriousness. The House of Lords decided that condition was a word that had more than one specific meaning, and in this particular contract it was not being used as a term of art to denote that any breach could lead to repudiation. Taken as a whole, the contractual document showed that this was not the discernible intention of the parties.

Even if the parties do not expressly or by implication (for example by their emphasis upon or failure to consider some point) make clear the status of a term, it may sometimes be possible to discover this by reference to a rule of law. For example, the Sale of Goods Act 1979 provides in sections 12–15 that certain terms such as those relating to title to the goods or their fitness for the purpose for which they are sold are not only implied into such an agreement, but are regarded as conditions as opposed to warranties. Where a statute fails to give guidance, the problem may be solved by reference to judge made law. In *The Mihalis Angelos* (1970) the owners of a vessel let it on charter (in other words on hire) in a charterparty (the name for the contract document in such a case) which contained the clause, "expected ready to load under this charter about July 1, 1965." It transpired that the ship could not have been ready by this time when the agreement was made, and in the event was not ready until July 23. Clearly, the owners were in breach of the term, but what sort of term was it? The House of Lords decided that the distinction between conditions and warranties was a valuable one, and that this "expected readiness" clause in charterparties was a condition. An important consideration in reaching their conclusion was undoubtedly that in commercial agreements where bargains are struck by people who meet on an equal footing, predictability and certainty are ultimately the crucial factors. No businessman wants to await the vagaries of a complicated and uncertain course of litigation.

The final possibility, is that the term is classed as an "innominate" or "intermediate term." Because this approach is one that has only lately been adopted by the courts, there is a considerable degree of uncertainty in this area which could only be dispelled by an authoritative review from the House of Lords. While we await such a statement, the starting point for this doctrine is the decision in *Hong Kong Fir Shipping Co. Ltd.* v. *Kawasaki Kisen Kaisha Ltd.* (1962). The plaintiffs chartered a ship to the defendants for two years by an agreement that contained a clause stating that the ship was "in every way fitted for ordinary cargo service." In fact, the engines were dilapidated and the crew was incompetent. The result was that several months of the charter were wasted whilst the ship underwent various repairs. The defendants accordingly claimed that the agreement was at an end and repudiated the charter. The plaintiffs, whose ship it was, sued for damages for wrongful repudiation and the Court of Appeal upheld their claim. At first sight it might appear that the court merely regarded this as a simple case of a breach of warranty as opposed to breach of a condition. However, the importance of the case lies in the fact that the Court of Appeal expressed the view that some terms, and this was one of them, did not lend themselves to the traditional form of legal analysis. Diplock L.J. stated: "the problem in this case is, in my view, neither solved nor soluble by debating whether the shipowner's express or implied undertaking to tender a seaworthy ship is a 'condition' or 'warranty'." The correct approach was to look at what had happened as a result of the breach and then decide if the charterers had been deprived of "substantially the whole benefit which it was the intention of the parties they should obtain."

The significance of this decision goes further than giving rise to a new type of "innominate" term. In the past, as we have seen, the courts have set out to determine what was the status of a particular term at the time the parties made their contract, and having decided that, to assess the consequences of the breach. In the *Hong Kong Fir* case the court has approached the problem, so to speak, the other way round. The relative importance of the term is derived from the consequences, whatever they turn out to be, which perhaps much later emanate from the breach. This approach was clearly thought to be valuable when one is dealing with a term, like the seaworthiness clause in a charterparty, which can be broken in a wide variety of ways ranging from the trivial to the really serious. However, the obvious difficulty in such a doctrine is its inherent uncertainty. Until the breach has occurred, it may not be clear what kind of term is involved. As between commercial parties of equal standing, the benefits of such an approach are less certain.

In subsequent cases the courts seem to have determined not to give the doctrine too wide a scope. In the *Mihalis Angelos* (above) which was decided after the *Hong Kong Fir* case, the court decided the common "expected readiness to load" clause was a condition, not an innominate term. However, in *Cehave N.V.* v. *Bremer Handelsgesellschaft mbH. (The Hansa Nord)* (1975), a dispute arose over 12,000 tons of citrus pellets which under the contract were to be shipped "in good condition." Some of the cargo was damaged, though it seems that the defects were not particularly serious. It was argued that in a contract for the sale of goods which is therefore governed by the Sale of Goods Act from which the classic modern distinction between conditions and warranties is derived, there was no place for the "intermediate" or "innominate" term. The Court of Appeal rejected this and held that the clause was indeed an "intermediate" term following the principles of the *Hong Kong Fir* case. On this basis, because the breach was not serious, the buyers were not entitled to repudiate the contract. In other words, this was equivalent only to a breach of warranty since it did not deprive the buyers of substantially the whole benefit intended under the contract.

Clearly the invocation of the notion of an innominate term does serve a valuable purpose in cases where the parties are not of equal bargaining power or where the breach is of a very technical nature and is being used, in effect, as a way of escape from what has simply become a bad bargain. In *Reardon Smith Line* v. *Hansen Tangen* (1976) the respondents agreed to charter an as yet unbuilt tanker identified as "Osaka No. 354." This description merely related to who had built the ship and the yard number. In fact, due to pressure of work, the ship was satisfactorily completed by another shipyard who acted as sub-contractors, so that the vessel became known as "Oskima 004." The appellants, to whom the vessel had been sub-chartered, wished to reject the vessel as the tanker market had collapsed in the meantime. Accordingly, they claimed that the vessel did not accord with its contract description. Although it might be thought there was little merit in the argument, it could be supported to some extent by reference to cases on description in the sale of goods. The House of Lords decided that the breach was of a very technical nature and did not entitle the appellants to reject the ship. Although the case does not squarely raise the issue of innominate terms, the House endorsed the reasoning and approach of *The Hansa Nord* (above) which clearly in a case such as this is calculated to try and ensure that an injustice is not perpetrated by a mechanical application of rigid rules.

Nevertheless, in commercial dealings between parties of equal bargaining power, a different approach may be justified. For example in *A/S Awilko* v. *Fulvia SpA di Navigazione (The Chikuma)* (1981) a charterparty, in a form commonly used, provided that unless "punctual and regular payment" of the hire charge was made, the owners were entitled to withdraw the vessel from the chaterers. On one occasion, the charterers paid in a way that in effect gave the owners an overdraft facility for the amount of the monthly hire as opposed to an equivalent to an unconditional cash payment. Had the owners wished to draw on the money immediately, it would probably have cost them no more than $100 in interest charges in the context of a monthly payment from the charterers of nearly $69,000. The owners, however, claimed that because of the technical failure to make an unconditional payment, they had not been punctually paid and were entitled to withdraw the ship. The House of Lords agreed. Even though the decision appeared to work harshly in this particular case, the overriding consideration in a comercial agreement such as this was that legal effect of any term should be quite clear, so that the parties should know exactly where they stand and a long course of expensive and uncertain litigation could be avoided in other cases.

Chapter 6

MISREPRESENTATION

In the last chapter reference was made to the distinction between "representations" and "terms." Although much of the discussion was concerned with the way in which the law classifies various statements or promises made in the course of negotiations into one or other of these categories, it is important to grasp that breach of a term is not the only way in which a contract can come to an end or a plaintiff recover compensation. If one party has been induced to enter into a contract by some factual statement which turns out to be untrue, (in other words a misrepresentation) the injured party may have a remedy despite the fact that the inaccurate statement never actually became a term of the agreement. It is this situation with which we are now concerned and which has given rise to the cluster of overlapping legal principles brought together under the heading of "Misrepresentation."

The justice of allowing someone who has been misled into entering a contract the opportunity of escaping from it is more obvious than the legal devices which try to achieve this aim. It is unfortunate that the Misrepresentation Act 1967 far from clarifying and codifying the various legal remedies at that date appears to have added another layer of complexity on the uncertain foundation of the previous common law. Nevertheless, there are clearly two issues which require attention, namely: (1) What sort of statement or conduct will amount to a misrepresentation? and (2) What redress does a plaintiff have in these circumstances? The rather complex range of remedies available is a reflection of the fact that a misrepresentation can range from the outrageously fraudulent to the entirely innocent and therefore more than one solution may be appropriate.

1. The Meaning of Misrepresentation

In the simplest type of case nobody could doubt the existence of a misrepresentation. Suppose that A wishes to sell his armchair to B. A untruthfully tells B that it was a personal gift by the Queen to A, and B thereupon buys it. Assuming that this was not a term of the contract of sale (an assumption that is made of any misrepresentation throughout this chapter) and that it was an inducement to B's purchase, then clearly this is a misrepresentation which gives rise to legal consequences. In some areas, however, the legal usage of the term "misrepresentation" is rather narrower than its use in every day speech, in others perhaps a little wider. A misrepresentation to be of legal effect must be of fact, not of opinion, intention or law; but in some cases silence itself will be regarded as a misrepresentation. These areas now require to be examined in more detail.

(1) Fact rather than law

To come within the legal definition of a misrepresentation, the statement must relate to a matter of fact not law. At first sight this appears perfectly straightforward. To say that the Sale of Goods Act 1979 relates to consumer as well as commercial contracts is a clear statement of law; to state that this blanket has a hole in it is a statement of fact. But suppose one makes a statement which combines fact and law, such as "these blankets can be rejected because they are not of merchantable quality." Is this a statement of fact or law? Probably this can best be regarded as a statement of fact about the condition of the blankets, and of law in relation to the consequence of rejection. In daily life, where such statements are comparatively common, it may frequently be difficult to disentangle the two.

(2) Fact rather than opinion

The statement of an opinion, that is to say a view expressed on a matter that is either incapable of proof or as to which the speaker does not have conclusive evidence, cannot found an action for misrepresentation. So in *Bisset* v. *Wilkinson* (1927) Bisset was selling two plots of land in New Zealand to Wilkinson for the purpose of sheep farming. Bisset expressed the view in the course of negotiations that if the land were worked properly it could carry 2,000 sheep. Ordinarily one would regard such a statement as giving rise to a remedy on the grounds of misrepresentation. A farmer's statement as to the quality of his land in some particular area looks very much like a statement of fact. Nevertheless in this case it was regarded merely as a matter of opinion. Both parties knew that the land concerned had never been used before for sheep-farming. Consequently, in the circumstances of this case, the statement could only be regarded as one of opinion not fact.

This case must be distinguished from the facts in *Smith* v. *Land and House Property Corporation* (1884). The plaintiffs wished to sell an hotel and claimed that it was let to a "Mr. Frederick Fleck (a most desirable tenant)." This, on any view, was an optimistic assessment of Mr. Fleck's solvency since it was discovered that he had been seriously in arrears with his rent and had only paid "by driblets under pressure." Here the Court of Appeal allowed the action for rescission (a remedy for misrepresentation where the pre-contractual position of the parties is restored which will be discussed later). Bowen L.J. explained this by saying, "In a case where the facts are equally well known to both parties, what one of them says to the other is frequently nothing but an expression of opinion . . . but if the facts are not equally well known to both sides, then a statement of opinion by one who knows the facts best makes very often a statement of a material fact, for he impliedly states that he knows facts which justify his opinion." The material facts known by the vendors about Mr. Fleck clearly did not justify the expression of an opinion of him as a good tenant.

(3) Fact rather than intention

A promise to do something in the future is not regarded as a representation. If the promise is a contractual term then it may give rise, for example, to an action for breach but it will not lead to rescission on the grounds of misrepresentation. Nevertheless, a statement of intention to do something in the future may sometimes imply a present state of mind which can be regarded as a fact. A famous example was provided in *Edgington* v. *Fitzmaurice* (1885). The directors of a company sought to raise money on the basis that this would be used to improve and extend their buildings. In truth they intended all along to pay off the company's existing debts. The court regarded this as a dishonest statement of fact. As Bowen L.J. said. "There must be a misstatement of an existing fact: but the state of a man's mind is as much a fact as the state of his digestion."

(4) Silence

It may seem strange that silence could ever be regarded as a representation, and normally as one would expect it signifies nothing. Hence the general rule is *caveat emptor* (let the buyer beware), although of course that maxim is not a licence to make false replies to a purchaser's questions. Even if one contracting party knows that the other is labouring under a misapprehension there is not necessarily any duty to disabuse him. In *Fletcher* v. *Krell* (1873), at a time when such things were felt to be important, a woman applied for a post as a governess without revealing the fact that she had previously been married. The court held that silence in that case did not amount to a misrepresentation.

In some instances, however, the law does impose a duty to disclose information and to remain silent can therefore amount to a misrepresentation.

(a) *Contracts uberrimae fidei*

Certain types of contract are said to require the utmost good faith (*uberrima fides*) and so to involve a duty to disclose certain information. For practical purposes, the most important example of this type is the insurance contract. The basis for the rule is that the relevant facts are likely to be peculiarly within the knowledge of the insured and it is therefore necessary to ensure that one party does not have an unfair bargaining position over the other. Ironically, the rule has sometimes been abused by those it was meant to protect. Insurance companies have been know to specify that the *accuracy* of the information supplied shall be a condition of the validity of the policy. Consequently a proposer who honestly but inaccurately answers a question, or fails to make a disclosure, may find that the policy is later avoided despite his own good faith and integrity. As always, care is necessary in assessing the precise terms of the contract.

The obligation to disclose "all material facts" in such a contract is interpreted by the courts to mean a factor which would, "influence the judgment of a prudent insurer in fixing the premium, or determining whether he will take the risk" (Marine Insurance Act 1906, s.18(2)). A clear example of the rule, which incidentally makes the point that the loss does not have to be a result of the non-disclosure, is the case of *Seaman* v. *Fonereau* (1743). The assured here concealed the fact that the ship involved was in a position of danger when last sighted. In fact it escaped from that difficulty but was subsequently captured by the Spaniards. It was held that the failure to disclose was sufficient to render the contract voidable.

(b) *Subsequent falsity*

A statement once made will generally be regarded as having effect up to the time the contract is made. If a statement although true when made subsequently becomes false, then silence under these circumstances can amount to a misrepresentation. In *With* v. *O'Flannagan* (1936) a doctor wished to sell his medical practice and quite truthfully stated in January that it was worth £2,000 a year. Subsequently the doctor became ill and by the time the contract was signed in May the value had dwindled to almost nothing. It was held that the failure to disclose the subsequent events amounted to a misrepresentation.

(c) *Partial revelation*

A slightly different problem is posed by the statement of one who literally tells the truth, but who thereby conveys a totally misleading impression of the real situation. In *Dimmock* v. *Hallett* (1866) a vendor of property stated that the farms on his land were let, but failed to reveal that the tenants had given notice of their intention to leave. This failure to disclose so distorted the positive information given that the court held there had been a misrepresentation.

(d) *Other cases*

Sometimes the relationship between the parties, as opposed to the type of contract concerned, gives rise to a duty to disclose. There may be such a "fiduciary relationship" in the case of for example a parent and child, solicitor and client or trustee and beneficiary. A similar relationship exists, by virtue of the Companies Act 1948, between the promoters of a company and the public.

2. The Misrepresentation must be Operative

A misrepresentation does not become actionable unless it is at least one of the reasons for which the plaintiff entered the contract. If the other party never heard or read the statement, even though it was made, then there is no cause of action. Similarly if even though there was a misrepresentation the other party did not rely on it then the contract cannot be avoided. This was the case in *Attwood* v. *Small* (1838). The vendors of a mine made exaggerated claims as to its capacity in order to sell it but the purchasers appointed their own surveyors to check the accuracy of the statements. They reported, quite wrongly, that the claims were correct and relying on this the purchasers bought the property. It was held by the House of Lords that an action for rescission must fail on the basis that no reliance had in fact been placed on the vendor's statement. The purchasers had relied on their own enquiries.

It should not be assumed from this that anyone who has had the opportunity to check the facts does not rely upon the misrepresentor's statements. Both in contract and in criminal deception it is no defence that the victim could have found out the truth had he gone to even a little more trouble.

Although the misrepresentation must be an inducement to enter the contract, it need not not be the only one. In *Edgington* v. *Fitzmaurice* (1885) the plaintiff loaned money to a company induced (1) by a misstatement in the prospectus about how the money would be used and (2) by a mistaken belief of his own that the type of transaction involved gave him a charge on the company's property. Even though he admitted that he would not have lent the money but for (2) it was held that (1) was still an operative misrepresentation.

3. Different Types of Misrepresentation

Depending upon the state of mind of the maker a misrepresentation may be either fraudulent, negligent or wholly innocent. The distinction matters because the remedies for each type of misrepresentation differ.

(1) Fraudulent misrepresentation

The classic definition of a fraudulent statement was provided by the House of Lords in *Derry* v. *Peek* (1889) as being a false statement made: (i) knowingly; or (ii) without belief in its truth; or (iii) recklessly whether it be true or false. More simply, this amounts to saying that a fradulent statement is one that the maker does not honestly believe to be true. It must be more than foolish, inaccurate or unreasonable; an allegation of fraud is a serious matter and there must, to borrow the language of the criminal law, be *mens rea*. Negligence, as the House of Lords made clear, is never sufficient to found an allegation of fraud although as in criminal law the fact that a belief was highly unreasonable may be evidence that it was not honestly entertained.

The remedy for fraud is twofold. The plaintiff may (1) claim damages, and (2) rescind the contract. Although damages and rescission are available as we shall see for other types of misrepresentation there are special features of both in their relation to fraud. The damages for fraud are not a contractual remedy as such but are recoverable under the tort of "deceit." The measure of damages is therefore that of tort not contract. In other words, the object of the award is to put the plaintiff in the position he would have been in had the fraud not been practised upon him, not the position he would have been in had the "contract" been properly carried out. More of this will be said later in Chapter 11. Quite apart from suing for damages, the injured party may also elect to avoid the contract and if necessary apply for an order of rescission to ensure that any property handed over is restored to him. There is, however, one special feature relating to fraud. If the fraudulent party sues for rescission the other can use fraud as a defence and decline to hand back what he has obtained under the contract. If for example someone defrauds an insurance company into giving him cover, then the company would be entitled not only to avoid any liability under the policy but also to keep any premium the fraudulent proposer had paid over.

(2) Negligent misrepresentation

Until recently the remedy provided by the law for a careless misrepresentation was extremely limited, but two developments have altered this. One is the development of the tort of negligent misrepresentation, the other, the Misrepresentation Act 1967. The first of these has had enormous ramifications in the law of tort and its consequences are still being explored by the courts. For present purposes only the way it impinges upon the law of contract is examined.

(a) *Negligence at common law*

At the time when *Derry* v. *Peek* was decided, and for long afterwards, it was assumed that no damages could be recovered at common law for loss due to a careless misstatement. This was part of a wider doctrine in tort that no damages were recoverable for pure economic loss because the consequences might be so far reaching. This orthodoxy was dramatically dispelled by the House of Lords in *Hedley Byrne & Co.* v. *Heller & Partners Ltd.* (1964). The plaintiffs here entered into certain advertising contracts on behalf of Easipower in a way which rendered them liable if Easipower failed to pay. They obviously wished to check the company's credit worthiness and so contacted their bankers for a credit reference which was not unfavourable. Easipower did in fact default and the plaintiffs sued the defendant bankers. Although the plaintiffs lost their action because the reference was given "without responsibility" (one wonders if the same result would be reached today after the passing of the Unfair Contract Terms Act 1977) the House of Lords decided that there could be liability for negligent misrepresentation on the normal tort principles enunciated in *Donoghue* v. *Stevenson* (1932) as long as there was a "special relationship" between the parties. It is still not completely clear what precisely this means, and the rationale behind such a qualification may be to limit liability within reasonable bounds. The essence of the relationship is perhaps that the person giving the information must be someone who can normally be expected to have knowledge of the kind required, and that it is reasonable for such information to be relied upon. Such a relationship was certainly held to exist in *Esso Petroleum Co. Ltd.* v. *Mardon* (1976). Here Esso's very experienced sales representative assured the defendant that a new garage development would have a throughput of petrol of some 200,000 gallons. The defendant doubted this but ultimately in reliance on the representative's estimate signed the tenancy agreement. In fact the throughput was less than half the estimate and in the course of the resultant litigation the defendant claimed for Esso's negligent misstatement and won. It seems clear then from this case that where a contract is brought about by the carless misstatement of an "expert" on whom the other party relies, then the victim has a cause of action in negligence. It does not matter that at the same time there may be liability in contract as well.

(b) *Negligence under the Misrepresentation Act 1967*

Section 2(1) of the Misrepresentation Act 1967, a piece of legal draftmanship not noted for its clarity or elegance, has the effect that a negligent misstatement provides a plaintiff with a remedy of damages and rescission unless the other party can prove that he had, "reasonable ground to believe and did believe up to the time the contract was made" that the facts represented were true. The great advantage for a plaintiff of proceeding under the 1967 Act is that it is for the party who made the misrepresentation to show that he did act reasonably, not the victim of the misstatement to prove negligence (see, *e.g.* the earlier discussion at p. 4. In fact unless some special circumstance exists such as the contract being void *ab initio* for mistake (on which see next chapter) or some advantageous difference in the level of damages as between tort and contract, it is unlikely that an action for negligent misstatement at common law will be brought.

Whilst the Act has not led to large numbers of reported cases a good example of the operation and difficulties inherent in the Act and its relationship to common law is *Howard Marine and Dredging Co. Ltd.* v. *A. Ogden & Sons (Excavations) Ltd.* (1978). In this case contractors wished to hire some barges for removing large quantities of clay. The carrying capacity of the barges to be used was crucial as this would affect for example how quickly the job could be done. The contractors approached a firm which hired out barges and on enquiring as to their capacity received an oral reply which turned out to be too high. The reason for the wrong estimate was that the person making it had relied on the entry in Lloyd's Register (which was usually accurate) instead of looking at the ship's documents in their possession. A majority of the Court of Appeal held that the maker of the inaccurate statement was liable under section 2(1) of the 1967 Act. The case suggests that the statement's maker must discharge a considerable burden. Bridge L.J. stated: "the statute imposes an absolute obligation not to state facts which the representor cannot prove he had reasonable ground to believe." On the further claim for common law negligence the Court was divided. Shaw L.J. thought there was liability in the context of a business transaction whose nature made it clear just how important was the capacity, but Lord Denning thought there was here no special relationship. Unfortunately this interesting point is left undecided by the case as the third member of the Court, Bridge L.J., did not reach a conclusion upon it.

(3) Innocent misrepresentation

In the event of an innocent misrepresentation then the injured party may still rescind the contract, but this right has now been qualified by section 2(2) of the 1967 Act which gives the court a discretion to award damages in lieu of rescission, "if of opinion that it would be equitable to do so." Presumably this would cover the case of a misrepresentation of comparatively minor importance where complete rescission would be a remedy out of all proportion to the damage done.

There is also an overlap at this point between subsections 2(1) and 2(2). A court could if it wished even in the case of a negligent misrepresentation award damages in lieu of rescission under section 2(2).

4. Rescission

Frequent mention has been made of this term in the preceeding pages since all three types of misrepresentation give rise to a right to recission and it is now helpful to look more closely at just what rescission is and how the right to it may be lost.

The effect of misrepresentation is generally to make a contract voidable not void, that is, the contract continues unless and until the injured party chooses to have it set aside. This may be done either (1) by the representee making it clear to the representor that he no longer intends to be bound by the contract's provisions, or (2) by doing domething which reasonably leads to that inference. Once the representee has done this the contract is terminated once and for all *ab initio* as if it had never existed. Not unnaturally the representor is sometimes hard or impossible to find and an example of the operation of (2) is provided by *Car and Universal Finance Co. Ltd.* v. *Caldwell* (1965). A rogue bought a car from its owner using a cheque which later was dishonoured. By the time the seller discovered this the rogue and his car had disappeared so he immediately requested the police and the A.A. to find the car. It was held that this showed a sufficient intention on the part of the seller to rescind the contract and so re-vest the property in the car in himself (in this particular case resulting in no one else being able to acquire ownership of the goods and a subsequent "sale" by the rogue therefore being invalid; *cf. Lewis* v. *Avery* (1972) *post*, p. 394.

It is not strictly necessary, as we have seen, for a victim of a misrepresentation to go to court to rescind the contract. He may do it himself and from that date the contract is a nullity and consequently any property exchanged re-vests in its former owner. If, however, the other party disputes the position or fails to hand back property which has been transferred under the previously existing contract then it is possible to apply to the court for a formal order of rescission. The court will then seek to put the parties back into the position they were in before the contract was made. This is sometimes described as restoring the *status quo ante* (the position before) or *restitutio in integrum* (complete restitution). Sometimes this can best be done by ordering a payment of money, but it is important to realise that this is not damages. The law draws a strict distinction (although its importance is lessened by for example the Misrepresentation Act 1967) between damages which can properly be recovered for breach of contract, and a mere indemnity which is designed to restore the position upon recission.

The point is illustrated by the case of *Whittington* v. *Seale-Hayne* (1900). The plaintiffs bred prize poultry and leased certain property from the defendants in order to carry on this business. Although it was not contained in the lease and therefore not a term of the contract, the plaintiffs had previously represented orally that the premises were in a sanitary condition. In fact the water was poisoned so that the poultry died, the manager of the farm became ill and the local authority required the drains to be repaired. The plaintiffs claimed for the lost stock, loss of profits and removal and medical expenses. In all, it was a claim of some £1,525. The defendants offered £20 to pay for the rent, rates and repairs to the drains which under the terms of the lease the plaintiffs were bound to pay. The court accepted the defendant's view. The other claims did not inevitably arise under the terms of the lease; there would have been no breach of contract if the plaintiffs had failed to carry on business. Unless therefore the expense is an inevitable part of the contract, it will not be compensated.

Although on these facts a different decision might be reached today (for example there may have been a negligent misstatement) the authority is still valid on the point that in the case of rescission only an indemnity, not damages, can be awarded.

5. Bars to Rescission

Rescission is in many ways a more drastic remedy than damages since it involves disentangling completely what may have become a complex web of connections. Not surprisingly therefore the right to rescind may be lost in certain circumstances where it would plainly be unreasonable to return to the *status quo ante*.

(1) Affirmation

If the victim of a misrepresentation decides to affirm the contract with full knowledge of what has happened either by declaring his intention to continue with the agreement or by doing some act from which such an intention may reasonably be inferred then the right to rescind is lost.

(2) Lapse of time

Lapse of time is not, in itself, a bar to rescission, but it may provide evidence that the representee in fact intended to affirm the contract. In any event, rescission is an equitable remedy and so a court would have a discretion to refuse to grant it if, for example, other people had altered their position on the reasonable understanding that the contract was to remain in existence. One case involving the sale of goods suggests that lapse of time without more can be a crucial factor. In *Leaf* v. *International Galleries* (1950) the plaintiff bought a painting of Salisbury Cathedral after being told that it was by Constable. Five years later when he wished to sell it he discovered that it was by someone else. There was no suggestion of fraud and the plaintiff applied for rescission of the contract as soon as he discovered the truth. Nevertheless the Court of Appeal refused to grant the remedy and stated that: "it behoves the purchaser either to verify or, as the case may be, to disprove the representation within a reasonable time, or else stand or fall by it," No doubt the position would have been quite different if the misrepresentation had been fraudulent. In that case it seems likely that time would only have started to run once the fraud had been discovered.

(3) Restitutio in integrum

The object of restitution is compensation in which each party gets back what it has given to the other. If the property has been consumed, destroyed or for example in the case of a mine, exhausted, then *restitutio in integrum* has become impossible and rescission will not then be granted. It does not, however, matter that the property is not still in its original pristine state. If substantial restitution is possible then the court may order return of the property with a further order of monetary compensation for any deterioration.

(4) Third party involvement

If a third party has acquired a title to the property under a contract made in good faith and for value (*i.e.* consideration) then the right to rescind is again lost. In effect someone else now owns the property and it is no longer there to be restored. The situation might arise in this way. If a contract is void *ab initio* for some reason, then no property can pass. But if the contract is merely voidable (that is valid until set aside) as in the case with a misrepresentation, then it is perfectly conceivable that before the victim has a chance to rescind the property has been sold on by one or other party to somebody else. Rescission has then become impossible.

6. Misrepresentations and Terms

The difficulties that were thought to exist in the law over the relationship between terms and representations have been swept away by section 1 of the Misrepresentation Act 1967. The result is that if a misrepresentation is made early in the negotiations which then later becomes a term of the contract then a plaintiff may have a cause of action both for misrepresentation and breach of contract. If the facts of *Leaf's* case were to recur, then the pleadings might well contain an allegation that a condition or warranty as to the painter's identity had been breached.

7. Exempting Liability

The remedies available to a plaintiff would clearly be of no use if it was possible to insert into a contract a term excluding all liability for misrepresentation. Section 3 of the 1967 Act as amended accordingly states that if a contract contains a term which would exclude or restrict any liability or remedy for misrepresentation, "that term shall be of no effect except in so far as it satisfies the requirement of reasonableness as stated in section 11(1) of the Unfair Contract Terms Act 1977; and it is for those claiming that the term satisfies that requirement to show that it does." More will be said of the Unfair Contract Terms Act 1977 in Chapter 14 but it is noteworthy that the onus rests firmly on the claimant relying upon it to show that it was reasonable, and that unlike the 1977 Act which excludes certain types of contract (*e.g.* insurance) from its ambit section 3 of the 1967 Act has general application.

A recent example of the application of section 3 occurred in *Walker* v. *Doyle* (1982). The vendor of a house made an innocent but incorrect statement that there were no disputes regarding the boundaries of the property. This was an incorrect misrepresentation which on the face of it gave a right to rescission of the contract. The contract had, however, been concluded using the National Conditions of Sale which contained a clause 17(1) stating, "no error, mis-statement or omission in any preliminary answer concerning the property . . . shall annul the sale." The vendor therefore relied on this term as excluding his liability. The court granted rescission. One of the grounds for the judgment was that clause 17(1) was an unreasonable exclusion clause. Not only does the case illustrate the operation of section 3 of the 1967 Act but it is also of interest in that the occurrence of the offending term in a common-form clause in a long used standard form contract did not prevent its demise in the circumstances of the case. As Dillon J. conmmented, "I do not think it can be said that its precarious survival until 1977 entitles it to the automatic accolade of fairness and reasonableness."

CHAPTER 7

MISTAKE

At first sight it might seem obvious that if an agreement has been concluded on the basis of a mistake by one or both of the parties then the law will release them from their obligations. Such an approach, however, could never represent the law. Some mistakes are trivial others fundamentally alter the basis of the contract. It would not be feasible or sensible to dissolve whole contracts merely because one party was labouring under a slight misapprehension as to some peripheral matter. Justice must not only embrace the interests of the immediate parties but also the requirements of certainty. If other parties have relied upon the existence of a contract which on the face of it is perfectly valid, it may cause inconvenience and hardship to declare it invalid. For all these considerations the operation of the legal doctrine of "mistake" is a much more circumscribed notion than the use of the word in common speech would suggest. The result is that when things go wrong with a contract the doctrine of mistake is not likely to be the first thing a lawyer turns to. In order for it to be relevant, there must in general be something very seriously defective about the agreement or the subject-matter of the contract. Even where there is quite serious error the only remedy may be equitable rather than legal.

"Mistake" covers a wide range of situations and some have doubted whether there really is a single doctrine of mistake at all. Many of the cases could be explained on the basis of a breakdown in the conjunction of offer and acceptance, albeit a breakdown of a serious kind. Some of them, however, would not readily lend themselves to this approach. If, for example, the parties reach perfect agreement on an entity which has ceased to exist then it is difficult to see how a failure of offer and acceptance is to blame for the resulting nullity. Moreover the willingness of courts of equity to intervene in certain circumstances does seem consistent with the growth of an equitable doctrine of mistake. In what follows therefore the subject will be treated in the traditional way as a topic in itself, but it should not be forgotten that many of the cases could with equal validity be analysed in a slightly different way.

One of the matters which makes this area of the law confusing is the quite separate legal rules developed by the courts of common law and equity for the resolution of the same problem. In many cases the distinction between equitable and legal rules is no longer central.

Professor Ashburner's statement in 1902 that: "the two streams of jurisdiction . . . , though they run in the same channel, run side by side and do not mingle their waters," was criticised by the House of Lords in *United Scientific Holdings Ltd.* v. *Burnley Borough Council* (1978). Lord Diplock commented, "this metaphor has in my view become both mischievous and deceptive. . . . If Professor Ashburner's fluvial metaphor is to be retained at all, the waters of the confluent streams of law and equity have surely mingled now." Despite this co-mingling the distinction still matters in the area of mistake. In those rare cases where the common law recognises the operation of mistake, the effect is that the contract is *void*. This has the drastic consequence that the whole transaction is a complete nullity so that not only the parties themselves will have to return to the status quo but others who have derived rights under the void agreement may also find themselves with no title or interest in the relevant property. Where equity intervenes the effect is to render the contract liable to be set aside on the grounds that it is "voidable." This means that the contract may be set aside but that those who have bona fide acquired rights under the temporarily valid agreement are protected. Indeed unless the voidability has crystallised into a declaration of invalidity the contract remains a perfectly valid agreement. Equity also has the further advantage that a contract may be set aside on terms. It is therefore not possible to inquire simply as to the ultimate solution provided by equity; it is still necessary to consider the effect of the mistake, if any, at common law.

There seem to be as many ways of describing types of mistake as there are judges or authors. Broadly speaking two threads can be followed through the web of terminology. One describes the situation where the parties agree between themselves but for some reason the contract is incapable of performance as they envisage it. In a sense the contract is frustrated (on which see Chapter 10) before it has even got off the ground. The second situation that may arise is where there is in fact no real *consensus ad idem* between the parties. These situations will be examined in turn.

1. Mistake as to the Basis of the Contract

The essence of this type of mistake is that although the parties may be in complete accord as to the terms of an agreement, neither party would have entered a contract if they had realised the falsity of some underlying assumption.

(1) Absence of subject-matter

Perhaps the clearest example of a fatal common mistake is that the very subject matter of the contract never or no longer exists. The matter is then described as *res extincta* (the thing is destroyed). An example is provided by *Scott* v. *Coulson* (1903). Both parties entered into a contract for the sale of a life policy in the belief that the assured, Mr. A.T. Death, was alive. Unfortunately Mr. Death was dead at the time of the contract. The agreement was therefore held to be completely void at common law. Similarly in *Galloway* v. *Galloway* (1914) a man and woman entered into a separation agreement on the assumption they were married to each other. Rather surprisingly to them, it transpired that they were not. The wife of the husband by an earlier marriage turned out to be still alive. Such a common mistake led to the agreement being void.

In *Couturier* v. *Hastie* (1852) it was found that the parties had agreed the sale of a specific cargo of corn which they believed to be on board a boat from Salonica to the United Kingdom. In fact the cargo had by then already been sold by the ship's master to a buyer at Tunis. Although the language of mistake is never actually used by the House of Lords, the finding that there was no contract here is generally thought to rest on the basis that as the entire content of the contract no longer existed, it must be void.

The common law relating to the sale of goods in such circumstances is now contained in section 6 of the Sale of Goods Act 1979 which declares: "Where there is a contract for the sale of specific goods, and the goods without the knowledge of the seller have perished at the time when the contract is made, the contract is void."

An analogous case which extended the principle of *res extincta* to the slightly different circumstances of *res sua* (the thing is his own) is shown in *Cooper* v. *Phibbs* (1867). Here one party took a lease of property from another which, unknown at the time to both of them, actually already belonged to the lessee. It was said by the court that the agreement "ought to be set aside" which Lord Atkin at least, in a later case, understood to mean was void at common law. It is simply quite impossible to give someone something he already has.

Two other decisions of the courts at first sight similar raise slightly different issues. In *Amalgamated Investment & Property Co. Ltd.* v. *John Walker & Sons Ltd.* (1977) the plaintiffs negotiated the purchase of a warehouse, which they wished to redevelop, for £1,710,000. In fact the day after the signing of the contract the Department of the Environment made the property a listed building (a planning device restricting development of buildings of special interest) so reducing its value to some £210,000. Neither party were aware of this during their negotiations, but the Court of Appeal refused to intervene. The agreement was in fact valid; at the time of the agreement both parties were perfectly correct in their belief that the building was not listed. The mistake, quite apart from being sufficiently serious, at the very least must pre-date the contract. Even if the listing had taken place prior to the contract it seems likely that the agreement would not have been void at law, although it might have led to consideration of the application of equity's doctrine of mistake exemplified in *Solle* v. *Butcher* (which is considered later.)

Not every case of non-existence of the subject matter will lead to the contract being void. If in *Couturier* v. *Hastie* the agreement had been to purchase not specific goods but the risk that there were such goods then the contract would have been perfectly valid. The parties would have agreed where the risk of non-existence was to fall in that event. In the Australian case of *McRae* v. *Commonwealth Disposals Commission* (1951) the Commission agreed to sell the plaintiff "an oil tanker lying on Jourmand Reef, which is approximately 100 miles north of Samarai." The plaintiff fitted out an expensive salvage operation and it was then discovered that not only was there no oil tanker in such a place but there was also no place known as Jourmand Reef. The court decided that the Commission had in effect impliedly promised that such a tanker existed and could therefore be sued for breach of contract. The precise basis for this decision is questionable. Can it be reconciled with *Couturier* v. *Hastie*? If based upon a collateral contract, where is the consideration? Nevertheless it does illustrate that the existence of the subject matter could be made a term of any contract. Doubtless if the facts of *McRae's* case were to recur in England it could now be dealt with on the basis of a negligent misrepresentation.

(2) Mistake as to quality

It is not difficult to see that if the subject matter does not exist then the contract can be void for mistake. A more difficult problem arises where although the thing exists it lacks or possesses some quality which makes it impossible to achieve the result the parties originally envisaged. We shall see later that a mistake as to quality where there is a failure as to the agreement, as in *Smith* v. *Hughes* (1871), will not absolve the parties. What of a common mistake as to quality? The position is not altogether clear. It seems certain that the courts are, at the very least, reluctant to apply the doctrine of mistake in such circumstances. The difficulty arises over whether they are prepared to countenance it at all.

The crucial case upon which discussion turns is *Bell* v. *Lever Bros. Ltd.* (1932). Lever Brothers appointed Bell as managing director of a company in which they had a controlling interest at an annual salary of £8,000 for a period of five years. Due to a merger Bell became redundant and Lever Brothers paid him £30,000 as compensation for his loss of employment. They then discovered that during his employment he had committed various acts which would have entitled them to terminate his employment without any compensation at all, although it was found that Bell had not been fraudulent in failing to reveal these actions. Not surprisingly Lever Brothers sued for the recovery of the £30,000, amongst other things on the basis of a common mistake rendering the contract void. The mistake claimed was that this was a service contract which could only be terminated by paying substantial compensation. The trial judge and Court of Appeal held that it was void for mistake; the House of Lords decided by a majority of three to two that it wasn't. The difficulty that arises is how to interpret the various speeches of their Lordships.

One view is that the case decides that there is no doctrine of operative mistake as to quality. There is no doubt that the parties had made a fundamentally wrong assumption about the factual basis of their agreement. If the doctrine of mistake did not operate in these circumstances, then when could it ever be relevant? This view could be supported by, amongst other cases, the Court of Appeal's judgment in *Solle* v. *Butcher* (1950). Here A agreed to let a flat to B for a rent of £250 a year on the assumption that the flat was not subject to the Rent Acts. On this they were mistaken, and the maximum rent permissable was only £140. Again this could hardly be denied to be a fundamental mistake as to quality since the application of the Rent Acts to property is a crucial consideration. Nevertheless the court purported to follow *Bell* v. *Lever Brothers* and held that the agreement was not void for mistake *ab initio* (from the beginning). In *Leaf* v. *International Galleries* (1950) the Court of Appeal also denied that the contract was void for mistake.

On the other hand the issue of mistake was never squarely raised in *Leaf's* case and the comments are therefore *obiter dicta*. Surely it is false apparently to regard a picture merely as a physical conglomeration of paint and canvas and not take account of the fact that it is often identified solely by reference to the painter? In *Nicholson* & *Venn* v. *Smith-Marriott* (1947) some table napkins were put up for sale as having been the authentic property of Charles I and consequently fetched £787. In fact they were much later and so only worth £105. Although the case was disposed of on other grounds Hallet J. said that the contract could have been held void for mistake. The buyers presumably wanted not just old napkins but an authentic Carolean relic. Surely this would come within Lord Atkin's statement in *Bell's* case that, " . . . a mistake will not affect assent unless it is the mistake of some quality which makes the thing without the quality essentially different from the thing as it was believed to be." Moreover, quite apart from dicta in *Bell's* case that are consistent with the wider view of there being a general doctrine of common law mistake there is at least one case decided since *Bell* v. *Lever Brothers* and *Solle* v. *Butcher* where the court did decide that a contract could be held void for a mistake as to quality. In *Sheikh Bros. Ltd.* v. *Ochsner* (1957) A agreed to to deliver at least 50 tons of sisal a month to B who would then process it and they would both share the profits. In fact the land could not produce at this rate; they had made a mistake as to its quality which was essential to the agreement. The Privy Council purporting to follow the decision in *Bell* decided that it was void. Although this decision is not technically binding on English courts, its persuasive value is surely very high.

Although there is no doubt that any doctrine of mistake at common law is extremely limited therefore, it would seem rather premature in the present state of the authorities to deny its existence altogether.

(3) The intervention of equity

The very narrow ambit of the doctrine of operative mistake at common law is to some extent relieved by the intervention of equity. Notwithstanding that an agreement is not *void* it may be set aside on the grounds that it is *voidable* in equity. Substantial justice between the parties is also aided by the fact that a court may set aside the agreement on terms.

A clear illustration is provided by *Solle* v. *Butcher*. Although as we have seen the agreement was held to be valid at law, the Court of Appeal declared it to be voidable. It did, however, set it aside on terms to ensure that neither party was unfairly prejudiced. Essentially, the tenant was given the choice of either leaving the flat or remaining on the same terms but at the increased rent of £250 a year. A similar approach was adopted in *Grist* v. *Bailey* (1967) where the mistake in a sale of property was as to the protection of the tenant under the Rent Acts and in *Magee* v. *Pennine Insurance Co. Ltd.* (1969) over mistakes in an insurance proposal.

The underlying rationale in the cases was explained in *Huddersfield Banking Co. Ltd.* v. *Henry Lister & Son Ltd.* (1895) by Kay L.J., ". . . both on principle and authority, when once the court finds that an agreement has been come to between the parties who were under a common mistake of a material fact, the court may set it aside." The obvious difficulty with this very important equitable jurisdiction is to know just when it will be exercised. Certainly a court will not intervene if any of the events which bar rescission for misrepresentation has occurred. Probably the courts would not wish to tie themselves too closely to a set of rigid principles when the whole object of the exercise is to do broad justice as between the parties, but this clearly produces an unfortunate degree of uncertainty. If the facts of *Bell's* or *Leaf's* cases were to recur, would they now be disposed of under this jurisdiction?

2. Mistake as to Agreement Between the Parties

As we saw in Chapter 2, when two parties are agreed on the same subject-matter in the same terms then they are bound. Sometimes, however, despite the appearance of agreement the parties are not really *ad idem*; a firm acceptance has not really connected on the same terms with the offer. For example, if I offer to sell you my "crop," meaning my riding whip, and you accept thinking you are buying the produce of my farm then there is no real *consensus* despite the apparent verbal conjunction of offer and acceptance. As we shall see, the law would provide a remedy for such a mistake. Nevertheless the operation of a doctrine of mistake in this area is severely limited. It is not sufficient that a party is not getting what he anticipated from the bargain. The test which the law applies to the parties' dealings is objective. As Blackburn J. said in *Smith* v. *Hughes* (1871): "If whatever a man's real intention may be, he so conducts himself that a reasonable man would believe that he was assenting to the terms proposed by the other party, and that other party upon that belief enters into the contract with him, the man thus conducting himself would be equally bound as if he had intended to agree to the other party's terms." Even if one party knows the other is labouring under a self-induced delusion this will not invalidate the agreement if to all outward purpose it is apparent that agreement has been reached. In the case itself the defendant was shown some oats by the plaintiff. He wanted old oats as the plaintiff apparently knew, but these were new oats. The defendant bought them labouring under the mistake that they were old oats which were the only kind he had any use for. There was no fraud and the plaintiff had done nothing at all to induce the erroneous belief in the defendant. The court held that the mere fact of the buyer's mistake as to the quality of the oats, even though known to the seller, did not invalidate the contract. Any reasonable onlooker would have drawn the reasonable inference that both parties were in agreement on the precisely identified subject-matter.

Nevertheless, there are certain circumstances where the mistake is so fundamental and important to the parties that the law will regard the apparent agreement as void.

(1) Mistake as to identity

A mistake as to identity renders the contract void if the true identity of the party is a crucial factor. If, for example, A visits his broker to take out an insurance policy on his car the actual identity of the insurance company may be a matter of complete indifference to him (see, *e.g. Mackie* v. *European Assurance Society* (1869) as long as his car is insured. Consequently a mistake as to the identity of the other contracting party would not have legal consequences. There may be other cases where identity is important, and not surprisingly some of the leading cases in the area involve confidence tricksters purporting to be well known and reputable figures.

In *Cundy* v. *Lindsay* (1878) a respectable firm of merchants called "Blenkiron & Co." carried on business at 123 Wood Street, London. A rogue called Blenkarn hired a room, also in Wood Street, and placed an order for handkerchiefs with Lindsay & Co. The order came on a letter which gave his address in Wood Street and contained a signature which might have been read as "Blenkiron & Co." The plaintiffs forwarded the handkerchiefs to the rogue on credit and needless to say received no payment. Blenkarn had sold the handkerchiefs to Cundy, who acted in good faith, and Lindsay sued Cundy for conversion (*i.e.* wrongful dealing with the handkerchiefs). If the contract between Lindsay and Blenkarn was only voidable for Blenkarn's fraud Cundy would have a defence because at the time of the sale to them Blenkarn had a title to pass on. If, however, that contract was *void* then Cundy was bound by the normal rule that a person cannot effectively sell something to which he has no title. The House of Lords decided that there was no contract. The plaintiffs, as the rogue well knew, intended only to deal with the respectable firm of "Blenkiron & Co." and nobody else. Blenkarn was a completely different entity and the contract was therefore void. This can be contrasted with the decision in *King's Norton Metal Co.* v. *Edridge, Merrett & Co. Ltd.* (1897). A rogue called Wallis adopted the name "Hallam & Co." His notepaper showed a large factory and claimed that "Hallam & Co." had depots and agencies in Belfast, Lille and Ghent. Using this notepaper he ordered goods from the plaintiffs which were delivered but never paid for. Again the issue arose as to the status of the agreement between the rogue and the plaintiffs. The court held that there was a contract. The plaintiffs intended to contract with the writer of the letter. There was nobody else. Their only mistake was not as to *identity* but as to the *attributes* of the rogue, in particular his credit-worthiness. This was not sufficient to render the contract *void*, but of course as was shown in Chapter 6 the agreement would be *voidable* for fraudulent misrepresentation. As was noted earlier, the vital difference is often in the rights that third parties will obtain in the latter but not in the former case.

Both the above cases involved parties dealing by letter. The situation is rather less clear where there is fraud and the parties are dealing *inter praesentes* (face to face). Does one look to the physical party standing in front of you, or to the entity he represents? The three crucial cases are not altogether easy to reconcile.

In *Phillips* v. *Brooks Ltd.* (1919) a rogue called North entered a jeweller's shop and selected some pearls worth £2,550 and a ring at £450. He wrote out a cheque saying, "You see who I am, I am Sir George Bullough." The plaintiff had heard of Sir George as being a rich man and asked if he wished to take the articles with him. With some aplomb North replied that he would give an opportunity for the cheque to be cleared and just asked to take the ring for his wife's birthday. The cheque was subsequently dishonoured and North pawned the ring. In suing the pawnbroker for its return the agreement between the plaintiff and North fell to be considered. Was it a contract? The court said it was because the plaintiff, "had contracted to sell and deliver the ring to the person who came into his shop. . . . His intention was to sell to the person present and identified by sight and hearing." The plaintiff had made a contract with the person in front of him, even though it might be voidable for fraud.

In *Ingram* v. *Little* (1961) three sisters advertised their car as for sale. They were visited by a rogue calling himself "Hutchinson" who made an offer of £717 for the car. As he was about to write a cheque, Elsie Ingram indicated that the deal was off as she was not prepared to take a cheque in payment. He thereupon falsely claimed to be a Mr. P.G.M. Hutchinson and gave an address. Hilda Ingram checked in the telephone directory that there was a person of that name at that address. They then allowed him to take the car. The cheque was later dishonoured and the rogue sold the car to a third party. The Court of Appeal held there was no contract. The plaintiffs intended only to deal with P.G.M. Hutchinson not the person who stood in front of them. It was not a mere mistake as to credit-worthiness, but as to identity.

Lewis v. *Averay* (1972) involved another rogue who claimed to be Richard Green, an actor who portrayed the part of Robin Hood. The rogue offered to buy the plaintiff's car and signed the cheque "R.A. Green." The plaintiff asked for evidence of his identity and the rogue produced a Pinewood Studios pass with his name and photograph on it. The plaintiff handed over the car, the cheque was dishonoured and the rogue sold the car. Here the Court of Appeal said there was a contract albeit voidable. The agreement was reached with the very person present.

How can one reconcile these three cases? Lord Denning at least thought that on their facts they were indistinguishable, but the court preferred the approach of *Phillips* v. *Brooks* to *Ingram* v. *Little*, which therefore seems to represent the present law. A further point of interest is that this appears to be an example of the Court of Appeal refusing to follow one of its own previous decisions.

The result is therefore that where parties are face to face at least, there is a presumption that the parties intend to deal with the person who is physically present.

(2) Mistake as to subject-matter

If A intends to sell commodity X, and B intends to buy commodity Y, then clearly both parties are labouring under a mistake as to the subject-matter of the contract. This is in effect what happened in *Scriven Bros. & Co.* v. *Hindley & Co.* (1913). An auction contained two lots of hemp and tow respectively. Tow is inferior in quality to hemp. The cataloguing and wording of the separate lots was not altogether clear and the bidder wrongly thought both lots contained hemp and made an extravagant bid for the inferior quality tow. The plaintiff therefore intended to sell tow, but the defendant bidder intended to buy hemp. Neither party realised the mistake of the other. Clearly there was no genuine *consensus* between the parties, but was there a contract when the situation was looked at objectively? The court decided there was no contract. The circumstances were so ambiguous that it was impossible to be certain what commodity was being contracted for. The parties were not *ad idem*.

A similar situation arose in the leading case of *Raffles* v. *Wichelhaus* (1864). The buyer agreed to purchase a consignment of cotton to arrive "ex Peerless from Bombay." Unfortunately, there were two ships called "Peerless" leaving Bombay at about the same time. The seller intended to deal in the cotton on board the ship leaving in December; the buyer intended to buy from the ship sailing in October. The case turned on the pleadings and the actual reason for the court's decision in favour of the buyer (when sued for refusing to accept the December shipment) is not clear, but it is commonly thought that there was no contract because it would not be open to a reasonable man to determine the sense of any agreement between the parties. The facts could be regarded as entirely ambiguous; the appropriate offer simply did not "connect" with the acceptance.

An agreement mistake merely as to the quality of the subject matter will not be sufficient as *Smith* v. *Hughes* (1871) shows. On the other hand if, as might be said in the case of *Nicholson & Venn* v. *Smith-Marriott* (1947), the mistake of quality was so great as to amount to a common mistake as to the identity of the subject matter then this would be an example of the other kind of operative mistake considered previously.

(3) Mistake over the terms of the contract

In general there is no relief if a party mistakenly interprets the effect of the agreement or one of its terms. So in *Wood* v. *Scarth* (1858) the plaintiff accepted the defendant's offer to lease a public house for £63 a year. The defendant thought his clerk had made it clear that a premium of £500 should be payable in addition, but he had in fact failed to do this. The court held that the agreement must stand. Any reasonable observer would have seen a precise and unambiguous offer and acceptance which the defendant's mistake could not be seen to vitiate.

However, the position is different where a party's mistake as to the terms of the deal is known to the other party. In *Hartog* v. *Colin & Shields* (1939) the defendants intended to sell skins at a certain price "per piece" as was apparently the custom in the trade and the basis of their negotiations. By a mistake they offered them "per pound" which worked out much cheaper. The buyers accepted this offer. The court held that there was no contract. The buyers were aware of the seller's mistake.

(4) Intervention of equity

In principle the intervention of equity in this type of mistake is much more limited. The court has looked at the bargain and determined for itself the sense of the promise. Either there has been no real offer and acceptance so the contract is void, or there has so that it will be valid. One area where equity can, however, intervene is in refusing a decree of specific performance. Since like all equitable remedies it is discretionary the court may always withhold it if it is thought fairer to do so, but this would not prevent a claim for damages at law as indeed happened in *Wood* v. *Scarth*. Equity even so would not refuse specific performance merely because one party found he had made a worse bargain than he thought as for example in *Tamplin* v. *James* (1880).

3. Rectification and Non Est Factum

In the case of written documents the law provides two further remedies where there has been a mistake.

(1) Rectification

In general a person who signs a document is bound by its terms whether or not he has understood or even read them, and no oral evidence is admitted to contradict such written terms. The former is sometimes described as the rule in *L'Estrange* v. *Graucob* (1934) which provided a particularly harsh illustration of the principle, and the latter the parol evidence rule. Sometimes however a document will be drawn which does not accurately reflect the prior agreement of the parties. In that case an application can be made to have the document rectified. As Cozens-Hardy M.R. stated in *Lovell & Christmas Ltd.* v. *Wall* (1911): "The essence of rectification is to bring the document which was expressed and intended to be in pursuance of a prior agreement into harmony with that prior agreement." It is important to note that the court is not varying the agreement or remaking the bargain. It is merely ensuring that the document is an accurate record of the agreement already reached. In *Joscelyne* v. *Nissen* (1970) for example, a father and daughter who shared the same house agreed that the daughter should take over the father's car hire business and in return pay certain household expenses including gas, electricity and coal. The subsequent written document did not specifically refer to these expenses. After paying them for a while she refused to continue. The father brought an action for rectification of the agreement to include these specific payments. The Court of Appeal found for the plaintiff. There was a common continuing intention up to the time when the written document was executed. It could therefore be amended to ensure that it accurately reflected what the parties had in fact agreed.

(2) Non est factum

The plea of *non est factum* (this is not my deed) provides another exception to the rule that a person is bound by the terms of any document he has signed. The plea originated in the mediaeval common law to protect, for example, people who might have signed a document which they could not read and whose effect had been misrepresented to them. As social conditions have changed the ambit of the plea has been steadily reduced. It now operates only in somewhat extreme cases but it still remains a specific common law plea quite distinct from the law of misrepresentation and mistake. Its effect is that the purported agreement is completely void.

The whole area was thoroughly considered by the House of Lords in *Saunders* v. *Anglia Building Society* (1971). Mrs. Gallie was a 78 year old widow who had a nephew called Wally Parkin. She had left the house to Parkin in her will and handed over the deeds to him so that he could raise some money on the security of the house. Parkin and an acquaintance called Lee called at the house and asked her to sign a document. She was told that the deed was an assignment of the lease to her nephew to enable him to raise the money. Because she had broken her glasses she did not read the document, but did not object to her nephew raising money in that way. In fact it was a deed of sale to the dishonest Mr. Lee who failed to pay Mrs. Gallie or Parkin and mortgaged the house to a building society. After Lee defaulted on the mortgage repayments the building society sought possession of the house (the normal result of failure to keep up mortgage payments). Mrs. Gallie claimed that the assignment to Lee was void on the ground of *non est factum*. The House of Lords decided that the assignment was valid. Certainly Mrs. Gallie had been tricked, but she was not mistaken as to the "object of the exercise." She intended to enable Parkin to raise money. If Lee had not been dishonest, the transaction would have achieved this. The burden on a plaintiff to establish the plea is therefore a very heavy one. The Law Lords used various terms to describe the type of mistake required but it seems that the document must be fundamentally different in character from that which the signatory believed it to be. An example of the type of mistake required is provided by the case of *Lewis* v. *Clay* (1897). Here one Neville showed some documents to Clay which were largely covered by blotting paper except for some small gaps. Clay was told that his signature was required as a witness to a family arrangement; in fact they were documents which on their face made Clay liable for a payment of £11,113 to one Lewis. The court here in effect upheld a plea of *non est factum*.

The House of Lords also laid down a second requirement that a plaintiff would have to satisfy, in effect overruling an earlier case which had cast doubt on the matter. He must prove that he did not act negligently (not in the technical way that word is used on the tort of negligence but simply meaning "carelessly") in signing the document.

Identical principles apply to the person who signs an agreement in blank leaving someone else to fill in the details as in *United Dominions Trust* v. *Western* (1976). In such a case one would have thought that it will be almost impossible to prove that the person had not been careless in signing such a document. The result will be, as happened in the case, that the signatory will be bound by a contract which does not necessarily represent what he had agreed to.

Chapter 8

PRIVITY

1. The Meaning of Privity

The doctrine of privity of contract requires that no one who is not a party to the contract can either enforce it or be made liable upon it. It is something that was mentioned in Chapter 2 in the context of the requirement that consideration must move from the promisee. In other words, it is an aspect of the emphasis in English contract law on the element of "bargain." No one who has not put something into the contract can either take action or be sued upon it. We now need to examine this concept in more detail.

If A and B make a contract which purports to place some obligation upon C, it is not difficult to see why the law would not enforce it. No one would think it right that C should have some obligation foisted upon him. But suppose A and B agreed that B should confer some benefit on C. Can C compel B's adherence to the contract? In this situation it is more difficult to see why C should not have a right of action. Nevertheless, the result of the doctrine of privity at common law is that C cannot enforce the agreement. He is a "stranger" as it is said to the contract. The case of *Tweddle* v. *Atkinson* (1861) (discussed in Chapter 3 *ante* p. 338) provides a simple illustration of that situation, and the House of Lords has on a number of occasions re-affirmed the general principle. In *Dunlop* v. *Selfridge* (1915) the plaintiffs, Dunlop, sold tyres to Dew & Co. under a contract which stated that the buyers would not sell the tyres below a certain price and that a similar term would be part of any agreement between Dew & Co. and subsequent purchasers. Dew & Co. sold tyres to Selfridge who agreed not to sell below the fixed price and to pay Dunlop £5.00 for every tyre sold in breach of this agreement. Selfridge later supplied tyres to customers below the fixed price. Dunlop brought an action against Selfridge for damages and an injunction to restrain further breaches of contract. The House of Lords gave judgment for Selfridge. There were in fact three distinct contracts; the first between Dunlop and Dew, the second between Dew and Selfridge, and the third between Selfridge and their customer. No doubt Dew could have sued Selfridge in failing to keep the contract made with them but Dunlop could sue neither Dew nor Selfridge. They could not sue Dew because Dew had honoured their contract by extorting a promise from Selfridge that they would not sell the tyres below the stated price (note that Dew had not as part of that bargain with Dunlop promised that they would additionally seek to restrain Selfridge from selling below the stated price) and they could not directly proceed against Selfridge because they had struck no bargain with them. Their reasoning can easily be grasped by looking at the diagram.

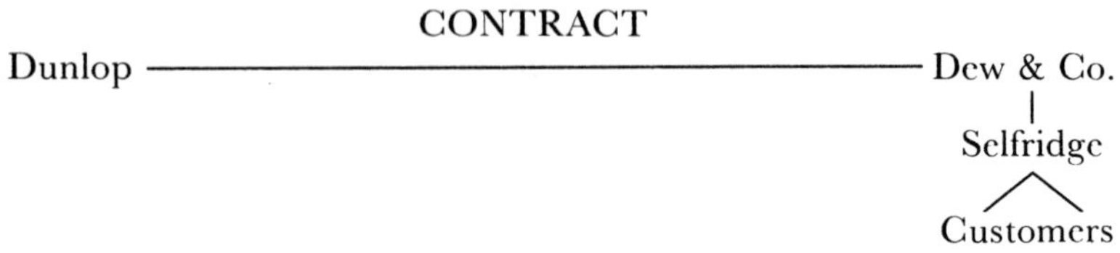

It was as if Dunlop were trying to take advantage of somebody else's agreement.

Like many legal rules, much of the complication arises from attempts by the courts to relieve parties from the injustice of an over strict application of the general principle. An example of the difficulties imposed by the doctrine of privity is provided by *Jackson* v. *Horizon Holidays Ltd.* (1975). The plaintiff contracted with the defendants for a holiday in Ceylon for himself, his wife and children. It was a less than euphoric experience. The hotel plumbing did not work properly and there was mould growing up the walls. The defendants were clearly in breach of contract, but the damage extended not only to the maker of the agreement but also his family who were not parties to the contract. Lord Denning at least thought that the plaintiff could recover damages on behalf of his family, but this clearly appears to fly in the face of orthodox privity of contract. The House of Lords in *Woodar Investment Development Ltd.* v. *Wimpey Construction U.K. Ltd.* (1980) criticised Lord Denning's reasoning although without overruling the case. It could, for example, be supported on the basis that his family's failure to enjoy their holiday was itself a loss to the original contracting party, Mr. Jackson. One might think, however, that there is something slightly artificial about such an approach although it does produce a more or less satisfactory practical result within the confines of the doctrine of privity. Not surprisingly perhaps Lord Scarman commented: "If the opportunity arises, I hope the House will reconsider *Tweddle* v. *Atkinson* and the other cases which stand guard over this unjust rule."

Pending such a major review by the House of Lords it is necessary to examine the various ways in which the Law has sought to mitigate the effects of the doctrine of privity or to recognise legitimate limitations upon it such as the doctrine of agency.

2. Limitations to the Doctrine of Privity

(1) Implying a trust

Suppose A gives £1,000 to B with instructions that while A is abroad the money is to be spent on C's welfare. This creates the legal mechanism of a "trust." B (the trustee) holds the money on trust for C (the beneficiary of the trust). C as the person entitled under the trust can sue B in equity for the performance of his obligation as trustee. One of the contributions of equity to the problems created by the doctrine of privity is to extend the notion of a trust affecting property such as money to that of the benefit of a promise. The promise is the "property" which is the subject matter of the trust. Accordingly a beneficiary, C, can enforce the trust against say, B, where A has contracted to vest some property or benefit in B for the benefit of C. The principle becomes clearer if we examine a case where the House of Lords approved it.

In *Les Affréteurs Réunis S.A.* v. *Walford* (1919) Walford, a broker, negotiated a a charterparty (a contract for the use of a ship) between the owners of a ship and the charterers (the people who wanted to use it). The agreement made between the owners and the charterers contained a term that the owners would pay Walford a 3 per cent. commission on the estimated gross amount of hire, which was not in fact paid. Walford sued the owners for this commission. He also applied to join the charterers as parties and the action proceeded as if this had been done. The House of Lords gave judgment for Walford, Lord Birkenhead declaring "in such cases charterers can sue as trustees on behalf of the broker." The reasoning, as can be seen from the diagram, was that since the charterers were trustees of the promise to pay Walford commission, Walford as the beneficiary could enforce his claim either by getting the charterers to join him as co-plaintiff or by compelling them to act by joining them as co-defendant. Either way the beneficiary could enforce his interest despite not being a party to the original contract between the owners and charterers.

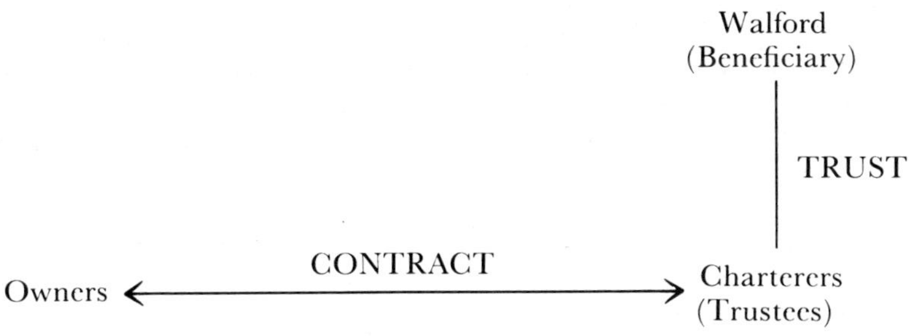

If this idea had been developed then there is no doubt that the doctrine of privity could have been robbed of much of its effect. The behaviour of the courts since *Walford's* case has, however, been to make scant use of the machinery of the constructive trust as it is called. No doubt this is partially owing to the fact that a trust must be irrevocable (in other words, it cannot subsequently be altered) and many of the situations which at first sight might be thought to be amenable to the constructive trust analysis turn out to contain elements which the parties would never wish to make unalterable. For example, in *Re Schebsman, Official Receiver* v. *Cargo Superintendents (London) Ltd. and Schebsman* (1944) Schebsman had been employed by two companies. He entered into an agreement with them whereby he, or in the event of his death his wife and daughter, was to receive a sum of £5,500. Schebsman first went bankrupt then died and one of the arguments advanced in the subsequent litigation was that the deceased held the company's promise as trustee on trust for his wife and daughter. This argument, if it had succeeded, would have enabled them directly to enforce the trust. The Court of Appeal rejected the argument. Lord Greene M.R. said: " . . . it is not legitimate to impart into the contract the idea of a trust when the parties have given no indication that such was their intention. To interpret this contract as creating a trust would, in my judgment, be to disregard the dividing line between the case of a trust and the simple case of a contract made between two persons for the benefit of a third."

Such a view seems to indicate that the constructive trust is not likely to pose much of a threat to the orthodox doctrine of privity.

(2) The Restrictive Covenant

Land and interests over land generally have a degree of permanence that people do not. The results of the doctrine of privity if applied mechanically to land would have produced highly inconvenient consequences and even the common law made an exception in the case of leases. If A lets property to B, and B later assigns his lease to C, then C can be bound by the covenants and terms that originally bound B. C would still be bound to the new lessor if A sold his interest to D. Equity, however, has made a later and separate contribution which clearly operates in the case of land and which some have sought to extend further to other types of contract.

In the famous case of *Tulk* v. *Moxhay* (1848) the plaintiff owned several plots of land in the middle of Leicester Square. He sold the garden in the centre to one Elms who agreed as part of the contract not to build upon the garden. The land was conveyed a number of times until it eventually came into the possession of one Moxhay who knew of the original covenant but nevertheless proposed to build on the land. The plaintiff realised that on orthodox principles he could not succeed at common law so he sought an injunction in equity to restrain the building. The court granted the injunction on the basis that it would be unconscionable to allow the defendant to disregard a contractual obligation which he knew about at the time of purchase. Although the doctrine has been modified and developed somewhat since then, the case provides a basis for the principle that negative covenants (*e.g.* a restriction on building) can be made to run with the land itself so as to bind subsequent purchasers who have notice of the restriction, even though they were not parties to the original agreement.

In two areas in particular, that of price control and the use of a chattel (in this sense any property other than land), an attempt has been made to apply similar principles to those which restrict the use of land.

(a) *Price control*

The difficulty in imposing price control as a result of the doctrine of privity has already been seen in *Dunlop* v. *Selfridge*. In *Taddy* v. *Sterious* (1904) a more determined attempt was made. The plaintiffs, tobacco manufacturers, attached a printed sheet to each packet stating, as a term of the contract of sale, that the tobacco was only sold "on the express condition that retail dealers do not sell it below the prices above set forth." If the retail dealer had bought through a wholesaler, then the latter was stated to be regarded as the plaintiff's agent (more will be said of agency later). The agency argument was rejected, but the second argument advanced was that the principle of *Tulk* v. *Moxhay* should be applied to the price restriction. The court roundly rejected this. Swinfen Eady J said: "Conditions of this kind do not run with goods and cannot be imposed upon them. Subsequent purchasers, therefore, do not take subject to any conditions which the court can enforce."

This area is now in any event governed by statute. After a rather complicated legislative history the law has been consolidated in the Resale Prices Act 1976. The effect of Parts I and II of the Act is that minimum price clauses are void unless they fall within a class of goods which the Restrictive Practices Court is prepared to exempt. To date, the only classes of goods so exempted are books and medicaments. So at common law the rule was that while A could by contract with B enforce a minimum price at which B was to sell the goods, A could nor enforce a similar undertaking given by C who bought the goods from B. Now, as the result of statutory provisions directed against resale price maintenance, A cannot oblige B to sell the goods at any particular price.

(b) *Use of a chattel*

An attempt was made to apply the doctrine of *Tulk* v. *Moxhay* to a ship in *De Mattos* v. *Gibson* (1858). Knight Bruce L.J. expressed himself in broad terms that certainly favoured the application, although it should perhaps be borne in mind that at the time of this statement the principle in *Tulk* v. *Moxhay* was comparatively recent and had not yet reached the degree of development it has later achieved. In particular, requirements have been appended to the notion of the restrictive covenant in respect of land which were not apparent in the years after 1845 and which suggest that it is a doctrine of narrower application than might have been thought soon after the decision. Nevertheless, the Privy Council in *Lord Strathcona Steamship Co.* v. *Dominion Coal Co.* (1926) approached another shipping case in a way that suggests they were seeking to apply the restrictive covenant doctrine. The case has, however, been heavily criticised. One of the requirements of a restrictive covenant in land is that it must protect a proprietary interest (*i.e.* a right over the object itself and not merely against an individual) which the type of charterparty involved did not bestow. In a subsequent case *Clore* v. *Theatrical Properties Ltd.* (1936) Lord Wright M.R. commented that the *Strathcona* principle should be restricted "to the very special case of a ship under a charterparty" and in *Port Line Steamers Ltd.* v. *Ben Line Steamers Ltd.* (1958) Diplock J. (later Lord Diplock) expressed the view that the *Strathcona* case was wrongly decided. Even so, the doctrine gets some support from the observations of Browne-Wilkinson J. in *Swiss Bank Corp.* v. *Lloyds Bank Ltd.* (1979).

The result of the cases therefore seems to be that whilst the doctrine of the restrictive covenant is not altogether unarguable in the case of charterparties, it would require a substantial dose of artificial respiration to bring it back to full vigour. Outside this area it seems unlikely that the doctrine has any application.

(3) Statutory interventions

In some cases Parliament has intervened to resolve the problems posed by the doctrine of privity, especially in the area of insurance. For example section 11 of the Married Women's Property Act 1882 states that where a husband or wife insures his or her life for the benefit of their spouse or children this will create a trust in favour of the objects of the policy. This section therefore provides the spouse or children with an enforceable right of action even though they are not parties to the original agreement.

One statutory provision which has caused difficulty in the past is section 56(1) of the Law of Property Act 1925. On the face of it, this provision appears to state that someone who is not named as a party to a "conveyance or other agreement" can take the benefit of the agreement. Lord Denning interpreted the section as making at least a large dent in the orthodox doctrine of privity but, unfortunately, the House of Lords did not agree. The point arose for determination in *Beswick* v. *Beswick* (1968). Peter Beswick sold his business to his nephew John on terms that Peter would receive a weekly payment for the rest of his life and in the event of his death his widow was to receive £5 per week. After Peter's death John made only one payment to his widow. She thereupon sued (i) as administratrix (a person appointed to administer the estate of the deceased) of her husband's estate, and (ii) in her personal capacity. In the House of Lords the second argument was rejected. Section 56(1), their Lordships decided, was limited in effect to covenants relating to land. Although the words could literally have supported Lord Denning's contention it was felt that Parliament could not possibly have intended to make such a major change in the doctrine of privity in contract generally in a statute devoted to reforming the law of real property (see *ante*, p. 57). Nevertheless the House upheld the claim on the first argument, and granted a decree of specific performance of the agreement. In effect Mrs. Beswick was not suing as a third party benefiting under a contract, but rather as the representative of the original promisee. The result therefore was satisfactory and within the spirit of the doctrine of privity.

(4) Agency

The law of agency is an extensive legal topic which warrants a book to itself but it does have an important relevance to the present discussion.

The essence of agency is that one person is appointed to be the representative of another. The commercial convenience of such an arrangement has long been recognised and indeed the present law of agency is largely derived from the custom of merchants. To some extent however, it does appear to conflict with the doctrine of privity and this is why it needs to be considered at this point. Normally, as we have seen, if A contracts with B, then these are the only two parties who can enforce the agreement. Yet if A is the agent of someone else, P (called in law the principal), then P becomes able to sue or be sued upon a contract which he has not personally made. In most cases this will not be thought of as offending anything but the strict letter of the privity doctrine. After all, B may know perfectly well that A always acts as the agent of P and therefore it accords with the expectations of everyone involved that the real contract is between P and B. A is simply an intermediary who drops out of the picture. In a sense, he is the crucial link in a chain that really binds only the parties P and B together. Such an approach accords with many of the situations in which the concept of agency operates, but the law goes somewhat further than this.

Quite apart from the occasions when A has actual authority to enter into a contract on behalf of P the law also recognises so-called "ostensible" or "apparent" authority. Lord Denning explained this concisely in *Hely-Hutchinson* v. *Brayhead Ltd.* (1968) when he said: "Ostensible or apparent authority is the authority of an agent as it appears to others. It often coincides with actual authority. Thus, when the board [of a company] appoint one of their number to be managing director, they invest him not only with implied authority, but also with ostensible authority to do all such things as fall within the usual scope of the office. Other people who see him acting as managing director are entitled to assume that he has the usual authority of a managing director. But sometimes ostensible authority exceeds actual authority. For instance, when the board appoint the managing director they may expressly limit his authority by saying he is not to order goods worth more than £500 without the sanction of the board. In that case his *actual* authority is subject to the £500 limiation, but his *ostensible* authority includes all the usual authority of a managing director. The company is bound by his ostensible authority in his dealings with those who do not know of the limitation." Accordingly if the director orders goods worth £5,000 in breach of his *actual* authority, the seller may still sue the company for payment if it appeared to the seller that he had apparent authority. This moves a little further from the doctrine of privity in that P finds himself bound by a contract that he at least had no wish to make as well as not being personally involved with the transaction.

An even greater deviation from the notion of privity is the doctrine of the undisclosed principal. If A has in fact been authorised to act as P's agent but A makes a contract with B where to all outward appearances A is acting entirely for himself, P can nevertheless sue and be sued as the undisclosed principal. In this case of course not only does B not intend to benefit or burden P, he does not even know he exists. The justification for such a rule appears to rest on the basis that it has been found a convenient practice in business. Diplock L.J. in one of the leading agency cases, *Freeman & Lockyer* v. *Buckhurst Park Properties Ltd.* (1964) explained it thus: "It may be that this rule relating to "undisclosed principals," which is peculiar to English law, can be rationalised as avoiding circuity of action, for the principal could in equity compel the agent to lend his name in an action to enforce the contract against the contractor, and would at common law be liable to indemnify the agent in respect of the performance of the obligations assumed by the agent under the contract." Whatever its explanation it is an undoubtedly valid doctrine which does not readily square with orthodox notions of privity.

(5) Assignment and negotiability

Both these topics would require extensive space to cover in any detail. They are here examined merely to see how they relate to the doctrine of privity.

(a) *Assignment*

In view of that we have seen about the way the doctrine of privity operates it may seem surprising that it is possible to assign the benefit of a contractual arrangement. This was a development of equity which has since been assisted by statute. For example, suppose A owes B £1,000. A is described as the debtor and B the creditor in this situation. It is possible for B to assign the debt to C who can then enforce it directly against A. B has in effect given away (as one might sell or give away any item of valuable property) his right to enforce the debt and so drops out of the picture. A debt is the most obvious form of such a right but there are others. Such "choses in action" as they are described (that is, intangible property or rights which can only be obtained or enforced by bringing an action in court) also include copyrights, patents, shares in a company, insurance policies or benefits under a trust. Of course it is possible for the parties to include a term in the contract that the rights or benefits arising under it shall not be assignable, and certain rights as a matter of policy cannot be assigned. For example, a wife cannot assign any right to maintenance payments. A further limitation is that although the benefit of a contract can be assigned, the burden cannot be. So in the above example A could not, even with D's consent, assign to D the obligation to pay B.

Equity's development of this area can again be explained by the common law's failure to meet the demands of business convenience. A simple and reliable machinery for assignment is supplied by section 136(1) of the Law of Property Act 1925. This provides that where an assignment of any chose in action is (i) absolute (*e.g.* complete and not, say, conditional upon something else happening), (ii) written, and (iii) notice in writing has been given to the debtor, then this will be effective to pass the whole legal interest in the thing in action to the assignee.

(b) *Negotiability*

Some types of contractual benefit are so readily assignable as to become negotiable, and such written choses in action are called negotiable instruments.

There are others, but the most common everyday form of negotiable instrument is a cheque. Assuming that one is not overdrawn, the relationship between a bank and a customer is that of debtor and creditor. The bank owes the sum in the account to the customer. If I write a cheque to a shopkeeper what I am in fact doing is to assign over to the shopkeeper some or all of the debt owed by the bank (the drawee) to me (the drawer). In such a case the shopkeeper could if he wished then indorse (*i.e.* sign) the cheque and deliver it over to someone else who in turn could simply pay it into his account or negotiate it further to yet another party. Negotiable instruments therefore provide a streamlined version of ordinary contractual assignment. They arose out of business convenience and special rules relating to them are found largely in the Bills of Exchange Act 1882. The distinction and advantage of negotiable instruments over normal assignments is that various technicalities which might inhibit exchange do not apply to them. For example, it is never necessary to inform the debtor that there has been a transfer.

3. Conclusion

Despite Lord Scarman's dictum in the *Woodar Investment* case (above p. 400) the doctrine of privity has shown considerable resilience. It has not suffered the erosion of subsequent cases which sometimes renders a general principle the insubstantial ghost of its original form. Most of the authoritative decisions of the courts, such as for example *Beswick* v. *Beswick,* have in the end tended to reaffirm the orthodox doctrine rather than to undermine it. There are, as we have seen, various inroads both common law and statutory into the integrity of the principle, but they tend to be well established and relatively clearly demarcated. For an old doctrine, it still shows a youthful vigour.

CHAPTER 9

INCAPACITY AND ILLEGALITY

So far we have examined the various ingredients which are required to constitute a contract and some of the things that can go wrong so as to make it defective. Before leaving consideration of how contracts are formed we need to examine briefly a further set of rules which may come into play. Notwithstanding that all the formal requirements of a contract are present and that there has been no question of misrepresentation or mistake a contract may still be invalid, either in part or in whole, as a result of the incapacity of a party to make a contract or the illegality of the transaction itself. In both these areas the underlying rationale is that of public policy. Certain classes of person are thought of as requiring protection or special consideration and certain types of transaction break the law because they offend moral or economic values which society considers to be worth protecting.

I. *INCAPACITY*

Generally speaking anyone is capable and competent to bind himself by any contract which is not in itself illegal or contrary to public policy. Certain persons, however, are said to lack capacity to contract freely. The unlikely assortment which makes up this group includes minors, corporations, the mentally disordered and drunkards. Of these only the first will be looked at in any detail.

1. MINORS

The term "infant" used to be applied to anyone under the age of 21 but by virtue of the Family Law Reform Act 1969 the age of majority was reduced to 18. The Act also replaces the rather outworn terminology "infant" with "minor" and although these terms are effectively interchangeable, the latter is the one used in modern statutes. One might have expected the law in such a basic area to be straightforward and long settled. Unfortunately it is somewhat involved and archaic. The result is that contracts with minors fall into three broad categories. There are those that are perfectly valid; those that can be disaffirmed; and those that are "void" within the Infants' Relief Act 1874. These will be examined in turn. It is the special rules relating to contract with minors which explain why so many order and booking forms include a term that the signatory must be over 18. No supplier of goods or services wants to find himself in difficulties recovering the price because he has sought to contract with a minor.

(1) Contracts which are valid

These are agreements where the minor's liability to sue or be sued is effectively the same as anyone else of full capacity. They fall into two categories; (a) contracts for so-called "necessaries," and (b) contracts of service.

(a) *Contracts for necessaries*

It has long been the law that a minor can be sued for the price of "necessaries." These not only include such essentials as food and clothing but also those articles or services which are appropriate to one in his station in life. As regards goods, the Sale of Goods Act 1979, s. 3(2) states that: " 'necessaries' means goods suitable to the condition in life of the minor or other person concerned and to his actual requirements at the time of sale and delivery." The common law applies a similar test to services.

The operation of the law is illustrated by the leading case of *Nash* v. *Inman* (1908). A Savile Row tailor supplied a Cambridge undergraduate with, "eleven fancy waistcoats at two guineas each." When he sued for payment he was met with the plea of infancy. The Court of Appeal gave judgment for the defendant. Although he was, "the son of an architect of good position" so that the clothing might well have been "suitable to the condition in life of the minor," the plaintiff failed to satisfy the second limb of the statutory definition. They were not suitable to his actual requirements at the time. His father had given uncontradicted evidence that he was already adequately supplied with clothes.

Necessary services includes such matters as legal and medical advice and education. A further illustration is supplied by *Chapple* v. *Cooper* (1844). An undertaker sued a widow, who was an infant, for the cost of her husband's funeral. It was held that this was a necessary for which the widow was liable. Obviously this involves a slight, though doubtless sensible, extension to the concept of what is necessary since in a sense there is no direct personal benefit to an infant in the burial of a deceased person.

The range of necessaries clearly cannot be a closed category and will vary with the status of the minor and the subject-matter of the contract.

The precise legal basis for a minor's liability is strangely not entirely clear. Some have suggested it is simply contract; others quasi-contract. In other words, liability rests on the basis that the infant has been supplied with goods and should not be unfairly enriched (see for example Fletcher Moulton L.J. in *Nash* v. *Inman*). Whatever view is correct there is one other anomaly concerning contracts with minors at least in respect of the sale of goods. Section 3(2) states that a minor need only pay "a reasonable price" for goods delivered. Hence an agreed contract price may turn out to be more than that which the minor can lawfully be compelled to pay.

(b) *Beneficial contracts of service*

The law is designed to protect a minor, not prevent him from earning a living. Hence it has long been the case that a minor can bind himself by a so-called beneficial contract of service. This really means a contract of employment which, taken as a whole, is substantially to his advantage even though it may contain some term or terms which are disadvantageous to him. Two contrasting cases bring out the principle which a court applies.

In *De Francesco* v. *Barnum* (1890) a 14 year old girl entered into an indenture (meaning agreement) of apprenticeship with De Francesco to be taught stage dancing. The agreement was, to say the least, somewhat one-sided. She was not to marry during the seven year period of the agreement; she could not contract professional engagements without written consent; she was entirely at the disposal of her master. He on the other hand made no commitment to employ her and even when he did the rate of pay was very low; he could send her to work abroad; if at any time he considered her unfit he could put an end to the agreement. Fry L.J. concluded: "Those are stipulations of an extraordinary and unusual character, which throw, or appear to throw, an inordinate power into the hands of the master without any correlative obligation on the part of the master." The court held the contract to be invalid as not being for the infant's benefit.

In *Clements* v. *London and N.W. Rail Co.* (1894) an infant was employed by a railway company as a porter. The company operated an insurance scheme amongst its employees whereby in exchange for giving up his right to sue the employer for personal injuries under the Employers' Liability Act 1880 he received certain benefits. Although the level of compensation was lower than that which might be obtained under the Act, it did not depend upon proving negligence and embraced a wider range of possible accidents. When the infant was injured in an accident the validity of the agreement fell to be considered. It was held to be valid. Taken as a whole, the contract was for the infant's benefit and binding upon him.

The trend in recent cases has been to extend the notion of contract of service to analogous situations. So in *Doyle* v. *White City Stadium Ltd.* (1935) the infant plaintiff entered into an agreement with the British Boxing Board to obtain a fighter's licence. One of the terms of the licence was that in the event of a foul and disqualification the fighter should only receive his travelling expenses and not the "purse." Doyle was disqualified for hitting below the belt. The court held that even though in this case the contract had deprived him of a £3,000 "purse" the agreement as a whole was analogous to a beneficial contract of service and was therefore binding upon him.

(2) Contracts which are voidable

These are contracts which although valid at the moment they are made, the minor may repudiate before he is 18 or within a reasonable time afterwards. There is no sanction against his repudiation as would be the case with anyone else. The types of contract which come within this category include contracts concerning land (for example for a lease of property), company shares, partnership and marriage settlements. The common denominator in all these transactions is that they concern relatively durable arrangements in respect of property.

If the minor repudiates the agreement before any obligations have arisen under it then there is no doubt that the whole arrangement is a nullity. It is as if it has never happened. Two problems, however, may arise: (i) what of obligations that have accrued before the minor's repudiation, and (ii) what of money that the minor may have paid over under the avoided contract?

As regards (i), there is a curious lack of conclusive authority and conflicting dicta in cases and textbook writers alike. Pending a conclusive decision the balance of opinion favours the view that a minor is liable on a contract debt that has arisen *before* repudiation. Such a view would seem at least to minimise the disruptive effect of a minor's privilege to repudiate.

The recovery of money paid under the "contract" depends upon whether or not there has been what is called a total failure of consideration. In other words, he must have got nothing at all out of the arrangement. Two contrasting cases make the point. In *Corpe* v. *Overton* (1833) a minor agreed to enter into a partnership and paid a £100 deposit which would be forfeited if he failed to execute (*i.e.* sign so as to make operative) the deed. Before the deed was executed the minor repudiated the agreement. He was held entitled to the return of his £100. At the time he repudiated, he had received nothing. The situation was different in *Steinberg* v. *Scala (Leeds) Ltd.* (1923). Here a minor bought shares in Scala which were not fully paid up. When shares are not fully paid up the company can subsequently require a shareholder to make payments up to the nominal value of the shares. This was done by Scala and the minor paid a further £250 on the shares. She now wished to repudiate the contract and reclaim the £250. Her claim failed. Even though she was freed from any future obligation to make payment, there had not been a total failure of consideration and she could not recover past payments. She had applied for the shares and she had got them.

(3) Contracts void under the Infants' Relief Act 1874

The complexities and uncertainties of interpretation which stem from the curious drafting of the Infants' Relief Act 1874 make it a statute overdue for repeal and replacement. It does at least provide a lesson in the contortions of statutory drafting and judicial interpretation.

Section 1 provides that certain classes of contract are "absolutely void," namely: (i) loans for money lent or to be lent; (ii) contracts for non-necessary goods; and (iii) accounts stated. Of these (iii) is of the least practical importance. An account stated is either an acknowledgment of a debt (but it is only some not conclusive evidence of such a debt) or a type of compromise between parties who may for example have been trading together and where each owes the other money.

The natural interpretation of the words "absolutely void" would be that such transactions are of no legal effect whatsoever. Accordingly, one would expect that neither party could sue on the "contract" and that any money paid over could be recovered. Unfortunately, doubt has been expressed by textbook writers and in cases on both these points. For example, before the Act of 1874 it was held that an infant could sue for failure to deliver goods. If it was an infant's *relief* Act surely the minor should not be in a worse position afterwards? On the other hand since the Act was meant to reform the law, might not this be regarded as a deliberate change in an Act which effects an overall improvement of the law for minors? As regards the recovery of money paid, one interpretation of the cases is that this is only possible where there has been a total failure of consideration of the kind considered in the previous section. An authority cited for this proposition is *Valentini* v. *Canali* (1889). An infant agreed to become a tenant of a house and to purchase certain furniture within it. He paid £68 on account, used the furniture for several months and then wished to repudiate the contract. It was held that he was not entitled to the return of £68. The words "total failure of consideration," however, are never actually used in the case and the judgment is somewhat brief. It therefore seems an uncertain authority and may be explicable on the basis that the plaintiff could not restore what he had received. The furniture was presumably by then somewhat worn.

A related question is whether in such a contract the property in goods passes to an infant. If the agreement is "absolutely void" then it seems not. Nevertheless, although there is no decided case on the point, there is a dictum of Lush J. in *Stocks* v. *Wilson* (1913) that property does pass in such a case.

The result is therefore hardly satisfactory and the precise meaning of "absolutely void" in this context remains unresolved. There is something to be said, however, for an interpretation which gives the phrase its obvious natural meaning. Those cases that deviate from this approach can hardly be said to effect an improvement in the law and what other justification can there be for an interpretation that flies in the face of the obvious?

Section 2 of the Act provides even greater difficulties of interpretation. It applies to all contracts that do not come within (1) and (2) above, and its intent seems to have been to prevent a contract that was unenforceable because of infancy being given a new lease of life by ratification or a fresh promise when the infant became an adult. Unfortunately the wording of the section is extremely obscure and draws a curious distinction between a ratification and a fresh promise. The result is that any later promise to pay a debt contracted in infancy or a ratification of any other sort of contract is completely unenforceable. Rather strangely (and accidentally?) a new promise supported by fresh consideration to perform a contractual obligation other than paying a debt is valid.

(4) Contract and tort

Generally speaking an infant is liable in tort in the same way as an adult. The significance of this is that in some contexts tort and contract overlap, and it has accordingly been held that where a tort is directly connected with a contract, suing the infant in tort cannot be used as a way to get round the unenforceability of the contract. An example is *Fawcett* v. *Smethurst* (1914). Here the infant defendant hired a car for a specific journey but in the event drove it further than was agreed. The car was damaged on the journey but the plaintiff's claim for damages in tort failed. Success would have meant that the plaintiff could get indirectly what he could not get directly (see also *Leslie Ltd.* v. *Sheill* (1914)).

(5) The intervention of equity

A law designed to safeguard minors against exploitation could easily work an injustice against people of full capacity who contract with them. Accordingly even the common law developed the doctrine of quasi-contract to allow recovery of money paid where the effect was to unjustly enrich the recipient, for example money paid over on a mistake of fact. Nevertheless an action in quasi-contract will not be enforceable against a minor if its effect is indirectly to enforce an unenforceable contract. So in *Leslie* v. *Sheill* an infant fraudulently represented that he was of full age and thereby obtained a loan of £400. Clearly this could not be recovered under contract law, but the plaintiffs also rested their claim on the tort of deceit and quasi-contract. Both these claims failed.

Equity has made an important contribution in the doctrine of restitution. The principle is that those who have been unjustly enriched should be made to disgorge their profits, and this principle can be applied to infants. So if an infant fraudulently obtains goods and remains in possession of them, an order for restitution will be made to restore them to the plaintiff. If however the infant having obtained goods or money no longer possesses them, then no order for restitution can be made as was indeed the case in *Leslie* v. *Sheill*. To do so would again have the effect of circumventing an unenforceable agreement, and statements to the contrary in the earlier case of *Stocks* v. *Wilson* (1913) can probably be regarded as overruled.

One equitable remedy not available to a minor is specific performance. Since mutuality is a precondition of this remedy, and specific performance cannot be enforced against a minor, so he cannot obtain this remedy against anyone else.

2. Corporations

A corporation is a legal entity which is treated by the law as being separate from the person or persons who constitute it. They may be created by Royal Charter or statute. Universities for example tend to be created by Royal Charter. The most common form of statutory corporation is a registered company under the Companies Acts 1948–1981. The law regards a corporation as just as much an individual as a natural person, but places certain restrictions on their capacity. Corporations created by statute may only contract *intra vires* (within the power) which the statute or memorandum of association of the company authorises, otherwise the contract is void. The rationale behind this is that shareholders and creditors should be protected against directors who employ company resources for unauthorised objectives. Nevertheless the practical effect of this doctrine is reduced by the fact that the memorandum of association of a company can be (and usually is) widely drafted. Further, section 9(1) of the European Communities Act 1972 states that a transaction is *deemed* to be within the capacity of the company where the other party deals in good faith. A company can no longer therefore escape from a contract on the grounds that it was *ultra vires*, at least where the other party acts bona fide. The wording of the section, "In favour of a person dealing with a company . . . " leaves open the possibility that *ultra vires* could be pleaded as a defence by a party against whom a company seeks to enforce a contract.

3. The Mentally Disordered

If a person was suffering from such a degree of mental disability that he was incapable of understanding the nature of the contract, then the contract is *voidable* at the election of the person of unsound mind provided he can show that the other party knew of his disability. The last proviso does not apply where the contract is for necessaries, but by virtue of section 3(2) of the Sale of Goods Act 1979 he is then only obliged to pay a "reasonable price."

4. Drunkenness

The general view appears to be that drunken persons are in a similar position to those suffering from a mental disorder, and section 3(2) of the 1979 Act also applies to them. One obvious difference is that it is never likely to be a problem to show that the other party was aware of the drunkenness. If one party was so intoxicated that he did not know what he was doing then this ought to be quite obvious to the other party.

II. *ILLEGALITY*

A full, or even adequate, treatment of the way in which certain transactions may offend some legal rule and thereby become defective lies outside the scope of the present work and is to some extent peripheral to the central principles of contract law. But it is still important to note that sometimes agreements which on the face of it might be thought of as binding are not recognised as effective by the courts for reasons other than the incapacity of the parties. The terminology of this complex area is not always used with complete accuracy or consistency but the major distinction which is normally drawn is that between contracts which are "void" and those that are "illegal." An illegal agreement cannot be enforced because it is of a kind that is in effect prohibited. A void contract (in this context) is one that is simply unenforceable or denied its full validity. One result of this distinction is that although an illegal contract taints any other transaction that depends upon it, a void one being only unenforceable does not necessarily do so. It is convenient to consider first void and then illegal contracts both of which can arise either by statute or common law.

1. Void Contracts

(1) Contracts which are void by statute

Numerous transactions are rendered void by statute and reference has to be made to specialised works to discover how statutory provisions affect a transaction. Two obvious examples are wagering and restrictive trading agreements.

(a) *Wagering agreements*

The whole area of wagering and gambling is heavily regulated by statute. An example is section 18 of the Gaming Act 1845 which provides:

> "All contracts or agreements, whether by parole or in writing, by way of gaming or wagering, shall be null and void, and no suit shall be brought or maintained in any Court of Law or Equity for recovering any sum of money or valuable thing alleged to be won upon any wager . . . ."

The result of such a provision is that although a wagering transaction is not illegal in the sense that it is proscribed, it simply cannot be enforced if a party to it refuses either to pay the agreed stake or hand over the winnings. For the purposes of this section a wagering contract is one where there are only two parties so that for example a football pool is not within the section. Nevertheless, as we saw in Chapter 4, such a transaction is usually unenforceable for the reason that the parties choose to exclude a legally binding relationship (see, *e.g. Jones* v. *Vernon's Pools Ltd.* (1938)). A further result of the section is that if the wagering transaction is paid by cheque which the drawer subsequently 'stops' then the payee cannot sue on the cheque even though this would normally be an ordinary recoverable contract debt.

Even an indirect way of enforcing such a transaction has been held to be invalid. In *Hill* v. *William Hill* (*Park Lane*) *Ltd.* (1949) a race horse owner owed some £3,635 in unpaid debts. He was ordered by Tattersalls to pay the debt by instalments or else, in effect, be blacklisted. He failed to pay. Later in exchange for a promise not to enforce the order he promised to pay. Even though there was therefore a separate agreement with fresh consideration the House of Lords held the arrangement to be void. In substance it was an agreement to recover a sum of money won upon a wager and therefore within the terms of the section.

(b) *Restrictive trading agreements*

Restrictive trading agreements are governed by several statutes and may also fall foul of the provisions of Article 85 of the Treaty of Rome if they result in unfair competition within the EEC. An example is section 1 of the Restrictive Trade Practices Act 1976 which requires certain agreements to be registered with the Director General of Fair Trading. This Act is intended to control agreements as to such matters as the price charged for goods or services or the persons or areas to be supplied. Once registered the Director General must submit the agreement to the scrutiny of the Restrictive Practices Court. Such an agreement is presumed to be contrary to the "public interest" and the parties have the onus of rebutting the presumption. If they fail to do this (and most such agreements are considered by the Court to be contrary to the public interest) then that provision is declared to be void.

A similar type of restriction (although the effect is actually to render the agreement *illegal* not just void) is that imposed by the Resale Prices Act 1976 (discussed in the context of privity *ante*, p. 403) which effectively renders unlawful restrictions intended to ensure that goods can only be sold by retailers at fixed prices.

(2) Contracts void at common law

The courts have long taken the view that certain classes of contract are void on the grounds of "public policy." As early as 1824 one judge described this notion as "a very unruly horse" and the result has been that there are three important areas where such a potentially nebulous concept has crystallised into a rule.

(a) *Contracts ousting the jurisdiction of the courts*

The courts have looked critically at any attempt to limit by contract a person's right of access to the courts. Consequently even though an agreement may make some domestic tribunal the ultimate arbiter on questions of fact, if it purports to limit the adjudication of the courts on matters of law it will be, to that extent at least, void. An agreement that in the first instance a dispute will go to arbitration rather than the courts is lawful (see, *e.g. Scott* v. *Avery* (1856)) although this area is now affected by the provisions of the Arbitration Act 1979.

(b) *Contracts prejudicial to marriage*

This head of policy renders void contracts which seek to restrict a person's right to marry, involve charging a fee for procuring a marriage partner or which make provision for a future separation between husband and wife. One might wonder whether in relation to the last two areas public opinion may have moved somewhat ahead of the law.

(c) *Contracts in restraint of trade*

This is an important area which frequently comes before the courts and the overall approach has been to lean against agreements which either place fetters on an individual's deployment of skills or the ability to trade freely.

The two areas where such contracts are most likely to be encountered are in the context of employment contracts or in the sale of a business. If an employee or apprentice has gained valuable commercial information or training there may be an understandable desire on the part of the employer to restrict his ability to set himself up in competition. Equally the purchaser of a business might wish to protect himself against a well-known and successful vendor simply setting up business again close by and so destroying the purchaser's custom.

The result of leading cases such as *Nordenfelt* v. *Maxim Nordenfelt Guns and Ammunition Co.* (1894) and *Esso Petroleum Co. Ltd.* v. *Harper's Garage (Stourport) Ltd.* (1968) is that every covenant in restraint of trade is prima facie void unless it can be shown that the agreement is reasonable as between the parties and that it is not unreasonable as regards the public interest.

Two contrasting cases illustrate the point. In *Mason* v. *Provident Clothing Co. Ltd.* (1913) the House of Lords held that a restriction on an employee against working in a similar capacity within 25 miles of London was void. It was wider that that which could reasonably be required to protect the business of the employer. In *Fitch* v. *Dewes* (1921) the restriction upon a solicitor's former managing clerk against being similarly employed for the rest of his life within a seven mile radius of Tamworth Town Hall was held to be valid. In the circumstances of this case it was reasonable. Nevertheless each case will depend upon its facts and covenants which are too widely drafted will be struck out. A prohibition against practising some trade or profession within seven miles of Tamworth Town Hall might be reasonable. A similar restriction measured as a five mile radius from, say, Leicester Square might be considered quite unreasonable embracing as it does a major portion of the business area of the capital.

2. Consequences of a Contract being Void

(1) By statute

This will depend upon the particular wording of the statute (for example there are special provisions relating to wagering contracts) but many of the principles applied are analogous to those of common law.

(2) At common law

(a) *Severance*

The fact that one part of a contract is void does not necessarily mean that the entire contract fails. If, of course, the entire promise is indeed void then there may be a total failure of consideration which renders the whole agreement void. If only one of several or merely part of a contractual promise is void, then the court may sever the void area and leave the rest of the contractual obligations intact. This will not be done however if the real effect of such severance is to alter the whole nature of the agreement (see, *e.g.* the contrasting cases of *Goldsoll* v. *Goldman* (1915) and *Attwood* v. *Lamont* (1920)).

(b) *Money paid over*

The prevailing view is that money paid over under a void term or contract can be recovered. There is a certain lack of authority, but the proposition is supported by the decision in *Hermann* v. *Charlesworth* (1905).

3. Illegal Contracts

(1) Contracts which are illegal by statute

Numerous transactions are rendered illegal by particular statutes which may often be concerned with such matters as economic controls or the licensing of certain activities. An example is that of an agreement for the collective enforcement of price control under Part I of the Resale Prices Act 1976 (see *ante*, p. 403).

Even if a statute does not specifically prohibit a transaction it may be construed as having that effect by implication. This is illustrated by the contrasting cases of *Cope* v. *Rowlands* (1836) and *Archbolds (Freightage) Ltd.* v. *S. Spanglett Ltd.* (1961). In the former a statute made it an offence for a stock broker to act in the City of London without first obtaining a licence. The broker did some work for the defendant and sued for payment. The action was dismissed for the reason given by Parke B. that, "The clause . . . must be taken . . . to imply a prohibition of all unadmitted persons to act as brokers, and consequently to prohibit by necessary inference all contracts which such persons make. . . . " In the latter the Road and Rail Traffic Act 1933 required a carrier of goods to have an "A" licence which permitted him to carry other people's goods. The carriers, who did not have such a licence, agreed to transport a cargo of whisky for the plaintiffs who were unaware of the defendants failure to obtain a licence. The defendants subsequently argued that the contract was prohibited under the Act. Clearly it was not expressly prohibited, but the Court of Appeal rejected the argument that it was even impliedly illegal. The object of legislation was to regulate those who provided transport. This could be done through criminal penalties against those in breach and did not require every agreement made contrary to the licensing provision to be invalid.

(2) Contracts illegal in their performance

Even though a contract may be perfectly valid at its inception, the mode of performance may subsequently render it illegal. This happened in *Anderson Ltd.* v. *Daniel* (1924) where a statute provided that in sales of artificial fertilisers the seller was required to give the buyer an invoice giving details of certain chemicals contained in it. The sellers delivered the fertiliser without such an invoice and the defendants successfully resisted an action for the price of the goods. Although there is, of course, nothing inherently wrong in selling fertiliser, the way it was actually done in this case rendered the transaction unlawful. This case may be contrasted with *Shaw* v. *Groom* (1970) where a landlord, in breach of statute, failed to provide a rent book. In an action for rent arrears the defendant alleged that the contract was unlawful but the Court of Appeal rejected this view. The Act might render the landlord liable to a fine for his failure, but the central intention of the legislature was not to prevent a landlord from recourse to the courts to recover payment.

Although the cases just considered involved statutes, similar considerations apply when a contract is illegal at common law.

(3) Contracts which are illegal at common law

In the same way that the courts have held certain agreements to be void, so more serious infringements of what have been regarded as rules of public policy will render the contract illegal. Broadly speaking, there are three main areas:

(a) *A contract for crime, tort or fraud*

A striking example of this category is the old case of *Everet* v. *Williams* (1725). An agreement between two highwaymen to rob a coach and share the loot was held to be illegal so that one could not sue the other for the appropriate share.

(b) *Contracts prejudicial to the state*

This includes a wide range of activities including agreements with enemy aliens or damaging to foreign relations; agreements prejudicial to the administration of justice; and agreements which encourage corruption in public life. An example of the latter was *Parkinson* v. *College of Ambulance* (1925) where the plaintiff unsuccessfully claimed the return of £3,000 paid to a charity for a knighthood he had "bought" and which was not forthcoming.

(c) *Contracts to promote sexual immorality*

This is an area where the courts may well be less willing to intervene now than in the different moral climate of, say, a hundred years ago. Nevertheless, it seems clear that a prostitute cannot sue for the price of her services nor could a landlord who supplied premises for prostitution sue for his rent (see, *e.g. Pearce* v. *Brooks* (1866)). Rather curiously a promise of money for past sexual immorality made under seal (otherwise the contract would fail on the grounds of "past consideration") is valid. This is perhaps explicable on the grounds that the provision of support for a former partner, for example, is something to be encouraged, not prohibited.

4. Consequences of a Contract Being Illegal

The crucial distinction here is not so much between law and statute as it is between a contract illegal from its inception and one that is only rendered illegal by its performance. Common to both types of illegality is the problem of whether it is possible to sever the illegal part of the contract from the rest. The orthodox view in the past has been that a contract tainted with illegality fails completely. A more recent view is that adopted by Templeman J. in *Ailion* v. *Spiekermann* (1976) who decided that severance was a possibility in a proper case stating that "the absence of precedent does not worry me so long as there is no lack of principle." The trend therefore seems to be in the direction of allowing severance in appropriate cases.

(1) Contracts illegal in themselves

The general result is that the contract is treated as a complete nullity, although there are various exceptions which are particularly necessary to protect an innocent party from the drastic effects of illegality.

(a) *Parties cannot sue*

Because the contract is treated as if it had never been made, neither party can sue or be sued upon the agreement. Consequently one might think that property can never pass under such a contract. In principle this seems correct, although the Court of Appeal (in *Belvoir Finance Co. Ltd.* v. *Stapleton* (1971)) seem to have cast doubt on this idea by stating that at least in an agreement involving the Sale of Goods Act property may pass under an illegal contract. The better view would seem to be that it cannot in general do so. In many cases where the property has already been delivered the decision would make no difference in any event since property handed over under an illegal contract is irrecoverable. So in the *Parkinson* case (above) Mr. Parkinson could not recover his £3,000. The principle is sometimes expressed in the maxim: *in pari delicto melior conditio defendentis* (where both parties are equally at fault, the defendant is in the better position).

There are exceptions to the above.

(i) *Illegality not vital to the cause.* If a plaintiff can rely on some cause of action not dependant upon the illegal contract, then the property can be recovered. So in *Bowmakers* v. *Barnet Instruments Ltd.* (1945) the parties entered into an illegal hire purchase agreement. Nevertheless, since the plaintiffs' rights as the hirer of goods did not depend upon the illegal agreement they were able to claim damages for the conversion of the goods.

(ii) *Parties not in pari delicto.* Where the parties are not equally at fault the court may sometimes allow the relatively innocent party to recover. Examples would be where one party has used fraud or oppression against another or where a rule is designed to protect a class of persons. Accordingly, a tenant can recover an illegal premium paid to a landlord.

(iii) *Repentance.* If a party to an executory contract repents before the contract has been substantially performed, he may also recover. (See, *e.g. Taylor* v. *Bowers* (1876)).

(b) *Related transactions*

Related transactions are tainted by the illegality and are also unenforceable. This problem may arise where one contract is dependant for its performance upon another. So in *Fisher* v. *Hughes* (1854) an illegal contract for debauchery invalidated the promissory note to pay for it.

(2) Contracts illegal in performance

Where both parties are equally guilty then the same considerations outlined in relation to initial illegality will govern this form of illegality. Repentance will not however be a problem since if a party repents before he has yet carried out an illegal performance, then of course no illegal performance will ever have happened.

The real distinction between the two types of illegality resides in the fact that in the case of illegal performance one party may be entirely innocent and quite unaware of the other's illegal mode of performance. In this situation the innocent party has all the usual contractual remedies against the other. An example is provided by *Marles* v. *Trant* (1954). Here X sold some seed as "spring wheat" to the defendants. In fact, in breach of contract, it was winter wheat. The defendants then sold the wheat on to the plaintiff failing to supply an invoice with the goods so rendering the contract illegal. The plaintiff, when he discovered he had been delivered the wrong type of wheat, was nevertheless able to sue the defendant for damages under the contract which was illegal as performed. So also could the defendant sue X for his breach of contract. One may contrast this case with *Anderson* v. *Daniel (ante*, p. 421). In that case the seller lost because he was not innocent; in this case the buyer won because he was.

Sometimes the difficulties may be circumvented by a collateral contract as in *Strongman* v. *Simcock* (1945). The plaintiff builders agreed with the defendant architect to do certain building work for the latter who would obtain the licences then required. He failed to do so with the result that the main contract was illegally performed. Although the builders could not recover on the main illegal contract, they were entitled to succeed on the collateral contract. There was a promise on the part of the architect to obtain the appropriate licence matched by the promise of the builders to do the work on that basis.

Chapter 10

DISCHARGE

So far we have been largely concerned with examining the way a contract may be formed. In this and the next chapter we need to consider the way a contract may come to an end and the remedies available to an injured party when things have gone wrong.

A contract may be discharged in any one of four ways, namely: performance, agreement, breach and frustration. We now need to consider these in turn.

1. Performance

If both parties to a contract properly carry out their respective obligations under it, then obviously their agreement will be completely discharged. The problems that arise centre around what precisely constitutes performance and what happens if one party, for a variety of possible reasons, does not carry out his side of the bargain within the precise terms of the contract.

The basic common law rule is that the performance must strictly and entirely match the terms of the contract. This is well illustrated by the case of *Cutter* v. *Powell* (1795). Cutter agreed to serve as second mate on a ship bound from Kingston, Jamaica to Liverpool for the sum of thirty guineas, "provided he proceeds, continues and does his duty . . . from hence to the port of Liverpool." Unfortunately, he died at sea before making port and his widow sued for the wages earned before his death on a *quantum meruit* (as much as he has deserved). Her action failed. The agreement constituted one entire contract which, albeit through no fault of his own, the deceased had failed to carry out. In fact, although the decision in the case seems harsh and somewhat unfair, the rate of pay was well above what a seaman could normally have expected to earn and accordingly the deceased was in a sense taking a deliberate gamble, (see also, *e.g.* *Vigers* v. *Cook* (1919)).

A similarly strict rule is applied in certain sections of the Sale of Goods Act 1979 (which was based upon the previous common law) and is illustrated by *Re Moore & Co. Ltd. and Landauer & Co.* (1921). The buyers agreed to take a quantity of canned fruits packed in cases with 30 tins in each. When delivered it was found that although the correct quantity had been dispatched about half the cases contained only twenty four tins each. This variation in the packaging made no difference to the market value of the goods. Nevertheless, this was a sale of goods by description under section 13 of (now) the Sale of Goods Act 1979; the goods did not strictly comply with their contract description and the buyers were therefore entitled to reject the whole consignment.

As with so many legal rules, however, it is in practice less important than the large number of exceptions which qualify it. The possible injustice and harshness of the rule is accordingly heavily mitigated.

(1) Exceptions

(a) *Substantial performance*

Where one party has substantially performed his part of the contract then he may be able to enforce it under the doctrine of substantial performance. The difference in approach between the strict doctrine and this approach can be explained on the basis that certain obligations within a contract are in reality *conditions* whereas others are merely *warranties* or even *innominate terms*. If the effect of the mis-performance is not equivalent to the breach of a condition then it is not surprising that the contract should be left intact but with some financial adjustment to compensate the injured party.

The operation of the so-called doctrine is well illustrated by comparing two cases. In *Hoenig* v. *Isaacs* (1952) an interior decorator agreed to decorate and furnish a flat for £750. The defendant paid £400 on account but refused to pay the remaining £350 on the basis that the design and workmanship was faulty. It was found that there were indeed defects but the cost of remedying these came to some £56. The defendant's claim that further payment could be resisted on the basis of *Cutter* v. *Powell* was rejected. There had been substantial performance of the contract which entitled the decorator to the balance of the money less the cost of remedying the defects. In *Bolton* v. *Mahadeva* (1972) on the other hand, a contractor agreed to install a central heating system for £560. On completion it was found that it emitted fumes, failed to heat the house properly and would cost £174 to put right. The Court of Appeal refused to allow the plaintiff's action for payment of the agreed lump sum as they did not regard the performance as substantial. In the context of the smaller contract price, the cost of remedying the defects was clearly proportionately very much higher than in *Hoenig*. Rather curiously, perhaps, if in this case the defendent had already paid over some of the contract price, then although the plaintiff could not obtain any further sums, the defendant could not recover the money she had by then paid. The reason is that there must be a *total* failure of consideration before such a payment can be recovered and in a case such as this the failure is clearly not total.

(b) *Acceptance of part performance*

Sometimes, although one party only partially performs his part of the contract, it may be possible to infer a new contract in place of the old under which the defaulting party is to be paid an appropriate amount for such work as has actually been carried out. This will only apply when the defendant really does have an option to take the benefit of the work done or to reject it. This is well illustrated in *Sumpter* v. *Hedges* (1898). A builder agreed to erect certain buildings on the defendant's land for £565. After completing £333 worth of work he abandoned the contract and the defendant had to complete the building himself. The builder's claim on a *quantum meruit* failed. The defendant was in possession of what he could not help keeping and had no real choice but to complete the work on what would otherwise be a useless eyesore on his land. What he did have to pay for was the material left on the site which he later incorporated into the building. In this case, there was a real option and he chose to use the materials.

(c) *Performance prevented*

If one party prevents the other from carrying out the contract as specified, then the law properly grants the innocent party a remedy. So in *Planché* v. *Colburn* (1831) the plaintiff agreed to write a book on *Costume and Ancient Armour* for a fee of £100. He wrote part of the book and the defendants then decided to abandon the series of which the book was to form a part. Accordingly, the author recovered £50 on a *quantum meruit*. Alternatively, it seems that he could have regarded the publishers' action as an anticipatory breach and having completed the book, might have sued for the full contract price (see *post*, pp. 435–436).

A somewhat similar situation is illustrated by those cases where the contract can only be performed in its entirety with the concurrence of the other party. If one party rejects the other's performance, then the mere fact that the latter has offered or, as is usually said in this context, "tendered performance", will be treated as equivalent to performance itself. A leading case on this point is *Startup* v. *Macdonald* (1843). The plaintiffs agreed to sell a quantity of oil to the defendants and to deliver it by the end of March. At 8.30 p.m. on March 31, the plaintiffs arrived with the oil but the defendants refused to accept the delivery owing to the lateness of the hour (section 29(5) of the Sale of Goods Act 1979 now provides that delivery must be made at a reasonable hour, and that this is a question of fact). In this particular case it was held that the plaintiffs had done all they could to comply with the contract and that consequently their tender of performance entitled them without more to sue the defendants for damages for their failure to take delivery.

The tender of money to pay a debt is treated slightly differently. Although the tenderer is not obliged to repeat the offer, the debt remains and can be sued upon. Payment must also be offered of the exact amount due and in "legal tender" as defined by statute. For example, "copper" coins are not strictly "legal tender" beyond 20 pence (see, *e.g.* Currency and Bank Notes Act 1954, s.1; Coinage Act 1972, s.2). The result is that one cannot legally tender payment of debts using impracticably large quantities of low denomination coinage.

(d) *Severable obligations*

Very often a contract will be construed as being comprised of severable obligations rather than a complete performance on the principle of *Cutter* v. *Powell*. A clear example is the type of standard term contracts used in the building industry. These will invariably provide for inspection and payment for the work as it progresses rather than in a lump sum payable upon completion. At each stage of the building therefore a contractor could sue for payment properly due at that stage. Such a provision circumvents (for the builder) the difficulties that would otherwise be placed in his way by a case such as *Sumpter* v. *Hedges* (*ante*).

(2) Vicarious performance

Has a contract been performed if one of the parties gets somebody else to do the work? The answer depends on the type of contract involved. If A contracts with B, a famous artist, to paint A's portrait, then B's sub-contracting of the work to C cannot constitute performance of the agreement. Clearly it is important, or even vital to A, that B himself should carry out the contract. Each contract will depend upon its own facts, but clearly, where there is a strong 'personal' element in the agreement, vicarious performance will not usually be enough. At the other extreme, if A is owed money by B and B gets C to pay over the money to A, then this will completely discharge the contract. It is presumably of no consequence to A how he is paid as long as he is paid. In between these two extremes, difficult questions may arise as to whether vicarious performance has discharged the contract (see, *e.g.* *British Waggon Co.* v. *Lea* (1880)).

However, even if the contract can be performed vicariously it is important to note that the original contractor is still liable for any default on the part of his sub-contractor, although he may of course join the sub-contractor as a third party. For example, if B agrees to carry out work for A which he sub-contracts to C, then, if the latter defaults, B is still liable to A as if he had carried out the faulty work himself. B can in turn, however, sue C for his breach of contract with B. C's only liability to A would be in tort, although the House of Lords have recently extended the scope of this tortious liability in *Junior Books* v. *Veitchi* (1982) (considered *post*, p. 482).

(3) Time

What happens if one party is late in carrying out his obligations under the contract? Not surprisingly this depends on what sort of agreement the parties envisage, or as it is usually stated, whether or not time is "of the essence" of the contract. At common law the rule was that time was of the essence unless the parties agreed otherwise whereas in equity it was not. The historical difference is rendered unimportant now by section 40 of the Law of Property Act 1925 which states:

> "Stipulations in a contract, as to time or otherwise, which according to rules of equity are not deemed to be or to have become of the essence of the contract, are also construed and have effect at law in accordance with the same rules."

The result is therefore, as the House of Lords have affirmed in *Raineri* v. *Miles* (1980), that although late performance does not automatically give rise to a right to terminate the contract, it is nevertheless a breach which may entitle the plaintiff to damages.

There are three occasions when time is of the essence in a contract. In the first place the parties themselves may specify expressly that this shall be so in their agreement. Secondly, the subject matter of the contract may make it clear that the performance time must be strictly adhered to. For example, if the transaction involves a commodity that fluctuates in value (such as shares) or which is perishable (such as fresh fruit) then performance on time may well be essential. Thirdly, if one party has been guilty of delay and the other then informs him that he will regard the contract as terminated unless it is completed within a reasonable time, this will again have the effect of making time "of the essence" (see, *e.g.* *Charles Rickards Ltd.* v. *Oppenheim* (1950)).

2. Agreement

Contracts are made by agreement. Not surprisingly, therefore, a contract can be varied or discharged by agreement. The orthodox distinction made is between bilateral and unilateral discharge which in effect means that in the former there is a mutual benefit to be derived from some variation or discharge in the performance whereas in the latter the modification is for the benefit of one party only. Although this is the normal way of classifying discharge by agreement it is important to realise that the underlying problems in this area are caused by two legal concepts, namely consideration and the requirements of "formality." In the discharge of a contract just as much as in its formation the law looks askance at a promise unsupported by the element of "bargain." As regards formality, particular problems are posed when the law stipulates that a contract must be drawn up in one way, as for example in writing, but the parties purport to discharge it by agreement without complying with the same formalities. Both problems are of course solved if the parties discharge the agreement under seal which, as we saw in Chapter 3, replaces the requirement of consideration.

(1) Bilateral discharge

In the case of an executory contract where neither party has completely performed his obligations then an agreement to discharge will clearly be effective. Consideration has been supplied by the parties in that both of them have exchanged promises not to enforce all the original obligations.

Complications arise when we consider the case of a transaction that by statute must be evidenced in writing. A common example is a contract for the sale or other disposition of land (see Law of Property Act 1925, s.40(1)). Must any agreement to vary or discharge the contract also conform to this formality? The answer is somewhat involved and depends upon what the agreement was seeking to achieve but there are three possible alternatives, namely: (a) the parties intend to discharge the agreement altogether; (b) the agreement is intended to vary the original contract; and (c) the parties intend to replace the original agreement by a completely new one. Quite what the parties intended will have to be inferred from their agreement or conduct if it is not clearly articulated. In the case of (a) an oral agreement to discharge, the contract will be effective even without written evidence. Section 40 is designed to regulate the formation of contracts not their discharge. In the case of (b) on the other hand their agreement will be completely ineffective. The "new" contract is simply not evidenced in writing and so the original contract continues in being. Where (c) occurs the effect is that the original agreement is completely rescinded but the new agreement fails because it is unenforceable through lack of written evidence. In this last case a difficult question of construction may arise as to whether the parties intended the result in (b) or (c). The crucial difference is that in one case the original agreement continues unaffected whereas in the other it is completely abrogated (the distinction is illustrated by the contrasting cases of *United Dominions Corporation (Jamaica) Ltd* v. *Shoucair* (1969) and *Morris* v. *Baron & Co.* (1918)).

A slightly different situation that frequently arises is that one party requests the other not to insist on the strict performance of a contract and the party so requested agrees. A simple illustration might arise in the sale of goods. Delivery has been agreed for April 1, but the supplier obtains an agreement that the goods will not actually be delivered until May 1. What is the effect of such a forbearance or "waiver" as it is usually called? Not unnaturally, the judges have reacted against the unfairness of allowing such a waiver to be evaded especially as it is a common business practice. Nevertheless, the rather unclear result has been an apparent sacrifice of principle to business expediency. At common law there has developed a doctrine of waiver which provides authority for the proposition that both the recipient and grantor of the waiver are bound by the indulgence. Despite the sensible result the obvious objection to such a doctrine is that it appears to dispense with the essential ingredient of consideration.

Equity provides a more elegant solution. In effect, it is an application of the doctrine of "promissory" or "equitable" estoppel (see *ante*, p. 344). The approach of equity to waiver is well illustrated by *Charles Rickards Ltd.* v. *Oppenheim* (1950). The defendant ordered a body to be built on a car chassis he had purchased, the work to be completed within "six or seven months." At the end of this time the work was not finished but he agreed to wait a further three months. The work was still by then unfinished so he gave final notice that unless it was completed within another four weeks the order would be cancelled. At the end of this period the body was still not complete and the car was only offered to him three months later when he refused to accept it. The plaintiffs thereupon sued him for his failure to accept the car. The Court of Appeal decided that although originally time had been of the essence the agreement to extend the performance time by three months operated as a waiver. If the car had been delivered within that time the defendant would have been bound to accept it. However, the defendant, by giving reasonable notice that time was once again of the essence, rendered the plaintiffs in breach of contract by their failure to complete the work. Accordingly, their action against the defendant failed. The result is satisfactory and in accordance with the principles enunciated in a case such as *Hughes* v. *Metropolitan Railway Co.* (*ante*, p. 345).

(2) Unilateral discharge

As the title suggests, a unilateral discharge occurs when only one party has an obligation left to perform and the other purports to release him from that obligation. For example, A owes B £1,000 for goods delivered. A is in financial difficulties and B agrees to accept £900 in discharge of the contract price. The difficulty with this arrangement is of course that it is a *nudum pactum*; there is no consideration for B's promise (see *ante*, p. 343). There needs to be a further element of bargain, no matter how notional, to make the agreement valid.

Where there is a fresh element of bargain this is known as "accord and satisfaction." "Accord" is the agreement that the contract should be performed in a modified way and "satisfaction" is the consideration to support the promise. If in the above example A paid over £900 and a bag of sweets then this would support the requirements of accord and satisfaction. It is not even necessary that the consideration be executed to make the agreement effective so that if it is the intention of the parties even an executory promise may be sufficient "satisfaction." This is illustrated in the case of *British Russian Gazette Ltd.* v. *Associated Newspapers Ltd.* (1933). A Mr. Talbot agreed to compromise (*i.e.* to settle) a libel action for a sum of money. His letter stated: "I accept the sum of one thousand guineas . . . in full discharge and settlement of my claims . . . and I will forthwith instruct my solicitors to end the proceedings now pending." Before he had actually received the money Mr. Talbot disregarded his agreement and continued with the action arguing that until the payment had actually been made there was no effective discharge. The Court of Appeal rejected this view. There was accord and satisfaction; a promise had been exchanged for a promise and Mr. Talbot was bound by the terms of the compromise. He had promised to discontinue the action; the newspaper had promised to pay him the money.

3. Breach

(1) Consequences of breach

It is something of a misnomer or at least an over simplification to talk of breach as discharging a contract. Nevertheless, it is convenient to consider it in the context of a chapter concerned with how contractual obligations can come to an end. What is said here also needs to be read in the context of what has already been said about terms in a contract in Chapter 5. Every failure to perform satisfactorily any of the obligations in a contract will entitle the innocent party to sue for damages. If it is the breach of a comparatively minor term, a breach of warranty, then damages will be all the innocent party is entitled to and the contract continues. If it is of a serious kind, a breach of condition, then this is a repudiatory breach which entitles the injured party not only to damages but also to regard himself as excused from further performance of the contract. It is in this area that many of the problems in breach have arisen partly as the result of confusing terminology.

The correct way of describing the situation has recently been emphasised by Lord Wilberforce in *Johnson* v. *Agnew* (1980) where he quoted with approval Lord Porter's comment that, "to say that the contract is rescinded or has come to an end or has ceased to exist may in individual cases convey the truth with sufficient accuracy, but the fuller expression that the injured party is thereby absolved from future performance of his obligations under the contract is a more exact description of the position."

Although it is usually clear what is in fact meant, it is therefore strictly quite wrong to say that a contract has come to an end as a result of a repudiatory breach (see, *e.g. Photo Production Ltd.* v. *Securicor* (1980) *post*, p. 434). In the first place this may be just the sort of occasion when an "agreed damages" clause in the contract will come into operation (on which see *post*, p. 450). Secondly, the injured party always has an option in the face of a repudiatory breach either to treat the contract as still in force or to accept the repudiation. Even a major repudiatory breach does not therefore operate automatically to end the innocent party's obligations. This is well illustrated by the old case of *Avery* v. *Bowden* (1855). Bowden effectively repudiated a contract to load Avery's ship in a way that would have doubtless given the latter an opportunity to sue immediately for breach of contract. Instead the ship waited in the hope that the agreement would be fulfilled but the contract was then frustrated before the time agreed for loading the cargo had expired owing to the outbreak of the Crimean War. The contract therefore remained in existence until the frustrating event preventing Avery from suing for breach (on which see 4. below).

(2) Forms of breach

Breach can take two forms, what one might call actual or anticipatory. Actual breach is the result of any failure by one of the parties to fulfil one or more of the obligations under the contract. This may arise as the result of non-performance, for example failure to deliver goods, or defective performance, if say the goods fall below the contract quality. Alternatively, a promissory statement of fact in the contract may turn out not to be true.

Anticipatory breach arises when one party gives notice of breach before performance has even started. Before considering this, it is necessary to examine what has sometimes been treated as a separate sub-heading, namely fundamental breach.

(a) *Fundamental breach*

One particular form of breach which has been a fruitful source of legal difficulty is so-called fundamental breach. The complications that surrounded this area even after the decision of the House of Lords in the *Suisse Atlantique* case (1967) have hopefully been largely swept away by the recent decision of their Lordships in *Photo Production Ltd.* v. *Securicor Transport Ltd.* (1980). It must now therefore be open to doubt whether it is strictly necessary to consider fundamental breach under a seperate heading at all. This case dispels any remnants of the view that a fundamental breach or a breach of a fundamental term means that the guilty party cannot rely on an exemption clause. The facts of the case vividly illustrate this point. Securicor had been employed to provide a night patrol service to their client's factory. In the course of such a visit one of Securicor's employees decided to light a small fire. The result was £615,000 worth of damage to the factory, although it was found that the employee did not intend to burn down the premises and that Securicor had not been negligent in employing or supervising him. It would be difficult to imagine a more serious breach of contract. Securicor had been employed to protect the premises; in fact they had been responsible for burning them down. Nevertheless a widely drafted exclusion clause stating that: "Under no circumstances shall the company be responsible for any injurious act or default by any employee of the company unless such act or default could have been foreseen and avoided by the exercise of due diligence on the part of the company as his employer" was held appropriate to cover the breach in question and exempt Securicor from liability.

In an appropriate case the victim of a fundamental breach may choose to treat the contract as ended. What constitutes such a breach? Lord Diplock in the *Photo Production* case said that it was a breach such as would effectively deprive the innocent party of substantially the whole benefit that it was intended he should receive under the contract. It must therefore be a very serious breach. Devlin J. in *Smeaton Hanscomb & Co. Ltd.* v. *Sassoon (I.) Setty, Son & Co.* (1953) stated that, "It is, I think, something which underlies the whole contract so that, if it is not complied with, the performance becomes something totally different from that which the contract contemplates." An example given by Devlin J. was delivering pine instead of mahogany logs in a contract for the supply of the latter.

The fact that a fundamental breach gives the innocent party the option or election to refuse to perform further his obligations under the contract is perhaps not surprising considering that this is the effect of any breach of a condition. By its very nature breach of a fundamental term or a fundamental breach goes to the root of the contractual nexus. What however the *Photo Production* case emphasises is that even in the case of such a fundamental breach the parties are at liberty to provide for its consequences in a suitably drafted provision. Again, there is nothing automatic about even a fundamental breach.

(b) *Anticipatory breach*

An anticipatory breach arises when before the due date for performance of the contract the party at fault gives notice of the fact that he has no intention of fulfilling his obligations. An example is the case of *Avery* v. *Bowden* already referred to. In the event of such a repudiatory anticipatory breach a plaintiff has a choice. He may either elect to treat the contract as thereby ended and sue immediately for breach or he may wait until the performance date has arrived and then sue for breach when the other party fails to comply with the contract.

The first possibility is illustrated by *Frost* v. *Knight* (1872) (and see also *Hochster* v. *de la Tour* (1853)). Mr. Knight agreed to marry a Miss Frost on the death of his father. Before this had occurred he broke off the engagement. Miss Frost successfully sued Mr. Knight for breach of promise of marriage. The case is a strong one because at the time of the action the right was still contingent since either of the parties might have predeceased Mr. Knight's father. Although actions for breach of promise have now been abolished by statute (Law Reform (Miscellaneous Provisions) Act 1970, s.1(1)) the principle of the case still remains perfectly valid.

The second possibility was the basis of *Avery* v. *Bowden* (*ante*, p. 433). In that case, as we have seen, the election to treat the contract as continuing led to the innocent party being probably worse off owing to the effect of frustration than he would have been had he sued immediately. In many cases there may not be much incentive for the innocent party to treat the contract as continuing because he will be unable to complete his side of the bargain without the co-operation of the contract breaker and hence will be unable to claim the full contract payment as opposed to damages. Sometimes, however, one of the parties may be able to fulfil his obligations without further reference to the other and so produce rather surprising results. In *White and Carter (Councils) Ltd.* v. *McGregor* (1962) advertising agents supplied litter bins to local authorities which were in effect paid for by the advertisements affixed to them. McGregor signed an agreement advertising his garage for three years but later on the same day purported to countermand the contract. Even though the agents realised that this was not what their client any longer wanted they refused to accept the repudiation, duly carried out the agreement for the three years of the contract, and sued for the price of their services. The House of Lords upheld their claim. Although the case is somewhat unusual on its facts and apparently strange in its result it is defensible in principle. Any other result would undermine the fact that the injured party has an election as to whether or not he will accept the repudiation.

4. Frustration

The early common law took the harsh view, also exemplified in *Cutter* v. *Powell* (*ante*), that contractual obligations must be strictly adhered to. In *Paradine* v. *Jane* (1647) a tenant was sued for arrears of rent notwithstanding the fact that for the last three years the King's enemies had prevented him from occupying the property. The court decided he still had to pay. He had voluntarily undertaken an obligation and must therefore go through with it. Had he wished to excuse himself from his liability under certain circumstances he could have made provision for this in the contract.

The rigour of this rule was partially relieved by the case of *Taylor* v. *Caldwell* (1863) out of which the modern doctrine of frustration has developed. In this case the parties had entered into an agreement for the use of the Surrey Gardens and Music Hall for a series of "grand concerts, and day and night fêtes." Before the day of the first concert the building was accidentally destroyed by fire. The claim against the defendants for breach of contract failed. Blackburn J. commented: "We think . . . that the Music Hall having ceased to exist, without fault of either party, both parties are excused, the plaintiffs from taking the gardens and paying the money, the defendants from performing their promise to give the use of the Hall and Gardens . . . . "

From this it can be seen that the doctrine of frustration operates to relieve the parties from further obligations when performance of the contract has become impossible. The practical sense behind this approach is obvious although its precise juristic basis is more controversial. The two most important explanations are what one might call the "implied term" and "imposed solution" theories.

Both require examination but the latter appears to be the currently preferred approach.

The "implied term" view was adopted by Blackburn J. in *Taylor* v. *Caldwell*, and is similar to the reasoning in cases such as *The Moorcock* (see p. 365) in that it rests on the supposed intention of the parties. If at the time when the contract was made the parties had contemplated the frustrating event then the assumption is that they would have regarded the contract as terminated upon that event. This may have been an approach attractive to adherents of nineteenth century laissez-faire individualism but it now rings as somewhat artificial. As Lord Radcliffe said in *Davis* v. *Fareham U.D.C.* (1956) there is "a logical difficulty in seeing how the parties could even impliedly have provided for something which *ex hypothesi* they neither expected nor foresaw." There is more to be said for the view that the law is intervening to impose a fair solution when events have happened that render the whole situation radically different from that originally envisaged by the parties. As Lord Radcliffe went on to say, "*Non haec in foedera veni*. It was not this that I promised to do."

Whatever the precise theoretical basis, two considerations arise in this area: (1) what events will lead to a contract being in law "frustrated"? and (2) what will be the consequences if it is?

(1) What amounts to frustration

The common factor in cases of frustration is that the contract has become impossible or at least pointless. Nevertheless there are various ways in which this situation may come about and certain restrictions on the availability of the doctrine which now need to be considered.

(a) *Contract illegal*

If after the formation of a contract its subsequent performance becomes illegal then the contract is frustrated. A frequent example is the outbreak of war which makes further performance illegal as "trading with the enemy." Another example is provided by *Denny Mott & Dickson Ltd.* v. *James B. Fraser & Co. Ltd.* (1944). Here an agreement for the sale of timber was linked with an option to take a long lease or to purchase a timber yard which was to be used in conjunction with the contract. The result of various importation orders was that it became impossible to perform the contract legally. The House of Lords accordingly held that since the main purpose of the contract, trading in timber, had become illegal, the whole contract, including the option, had been frustrated.

(b) *Death*

In a contract where the personality of one of the parties is vital, death is the ultimate frustrating event. Hence a contract of service or, for example, an agreement to paint a picture or write a book, will be frustrated by the death of the employee, painter or author.

(c) *Subject-matter destroyed*

Where all or a vital part of the subject-matter of the contract is destroyed so that performance of the contract is rendered impossible this will lead to frustration. The case of *Taylor* v. *Caldwell* (*ante*, p. 436) is an example of this.

(d) *Unavailability*

In the case of a contract for personal services death is the most extreme form of "unavailability" but there are other examples. Much will depend on the relationship between the length of time one party is unavailable and the time span contemplated by the contract. For example in *Morgan* v. *Manser* (1948) a music hall artiste known as "Cheerful Charlie Chester" signed a 10 year contract with his manager in 1938 but in 1940 he was called-up for military service. The court held that the contract had been frustrated. He was not in fact demobilised until 1946 and in the context of a 10 year contract this absence completely undermined the agreement. Perhaps if he had merely been called up for a short period of "national service" the result might well have been different. Another example of a frustrating event would be illness in an appropriate case (see, *e.g.* *Robinson* v. *Davison* (1871)).

Similar principles apply to anything else which through some extraneous cause is rendered unavailable for the purposes of the contract. Hence in *Bank Line Ltd* v. *Arthur Capel & Co.* (1919) the war-time requisitioning of a ship frustrated the charterparty of which it was the subject.

(e) *Mode of performance impossible*

Where the parties agree that the contract shall be carried out in a particular manner which subsequently becomes impossible then this will lead to the contract being frustrated. It is quite different, however, if the parties merely anticipate that a certain means of carrying out the contract will be adopted without it being a term of the agreement and that method subsequently becomes impossible. It is not sufficient to invoke the doctrine of frustration that it has simply become more onerous or expensive to carry out the contract.

This principle is well illustrated by the cases that arose out of the closure of the Suez Canal in 1956. In *Tsakiroglou & Co. Ltd.* v. *Noblee and Thorl GmbH* (1962) there was a contract for Sudanese groundnuts to be shipped from Port Sudan to Hamburg. Obviously the usual and quickest route between these two ports was via the Suez Canal. When this was closed to traffic the seller failed to make the shipment and claimed frustration as a defence to the buyers action for breach of contract. The House of Lords rejected the seller's claim. Even though the journey via the Cape of Good Hope would take four weeks longer and increase the cost of freightage the contract did not have a fixed delivery date and no route had been agreed upon. Consequently it was not a fundamentally different enterprise to take the longer route, merely a more expensive one for the seller. As a result of this many charterparties now contain some stipulation as to the route to be followed or a "Suez Canal clause."

(f) *Performance radically different*

This category represents the furthest limit of the doctrine in that the frustrating event is regarded as sufficient because it in effect renders the whole contract pointless or futile although not strictly impossible. The leading authorities on this area are the so-called "coronation cases" arising out of the postponement of Edward VII's coronation. In *Krell* v. *Henry* (1903) the defendant made a written agreement for the hire of a suite of rooms overlooking the coronation procession. Although the agreement did not expressly mention the procession both parties understood that this was the reason for the hire. When the procession was cancelled the plaintiff nevertheless sued for the balance of the fee. The court upheld the defendant's contention that the contract had been frustrated. Vaughan Williams L.J. extended the notion of *Taylor* v. *Caldwell*, saying, "English law applies the principle not only to cases where the performance of the contract becomes impossible by the cessation of existence of the thing which is the subject-matter of the contract, but also to cases where the event . . . is the cessation or non-existence of an express condition or state of things, going to the root of the contract, and essential to its performance." Although the defendant could have used the rooms on the relevant days it would clearly have been a futile and pointless exercise since the whole object of the contract was undoubtedly to view the coronation procession.

Nevertheless the courts are not quick to invoke this head of frustration as can be seen by contrasting the decision in *Herne Bay Steam Boat Company* v. *Hutton* (1903). The facts arose out of the same coronation celebrations but the object in this case was to charter a boat in order to view the naval review "and for a day's cruise around the fleet." The review was cancelled but the boat owners still recovered the cost of the hire. The distinction between the cases could be explained on the basis that seeing the naval review was only one of the purposes for hiring the boat. The fleet remained and could still be viewed so that the entire foundation of the contract was not destroyed.

Another more recent case which illustrates the reluctance of the courts to construe *Krell* v. *Henry* at all generously is *Davis Contractors Ltd* v. *Fareham U.D.C.* (1956). A building company contracted to build some houses in eight months for £92,425. Owing to shortages the work in fact took 22 months and £17,651 more to complete. The builders claimed that the contract had been frustrated but the House of Lords rejected this view. Lord Radcliffe commented; " . . . it is not hardship or inconvenience or material loss itself which calls the principle of frustration into play. There must be as well such a change in the significance of the obligation that the thing undertaken would, if performed, be a different thing from that contracted for."

(2) Self-induced frustration

It is often said that frustration cannot be self-induced, since its essence is that it comes about without the fault of either party. At first sight this may seem obvious since such an act would normally be a breach of contract in the ordinary way. It need not however always be so as is shown by *Maritime National Fish Ltd.* v. *Ocean Trawlers Ltd.* (1935). Here the charterers took a ship, the St. Cuthbert, for a year from the owners both parties knowing that the ship was of a type that could only be lawfully operated with a licence from the Canadian government. The charterers applied for five licences to cover the ships they were operating but were only granted three and were obliged to elect to which ships the licences granted were to apply. They decided not to include the St. Cuthbert and later claimed that the charter had been frustrated by the government's refusal to grant an adequate number of licences. The Privy Council rejected this view explaining that it was the act and election of the charterers themselves that led to the ship being inoperable even though it was not a term of the contract that the charterers would obtain a licence for the ship.

Where there is an allegation that the frustration was self-induced the onus of proving this rests upon the party who alleges it (see *Joseph Constantine Steamship Line Ltd.* v. *Imperial Smelting Corpn. Ltd.* (1942)).

(3) Foreseeing the event

If a contract contains a provision which expressly sets out what is to happen on the occurrence of what would otherwise be a frustrating event then there is generally no longer any question of the agreement having been frustrated. The difficulty will simply be resolved in accordance with the terms the parties have agreed upon. If the event was not foreseen then of course this is precisely what the doctrine of frustration is meant to cover. The difficulty that may arise exists in those cases which so to speak fall between these two extremes. What if the frustrating event is foreseen, but the scope or seriousness of the disaster is very much greater than that which the parties envisaged?

It is clearly a difficult matter of construction whether a term really does cover the events that have taken place as the leading case of *Jackson* v. *Union Marine Insurance Co. Ltd.* (1874) illustrates. A charter party provided that a ship was to proceed with all possible despatch "dangers and accidents of navigation excepted" from Liverpool to Newport. It had got no further that Carnarvon Bay before it ran aground and it took eight months for the ship to be repaired as a result. Notwithstanding the contract clause mentioned, the court held that the charter had been frustrated. At first sight the clause might have been thought apt to cover the delay but the court decided that it was never intended to cover so serious and extensive a delay as actually occurred. A similar problem arose in *Pacific Phosphate Co. Ltd* v. *Empire Transport Co. Ltd.* (1920). An agreement to provide ships contained a clause suspending the agreement in the event of war. This was nevertheless held not sufficient to cover the catastrophic dislocating effects of the First World War which was outside the ambit of anything which the parties had contemplated when they made the agreement. Consequently the contract was frustrated.

(4) Leases

Much controversy used to exist over the problem of whether the doctrine of frustration applied to a lease. The difficulty lay in the fact that a lease is a rather special type of contract in that it bestows an interest in the land itself, (or, as is usually said, *in rem*). The result is that an interest in the land survives even if, for example, a house being leased falls down. There may still be an obligation on the part of the tenant to pay rent and the landlord to repair. Despite this the House of Lords have recently resolved the controversy in *National Carriers Ltd.* v. *Panalpina (Northern) Ltd.* (1981) in favour of the view that the doctrine of frustration does apply to leases. They are after all essentially a special form of contract and *Taylor* v. *Caldwell* itself showed that the doctrine applied to the related concept of a licence to occupy land. Nevertheless the occasions on which frustration will be successfully invoked in the context of a lease are likely to be very rare.

(5) The consequences of frustration

When a frustrating event has occurred the contract automatically comes to an end. There is no question of the parties having any choice or election in the matter as there is in the case of a breach of condition. Nevertheless, the contractual obligations are only ended as from the date of frustration. There is no question, as may happen when there has been a fundamental mistake, of the contract being void *ab initio*. In analysing the legal consequences it is still necessary to consider both the common law and statutory provisions separately since, in theory at least, it is possible to exclude the operation of the Law Reform (Frustrated Contracts) Act 1943. This approach does however have the advantage of showing how the law in this area has been developed and reformed.

(a) *At common law*

The original rule at common law was strict and somewhat arbitrary in its effect. Since the rights and liabilities of the parties become fixed at the moment of the frustrating event, it was said that "the loss lay where it fell." This point is shown by *Chandler* v. *Webster* (1904), another of the so-called "coronation" cases. The plaintiff hired a room in Pall Mall in order to view the procession for a price of £141 15s payable at once. He paid £100 before the coronation was postponed and after this frustrating event sought to recover his money. Not only did he not succeed in doing so but he was also obliged to pay the balance of £41 15s. The reasoning was that since the frustrating event only terminated the contract from that time, and the money had been payable before this, then he was still liable on what was at that stage a valid contract. By contrast in *Krell* v. *Henry* (above) the balance of the money due for the hire of the room did not become payable until after the frustrating event. Accordingly the hirer of the room was unable to recover this amount because the contract had already been terminated before this right accrued. Consequently the application of the same principle produced different practical results in the two cases.

The injustice of this state of affairs was to some extent alleviated by the case of *Fibrosa Spolka Akcyjna* v. *Fairbairn Lawson Combe Barbour Ltd.* (1943). Fairbairn agreed to make some machinery for Fibrosa (a Polish company) in July 1939 for a price of £4,800. Of this, £1,600 was payable in advance and £1,000 was indeed paid over by Fibrosa. By September 1940 the place of delivery in Poland was under German occupation and the contract was therefore frustrated.

Fibrosa claimed the return of their £1,000 and succeeded. The House of Lords overruled *Chandler* v. *Webster* because it was inconsistent with the basic proposition that a person who has paid for something and received nothing in return is entitled to recover his money in a claim in quasi-contract. Historically, this is known as a claim "upon a total failure of consideration." Whereas in the context of formation of contract "consideration" may mean the *promise* to perform, in the context of a claim for recovery of advance payment it denotes the *actual* performance.

Although an improvement on the earlier law the case still leaves two areas of possible injustice. The manufacturer might well have expended time and money on the undelivered goods before the contract was frustrated for which he is prevented from being compensated. Secondly, unless the failure of consideration is total the other party cannot recover anything. This is so even if the consideration bestowed is trivial or nominal. Not surprisingly therefore there has been statutory intervention.

(b) *By statute*

The major objection to the *Fibrosa* case was that it produced an "all or nothing" solution, though of a different sort from that produced by *Chandler* v. *Webster*. Under the Law Reform (Frustrated Contracts) Act 1943 both parties, so far as is possible, can be compensated by the court so that any loss or benefit is fairly distributed between them. The Act does this by instituting two major reforms; (1) money already paid can be recovered, and (2) compensation can be awarded for partial performance. The Act says nothing about what actually constitutes "frustration" which is still entirely governed by common law.

Section 1(2) in effect provides that money already paid can be recovered, regardless of whether the failure of consideration is partial or total, subject to the court allowing deduction of any expenses which the payee has incurred before the time of the frustrating event. Equally if the sum was only payable but not paid before the termination of the contract, the court may allow the recovery of an amount equal to the expenses incurred by the prospective payee. The result therefore is that the common law rule of all or nothing is replaced by a wide discretion in the court to award expenses out of amounts paid or payable before the contract was frustrated.

Section 1(3) allows a claim for partial performance when the contract is frustrated. For example, if A installed machinery in B's factory which operated satisfactorily for several months but before the price became payable was destroyed by fire, then A may claim a sum from B to compensate for the fact that he has received nothing whereas B has received a valuable, albeit shortlived, benefit. Some difficulty, however, arises on the meaning of "a valuable benefit" in section 1(3). Take the facts of *Appleby* v. *Myers* (1867). The plaintiffs agreed to construct machinery in the defendant's factory and maintain it for two years for a price of £459. When the work was almost completed it was destroyed by fire. The contract was frustrated and as the law then stood the loss lay where it fell since the money was not payable at the moment of frustration. What would be the result of the case if it were decided today? Expenses could not be recovered since no money was paid or payable when the contract was terminated. Is recovery possible under section 1(3)? One view would be that partially completed machinery is of no use and therefore there was no benefit to Myers. Another is that he did have a benefit from the mere fact that work had been carried out on his property even though it had not been completed. Both views are tenable but it seems more sensible on these facts to say that Appleby should recover nothing. The effect of the fire on the "benefit" of the uncompleted machinery was surely to destroy it before it could be of the slightest real benefit to Myers. This is also the view expressed by Goff J. in *B.P. Exploration* v. *Hunt* (*No.* 2) (1982) which contains a helpful discussion of the 1943 Act.

The Act is restricted in that it does not apply to most charter parties or contracts for the carriage of goods by sea or policies of insurance. It also effectively excludes contracts for the sale of specific goods where the contract is frustrated by the perishing of those goods. For example A agrees to sell B all the present contents of his wine cellar but before delivery can take place the wine is destroyed by fire. The Act would not apply to such a frustrating event. Finally, as already referred to, the parties may themselves exclude the operation of the Act by the terms of their agreement.

CHAPTER 11

REMEDIES

In the course of discussing what can go wrong with the contractual bond certain remedies have already been mentioned in some detail. For example, in the cases of misrepresentation or mistake the remedies of rescission and rectification may be relevant. In other cases where there has been some form of unjust enrichment of one party at the expense of the other we have seen that there may be an action in quasi-contract as in the *Fibrosa* case (see *ante*, p. 443). What must now be examined are the remedies which the innocent party can obtain against a contract breaker for his breach of contract. These are: damages, specific performance and injunction. Finally it is necessary to consider the circumstances under which the plaintiff's remedy may be extinguished.

1. DAMAGES

An award of damages is the normal remedy in the law of contract. The object of the award is to put the plaintiff, so far as money can, in the same position that he would have been in had the contract been performed properly. In this regard it is different from the law governing tortious liability (on which see *post*, p. 480) where the object is to put the victim back into the position in which he would have been had the wrongful act never been carried out.

Assessing the level of damages in a case of breach really involves two quite separate considerations. First of all it has to be determined whether or not the damage that has occurred is a kind that the law will compensate. Secondly, if it is, it must be decided how the amount is to be calculated. This essentially involves asking: what for? and, how much? It is these two problems which we now need to consider.

(1) Remoteness of damage

The law could not possibly compensate a plaintiff for every result of a breach of contract. For example, A sells B a faulty vacuum cleaner which B decides to return to A's shop. On his way back to the shop he is run over by a careless motorist and injured. As a result he loses his job and his wife leaves him. In a sense, all of B's difficulties have flowed from A's breach of contract, but as a matter of common sense it would seem strange to link the sale of a domestic appliance to marital desertion. Accordingly, the law draws a line at some consequences which are said to be too remote from the damage to be compensable. Inevitably a general principle designed to do this must be couched in wide and perhaps rather vague terms but an examination of the cases shows the rules a court will apply. At the end of the day it is a question of policy rather than logic where the line is to be drawn.

The case which first laid down the modern rule as to remoteness of damage was *Hadley* v. *Baxendale* (1854), the facts of which provide a good illustration of the type of problem involved. The plaintiffs owned a mill in Gloucester and asked the defendant carrier to transport a broken mill shaft to Greenwich in order to provide a pattern for a new one. As a result of the defendant's fault the shaft was not delivered on time and work at the plaintiff's mill was held up for longer than it need have been. It was found that all the carrier knew was that he was transporting a broken mill shaft and that the plaintiffs were the millers of that mill. The rule laid down by Alderson B to assess damages in such a case was that:

> "Where two parties have made a contract which one of them has broken, the damages which the other party ought to receive in respect of such breach of contract should be such as may fairly and reasonably be considered either arising naturally, i.e. according to the usual course of things, from such breach of contract itself, or such as may reasonably be supposed to have been in the contemplation of both parties, at the time they made the contract, as the probable result of the breach of it."

The rule therefore has two elements. A defendant is always liable for the usual consequences of his breach. He is only liable for unusual consequences if he has special knowledge of them at the time when the contract was made.

Applying the rule to the facts of the case the court held that the defendant was not liable for the loss of profit when the mill was closed. In the majority of cases it was found that the absence of a mill shaft would not have caused a stoppage; for example, there might have been a spare. The special circumstance that this mill did not have a spare was not known to the defendant and so they could not be held liable even under the second limb of the rule.

Although the principle in *Hadley* v. *Baxendale* has frequently been discussed and reformulated the substance of the rule seems to have survived intact. For example, in *Victoria Laundry (Windsor) Ltd.* v. *Newman Industries Ltd.* (1949) the plaintiffs, who where launderers and dyers, wanted a larger boiler to expand their business. The defendants agreed to install a boiler on June 5, 1946 but owing to their breach of contract it was not delivered until November 8, 1946.

The plaintiffs claimed under two heads. (i) £16 a week damages for loss of profits for the extra custom they could have taken on, and (ii) £262 a week which they could have obtained under certain especially lucrative contracts with the Ministry of Supply. It was found that the defendants knew that the plaintiffs were anxious to have the boiler installed as soon as possible but not that they were aware of the lucrative supply contract. Accordingly, they were liable for the loss of profits arising from the failure to enlarge the business and carry out normal contracts but not for the much greater loss of profits obtainable from contracts with the Ministry of Supply. By contrast, in *Simpson* v. *London and North Western Rail Co.* (1876) the defendants knew that the plaintiffs' samples were to be exhibited at an agricultural show in Newcastle. Indeed the goods were labelled, "must be at Newcastle on Monday certain." They failed to arrive on time and the plaintiff claimed for the loss of profits he would have made had the contract been performed properly. The defendants were held liable since they knew of the special circumstances of the case and agreed to contract on that basis.

The rule in *Hadley* v. *Baxendale* was examined in some detail by the House of Lords in *Koufos* v. *C. Czarnikow Ltd.* (*The Heron* II) (1969). The result was a series of judgments which appear to generate more heat than light and leave the rule essentially intact. Much of the argument is concerned with what precisely is meant by a person's contemplation of future damage. The view which seems to have commanded the most general support is that it must be such that a reasonable man would regard it as "liable to result" although this does not require that it should be definitely more likely to result than not. There seems much to be said for the observation of Sellers L.J. in the Court of Appeal that, "the phrases and words of *Hadley* v. *Baxendale* have been hallowed by long user and gain little advantage from the paraphrases or substitutes. The ideas and factors conveyed by the words are clear enough."

Nevertheless the difficulties in applying these principles to specific cases are illustrated by *H. Parsons (Livestock) Ltd.* v. *Uttley Ingham & Co. Ltd.* (1978). None of the judgments of the Court of Appeal are entirely free from difficulty in their application of the rule of remoteness to contract damages. What the case does appear to decide is that if the loss is of a *type* that could reasonably have been contemplated, the defendant is liable even if the *extent* of the damage is greater than was reasonably foreseeable.

(2) Quantification

Once it has been decided that the loss is not too remote from the damage to be recoverable, the next question to decide is: how much?

It is important to note that the object of damages in contract is compensatory not punitive. If, despite the defendant's breach of contract, the plaintiff suffers no loss, then nothing except nominal damages will be recoverable and he may not even recover the costs of his action. For example, if B wrongfully dismisses A who immediately afterwards gets a similar but much better paid job then A, albeit fortuitously perhaps, has suffered no loss and will not be able to recover any more than nominal damages.

The general principle, as we have seen, is that the plaintiff will receive in damages such an amount as will put him in the same position as if the contract had been performed properly. Quite what this amount will be is entirely dependent on the subject matter of the contract, but there are certain general principles which the courts apply.

(a) *Goods*

There will generally be a market in goods that are bought and sold so that a loss can be quantified by reference to the market. For example, if a seller fails to deliver goods then the buyer's damages will be the difference between the contract price and the greater amount he has to pay for the same goods in the market. If it is the buyer who refuses to accept delivery then similarly the damages will be the difference between what he would have received under the contract and what he actually gets for the goods when he sells them in the market (see ss. 50 and 51 Sale of Goods Act 1979).

An example of how the courts proceed when there is no available market price is *W. L. Thompson Ltd.* v. *Robinson Gunmakers Ltd.* (1955). Here the buyers in breach of contract refused to accept delivery of a Vanguard car from the sellers who were car dealers. Because of resale price maintenance (see *ante*, p. 403) the car could not be sold at less than the manufacturer's list price. The result was effectively that the market and contract prices were the same. There was at that time no demand for this type of car but the sellers were able to mitigate their loss by persuading their suppliers to take it back. The buyers contended that although they were in breach, the plaintiffs had in fact suffered no loss. The court disagreed. Section 50 of the Sale of Goods Act only represents a prima facie rule which did not apply in this situation. The sellers were therefore entitled to £61, the profit they would have made on the bargain. The buyer's contention would have succeeded if, as in *Charter* v. *Sullivan* (1957), the car was of a type which was in such demand that the seller could easily sell it to another buyer.

The distinction between the two cases is clearer if one remembers that in *Charter* v. *Sullivan* the seller could not obtain a sufficient supply of cars to satisfy the demand. There was therefore no question of being able to make two sales instead of one. In *Thompson* v. *Robinson* the operation of Resale Price Maintenance prevented sale of the car at less than list price and there was an excess of supply over demand of this type of car. There was no question of being able to sell the car anywhere else.

(b) *Speculative damages*

Where evidence can be given on the quantity of a loss then the plaintiff must give it or risk recovering only nominal damages (see, *e.g.* *Clark* v. *Kirby-Smith* (1964)). A problem arises however when there has been a breach of contract but the precise measure of damages is difficult to calculate. This arose in an acute form in *Chaplin* v. *Hicks* (1911). The defendant agreed with the plaintiff that if she attended an audition along with 49 other actresses she would have the chance of being one of the 12 chosen for employment. The plaintiff failed to give her a reasonable opportunity to attend according to the agreement but claimed that only nominal damages could be recovered. She only had a one in four chance of obtaining the job and clearly there were many uncertainties involved in her being selected. Nevertheless, the court awarded the plaintiff what was then substantial damages of £100. She had suffered an actionable breach of contract and the mere fact that it might be difficult or impossible precisely to quantify the level of compensation was not a bar to the court making an attempt to do so.

A somewhat similar problem has arisen in the cases arising out of spoilt holidays. Although compensation will not generally be awarded merely for injured feelings the courts have held that where the whole object of the contract is providing pleasure, a breach of contract in failing to do so may lead to the recovery of substantial damages (see, *e.g.* *Jackson* v. *Horizon Holidays Ltd.* (1975) (*ante*, p. 400); *Jarvis* v. *Swans Tours Ltd.* (1973)).

(c) *Tax*

Where damages which are not themselves taxable are recovered as compensation for a loss that is, a question arises as to the amount the defendant should be obliged to pay. For example, A wrongfully dismisses B from his job. Can B recover his total loss of salary or should he be awarded only the net amount he would have received after deduction of tax? In *British Transport Commission* v. *Gourley* (1956) the House of Lords decided (although it was a tort case the same principle applies in contract) that a plaintiff may only recover the net amount of his loss. Since the principle of contractual damages is compensatory, any other result would in effect have allowed the plaintiff to make a profit. He would always normally receive payment only after tax had been deducted.

The position has been modified by statute in relation to wrongful dismissal awards in excess of £10,000. The effect of sections 187 and 188 of the Income and Corporation Taxes Act 1970 is that the *Gourley* principle applies to the first £10,000 and thereafter, although the damages are paid without deduction of tax, the amount received becomes taxable in the hands of the plaintiff. So-called "golden handshakes" are now therefore subject to tax.

(3) Agreed damages and penalties

It is very common, especially in building contracts and charter-parties, to have a clause in the agreement which sets out what damages are to be payable in the event of breach. This is known as "liquidated damages"; that is to say, the amount is fixed. Such a precaution is a sensible way to avoid the trouble and expense of the court making the calculation for itself. The effect is that whether the actual damage suffered is more or less than that envisaged in the agreed damages clause, the plaintiff will only be able to recover the specified amount.

Nevertheless, a party may challenge an agreed damages clause on the grounds that it is in fact a "penalty." It is common in everyday speech to talk of penalty clauses when what people strictly should refer to is a liquidated damages clause. A penalty clause is a term used in effect as a fine or threat against the other party to perform the contract and the courts will not enforce it. If the term is struck out as a penalty the amount of damages will once again be at large and the court will have to do the calculation for itself.

How will a court decide if a term is in reality a penalty? The essential question which the court must ask itself is: does the amount represent a genuine pre-estimate of any loss arising out of breach at the time the contract was made? Although this always remains the central question, Lord Dunedin in *Dunlop Pneumatic Tyre Co. Ltd.* v. *New Garage and Motor Co. Ltd.* (1915) laid down a number of useful guidelines to assist a court in determining this issue. They may be summarised as follows:

1. Even though the parties use the words "penalty" or "liquidated damages" this will not be conclusive. The court will look at the substance not just the form of the agreement and decide what the terms really amount to.

2. It is a penalty if the sum stipulated is extravagantly greater

than any loss which could conceivably flow from the breach. Clearly such a term, by definition, is not a genuine pre-estimate of loss.

3. It will be a penalty "if the breach consists only in not paying a sum of money, and the sum stipulated is a sum greater than the sum which ought to have been paid." This proposition is of course only a particular application of the previous one.

4. There is a presumption (but no more) that it is a penalty when "a single lump sum is made payable . . . on the occurrence of one or more or all of several events, some of which may occasion serious and others but trifling damage."

5. "It is no obstacle to the sum stipulated being a genuine pre-estimate of damage, that the consequences of the breach are such as to make precise pre-estimation almost an impossibility." That is just the situation when the parties would want to employ an agreed damages clause.

It may be a difficult matter of construction to decide whether or not a term operates as a penalty. In the *Dunlop* case itself the clause concerned stipulated a sum of £5 to be paid on each occasion if, amongst other things, a tyre was sold below the list price (such an arrangement would not now be possible, see *ante*, p. 403). The House of Lords decided in this case that the stipulation was reasonable. The potential damage to Dunlop of undercutting their prices was considerable although the quantification of such damage might be almost impossible. It was therefore reasonable to have a fixed but not extravagant level of damages. By contrast, in *Kemble* v. *Farren* (1829) the manager of the Covent Garden Theatre agreed to employ the defendant as "a principal comedian." One term of the contract was that in the event of a failure to fulfill the agreement "or any part thereof" the party at fault was to pay the other £1,000 as liquidated damages and not as a penalty. The court held, notwithstanding the way it had been described, that the clause was a penalty. A very large sum was payable on the occurrence of what might be a very trivial breach; the clause did not represent a genuine attempt at the pre-estimate of loss. Indeed the case is a good illustration of propositions 1–4 of the *Dunlop* case (see also *Ford Motor Co.* v. *Armstrong* (1915)).

A related, but quite different, concept to agreed damages is that of an "action for an agreed sum." The most obvious example is an action to recover the price of goods sold. Strictly speaking what is being claimed in such a case is not damages but the recovery of the debt owed by the defendant to the plaintiff. Because of this questions of mitigation (on which see below) and remoteness do not arise (for example see, *White and Carter (Councils) Ltd.* v. *McGregor* (1962), *ante*, p. 436).

(4) Mitigation

The victim of a breach of contract is not entitled merely to sit back and let the damage grow worse if, by taking reasonable steps, he can reduce it. He is under a duty to mitigate his loss although the onus is on the defendant to prove that he has not done so. For example, if A wrongfully refuses to supply goods to B, then B is under a duty to mitigate his loss by immediately going into the market and buying similar goods at the going rate. If he delays and the price rises further he cannot recover his now increased loss.

A fruitful source of mitigation problems has been actions for wrongful dismissal. In the leading case of *Brace* v. *Calder* (1895) the plaintiff was wrongfully dismissed by a partnership but then offered re-employment on the same terms as before. In the circumstances of this particular case the plaintiff had acted unreasonably in turning down the offer of employment and so recovered only nominal damages. This does not mean that a person in such a position has to accept any job that he is offered. It would only amount to a failure to mitigate if the job was of a kind which it would be appropriate and reasonable for the plaintiff to undertake.

The key-word in this area is "reasonable." If, for example, a plaintiff in reasonably attempting to mitigate his loss actually makes it worse then he will not be penalised for his actions. He will be able to recover his actual loss even though he has himself increased it. In *Pilkington* v. *Wood* (1953) a solicitor in breach of contract advised that the title to the plaintiff's house was good. The solicitor argued that the plaintiff should have mitigated his loss by bringing an action against the vendor for conveying a defective title. The court, in rejecting this argument, said that it was not reasonable to expect the plaintiff to "embark on a complicated and difficult piece of litigation" in order "to protect his solicitor from the consequences of his own carelessness."

2. Specific Performance

A decree of specific performance is an order by the court to the defendant compelling him to perform his obligations under the contract. The obvious question is perhaps, why is this not the standard remedy in every case? The rather unsatisfactory answer seems to be that it is for reasons of history rather than logic. The basic common law remedy for breach of contract was the award of damages, and the entirely equitable remedy of specific performance was developed by the courts in order to do justice in those cases where an award of monetary compensation would not be an adequate remedy. Various consequences flow from this historical development.

(1) Damages inadequate

An order for specific performance will not be made unless an award of damages would be inadequate to compensate the plaintiff for his loss. Hence a decree will rarely be issued for a contract to supply goods which are available in the open market since damages will always be an adequate substitute. The only case where an order is likely to be made (provided for by the Sale of Goods Act 1979, s.52) is when similar goods are unobtainable elsewhere. This was illustrated in *Behnke* v. *Bede Shipping Co.* (1927) where an order for specific performance was granted in relation to the purchase of a ship. In this case there was only one other ship of similar specifications afloat. The occasions on which such an order is made are therefore likely to be very rare.

Rather strangely perhaps, specific performance will always be granted in respect of a sale of land. This proceeds on the assumption that every parcel of land is unique and damages can never be an adequate remedy for its loss. This is so even if the land involved is, for example, merely one out of a street of identical terraced houses. A court will also make an order in respect of an obligation to pay money. This was done in *Beswick* v. *Beswick (ante*, p. 405) where owing to the particular circumstances of that case damages would not have been an adequate remedy.

(2) Mutuality

Although there are certain exceptions, it is generally true that an order of specific performance will not be made against a defendant unless such an order could, if their roles were reversed, have been made against the plaintiff. This is the reason that a minor cannot obtain specific performance; the other party cannot obtain such an order against him (see *ante*, p. 415).

(3) Discretion

Being an equitable remedy, specific performance is discretionary. This does not mean that it can be arbitrarily withheld, but the court might always refuse to grant such an order if it was just and equitable to do so. For example the plaintiff might have been guilty of unconscionable delay in bringing his action which had in some way prejudiced other parties.

Nevertheless, where a party claims specific performance, a court may always award damages in addition to or instead of making such an order.

(4) Non specifically enforceable contracts

Specific performance will not be granted in the case of a contract for personal service. Hence an employee cannot be compelled to serve his employer although there may be liability for damages. To make such an order would in most cases be impracticable and is an infringement of personal liberty.

Another case in which no order for specific performance will be granted is when the enforcement of the decree would require constant supervision by the court. In *Ryan* v. *Mutual Tontine Westminster Chambers Association* (1893) a lessor of a flat agreed to provide a porter to be "constantly in attendance." A lessee of the flat was unable to obtain an order of specific performance to enforce this obligation since it would clearly require constant supervision for its proper enforcement. For similar reasons a contract to carry out building will not generally be compelled by specific performance.

3. Injunction

An injunction is an order of the court restraining the defendant from committing a breach of contract. Normally this will simply be what one might call the negative of a decree of specific performance. The defendant is prevented from doing something that he has promised not to do. Sometimes, however, a so-called mandatory injunction can be obtained to restore the position to that which existed before the defendant's breach of contract. If, for example, the defendant has constructed a building in breach of contract, a mandatory injunction might be obtained to demolish it.

It has already been mentioned that a decree of specific performance cannot be used to compel the performance of a contract for personal services. Nevertheless, where there is an express negative stipulation in a contract an injunction can be obtained to restrain breach of that undertaking even though the effect of this is to *encourage* the defendant to perform his obligations under the agreement. In *Warner Bros. Picture Inc.* v. *Nelson* (1937) the actress Bette Davies entered into an agreement with the plaintiffs in which she agreed "to render her exclusive services" as an artiste and to perform only for them. In breach of this contract she signed an agreement with a third party and the plaintiffs sought an injunction to restrain her from acting elsewhere. They succeeded. The effect of the order was not to compel her to work for the plaintiffs although it might certainly have been a potent encouragement. She could after all have obtained employment in some other unrelated field which would not be within the enforceable terms of any negative stipulation in the contract. This can be contrasted with the decision in *Page One Records Ltd. and Another* v. *Britton* (1968). The defendants, a pop group known as "The Troggs," engaged the first plaintiff as their sole manager and agreed not to employ anyone else in the same capacity. The defendants wished to terminate the agreement and the plaintiffs sought an injunction restraining them from engaging another manager. The injunction was refused. The court held that to grant it would, in effect, be to compel the group to employ the plaintiff as manager or to remain idle. Of the two cases, it is difficult not to believe that the latter takes a more realistic view of the practicalities of the situation.

4. Limitation

Based upon the principle *interest rei publicae ut finis sit litium* (it is the concern of the state that there be an end to litigation) a right to a contractual remedy can be extinguished merely by effluxion of time.

In the case of a simple contract debt section 5 of the Limitation Act 1980 states that an action shall not be brought more than six years after the date on which the cause of action accrued. This means the time at which the facts giving rise to the action happened, not necessarily the date when the potential plaintiff discovered that he could bring an action. The result is that it is possible for a plaintiff to be "statute-barred," as it is called, before he even realised that he had any legal redress. Where personal injuries are claimed the limitation period is in general reduced to three years, and where the contract is under seal the period is 12 years (s.11 and s.8(1)). Where there is fraud or mistake section 32 of the 1980 Act stipulates that time does not begin to run until "the plaintiff has discovered the fraud, concealment or mistake . . . or could with reasonable diligence have discovered it."

When a person is acting under a disability (in legal terms), for example, a minor, time does not begin to run until the disability has been removed (s.28). In the case of a minor this would therefore be on his eighteenth birthday.

Even though the limitation period has expired, the action may be revived if a debtor either makes a written acknowledgement or part payment of the debt (s.29(5)). If he makes an acknowledgement it must be in writing and signed by the person making it (s.30(1)). The effect is that time begins to run again as from the date of the acknowledgement or part payment.

Although the 1980 Act does not apply to claims for equitable relief such as specific performance or injunction, similar rules are applied "by analogy to the statute" or by the application of the equitable doctrine of "laches" (delay). The result is therefore that if an equitable claim corresponds to a similar common law claim which would be barred by statute then no equitable relief will be granted "by analogy." In any event, courts of equity have always refused to grant relief if the plaintiff has been guilty of unconscionable delay. Accordingly the doctrine of "laches" will be applied if the plaintiff has, for example, acquiesced in the wrong done to him or his dilatoriness in bringing an action has unfairly prejudiced other parties.

CHAPTER 12

CONTRACTS FOR GOODS AND SERVICES

In the remaining chapters in this section more detailed attention will be given to *specific* contracts. While the general principles of the law of contract (concerning such matters as agreement, consideration, capacity and remedies) apply to all contracts and are still largely governed by the common law, Parliament has increasingly intervened to regulate the form and terms of *particular* contracts. Sometimes the aim of Parliament has been merely to codify the case law without effecting significant changes of substance. A good example of such legislation was the Sale of Goods Act 1893, the idea behind which was to reduce a mass of case law to an accessible form without major change. But in this century Parliament has been concerned to intervene in a much more drastic way with the broad view of ensuring that contracts are "fair." We have already touched on this matter (*ante*, p. 317) and now we turn to consideration of some specific contracts the form and terms of which are governed by legislation.

Legislation now closely regulates many kinds of contracts such as those for the sale of goods and hire-purchase, contracts of employment and the letting of houses. Past experience shows that in such contracts one party may take advantage of his superior bargaining power to secure terms which are unduly to his advantage and the purpose of such legislation is to ensure that parity is restored. Such legislation can be extremely detailed; the Hire Purchase (Documents) (Legibility and Statutory Statements) Regulations 1965 go to the length of regulating the colouring of paper and the size, colour and density of the type face which must be employed in contracts of hire-purchase and credit sale. Such legislation may therefore severely restrict freedom of contract in the sense that the essential terms of the contract, and its form, may be largely dictated by the relevant statute.

It is not possible here to give a detailed account of this very considerable body of statute law. Succeeding chapters in this section concentrate on that legislation which affects the consumer in relation to everyday transactions concerning the sale of goods and the provision of services. Even this is a formidable body of law and we can only highlight certain features of it.

1. Sale of Goods

The modern law of the sale of goods owes its origins to the victory of business expediency over the often technical and cumbersome restrictions placed upon buyers and sellers by the old common law. The first large scale statutory intervention was the Sale of Goods Act 1893. This largely codified the existing law although it did undoubtedly make some modifications. It confirmed the gradual movement away from a strict application of the maxim *caveat emptor* (let the buyer beware) in most cases to a position in which certain terms were always to be implied, subject to the intentions of the parties, for the protection of the buyer. In particular these were the implied conditions as to title, description, merchantable quality and fitness for purpose (ss.12–15). Opinions vary as to its success as a statute but its longevity and importance are undeniable. Until 1967 it had survived with only very minor alterations and has been substantially re-enacted in the Sale of Goods Act 1979.

The amendments to the Act effected by the Misrepresentation Act 1967, Criminal Law Act 1967 and Theft Act 1968 were of some significance but a more important change was brought about by the Supply of Goods (Implied Terms) Act 1973. This Act *inter alia* prevented the exclusion of the terms implied by sections 12–15 in the case of consumer sales. The Consumer Credit Act 1974 made amendments consequent upon the new terminology and scope of that Act.

The background to these recent changes was a growing awareness of the inadequacy of the traditional concepts of "commercial law" to meet the demands of a consumer society. The Sale of Goods Act 1893 was adapted to dealings between business men and equals, not to transactions between large corporations and small scale consumers. The powerful bargaining position of large organisations made the notion of "freedom of contract" increasingly unreal. Often the only choice the consumer had was to take some essential commodity on the seller's terms or not at all. The widespread use of so-called "standard form" contracts is an aspect of this development. In many cases it is of course an acceptable and sensible way to save time and money. Sometimes however it could (and to some extent still can) mean that unfair terms are foisted upon a reluctant purchaser who has no other real choice. Hence the recognition in the Supply of Goods (Implied Terms) Act 1973, that consumer contracts required special treatment and the provisions in the Unfair Contract Terms Act 1977 for rules relating to terms in standard form contracts.

2. Services

Contracts for the supply *of services* need to be distinguished from the notion of a contract *of service*. The latter is largely regulated by various Acts relating to employment and is concerned with the relationship between employer and employee. The former, with which we are alone concerned, is exemplified in a consumer context by an agreement to mend a leaking pipe or unblock a drain. In marginal cases the distinction is not always easy, but in most consumer contexts it will normally be fairly clear what the relationship is between the parties.

Statutory intervention in the area of supply of services has not been until recently so systematic as in the sale of goods. Nevertheless, the common law applied principles similar to those found in the Sale of Goods Act and the law has recently been codified and reinforced by the Supply of Goods and Services Act 1982 (see *post*, p. 469). In the field of consumer credit where the purchase of goods is linked with the provision of financial services the law has been largely reformulated and strengthened in favour of the consumer by the Consumer Credit Act 1974.

Although much of the law still bears the imprint of its origins in an earlier century with different economic philosophies, the trend, especially in recent years, has been firmly towards consumer protection. The strictness of the approach grounded in laissez-faire individualism appears to be yielding to a concern for the reasonable expectations of consumers in a market that is recognised as being unequal.

CHAPTER 13

SALES, SERVICES AND IMPLIED TERMS

The importance of the distinction between a sale of goods and a contract to supply services has been lessened by the recently enacted Supply of Goods and Services Act 1982 which is fully effective as from July 4, 1983. Nevertheless, the distinction is still of significance and it is necessary to decide what type of transaction we are dealing with before we can go on to consider its consequences.

1. THE DISTINCTION BETWEEN GOODS AND SERVICES

Section 2(1) of the Sale of Goods Act 1979 contains the basic definition of a sale under the Act and states that:

> "A contract of sale of goods is a contract by which the seller transfers or agrees to transfer the property in goods to the buyer for a money consideration, called the price."

In most consumer transactions the ingredients of this definition are likely to be readily satisfied (although for difficulties that can arise, see *Esso Petroleum Co. Ltd.* v. *Commissioners of Customs and Excise* (1976)). It is to be noticed that the reference to "property" means legal ownership of the goods in question. Although the passing of ownership to the buyer is often marked by physical delivery of the chattel this is not necessarily so. It is perfectly possible and normal for the sale of an article to be completed before it leaves the physical possession of the seller. This may be important because if property in the goods has passed to the buyer he will normally find himself responsible for them from that point onwards. In an appropriate case he may, for example, wish to insure the goods against the risk of damage or destruction.

A contract to supply services, which may or may not also involve the supply of goods and materials, is clearly outside the scope of section 2(1) of the 1979 Act. In most cases the distinction between goods and services is clear enough. Buying a radio in a shop is clearly a sale of goods, employing a plumber to unblock a pipe is equally clearly a contract for services. But what of a contract to paint a picture or replace the clutch on a car?

In *Robinson* v. *Graves* (1935) the court held that a contract to paint a portrait was a contract for services. Greer L.J. said that the substance of the contract was the deployment of skill and labour for the production of the article and the fact that some materials might also pass to the buyer was an ancillary consideration.

Applying this test to the facts of individual cases is not entirely easy. For example in *Cammell Laird & Co. Ltd.* v. *Manganese Bronze & Brass Co. Ltd.* (1934) it was held that a contract to construct two ships' propellers was a contract of sale. A meal in a restaurant has also been held to be a contract of sale, *Lockett* v. *A. & M. Charles Ltd.* (1938). On the other hand, repairing a car has been held to be a contract of services, *G. H. Myers & Co.* v. *Brent Cross Service Co.* (1934), as was a vet's injection of serum, *Dodd and Dodd* v. *Wilson and McWilliam* (1946). Where there is a contract to install material into a building or to incorporate a new part into a chattel the courts have tended to the view that this is a contract for services. This would cover, for example, an agreement to install central heating or repair some consumer appliance.

2. Implied Terms

(1) Goods

Sections 12–15 of the Sale of Goods Act 1979 contain the special implied terms relating to goods. Together they form an important body of protection for the consumer which has been further strengthened by the limits imposed upon their exclusion.

(a) *Title*

Central to the sale of goods is the transfer of ownership or property in the goods to the buyer. Not surprisingly section 12(1) implies a condition that the seller has a right to sell the goods and so will pass a good title to the buyer. Section 12(2) allows for the possibility that the seller may be uncertain as to his title but the buyer may nevertheless wish to take the risk and purchase the goods with whatever title he has.

If there has been a breach of section 12(1), this will amount to a "total failure of consideration." The buyer is then entitled to recover the price of the goods even though he may by then have used the goods for a considerable time (see *Rowland* v. *Divall* (1923)).

(b) *Sale by description*

Section 13(1) states that, "Where there is a contract for the sale of goods by description, there is an implied condition that the goods will correspond with the description." This section is further clarified by section 13(3) which provides: "A sale of goods is not prevented from being a sale by description by reason only that, being exposed for sale or hire, they are selected by the buyer."

In many cases it may seem rather strange to talk of an implied term as to description. If I buy a pair of all leather shoes which are in fact made of plastic there has been a breach of section 13 but there is also likely to be a breach of an express term of the contract, *i.e.* that the shoes are "all leather." Indeed Professor Goode casts doubt on the utility of retaining section 13 in its present form.

Two related problems arise in evaluating the effect of section 13, namely, (1) what is meant by a sale by description? and (2) what is required to bring about a breach of the section?

A very wide meaning has been given to the term "sale by description." Not only does this include goods of a generic kind, for example a packet of Brand X cigarettes, but also specific goods when they are sold as a thing corresponding to a description. In *Grant* v. *Australian Knitting Mills* (1936) the sale of woollen underwear was held to be a sale by description "even though the buyer is buying something displayed before him on the counter." Section 13(3) covers the situation which might arise at, say, a supermarket where the shopper himself selects goods from the shelf. If a customer chooses a packet labelled "Ceylon Tea" which in fact turns out to be China Tea this is a breach of section 13. Similarly, if there is an inaccuracy as to the quantity or provenance of the goods this could amount to a breach. It does not matter that the description was not the sole reason for purchasing the goods as long as it was a factor. In *Beale* v. *Taylor* (1967) the plaintiff saw an advertisement for a "Herald, convertible, white, 1961." He went to inspect the car and also noticed on its rear a disc marked "1200." In fact the car consisted of the rear portion of a 1961 Herald 1200 welded to the front part of an earlier model. The Court of Appeal held that the advertisement and disc together constituted a sale by description to which the vehicle clearly did not conform. There was therefore a breach of section 13.

The width of application of section 13 is combined with a strict approach to any deviation from the description. In *Arcos Ltd.* v. *Ronaasen* (1933) the sellers agreed to sell wooden staves half an inch thick to the buyers. A large proportion of the staves were between half and nine sixteenths of an inch thick although it was found that they were fit for their purpose and merchantable. Nevertheless, the House of Lords decided that there was a breach of section 13. As Lord Buckmaster said:

> "If the article they have purchased is not in fact the article that has been delivered, they are entitled to reject it, even though it is the commercial equivalent of that which they have bought."

Similarly in *Re Moore & Co. and Landauer & Co.* (1921) (see *ante*, p.

425) there was a breach of section 13 because the packaging failed to comply with the contract description even though the market value of the goods was not affected by this breach. By contrast, in *Ashington Piggeries* v. *Hill* (1972) the contract was for "herring meal." What was delivered contained a preservative producing a chemical toxic to the mink for which it was supplied as feed. It was decided that there was no breach of section 13. Even though the feed might be unsuitable or useless for mink, the contract description did accurately identify what had been supplied. The essence of section 13 was "identification" and the fact that there may be a failure as to "quality" did not necessarily involve a breach of the section.

One result of a wide interpretation of section 13 in the area of consumer sales is that it might be used to circumvent any requirement that goods be sold "in the course of a business." In effect, if a quality of the goods relating to its fitness for a purpose can be regarded as part of its contract description then there may be an action for breach of this condition even in the case of a private sale. For example, could a "car" with an engine which had irrevocably seized up and will not go really be described in any meaningful sense as a "car"?

(c) *Merchantable quality*

Section 14(2) states:

> "Where the seller sells goods in the course of a business, there is an implied condition that the goods supplied under the contract are of merchantable quality except that there is no such condition—
>
> (*a*) as regards defects specifically drawn to the buyer's attention before the contract is made; or
>
> (*b*) if the buyer examines the goods before the contract is made, as regards defects which that examination ought to reveal."

Unlike section 13, section 14(2) only applies to goods sold "in the course of a business." Although the concept is widely defined by section 61(1) to include sales by local and public authorities, and government departments, this requirement excludes private sales. A normal consumer purchase from a shop or retail outlet will of course present no difficulty.

The reference to goods "supplied under the contract" is to make clear that it is the entirety of what is supplied that must be considered. This therefore includes packaging or other material mixed in with the consignment. For example, in the spectacular case of *Wilson* v. *Rickett Cockerell & Co. Ltd.* (1954) the plaintiffs purchased a ton of Coalite. This particular delivery gave new meaning to the slogan "come home to a real fire." Part of the consignment contained an explosive substance which detonated when the Coalite was burnt so damaging the plaintiff's house. The notion that the coal *qua* coal was perfectly merchantable and it was merely the presence of an unrelated foreign body that had caused the damage was rejected. Taking the consignment as a whole the goods supplied were not fit for burning in a domestic grate.

The first exception to the provision is clear enough. If the seller points out to the prospective buyer that, say, the clutch in the car being purchased is about to break down then no complaint about lack of merchantable quality can be made if it does. The second exception relates to when the buyer himself examines the goods before the contract is made. The first point to make is that it only applies if the buyer chooses to inspect the goods. If he fails to do so he is not prevented from complaining about lack of merchantable quality. Secondly, the use of the formula "that examination" suggests that it is the form of inspection actually adopted by the buyer which matters. If he only inspects the outside of the article and the defect would only have been visible by an internal inspection then again he is not prevented from complaining about the internal defect. On the other hand, if he merely adopts a cursory inspection, whereas a properly conducted examination would have shown up the defect, the exception comes into play (see *Thornett & Fehr* v. *Beers* (1919)). The result is therefore that no inspection at all may be better than one which is conducted carelessly.

The term "merchantable quality" is now defined in section 14(6) which states that goods must be "as fit for the purpose or purposes for which goods of that kind are commonly bought as it is reasonable to expect having regard to any description applied to them, the price (if relevant) and all the other relevant circumstances." The application of this test to the facts of particular problems is not always easy.

If an article is only sold for one use then it clearly must be fit for that use. If underwear produces an unpleasant rash when worn it can hardly be of merchantable quality (see, *e.g.* Lord Wright in *Grant* v. *Australian Knitting Mills Ltd.* (1936)). But what of "cosmetic" defects such as a scratch on a car or a chip in the enamel covering of a refridgerator? If such defects, which do not necessarily affect the functioning of the product, are excluded the consumer may well be in difficulties in the absence of an express contractual undertaking. The general view appears to be that such defects may be breaches of merchantable quality unless they are merely trivial or microscopic. People purchase products not only for their function but also (especially in the case of cars) for their aesthetic qualities and the pleasure a well-finished product will give. This is arguably part of the "purpose" for which the purchase is made.

The fact that an article is second-hand may also be relevant. Nobody would normally expect a second-hand car to be as reliable or in such good condition as the same car when new. This point was made by Lord Denning M.R. in *Bartlett* v. *Sidney Marcus* (1965). The plaintiff purchased a second-hand Jaguar car for £950, it being pointed out that the clutch needed repair. After 300 miles it was found that the defect was more serious than the plaintiff had anticipated and it cost £84 to put right. Nevertheless, the Court of Appeal said there was no breach of section 14(2). The car was in usable condition if not perfect; defects are likely to occur in second-hand cars and having regard to the description of the car as having a defective clutch it was merchantable. By contrast, in *Crowther* v. *Shannon Motor Co.* (1975) the buyer bought a Jaguar in which the engine had done 82,165 miles. After another 2,300 miles the engine seized up. It was found that the engine was "clapped out" at the date of sale and that the buyer of a Jaguar car could reasonably expect 100,000 miles from such an engine. The Court of Appeal held in fact that there had been a breach of the implied term as to fitness for purpose under section 14(3) (see *post*), but it seems likely that a claim under section 14(2) would also have been successful.

Price is another factor in assessing merchantable quality which was discussed in *Brown & Son Ltd.* v. *Craiks* (1970). Lord Reid commented that if the price for better quality goods was substantially higher than that for the lower quality, a buyer who pays the higher price can reasonably expect to receive the better quality. If he received the inferior quality he would be entitled to regard the goods as "unmerchantable" at that price even though they could be sold at the rate appropriate to the inferior goods. When goods are sold at a discount in a "sale" this is a quite different situation. The retailer is merely claiming to sell his ordinary goods more cheaply and should not be allowed to use this as a cloak for selling inferior or "unmerchantable" goods. It would be another matter if the goods were sold cheaply and described as "seconds" or "rejects."

A difficult problem arises in the case of latent defects. If the goods sold have at that time a latent defect which is known to be of an injurious kind then there is clearly a breach. For example, the fact that something breaks down or wears out very soon after purchase may well be evidence that, at the time of sale, it was not of merchantable quality. But what of the situation where goods are sold, and it subsequently emerges that the product as then sold was dangerous? It seems on the face of it unreasonable to make a seller responsible for what he could not at the time have known. On the other hand, liability in contract is strict and it appears on present authority that he would still be liable (see *Henry Kendall & Sons* v. *William Lillico & Sons Ltd.* (1969)).

(d) *Fitness for purpose*

Section 14(3) states:

> "Where the seller sells goods in the course of a business and the buyer, expressly or by implication, makes known—
> (*a*) to the seller, . . .
> (*b*) . . . any particular purpose for which the goods are being bought, there is an implied condition that the goods supplied under the contract are reasonably fit for that purpose, whether or not that is a purpose for which such goods are commonly supplied, except where the circumstances show that the buyer does not rely, or that it is unreasonable for him to rely, on the skill or judgment of the seller . . . "

Some of the terminology of this subsection has already been explained in relation to section 14(2), but the similarity goes further than this. In many cases there will be an overlap between section 14(2) and (3). When the goods have only a single purpose then the concept of fitness for purpose will be an integral part of the requirement for merchantable quality. Hence a hot water bottle that bursts or clothing which causes a rash when worn will not satisfy the requirements of either section 14(2) or (3) (see, *e.g. Priest* v. *Last* (1903); *Grant* v. *Australian Knitting Mills Ltd.* (1936)). Similarly the sale of a secondhand car which is defective may well give rise to a breach of both provisions.

If the buyer requires the goods for a special purpose then this fact must be expressly or impliedly communicated to the seller. For example, in *Griffiths* v. *Peter Conway Ltd.* (1939) the buyer, who had an abnormally sensitive skin, purchased a Harris tweed coat. It was found that the coat would not have caused any harm to a normal user but it produced dermatitis in the buyer. Her action for breach of fitness for purpose failed. She had not made known her special sensitivity and it was something no seller could assume to exist. Of course if the purpose in purchasing the article is obvious, as in the case of a hot water bottle, it is not necessary to spell out the purpose for which the goods are bought. In such a case the courts will readily imply it (see *Priest* v. *Last*).

The requirement that the goods be "reasonably fit for that

purpose" reflects the fact that price, age, and the condition of the goods all have to be taken into account. This point has already arisen in the discussion of section 14(2), and in the case of *Bartlett* v. *Sidney Marcus Ltd.* (*ante*, p. 465) the alternative claim under section 14(3) also failed. The car was as fit for its purpose as one could reasonably expect a second-hand car to be. On the different facts of *Crowther* v. *Shannon* (*ante*, p. 465, however, the claim under section 14(3) was upheld. Rather strange as it may seem, the fact that reliance is placed on the seller's skill and judgment does not mean that he is liable only if there has been some carelessness or lack of judgment in his sale of a defective product. Once there has been reliance on the seller's skill and judgment liability is absolute. It is no defence that if the seller had exercised all possible diligence he still could not possibly have discovered the defect (see, *e.g.* *Frost* v. *Aylesbury Dairy Co. Ltd.* (1905)).

The condition of fitness for purpose is not implied where the buyer has not relied on the seller's skill or judgment. Nevertheless the courts have readily inferred the existence of reliance and the onus rests on the seller to prove that there was no such reliance. If however the buyer asks for a product by its trade or brand name, in a way that makes it clear he is not relying on the seller's skill and judgment regarding the suitability of the product, the effect would be to exclude section 14(3) (see *e.g.* *Baldry* v. *Marshall* (1925)). If the buyer relies upon the seller's skill in some areas but his own specifications in others it will have to be decided whether the unsuitability arose from the actions of the former or the latter. Only if the defect arose in an area where the seller was expected to use his own skill and judgment will there be liability under section 14(3) (see, *e.g.* *Cammell Laird* v. *Managanese Bronze & Brass* (1934); *Ashington Piggeries* v. *Hill* (1972)).

A further ground for the non-application of section 14(3) is that the reliance is unreasonable. This might arise where, for example, the buyer knows that the seller has no expertise in relation to the goods or where the buyer conducts an examination of the goods which ought to have made it abundantly clear that the goods were unsuitable.

(e) *Correspondence with sample*

Section 15 provides:

> "(1) A contract of sale is a contract for sale by sample where there is an express or implied term to that effect in the contract.
>
> (2) In the case of a contract for sale by sample there is an implied condition—

(*a*) that the bulk will correspond with the sample in quality;
(*b*) that the buyer will have a reasonable opportunity of comparing the bulk with the sample;
(*c*) that the goods will be free from any defect, rendering them unmerchantable, which would not be apparent on reasonable examination of the sample."

Like section 13 the condition is not limited to business sales. This reflects the similarity in concept between the two provisions. "Unmerchantable" has the same meaning as in section 14(6).

Merely to exhibit a sample in the course of negotiations does not make it a sale by sample. For example, if I see an article in a shop window and ask to buy one that is just the same this will not invoke section 15. What is required is that the sample be used as the basis for comparison with the goods which are purchased. The purpose behind a sale by sample was explained by Lord Macnaghten in *Drummond* v. *Van Ingen* (1887) when he said:" . . . the office of a sample is to present to the eye the real meaning and intention of the parties with regard to the subject-matter of the contract which, owing to the imperfection of language, it may be difficult or impossible to express in words."

Even if a buyer is prevented by the operation of section 15(2)(*c*) from alleging a breach of correspondence with sample, this will not necessarily prevent reliance under section 14(2) or (3).

Excluding sections 12–15

Reflecting the laissez-faire policy of the time, the Sale of Goods Act 1893 as originally drafted permitted contracting out of the statutory implied terms. Despite the protection which had been given to credit buyers under the Hire Purchase Act 1938 it was not until the passing of the Supply of Goods (Implied Terms) Act 1973 that the cash sale of goods was put upon a similar footing.

Section 12 of the Sale of Goods Act cannot be excluded in any contract regardless of whether it is a commerical, consumer or private sale (Unfair Contract Terms Act 1977, s.6(1)(*a*)). In relation to consumer transactions only (on which see further p. 476), any term which purports to exclude the provisions of sections 13–15 is void (Unfair Contract Terms Act 1977, s.6(2)), and even in non-consumer transactions the terms can only be excluded in so far as they satisfy the 1977 Act's test of "reasonableness" (s.6(3)). In order to prevent unscrupulous traders from misleading buyers as to their statutory rights, these provisions have been strengthened by the Consumer Transactions (Restrictions on Statements) Order 1976 (as amended). This order, made under the authority of the Fair

Trading Act 1973, section 22, makes it a criminal offence to purport to introduce a term into a consumer transaction which is void by virtue of section 6 of the Unfair Contract Terms Act 1977.

(2) Services

The law relating to implied terms in contracts for services has received a major overhaul in the Supply of Goods and Services Act 1982. The Act is somewhat less radical than a superficial reading of it might suggest since many of its terms were already part of the pre-existing common law. Nevertheless there are obvious advantages in such a reform. It promotes clarity and certainty, does away with the need to construe the previous common law, and perhaps strengthens the position of the consumer by drawing attention to the obligations placed upon those who supply services. The appropriate implied terms under the Act apply whether or not materials are also provided by the contract.

(a) *Care and skill*

Section 13 provides that: "where the supplier is acting in the course of a business, there is an implied term that the supplier will carry out the service with reasonable care and skill."

This section is essentially a statutory application of the principle illustrated by *The Moorcock* (*ante*, p. 365) which stressed the willingness of courts to give "business efficacy" to the parties' agreement. The limitation both here and in section 14 of the Act to business contracts is a concept that has already been noted in the Sale of Goods Act.

What is "reasonable" will depend entirely on the facts and circumstances of the case. A supplier is expected to be both competent and use his best endeavours to produce the desired result but there is nothing to prevent the contract laying down even stricter terms. If a contract is for the supply of central heating not only must it be installed reasonably but there may also be a stipulation by the purchaser that a certain higher level of temperature or efficiency will be achieved. Liability for such a term would then be strict and it would not be sufficient if the supplier used reasonable care and skill but failed to produce the specified result.

It is noteworthy that both sections 13 and 14 speak of an implied "term" not "condition." The gravity of the term must therefore depend upon the circumstances of the breach.

(b) *Time*

Section 14(1) provides that in a business transaction where the time for completion of the service is not fixed, "there is an implied term that the supplier will carry out the service within a reasonable time." What is a reasonable time is a question of fact.

This section is a response to the frequent complaints about delay in the performance of contracts for services, and needs to be considered in conjunction with the observations already made in respect of such cases as *Charles Rickards Ltd.* v. *Oppenheim* (1950) (see *ante*, p. 429).

(c) *Price*

Where the price has not been fixed, section 15(1) states that, "there is an implied term that the party contracting with the supplier will pay a reasonable price." Again, what is a reasonable charge is a question of fact.

The result of this section is that, where there has been no agreement as to price, a customer would not be obliged to pay an extortionate bill for the services. It does not mean that a consumer can challenge the price if it has already been agreed, even though it might in fact have been excessive.

(d) *Property*

Where as part of a contract for services property is also transferred to the customer, sections 2–5 of the 1982 Act imply terms as to title, description, merchantable quality, fitness for purpose and sample which are substantially the same as those already implied by sections 12–15 of the Sale of Goods Act 1979. Corresponding provisions are made to apply to contracts of hire by sections 6–10.

The result of many of the cases decided before the passing of the 1982 Act would not be different although they would now be decided on the basis of the statute rather than the common law. For example, in *Dodd and Dodd* v. *Wilson and McWilliam* (1946) a vetinary surgeon innoculated the plaintiff's cattle with a preparation which in fact caused them to become sick. There was no question of negligence and since it was regarded as a contract for services the Sale of Goods Act did not apply. The court decided that there was an implied condition that the serum was fit for its purpose. If the case arose for decision today, the same result would be reached by the application of section 4(5) of the 1982 Act.

Excluding the statutory terms

As regards consumer transactions it is perhaps arguable that sections 13–15 of the 1982 Act could never be excluded owing to the effect of section 3 of the Unfair Contract Terms Act 1977 in that both Acts adopt a standard of reasonableness. This is made to apply by virtue of section 16(1) of the 1982 Act.

Section 2 of the 1982 Act cannot be excluded by a term of any contract (Unfair Contract Terms Act 1977, s.3A). Sections 3–5 cannot be excluded as against a person dealing as a consumer (Unfair Contract Terms Act 1977, s.7(2)), and in all other cases can only be excluded in so far as they satisfy the 1977 Act's test of "reasonableness."

Chapter 14

EXEMPTION CLAUSES, UNFAIR TERMS AND UNSOLICITED GOODS

The common link in the title to this chapter is that these areas have posed special problem for businessmen and consumers alike with the result that the law has formulated a number of specific rules to deal with them.

1. Exemption Clauses

An exemption clause is a term in a contract which seeks to exempt one of the parties from liability for what would otherwise be a breach of contract. Closely related is the concept of a limitation clause which is designed to limit rather than extinguish the party's liability in the event of breach. Although "exclusion clause" might be a more accurate description, the terms "exemption clause" is commonly used to denote both types of clause. What is said here about such clauses is just as important to the general law of contract as it is to the sale of goods. It is however convenient to deal with them at this point both because of their relationship to the Unfair Contract Terms Act 1977 (see below) and because many of the worst excesses of exemption clauses have arisen in the consumer context. This is to a considerable degree the result of the introduction of standard form contracts and their use in situations of grossly unequal bargaining power.

Before an exemption clause even falls to be construed it must be incorporated into the contract. This area has been examined in Chapter 5 and applies equally to exemption clauses as to any other type of clause. An exemption clause may also be defeated by the device of the collateral contract (see *ante*, p. 366). For example, in the case of *Andrews* v. *Hopkinson* (1957) the plaintiff wished to purchase a second-hand car and was told by the dealer, "It's a good little bus. I would stake my life on it." Unfortunately perhaps it was not his life that was at stake. The plaintiff purchased the car on hire-purchase which involved the dealer selling it to a finance company who hired it back to the plaintiff. The plaintiff had signed a delivery note from the finance company stating that he was "satisfied as to its condition" and accordingly would have been in difficulties in bringing an action against the company. Nevertheless, he was able to sue the dealer on the collateral contract. The exemption clause was accordingly successfully circumvented rather than defeated.

Misrepresentation may also have the same effect. In *Curtis* v. *Chemical Cleaning and Dyeing Co.* (1951) a shop assistant misrepresented the effect of a form which the customer was asked to sign. Accordingly, the rule in *L'Estrange* v. *Graucob* (*ante*, p. 362) was ousted by the misrepresentation, albeit one that was not fraudulent. If it had been fraudulent then *a fortiori* would the clause have failed.

If after the application of the above considerations the exemption clause still stands there are a number of other factors that may then come into play in order to defeat its effect, and these will be examined in turn. It is important to stress that, as we have already seen (*ante*, p. 434), there is no longer any question of a substantive rule of law preventing exemption clauses from surviving a fundamental breach. This was made quite clear in the *Photo Production* case.

Failure of exemption clauses

(a) *Third parties*

In examining the doctrine of Privity (Chapter 8) we saw that C, for example, cannot normally enforce a contract made between A and B even if it is for C's benefit. Similarly, a third party cannot take the benefit of an exemption clause. The leading case is *Scruttons Ltd.* v. *Midland Silicones Ltd.* (1962). The case is not without difficulty in its reasoning and has been circumvented in its practical effect to some extent by *New Zealand Shipping Co. Ltd.* v. *Satterthwaite & Co. Ltd.* (1975) but its basic principle is defensible. Midland Silicones had employed carriers to transport a drum of chemicals under a contract which limited the liability of the carrier to £599 per packet. The drum was damaged to the extent of £593 by the negligence of Scruttons, the stevedores whom the carriers had employed to unload the ship. It was decided that the stevedores could not take the benefit of a limitation clause contained in a contract to which they were not parties (see also, *e.g.* *Adler* v. *Dickson* (1955)).

(b) *Contra proferentem rule*

This is a rule of construction which states that where there is an ambiguity in the meaning of an exemption clause it will be resolved *contra proferentem*, that is, against the person who is putting it forward and relying on it. Where there is an exemption clause which a court regards as unfair, the judges have been quick to find ambiguity in the term and then construe it very strictly.

In *Baldry* v. *Marshall* (1925) the buyer wished to purchase a car "suitable for touring purposes." The dealers recommended a

Bugatti which turned out to be unsuitable and the buyer sought to recover his money. The written contract expressly excluded "any other guarantee or warranty, statutory or otherwise" apart from a year's guarantee against mechanical defects. The Court of Appeal held that the requirement that the car should be for touring purposes was a condition not a warranty and the exemption clause did not therefore apply (see also, *e.g. Andrews* v. *Singer* (1934)).

The courts have also taken a strict view of attempts to exclude liability for negligence (on which see further Unfair Contract Terms Act 1977, s.2 *post*, p. 476). In *Hollier* v. *Rambler Motors* (*A.M.C.*) *Ltd.* (1972) the plaintiff's car was damaged at the defendant's garage as a result of a fire caused by their negligence. Their usual terms included a condition that "The company is not responsible for damage caused by fire to customer's cars on the premises." The Court of Appeal said that such a clause would not have protected the defendants in the light of what had happened. The court took the view that the clause could be taken to mean that they could not be liable only in the event of a fire caused without negligence. Accordingly, the clause was not sufficiently unambiguous to protect the defendants (for a similarly minded approach see *White* v. *John Warwick & Co. Ltd.* (1953)).

(c) *Legislation*

Various statutes in specific areas have attempted to restrict the efficacy of exemption clauses, for example, section 3 of the Misrepresentation Act 1967. The most important statute in this area is now however the Unfair Contract Terms Act 1977 (considered below).

The whole area of limitation and exemption clauses has been recently reviewed in two cases which repay examination.

In *Ailsa Craig Fishing Co. Ltd.* v. *Malvern Fishing Co. Ltd.* (1983) Securicor agreed to provide security services for certain vessels moored in Aberdeen harbour. As a result of their failure two ships sank. They sought to rely on a limitation clause which restricted their liability "for any loss or damage of whatever nature arising out of the provision of, or purported provision of, or failure in provision of" their services. The House of Lords upheld Securicor's reliance on the limitation clause. In particular it is noteworthy that they rejected the submission that because there had been a total failure on the part of Securicor to carry out the contract the clause could not be held to apply. Construing the clause in the context of the contract as a whole it did indeed cover Securicor's actions. The point was also made that a clause limiting liability was not to be construed as strictly as one exempting it. The former was much more likely to correspond with the intentions of the parties than the latter.

In *George Mitchell (Chesterhall) Ltd.* v. *Finney Lock Seeds Ltd.* (1983) the Court of Appeal had to construe the effect of an exemption clause in a contract for the sale of goods. In a characteristic judgment Lord Denning M.R. reviews the treatment of exemption and limitation clauses in recent years, and the case provides an illustration of many of the contract principles that can arise in this situation and the different approaches of judges in dealing with the problems raised. The defendants had sold seed to the plaintiffs which turned out to be both unmerchantable and not of the agreed variety. The seed merchants relied on an exemption clause which purported to "exclude all liability for any loss or damage arising from the use of any seeds . . . supplied by us and for any consequential damage whatsoever." The precise ratio is not easy to discern but clearly the defendants had been negligent and on its true construction it could be said that the term was not sufficient to exempt the defendants from the consequences of their own negligence. Lord Denning M.R. would apparently have reached the same result on the basis that there is a general power to prevent reliance on an unreasonable exclusion clause.

2. Unfair Terms

The passing of the Unfair Contract Terms Act 1977 is the most important statutory inroad yet made into the orthodox doctrine of freedom of contract, and very greatly strengthens the hand of the consumer against the imposition upon him of unfair bargains. Some of its provisions, especially sections 6 and 7, have already been considered in the context where they arise but it is now necessary to examine in more detail the overall scope and effect of the Act.

The title of the Act is misleading. It has application to the law of tort as well as contract and does not simply outlaw agreements which a court considers to have been a bad or an unfair bargain. Its application is limited to countering the effect of unfair exemption clauses. This effect is achieved in a number of ways by a statute of some complexity in the way its internal elements interact. First of all a basic distinction is made between consumer and other transactions. Secondly, some terms are completely outlawed. Thirdly, certain terms are exposed to a test of "reasonableness" within the meaning of the Act. Nothing in the Act, of course, affects what has already been said about the incorporation of an exemption clause into the contract in the first place.

Dealing as a consumer

Section 12(1) of the Act defines a consumer transaction as one where: (a) the person neither makes the contract in the course of business nor holds himself out as doing so; and (b) the other party does make the contract in the course of business; and (c) the goods supplied are of a type ordinarily supplied for private use or consumption. This last condition only applies to sections 6 and 7 of the Act (see *ante*, pp. 468, 471). "Business liability" is dealt with in section 1 (3) and is widely defined to include transactions conducted by a person in the course of a business or from the occupation of business premises.

The distinction is necessary because of the extra protection which is given to consumers. Ordinary high street contracts will therefore fall within the ambit of a consumer transaction but, for example, a sale between two private individuals of a second-hand car will be outside the scope of section 12(1). Auction sales are specifically excluded by virtue of section 12(2).

Negligence

Section 2(1) makes void any attempt to limit or exclude liability for personal injury or death. This section applies both in contract and in tort and regardless of whether it is a consumer or business contract.

In the case of other negligent loss or damage, section 2(2) states that exclusion or restriction is only permitted in so far as it satisfies the Act's requirement of "reasonableness."

Contracts generally

Section 3 makes general provision for the problem of exemption clauses. This states that where one party deals as consumer *or* on the other's written standard terms of business, the other cannot exclude or restrict his liability for breach of contract or render a contractual performance substantially different from that which was reasonably expected of him or render no performance at all except in so far as the term satisfies the Act's requirement of "reasonableness." This crucial provision accordingly provides a wide power to strike out unfair exemption clauses in consumer transactions.

Goods and services

These are affected by sections 6 and 7 discussed earlier.

Reasonableness

"Reasonableness" is a key concept in the Act and some guidance on its meaning is provided by section 11 which states that the term must be "a fair and reasonable one ... having regard to the circumstances which were, or ought reasonably to have been, known to or in the contemplation of the parties when the contract was made." The relevant time is therefore when the contract was made, not when it was breached. In determining the issue of fairness and reasonableness regard will be had to the matters set out in Schedule 2 of the Act. These matters include the relative bargaining strengths of the parties; whether the customer had an inducement to enter the contract; whether the customer knew of the nature of the term and also whether the goods had been made to the special order of the customer.

The onus in every case is on the party claiming that the term is reasonable to show that it is (s.11(5)).

Contracts where the Act does not apply

Schedule 1 places some important limits on the scope of the Act. In particular, the Act does not apply to international supply contracts, a contract in relation to land or to any contract of insurance. The latter exclusion means that the Act has no application in an important consumer area.

The meaning of "exemption clause"

The Act makes no attempt at an authoritative definition of an exemption or limitation clause although section 13 suggests a fairly wide interpretation of the concept. This may be because the concept is simply not susceptible to such an approach. How is it possible on a completely logical basis to distinguish between a term that restricts the contractor's liability and one that merely sets out the limits of the contractor's duty? Are they both different ways of looking at the same thing? If so, how will a court decide that it is an unfair exclusion clause and not simply a legitimate means for both parties to set out their respective obligations? Clearly this is an area at the heart of the 1977 Act which seems likely to provide the courts with some difficulty.

3. Unsolicited Goods

There have been occasions, especially in the recent past, when unscrupulous suppliers have delivered goods which have never been ordered and followed this by sending a demand for payment. It has already been seen in the discussion of *Felthouse* v. *Bindley* (1862) (*ante*, p. 5) that one person cannot impose a contract upon another but it was thought appropriate to embody this principle in a clear statutory form which gave additional protection to the victim of such sales techniques. The result was the Unsolicited Goods and Services Act 1971.

This Act provides that a recipient of unsolicited goods (that is goods sent without his request and with a view to his acquiring them) is entitled to treat them as an unconditional gift if the sender does not reclaim the goods within six months of their receipt (s.1(2)(*a*)). Alternatively, the recipient can give written notice to the sender stating that the goods were unsolicited and giving the address from where they can be collected. If the sender does not come to collect the goods within 30 days of the notice, the property in the goods will pass to the recipient (s.1(2)(*b*)). If the goods are accidently lost or damaged before the expiration of either of the statutory periods the recipient as an "involuntary bailee" of the goods will not generally be liable. It might be different if he deliberately destroyed them.

Section 2 of the Act imposes criminal sanctions on a trader who demands payment for unsolicited goods where he has no reasonable cause to believe that there is a right to it. It is also a criminal offence in similar circumstances to threaten legal proceedings to enforce such a payment.

Chapter 15

MANUFACTURERS' LIABILITY

Most people (who have not read this book) when buying consumer durables tend to regard the manufacturer as the primary person to whom any complaint about the product should be addressed. This is a view that some retailers do little to dispel, but we have seen that as a matter of law it is entirely unfounded. Unless he buys direct from the manufacturer, the consumer's contract is with the retailer, not the manufacturer, and it is against him that in the first instance a remedy should be sought. The provisions of sections 12–15 of the Sale of Goods Act 1979 will often provide valuable assistance and the retailer may always recoup his loss by in turn bringing an action for breach of contract against his supplier. Similarly, if A gives B as a present an article he has bought from a retailer C, then the doctrine of privity ensures that although of course A can bring an action, B cannot sue C if the product turns out to be defective. The only effective way in which B could do this would be for A to transfer to B his rights against C using the machinery of section 136 of the Law of Property Act 1925 (see *ante*, p. 407). This may sometimes be prudent but is a somewhat unusual precaution.

There are however certain circumstances when the manufacturer is directly liable to the consumer. These are: (1) under a manufacturer's guarantee; (2) as a result of negligence; and (3) under the terms of the Consumer Safety Act 1978. These possibilities will now be examined.

1. Manufacturers' Guarantees

Everyone is familiar with the "guarantee" cards which often arrive with consumer goods and in which the manufacturer typically undertakes to repair or replace defective goods within a certain period of time. Rather curiously their precise legal status is somewhat uncertain and the point will presumably only fall for consideration in the unlikely event of a manufacturer refusing to honour a guarantee. The difficulty arises from the requirements of offer, acceptance and consideration. On the face of it the undertaking from the manufacturer appears to be a gratuitous promise from someone with whom the consumer has no direct contractual relationship. One way round this difficulty is to regard the manufacturer's promise as the basis of a collateral contract with the consumer for which the consideration is supplied by purchasing the goods from the retailer. This view could be supported by reference to *Carlill* v. *Carbolic Smoke Ball Co.* (see *ante*, p. 320). Even though Mrs. Carlill had not bought the smoke ball directly from the company it was held that there was a contract between them quite apart from any contract of sale with the retailer (see also *Shanklin Pier Ltd.* v. *Detel Products Ltd.* (1951)). Provided the plaintiff knew of the guarantee before purchasing the product *Carlill's* case provides a strong analogy.

In the past some manufacturers included "guarantees" which the customer was invited to sign and return but which in fact had the effect, because of their restrictive terms, of depriving the customer of rights against the manufacturer. In relation to damage or defects caused through the manufacturer's negligence, this practice is now prevented by section 5 of the Unfair Contract Terms Act 1977. Such a clause will be ineffective if the requirements of the section are satisfied. These are: (1) that the goods are of a type ordinarily supplied for private use; (2) they prove defective while in consumer use; and (3) the manufacturer did not sell the goods directly to the consumer. The effect is therefore that as regards defects or damage arising from negligence the manufacturer may provide the consumer with additional rights or remedies, but he cannot take away such rights as the consumer already has.

2. Negligence

If the goods actually cause harm or damage to the ultimate consumer then the manufacturer may be liable in the tort (that is, civil wrong) of negligence. This basis of the modern law was laid down in the classic case of *Donoghue* v. *Stevenson* (1932). Mrs. Donoghue was bought a bottle of ginger beer by a friend at a café in Paisley. She drank some of the contents, and when her friend refilled her glass, out floated the remains of a decomposing snail. Mrs. Donoghue claimed damages from the manufacturer (she of course had no contractual relationship with the café or the manufacturer) for the resultant nervous shock and gastro-enteritis. The House of Lords upheld the claim. Lord Atkin made the now famous comment that " . . . a manufacturer of products which he sells in such a form as to show that he intends them to reach the ultimate consumer in the form in which they left him with no reasonable possibility of intermediate examination, and with the knowledge that the absence of reasonable care in the preparation . . . of the products will result in an injury to the consumer's life or property, owes a duty of care to the consumer to take that reasonable care."

This decision has been generously interpreted over the last 50 years. There is no limit to the type of goods to which it relates and it has been extended to cover the analogous case of those who supply services. It is also possible to make a claim both for breach of contract and negligence in the same proceedings (see *e.g. Andrews* v. *Hopkinson* (*ante*, p. 472) where both claims were successful).

There are however considerable hurdles in the way of a consumer who seeks to prove negligence all of which he must successfully surmount.

No intermediate inspection

Only if there was a real possibility of an intermediate inspection before use that would have shown up the fault is the manufacturer exempted from liability. In modern conditions of consumer marketing this is unlikely to present much of a problem.

Goods must be defective

Normally this should not present a difficulty. A bun with a stone in it or a car with a dangerous steering mechanism is clearly defective. Difficulties may however arise in proving that the goods were defective at the time they left the manufacturer (see *e.g. Evans* v. *Triplex Safety Glass Co.* (1936)).

There must be negligence

The onus of proving negligence is on the plaintiff and this may be an onerous and expensive task. Sometimes if the negligence is flagrant the plaintiff will be helped by the application of the maxim *res ipsa loquitur* (the thing speaks for itself). If bags fall out of a warehouse onto the plaintiff in the street below (*Scott* v. *The London Dock Co.* (1865)), or a consumer finds a stone in the middle of a bath bun (*Chaproniere* v. *Mason* (1905)) then the onus shifts to the defendant to prove that he was not negligent. More often than not the negligence is far from obvious and it is at this point that a plaintiff may well decide that it is unprofitable to pursue the claim.

It is also important to note that the manufacturer need only show *reasonable* care and skill. He is not guaranteeing the goods. Nevertheless in cases where a manufacturer seeks to establish a careful and thorough means of producing or checking goods, the courts have sometimes turned this to the plaintiff's advantage. If the system really is so efficient it might be said that the only explanation for a defective product is that someone has been negligent.

The negligence must cause the damage

If the damage to the plaintiff would have occurred in any event, the manufacturer will not be liable even though the product happened to be defective. If a car is manufactured with dangerous steering but the accident is caused entirely by another motorist's careless driving the manufacturer will not attract liability for the accident.

Establishing causation can sometimes be a serious problem as cases involving, for example, the effect of drugs have shown.

The kind of damage must be recoverable

There is no doubt that if the plaintiff or his property is physically damaged by the product he may recover damages for his injury or loss. For example, if the central heating boiler explodes a plaintiff can recover for damage to the house and furniture as well as the conventional sum awarded for any personal injury suffered. Beyond this the law as it affects consumers is not entirely clear.

The orthodox view has always been that a plaintiff cannot recover for pure economic loss which does not involve physical damage (*S.C.M.* (*United Kingdom*) *Ltd.* v. *Whittall* (1971)). Accordingly, if the consumer suffers financial loss because the product will just not work, it seems that no damages are recoverable on the grounds of negligence. What if the product goes wrong and, so to speak, damages itself? The Law Commission considered that a plaintiff could not recover in this situation unless the defect is likely to cause personal injury or damage to other property.

Nevertheless this may be an area where the courts are gradually moving towards a more generous view of what loss is recoverable. This view can be supported by, amongst others, the recent decision of the House of Lords in *Junior Books Ltd.* v. *Veitchi Co. Ltd.* (1982). Here the plaintiffs engaged a building company to construct a factory. The building company sub-contracted the laying of a special floor to another firm which had been nominated by the plaintiffs' architects. There was therefore no direct contractual link between the plaintiffs and the sub-contractors. The floor proved to be defective and the plaintiffs brought an action in tort against the sub-contractors for the cost of replacing the floor and the consequential economic loss this would involve. There was no allegation that the floor presented a danger to health or that there was a risk of damage to other property of the plaintiffs. The House of Lords decided that the plaintiffs had a right to recover against the sub-contractors. A producer of a faulty article owed a duty of care, at least where the proximity between the parties was sufficiently close, which went beyond merely preventing harm and included a duty not to produce a defective article. A producer is therefore liable, in a case such as this, for the cost of remedying the defective floor and the consequential economic loss this would involve.

This case represents a very important extension of the principle laid down in *Donoghue* v. *Stevenson*. Much will depend on how the courts interpret or limit the application of this decision but the case appears on the face of it to provide a significant widening of the concept of recoverable damage in favour of the consumer.

3. The Consumer Safety Act 1978

The Consumer Safety Act 1978 repeals the Consumer Protection Acts of 1961 and 1971 and replaces them with strengthened provisions to encourage safety in consumer goods. This is achieved in three ways. First of all the Secretary of State is empowered to make regulations regarding the composition, design and labelling of goods. For example, regulations have dealt with such diverse things as cosmetics, nightdresses, electric blankets and the colour coding of electrical appliances. A manufacturer who fails to comply with these regulations commits an offence.

Secondly, the Secretary of State can take action against the marketing of a product after it has been produced. A "prohibition order" can be issued to prevent the supply of a specified class of goods. Similarly a "prohibition notice" directs a particular trader to cease supplying goods. A "notice to warn" can be issued where the goods have already been sold ordering the trader to warn consumers about an unsafe product.

If a trader fails to comply with a regulation or prohibition order or notice, section 6(1) of the 1978 Act provides the injured party with a civil remedy. By section 6(2) this cannot be excluded by any exemption clause. The remedy is available to anyone who suffers damage as a result of the breach in addition to any contractual right of action he may have and regardless of the existence of negligence although subject to certain statutory defences. It is important to realise however that only those classes of goods which are the subject of an order by the Secretary of State are relevant to a claim for compensation under section 6(1).

CHAPTER 16

CONSUMER CREDIT

Since the turn of this century there has been an enormous growth in the use of hire-purchase to buy consumer durables such as cars, washing machines and almost every kind of electrical appliance. More recently the advent of the credit card has meant that services such as holidays or car hire can also be purchased on credit. The result is that any survey of the consumer field which failed to take account of legislation regulating credit transactions would be substantially incomplete. Having said this, in what follows an attempt is made merely to identify in outline those areas of the law which are of special importance to a consumer involved in everyday transactions.

Two factors require the law's positive intervention in the field of consumer credit. In the first place, the agencies which supply credit facilities such as banks or finance houses are often large and powerful organisations which present a classic case of inequality of bargaining power. Secondly, consumers may be tempted to over-reach their resources by the apparently easy expedient of a credit sale, especially if they are the subject of sales pressure.

Recognising these problems the Hire Purchase Act 1938 instituted a degree of protection for the consumer. Subsequent hire-purchase legislation, in a somewhat piecemeal way, reacted to individual abuses and gradually increased the protection offered to the consumer. The culmination of this process is the Consumer Credit Act 1974, a response to the findings of the Crowther Committee. The rationale behind the legislation is to provide regulation of those transactions which in substance if not in legal form are ways in which the consumer receives credit. For example, hire-purchase is not (as we shall see) in its outward legal form a means of supplying credit, but in truth it is in substance just that. The Act therefore embraces a very wide range of transactions. In view, however, of the fact that hire-purchase and credit card sales are probably the two areas most likely to be encountered in the normal run of consumer transactions the emphasis will be on examining these areas.

Although the ultimate aim of the 1974 Act is to repeal and replace the earlier consumer legislation, this object has so far only been partially realised. Substantial portions of the statute have not been brought into force. In particular, the Act provides a framework for the making of numerous orders and regulations to control every detail of credit transactions. Many of these statutory instruments have still not appeared; others appear at irregular intervals. The result is that establishing the current law is a matter of some complexity. Not only must careful regard be had to what parts of the Act are in force and what regulations have been made under it, but also the fact that the Act is not fully implemented means that much of the old legislation still stands for the time being. In what follows the general assumption is made that the Act is fully in force. Where this is not the case, the present law is generally to be found in the corresponding provisions of the Hire Purchase Act 1965.

Before examining what rights and remedies the present legislation gives it is necessary to grasp the legal mechanics of such phenomena as hire-purchase or credit card sales. It was long ago decided that a hire-purchase agreement was not a straightforward contract of sale (*Helby* v. *Mathews* (1895)). In the typical situation of a car purchase the consumer asks the dealer to arrange the finance. The dealer then makes an offer to a finance company offering to sell them the car. At the same time the prospective purchaser makes an offer to the finance company to take the car on hire-purchase; that is, he will hire the car paying certain regular instalments but have an option to purchase the car outright after all the payments have been made. This right is, of course, invariably exercised. If the finance company accept the offers the arrangement is complete (see fig. 1).

(Fig. 1)

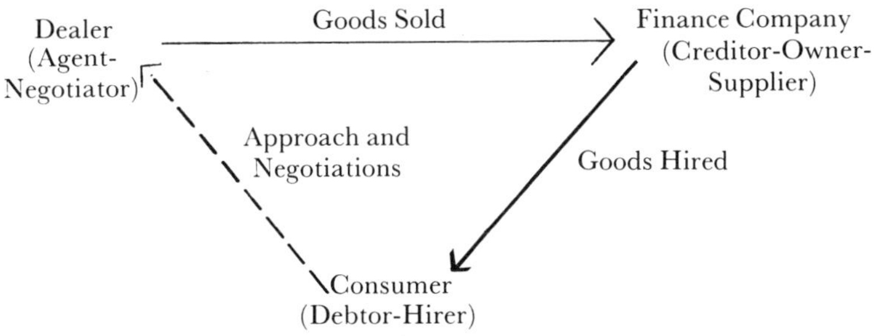

To use the language of the 1974 Act, the dealer is the agent or negotiator of the finance company (he is the supplier of the goods only in a physical sense); the finance company is the legal owner of the goods until their purchase, and the creditor to whom payments are owed as well as the legal supplier; the consumer is the hirer of the goods and the debtor who owes the payments to the company.

It might be asked, why not simply mortgage the chattel as one mortgages a house in order to purchase it? The reason is that to mortgage a chattel requires that the parties comply with the obscure and technical provisions of the Bills of Sale Acts 1878–82 which has been considered too cumbersome a machinery.

In the case of a credit card sale the machinery is somewhat different. The comsumer will normally get immediate ownership of the goods and the dealer will be paid by the credit card company with whom he will have an agreement. The card company will then at a subsequent time seek reimbursement from the consumer (see fig. 2).

(Fig. 2)

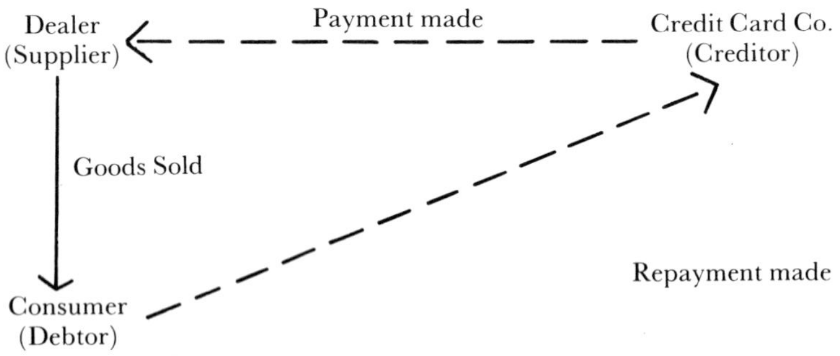

Rights and obligations in hire-purchase

There is no doubt that a hire-purchase agreement between a consumer and a dealer is ordinarily a consumer credit agreement under section 8 of the 1974 Act. The credit must not exceed £5,000 (s.8(2)), although this is one of the major departures from former hire-purchase legislation. It is the level of *credit* which is important, not the price of the goods, and this figure also excludes any deposit and the total charge for credit such as interest. Once it is established that a transaction is regulated by the 1974 Act and not exempt by reason of section 16 (for example land mortgages have special provisions relating to them) the consumer is protected in a number of ways.

Formalities

The formalities regarding a hire-purchase agreement are strict (see *ante*, p. 457). Not only must the agreement be in writing but even the type of paper and print are controlled. Section 62 and 63 of the 1974 Act ensure that the debtor or hirer is entitled to at least one copy of the agreement. For something like the hire-purchase of a car, as described above (fig. 1) he will be entitled to two copies. First of all he will receive a copy of the unexecuted agreement. Once his offer has been accepted by the creditor or owner a copy of the executed agreement must be sent to him within seven days of the making of the agreement (s. 63(2)). Failure to comply with these formalities may render the agreement unenforceable by the owner or creditor.

Cancellation

Just like any contract the hirer can withdraw from the agreement by revoking his offer at any time before it has been accepted. In addition the consumer has a right to cancel after acceptance in some circumstances (ss. 67–73 of the 1974 Act). The obvious purpose here is to allow a consumer who may have been subject to sales pressure a "cooling off" period when he can reconsider the position. The statute provides an exception to the normal rule that a contract once made binds the parties irrevocably.

In order to come within the cancellation provisions it is necessary that oral representations were made to the hirer by the negotiator (the dealer in our example) for the finance company and that the agreement was not signed at the business premises of either the creditor or owner, or the negotiator in any antecedent negotiations, or at the premises of a party to a linked transaction (for example it may be a condition of an agreement that the party take out an insurance policy). The effect is therefore that agreements signed by the consumer in his own home are clearly cancellable. The period of "cooling off time" is five days following the actual receipt of his copy of the final executed agreement (s. 68). Cancellation is effected by giving written notice to the creditor or owner, or to his agent. For this purpose a dealer in a normal three party arrangement is deemed to be the creditor's agent (s. 56) and the cancellation is effective from the date of posting. Once a cancellation has been made, the agreement and any other transaction linked to it is treated as if it had never been made (s. 64(4)). The hirer is entitled to the return of his money and the owner to the return of his goods.

Termination

At any time before the last instalment is due a hirer may terminate a hire purchase agreement (ss. 99–100). Of course it may often be highly disadvantageous to do so if he has already paid a substantial amount in instalments. In order to prevent the owner being left with goods that may have heavily depreciated in value, section 100(1) of the 1974 Act requires the debtor to pay such sum (as when for example the agreement has been terminated early on) as will bring the total payments to one half of the total price. If a court thinks it just it may order the payment of a lesser sum than this as when, for example, the agreement is ended before the goods have depreciated in value to any extent.

Defective goods

In the typical transaction outlined in figure 1 above the goods have been hired from the owner finance company. In such a case the effect of sections 8–11 of the Supply of Goods (Implied Terms) Act 1973 and the Unfair Contract Terms Act 1977 is that there are implied terms on the model of sections 12–15 of the Sale of Goods Act 1979 as against the owner or creditor in respect of defective goods.

In addition the consumer may have an action in negligence (as in *Andrews* v. *Hopkinson* (*ante*, p. 472)) or on a collateral contract against the dealer. Because such a dealer will be a "credit broker" or "negotiator" within section 56 of the Act, and so in effect an agent of the finance company, any representations made by the dealer are treated as those of the company. Accordingly, any misrepresentation made by the dealer will ground an action against the finance company. The obvious advantage to the consumer of this arrangement is that he can be reasonably sure of having someone solvent to sue.

Enforcement by the owner/creditor

The most obvious obligation placed upon the consumer is to make the regular instalment payments. If he fails to do so then the agreement will invariably contain a term entitling the hirer to terminate the agreement and repossess the goods. Even at this stage however the consumer enjoys a level of protection. By section 87 of the 1974 Act the owner must serve a default notice on the hirer. This effectively sets out the nature of the breach. If the debtor or hirer rectifies the breach it is treated as never having happened (s. 89). Alternatively he may apply for a "time order" under section 129 which gives the court power to extend the repayment period.

In the last resort the law will protect the consumer against the owner or creditor "snatching back" the goods. The creditor cannot enter any premises to repossess the goods without a court order (s. 92(1)). Often the debtor may already have paid a substantial amount for the goods. Accordingly section 90 states that if he is in breach, has not terminated the agreement and has paid or tendered one-third or more of the total price, then the goods are "protected goods". The creditor cannot then take possession of them without a court order. A potent reason for complying with this provision is provided by section 91. If the creditor does repossess the agreement is terminated, the debtor is released from further liability, and he can recover all sums which have been paid under the agreement.

Credit card sales

As we saw from figure 2 above, in a credit card sale the property is normally transferred directly from the supplier (in both the legal and physical senses) to the consumer. All the terms that are normally implied as part of a sale of goods are therefore implied into this contract.

The Act however goes further than this. Such a transaction is a debtor-creditor-supplier agreement to which sections 56 and 75 of the 1974 Act apply. The thinking behind these provisions is that the credit card company is in business terms closely connected to the supplier and should share his liability. Consequently section 75 states that if the debtor has any claim for misrepresentation or breach of contract against the supplier, he shall have a like claim against the creditor; section 56 treats the supplier as the agent of the creditor for such purposes. This provision is of great potential use to a consumer. If the shop from which the customer bought the goods has ceased trading or become bankrupt there may still be a claim against a fully solvent credit card company.

There are limitations to the application of this provision set out in section 75(3). It will not apply if the cash price of the item is less than £30 or more than £10,000. There is a further uncertainty about the extent to which the credit card company is liable in the case of those whose cards were issued before July 1, 1977 when this part of the Act was brought into force. Several authors have expressed the view that there would still be liability but the situation would benefit from being clarified.

Extortionate credit bargains

In the last resort a debtor may use the machinery provided by section 137–140 of the 1974 Act to claim that the credit agreement is extortionate. These provisions apply to most "credit bargains," even those that might otherwise be exempt under section 16, and has retrospective effect.

A bargain is extortionate under section 138 if it requires the debtor to make payments which are grossly exorbitant or otherwise grossly contravene ordinary principles of fair trading. It is difficult to be sure how generously the courts will interpret their wide power to set aside or alter the agreement between the parties. Factors which can be taken into account include the prevailing interest rates and the age, experience, health and circumstances of the debtor. The matter can be raised either in the county court (s.139(5)) or in other proceedings where consideration of the credit agreement is relevant.

Licensing provisions

Many individual business activities, such as advertising, are controlled by the Act through criminal sanctions. In addition sections 22–24 and 147–150 set up a centrally administered system of licensing of all those involved in extending credit. This will enable the whole industry to be carefully monitored and effectively controlled. Even if there has been no criminal offence committed the Director General of Fair Trading may take into account the business practices of the licensee in deciding whether to grant or refuse a licence. This clearly enables the system to be made sensitive to consumer complaints in the operation of credit facilities.

The complex provisions of the 1974 Act will, when fully implemented, provide a degree of protection to the consumer which few countries can presently rival. It is unfortunate that, as yet, so much of it still remains at a transitional stage.

Appendix I

A LAW LIBRARY FOR "A" LEVEL LAW

A law library is of central importance to the lawyer and therefore to the teacher and student of law. This importance derives from the fact that lawyers need to refer to their books as authorities and their usage of books tends to be very much more extensive than is the case with other disciplines. A good law library at a university will run to tens of thousands of volumes. It would of course be quite unrealistic to expect that the schools and institutions teaching law at "A" level can have the resources to purchase books on anything like this scale. Nevertheless, and since the subject cannot be properly taught and studied from a single course-book, teachers and students must have available to them some additional texts. In this appendix suggestions are made for an "A" level library under three heads: Classes A, B and C. Class A is comprised of texts which are an essential basis of, and supplement to, the proper study of the subject at this level. While it would not be expected that a student would read all of the Class A books in their entirety, it would be expected that frequent reference would be made to them as appropriate to supplement the course-book and the teaching. Class B is comprised of texts which it is very desirable to have available if resources permit their purchase. Class C comprises certain materials to which it is important that at least the teacher should have access if he is, as he must, to keep up to date with developments in, and changes of, the law.

The prices indicated are those charged at the time of going to press. Prices in parentheses indicate the cost of the paperback edition where available.

CLASS A

Title	*Ed.*	*Date*	*Author(s)*	*Publisher*	*HB*	*Price*	*(PB)*
English Legal System	5th	1980	Walker, R., and Walker, M.	Butterworths	£21.00		(£13.95)
The English Legal System	3rd	1982	Eddey, K.J.	Sweet & Maxwell	£11.95		(£5.95)
Essential Business Law: Law and the Legal System	1st	1979	Smith, Peter	Sweet & Maxwell			(£1.25)
The Law Machine	1st	1982	Berlins, M. and Dyer, C.	Pelican			(£2.50)
Outlines of English Law	3rd	1982	Marsh, S.B., and Soulsby, J.	McGraw Hill			(£5.95)
Constitutional and Administrative Law	4th	1981	De Smith (edited by Street, H., and Brazier, R.)	Penguin Education			(£6.95)
Essential Business Law: Arbitration	1st	1980	Kay, Maurice	Sweet & Maxwell			(£1.25)
Cases and Materials on the English Legal System	3rd	1980	Zander, Michael	Weidenfeld & Nicholson			(£8.95)
Freedom, the Individual and the Law	5th	1982	Street, Harry	Penguin Books			(£3.50)
The Sentence of the Court	3rd	1978		H.M.S.O.			(£2.00)

CLASS A

Title	*Ed.*	*Date*	*Author(s)*	*Publisher*	*HB*	*Price*	*(PB)*
Social Security in Great Britain	4th	1977		H.M.S.O.			(£0.90)
Social Services in Britain	11th	1977	Central Office of Information, pamphlet No. 3	H.M.S.O.			(£1.50)
The European Community: How it Works		1979	Noël, Emile	European Perspective Series			(£2.60)
Osborn's Concise Law Dictionary	7th	1983	(edited by Bird, R.)	Sweet & Maxwell	£7.50		(£4.50)
Contract	4th	1981	Davies, F.R.	Sweet & Maxwell	£7.00		(£3.95)
Cases and Statutes on Contract	3rd	1979	Brazier, R.	Sweet & Maxwell			(£4.75)
Criminal Law	1st	1981	Seago, Peter	Sweet & Maxwell	£13.00		(£8.50)
Introduction to Criminal Law	9th	1980	Cross, A.R.N. and Jones, A. (edited by Card, R.E.T.)	Butterworths	£16.25		(£9.95)
Cases and Statutes on Criminal Law	6th	1977	,,	Butterworths	£13.00		(£8.95)
Sale of Goods and Consumer Credit	2nd	1980	Dobson, A.P.	Sweet & Maxwell			(£7.25)
Consumer Law and Practice	1st	1980	Lowe, R. and Woodroffe, G.F.	Sweet & Maxwell	£19.50		(£12.00)
Students' Law Reporter			Published three times a year by	Sweet & Maxwell			(£0.45 per issue)

CLASS B

Title	*Ed.*	*Date*	*Author(s)*	*Publisher*	*Hb.*	*Price*	*(Pb.)*
The Oxford Companion to Law	1st	1980	Walker, David M.	Clarendon Press	£20.00		
Learning the Law	11th	1982	Williams, Glanville	Sweet & Maxwell	£5.00		(£3.55)
The Law of Contract	10th	1981	Cheshire, G.C., and Fifoot, C.H.S. (edited by Furmston, M.P.)	Butterworths	£22.50		(£14.95)
A Casebook on Contract	7th	1982	Smith, J.C., and Thomas, J.A.C.	Sweet & Maxwell	£17.00		(£12.95)
Criminal Law	4th	1978	Smith, J.C., and Hogan, Brian	Butterworths	£13.95		(£12.95)
Textbook of Criminal Law		1978	Williams, Glanville	Stevens			(£14.25)
Casebook on Criminal Law	4th	1982	Elliott, D.W., and Wood, J.C. (edited by Elliott, D.W. and Wells, Celia)	Sweet & Maxwell	£28.00		(£18.50)
Cases and Materials on Criminal Law	2nd	1980	Smith, J.C., and Hogan, Brian	Butterworths	£22.50		(£14.95)
The Machinery of Justice in England	7th	1977	Jackson, R.M.	Cambridge University Press			(£16.50)

CLASS C

Title	*Publisher*	*Annual Subscription (1983)*	*Students' Concessionary Price*
New Law Journal	Butterworths	£41.50	£20.75
Current Law Statutes	Sweet & Maxwell	£90.00	£49.50
EITHER			
Weekly Law Reports	Incorporated Council of Law Reporting	£70.00	£24.00
OR			
All England Law Reports	Butterworths	£82.00	£32.80

Appendix II

SPECIMEN QUESTIONS

A. Legal System

1. The House of Lords has declared that while precedent is an indispensable foundation upon which to decide what the law is, it has also recognised that a too rigid adherence to the doctrine may lead to injustice in particular cases and may hamper the proper development of the law.

Consider the operation of the doctrine of precedent in (i) the House of Lords, and (ii) the Court of Appeal (Civil Division) in the context of this view.

2. "The only sure guide to statutory interpretation is that words and phrases must be given their natural and ordinary meaning in the context in which they appear."

Discuss.

3. Describe the role of (a) magistrates, and (b) juries in criminal trials. What are the advantages and disadvantages of lay participation in the criminal justice system?

4. (a) What, in your view, are the principal justifications for the introduction of Administrative Tribunals into the legal system?

(b) What are the advantages and disadvantages of two such tribunals in comparison with the ordinary civil courts?

5. Alan, who is alleged to have fallen asleep while driving his car, collides with a motor-cyclist, who is seriously injured. Alan is charged with the offence of reckless driving and is sued for damages by the motor-cyclist.

(a) Discuss the considerations affecting the choice of venue for the hearing of the prosecution and civil action, respectively.

(b) What right of appeal is there from the decisions of these courts?

6. Legal aid and advice in civil matters has been described as a "safety net" intended to ensure that no one fails to pursue a rightful claim or defence through lack of funds.

(a) To what extent does the present scheme of legal aid and advice achieve this aim?

(b) What are the remaining areas of greatest need?

7. (a) What effect has the European Communities Act 1972 had on the traditional doctrine that the British Parliament may enact what it wishes?

(b) In what circumstances (i) may and (ii) must an English court refer a question of law to the Court of Justice of the European Community?

8. "Janus-like we have always turned two faces towards a policeman. We expect him to be human and yet inhuman. We employ him to administer the law, and yet ask him to waive it."

Discuss with reference to the exercise and control of police powers in this country.

9. Following a series of burglaries the police suspect that Ben is the burglar.

(a) The police believe that if they search Ben's house they will find evidence relating to the burglaries. What powers do they possess to search his house and to question him about the burglaries?

(b) Assume that Ben is subsequently charged with burglary and wishes to apply for bail. What factors will influence the court's decision to grant or withhold bail?

10. What are the purposes of punishment? Do the punishments which the courts impose achieve these purposes?

B. Criminal Law

1. Harriet taxes her husband, George, with having a mistress; he laughs in her face and boasts that he has, in fact, two mistresses.

Harriet is so incensed that she grabs the bread knife and lunges at George with it, wounding him in the throat. Harriet is horror-stricken when she sees that George is severely wounded and unconscious. She rings for an ambulance and bandages his wound. George is dead.

(a) Consider Harriet's criminal liability for George's death.

(b) Would it make any difference to your answer if George died two days after reaching hospital where his death was caused by his throat being bandaged too tightly?

2. Discuss the criminal liability, if any, of Sam, a shopkeeper, in the following circumstances. Give reasons for your answer.

(a) Thelma hands Sam a £1 note, which she asks him to pay into the Christmas club which Sam has organised. Sam does not pay the money into the club but, instead, uses it to pay a bet.

(b) Una gives Sam £5 as a deposit on some goods which she has ordered. Sam, who has no intention of supplying the goods, gives the £5 to his son as a present.

(c) Sam discovers a purse lying on the floor of his shop. There have only been three customers in the shop since he swept it out and sam at first decides to ask each of them if they have lost a purse. Later, he changes his mind, takes the money from the purse for his own use and sells the purse in his shop.

3. Arthur wants to kill Peter and has been drinking heavily in order to summon up the courage to do so. He tells Bert, who is very inebriated, about his plan and Bert decides that he would like to watch the event. Arthur then realises that he needs Cyril's gun to shoot Peter. Arthur buys Cyril several large whiskies and then explains why he wants to borrow the gun. Cyril, who is by now drunk, gives Arthur his gun. Arthur and Bert approach Peter and Arthur fires the gun. As a result of his drunken state, Arthur's shot misses Peter but kills Paul.

Consider the criminal liability, if any, of Arthur, Bert and Cyril.

4. You are told that the Ancient Book Act 1977, has just received the Royal Assent, and that section 1 provides, "It shall be an offence to destroy any book printed before 1800."

(a) Arthur owns 200 books, which he thinks are worthless. He is concerned in case any of the books were printed before 1800 and consults Ben, an expert on old books, who assures him that all the books were printed long after 1800. Arthur destroys the books and is now horrified to discover that three of them were printed in 1750.

(b) Colin is an alcoholic, who suffers from bouts of *delirium tremens*. During one particularly severe bout, he thinks that a bookcase is alive and is going to crush him. He burns the books in the bookcase, which include two books published before 1800.

(c) David is disgusted by a book which has the date 1670 on the fly-leaf and deliberately burns the book as an example of Restoration immorality. It turns out that the book was not, in fact, printed until 1902.

Consider whether Arthur, Ben, Colin and David are guilty of an offence under the Ancient Books Act 1977.

5. George, an avid "do it yourself" enthusiast, decides to take the opportunity of his wife's visit to her mother, to install a sunken bath at their bungalow. He digs a six foot hole just inside the bathroom door and is about to begin work on fitting the bath when he is summoned to London on a business meeting. As he is sitting on the train as it speeds towards London he suddenly remembers that his wife will be returning that afternoon and might well be seriously injured by falling into the hole. George, who hates his wife, decides to do nothing, hoping that any serious injury might keep her in hospital for several months.

His wife, Flo, does, in fact, fall into the hole and is very seriously injured.

Consider George's criminal liability. What would be the position if Flo later died from her injuries?

6. (a) Mike, a plain clothes police officer, is travelling on a local bus. He sees that William, the bus conductor, is waiting until passengers are leaving the bus before he collects their fares. He puts the money into his official punch but does not issue any ticket. Mike arrests William who admits that he was planning later to separate the money collected in this way from the money collected with the issue of a ticket and keep it.

(b) Joe travels home each evening on a pay train where the fares are collected by the guard. One Wednesday he arrives at his station, which has no ticket collector, before the guard has collected his fare. As he gets off the train he sees the guard standing further down the platform, issuing tickets. Joe, muttering to himself "Why should I go out of my way to pay? It's his fault he hasn't got my money," simply walks out of the station.

Discuss the criminal liability of William and Joe.

7. Albert, Brian and Charles are mountain climbers. On the occasion in question they were roped together as they climbed a particularly steep and high slope. As they neared the top, Charles who was at the bottom negligently lost his footing and slipped pulling Brian away from the surface. Albert managed to keep his hold, but realises he cannot support the weight of the other two for long. He therefore tells Brian to cut Charles adrift. Brian refuses, but Albert replies that if Brian does not cut Charles loose then he will cut both Brian and Charles adrift. Reluctantly Brian cuts the rope below him, being sure Charles will fall to his death.

Charles is killed and Albert and Brian are charged with murder. Discuss their criminal liability.

8. How far can mistake of (a) fact and (b) law provide a defence to a criminal charge?

9. "To that, I can only say that on the question what amounts to insanity that would prevent a person being punishable or not, I have read every definition which I could ever meet with, and was never satisfied with one of them." (Lord Blackburn in 1874.)

(a) What criticisms would you make of the M'Naghten Rules?

(b) How far does the defence of diminished responsibility help to remedy the position?

10. "The decision in *D.P.P. v. Morgan* illustrates the insensitivity of the law to the legitimate views of women."

Discuss, with reference both to *D.P.P. v. Morgan* and subsequent legislation concerning rape.

C. Contract

1. Oliver wrote to Arnold on 1 May offering to sell him a specified clock for £50. Oliver's letter said: "This offer may be accepted by written notice to me before 8 May." On 6 May Arnold wrote and posted a letter of acceptance, but this was not received by Oliver until 11 May. On 7 May Arnold heard there were delays in the post so he rang Oliver but was only able to speak to his wife. She said that Arnold's letter had not yet arrived, but that she would tell her husband that Arnold was accepting the offer. Oliver did not get home until 10 May and his wife immediately told him of Arnold's telephone call. On 23 May Geoffrey offered Oliver £60 for the clock.

Advise Arnold who wishes to accept Geoffrey's offer.

2. "English law's almost obsessive concern with the element of bargain or consideration in the formation of a contract has led to inadequate provision for the frequent occasions when the parties wish to modify or vary the terms of their agreement."

Discuss.

3. Clark, wearing the uniform of a Chief Constable, entered a shop in Cambridge owned by Smith, agreed to buy a watch and tendered a cheque in payment. The cheque was signed by Clark in the name of the Chief Constable of the City, who was called Clark. Smith was reluctant to accept the cheque but did not say so to Clark. He asked him if he would write his private address on the back of the cheque. Clark wrote the Chief Constable's address on the cheque. Smith telephoned the Police Station and the Station Officer confirmed that the address given was the address of the Chief Constable. Smith accepted the cheque and delivered the watch to Clark.

Clark sold the watch to James and disappeared. There were no funds available to meet the cheque.

Smith wishes to recover the watch from James. What is Smith's legal position?

4. (a) When will a court order a decree of specific performance to enforce a contract?
   (b) John agreed with Peter that Peter would give him a course of 12 one hour driving lessons on alternate days in John's car. The price for the lessons was £60, to be paid at the end

of the course. After one lesson John decided that he did not enjoy driving and would have no further lessons. Peter said "You can't do that to me." Peter presented himself at John's door on eleven further occasions, rang the doorbell, waited for one hour and then left.

Advise Peter.

5. Jim has advertised cheap holidays at a villa he owns in Ruritania and two British students, Kevin and Sarah, book a holiday to commence immediately after their summer examination. Unfortunately, a law is passed in Ruritania in May making it illegal for British students to visit Ruritania.

Kevin has paid £100 in advance, Sarah paid a deposit of £50, and Jim appropriated this deposit when Sarah told Jim at Easter she would not be able to make the trip. Advise Jim, on the assumption that English law applies to the contract.

Would it make any difference if Jim had sold the villa at Easter, a month before the Ruritanian law was passed?

6. The Fixwell Garage agrees with Alison to do a full 10,000 mile service on Alison's car. The service manual of the car requires that, at this service, the oil should be changed and certain parts of the car greased. After Alison has collected her car from the Fixwell Garage she discovers that the oil has not been changed. She refuses to pay the Fixwell Garage any of the charge of £40 in respect of the service even though all other elements of the service have been satisfactorily carried out.

Advise the Fixwell Garage. Would it make any difference to your advice if the only element of the service not satisfactorily carried out was that one door hinge had not been greased?

7. Mr. Flint takes his family to Brownpool, a local seaside resort. Because of dangerous currents, Brownpool Corporation employ a full-time life-guard to patrol the beach. Whilst swimming, one of the Flint children gets into difficulty and is only rescued from drowning by the prompt action of the life-guard.

The grateful Flint promises to employ the life-guard as security officer at one of his factories, when the summer season at Brownpool is finished.

The life-guard hears nothing further from Flint and, on making enquiries, is told that the post is now filled.

Advise the life-guard on his legal rights.

8. To what extent does the Consumer Credit Act 1974 give effective protection to the individual consumer?

9. Molly bought a freezer so that she could freeze meals for her family, and also freeze vegetables from her allotment. The freezer had a placard on it which read "with quick-freeze compartment." She signed a contract for the purchase of the freezer, in which the seller had inserted the following clause: "All conditions implied by statute or common law are hereby excluded."
When the freezer was delivered to her home, Molly read the manufacturer's booklet and found that the small compartment in the freezer was in fact not a quick-freeze section. A quick-freeze section was essential to Molly if she were to freeze vegetables successfully.

The retailers refused to take back the freezer. Describe the possible courses of action Molly might take in order to solve her problem.

10. Fred agrees to install a central heating system in Alan's house. Alan signs a contract in which it is stated that the cost of the work will be £800, but nothing is said about how long it will take to complete. Six months later Fred finishes the installation and sends in a bill for £900, "because the job proved more difficult than expected." In fact several of the rooms in the house are no warmer than before. The water pump breaks down after three weeks and the boiler explodes, owing to a design fault, injuring Alan.

Advise Alan.

INDEX